FRANK WOOD'S
BUSINESS ACCOUNTING 1

Frank Wood

1926–2000

FRANK WOOD'S
BUSINESS ACCOUNTING

1

FOURTEENTH EDITION

ALAN SANGSTER BA, MSc, PhD, Cert TESOL, CA

with Lewis Gordon BSc, FCA, FHEA

Formerly authored by Frank Wood BSc (Econ), FCA

 **Pearson**

Harlow, England • London • New York • Boston • San Francisco • Toronto • Sydney • Dubai • Singapore • Hong Kong
Tokyo • Seoul • Taipei • New Delhi • Cape Town • São Paulo • Mexico City • Madrid • Amsterdam • Munich • Paris • Milan

PEARSON EDUCATION LIMITED
KAO Two
KAO Park
Harlow CM17 9NA
United Kingdom
Tel: +44 (0)1279 623623
Web: www.pearson.com/uk

First edition published 1967 (print)
Second edition published under the Longman imprint in 1972 (print)
Third edition published 1979 (print)
Fourth edition published 1984 (print)
Fifth edition published 1989 (print)
Sixth edition published 1993 (print)
Seventh edition published 1996 (print)
Eighth edition published under the Financial Times Pitman
    Publishing imprint in 1999 (print)

Ninth edition published 2002 (print)
Tenth edition published 2005 (print)
Revised tenth edition published 2007 (print)
Eleventh edition published 2008 (print)
Twelfth edition published 2012 (print and electronic)
Thirteenth edition published 2015 (print and electronic)
Fourteenth edition published 2018 (print and electronic)

The Financial Times. With a worldwide network of highly respected journalists, *The Financial Times* provides global business news, insightful opinion and expert analysis of business, finance and politics. With over 500 journalists reporting from 50 countries worldwide, our in-depth coverage of international news is objectively reported and analysed from an independent, global perspective. To find out more, visit www.ft.com/pearsonoffer.

ISBN: 978-1-292-20862-6 (print)
        978-1-292-20864-0 (PDF)
        978-1-292-20865-7 (ePub)

British Library Cataloguing-in-Publication Data
A catalogue record for the print edition is available from the British Library

Library of Congress Cataloging-in-Publication Data
Names: Sangster, Alan, author. | Gordon, Lewis (Financial accounter), author.
    | Wood, Frank, 1926-2000, author. | Wood, Frank, 1926-2000. Frank Wood's
    business accounting 1.
Title: Frank Wood's business accounting 1 : Frank Wood 1926-2000 / Alan
    Sangster with Lewis Gordon ; formerly authored by Frank Wood BSc (Econ),
    FCA.
Description: Fourteenth Edition. | New York : Pearson, 2018 | Revised
    edition of Frank Wood's business accounting 1, 2015. | Includes
    bibliographical references and index.
Identifiers: LCCN 2017057685| ISBN 9781292208626 (print) | ISBN 9781292208640
    (PDF) | ISBN 9781292208657 (ePub)
Subjects: LCSH: Accounting.
Classification: LCC HF5635 .W863 2018 | DDC 657--dc23
LC record available at https://urldefense.proofpoint.com/v2/url?u=https-3A__lccn.loc.gov_2017057685&d=DwIFAg&c=0YLnzTkWOdJ
lub_y7qAx8Q&r=Q1huLr_hfN5hBmNkITyEbqNkqKPJUy4ujVl9zNDFILM&m=kufTPQuX-exTVIdzjsa2LPgbC2py-wDuIpP3t6FuU_c&s=NLJe
uh5xH9Uz1fSM8QvxpjMcz_Z51Ah_dkIlAhOk_Yk&e=

10 9 8 7 6 5 4 3 2 1
22 21 20 19 18

Cover image © Shutterstock
Print edition typeset in 9.5/11.5pt Sabon LT Pro by SPi Global
Printed by Grafica Veneta S.p.A., Italy

NOTE THAT ANY PAGE CROSS REFERENCES REFER TO THE PRINT EDITION

Contents

part 1 Introduction to financial accounting

part 2 Books and transactions

part 3 Financial statements

part 4 Accounting today

Appendices

Lecturer Resources

For password-protected online resources tailored to support
the use of this textbook in teaching, please visit
www.pearsoned.co.uk/wood

Notes for teachers and lecturers

This textbook has been written to provide a very thorough introduction to accounting in two volumes. The split into two volumes is a recognition of the fact that many students will find that Volume 1 contains all that they require. Volume 2 takes the studies of the topic of this book to a more advanced stage.

Anyone seeking to obtain a good grounding in financial accounting will find this book suitable to their needs. This includes those studying accounting on courses at school, college or university; or studying for qualifications from the LCCI, Association of Accounting Technicians, the Institute of Secretaries and Administrators; or for qualifications of any of the six UK and Irish Chartered Accountancy bodies. The financial accounting requirements for National Vocational Qualifications and Scottish Vocational Qualification are also fully covered.

The book has the following features:

1 Each chapter:
   - starts with Learning Objectives;
   - contains Activities designed to broaden and reinforce students' understanding of the concepts being covered and, in some cases, to introduce new concepts in such a way that they do not come as a surprise when introduced formally later in the book;
   - ends with Learning Outcomes that can be mapped back to the Learning Objectives, reinforcing the major topics and concepts covered in the chapter;
   - contains answers to all the Activities immediately after the Learning Outcomes.
2 There is an alphabetical Glossary in Appendix 3 of all the significant terms introduced. Each entry is referenced back to the chapter in which it appeared.
3 Five sets of twenty multiple choice questions are positioned in the book (at the end of Chapters 6, 16, 22, 31 and 42) at the point at which they should be attempted, rather than as a group at the end of the book. All the answers are at the back of the book in Appendix 2.
4 At the end of Part 6 (*Check and errors*), there are five Scenario Questions designed to reinforce learning of the adjustments through their application in the preparation of financial statements previously learnt in Parts 1–6.
5 A set of Notes for Students appears at the front of the book. This covers how to use this book, how to tackle the end-of-chapter Review Questions, and how to study for and sit examinations. **It should be read by students before they start working through the main text.**
6 Blue is used in the text to enhance readability and bring out key points.

A new approach

A further change has been made in this edition in the presentation of *Double Entry*. This topic has always been a problem for students, and continues to be so. In the previous edition a new approach was presented. This approach has been modified following feedback from teachers and students. In this edition, we now focus on the *form of settlement* rather than the *item exchanged*. I believe that you will find it easier to teach, learn and understand. This principles-based approach to double entry has been fully adopted and is the focus of Chapter 2 (*Recording transactions*).

When a colleague and I used this principles-based approach with 250 students, their learning and understanding of double entry improved by more than 150 per cent; this is shown in Exhibit 1. The histogram shows the percentage of students in that group who selected the correct answer to each of 10 multiple choice questions compared with the percentage of 250 students in another group who had learnt double entry by rules, such as 'debit the receiver and credit the giver'. The multiple

Exhibit 1 The result of a switch to a principles-based approach to double entry

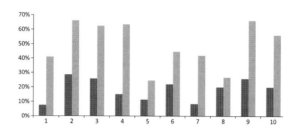

choice questions required them to identify the correct double entry for each of 10 transactions. This is why the approach adopted in this text has been changed: students find it far easier to learn!

The underlying truth behind the approach is that there are two elements to every transaction and *all* transactions involve at least one thing belonging to a business, either before, or as a result of the transaction. The other thing involved in the transaction is the *form of settlement,* e.g. cash, bank, a debt or capital. The approach adopted in this edition is simple: if you know how to record cash received or cash given, you can record receipts or givings of any *form of settlement*. A *form of settlement,* e.g. cash, is credited when it is given and debited when it is received. The entry for the *item exchanged* is the opposite. It is a straightforward method. And it never fails to give the correct treatment for a transaction, not least because you only have to identify the *form of settlement* and the *item exchanged* in a transaction to know how what to debit and what to credit.

In another change in this edition, when a transaction involves credit, the credit is identified using the term 'IOU'. In classes over the past three years, this has been found to make it easier for students to understand the principles of recording transactions.

In addition, in order to avoid confusion between 'credit' as a term in double entry and 'credit', when a transaction is not immediately paid for, during the first 10 chapters 'credit transactions' are referred to as transactions settled '*on time*'. In Chapter 11, the term 'credit sale' is introduced. Thereafter, 'credit' is used in place of '*on time*'. Focusing on the single use of 'credit' as a term in double entry up until that point has been found to make learning double entry easier.

I hope that you will find this innovation of help in the teaching of this topic; and I am sure that your students will find it much easier to learn from it. Please let me know your views on it, and those of your students.

Other changes, some major, others less so have also been made to the content of this textbook since the last edition:

- In response to many requests, the names of the two main financial statements have reverted to *Income Statement* and *Balance Sheet*.
- Part 2 has been renamed, *Books and transactions*.
- Part 3 has been renamed, *Financial statements*
- Part 4, *Accounting today,* is new to this edition. It replaces Chapters 22 and 23 of the thirteenth edition, which are now available online.
- Part 6 has been renamed, *Checks and errors*.
- Chapters 15 (*Accounting for purchases*) and 16 (*Accounting for returns*) from the last edition have been incorporated in abbreviated form in Chapter 11 (*Accounting for sales, purchases and returns*) along with all of Chapter 14 from the thirteenth edition, *Accounting for sales*.
- The full versions of Chapters 15 (*Accounting for purchases*) and 16 (*Accounting for returns*) have been placed online.
- Chapters 12 (*The banking system in the UK*), 20 (*Columnar day books*), and 21 (*Payroll accounting*) in the thirteenth edition have also all been removed from the book and placed online.

- Chapter 13 (*Value added tax*) has been revised.
- Chapter 38 (*Maths for accounting*) is new. It covers the arithmetic and algebra needed at this level and focuses on those misunderstandings and errors that cause students the most problems.
- There are over 100 new end of chapter *Review Questions* in this edition.
- The text is fully compliant with International GAAP.

People generally view financial accounting as a never-changing subject. This is not true; despite appearances, accounting is a dynamic subject. The current major ongoing change, begun in 2005 and still in progress, is the switch from domestic accounting rules to international rules. Specifically, the rules that have been developed in the UK since 1970, known as Statements of Standard Accounting Practice (SSAPs) and Financial Reporting Standards (FRSs) have been phased out. In their place, most businesses are now using International Financial Reporting Standards (IFRSs) and International Accounting Standards (IASs).

Some small and medium-sized businesses continue to use UK standards. These have simpler requirements, more in keeping (in terms of length and detail, but not in substance) with those issued under International GAAP.

It seems likely that all businesses will eventually move to using international standards and that the UK standards will disappear.

I hope that you find these changes helpful and appropriate and would welcome comments on these and any other changes you feel ought to be made in future editions. You can contact me by email at a.j.a.sangster@btinternet.com

Finally, I would like to thank all those teachers and lecturers who gave me their advice as to the changes they would like to see incorporated in this edition. Above all, I would like to acknowledge the assistance received from Graeme C. Reid and Christopher Foo for all their help and advice over my 25 years as author of *Frank Wood's Business Accounting*.

Alan Sangster

Notes for students

This textbook presents your topics in what has been found to be the most appropriate sequencing to build the foundations of your accounting knowledge. You will find that a number of features of the book, properly used, will enhance your understanding and extend your ability to cope with what will possibly appear, at first, to be a mystifying array of rules and procedures.

To make best use of this resource, you should consider the following as being a proven path to success:

- At the start of each chapter, **read the Learning Objectives**. Then, while you work through the material, try to detect when you have achieved each of these objectives.
- At the end of each chapter, **check what you have learnt against the Learning Outcomes** that follow the main text.
- If you find that you cannot say 'yes, I have learnt that' to any of the Learning Outcomes, look back through the chapter and reread the topic you have not yet learnt.
- **Learn the meaning of each new term as it appears.** Do not leave learning what terms mean until you are revising for an exam. Accounting is best learnt as a series of building blocks. If you don't remember what terms mean, your knowledge and ability to 'do' accounting will be very seriously undermined, in much the same way as a wall built without mortar is likely to collapse the first time someone leans against it.
- Attempt each of the **Activities** in the book *at the point at which they appear*. This is *very* important. They will reinforce your learning and help set in context some of the material that may otherwise appear very artificial and distant from the world you live in. The answers are at the end of each chapter. **Do not look at the answers before you attempt the questions – you'll just be cheating yourself.** Once you have answered one, check your answer against the answer provided in the book and be sure you understand it before moving on.
- Attempt each of the sets of multiple choice questions when you reach them in the book. There are five sets of twenty questions, one at the end of each of Chapters 6, 13, 27, 33 and 45. The answers are in Appendix 2 at the back of the book. **Do not look at the answers before you attempt the questions – you'll just be cheating yourself.** If you get any wrong, be sure you understand why before moving on to new material.
- Attempt the Scenario Questions at the end of Part 5. They will help you see how the items covered in Part 5 affect the preparation of financial statements.
- **Learn the *accounting equation* when you first come across it in Chapter 1.** It is *the* key to understanding many of the aspects of accounting that students find difficult. Make sure that you learn it in both the forms presented to you or that you can rearrange it to produce the alternate form when appropriate.
- Do not be disillusioned by the mystery of double entry. The technique has been in common use for over 700 years and is probably the most tried and trusted technique for doing anything you are ever likely to encounter. It really is not difficult, so long as you remember to identify what to do with the form of settlement you learn about in Chapter 1. Like riding a bike, once you understand it, you'll never forget it and, the more you do it, the easier it gets.
- Because of time pressure, some teachers and lecturers will need to omit Chapter 31 (*Joint ventures*). Make sure that you work through it on your own before you look at the material in Chapter 32, the first chapter on accounting for partnerships. This is very important, as accounting for joint ventures bridges the gap between accounting for sole proprietors and accounting for partnerships and will make it much easier for you to understand the differences between them.

● Above all, remember that accounting is a vehicle for providing financial information in a form that assists decision-making. Work hard at presenting your work as neatly as possible and remember that pictures (in this case, financial figures) only carry half the message. When you are asked for them, words of explanation and insight are essential in order to make an examiner appreciate what you know and that you actually understand what the figures mean.

There are two subjects I would like you to consider very carefully – making best use of the end-of-chapter Review Questions, and your examination technique.

Review questions: the best approach

Review questions are included at the end of most chapters. They are there for you to gauge how well you understand and can apply what you have learnt. **If you simply read the chapters without attempting the questions, you will not pass your examinations.** You should first attempt each question, then check your answer fully against the answers at the back of the book. **Do not simply compare the question with the answer and tick off the bits of the answer against the relevant part of the question.** No one ever learnt to do accounting properly that way. It is tempting to save time, but you will regret it eventually.

Need for practice

Try to find the time to answer as many exercises as possible. This is why:

1 Even though you may think you understand, when you come to answer the questions you may find you don't. The true test of understanding is whether or not you can tackle the questions competently.
2 Practice makes perfect. If you don't practice doing accounting questions, you will almost certainly not become good at accounting.
3 You need to be able to answer questions quickly: many fail accounting exams because they run out of time. A lot is expected from you in an accounting exam in a very short time because examining boards believe, and have always believed, that an 'adequately prepared' student will be able to work quickly on the problems set. By an 'adequately prepared' student, they mean a student who not only has the knowledge, but has been trained to work quickly and, at the same time, maintain accuracy and neatness.
4 Speed is not enough. You also have to be neat and tidy, and follow all the proper practices and procedures while working at speed. Fast, correct, but really scruffy and unreadable work can also cause you to fail the exam. Why? At this level, the accounting examiner is mainly concerned about your practical ability in the subject. Accounting is a practical subject, and your practical competence is being tested. The examiner will, therefore, expect the answers to be neat and well set out. Untidy work with numbers spread over the page in a haphazard way, badly written numbers, and columns of figures in which the vertical columns are not set down in straight lines, will be penalised and can easily mean the difference between a pass and a fail.
5 Appropriate presentation of information is important. Learn how to present the various financial statements you may need to produce in an examination. Examiners expect to see the items in statements of profit or loss, statements of financial position, and statements of cash flow in the correct order and will probably deduct marks if you don't do this. Practise by writing down examples of these statements without any numbers until you always get the layout correct. One exam trick most students overlook is that the layout of a financial statement is often included in an examination paper as part of one question yet another question asks you to produce an answer using the format of that financial statement. **The one you need to produce will contain different numbers but the general layout should be very similar.**

Need for headings

Your work should not only be neat, it should be well presented. Headings should always be given, and any dates should be inserted. The test you should apply is to imagine that you are a partner in a firm of professional accountants and have taken a few weeks holiday. During that time your assistants have completed all sorts of work including reports, drafting final accounts, various forms of other computations, and so on. All of this is waiting for you when you return. When you return you look at each item in the pile. Suppose the first one looks like a balance sheet as at 31 December in respect of one of your clients. When you look at it you can see that it is a balance sheet, but you don't know for which client, neither do you know which year it is for. Would you be annoyed with your assistant who prepared it? Of course you would. So, in an exam, why should the examiner give you high marks if you prepare a balance sheet answer without the date, or the name of the business, or the fact that it is a balance sheet position written clearly across the top? If proper headings are not given you will lose a lot of marks. Don't wait until your examination to do this. You also need to take similar care with sub-totals and sub-headings that need to be shown, such as those for non-current assets or for current liabilities

The examiner

When answering an examination question, think about what you would say if you were employing an accounts assistant who gave you a sheet of paper with accounting entries written in the same style as your own efforts in answering the exam question. Would you have told your assistant to go back and do the work again because it is untidy? If you say that about your own work, why should the examiner think any differently?

Anyone who works in accounting knows that untidy work leads to completely unnecessary errors. This is why examiners penalise unclear, untidy, poorly-presented work. Examiners want to ensure that you are not going to mess up the work of an accounting department. Even today, accountants still write down many things on paper, so don't imagine that examiners will overlook such messy work just because most accounting is now done using a computer. Imagine going to the savings bank and the manager saying to you: 'We don't know whether you've got £5 in the account or £5,000. You see, the work of our clerks is so untidy that we can never sort out exactly how much is in anybody's account.' We would guess that you would not want to put a lot of money into an account at that bank. How would you feel if someone took you to court for not paying a debt of £100 when, in fact, you owed them nothing? This sort of thing would happen all the time if we simply allowed people to keep untidy accounts. The examiner is there to ensure that the person to whom they award a pass will be worthy of it, and will not continually mess up the work of any firm at which they may work in the future.

If you want to pass your accounting exam, and your work is untidy, what can you do about it? Well, the answer is simple enough: start right now to be neat and tidy in your work. I did. My writing was so bad that my accounting teacher at school told me to print everything in capital letters. I thought he was mad, but my marks improved immediately, and so did my handwriting and my overall neatness in preparing answers. Start being neat now. You cannot suddenly become neat in an examination.

The structure of the questions

The review questions in each chapter generally start with the easiest and then get gradually more difficult. Some are very difficult and time consuming. If all the questions were easy, the shock of meeting more complicated questions for the first time in an examination could lead you to fail it. By giving you a mixture of straightforward and complicated questions, you will learn how to deal with the complex issues before meeting them in an exam. It's in your best interests not to ignore review questions you find hard. Put in the effort, the practice will increase your knowledge and understanding, and your performance in the exam will improve as a result.

The answers

At the back of the book, you will find answers to approximately half of the Review Questions. The answers to the other review questions (indicated by the letter 'A' after the question number) are only available to you from your teacher or lecturer. Don't worry if you are studying this subject on your own. There are still more than sufficient review questions with answers in the book to ensure you know and understand the material you are learning.

Examination technique

By the time you sit your first accounting exam, you will have spent a lot of hours trying to master such things as double entry, balance sheet and final adjustments. Learning accounting demands a lot of discipline and practice. Compared with the many hours learning the subject, most students spend very little time actually considering in detail how to tackle the examination. You may be one of them. Start changing this now by planning for the day when you will need to be able to demonstrate that you have learnt and understood, and can apply, the material in this book. Here are some of the things you should be thinking about:

Understanding examiners

If you want to understand anything about examinations then you have to understand examiners. Let's look at what these peculiar creatures get up to in an examination. The first thing is that when they set an examination they are looking at it on the basis that they want good students to get a pass mark. Obviously anyone who doesn't achieve the pass mark will fail, but the object of the exercise is to find those who will pass, not find the failures. This means that if you have done your work properly, you should manage to get a pass mark. It is important to stress this: if you study and practice properly, you should pass, no matter what questions you are asked.

Unfortunately, some students who should pass will fail, not because they haven't put in enough hours on their studies, nor because they are unintelligent, but simply because they throw away marks unnecessarily by poor examination technique. If you can read the rest of this and then say honestly that you wouldn't have committed at least one of the mistakes that are mentioned, then you are certainly much more aware of how to approach an exam than most students I have met. These things appear obvious, but most students never think them through and prepare for them.

Punctuality

Before you even think about the examination paper and what you should do with it, think about how you are going to get to the exam room. Do you know where it is? How are you going to get there? If you are going by bus or train, do you know which bus or train to catch? Will it be the rush hour when it may well take you much longer than if it were held at midday? How much time will you allow for the journey in case anything should go wrong?

Quite a large proportion of students lose their way to the examination room, or else arrive, breathless and flustered, at the very last minute. They then start the exam anxious and nervous: a recipe for disaster for a lot of students. So plan how you are going to get there and give yourself enough time.

Cramming

Trying to learn everything at the last minute rarely works. The last few days before the exam should not be spent cramming. You can look at past examination papers and rework some of them, but this is totally different from trying to cram new facts into your head. Worst of all, don't try to learn anything during the night before the exam, especially if you don't get any sleep. You may get away with this a few times, but you will be found out eventually, fall asleep during the exam, or simply find that you cannot think straight. Apart from the risk of failing the exam because you are exhausted, it is well known that anything you learn before you go to bed the night before an exam will be remembered far better than anything you try to learn on the day of the exam. Studying through the night means you are learning things in the 'morning' of the exam. Your mind needs a rest, even if you don't.

On your way to the exam, try to relax. Try taking your mind off the exam by doing something else, such as chatting with friends, listening to music, or scanning *Facebook* or other social media for something entertaining to pass the time. Of course, everyone needs some adrenalin to spur them into action when they begin to answer an exam paper, but you do not want to waste your adrenalin before the examination by doing something stressful, like learning something important you've not yet looked at. Doing so will only make you more nervous and less able to cope in the exam. If you haven't learnt something when you leave home, its not likely you'll be able to concentrate enough to do so on your way to the exam.

Read the rubric carefully and follow its instruction

The rubric appears at the start of the examination paper, and says something such as:

'Attempt five questions only: the *three* questions in Section A and *two* from Section B.'

That instruction from the examiner is to be followed *exactly*. You cannot change the instruction – it means what it says. You have to do what it says.

You may think that is so simple that it is not worthwhile my pointing it out to you, but I cannot remember an exam I have marked when at least some students failed to follow the instructions they were given. Let's look at two typical examples where students have ignored the rubric above and what will happen to their mark:

(a) Instead of answering three questions from Section A and two from Section B, a student answered *two* questions from Section A and *three* from Section B. Here the examiners will mark the two Section A answers plus the first two answers shown on the student's script in respect of Section B. They will not read any part of the third answer to Section B. The student can therefore only get marks for four answers.

(b) A student answered *three* questions from Section A and *three* from Section B. Here the examiners will mark the three answers to Section A plus the first two answers to Section B. They will not look at the third answer to Section B.

In the case of (b), the student may have done it that way deliberately, thinking that the examiner would mark all three Section B answers, and then award the student the marks from the best two answered questions. Examiners will not waste time marking an extra answer.

If you have time and want to give an extra answer, thinking that you will get better marks for it than one answered previously, then do. But, if you do, make certain that the examiner is fully aware that you have deleted the answer that you do not want to have marked. Strike lines right through it, and also state that you wish to delete it. Otherwise, it is possible that the first answers only will be marked and your new answer ignored.

Always remember in examinations that you should try to make life easier for the examiner. Give examiners what they want, in the way that they want it. If you do, you will get better marks.

Make their job harder than it needs to be and you will suffer. Examiners are only human. They do their job and their job is to mark what they asked you to do. Do something else and they will ignore it.

Time planning

Let's look at the way in which you should tackle the examination paper. One of the problems with accounting exams is that students are expected to do a lot of work in a relatively short time. It will be the same for every other student taking your exam, so it is not unfair so far as any one student is concerned. Working at speed does bring various disadvantages, and makes the way you tackle the examination of even greater importance.

Time per question

The marks allotted to each question will indicate how long you should take in tackling it. Most exams are of two hours, i.e. 120 minutes. This means that in a normal examination, with 100 marks in total, a twenty-mark question should be allocated 20 per cent of the time, i.e. $20\% \times 120 = 24$ minutes. Similarly, a question worth 30 marks should take up 30 per cent of the time, i.e. $30\% \times 120 = 36$ minutes, and so on. Alternatively, it is 1.2 minutes for each mark awarded for the question.

If the question is in parts, and the marks awarded are shown against each part, then that will tell you what time you should spend on each part. If part of the question asks for a description, for instance, and only three marks are awarded to that part, then you should not spend twenty minutes on a long and detailed description. Instead a brief description, taking about four minutes, is what is required.

Do the easiest questions first

Always tackle the easiest question first, then the next easiest question and so on. It is amazing how many students do not do this! Leave the most difficult question as the last one to be attempted. Why is this good advice? The fact is, most exams include what might be called 'warm-up' questions. These are usually fairly short, and not very difficult.

You may be able to do the easiest question in less than the time allocated. The examiner is trying to be kind to you. The examiner knows that there is a certain amount of nervousness on the part of a student taking an examination, and wants to give you the chance to calm down by letting you tackle these short, relatively easy questions first of all, and generally settle down to your work.

Even where all the questions are worth equal marks, you are bound to find some easier than others. It is impossible for an examiner to set questions which are exactly equal in difficulty. So, remember, start with the easiest question. This will give you a feeling of confidence that will help you when you get to the more difficult questions later.

Do not expect that these 'warm-up' questions will be numbered 1 and 2 on your exam paper. Most accounting exams start with a rather long question, worth quite a lot of marks, as the first question on the paper. A lot of students are fascinated by the fact that such a question is number 1, that it is worth a lot of marks, and their thinking runs: 'If I do this question first, and make a good job of it, then I am well on the way to passing the examination.'

There is no doubt that a speedy and successful attempt at such a question could possibly lead to a pass. The trouble is that this doesn't usually happen, and many students have admitted afterwards that their failure could be put down to simply ignoring this advice. What happens very often is that the student starts off on such a question, things don't go very well, a few mistakes are made, the student then looks at the clock and sees that they are not 'beating the clock' in terms of possible marks, and then panic descends. Leaving that question very hastily, the student then proceeds to the next question, which normally might have been well attempted but, because of the student's state of mind, a mess is made of that one as well, and so the student fails an exam that ought to have been passed.

Attempt every required question

Attempt each and every question you are required to do. If you are asked to do four questions, don't just do three. On each question the first few marks are the easiest to get. For instance, on a 20-mark essay question it is reasonably easy to get the first five marks. Managing to produce a perfect answer to get the last five marks, from 15 to 20, is extremely difficult. This applies also to computational questions.

This means that in an examination of, say, five questions with 20 marks for each question, there is not much point in tackling only three questions and trying to make a good job of them. Your maximum possible mark would be 60, and if you had not achieved full marks for each question, in itself extremely unlikely, you could easily fall below the pass mark. It is better to leave questions unfinished when your allotted time, calculated as described above, has expired, and to then go on immediately to the other questions. It is so easy, especially in an accounting exam, to find you have exceeded the time allowed for a question by a considerable margin. So, although you may find it difficult to persuade yourself to do so, move on to the next question when your time for a question has expired.

Computations

When you sit an exam, you should be attempting to demonstrate how well you know the topics being examined. In accounting exams, there are three things in particular to remember. If you fail to do so, you will probably earn less marks than your knowledge deserves. One of these things has already been mentioned – be neat and tidy. The other two have to do with computations: *show all your workings* and *don't worry if your balance sheet does not balance*.

Workings

One golden rule which should *always* be observed is to **show all of your workings**. Suppose you have been asked to work out the Cost of Goods Sold, not simply as part of a Trading Account but for some other reason. On a scrap of paper you do the (incorrect) calculation shown below:

	£
Opening inventory	4,000
Add Purchases	11,500
	15,500
Less Closing inventory	(3,800)
	12,700

You then use this wrong answer of £12,700 in your exam script. The scrap of paper with your workings on it is then crumpled up by you and thrown in the wastepaper basket as you leave the room. This answer should have been £11,700 and not £12,700 and the examiner may well have allocated four marks for this bit of the question. What will the examiner do when marking your answer? Will the examiner think. 'I should imagine that the candidate mis-added to the extent of £1,000 and, as I am not unduly penalising students for poor arithmetic, I will give the candidate 3½ marks'? Unfortunately, the examiner cannot do this. You will get a mark of zero. If you had attached the workings to your answer, then you would have got 3 or even 3½ marks.

It is a good idea to put the workings of any calculated sum on the face of the any financial statements you have been asked to prepare. For instance, if rent paid is £1,900 and £300 of it has been paid in advance, you can show it on the face of the income statement as:

Rent (1,900 – 300)   £1,600

By showing the workings in brackets you are demonstrating that you realise that they would not be shown on the published accounts. It also makes it easier for the examiner to mark, and it is always a good idea to make the examiner think you are trying to help.

Do balance sheets have to balance?

Many students ask: 'What should I do if my balance sheet doesn't balance?' The answer is quite simple: leave it alone and get on with answering the rest of the exam paper.

One of the reasons for this is to try and ensure that you answer the required number of questions. You might take twenty minutes to find the error, which might save you one mark. If, instead, you had tackled the next question, in that time you might have gained, say, ten marks, for which you would not have had time if you had wasted it by searching for the error(s). That assumes that you actually find the error(s)! Suppose you don't, you have spent twenty minutes looking for it, have not found it, so how do you feel now? The answer is, of course: worried. You may make an even bigger mess of the rest of the paper than you would have done if you had simply ignored the fact that the balance sheet did not balance. In any case, it is quite possible to get, say, 29 marks out of 30 even though the balance sheet does not balance. The error may be a very minor one for which the examiner deducts one mark only.

Of course, if you have finished all the questions, then by all means spend the rest of your time tracing the error and correcting it. Be certain, however, that your corrections are carried out neatly. Untidy crossings-out can result in the loss of marks. So, sometimes, an error found can get back one mark, which is then lost again because the corrections make an untidy mess of your paper, and examiners often deduct marks for untidy work. It might be better to write against the error 'see note', indicating exactly where the note of the correction you wish to make is shown. You can then illustrate to the examiner that you know what the error is and how to correct it.

Essay questions

There are some basic things about essay questions that every student should know.

Typical questions

Let's look at two typical exam questions. In doing so, visualise carefully what you would write when answering them.

(a) You are employed as a bookkeeper by G. Jones, a trader. State briefly what use you would make of the following documents in relation to your bookkeeping records.
   (i)   A bank statement.
   (ii) A credit note received to correct an overcharge on an invoice.
   (iii) A pay-in slip.
   (iv) A petty cash voucher.

(b) Explain the term 'depreciation'. Name and describe briefly two methods of providing for depreciation of non-current assets.

Now let's see whether you would have made a reasonably good attempt at the questions. With question (a) a lot of students would have written down what a bank statement is, what a pay-in slip is, what a petty cash voucher is, and so on. Marks gained by you for an answer like that would be . . . virtually nil. Why is this? Well, you simply have not read the question properly. The question asked what *use* you would make of the documents, not to *describe* what the documents were. The bank statement would be used to check against the bank column in the Cash Book or cash records to see that the bank's entries and your own are in accordance with one another, with a bank reconciliation statement being drawn up to reconcile the two sets of records. The petty cash voucher would be used as a basis for entering up the payments columns in the Petty Cash Book. The *use* of the items was asked for, not the *descriptions* of the items.

Let us see if you have done better on question (*b*). Would you have written down how to calculate two methods of depreciation, probably the reducing balance method and the straight line method? But have you remembered that the question also asked you to *explain the term depreciation*? In other words, what is depreciation generally? Some students will have omitted that part of the question. More students would have made a poor attempt at question (*a*), but some will have made the mistake described above with question (*b*).

Underline the key words

I have already described how a large percentage of students fail to answer the question set, instead answering the question they imagine it to be. Too many students write down everything they know about a topic, rather than what the examiner has asked for.

To remedy this defect, *underline the key words* in a question. This brings out the meaning so that it is difficult to misunderstand the question. For instance, let's look at the following question:

'Discuss the usefulness of departmental accounts to a business.'

Many students will write down all they know about departmental accounts, how to draw them up, how to apportion overheads between departments, how to keep columnar sales and purchases journals to find the information, etc.

Number of marks gained . . . virtually nil.

Now underline the key words. They will be:

Discuss usefulness departmental accounts

The question is now seen to be concerned not with *describing* departmental accounts, but instead discussing the *usefulness* of departmental accounts.

Lastly, if the question says 'Draft a report on . . . ' then the answer should be in the form of a *report*; if it says 'List the . . . ' then the answer should consist of a *list*. Similarly 'Discuss . . . ' asks for a *discussion*. 'Describe . . . ' wants you to *describe* something, and so on.

You should ensure, therefore, that you are going to give the examiners

(*i*) what they are asking for; *and*

(*ii*) in the way that they want it.

If you do not comply with (*i*), you may lose all the marks. If you manage to fulfil (*i*) but do not satisfy the examiner on (*ii*), you will still lose a lot of marks.

It is also just as important in computational questions to underline the key words to get at the meaning of a question, and then answer it in the manner required by the examiner. With computational questions it is better to look at what is required first before reading the rest of the question. That way, when you are reading the rest of the question, you are able to decide how to tackle it.

Never write out the question

Often – too often – students spend time writing out the text of essay questions before they set about answering them. This is a complete waste of time. It will not gain marks and should *never* be done. It is probably the most common way that students waste time in an exam. Why waste time when you have only a limited amount of it available to you?

Running out of time?

If your plans don't work out, you may find yourself with a question you could answer, but simply do not have the time to do it properly. It is better to write a short note to the examiner to that effect, and put down what you can of the main points in an abbreviated fashion. This will show that you have the knowledge and should gain you some marks.

Summary

Remember:

1 Read the instructions.
2 Plan your time before you start.
3 Tackle the easiest questions first.
4 Finish off answering each question when your time allocation for the question is up.
5 Hand in all your workings.
6 Do remember to be neat, and to include all proper headings, dates, sub-totals, etc. A lot of marks can be lost if you don't.
7 Only answer as many questions as you are asked to tackle by the examiner. Extra answers will not normally be marked and certainly won't get credit.
8 Underline the *key* words in each question to ensure that you answer the question set, and not the question you wrongly take it to be.
9 Never copy the question onto your answer.

Good luck with your exam. I hope you get the rewards you deserve!

Alan Sangster

The Last Lecture

Our course is run, our harvest garnered in,
And taking stock of what we have, we note how life,
This strange, mysterious life which now we hold and now
eludes our grasp,
Is governed still by natural law, and its events
Tread on each other's heels, each one compelled to follow
where the first has led.
Noting all this, and judging by the past,
We form our plans, until we know at last
The treasure in the future's lap.

The man, the plant, the beast, must all obey this law,
Since in the early dawn of this old world
The law was given, and the stuff was made
Which still alone can hold the breath of life:
Whereby we know that grass and man are kin,
The bond a common substance which within
Controls their growth.

Can we know all? Nay, but the major part
Of all that is must still elude our grasp,
For life transcends itself, and slowly noting what it is,
Gathers but fragments from the stream of time.
Thus what we teach is only partly true.
Not knowing all, we act as if we knew,
Compelled to act or die.

Yet as we grow in wisdom and in skill
The upward path is steeper and each step
Comes nigher unto heaven, piercing the clouds
Which heretofore have hid the stars from view.
The new-gained knowledge seems to fill the air,
It seems to us the soul of truth is there.
Our quest is won.

Bold climber, all that thou hast won
Lies still in shadow of the peaks above;
Yet in the morning hours the sun
Rewards thy work of love,
Resting a moment on thy lesser height,
Piercing the vault with rays too bright to face,
Strengthens thy soul and gives thee ample might
To serve thy human race.

Theodore Dru Alison Cockerell (1866–1948)

Zöology: A Textbook for Colleges and Universities, Yonkers-on-Hudson, NY: World Book Company, 1920, pp. 538–539

Publisher's acknowledgements

We are very grateful to teachers of accounting in many schools, colleges of further education and universities whose generous advice has contributed to the development of this new edition. We wish to thank, in particular, Adriana Korczak (University of Bristol); Martin Kelly (Queens University Belfast); Christopher Coles (University of Stirling); Christopher Barlow (University of Liverpool); Angela Cairns (Glasglow Caledonian University); Jonas Truedsson (Malardalen University) and Steve O'Connor (London South Bank University).

We are grateful to the following for permission to reproduce copyright material:

Figures

Figure 7.1 from *The Statement of Principles for Financial Reporting*, ASB Publications (1999) p.34, © Financial Reporting Council. Adapted and reproduced with the kind permission of the Financial Reporting Council. All rights reserved. For further information please visit www.frc.org.uk/asb or call +44 (0)20 7492 2300.

Text

Exam Board Questions from Edexel Foundation, © Pearson Education; Association of Chartered Certified Accountants (ACCA), © The Association of Chartered Certified Accountants; Association of Accounting Technicians (AAT); Midland Examining Group, reproduced by kind permission of OCR; Institute of Chartered Secretaries and Administrators (ICSA); Scottish Qualifications Authority (SQA); AQA examination materials are reproduced by permission of AQA.

All answers to questions are the author's own work and have not been supplied by any of the examining bodies.

Cover images: Front: Shutterstock

All other images © Pearson Education

part
1

INTRODUCTION TO FINANCIAL ACCOUNTING

Introduction

This part is concerned with the basic principles underlying the double entry system of bookkeeping and the impact of each transaction upon the financial performance and financial position of a business.

The background and the main features of financial accounting

Learning objectives

After you have studied this chapter, you should be able to:

- explain what accounting is about
- briefly describe the history of accounting
- explain the relationship between bookkeeping and accounting
- list the main users of accounting information and what accounting information they are interested in
- describe the main difference between financial accounting and management accounting
- present and explain the accounting equation
- explain the relationship between the accounting equation and the layout of the balance sheet
- explain the meaning of the terms assets, capital, liabilities, accounts receivable and accounts payable
- describe how accounting transactions affect the items in the accounting equation
- draw up balance sheets after different accounting transactions have occurred

Introduction

In this chapter, you will learn: what accounting is; what led to its development into what it is today; who uses accounting information; and the relationship between the various components that, together, comprise what is known as the 'accounting equation'.

1.1 What is accounting?

What do you think of when you read or hear the word, 'accounting'? What do you believe it means or represents?

If you have already attended some accounting classes or if you have spoken to someone who knows something about accounting, you will probably have a fairly good idea of what accounting is and what it is used for. If not, you may find it useful to have this knowledge before you start studying the subject. During the course of the next few pages, let's see if you can gain that knowledge and learn what accounting is.

Accounting can be defined as:

The process of identifying, measuring, and communicating economic information to permit informed judgements and decisions by users of that information.

A bit of a mouthful really but, what it means is that accounting involves deciding what amounts of money are, were, or will be involved in transactions (often buying and selling transactions) and then organising the information obtained and presenting it in a way that is useful for decision-making.

Despite what some people think, accounting is not a branch of mathematics, although the man credited with writing the first book to be printed on the subject, Luca Pacioli (c. 1446/7–1517), was a mathematician and teacher. He wrote on the topic *'in order that the subjects of the most gracious Duke of Urbino* [his sponsor or benefactor] *may have complete instructions in the conduct of business'*, and to *'give the trader without delay information as to his assets and liabilities'*. ('Assets' are things that you own; 'liabilities' are things that you owe.)

What Pacioli wrote is contained in 27 pages of a textbook and reference manual for merchants on business and mathematics (*Summa de arithmetica, geometria, proportioni et proportionalita – Everything about Arithmetic, Geometry and Proportion*). It was first published in Italy in 1494. His bookkeeping treatise has been translated into many languages, including English, and is acknowledged as the chief reason why we maintain accounts in the way we do today.

Accounting may not require a knowledge of mathematics but you do need to be able to add, subtract, multiply and divide – things you need to be able to do in your daily life anyway. Otherwise, you would not know how much money you had with you, how much you would have if you spent some of it, or whether the change you received was correct. To help you with the mathematics you do need to be able to do, Chapter 38 (*Maths for accounting*) sets down the basics you will need to know.

1.2 The history of accounting

Accounting began because people needed to:

● record business transactions; and
● know how much they owed others and how much others owed them.

It is known to have existed in one form or another for at least 10,000 years. (Records exist which indicate its use at that time in Mesopotamia – modern-day Iraq.) There is also considerable evidence of accounting being practised in ancient times in Egypt, China, India, Greece and Rome. In England, the 'Pipe Roll', the oldest surviving accounting record in the English language, contains an annual description of rents, fines and taxes due to the King of England, from 1130 to 1830.

In India, a system of accounting, called *Bahi-khata*, was developed many centuries ago but it did not spread beyond that region, probably because a description of it was never written down until the twentieth century. It spread by word of mouth and, even today, is a standardised method of keeping accounting records in parts of that region.

In the rest of the world, accounting appears to have developed slowly for thousands of years. The first known example of business records maintained for a whole business using what we call 'double entry bookkeeping' – the method described by Pacioli and the method used universally today – was in a branch of an Italian firm in southern France in 1299. But, it was another 150 years before it became relatively commonly used by northern Italian partnerships and joint ventures. The rest of the world took considerably longer to adopt the method. It is due to Pacioli and what he wrote about it in 1494 that this system of double entry book keeping came to be universally adopted.

It has been suggested that no standard system for maintaining accounting records had been developed before this because the circumstances of the day did not make it practicable for anyone to do so. There was little point, for example, in anyone devising a formal system of accounting if the people who would be required to 'do' accounting did not know how to read or write.

One accounting scholar (A. C. Littleton) suggested that seven key ingredients were required before a formal system like double entry bookkeeping could be developed and that all seven existed when Pacioli wrote his treatise:

- *Private property*. The power to change ownership exists and there is a need to record the transaction.
- *Capital*. Wealth is productively employed such that transactions are sufficiently important to make their recording worthwhile and cost-effective.
- *Commerce*. The exchange of goods on a widespread level. The volume of transactions needs to be sufficiently high to motivate someone to devise a formal, organised system that could be applied universally to record transactions.
- *Credit*. The present use of future goods. Cash transactions, where money is exchanged for goods, do not require that any details be recorded of who the customer or supplier was. The existence of a system of buying and selling on time (i.e. paying later for goods and services purchased today) led to the need for a formal organised system that could be applied universally to record credit transactions of this type.
- *Writing*. A mechanism for making a permanent record in a common language. Writing had clearly been around for a long time prior to Pacioli but it was, nevertheless, an essential element required before accounting could be formalised.
- *Money*. There needs to be a common denominator for exchange. So long as barter was used rather than payment with currency, there was no need for a bookkeeping system based upon transactions undertaken using a uniform set of monetary values.
- *Arithmetic*. As with writing, this has clearly been in existence far longer than accounting. Nevertheless, it is clearly the case that without an ability to perform simple arithmetic, there was no possibility that a formal organised system of accounting could be devised.

Of these, the most important catalyst for the emergence of double entry bookkeeping was the use of credit in business. In the Middle Ages, a businessman who did not know how much was owed to him and how much he owed, could lose his business, his home and everything he owned.

During the Crusades (1096–1292), trade routes to the east were opened and merchants, many from the Italian ports like Venice, began to expand their activities along the new routes. Venice dominated trade and another Italian city, Florence, was the major banking centre in the western world up to at least the mid-fifteenth century.

This expansion of trade led merchants to start operating in joint ventures (where they shared costs and profits) with businessmen located elsewhere. They were heavily involved in importing raw materials and exporting finished goods, particularly in Florence. Many merchants also employed agents to conduct business on their behalf. The need to record details of these transactions and arrangements was obvious.

This did not transform into double entry bookkeeping for many years. In the Middle Ages, when accounting information was recorded it initially took the form of a note of the details of each credit transaction that had not been paid and each receipt and payment. These notes were used by the owner mainly in order to keep track of payments outstanding. However, in Florence, merchants were more accustomed to keeping details of their activities than elsewhere. Many of them already maintained a record of important personal events in a book called a *Ricordanze*. It was a very popular practice and Florentine merchants started to record transactions, receipts and payments in their *Ricordi*.

The larger the business, the greater the number of entries that were made. They were prepared when they occurred and it could be some time before the next transaction with the same person occurred. Even with these records in a *Ricordanze*, it became difficult to tell what total amounts were owed and due.

To address this problem, merchants started transferring details from the *Ricordanze* into another book and entries in that book were organised into what we now call 'accounts', one for each person or item.

This was the beginning of the system of double entry bookkeeping described by Pacioli. In his system, a book called a *Memorandum* replaced the *Ricordanze*. The details recorded in it were abbreviated, organised and transferred into another book called a *Journal*. Details from that book were then further summarised and entered into accounts maintained in a third book called a *Ledger*.

The accountant of the Middle Ages was someone who knew how to enter data relating to financial transactions into the accounting books. He was what we call a 'bookkeeper'. Quite often, it would be the owner of the business who performed all the accounting tasks. Otherwise, an employee would be given the job of maintaining the accounting records.

As businesses grew in size, it became less common for the owner to personally maintain the accounting records and more usual for someone to be employed as a bookkeeper. Then, as companies began to dominate the business environment, managers became separated from owners – the owners of companies (shareholders) often have no involvement in the day-to-day running of the business. This led to a need for some monitoring of the managers. Auditing of the financial records became the norm and this, effectively, established the accounting profession.

The first association of accountants, the *Collegio dei Rexonati*, was formed in Venice in 1581 and had a role in training auditors, but the widespread emergence of an accounting profession was slow. It was not until the nineteenth century that the majority of Italian states required accountants to be members of a recognised association, but organisation was regional not national.

In 1854, the first national body of accountants was formed: the Institute of Chartered Accountants of Scotland. Thereafter, other national bodies began to emerge gradually throughout the world, with the English Institute of Chartered Accountants being formed in 1880 and the first US national accounting body being formed in 1887.

If you wish to discover more about the history of accounting, you will find that it is readily available on the Internet. Perform a search on either of the terms 'history of accounting' or 'accounting history' and you should find more information than you could ever realistically read on the subject.

1.3 Accountants

From its roots among the scribes of Mesopotamia, accounting is one of the oldest professions in the world. Today, there are around 200 professional accountancy bodies, each with its own requirements to be met before anyone can become a member. While there are notable exceptions, nowadays these generally consist of a series of examinations plus relevant work experience, the same requirement as applied to anyone seeking admission to the Venetian *Collegio dei Rexonati* in 1581.

Today, accountants go beyond the role of the bookkeepers of the Middle Ages. As they did then, accountants record and manipulate financial data in order to provide financial information. In addition, today's accountants are also expected to interpret the information they produce, all in order to assist in decision-making.

It is not necessary to be a member of a professional accountancy body in order to work as an accountant, although few who are not are likely today to rise above the level of a bookkeeper.

Being a member of a professional accountancy body indicates a minimum level of knowledge and expertise that would be expected and upon which employers and others using information provided by such accountants may rely. Because membership of such a body presents an image of professional expertise and understanding, it is important that accountants act in a manner that is consistent with what is expected of them. Any failure to do so places the image of the profession at risk. In Chapter 36, you will learn how the profession seeks to maintain this image by presenting its members with an Ethical Code that they must follow.

1.4 The objectives of financial accounting

Financial accounting is the branch of accounting that is concerned with (i) recording business transactions, (ii) preparing financial statements that report on how an entity (a business, charity, club, society, government department, etc.) has performed and, (iii) reporting on its financial position. It has many objectives, including letting people and entities know:

● if they are making a profit or a loss;
● what the entity is worth;
● what a transaction was worth to them;
● how much cash they have;
● how wealthy they are;
● how much they are owed;
● how much they owe;
● enough information so that they can keep a financial check on the things they do.

However, the primary objective of financial accounting is to provide information for decision-making. The information is primarily financial, but it can include data on volumes, for instance the number of cars sold in a month by a car dealership or the number of cows in a farmer's herd.

So, for example, if a business recorded what it sold, to whom, the date it was sold, the price at which it was sold, and the date it received payment from the customer, along with similar data concerning the purchases it made, information could be produced summarising what had taken place. The profitability of the business and the financial status of the business could also be identified, at any time. It is the primary task of financial accounting to take such information and convert it into a form that is useful for decision-making.

People and businesses

Accounting is something that affects people in their personal lives just as much as it affects very large businesses. We all use accounting ideas when we plan what we are going to do with our money. We have to plan how much of it we will spend and how much we will save. We may write down a plan, known as a **budget**, or we may simply keep it in our minds.

Recording accounting data

However, when people talk about accounting, they are normally referring to financial accounting performed by businesses and other entities. No-one can remember all the details of what has taken place, so records of it have to be kept. These records contain the accounting data.

Entities not only record cash received and paid out. They will also record goods bought and sold, items bought to use rather than to sell, and so on. This part of accounting is usually called the *recording of data*.

Classifying and summarising

Once the accounting data has been recorded, it has to be organised so as to be most useful to the entity. In doing so, we *classify* and *summarise* the accounting data.

Once data has been classified and summarised, it is much easier to work out how much profit or loss has been made by the entity during a particular period. It is also much easier to show what resources are owned by it, and what it owes on the closing day of the period.

Communicating information

From this data and the information it can be used to produce, people skilled in financial accounting should be able to tell whether or not an entity is performing well financially. They should be able to ascertain the strengths and weaknesses of the business, and what it is worth.

Finally, they should be able to tell or *communicate* their results to the owners of the entity, or to others allowed to receive this information.

Financial accounting is, therefore, concerned with:

● recording data;
● classifying and summarising data;
● communicating what has been learnt from the data.

This is also the case for the other main branch of accounting, **Management accounting**, which is accounting undertaken to assist managers within a business to take effective decisions. You will learn about this branch of accounting in Section 1.8

1.5 What is bookkeeping?

Until about one hundred years ago, records of all accounting data was *kept* manually in *books*. This is why the part of accounting that is concerned with recording data is often known as **bookkeeping**.

● Nowadays, although handwritten books may sometimes be used (particularly by very small entities), most accounting data is recorded and stored electronically.

Bookkeeping is the process of recording data relating to accounting transactions in the accounting books. You'll learn more about this in Chapter 2.

1.6 Financial accounting is concerned with . . .

Financial accounting is concerned with how accountants use bookkeeping data. This book will cover many such uses.

1.7 Users of financial accounting information

Possible users of financial accounting information include:

● *Managers.* These are the day-to-day decision-makers. They need to know how well things are progressing financially and about the financial status of the business.
● *Owner(s) of the business.* They want to be able to see whether or not the business is profitable. In addition they want to know what the financial resources of the business are.
● *A prospective buyer.* When the owner wants to sell a business the buyer will want to see such information.
● *The bank.* If the owner wants to borrow money for use in the business, then the bank will need such information.
● *Tax inspectors.* They need it to be able to calculate the taxes payable.
● *A prospective partner.* If the owner wants to share ownership with someone else, then the would-be partner will want such information.
● *Investors,* either existing ones or potential ones. They want to know whether or not to invest their money in the business.
● *Creditors.* They want to know if there is any risk of not being paid what they are due.

There are many other users of financial accounting information – suppliers and employees, for example. It is obvious that without properly recorded accounting data a business would have many difficulties providing the information these various users (often referred to as '**stakeholders**') require.

Activity 1.1 Which two of these stakeholder groups do you think are considered to be the most important? Why?

However, the information produced by financial accounting needs to be a compromise – the existence of so many different groups of stakeholders make it impossible to produce accounting information at a reasonable cost in a form that suits them all. As a result, financial accounting focuses on producing information for owners and creditors. The other stakeholder groups often find the accounting information provided fails to tell them what they really want to know. As any accountant would tell you, if organisations made the effort to satisfy the information needs of all their stakeholders, financial accounting would be a very costly exercise indeed!

1.8 The two branches of accounting

So far, you have learned that financial accounting is accounting performed for the owners of a business. It is used to show them how much profit has been made and what their business is worth. There is also another branch of accounting that is used by managers and decision makers within a business. It is called '**management accounting**'. A management accountant produces reports that help managers *plan* and enable managers to *control* what the business is doing. Qualified accountants know how to do both forms of accounting, though some specialise more in financial accounting while others specialise in management accounting.

Financial accounting is concerned with what has already happened assessing performance and considering where we are now. Management accounting is interested in explaining what has happened and in looking into the future.

The reports produced by each of these two branches of accounting are mainly expressed in terms of money, though there are some exceptions, particularly in management accounting. For example, units of a product bought, manufactured, or sold may be the focus of a report on how much of a product to manufacture. However, even then, the amounts involved financially will also be presented and will be used to justify any conclusions drawn in the report.

Management accounting is introduced in the final chapter of this book so that you can understand what it is used for, and why. The other chapters in this book are about financial accounting.

Let's now look at the framework upon which financial reporting is based, the **Accounting Equation**.

1.9 The accounting equation

By adding up what the accounting records say belongs to a business and deducting what they say the business owes, you can identify what a business is worth according to those accounting records. The whole of financial accounting is based upon this very simple idea. It is known as the *accounting equation.*

It can be explained by saying that if a business is to be set up and start trading, it will need resources. Let's assume first that it is the owner of the business who has supplied all of the resources. This can be shown as:

> Resources supplied by the owner = Resources in the business

In accounting, special terms are used to describe many things. The amount of the resources supplied by the owner is called **capital**. The actual resources that are then in the business are called **assets**. This means that when the owner has supplied all of the resources, the accounting equation can be shown as:

$$\boxed{\text{Capital} = \text{Assets}}$$

Usually, however, people other than the owner have supplied some of the assets. **Liabilities** is the name given to the amounts owing to these people for these assets. The accounting equation has now changed to:

$$\boxed{\text{Capital} = \text{Assets} - \text{Liabilities}}$$

This is the most common way in which the accounting equation is presented. It can be seen that the two sides of the equation will have the same totals. This is because we are dealing with the same thing from two different points of view – the value of the owners' investment in the business and the value of what is owned by the owners.

Activity
1.2

What piece of useful information that is available from these three items is not directly shown by this equation? (*Hint*: you were introduced to it at the start of this section.)

Unfortunately, with this form of the accounting equation, we can no longer see at a glance what value is represented by the resources in the business. You can see this more clearly if you switch assets and capital around to produce the alternate form of the accounting equation:

$$\boxed{\text{Assets} = \text{Capital} + \text{Liabilities}}$$

This can then be replaced with words describing the resources of the business:

$$\boxed{\begin{array}{cc} \textbf{Resources: what they are} = & \textbf{Resources: who supplied them} \\ \textbf{(Assets)} & \textbf{(Capital} + \textbf{Liabilities)} \end{array}}$$

It is a fact that no matter how you present the accounting equation, the totals of both sides will *always* equal each other, and that this will *always* be true no matter how many transactions there may be. The actual assets, capital and liabilities may change, but the total of the assets will always equal the total of capital + liabilities. Or, reverting to the more common form of the accounting equation, the capital will always equal the assets of the business *minus* the liabilities.

Assets consist of property of all kinds, such as buildings, machinery, inventories of goods and motor vehicles. Other assets include debts owed by customers and the amount of money in the business's bank account.

Liabilities include amounts owed by the business for goods and services supplied to it and for expenses incurred by it that have not yet been paid for. Liabilities also include funds borrowed by the business.

Capital is often called the owner's **equity** or net worth. It comprises (i) the funds invested in the business by the owner *plus* (ii) any profits retained for use in the business *less* (iii) any share of profits paid out of the business to the owner.

Activity
1.3

What else would affect capital? (*Hint*: this item causes the value of capital to fall.)

1.10 The balance sheet and the effects of business transactions

The accounting equation is expressed in a financial report called the **balance sheet**.

Activity 1.4 Without looking back, write down the commonly used form of the accounting equation.

The balance sheet shows the financial position of an organisation *at a point in time.* In other words, it presents a snapshot of the organisation at the date for which it was prepared. The balance sheet is not the first accounting report to be prepared, nor the first that you will learn how to do, but it is a convenient place to start to consider accounting.

Let's now look at how a series of transactions affects the balance sheet.

1 The introduction of capital

On 1 May 2018, B. Blake started in business and deposited £60,000 into a bank account opened specially for the business. The balance sheet would show:

B. Blake
Balance Sheet as at 1 May 2018

	£
Assets: Cash at bank	60,000
Capital	60,000

Note how the top part of the balance sheet contains the assets and the bottom part contains the capital. This is always the way the information is presented in a balance sheet.

2 The purchase of an asset

On 3 May 2018, Blake buys a kiosk (a small shop) for £32,000 and pays for it by Internet transfer from the business bank account. The effect of this transaction on the balance sheet is that the cash at the bank is decreased and the new asset, the shop, is added:

B. Blake
Balance Sheet as at 3 May 2018

Assets	£
Shop	32,000
Cash at bank	28,000
	60,000
Capital	60,000

Note how the two parts of the balance sheet 'balance'. That is, their totals are the same. This is always the case with balance sheets, and is why they have that name.

3 The purchase of an asset and the incurring of a liability

On 6 May 2018, Blake buys some goods on time for £7,000 from D. Smith. 'On time' means that Blake has not yet paid for them, but will do so at some time in the future. The effect of this is that a new asset, **inventory**, is acquired, and a liability for the goods is created. A person to whom money is owed for goods is known as a **creditor**, and is described in the balance sheet as an **account payable**. The balance sheet becomes:

B. Blake
Balance Sheet as at 6 May 2018

Assets	£
Shop	32,000
Inventory	7,000
Cash at bank	28,000
	67,000
Less: Account payable	(7,000)
	60,000
Capital	60,000

Note how the liability (the account payable) is shown as a deduction from the assets. This is exactly the same calculation as is presented in the most common form of the accounting equation.

 Activity 1.5 Why do you think the £7,000 value for account payable is shown in brackets?

Now, let's return to our example.

4 Sale of an asset on time

On 10 May 2018, goods that cost £600 were sold on time to J. Brown for the same amount. 'On time' means that Brown will pay for them later. The effect is a reduction in the amount of goods held, i.e. inventory, and the creation of a new asset. A person who owes the business money is a **debtor**, and is described in the balance sheet as an **account receivable**. The balance sheet is now:

B. Blake
Balance Sheet as at 10 May 2018

Assets	£
Shop	32,000
Inventory	6,400
Account receivable	600
Cash at bank	28,000
	67,000
Less: Account payable	(7,000)
	60,000
Capital	60,000

5 Sale of an asset for immediate payment

On 13 May 2018, goods that cost £400 were sold to D. Daley for the same amount. Daley paid for them immediately by debit card. Here one asset, inventory, is reduced, while another asset, cash at bank, is increased. The balance sheet becomes:

B. Blake
Balance Sheet as at 13 May 2018

Assets	£
Shop	32,000
Inventory	6,000
Account receivable	600
Cash at bank	28,400
	67,000
Less: Account payable	(7,000)
	60,000
Capital	60,000

6 The payment of a liability

On 15 May 2018, Blake pays D. Smith £3,000 by Internet transfer in part payment of the amount owing. The asset of cash at bank is therefore reduced, and the liability to the creditor is also reduced. The balance sheet is now:

B. Blake
Balance Sheet as at 15 May 2018

Assets	£
Shop	32,000
Inventory	6,000
Account receivable	600
Cash at bank	25,400
	64,000
Less: Account payable	(4,000)
	60,000
Capital	60,000

Note how the total of each part of the balance sheet has not changed. The capital is still £60,000 and that is what the business is worth to the owner.

7 Collection of an asset

J. Brown, who owed Blake £600, makes a part payment of £200 by cheque on 31 May 2018. The effect is to reduce one asset, account receivable, and to increase another asset, cash at bank. The balance sheet becomes:

B. Blake
Balance Sheet as at 31 May 2018

Assets	£
Shop	32,000
Inventory	6,000
Account receivable	400
Cash at bank	25,600
	64,000
Less: Account payable	(4,000)
	60,000
Capital	60,000

1.11 Equality of the accounting equation

It can be seen that every transaction has affected two items. Sometimes it has changed two assets by reducing one and increasing the other. In other cases, the effect has been different. However, in each case other than the very first (when the business was started by the owner injecting some cash into it), no change was made to the total of either section of the balance sheet and the equality between their two totals has been maintained. The accounting equation has held true throughout the example, and it always will. The effect of each of these seven accounting transactions upon the two sections of the balance sheet is shown below:

Number of transaction as above	Assets	Capital and Liabilities	Effect on balance sheet totals
1	+	+	Each side added to equally
2	+ −		A *plus* and a *minus* both on the assets side cancelling each other out
3	+	+	Each side has equal additions
4	+ −		A *plus* and a *minus* both on the assets side cancelling each other out
5	+ −		A *plus* and a *minus* both on the assets side cancelling each other out
6	−	−	Each side has equal deductions
7	+ −		A *plus* and a *minus* both on the assets side cancelling each other out

These are not the only types of accounting transactions that can take place. Two other examples arise when

(8) the owner withdraws resources from the business for his or her own use; and where
(9) the owner pays a business expense personally.

A summary of the effect upon assets, liabilities and capital of each type of transaction you've been introduced to so far is shown below:

Example of transaction	Effect	
(1) Owner pays capital into the bank	↑ Increase asset (Bank)	↑ Increase capital
(2) Buy inventory by cheque	↓ Decrease asset (Bank)	↑ Increase asset (Inventory)
(3) Buy inventory on time	↑ Increase asset (Inventory)	↑ Increase liability (Accounts payable)
(4) Sale of inventory on time	↓ Decrease asset (Inventory)	↑ Increase asset (Accounts receivable)
(5) Sale of inventory for cash (cheque)	↓ Decrease asset (Inventory)	↑ Increase asset (Bank)
(6) Pay creditor	↓ Decrease asset (Bank)	↓ Decrease liability (Accounts payable)
(7) Debtor pays money owing by cheque	↑ Increase asset (Bank)	↓ Decrease asset (Accounts receivable)
(8) Owner takes money out of the business bank account for own use	↓ Decrease asset (Bank)	↓ Decrease capital
(9) Owner pays creditor from private money outside the firm	↓ Decrease liability (Accounts payable)	↑ Increase capital

Transactions (8) and (9) cause the totals of each part of the balance sheet to change (as did the very first, when capital was introduced to the business by the owner). When the capital changes, the totals of the two parts of the balance sheet both change.

1.12 More detailed presentation of the balance sheet

Let's now look at the balance sheet of B. Blake as at 31 May 2018, presented according to how you will learn to present the information later in this book:

B. Blake
Balance Sheet as at 31 May 2018

	£	£
Non-current assets		
Shop		32,000
Current assets		
Inventory	6,000	
Account receivable	400	
Cash at bank	25,600	
		32,000
Total assets		64,000
Less: Current liabilities		
Account payable		(4,000)
Net assets		60,000
Capital		60,000

You will have noticed in this balance sheet the terms 'non-current assets', 'current assets' and 'current liabilities'. **Chapter 15 contains a full explanation of these terms.** At this point we will simply say:

● **Non-current assets** are assets which have a long life bought with the intention to use them in the business and not with the intention to simply resell them, e.g. buildings, machinery, fixtures & fittings (e.g. shelves), motor vehicles.
● **Current assets** are assets consisting of cash, goods for resale or items having a short life (i.e. no more than a year remaining on the date of the balance sheet). For example, the amount (and so the value) of inventory goes up and down as it is bought and sold. Similarly, the amount of money owing to a business by debtors will change quickly, as the business sells more to them on time and when they pay their debts. The amount of money in the bank will also change when it is received or paid out.
● **Current liabilities** are those liabilities which have to be paid within no more than a year from the date on the balance sheet, e.g. accounts payable for goods purchased.

Don't forget that there is a Glossary of accounting terms at the back of the book.

Learning outcomes

You should now have learnt:

1 Accounting is concerned with the recording, classifying and summarising of data, and then communicating what has been learnt from it.

2 Accounting has existed for at least 10,000 years but a formal, generally accepted method of recording accounting data has only been in existence for the last 500 years.

3 It may not only be the owner of a business who will need the accounting information. It may need to be shown to others, e.g. the bank or the Inspector of Taxes.

4 Accounting information can help the owner(s) of a business to plan for the future.

5 Financial accounting is performed for the owners of a business so that they can assess its performance and financial position. Management accounting is prepared for those running a business so that they can plan and control its activities.

6 The accounting equation is: Capital = Assets − Liabilities.

7 The two sides of the accounting equation are represented by the two parts of the balance sheet.

8 The total of one part of the balance sheet should always be equal to the total of the other part.

9 Every transaction affects two items in the accounting equation. Sometimes that may involve the same item being affected twice, once positively (going up) and once negatively (going down).

10 Every transaction affects two items in the balance sheet.

Note: Generally, the values used in exhibits and exercises are relatively small amounts. You may think this wrong, that it is unrealistic, and it is, but it has been done to make your work easier. It means that you can concentrate on learning accounting rather than having to also cope with complex calculations. Constantly handling large figures does not add anything to the study of the principles of accounting. It simply wastes a lot of your time. This is especially true today because in the 'real world' most of what you are going to learn is done using computers, and they deal with all the complex mathematics for you, so you don't really need to learn that aspect at all.

Answers to activities

1.1 Owners and creditors are considered to be the most important stakeholders because they have most to lose if the business fails.

1.2 Who supplied the resources of the business.

1.3 Capital will be reduced if a business makes a loss. The loss means that assets have been reduced and capital is reduced by the same amount so as to maintain the balance in the accounting equation.

1.4 Capital = Assets − Liabilities

1.5 It is a negative number. In accounting, we *always* use brackets to indicate negative numbers.

Review questions

If you haven't already started answering them, you now have a set of graded review questions to try. 'Graded' means that they get more difficult as you go through them. Ideally, they should be done in the sequence they appear. *However, don't forget that the questions with an 'A' after the question number do not have any answers provided in this book.* Your teacher or lecturer will be able to provide you with the answers to those questions but be sure to attempt them first before asking for the answers! The answers to the other questions can be found at the back of the book.

We realise that you would like to have *all* the answers in the book. However, teachers and lecturers would not then be able to test your knowledge with questions from this book, as you would already possess the answers. It is impossible to please everyone, and the compromise reached is that of putting a large number of review questions in the book.

This means that appropriate reinforcement of what you have learnt can take place, even if you are studying on your own and have to miss out all the 'A' questions because you have no access to the answers.

Multiple choice questions. In addition to these Review Questions, there are questions relating to the material in this chapter in a bank of multiple choice questions at the end of Chapter 6. You should wait and attempt them when you reach them, not before.

1.1 Complete the gaps in the following table:

	Assets	Liabilities	Capital
	£	£	£
(a)	30,000	18,000	?
(b)	69,400	32,100	?
(c)	47,500	?	11,700
(d)	71,800	?	19,400
(e)	?	30,500	28,100
(f)	?	47,200	36,500

1.2A Complete the gaps in the following table:

	Assets	Liabilities	Capital
	£	£	£
(a)	93,000	44,000	?
(b)	?	36,200	38,900
(c)	107,300	?	41,500
(d)	125,500	77,400	?
(e)	114,700	?	33,400
(f)	?	64,600	21,300

1.3   Which of the items in the following list are liabilities and which of them are assets?

(a)   Motor vehicle
(b)   Amounts owed to us by customers
(c)   Land

(d)   Bank overdraft
(e)   Inventory of goods held for sale
(f)   Amounts owed by us to suppliers

1.4A   Classify the following items into liabilities and assets:

(a)   Computers
(b)   Buildings
(c)   Accounts payable
(d)   Inventory
(e)   Accounts receivable

(f)   Cash in bank
(g)   Bank overdraft
(h)   Loan from bank
(i)   Vans

1.5   State which of the following are wrongly classified:

Assets	Liabilities
Loan from K. Jones	Delivery van
Bank overdraft	Accounts payable
Accounts receivable	Computer equipment
Warehouse	Machinery
Office furniture	Cash in hand

1.6A   Which of the following are shown under the wrong headings?

Assets	Liabilities
Cash at bank	Bank overdraft
Fixtures and fittings	Equipment
Accounts payable	Computers
Premises	Loan from building society
Inventory	
Accounts receivable	
Capital	

1.7   J. Noakes is setting up a new business. Before selling anything, he bought a van for £8,750; a transportable market stall for £2,400; a computer for £490; and an inventory of goods for £12,300. He did not pay in full for his inventory of goods and still owes £8,200 for them. He borrowed £3,000 from L. Fox. After the events just described, and before trading starts, he has £200 cash in hand and £1,440 in the bank. Calculate the amount of his capital.

1.8A   R. Hill is starting a business. Before starting to sell anything, he bought fixtures for £3,200, a van for £4,750 and an inventory of goods for £2,340. Although he has paid in full for the fixtures and the van, he still owes £1,910 for some of the inventory. P. Harding lent him £5,000. After the above, Hill has £520 in the business bank account and £100 cash in hand. You are required to calculate his capital.

1.9 Draw up E. McNiven's balance sheet from the following information as at 31 December 2019:

	£
Capital	40,000
Accounts receivable	11,380
Motor vehicle	9,250
Accounts payable	14,700
Equipment	17,890
Inventory	15,260
Cash at bank	920

1.10A Draw up G. Cook's balance sheet as at 30 June 2019 from the following items:

	£
Capital	17,460
Equipment	9,720
Accounts payable	8,380
Inventory	6,430
Accounts receivable	9,280
Cash at bank	410

1.11 Complete the columns to show the effects of the following transactions:

	Assets	Liabilities	Capital
(a) We pay a creditor £310 by cheque.			
(b) Bought fixtures £175 paying in cash.			
(c) Bought goods on time £630.			
(d) The proprietor introduces another £1,200 cash into the business.			
(e) J. Walker lends the business £2,500 in cash.			
(f) A debtor pays us £50 in cash.			
(g) We return goods costing £90 to a supplier whose bill we had not paid.			
(h) Bought an office computer paying £610 by cheque.			

Effect upon

1.12A Complete the columns to show the effects of the following transactions:

	Assets	Liabilities	Capital
(a) Bought a van on time £8,700.			
(b) Repaid by cash a loan owed to F. Duff £10,000.			
(c) Bought goods for £1,400 paying by cheque.			
(d) The owner puts a further £4,000 cash into the business.			
(e) A debtor returns to us goods worth £150. We agree to make an allowance for them.			
(f) Bought goods on time £760.			
(g) The owner takes out £200 cash for his personal use.			
(h) We pay a creditor £1,150 by cheque.			

Effect upon

→

1.13   T. Ross has the following items in his balance sheet on 30 April 2019: Capital £29,800; Accounts payable £10,200; Fixtures £18,600; Motor vehicle £8,200; Inventory £3,900; Accounts receivable £7,600; Cash at bank £1,550; Cash in hand £150.

During the first week of May 2019:

(a)   He bought extra inventory for £850 on time.
(b)   One of the debtors paid him £500 by cheque.
(c)   He bought a computer by cheque £690.

You are asked to draw up a balance sheet as at 7 May 2019 after the above transactions have been completed.

1.14A   J. Hill has the following assets and liabilities on 30 November 2019: Accounts payable £2,800; Equipment £6,200; Motor vehicle £7,300; Inventory £8,100; Accounts receivable £4,050; Cash at bank £9,100; Cash in hand £195.

You are not given the capital amount at that date.

During the first week of December 2019:

(a)   Hill bought extra equipment on time for £110.
(b)   Hill bought extra inventory by cheque £380.
(c)   Hill paid creditors by cheque £1,150.
(d)   Debtors paid Hill £640 by cheque and £90 by cash.
(e)   Hill put an extra £1,500 into the business, £1,300 by cheque and £200 in cash.

You are to draw up a balance sheet as at 7 December 2019 after the above transactions have been completed.

Recording transactions

Learning objectives

After you have studied this chapter, you should know that:

- there are two elements to every transaction: an *Item exchanged* and a *Form of settlement*
- double entry bookkeeping requires that for each transaction, an entry is made once for the *Item exchanged;* and once for the *Form of settlement*
- the treatment of the *Item exchanged* is always the opposite of the treatment of the *Form of settlement*
- debit means 'place on the left of the account called'
- credit means 'place on the right of the account called'
- the total of the debit must always equal the total of the credit
- capital is what the owner contributes to a business
- capital does not belong to a business. It belongs to the owner of the business
- liabilities are all other items that do not belong to a business, such as loans from banks
- debtors are people who owe money to a business
- creditors are people who are owed money by a business. The owner of a business is not a creditor of the business. The owner is an investor in the business
- expenses are immediately used up but they belong to the business and are treated the same way as all other possessions
- possessions that last some time are called 'assets'
- when the *Form of settlement* is given, it is a credit
- when the *Form of settlement* is received, it is a debit
- the entry for the *Item exchanged* is always the opposite of the entry for the *Form of settlement.*
- to identify the accounts to debit and credit, you *always* focus upon the *Form of settlement*

Introduction

In this chapter, you will learn the *Principles of double entry:* how to do double entry bookkeeping. You will learn how double entry is used to record financial transactions. You will also learn how to use T-accounts, the traditional way to make such entries under the double entry system.

Part One The principles of double entry

2.1 The nature of a transaction

In Chapter 1, you saw how various events had each changed two items in the statement of financial position. These events are known as 'transactions'. Transaction involves two things: the **Item exchanged** and a **Form of settlement** that is either cash, an **IOU**, or capital. 'IOU' is usually called 'credit,' but 'IOU' is easier to learn to use at this stage of your studies. ('Capital' is what has been invested by the owner in a business.) These two things are called the *'elements of a transaction'*. If there is no *Item exchanged* (i.e. bought or sold), there is no transaction:

● If a businessman asks the price of something, but does not buy it, there is no transaction.
● If a businessman asks the price of something and then buys it, that event is a transaction.

When we enter the data relating to a **transaction** in the accounting records we need to ensure that the items that were affected by the transaction, *and only those items*, are shown as having changed. Bookkeeping is the first stage in doing so. It can take many forms, but the one that is most used is called **double entry bookkeeping**.

Activity 2.1 What do you think likely names might be for other forms of bookkeeping? (Hint: double beds and _____ beds.)

Double entry bookkeeping is therefore all about recording the financial results of transactions. Examples of transactions include a purchase of a machine, payment of an electricity bill, sale of a sandwich, and interest received from a bank for money deposited.

There is a wide range of possible transactions for any business, and we need a system of bookkeeping that is flexible enough to record any of them. We do this by having places where we record each entry. These are called **accounts**. We can add a new account whenever we want and there is no limit to the number of accounts we can have.

What we record in accounts are the two 'elements of transactions'.

2.2 The elements of a transaction

As mentioned above, in accounts we record the outcome of transactions involving two elements: the *Item exchanged,* such as a car or a computer; and the *Form of settlement,* such as cash.

So, if you buy a computer with cash, the *Item exchanged* is the computer. You need to create an account called 'computer account'. In that account, you record that you now own a computer, which means that the total value of the account has increased.

You also need an account for the *Form of settlement*, in this case 'cash'. You call that account, 'cash account'. In that account, you record that your cash has been reduced because you used some cash to become the owner of a computer.

Traditionally, each account has a left-hand side and a right-hand side. You can see one for a computer in Exhibit 2.1

Exhibit 2.1

Computer account

Activity 2.2 What do you think we call this form of account? (*Hint:* what shape do the lines make?)

The amount of each transaction is entered on one of those two sides in the account for the *Form of settlement*; and on the other side in the account for the *Item exchanged*. That is the **double entry**: one entry made in two different accounts for each transaction. When we make these entries, we describe one as a **debit** and the other as a **credit**. Let's see what these terms mean.

2.3 Debit and credit

Debit means '*place on the left of the account called*' and credit means '*place on the right of the account called*'. You can see why we just use the words 'debit' and 'credit', instead of the whole eight-word phrase each time, can't you?

These two words '*debit*' and '*credit*' are central to understanding double entry bookkeeping. Every time you record a transaction, you *debit* one account, and you *credit* another account. The amount you *debit* to the first account will always be equal to the amount you *credit* to the other account. This is why we call this form of bookkeeping, 'double entry'.

> Debit ALWAYS *equals* Credit

Activity 2.3 Why do you think debit always equals credit?

Let's now look at what guides you in making these 'double entries': the *Principles of double entry bookkeeping*.

2.4 The principles of double entry bookkeeping

When recording a transaction, you need to decide which account to *debit* and which account to *credit* for each entry. In order to do so, there are three things that are always correct:

1 a *Form of settlement* given is always a credit
2 a *Form of settlement* received is always a debit
3 the entry for the *Item exchanged* is always the opposite to the entry for the *Form of settlement*.

These are what ensure you make the correct entries *every* time.

Now that you know what an account is, what *debit* and *credit* mean, and the principles to follow, let's see what happens when we record the elements of a transaction.

> If you remember these principles, you will *always* know which account to *debit* and which account to *credit*.

2.5 Recording the elements of a transaction

The amount of each transaction is entered in the accounts of the two elements of the transaction: on one side in the account for the *Form of settlement*, and on the other side in the account for the *Item exchanged*.

So, imagine that you entered into a transaction worth £100. After the entries for the transaction have been made, the two accounts would *either* look like this:

Exhibit 2.2

Item exchanged account		Form of settlement account	
£100			£100

or like this:

Exhibit 2.3

Item exchanged account		Form of settlement account	
	£100	£100	

These are the only two possibilities. **The *Form of settlement* will tell you which of these to use:**

● If you *purchased* something for cash, you would record the entries as in Exhibit 2.2: the *Form of settlement* was given, so it must be credit; the *Item exchanged* must be debit.
● If you *sold* something for cash, you would record the entries as in Exhibit 2.3: the form of settlement was received, so it must be debit; the *Item exchanged* must be a credit.

Do you see how the *Form of settlement* guides you in how to make these entries?

> *Always* use the *Form of settlement* to guide you in what to *debit* and what to *credit*.

This is straightforward when cash is involved. And it is the same when it is not. When you purchase goods that you will pay for later, you have given the seller an IOU, i.e. a promise to pay later. So, you must credit the *Form of settlement* and debit the goods account. What account do you use to record this IOU?

2.6 When the form of settlement is an IOU

An IOU is a 'debt'. A '**debt**' is created whenever a seller agrees to wait for the payment until some time in the future. In the accounts of the seller, whenever a new debt is created, it is the *Form of Settlement* in the transaction.

Whenever a debt is repaid, it is the *Item exchanged*. This is because you pay a debt using a *Form of settlement*. Let's assume that the *Form of settlement* in both Exhibit 2.2 and Exhibit 2.3 is an IOU:

● In Exhibit 2.2 (a purchase): a *Form of settlement* has been given, so it is a credit. That is, the debt *due to the seller* is a credit.
● In the case of Exhibit 2.3 (a sale): a *Form of settlement* has been received so it is a debit. That is, the debt *due from the customer* must be a debit.

Activity 2.4 Describe the two entries in Exhibit 2.2 using 'debit' and 'credit'; and give an example of a transaction that fits this description.

2.7 Balance

Once you have made some transactions, you may want to find out how much an account is worth. For example, how much a debtor owes you, or how much you owe someone else. You do this by calculating the difference between the totals of the debits and the total of the credits entered in that account. We call that difference, the '**balance**'. In Exhibit 2.2, the *Item exchanged* account has £100 more on the debit side: it has a 'debit balance' of £100; and the *Form of settlement* account has £100 more on the credit side: it has a 'credit balance' of £100.

Let's now use the *Principles of double entry bookkeeping* to see what happens when you have a list of balances and want to know what your business is worth. We'll use an example that involves 'capital'. Capital is a *Form of settlements*.

2.8 Drawing-up a list of what a business is worth

Imagine you have been in business for a few months but you have not kept any proper records of your transactions. You have decided to end that business and start a new one by transferring everything to the new business. You now also want to start using double entry bookkeeping.

The first step is to write down a list of everything belonging to the old business and everything the old business owes. Here is the list you prepared:

Exhibit 2.4

		£
1	Cash	600
2	Cash in US dollars worth	200
3	Cash in the bank	1,200
4	Cash in the bank in euros worth	430
5	Computer	500
6	Mobile phone	240
7	Sales register	320
8	Printer	150
9	Printing supplies	40
10	Goods for sale	18,000
11	Amount due by Fred Palmer	300
12	Amount due by Winnie Woo	370
13	Loan from bank	10,000

Activity 2.5 If you now enter these items in T-accounts of the new business, what do you think the *Form of settlement* will be for each one?

You are exchanging all of these items shown in Exhibit 2.1. That is, you are giving them to the new business and it will give you something in return for each of them. In each case, the *Form of settlement* account will be one called '**capital account**'. You, the business owner, have transferred all these items from your old business into your new business. They are now all possessions of your new business. We use a capital account to record what the business owner has put into the business.

Once the business is active, making purchases and sales, we add any profits to that account, subtract any losses from it, and also subtract any items taken out of the business for the owner's own personal use. We call the balance on that account, 'capital.' It is what the business is worth to the owner on the date when the balance is calculated. In other words, it is what the owner has invested in the business at that point in time.

> 'Capital' at any point in time is equal to the amount the owner has invested in the business plus any profits, less any losses, less everything taken out of the business by the owner, such as cash or goods.

Activity 2.6

What do you think the balance on the capital account will be once you have entered each of these 13 items into the correct accounts?

> It is important to remember: it is the transactions of the business that you are recording. The business is *not* you. When you begin a business, you give it many things. It settles each of those transactions by giving you capital. The only exceptions are debts owing to someone else. When you give the new business a debt that you owe someone else, that transaction is settled by you giving the business back some of the capital it has given you. When you give back capital the business receives it and enters receipt of this *Form of settlement* as a debit.

Let's now look at how you make these 'double entries'.

2.9　Making double entries

You need to decide which account to debit and which account to credit for each entry. In order to do so, we consider the *Form of settlement*.

Activity 2.7

What is the entry to the capital account when it has decreased?
Is it a debit or a credit?

Let's see what the double entries are for the first four items you are transferring into the new business from your list in Exhibit 2.4. In each case, these things being transferred to the new business are the *Item exchanged*. You give them to the business and it settles each of these transactions using the *Form of settlement,* capital.

Exhibit 2.5

Item Exchanged	Debit	Credit
1 Cash	Cash account	Capital account
2 Cash in US dollars	Cash in US dollars account	Capital account
3 Cash in the bank	Cash in the bank account	Capital account
4 Cash in the bank in euros	Cash in the bank in euros account	Capital account

In each case, the *Form of settlement* (capital) is given to you by the business. That is why it is a credit. Do you see how the debit is always to a cash account? (You have four accounts in which 'cash' is kept: one for cash; one for cash held at your bank; one for cash in US dollars; and one for cash in euros.) These four entries are all debits because the *Form of settlement* is a credit.

What do you think the credit entry will be for items 5 to 12? Let's see:

Exhibit 2.6

Item Exchanged	Debit	Credit
5 Computer	Computer account	Capital account
6 Mobile phone	Mobile phone account	Capital account
7 Sales register	Sales register account	Capital account
8 Printer	Printer account	Capital account
9 Printing supplies	Printing supplies account	Capital account
10 Goods for sale	Goods for sale account	Capital account
11 Amount due by Fred Palmer	Amount due by Fred Palmer account	Capital account
12 Amount due by Winnie Woo	Amount due by Winnie Woo account	Capital account

Capital given is always a credit.

Activity 2.8 What does the fact that capital is credited for each of these items tell you about the debits?

Items 5 to 12 confirm to you that **any increase in something that belongs to the business is a debit.** You should remember that in accounting we call all these items that belong to the business 'assets'.

Activity 2.9 Look carefully at the wording of the debit entry for items 11 and 12. What is being debited, the amount due, or the people who owe the business these amounts? *(Hint:* these are entries for the 'item' exchanged.)

Think back to items 1 and 2 ('cash' and 'cash in US dollars'). They are both items of **cash** but they each have their own account *because they are different types of cash* – you cannot spend the US dollars in a shop unless you are in the United States, but you can spend cash that is in your local currency in any shop in your country. For this reason, you need two accounts to record these different types of cash.

Similarly, items 11 and 12 are both **debts** owed by other people that have been transferred from the old business but *they are debts of different people* so each of them must have its own account. By including the identity of the person who owes you the money in the name of the account, you know who is in debt to you. We call a person who owes you money a 'debtor'.

In Exhibit 2.7, we have entered the debt owed to us by Winnie Woo (Item 12) into her account.

Exhibit 2.7

Amount due by Winnie Woo	
£370	

You can see that the debit side of Winnie Woo's account (£370) is a higher amount than the credit side (£0). The account has a debit balance, so Winnie Woo is a debtor. **When a person's account has a debit balance, that person is a debtor.**

Activity 2.10 What do you think we call someone whose account has a credit balance?

Now let's look at the final item, Loan from bank. What does this mean? Does it mean that you have £10,000 in the bank? Or, does it mean that you owe the bank £10,000?

It means that you owe the bank £10,000. So, this is an amount your old business owes the bank. **It is not a possession of the business.** The loan is the *Item exchanged*. It is being transferred into the new business and the *Form of settlement* is *capital*, just as it was with all the other items in Exhibit 2.4. But, the business is not giving capital is exchange for the loan,. it is receiving it, so the entry for the *Form of settlement* (capital) is a debit.

And, this loan is not a possession of the business, so it is treated in the opposite way to a possession of the business. That is, it is a credit.

The double entries for item 13 therefore go in the opposite direction to those for the 12 items that did belong to the business. It has reduced your investment in the new business, so you must settle this transaction with capital. Because the business receives the *Form of settlement* (capital), it is a debit, and the entry for the *Item exchanged* is a credit.

Exhibit 2.8

Item Exchanged	Debit	Credit
13 Loan from bank	Capital account	Loan from bank account

As you learnt in Activity 2.10, we call a person or an organisation that we owe money a 'creditor.' The credit side of their account is a higher amount than the debit side. You can confirm this by looking at the 'Loan from bank' account in Exhibit 2.9: the credit side (£10,000) is higher than the debit side (£0).

Exhibit 2.9

Loan from bank account	
	£10,000

All items that do *not* belong to the business are called '**liabilities**'. These are things the business *must* pay to its *creditors*. **The only exception is capital.** It is *not* a liability because it belongs to the owners of the business and the business does not have to pay its owners back what they have invested.

So far, you have only seen a few entries in **T-accounts**. Let's now look at two of these accounts with the amounts from Exhibit 2.4 entered on the correct side and then look at what happens when we make a new transaction involving those two accounts.

2.10 Making double entries into existing accounts

Exhibit 2.10 shows you the entries for the printing supplies and the cash from Exhibit 2.4 in their T-accounts.

Exhibit 2.10

Printing supplies account	Cash account
£40	£600

Now, let's imagine that you decide you need some more printing supplies for your new business. You go to a shop and pay £50 in cash for what you need. What would the double entries be?

The *Form of settlement* is cash. It has been given, so it is a credit. The *Item exchanged* is printing supplies (e.g. toner, ink, paper, etc.). It must be the opposite: a debit.

> Debit Printing supplies account   Credit Cash account

Let's now look at those two accounts with the amount of the purchase entered.

Exhibit 2.11

Printing supplies account	Cash account	
£40	£600	£50
50		

What are the balances on these two accounts?

The balance – the difference between the total of the debits and the total of the credits – on the Printing supplies account has now increased from £40 to £90. At the same time, the balance on the Cash account has reduced from £600 to £550. The total belonging to the business has not changed. You have simply entered a transaction where printing supplies were exchanged for cash: the supplier gave them to you and you gave the supplier cash.

What would the double entries be if you now sold some of your goods? Let's see.

2.11 Recording a sale

Let's assume an old friend contacts you asking to buy some of your goods. You decide to sell him the goods at the same price as they cost you to purchase them. They cost you £60. You give him the goods and he gives you £60 in cash.

In Activity 2.11, you prepared the two T-accounts. Once you had entered the items from Exhibit 2.4 and the purchase of printing supplies for £50, they looked like this:

Goods for sale account	Cash account	
£18,000	£600	£50

The double entries for this sale transaction would be:

> Debit Cash account   Credit Goods for sale account

The *Form of settlement* (cash) has been received, so it must be debited. The *Item exchanged* ('Goods for sale') must be the opposite, so you must credit the Goods for sale account. The two accounts now contain:

Goods for sale account		Cash account	
£18,000	£60	£600	£50
		60	

Your Cash has increased and your Goods for sale have decreased. Your accounts continue 'in balance'. That is, the total of all the debits in all your accounts equals the total of all the credits in all your accounts.

 Activity 2.11 Confirm that the total of all the debit balances of the accounts listed in Exhibits 2.5 and 2.6 is the same as the total of all the credit balances. Why is this?

> Remember the Principles of double entry bookkeeping:
>
> 1 A *Form of settlement* given is always a credit.
>
> 2 A *Form of settlement* received is always a debit.
>
> 3 The entry for the *Item exchanged* is always the opposite to the entry for the *Form of settlement*.

These principles are all you need to know so that you *always* select the correct account to debit and the correct account to credit for any transaction. Apply them correctly to the *Form of settlement* and your debits and credits should always be in the correct account.

The examples above will guide you if you ever forget the principles.

 Activity 2.12 What are the double entries if you repay a loan by paying the creditor in cash?

You can also be guided by the item received. Whenever something is received that belongs to the business, it is a debit. When something received does not belong to the business, like a loan from a bank, it is always a credit. This is very useful to know when you are recording adjustments to accounts. We will do that later in this book. When recording transactions, if you always use the principles, you should always make the correct decisions on the debits and credits.

So far, we have not mentioned expenses. Let's look at how they are recorded in double entry.

2.12 Expenses and double entry

When you incur an expense, *it belongs to the business* in the same way that a computer, a machine, or a building belongs to the business. The difference is that an expense is used-up immediately whereas a computer is used for a long time. (We call possessions that you keep for some time 'assets'. We call possessions that are used-up immediately 'expenses'.)

For example, if you pay an electricity bill for £120 by cash, the *Item exchanged* is electricity. Cash was the *Form of settlement* and it was given, so must be a credit. The *Item exchanged* (the expense) must be the opposite, so you debit electricity. You will learn later that expenses are always debits.

2.13 Purchases accounts and Sales accounts

Instead of recording purchases and sales in an account for the *Item exchanged*, many businesses use accounts for purchases and accounts for sales. In that case, if you purchase something to sell in your shop, you make the entry in the 'Purchases account'. When you sell it, you make the entry in the 'Sales account'.

The purchases and the sales are kept apart. This is done because the balances on both these accounts are needed when you prepare an 'Income Statement', the report accountants produce that shows how profitable the business has been.

Purchases are possessions so, when they increase, the entry is a debit.

Sales are also possessions (that you have exchanged for money or a debt). When your possessions decrease (as they do when you make a sale), the entry is a credit.

2.14 Finally

You now know all you need to know about debits and credits. You will use this knowledge a lot during the rest of this book. If you ever get confused and cannot remember the *Principles of double entry* or how to record an entry, return to this chapter. You will soon know again how to do double entry.

Remember:

Always start by looking at the *Form of settlement*.

Remember:

When a *Form of settlement* is given, it is a credit.

Remember:

When a *Form of settlement* is received, it is a debit.

Remember:

The entry for the *Item exchanged* is always the opposite.

Remember:

The amount of the debit always equals the amount of the credit.

Part Two Some worked examples

Before showing you how a series of transactions are recorded, we'll first look at what else needs to be included when an entry is made in an account.

2.15 Completing the entry in an account

So far you have learnt how to decide which account to debit and which account to credit. You know where to enter the value of each transaction. Now, we shall add the other items that also need to be included when you make an entry:

● the date
● the name of the other account in which the transaction is being entered.

When you make your first entry in an account, you need to enter the year, month and day, plus the name of the other account involved in the transaction. Let's assume that you transferred all the items into the new business on 1 January 2019. To make the entries for Item 1 in Exhibit 2.4, you need to create an account for Cash and an account for Capital. Here is how the entries would look after you have made them.

Exhibit 2.12

Cash Account				Capital Account		
2019		£		2019		£
January 1 Capital		600		January 1 Cash		600

You only enter the year when you make the first entry on each side. So, if on the same day you used £10 of the cash to buy some stamps, the entries would be made as shown in Exhibit 2.13.

Exhibit 2.13

Cash Account			Cash Account			Stamps Account		
2019		£	2019		£	2019		£
January 1 Capital		600	January 1 Stamps		10	January 1 Cash		10

The year only appears once on each side of the account, no matter how many entries are made. Now we'll go through some worked examples.

2.16 Worked examples

1 Imagine that the owner of a new business has invested £10,000 in cash in the business on 1 August 2019. The result of this transaction is entered in the two accounts as follows. First, a debit entry is made in the Cash account. The entry includes the name of the other account involved. In this case, it is the Capital account:

Cash			
2019			£
Aug	1	Capital	10,000

Similarly, the double entry to the item in the capital account is completed by an entry in the cash account, so the word 'Cash' will appear in the capital account:

Capital

					2019				£
					Aug	1	Cash		10,000

2 A van is bought for £4,500 cash on 2 August 2019.

Van

2019				£	
Aug	2	Cash		4,500	

Cash

2019				£	2019				£
Aug	1	Capital		10,000	Aug	2	Van		4,500

3 Fixtures (e.g. shelves) are bought on time from Shop Fitters for £1,250 on 3 August 2019.

Fixtures

2019				£	
Aug	3	Shop Fitters		1,250	

Shop Fitters

					2019				£
					Aug	3	Fixtures		1,250

Note how a separate account is maintained for each person or organisation to whom you owe money. Each of these creditor accounts is known as an 'account payable'.

4 Paid the amount owing to Shop Fitters in cash on 17 August 2019.

Shop Fitters

2019				£	2019				£
Aug	17	Cash		1,250	Aug	3	Fixtures		1,250

Cash

2019				£	2019				£
Aug	1	Capital		10,000	Aug	2	Van		4,500
						17	Shop Fitters		1,250

Combining all four of these transactions, the accounts now contain:

Cash

2019				£	2019				£
Aug	1	Capital		10,000	Aug	2	Van		4,500
						17	Shop Fitters		1,250

Capital

				2019				£
				Aug	1		Cash	10,000

Van

2019			£					
Aug	2	Cash	4,500					

Shop Fitters

2019			£	2019				£
Aug	17	Cash	1,250	Aug	3		Fixtures	1,250

Fixtures

2019			£					
Aug	3	Shop Fitters	1,250					

Note how you enter each transaction in an account in date order and how, once you open an account (e.g. Shop Fitters), you continue to make entries in it rather than opening a new account for every entry.

Before you read further, work through Review Questions 2.10 and 2.11A.

2.17 A further worked example

Have you noticed how each column of figures is headed by a '£' sign? This is important. You always need to indicate what the figures represent. In this case, it is pounds; in other cases you will meet during this book, the figures may be thousands of pounds (represented by '£000') or they could be in a different currency altogether. **Always include appropriate column headings.**

Let's now go carefully through the following example. Make certain you can understand every entry and, if you have any problems, reread Part One of this chapter until you are confident that you know and understand what you are doing.

First, here is a table showing a series of transactions of a new business and the double entry action to take:

Transactions			Debit	Credit
2019 May	1	Started a household machines business putting £25,000 into a bank account.	Bank account	Capital account
	3	Bought equipment on time from House Supplies £12,000.	Equipment account	House Supplies account
	4	Withdrew £150 cash from the bank and placed it in the cash box.	Cash account	Bank account

		Transactions	Debit	Credit
	7	Bought a van for £6,800 and paid by Internet transfer from the bank account	Van account	Bank account
	10	Sold some equipment that was not needed at cost of £1,100 on time to J. Rose	J. Rose account	Equipment account
	21	Returned some of the equipment costing £2,300 to House Supplies	House Supplies account	Equipment account
	23	J. Rose pays the amount owing of £1,100 by cheque	Bank account	J. Rose account
	28	Bought another van for £4,300 paying by cheque.	Van account	Bank account
	31	Paid £9,700 to House Supplies by Internet transfer from the bank account.	House Supplies	Bank account

You may find it worthwhile trying to enter all these transactions in T-accounts before reading any further. You will need to know that, similarly to accounts payable (i.e. accounts of creditors), a separate account receivable (i.e. accounts of debtors) is kept for each debtor. You will need accounts for Bank, Cash, Capital, Equipment, Vans, House Supplies, and J. Rose.

In T-account form this is shown below:

Bank

2019			£	2019			£
May	1	Capital	25,000	May	4	Cash	150
	28	J. Rose	1,100		7	Van	6,800
					30	Van	4,300
					31	House Supplies	9,700

Cash

2019			£				
May	4	Bank	150				

Capital

				2019			£
				May	1	Bank	25,000

Equipment

2019			£	2019			£
May	3	House Supplies	12,000	May	10	J. Rose	1,100
					21	House Supplies	2,300

Vans

2019			£	
May	7	Bank	6,800	
	30	Bank	4,300	

House Supplies

2019			£	2019			£
May	21	Equipment	2,300	May	3	Equipment	12,000
	31	Bank	9,700				

J. Rose

2019			£	2019			£
May	10	Equipment	1,100	May	28	Bank	1,100

If you tried to do this before looking at the answer, be sure you understand any mistakes you made before going on.

2.18 Abbreviation of 'limited'

In this book, when we come across transactions with limited companies the letters 'Ltd' are used as the abbreviation for 'Limited Company'. So, if you see that the name of a business is 'W. Jones Ltd', it is a limited company. In our accounting books, transactions with W. Jones Ltd will be entered in the same way as for any other customer or supplier. It will be seen later that some limited companies use plc (which stands for 'public limited company') instead of Ltd.

2.19 Value added tax (VAT)

You may have noticed that VAT has not been mentioned in the examples covered so far. This is deliberate, so you are not confused as you learn the basic principles of accounting. In Chapter 13, you will be introduced to VAT and shown how to make the entries relating to it.

2.20 The mystery of making double entries

Double entry bookkeeping appears very simple: for every debit entry there is an equal credit entry. However, students often find that they cannot decide which account to debit and which account to credit. If you have this problem, you are not alone – virtually everyone struggles with this from time to time. But, you don't need to find this difficult.

> If you focus upon the *Form of settlement* and remember that when it is given it is a credit and when it is received it is a debit you'll get it right, time after time.

This approach was first proposed in 1494 by an Italian friar and teacher called Luca Pacioli. He did so in the first ever printed book to contain a detailed description of double entry bookkeeping. In his book, he describes double entry from three perspectives: capital of the owner; cash; and obligations (i.e. debt). All transactions involve at least one of these. That is what to focus upon when you are deciding which account to debit and which account to credit.

Learning outcomes

You should now have learnt that:

1 There are two elements to every transaction: an *Item exchanged* and a *Form of settlement*.

2 Double entry bookkeeping requires that for each transaction, an entry is made once for the *Item exchanged*; and once for the *Form of settlement*.

3 The treatment of the *Item exchanged* is always the opposite of the treatment of the *Form of settlement*.

4 Debit means 'place on the left of the account called'.

5 Credit means 'place on the right of the account called'.

6 The total of the debit must always equal the total of the credit.

7 Capital is what the owner contributes to a business.

8 Capital does not belong to a business. It belongs to the owner of the business.

9 Liabilities are all other items that do not belong to a business, such as loans from banks.

10 Expenses are immediately used-up but they belong to the business and are treated the same way as all other possessions.

11 Possessions that last some time are called 'assets'.

12 Debtors (accounts receivable) are people or organisations that owe money to a business.

13 Creditors (accounts payable) are people or organisations that are owed money by a business. The owner of a business is *not* a creditor of the business. The owner is an investor in the business.

14 When the *Form of settlement* is given, it is a credit.

15 When the *Form of settlement* is received, it is a debit.

16 The entry for the *Item exchanged* is always the opposite of the entry for the *Form of settlement*.

17 To identify the accounts to debit and credit, you *always* focus upon the *Form of settlement*: identify whether it is a debit or a credit; the *Item exchanged* will be the opposite.

Answers to activities

2.1 Other forms of bookkeeping include 'single entry bookkeeping' and 'triple entry bookkeeping'. You will be told about single entry bookkeeping soon. Triple entry bookkeeping was a technique recommended a few years ago that records more information than double entry bookkeeping. It did not catch on, accountants preferring to stick with what they knew.

2.2 This is known as a 'T-account'.

2.3 Each transaction you record involves two things, the *Item exchanged* and the *Form of settlement*. They have the same value because they are the two elements involved in the transaction. The amount debited will, therefore, always equal the amount credited.

2.4 Debit *Item exchanged* account £100. Credit *Form of settlement* account £100. An example would be the purchase of an external drive for a laptop computer, paid in cash, but many, many other items could have been exchanged. Instead of cash, another *Form of settlement* could be involved, such as doing so using an IOU.

2.5 The *Form of settlement* is 'capital'. These items all belong to you and you are now transferring them into your new business using double entry. When you do this, they become possessions of the business. The business pays for them by giving you capital. We call your account, the 'capital account'. Your 'capital' does not belong to the business. It belongs to you. So, every time you record one of these items, you are going to credit your Capital account. The capital account tells you how much you have invested in the business.

2.6 £12,350. You have added 12 items belonging to the business totalling £22,350 and one item worth £10,000 that is owed by the business. The balance on the capital account is therefore £22,350 minus £10,000 = £12,350. This is what your business is worth.

2.7 It is a debit. Your capital account decreases if you make a loss. It also decreases if you withdraw resources (cash or goods, for example) from the business for your own use. In Exhibit 2.4, you have transferred a loan you received from the bank to the business. This also reduces your investment in the business (see Activity 2.6) and so that item was entered as a debit to the capital account. Capital is a *Form of settlement*. It has been received from you when you gave the business your debt owing to the bank. By giving this capital back to the business, you compensated it for the debit it took over from you.

2.8 Whenever capital increases, the *Item exchanged* is debited. So, all items belonging to a business are debited when they increase, not just cash. The item exchanged now belongs to the business. This tells you that when a business receives something that belongs to it that it can use in the business, it will be a debit.

2.9 It is the amount due. We call this a 'debt'.

2.10 A 'creditor'.

2.11

Cash account	
£600	£50

Cash in US dollars account	
£200	

Cash in the bank account	
£1,200	

Cash in the bank in euros account	
£430	

Computer account	
£500	

Mobile phone account	
£240	

Sales register account	
£320	

Printer account	
£150	

Printing supplies account	
£40	
50	

Goods for sale account	
£18,000	

Amount due by Fred Palmer account	
£300	

Amount due by Winnie Woo account	
£370	

Loan from bank account		Capital account	
	£10,000	£10,000	£600
			200
			1,200
			430
			500
			240
			320
			150
			40
			18,000
			300
			370

£22,350. Yes. The total of the debit balances is the same as the total of the credit balances because each transaction is entered twice, once as a debit and once as a credit.

2.12 Debit loan from creditor account; credit cash account.

Review questions

2.1 Imagine you have been in business for a few months but you have not kept any proper records of your transactions. You have decided to end that business and start a new one by transferring everything to the new business. You now also want to start using double entry bookkeeping.

		£
1	Cash	400
2	Cash in US dollars worth	280
3	Cash in the bank	900
4	Cash in the bank in Euros worth	350
5	Computer	710
6	Mobile phone	590
7	Office furniture	840
8	Printer	160
9	Delivery van	2,950
10	Goods for sale	12,300
11	Amount due from J. Gidman	560
12	Amount due from K. Bailey	230
13	Loan from bank	6,000

The first step is to write down a list of everything belonging to the old business and everything the old business owes. Here is the list you prepared:

Required:

What is the debit and credit entry for each of these items? (Ignore the amounts.)

→

1	Cash	Debit	account	Credit	account
2	Cash in US dollars worth	Debit	account	Credit	account
3	Cash in the bank	Debit	account	Credit	account
4	Cash in the bank in euros worth	Debit	account	Credit	account
5	Computer	Debit	account	Credit	account
6	Mobile phone	Debit	account	Credit	account
7	Office furniture	Debit	account	Credit	account
8	Printer	Debit	account	Credit	account
9	Delivery van	Debit	account	Credit	account
10	Goods for sale	Debit	account	Credit	account
11	Amount due from J. Gidman	Debit	account	Credit	account
12	Amount due from K. Bailey	Debit	account	Credit	account
13	Loan from bank	Debit	account	Credit	account

2.2 Make the entries in the T-accounts for the items in question 2.1

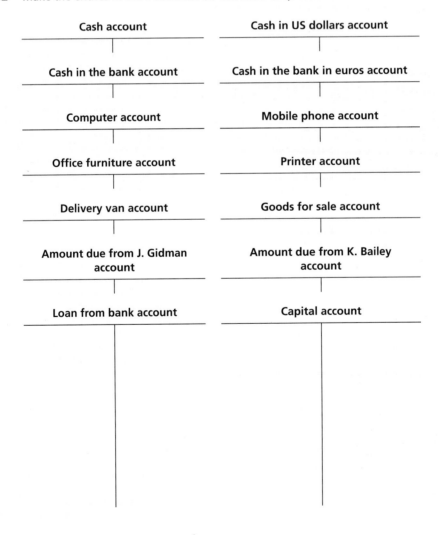

2.3   What are the two elements of every transaction?

2.4   If a customer pays you the amount she owes in cash, what is the item exchanged?

2.5   If you use cash to pay a supplier of goods the amount you owe him for goods you purchased two months ago, what is the item exchanged?

2.6   If you obtain a loan of £5,000 from a bank, what is the item exchanged?

2.7   What is the form of settlement in each of questions 2.4, 2.5 and 2.6?

2.8   What are the principles of double entry bookkeeping?

2.9   What is the debit entry and the credit entry in each of questions 2.4, 2.5 and 2.6?

2.10   Complete the following table:

	Account to be debited	Account to be credited
(a) Bought laptop computer on time from Timeless Ltd.		
(b) The proprietor paid a creditor, B. Burt, from his private funds.		
(c) A debtor, T. Robb, paid us by cheque.		
(d) Repaid part of loan from I. Simms in cash.		
(e) Returned the computer to Timeless Ltd.		
(f) A debtor, P. Bell, pays us by cheque.		
(g) Bought van on time from Tangle Motors.		

2.11A   Complete the following table:

	Account to be debited	Account to be credited
(a) Bought trailer for cash.		
(b) Paid creditor, J. Tough, by cheque.		
(c) Repaid W. Small's loan by cash.		
(d) Sold trailer for cash.		
(e) Bought office equipment on time from Dexter Ltd. It will be paid later.		
(f) A debtor, T. Walls, pays us by cash.		
(g) A debtor, L. Tait, pays us by cheque.		
(h) Proprietor puts a further amount into the business by cheque.		
(i) A loan of £650 in cash is received from F. Burns.		
(j) Paid a creditor, J. Fife, by cash.		

→

2.12 Write up the asset, liability and capital accounts to record the following transactions in the records of B. Spector's business:

July   1   Started business by putting £15,000 of his own money into a business bank account.
        2   Bought office furniture by Internet transfer from bank account £2,800.
        3   Bought computer equipment £1,260 on time from TVC Ltd.
        5   Bought a car paying by cheque £4,950.
        8   Sold some of the office furniture – original cost £750 – for £750 on time to Jevons & Co.
      15   Paid the amount owing to TVC Ltd £1,260 by Internet transfer from bank account.
      23   Received the amount due from Jevons & Co £750 by cheque.
      31   Bought machinery using the business's debit card £710.

2.13 You are required to open the asset and liability and capital accounts and record the following transactions for June in the records of P. Bernard:

June   1   Started business with £17,500 in cash.
        2   Paid £9,400 of the opening cash into a bank account for the business.
        5   Bought office furniture on time from Dream Ltd for £2,100.
        8   Bought a van paying by Internet transfer from the bank account £5,250.
      12   Bought equipment from Pearce & Sons on time £2,300.
      18   Returned faulty office furniture costing £260 to Dream Ltd.
      25   Sold some of the equipment for £200 cash (its original cost).
      26   Paid amount owing to Dream Ltd £1,840 by Internet transfer from the bank account.
      28   Took £130 out of the bank and added to cash.
      30   F. Brown lent us £4.000 – sending us the money by Internet transfer.

2.14A Write up the asset, capital and liability accounts in the books of D. Gough to record the following transactions:

2019
June   1   Started business with £16,000 in the bank.
        2   Bought van paying by cheque £6,400.
        5   Bought office fixtures £900 on time from Old Ltd.
        8   Bought van on time from Carton Cars Ltd £7,100.
      12   Took £180 out of the bank and put it into the cash till.
      15   Bought office fixtures paying by cash £120.
      19   Paid Carton Cars Ltd by Internet transfer from the bank account.
      21   A loan of £500 cash is received from B. Berry.
      25   Paid £400 of the cash in hand into the bank account.
      30   Bought more office fixtures paying with the business debit card £480.

2.15A   Write up the accounts to record the following transactions:

May   1   Started business with £1,500 cash and £18,000 in the bank.
2   Received a loan of £4,000 from T. Fox by cheque.
3   Bought a computer for cash £1,200.
5   Bought display stands on time from Drop Ltd £840.
8   Took £400 out of the bank and put it in the cash till.
15   Repaid part of Fox's loan using the business debit card £1,000.
17   Paid amount owing to Drop Ltd £840 by Internet transfer from the bank account.
24   Repaid part of Fox's loan by cash £500.
31   Bought a colour laser printer on time from P. Blake for £400.

Inventory

Learning objectives

After you have studied this chapter, you should be able to:

- explain why it is inappropriate to use an inventory account to record increases and decreases in inventory
- describe the two causes of inventory increasing
- describe the two causes of inventory decreasing
- explain the difference between a purchase account and a returns inwards account
- explain the difference between a sales account and a returns outwards account
- explain how to record increases and decreases of inventory in the appropriate accounts
- explain the meanings of the terms 'purchases' and 'sales' as used in accounting
- explain what is meant when the term 'on time' is used to describe a purchase or a sale
- explain the differences in recording purchases on time as compared to recording purchases that are paid for immediately in cash
- explain the differences in recording sales on time as compared to recording sales that are paid for immediately in cash

Introduction

In this chapter, you will learn how to record movements in inventory in the appropriate ledger accounts and how to record purchases and sales on time, as opposed to purchases and sales for cash.

3.1 Inventory movements

In the examples in Section 1.10 of Chapter 1, inventory was sold at the same price at which it was bought. When this happens and an inventory account is used rather than having separate accounts for purchases and sales (refer back to Section 2.12 if this is unclear), the difference between the two sides of the inventory account represents the cost of the goods unsold at that date. This is, of course, extremely unusual. In fact, any new business selling its inventory at 'cost' wouldn't last long. Businesses need to make profits to survive, as many 'dot.com' internet companies discovered a few years ago when their bubble burst and all the losses they had been making took effect.

Activity 3.1

Let's think about the double entry implications if all sales were at cost price. Fill in the blanks in the following:

As we did in Chapter 1, it would be possible to have an inventory account with goods purchased being _____ to the inventory account (as purchases represent _____ in the asset, inventory) and goods sold being _____ to it (as sales represent _____ in the possession, inventory).

At face value, maintaining an inventory account on this basis would serve no useful purpose. However, as pointed out by the distinguished scholar and accounting historian, G.N. Stoner, this 'early perpetual inventory records' system served a very useful purpose: it reveals the basic profit to date on each item of inventory once all the units of the item have been sold – a very useful piece of information for the managers of a business, which can be extended to be even more useful if the number of units of inventory involved in each transaction is also noted in the account.

Activity 3.2

How does adding the units to the entry in the account result in more useful information?

Normally, however, goods and services are sold at above cost price, so that the selling price includes elements of **profit**. When goods and services are sold for less than their cost, the difference is a **loss**.

Because businesses usually sell goods for more than their cost, the difference between the two sides of the inventory account would not represent the cost of the unsold goods. It would represent the cost of what remained *less* the profit earned on the goods that have been sold.

However, when preparing the financial statements of a business, we want the overall picture. We do not wish to know the profit on each type of good of service we have sold. (That is something management accountants would be involved in calculating so that the managers of the business know how profitable each item sold is. That topic is presented in Chapter 42.)

Thus, when preparing the financial statements of a business, we seek to identify the overall profit, on all items sold. Consequently, rather than using the 'early perpetual inventory records' system, many businesses use what is known as the 'periodic inventory valuation' system. Under this approach, we subdivide the way inventory is reported into several accounts, each one showing a movement of inventory. As you will see, under this approach one account is used for all purchases of goods for resale and another account is used for all sales of those goods.

Firstly, we must distinguish between transactions that cause inventory to increase and those that cause it to decrease. Let's deal with each of these in turn.

1 **Increase in inventory.** This can be due to one of two causes:

   (*a*) The purchase of additional goods.

   (*b*) The return in to the business of goods previously sold – there are many reasons why this may happen. For example, they may have been the wrong type not required or faulty.

To distinguish the two causes of an increase in inventory, two accounts are opened:

   (*i*) **a Purchases account** – in which purchases of goods are entered; and

   (*ii*) **a Returns Inwards account** – in which goods being returned into the business are entered. (Another name for this account is the **Sales Returns account.**)

We then *debit* the appropriate one of these two accounts.

2 **Decrease in inventory.** Ignoring things like wastage and theft, this can be due to one of two causes:

(a) The sale of goods.
(b) Goods previously bought by the business now being returned to the supplier.

Once again, in order to distinguish the two causes of a decrease in inventory, two accounts are opened:

(i) **a Sales account** – in which sales of goods are entered; and
(ii) **a Returns Outwards account** – in which goods being returned out to a supplier are entered. (This is also known as the **Purchases Returns account**.)

We then *credit* the account from these two alternatives that is the appropriate one to use in the context of what caused the inventory to decrease.

As inventory is a possession (and an asset), and these four accounts are all connected with this asset, the double entries are those used for possessions.

Activity 3.3 If assets are all possessions, what are the double entries for assets?

Accounts	To record	Entry in the account
Assets	an increase a decrease	_____ _____

Let's now look at some inventory entries in the following sections. We'll use the *Principles of double entry* to guide us.

3.2 Purchase of inventory to be paid for later

On 1 August 2019, goods for resale costing £165 are bought on time from D. Henry. **(Remember: when something is bought or sold 'on time' it means that it will be paid for later.)** First, the two elements of the transaction must be considered so that the bookkeeping entries can be made: the *Item exchanged* and the *Form of settlement*.

1 The *Form of settlement* is an IOU. It has been given, so it is a credit. The IOU is a debt owed to D. Henry, so it goes in that account.
2 The *Item exchanged* is goods for resale. It is the opposite of the *Form of settlement*. It is a debit. Goods for resale received are purchases, so the entry goes in that account.

These two entries appear in the T-accounts as:

Purchases

2019 Aug 1 D. Henry	£ 165	

D. Henry

	2019 Aug 1 Purchases	£ 165

Note that these entries are identical to those you would make if you were using an account for the goods rather than a purchases account. (If an account for the goods were being used, the name of the goods would replace 'Purchases'.)

3.3 Purchases of inventory for cash

On 2 August 2019, goods costing £310 are bought, cash being paid for them immediately at the time of purchase.

1 This time the *Form of settlement* is cash. It has been given, so it is a credit.
2 As before the *Item exchanged* is goods for resale. The movement of inventory is the result of a 'purchase', so the purchases account is used. The entry is the opposite of the entry for the *Form of settlement*, so it is a debit.

Purchases

2019	£	
Aug 2 Cash	310	

Cash

	2019	£
	Aug 2 Purchases	310

3.4 Sales of inventory on time

On 3 August 2019, goods were sold on time for £375 to J. Lee.

1 The *Form of settlement* is an IOU. It has been received, so it is a debit. The IOU is owed by J. Lee, so it goes in that account.
2 The *Item exchanged* is goods for resale. The movement of inventory is the result of a 'sale', so the sales account is used. The entry is the opposite of the entry for the *Form of settlement*, so it is a credit.

Sales

	2019	£
	Aug 3 J. Lee	375

J. Lee

2019	£	
Aug 3 Sales	375	

3.5 Sales of inventory for cash

On 4 August 2019, goods are sold for £55, cash being received immediately at the time of sale.

1 This time the *Form of settlement* is cash. It has been received, so it is a debit.
2 As before the *Item exchanged* is goods for resale. The movement of inventory is a 'sale', so the sales account is used. The entry is the opposite of the entry for the *Form of settlement*, so it is a credit.

Sales

				£
		2019		
		Aug 4 Cash		55

Cash

2019		£		
Aug 4 Sales		55		

So far, so good. Apart from replacing the account in the name of the goods with the purchases account when inventory increases and the sales account when it decreases, you've done nothing different in your entries to the accounts compared with what you learnt in Chapters 1 and 2.

> **Go back to Chapters 1 and 2, and refresh your understanding of account entries.**

Now let's look at the other inventory-related transactions that cause inventory to increase and decrease – returns inwards (sales that are being returned) and returns outwards (purchases that are being returned to the supplier).

3.6 Returns inwards

On 5 August 2019, goods which had been previously sold to F. Lowe for £29 are now returned *to the business*. This could be for various reasons such as:

● you sent goods of the wrong size, the wrong colour or the wrong model;
● the goods may have been damaged in transit;
● the goods are of poor quality.

As shown below, the account we use to record the return of the goods is the 'Returns inwards account':

1 The *Form of settlement* is an IOU. In this case, it is part of the debt owed by F. Lowe. As the IOU bas been given to F. Lowe (to reduce her debt to the business), it is a credit in the account of F. Lowe.
2 The *Item exchanged* is goods for resale. The movement in inventory is that of a 'returns inwards', so it is made to that account. It is the opposite of the entry for the *Form of settlement*, so it is a debit.

Returns inwards

2019		£		
Aug 5 F. Lowe		29		

F. Lowe

				£
		2019		
		Aug 5 Returns inwards		29

(Remember, another name for the Returns Inwards account is the 'Sales Returns account'.)

3.7 Returns outwards

On 6 August 2019, goods previously bought for £96 are returned *by the business* to K. Howe.

1 The *Form of settlement* is an IOU. In this case, it is part of the debt owed to K. Howe. As the IOU was received from K. Howe it is a debit in the account of K. Howe.
2 The *Item exchanged* is goods for resale. The movement in inventory is that of a 'returns outwards', so it is made to that account. It is the opposite to the entry for the *Form of settlement*, so it is a credit.

Returns outwards

		2019		£
		Aug 6 K. Howe		96

K. Howe

2019		£		
Aug 6 Returns outwards		96		

(Remember, another name for the Returns Outwards account is the 'Purchases Returns account'.)

You'll have seen how using the *Principles of double entry* made the selection of the accounts to debit and credit very easy. You only had to decide what to do with the account of the *Form of settlement*. The second part of the double entry is always the opposite of the first so, if the account of the *Form of settlement* is a debit, the account of the *Item exchanged* is a credit.

You may now be thinking this is all very straightforward. Check to see if that's the case by looking at two review questions. Once you've done that, I'll show you a worked example.

Before you read further, work through Review Questions 3.1 and 3.2.

3.8 A worked example

2020
May	1	Bought goods on time £220 from D. Small.
	2	Bought goods on time £410 from A. Lyon & Son.
	5	Sold goods on time to D. Hughes for £60.
	6	Sold goods on time to M. Spencer for £45.
	10	Returned goods £15 to D. Small.
	11	Goods sold for cash £210.
	12	Goods bought for cash £150.
	19	M. Spencer returned £16 goods to us.
	21	Goods sold for cash £175.
	22	Paid cash to D. Small £205.
	30	D. Hughes paid the amount owing by him £60 in cash.
	31	Bought goods on time £214 from A. Lyon & Son.

You may find it worthwhile trying to enter all these transactions in T-accounts before reading any further. You will need the following accounts: Purchases, Sales, Returns Outwards, Returns Inwards, D. Small, A. Lyon & Son, D. Hughes, M. Spencer and Cash.

Here are the entries in the T-accounts:

Purchases

2020			£		
May	1	D. Small	220		
	2	A. Lyon & Son	410		
	12	Cash	150		
	31	A. Lyon & Son	214		

Sales

				2020			£
				May	5	D. Hughes	60
					6	M. Spencer	45
					11	Cash	210
					21	Cash	175

Returns outwards

				2020			£
				May	10	D. Small	15

Returns inwards

2020			£		
May	19	M. Spencer	16		

D. Small

2020			£	2020			£
May	10	Returns outwards	15	May	1	Purchases	220
	22	Cash	205				

A. Lyon & Son

				2020			£
				May	2	Purchases	410
					31	Purchases	214

D. Hughes

2020			£	2020			£
May	5	Sales	60	May	30	Cash	60

M. Spencer

2020			£	2020			£
May	6	Sales	45	May	19	Returns inwards	16

Cash

2020			£	2020			£
May	11	Sales	210	May	12	Purchases	150
	21	Sales	175		22	D. Small	205
	30	D. Hughes	60				

Did you get this right? Be sure you understand any mistakes you made before going on.

3.9 Special meaning of 'sales' and 'purchases'

You need to remember that 'sales' and 'purchases' have a special meaning in accounting when compared to ordinary language usage.

Purchases in accounting means the *purchase of those goods which the business buys with the sole intention of selling.* (i.e. goods for resale). Obviously, sometimes the goods are altered, added to, or used in the manufacture of something else, but it is the element of resale that is important. Thus, to a business that deals in computers, computers are treated as purchases. To most businesses, they are not. They are treated as assets *because* they are bought to be kept.

Thus, if something is bought *that the business does not intend to sell*, such as a van, it *cannot* be called a 'purchase', even though in ordinary language you would say that a van has been purchased. The van was bought to be used and *not* for resale. You *must* use an account for the van for any entries, *not* the purchases account.

Similarly, **sales** means the *sale of those goods in which the business normally deals and which were bought with the sole intention of resale.* The word 'sales' must never be given to the disposal of other items, such as vans or buildings that were purchased to be used and *not* to be sold.

If we did not keep to these meanings, we would find it very difficult to identify which of the items in the purchases and sales accounts were inventory and which were assets that had been bought to be kept and then sold once they were no longer of use to the business.

Learning outcomes

You should now have learnt:

1 That it is *not* appropriate to use an inventory account to record increases and decreases in inventory because inventory is normally sold at a price greater than its cost.

2 That inventory increases either because some inventory has been purchased or because inventory that was sold has been returned by the buyer.

3 That inventory decreases either because some inventory has been sold or because inventory previously purchased has been returned to the supplier.

4 That a purchase account is used to record purchases of inventory (as debit entries in the account) and that a returns inwards account is used to record inventory returned by customers (as debit entries in the account).

5 That a sales account is used to record sales of inventory (as credit entries in the account) and that a returns outwards account is used to record inventory returned to suppliers (as credit entries in the account).

6 How to record increases and decreases of inventory in the appropriate accounts.

7 When an item is not paid for at the time when it is purchased or sold, we can say that it was purchased (or sold) 'on time'.

8 That in accounting, the term 'purchases' refers to purchases of inventory. Acquisitions of any other assets, such as vans, equipment and buildings, are *never* described as purchases.

9 That in accounting, the term 'sales' refers to sales of inventory. Disposals of any other assets, such as vans, equipment and buildings, are *never* described as sales.

10 That purchases for cash are *never* entered in the supplier's account.

11 That purchases on time are *always* entered in the supplier's (creditor's) account.

12 That sales for cash are *never* entered in the customer's account.

13 That sales on time are *always* entered in the customer's (debtor's) account.

Answers to activities

3.1 As we did in Chapter 1, it would be possible to have an inventory account with goods purchased being DEBITED to the inventory account (as purchases represent AN INCREASE in the possession, inventory) and goods sold being CREDITED to it (as sales represent A DECREASE in the possession, inventory).

3.2 If the inventory account shows a debit of £100 and two credit entries totalling £120, the basic profit so far on the goods is £20. If there are no units left, the figure of £20 represents the basic profit earned from that good – a 20 per cent profit.

Assume that the debit entry includes a note that 5 units were purchased, and the credit entries include notes indicating that 1 unit was sold for £40 and then 2 units were sold for £80. Overall basic profit would still be £20 but there are still 2 units in inventory.

Managers know a profit has already been made on the item. They may decide to sell off the remaining units at a lower price, or to increase the selling price, or to do nothing to the selling price. The point is that they have the information in the inventory account with which to make such a decision.

An extra column could be added to each side of the account in order to do this, and this was often done during the 300 or so years when this method of recording inventory was widely used. It is no longer used in financial accounting.

3.3

Accounts	To record	Entry in the account
Assets	an increase	Debit
	a decrease	Credit

Review questions

3.1 Complete the following table:

		Account to be debited	Account to be credited
(1)	Goods sold for cash.		
(2)	Vehicles bought on time from F. Smith.		
(3)	Computer sold for cash.		
(4)	Goods sold on time to J. Lilly.		
(5)	Goods purchased by us returned to supplier, M. Peel.		
(6)	Goods bought on time from F. Day.		
(7)	Goods sold, a cheque being received immediately.		
(8)	Goods we returned to W. Brown.		
(9)	Goods sold returned to us by customer, I. Gray.		
(10)	Goods bought on time from T. Gow.		

3.2A Complete the following table for a business that buys and sells cleaning products:

		Account to be debited	Account to be credited
(a)	Goods bought on time from B. Cowan.		
(b)	Goods returned to us by L. Keith.		
(c)	Filing cabinets returned to C. Riddle Ltd.		
(d)	Goods bought for cash.		
(e)	Lorry bought on time from M. Davis Ltd.		
(f)	Goods returned by us to J. Hicks.		
(g)	N. Peters paid us his account by cheque.		
(h)	Goods bought by cheque.		
(i)	We paid creditor, F. Toms, by cheque.		
(j)	Goods sold on time to S. Mulligan.		

3.3 You are to write up the following in the books:

2019
July 1 Started in business with £3,800 cash.
3 Bought goods for cash £480.
7 Bought goods on time £1,200 from J. Gill.
10 Sold goods for cash £172.
14 Returned goods to J. Gill £240.
18 Bought goods on time £1,460 from F. Genesis.
21 Returned goods to F. Genesis £104.
24 Sold goods to A. Prince £292 on time.
25 Paid J. Gill's account by cash £960.
31 A. Prince paid us his account in cash £292.

3.4A Enter the following transactions in the appropriate accounts:

2019
Aug 1 Started in business with £7,400 cash.
2 Paid £7,000 of the opening cash into the bank.
4 Bought goods on time £410 from J. Watson.
5 Bought a van by cheque £4,920.
7 Bought goods for cash £362.
10 Sold goods on time £218 to L. Less.
12 Returned goods to J. Watson £42.
19 Sold goods for cash £54.
22 Bought fixtures on time from Firelighters Ltd £820.
24 F. Holmes lent us £1,500 paying us the money by cheque.
29 We paid J. Watson his account by cheque £368.
31 We paid Firelighters Ltd by cheque £820.

→

3.5   Enter the following transactions in the accounts of L. Linda:

July   1   Started in business with £20,000 in the bank.
2   D. Rupert lent us £5,000 in cash.
3   Bought goods on time from B. Brown £1,530 and I. Jess £4,162.
4   Sold goods for cash £1,910.
6   Took £200 of the cash and paid it into the bank.
8   Sold goods on time to H. Rise £1,530.
10   Sold goods on time to P. Taylor £341.
11   Bought goods on time from B. Brown £560.
12   H. Rise returned goods to us £65.
14   Sold goods on time to G. Farm £535 and R. Sim £262.
15   We returned goods to B. Brown £94.
17   Bought van on time from Aberdeen Cars Ltd £9,100.
18   Bought office furniture on time from J. Winter Ltd £1,800.
19   We returned goods to I. Jess £130.
20   Bought goods for cash £770.
24   Goods sold for cash £110.
25   Paid money owing to B. Brown by cheque £1,924.
26   Goods returned to us by G. Farm £34.
27   Returned some of office furniture costing £180 to J. Winter Ltd.
28   L. Linda put a further £2,500 into the business in the form of cash.
29   Paid Aberdeen Cars Ltd £9,100 by cheque.
31   Bought office furniture for cash £365.

3.6A   Enter the following transactions in the accounts:

2020
May   1   Started in business with £18,000 in the bank.
2   Bought goods on time from B. Hind £1,455.
3   Bought goods on time from G. Smart £472.
5   Sold goods for cash £210.
6   We returned goods to B. Hind £82.
8   Bought goods on time from G. Smart £370.
10   Sold goods on time to P. Syme £483.
12   Sold goods for cash £305.
18   Took £250 of the cash and paid it into the bank.
21   Bought a printer by cheque £620.
22   Sold goods on time to H. Buchan £394.
23   P. Syme returned goods to us £160.
25   H. Buchan returned goods to us £18.
28   We returned goods to G. Smart £47.
29   We paid B. Hind by cheque £1,373.
31   Bought machinery on time from A. Cobb £419.

The effect of profit or loss on capital and the double entry system for expenses and revenues

Learning objectives

After you have studied this chapter, you should be able to:

- calculate profit by comparing revenue with costs
- explain how the *Principles of double entry* can guide you in identifying whether an account should be debited or credited
- explain how the accounting equation is used to show the effects of changes in assets and liabilities upon capital after goods or services have been traded
- explain why separate accounts are used for each type of expense and revenue
- explain why an expense is entered as a debit in the appropriate expense account
- explain why an item of revenue is entered as a credit in the appropriate revenue account
- explain how to identify the correct double entry for service revenue, such as commission received and rent received.
- enter a series of expense and revenue transactions into the appropriate T-accounts
- explain how the use of business cash and business goods for the owner's own purposes are dealt with in the accounting records

Introduction

In this chapter, you will learn how to calculate profits and losses and how to enter expense and revenue transactions into the ledger. You will also learn about drawings (i.e. amounts withdrawn from the business by the owner), and how to record them.

4.1 The nature of profit or loss

To an accountant, **profit** means the amount by which **revenue** is greater than the cost of a set of transactions. The term 'revenue' means the sales value of goods and services that have been supplied to customers. The 'cost' is the total monetary amount of all the possessions (assets and expenses) that were used up in obtaining those revenues – i.e. it is the cost incurred in generating the revenue.

For example, if our customers pay us £100,000 for goods and services and the cost we incurred in providing those goods and services was £70,000 the result would be a profit of £30,000:

		£
Revenue:	goods and services supplied to our customers for the sum of	100,000
Less Costs:	value of all the assets and expenses used up to enable us to supply these goods and services	(70,000)
Profit is therefore:		30,000

On the other hand, it is possible for our costs to exceed our revenues for a set of transactions. In this case the result is a **loss.** For example, a loss would be incurred given the following:

		£
Revenue:	what we have charged to our customers in respect of all the goods and services supplied to them	60,000
Less Costs:	value of all the assets and expenses used up to supply these goods and services to our customers	(80,000)
Loss is therefore:		(20,000)

Activity 4.1 In each of these two examples, a different explanation was given for the terms 'revenue' and 'costs'. What is the difference between the two explanations given for 'revenue'? What is the difference between the two explanations given for 'costs'?

4.2 The effect of profit and loss on capital

Businesses exist to make a profit and so increase their capital. Let's look at the relationship between profit and capital in an example.

On 1 January the assets and liabilities of a business are:

Assets: Fixtures £10,000; Inventory £7,000; Cash at the bank £3,000.

Liabilities: Accounts payable £2,000.

The capital is found from the accounting equation:

$$\boxed{\text{Capital} = \text{Assets} - \text{Liabilities}}$$

In this case, capital is £10,000 + £7,000 + £3,000 − £2,000 = £18,000.

During January, the whole of the £7,000 inventory is sold for £11,000 cash. On 31 January the assets and liabilities have become:

Assets: Fixtures £10,000; Inventory nil; Cash at the bank £14,000.

Liabilities: Accounts payable £2,000.

The capital is now £22,000:

$$\text{Assets (£10,000 + £14,000)} - \text{Liabilities £2,000}$$

So capital has increased by £4,000 from £18,000 to £22,000. It has increased by £4,000 because the £7,000 inventory was sold at a profit of £4,000 for £11,000. Profit, therefore, increases capital:

$$\boxed{\text{Old capital} + \text{Profit} = \text{New capital}}$$

£18,000 + £4,000 = £22,000

A loss, on the other hand, would reduce the capital:

$$\text{Old capital} - \text{Loss} = \text{New capital}$$

4.3 Profit or loss and sales

Profit will be made when goods or services are sold for more than they cost, while the opposite will result in a loss.

(You will learn later that there are different types of profit, some of which you may have heard of, such as 'gross profit' and 'net profit'. For now, we're not going to complicate things by going into that level of detail. So, whatever you may already know about these different types of profit, try to focus for the time being on the simple definition of profit presented here.)

4.4 Profit or loss and costs

Once profits or losses have been calculated, you can update the capital account. How often this will be done will depend on the business. Some only attempt to calculate their profits and losses once a year. Others do it at much more frequent intervals. Generally speaking, the larger the business, the more frequently profits are calculated.

In order to calculate profits and losses, revenue and costs must be entered into appropriate accounts. All the costs could be charged to one 'Costs Account', but you would be able to understand the calculations of profit better if full details of each type of cost were shown in those profit calculations. The same applies to each type of revenue.

For this reason, a separate account is opened for each type of revenue and each type of cost. For example, accounts relating to the costs of expenses may include:

Commissions account	Subscriptions account	Rent account
Bank interest account	Motor expenses account	Postages account
Royalties receivable account	Telephone account	Stationery account
Rent receivable account	General expenses account	Wages account
Overdraft interest account	Audit fees account	Insurance account

Note: The costs of assets used-up in generating revenue are known as 'depreciation'. Depreciation is also included in total costs when calculating profit. You will learn about those costs later in this book.

The title of each cost or revenue account is a matter of choice – they can be called anything – but it is best to give them names that reflect what they are for. For example, an account for postage stamps could be called 'Postage stamps account', 'Postages account', 'Communication expenses account', and so on. Also, different businesses combine different types of expenses into one account, such as having a 'Rent and telephone account', or a 'Rent, telephone and insurance account', Rare or small value items of expense are usually put into a 'Sundry expenses account' or a 'General expenses account'.

Most organisations do use names for their accounts that make it obvious which accounts are for revenue and which accounts are for expenses. However, some don't: an account for commission, for example, may be for commission income or for commission expenses. When in doubt as to whether an account is for revenue or expenses, you have two obvious indicators to consult. The first is on which side the entries are mainly appearing in the account. If it is the debit side, the account is almost certainly an expense account. The other indicator is the nature of the business. For example, a commission account in the accounting books of a firm of stockbrokers is almost certainly a revenue account.

Activity 4.2 Identify which of the accounts listed in the table above are expense accounts and which ones are revenue accounts.

4.5 Debit or credit

You need to know whether cost accounts for expenses should be debited or credited with the amounts involved. You already know that an increase in any possession of the business is a debit. And you know from Section 2.11 that when you incur an expense, it belongs to you but it is used-up immediately. So, you treat expenses the same way as you treat any other possession.

Before reading any further, answer Activity 4.3:

Activity 4.3 When you pay an expense using cash, which account do you debit? The expense account or the cash account?

As you found in Activity 4.3, expenses are *always* debited to the expense account. Apart from the guidance you have from what the *Principles of double entry* tell you about debits (and credits) for possessions, what other reason can you think of to explain this?

Well, if you think about how businesses obtain assets and incur expenses, transactions for them both have to be settled by giving something for the item received in the exchange (i.e. the asset or the expense). The *form of settlement*, for example cash or an IOU owed to the supplier (if the supplier allowed you time to pay), will always be the credit because they are given to the supplier in settlement of the transaction. You must, therefore, make the same type of entry in an expense account as you would in an account for an asset.

Putting it another way, looking at how businesses generate revenue, they use resources to pay for expenses and to pay for assets. These are then used to provide goods and services that are sold, so generating revenue. Expenses are used-up in the short term, while assets are used up in the long term. Because both expenses and assets are utilised in order to get revenue, the entries in their accounts are the same. Increases in assets and increases in expenses are entered on the debit side of the appropriate accounts and the form of settlement is credited.

So, for example, if you pay rent of £500 in cash, the rent account will be debited, because the total rent expense has increased by £500. The account for the *Form of settlement*, cash, will be credited. If you had not yet paid the £500, you would still debit the account for the item exchanged, the rent. The credit for the unpaid debit, i.e. an IOU, would be to the account of the creditor who you have not yet paid.

Activity 4.4 You can use the accounting equation to confirm this. Write down the accounting equation and see if you can work out what happens to it if (a) a business spends £30 in cash hiring a van for a day and (b) if a business hires a van for a day at a cost of £30 and is given 1 month to pay the bill. Assume in each case that the business has assets of £200, liabilities of £80 and capital of £120 before the transaction. What happens to capital in each case?

4.6 Revenue from services

You already know how to record revenue from Sections 3.4 and 3.5, where we looked at the double entries for sales. We entered the sales as credits into the sales account because they represented the value of the items exchanged with (i.e. sold to) your customers. Like costs, revenue is collected together in appropriately named accounts, such as a 'sales account', where it is shown as a credit until it is used in the profit calculations at the end of the period.

When revenue is from the sale of services, not from the sale of goods, the treatement of the debits and credits does not change. However, it can be difficult to understand why.

In the case of virtually all services, what is being paid for is the time of the seller: **time is the item exchanged**. If you want to think of this in terms of units, imagine that you have an inventory of units of time. You can only provide a few each day and, once provided, you have less units available to sell during the rest of that day. Think of an auctioneer. The auctioneer has only a certain amount of time each day in which to sell items on behalf of clients. When she sells one, the client pays commission to compensate the auctioneer for her time. Time is the item exchanged.

So, think of each unit of time you sell as being like a unit of a good. If you have 10 units and you sell one, you only have nine left. If you have sold one of your 10 units of time, you have less to offer, but only temporarily because services are provided 'against the clock' – an auctioneer can only auction so many things in a day, a plumber can only fix so many broken pipes in a day, an accountant can only do work for clients for so many hours in the day, a taxi driver can only drive his taxi for so many hours in the day, and so on.

The next day, the auctioneer, the plumber, the accountant, and the taxi driver are again able to provide a full day of services, no matter how many units of their time were sold the day before.

So, the sale of a service decreases your possession of time temporarily and this must be recorded. However, we do not record this in an account for time. When we record the units of service sold, we use account names that describe the type of service provided: 'commission received' for the auctioneer, 'plumbing fees' for the plumber, 'accountancy fees' for the accountant, 'taxi fares' for the taxi driver. This allows us to distinguish between the revenues and costs of providing or obtaining each form of service that our business sells or purchases. As a result of doing this, it is a straightforward process discovering if the services we sell are each being sold at a profit or at a loss.

Keep all this in mind and you will be able to apply the *Principles of double entry* to guide you in the double entry for any services you purchase or sell.

Activity 4.5 If they increase, which of the following items are debited and which are credited: expenses, revenue, assets, liabilities, capital, profits, and losses?

4.7 Double entries for expenses and for revenue from sale of services

Let's look at some examples that demonstrate the double entry required:

1 Rent of £200 is paid in cash.

  (*a*) The *Form of settlement*, cash, is given so it is a credit.

  (*b*) The total of the *Item exchanged* (the expense of rent) is increased, and so is a debit.

  Summary: Debit the *rent account* with £200.
              Credit the *cash account* with £200.

2 Motor expenses of £355 are paid by debit card.

  (*a*) The *Form of settlement*, bank, is given so it is a credit.

  (*b*) The total of the *Item exchanged* (motor expenses) has increased, and so is a debit.

  Summary: Debit the *motor expenses account* with £355.
              Credit the *bank account* with £355.

3 £60 cash is received for commission earned by the business.

(a) The *Form of settlement*, cash, is received so it is a debit.

(b) The *Item exchanged*, your time, has been decreased (see Section 4.6). The appropriate name for the revenue account is 'commission received', and it is a credit.

Summary: Debit the *cash account* with £60.
Credit the *commission received account* with £60.

Before you look at the next example, you need to know that if you rent out an asset of your business, the rent you receive is paid for the use of that asset of the business, such as a building, a storage unit in a warehouse, or an office. It is compensation for the service you have provided. Providing the service (in this case renting out an asset) has decreased the availability of that asset to the business and is recorded in the same way as any other service you sell. So, when rent is received, the *Item exchanged* is the asset provided on loan to the customer. When recording rent received, we use a revenue account with the name 'Rent received'. No entries are ever made in the account of the asset you have rented out because, just like the auctioneer's units of time from Section 4.6, you will have the asset back and fully available to you very soon.

Now look at some more transactions and their effect upon the accounts in the following table:

		Form of settlement	Increase or Decrease	Account debited	Account credited
June 1	Paid for postage stamps by cash £50	Cash	Decrease	Postage stamps	Cash
2	Paid for electricity by debit card £229	Bank	Decrease	Electricity	Bank
3	Received rent in cash £138	Cash	Increase	Cash	Rent
4	Paid insurance by debit card £142	Bank	Decrease	Insurance	Bank

Entering these four examples into the appropriate accounts results in:

Cash

		£				£
June 3	Rent received	138	June 1	Postage		50

Bank

				£
	June 2	Electricity		229
	4	Insurance		142

Electricity

	£	
June 2 Bank	229	

Insurance

		£		
June 4	Bank	142		

Postage

		£		
June 1	Cash	50		

Rent received

				£
		June 3	Cash	138

4.8 Drawings

Sometimes the owners of a business will want to take cash out of it for their private use. This is known as **drawings**. Drawings are *never* expenses of a business.

In the case of drawings, the *Form of settlement* is 'capital' but we use a 'drawings account' for the entry. The reason for this is that if we made the entry in the capital account, it could become very full with lots of small drawings transactions. As a result, it is normal practice to maintain a separate account for drawings and to deduct the total of the drawings account from capital at the end of each year.

The *Form of settlement* is drawings. They are received by the business from the owner in exchange for the *Item exchanged*, which was cash. Drawings are debited and cash is credited.

The following example illustrates the entries for drawings:

On 25 August, the owner takes £50 cash out of the business for his own use.

Form of settlement and entry	Item exchanged and entry
Drawings; debit	Cash; credit

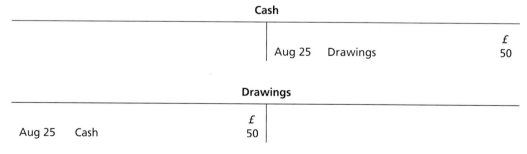

Cash

				£
		Aug 25	Drawings	50

Drawings

		£		
Aug 25	Cash	50		

Sometimes goods are taken for private use. This form of withdrawal by the owner is also known as *drawings*. In Sections 3.2 and 3.3, you learnt that when goods are purchased, the purchases account is debited. As a result, when goods are withdrawn it is the purchases account that should be credited.

The following example illustrates the entries for this form of drawings:

On 28 August, the owner takes £400 of goods out of the business for his own use.

Form of settlement and entry	Item exchanged and entry
Drawings; debit	Inventory; credit Purchases

Purchases

			£
	Aug 28	Drawings	400

Drawings

		£	
Aug 28	Purchases	400	

Learning outcomes

You should now have learnt:

1 How to calculate profit by comparing revenue with costs.

2 That the *Principles of double entry* can guide you to always know whether an account should be debited or credited.

3 That the accounting equation is central to any explanation of the effect of trading upon capital.

4 Why every different type of expense is shown in a separate expense account.

5 Why every different type of revenue is shown in a separate revenue account.

6 Why an expense is shown as a debit entry in the appropriate expense account.

7 Why revenue is shown as a credit entry in the appropriate revenue account.

8 How to identify the correct double entry for service revenue, such as commission received and rent received.

9 How to enter a series of expense and revenue transactions into the appropriate T-accounts.

10 What is meant by the term 'drawings'.

11 That drawings are *always* a reduction in capital and *never* an expense of a business.

12 How to record drawings of cash in the accounting books.

13 How to record drawings of inventory in the accounting books.

Answers to activities

4.1 There is no difference between either the two meanings given for revenue or the two meanings given for expenses. In each case, you are being given a slightly different wording so as to help you understand what the two terms mean.

4.2 *Expense accounts*
Rent account
Postages account
Commissions account
Stationery account
Wages account
Insurance account
Bank interest account
Motor expenses account
Telephone account
General expenses account
Overdraft interest account
Audit fees account

Revenue accounts
Subscriptions account
Rent receivable account
Royalties receivable account

Note that the answer has assumed that *unless* words like 'received' or 'receivable' follow the name of an account, the account is an expense. For example, the Commission Account and the Bank Interest Account could easily be for revenue rather than expenses. However, accounting practice is that as most accounts are for expenses, where there may be some confusion as to whether an account is for revenue or expenses, the name of the revenue account should make it clear that it is for revenue, not expenses. You can see an example in this question if you compare the names of the two rent accounts. Accounts like Subscriptions tend to appear mainly in the accounting books of clubs and societies and so there is no need in that case to indicate in the name that it is a revenue account. You can tell whether subscriptions are revenue or expenditure items from the type of organisation whose accounting books you are looking at. The same would apply, but even more so, to Audit Fees which are only ever revenue accounts in the accounting books of a firm of accountants. In all other cases, they are expense accounts.

4.3 When your cash decreases, you credit the cash account. This means that you must debit the expense account. This will always be the case whenever you incur expenses. It does not matter how you settle the transaction, the expense account will always be debited because it has increased.

4.4 The accounting equation is Capital = Assets − Liabilities. In this example, it starts as £120 = £200 − £80. Each transaction is entered twice. In both cases, the debit entry is £30 to a van hire expense account. The credit in (a) is to the cash account. In (b) it is to the car hire company's account (the creditor's account). In order for the accounting equation to balance, in (a) an asset (i.e. cash) has been reduced by £30 so capital must be reduced by the same amount, £30. In the case of (b) liabilities (i.e. the van hire company's account) have increased by £30 and so capital must also be reduced by that amount, £30. In the case of (a) the accounting equation becomes £90 = £170 − £80. In (b) it becomes £90 = £200 − £110. The effect on capital in both cases is that it decreases by the amount of the expense.

4.5 *Profit* is a form of *revenue*, so an increase in profit is a credit.

Losses are a form of *expense*, so an increase in losses is a debit.

Increases in *capital* are always a credit.

Profits and losses are both entered in the capital account at the end of the period. So if there is a profit, *capital* increases and you know from the *Principles of double entry* that this means the capital account must be credited. If there is a loss, the *Principles of double entry* tell you that the capital account must be debited.

Liabilities, such as loans, are the opposite of *assets,* so they are treated the opposite way from assets: increases in liabilities are credited to the appropriate liability account, and decreases are debited.

In other words, when they increase, the following are the debits and credit for the seven items.

Debit	Credit
Expenses	Revenues
Losses	Profits
Assets	Liabilities
	Capital

Review questions

4.1 Enter the following transactions, completing the double entry in the books for the month of August:

August	1	Started in business with £31,000 in the bank and £4,000 in cash.
	2	Purchased goods £1,160 on time from A. Cliff.
	3	Bought fixtures and fittings £4,600 paying by cheque.
	5	Sold goods for cash £600.
	6	Bought goods on time £1,300 from S. Bell.
	10	Paid rent by cash £800.
	12	Bought stationery £180, paying in cash.
	18	Goods returned to A. Cliff £164.
	21	Received rent of £480 by cheque for sublet of corner space.
	23	Sold goods on time to R. Coat for £3,200.
	24	Bought a van paying by cheque £16,400.
	30	Paid the month's wages by cash £1,220.
	31	The proprietor took cash for her own personal use £1,020.

4.2 Write up the following transactions in the books of J. Dunn:

May	1	Started in business with cash £30,000.
	2	Bought goods on time from T. Lamb £700.
	3	Paid rent by cash £1,740.
	4	Paid £25,000 of the cash of the business into a business bank account.
	5	Sold goods on time to R. Still £384.
	7	Bought stationery £170 paying by cheque.
	11	Cash sales £624.
	14	Goods returned by us to T. Lamb £80.
	17	Sold goods on time to R. Davis £424.
	20	Paid for repairs to the building by cash £156.
	22	R. Still returned goods to us £62.
	27	Paid T. Lamb by cheque £620.
	28	Cash purchases £940.
	29	Bought a van paying by cheque £7,000.
	30	Paid motor expenses in cash £432.
	31	Bought a computer £1,460 on time from S. Tims.

4.3A Prepare the double entries (*not* the T-accounts) for the following transactions using the format:

Date		Dr	Cr
	Account name	£x	
	Account name		£x

July	1	Started in business with £5,000 in the bank and £1,000 cash.
	2	Bought stationery by cheque £75.
	3	Bought goods on time from T. Smart £2,100.
	4	Sold goods for cash £340.
	5	Paid insurance by cash £290.
	7	Bought a computer on time from J. Hott £700.
	8	Paid electricity by cheque £32.
	10	Sold goods on time to C. Biggins £630.
	11	Returned goods to T. Smart £550.
	14	Paid wages by cash £210.
	17	Paid rent by cheque £225.
	20	Received cheque £400 from C. Biggins.
	21	Paid J. Hott by cheque £700.
	23	Bought stationery on time from News Ltd £125.
	25	Sold goods on time to F. Tank £645.
	31	Paid News Ltd by cheque £125.

4.4A Write up the following transactions in the T-accounts of F. Fernandes:

Feb	1	Started in business with £11,000 in the bank and £1,600 cash.
	2	Bought goods on time: J. Biggs £830; D. Martin £610; P. Lot £590.
	3	Bought goods for cash £370.
	4	Paid rent in cash £75.
	5	Bought stationery paying by cheque £62.
	6	Sold goods on time: D. Twigg £370; B. Hogan £290; K. Fletcher £410.
	7	Paid wages in cash £160.
	10	We returned goods to D. Martin £195.
	11	Paid rent in cash £75.
	13	B. Hogan returns goods to us £35.
	15	Sold goods on time to: T. Lee £205; F. Sharp £280; G. Rae £426.
	16	Paid business rates by cheque £970.
	18	Paid insurance in cash £280.
	19	Paid rent by cheque £75.
	20	Bought van on time from B. Black £6,100.
	21	Paid motor expenses in cash £24.
	23	Paid wages in cash £170.
	24	Received part of amount owing from K. Fletcher by cheque £250.
	28	Received refund of business rates £45 by cheque.
	28	Paid by cheque: J. Biggs £830; D. Martin £415; B. Black £6,100.

$\rightarrow$

4.5 From the following statements which give the cumulative effects of individual transactions, you are required to state as fully as possible what transaction has taken place in each case. That is, write descriptions similar to those given in Review Questions 4.1–4.4. There is no need to copy out the table. The first column of data gives the opening position. Each of the other columns represents a transaction. It is these transactions (A–I) that you are to describe.

Transaction:		A	B	C	D	E	F	G	H	I
Assets	£000	£000	£000	£000	£000	£000	£000	£000	£000	£000
Land and buildings	450	450	450	450	575	575	275	275	275	275
Motor vehicles	95	100	100	100	100	100	100	100	100	100
Office equipment	48	48	48	48	48	48	48	48	48	48
Inventory	110	110	110	110	110	110	110	110	110	93
Accounts receivable	188	188	188	188	188	108	108	108	108	120
Bank	27	22	22	172	47	127	427	77	77	77
Cash	15	15	11	11	11	11	11	11	3	3
	933	933	929	1,079	1,079	1,079	1,079	729	721	716
Liabilities										
Capital	621	621	621	621	621	621	621	621	621	616
Loan from Lee	200	200	200	350	350	350	350	–	–	–
Accounts payable	112	112	108	108	108	108	108	108	100	100
	933	933	929	1,079	1,079	1,079	1,079	729	721	716

Note: The heading *£000* means that all the figures shown underneath it are in thousands of pounds, e.g. Office Equipment book value is £48,000. It saves constantly writing out 000 after each figure, and is done to save time and make comparison easier.

4.6A The following table shows the cumulative effects of a succession of separate transactions on the assets and liabilities of a business. The first column of data gives the opening position.

Transaction:		A	B	C	D	E	F	G	H	I
Assets	£000	£000	£000	£000	£000	£000	£000	£000	£000	£000
Land and buildings	500	500	535	535	535	535	535	535	535	535
Equipment	230	230	230	230	230	230	230	200	200	200
Inventory	113	140	140	120	120	120	120	120	119	119
Trade accounts receivable	143	143	143	173	160	158	158	158	158	158
Prepaid expenses^{Author's Note}	27	27	27	27	27	27	27	27	27	27
Cash at bank	37	37	37	37	50	50	42	63	63	63
Cash on hand	9	9	9	9	9	9	9	9	9	3
	1,059	1,086	1,121	1,131	1,131	1,129	1,121	1,112	1,111	1,105
Liabilities										
Capital	730	730	730	740	740	738	733	724	723	717
Loan	120	120	155	155	155	155	155	155	155	155
Trade accounts payable	168	195	195	195	195	195	195	195	195	195
Accrued expenses*	41	41	41	41	41	41	38	38	38	38
	1,059	1,086	1,121	1,131	1,131	1,129	1,121	1,112	1,111	1,105

Required:

Identify clearly and as fully as you can what transaction has taken place in each case. Give two possible explanations for transaction I. Do not copy out the table but use the reference letter for each transaction.

(Association of Accounting Technicians)

Author's Note: You have not yet been told about 'prepaid expenses' and 'accrued expenses'. Prepaid expenses are expenses that have been paid in advance, the benefits of which will only be felt by the business in a later accounting period. Because the benefit of having incurred the expense will not be received until a future time period, the expense is not included in the calculation of profit for the period in which it was paid. As it was not treated as an expense of the period when profit was calculated, the debit in the account is treated as an asset when the balance sheet is prepared, hence the appearance of the term 'prepaid expenses' among the assets in the question. Accrued expenses, on the other hand, are expenses that have not yet been paid for benefits which have been received. In F, £8,000 was paid out of the bank account (50–42) of which £3,000 was used to pay off some of the accrued expenses (41–38).

Balancing-off accounts

Learning objectives

After you have studied this chapter, you should be able to:

- close-off accounts when appropriate
- balance-off accounts at the end of a period and bring down the opening balance to the next period
- distinguish between a debit balance and a credit balance
- describe and prepare accounts in three-column format

Introduction

In this chapter, you'll learn how to discover what the amount outstanding on an account is at a particular point in time. You'll also learn how to close accounts that are no longer needed and how to record appropriate entries in accounts at the end and beginning of periods. Finally, you'll learn that T-accounts are not the only way to record accounting transactions.

5.1 Accounts for debtors

Where debtors have paid their accounts

So far you have learnt how to record transactions in the accounting books by means of debit and credit entries. At the end of each accounting period the figures in each account are examined in order to summarise the situation they present. This will often, but not always, be once a year if you are calculating profit. If you want to see what is happening with respect to particular accounts, it will be more frequently done. For example, if you want to find out how much your customers owe you for goods you have sold to them, you would probably do this at the end of each month.

Activity 5.1 Why do you think we would want to look at the accounts receivable in the accounting books as often as once a month?

Let's look at the account of one of our customers, K. Tandy, for transactions in August 2019:

K. Tandy

2019			£	2019			£
Aug	1	Sales	144	Aug	22	Bank	144
	19	Sales	300		28	Bank	300

If you add up the figures on each side, you will find that they both sum to £444. In other words, during the month we sold a total of £444 worth of goods to Tandy, and have been paid a total of £444 by her. This means that at the end of August she owes us nothing. As she owes us nothing, we do not need her account to prepare the balance sheet (there is no point in showing a figure for accounts receivable of zero in the balance sheet). We can, therefore, **close off** her account on 31 August 2019. This is done by inserting the totals on each side:

K. Tandy

2019			£	2019			£
Aug	1	Sales	144	Aug	22	Bank	144
	19	Sales	300		28	Bank	300
			444				444

Notice that totals in accounting are always shown with a single line above them, and a double line underneath. As shown in the following completed account for C. Lee, totals on accounts at the end of a period are always shown on a level with one another, even when there are fewer entries on one side than on the other.

Now, let's look at the account for C. Lee.

C. Lee

2019			£	2019			£
Aug	11	Sales	177	Aug	30	Bank	480
	19	Sales	203				
	22	Sales	100				
			480				480

In this account, C. Lee also owed us nothing at the end of August 2019, as he had paid us for all the sales we made to him.

Note: In handwritten accounts, you will often see this layout enhanced by two intersecting lines, one horizontal and one diagonal on the side which has less entries. If this were done, C. Lee's account would look like this:

C. Lee

2019			£	2019			£
Aug	11	Sales	177	Aug	30	Bank	480
	19	Sales	203				
	22	Sales	100				
			480				480

We won't use this layout in this book, but your teacher or lecturer may want you to use it When you are preparing T-accounts.

Activity 5.2 Why do you think we would want to draw these two extra lines onto the hand-written account?

If an account contains only one entry on each side and they are equal, you don't need to include totals. For example:

K. Wood

2019			£	2019			£
Aug	6	Sales	214	Aug	12	Bank	214

Now let's look at what happens when the two sides do not equal each other.

Where debtors still owe for goods

It is unlikely that everyone will have paid the amounts they owe us by the end of the month. In these cases, the totals of each side would not equal one another. Let's look at the account of D. Knight for August 2019:

D. Knight

2019			£	2019			£
Aug	1	Sales	158	Aug	28	Bank	158
	15	Sales	206				
	30	Sales	118				

If you add the figures you will see that the debit side adds up to £482 and the credit side adds up to £158. You should be able to see what the difference of £324 (i.e. £482 – £158) represents. It consists of the last two sales of £206 and £118. They have not been paid for and so are still owing to us on 31 August 2019.

In double entry, we only enter figures as totals if the totals on both sides of the account agree. We do, however, want to **balance-off** the account for August showing that Knight owes us £324. (While there would be nothing wrong in using the term 'close off', 'balance-off' is the more appropriate term to use when there is a difference between the two sides of an account.)

If Knight owes us £324 at close of business on 31 August 2019, then the same amount will be owed to us when the business opens on 1 September 2019.

Balancing the accounts is done in five stages:

1 Add up both sides to find out their totals. Note: do not write anything in the account at this stage.
2 Deduct the smaller total from the larger total to find the balance.
3 Now enter the balance on the side with the smallest total. This now means the totals will be equal.
4 Enter totals level with each other.
5 Now enter the balance on the line below the totals on the *opposite* side to the balance entered above the totals.

Against the balance above the totals, complete the date column by entering the last day of that period – for August, this will always be '31' even if the business was shut on that date because it fell on a weekend or was a holiday. Below the totals, show the first day of the next period against the balance – this will always be the day immediately after the last day of the previous period, in this case, September 1. The balance above the totals is described as the **balance *carried down*** (often abbreviated to 'balance c/d'). The balance below the total is described as the **balance *brought down*** (often abbreviated to 'balance b/d').

Knight's account when 'balanced-off' will appear as follows:

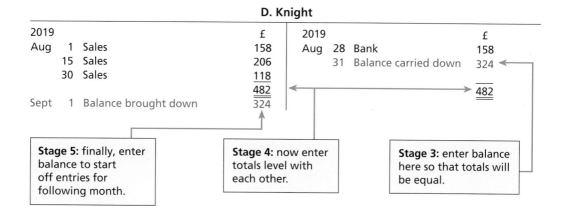

D. Knight

2019			£	2019			£
Aug	1	Sales	158	Aug	28	Bank	158
	15	Sales	206		31	Balance carried down	324
	30	Sales	118				
			482				482
Sept	1	Balance brought down	324				

Stage 5: finally, enter balance to start off entries for following month.

Stage 4: now enter totals level with each other.

Stage 3: enter balance here so that totals will be equal.

Note for students

- From now on, we will use the abbreviations 'c/d' and 'b/d'.
- The date given to balance c/d is the last day of the period which is finishing, and balance b/d is given the opening date of the next period.
- As the total of the debit side originally exceeded the total of the credit side, **the balance is said to be a 'debit balance'.** This being a personal account (for a person), the person concerned is said to be a debtor – the accounting term for anyone who owes money to the business.

Just as when the two sides each have only one entry and the two sides are equal, if an account contains only one entry it is unnecessary to enter the total after entering the balance carried down (because the balance becomes the only entry on the other side and it is equal to the other entry). A double line ruled under the entry will mean that the entry is its own total. For example:

B. Walters

2019			£	2019			£
Aug	18	Sales	51	Aug	31	Balance c/d	51
Sept	1	Balance b/d	51				

Note: T-accounts should *always* be balanced-off at the end of each period, even when they contain only one entry.

5.2 Accounts for creditors

Exactly the same principles will apply when the balances are carried down to the credit side. **This balance is known as a 'credit balance'.** We can look at the accounts of two of our suppliers which are to be balanced-off:

E. Williams

2019			£	2019			£
Aug	21	Bank	100	Aug	2	Purchases	248
					18	Purchases	116

K. Patterson

2019			£	2019			£
Aug	14	Returns outwards	20	Aug	8	Purchases	620
	28	Bank	600		15	Purchases	200

We now add up the totals and find the balance, i.e. Stages 1 and 2. When balanced-off, these will appear as:

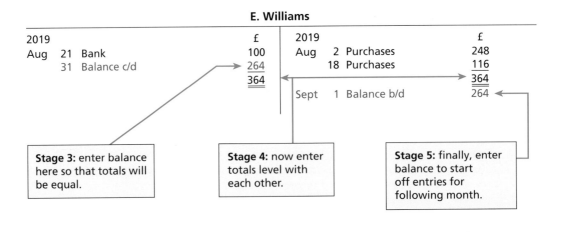

E. Williams

2019			£	2019			£
Aug	21	Bank	100	Aug	2	Purchases	248
	31	Balance c/d	264		18	Purchases	116
			364				364
				Sept	1	Balance b/d	264

Stage 3: enter balance here so that totals will be equal.

Stage 4: now enter totals level with each other.

Stage 5: finally, enter balance to start off entries for following month.

K. Patterson

2019			£	2019			£
Aug	14	Returns outwards	20	Aug	8	Purchases	620
	28	Bank	600		15	Purchases	200
	31	Balance c/d	200				
			820				820
				Sept	1	Balance b/d	200

The accounts of E. Williams and K. Patterson have credit balances. They are 'creditors' – the accounting term for someone to whom money is owed.

Before you read further attempt Review Questions 5.1 and 5.2.

5.3 Three-column accounts

Through the main part of this book, the type of account used is the T-account, where the left-hand side of the account is the debit side, and the right-hand side is the credit side. However, when computers are used the style of the ledger account is sometimes different. It appears as three columns of figures, one column for debit entries, another column for credit entries, and the last column for the balance. If you have an account at a bank, your bank statements will often be shown using this three-column format.

The accounts used in this chapter will now be redrafted to show the ledger accounts drawn up in this way.

K. Tandy

			Debit	Credit	Balance (and whether debit or credit)	
2019			£	£	£	
Aug	1	Sales	144		144	Dr
	19	Sales	300		444	Dr
	22	Bank		144	300	Dr
	28	Bank		300	0	

C. Lee

			Debit	Credit	Balance	
			£	£	£	
2019						
Aug	11	Sales	177		177	Dr
	19	Sales	203		380	Dr
	22	Sales	100		480	Dr
	30	Bank		480	0	

K. Wood

			Debit	Credit	Balance	
			£	£	£	
2019						
Aug	6	Sales	214		214	Dr
	12	Bank		214	0	

D. Knight

			Debit	Credit	Balance	
			£	£	£	
2019						
Aug	1	Sales	158		158	Dr
	15	Sales	206		364	Dr
	28	Bank		158	206	Dr
	31	Sales	118		324	Dr

B. Walters

			Debit	Credit	Balance	
			£	£	£	
2019						
Aug	18	Sales	51		51	Dr

E. Williams

			Debit	Credit	Balance	
			£	£	£	
2019						
Aug	2	Purchases		248	248	Cr
	18	Purchases		116	364	Cr
	21	Bank	100		264	Cr

K. Patterson

			Debit	Credit	Balance	
			£	£	£	
2019						
Aug	8	Purchases		620	620	Cr
	14	Returns	20		600	Cr
	15	Purchases		200	800	Cr
	28	Bank	600		200	Cr

Note how the balance is calculated after every entry. This can be done quite simply when using a computer because the software can automatically calculate the new balance as soon as an entry is made.

When manual methods are being used it is often too much work to have to calculate a new balance after each entry. Also, the greater the number of calculations, the greater the possibility of errors. For these reasons, it is usual for students to use T-accounts *except* when required to use three-column accounts in an exam! However, it is important to note that there is no difference in principle – the final balances are the same using either method.

Learning outcomes

You should now have learnt:

1 How to close off accounts upon which there is no balance outstanding.

2 How to balance-off accounts at the end of a period.

3 How to bring down the opening balance on an account at the start of a new period.

4 That when an opening balance on an account is a debit, that account is said to have a debit balance. It also has a debit balance during a period whenever the total of the debit side exceeds the total of the credit side.

5 That when an opening balance on an account is a credit, that account is said to have a credit balance. It also has a credit balance during a period whenever the total of the credit side exceeds the total of the debit side.

6 That 'debtors' are people or organisations whose account in your accounting books has a greater value on the debit side. They owe you money. They are included in the amount shown for accounts receivable in the balance sheet.

7 That 'creditors' are people or organisations whose account in your accounting books has a greater value on the credit side. You owe them money. They are included in the amount shown for accounts payable in the balance sheet.

8 That T-accounts and three-column accounts disclose the same balance, given identical information about transactions.

9 That three-column accounts update and show the balance on the account after every transaction.

10 How to prepare three-column accounts.

Answers to activities

5.1 In order to survive, businesses must, in the long term, make profits. However, even profitable businesses go 'bust' if they do not have enough funds to pay their bills when they are due. Debtors represent a resource that is not yet in the form of funds (e.g. cash) that can be used to pay bills. By regularly monitoring the position on the account of each debtor, a business can tell which debtors are being slow to pay and, very importantly, do something about it.

5.2 The purpose is to prevent any more entries being made in the account. The entries would *always* be made in ink, so as to prevent their being erased and replaced with different entries. In a computerised accounting system, there is no need for measures such as these, because the controls and checks built into the computerised system prevent such things from happening.

Review questions

5.1 Enter the following items in the appropriate debtors' accounts (i.e. your customers' accounts) only; do *not* write up other accounts. Then balance-off each of these personal accounts at the end of the month. (Keep your answer; it will be used as a basis for Review Question 5.3.)

May	1	Sales on time to B. Flyn £810; F. Lane £1,100; T. Fey £413.
	4	Sales on time to F. Start £480; B. Flyn £134.
	10	Returns inwards from B. Flyn £124; T. Fey £62.
	18	F. Lane paid us by cheque £1,100.
	20	T. Fey paid us £351 by cheque.
	24	B. Flyn paid us £440 by cash.
	31	Sales on time to F. Start £240.

5.2 Enter the following in the appropriate creditors' accounts (i.e. your suppliers' accounts) only. Do *not* write up the other accounts. Then balance-off each of these personal accounts at the end of the month. (Keep your answer; it will be used as the basis for Review Question 5.4.)

June	1	Purchases on time from J. Wilson £240; P. Todd £390; J. Fry £1,620.
	3	Purchases on time from P. Todd £470; P. Rake £290.
	10	We returned goods to J. Fry £140; J. Wilson £65.
	15	Purchases on time from J. Wilson £210.
	19	We paid P. Rake by cash £290.
	28	We paid J. Wilson by cash £300.
	30	We returned goods to P. Todd £39.

5.3 Redraft each of the accounts given in your answer to Review Question 5.1 in three-column style.

5.4 Redraft each of the accounts given in your answer to Review Question 5.2 in three-column style.

5.5 Enter the following in the personal accounts (i.e. the creditor and debtor accounts) only. Do *not* write up the other accounts. Balance-off each personal account at the end of the month. After completing this, state which of the balances represent debtors and which represent creditors.

Sept	1	Sales on time to J. Bee £1,040; T. Day £1,260; J. Soul £480.
	2	Purchases on time D. Blue £780; F. Rise £1,020; P. Lee £560.
	8	Sales on time to T. Day £340; L. Hope £480.
	10	Purchases on time from F. Rise £92; R. James £870.
	12	Returns inwards from J. Soul £25; T. Day £190.
	17	We returned goods to F. Rise £12; R. James £84.
	20	We paid D. Blue by cheque £780.
	24	J. Bee paid us by cheque £900.
	26	We paid R. James by cheque £766.
	28	J. Bee paid us by cash £80.
	30	L. Hope pays us by cheque £480.

5.6A Enter the following transactions in personal accounts only. Bring down the balances at the end of the month. After completing this, state which of the balances represent debtors and which represent creditors.

2020

May	1	Credit sales F. Black £620; G. Smith £84; L. Sime £1,200; J. Teel £608.
	2	Credit purchases from P. Best £190; I. Donovan £63; G. Lime £210; T. Still £360.
	8	Credit sales to G. Smith £322; L. Sime £448.
	9	Credit purchases from I. Donovan £215; T. Still £164.
	10	Goods returned to us by L. Sime £62; J. Teel £164.
	12	Cash paid to us by J. Teel £444.
	15	We returned goods to P. Best £25; T. Still £21.
	19	We received cheques from L. Sime £180; F. Black £620.
	21	We sold goods on time to F. Black £180; G. Smith £860.
	28	We paid by cheque the following: P. Best £165; T. Still £100; G. Lime £180.
	31	We returned goods to T. Still £40.

5.7A Redraft each of the accounts given in your answer to Review Question 5.6A in three-column style.

The trial balance

Learning objectives

After you have studied this chapter, you should be able to:

- prepare a trial balance from a set of accounts
- explain why the debit and credit trial balance totals should equal one another
- explain why some of the possible errors that can be made when double entries are being entered in the accounts do not prevent the trial balance from 'balancing'
- describe uses for a trial balance other than to check for double entry errors

Introduction

In this chapter, you'll learn how to prepare a trial balance from the accounts in the accounting books. You'll discover that the alternate version of the accounting equation can be a useful guide to understanding why a trial balance must balance if all the double entries in the accounts are correct. You'll also learn that the trial balance is no guarantee that the double entries have all been recorded correctly. Finally, at the end of the chapter, you'll have the opportunity to do twenty multiple choice questions covering the material in Chapters 1–6.

6.1 Total debit entries = Total credit entries

You've learnt that under double entry bookkeeping:

- for each debit entry there is a credit entry
- for each credit entry there is a debit entry.

Let's see if you can remember the basics of double entry.

Activity 6.1

What is the double entry for each of the following transactions:

(a) Purchase of a new van for £9,000 which was paid in full by cheque

Dr   £

        Cr   £

(b) Goods which cost £40 taken out by the owner for her own use

Dr   £

        Cr   £

The total of all the items recorded in all the accounts on the debit side should equal the total of all the items recorded on the credit side of the accounts.

Activity 6.2 Do you remember the alternate form of the accounting equation you were shown in Chapter 1? What does it tell you has happened when it does not balance?

We need to check that for each debit entry there is also an equal credit entry. In order to check that there is a matching credit entry for every debit entry, we prepare something called a **trial balance**.

A type of trial balance could be drawn up by listing all the accounts and then entering the total of all the debit entries in each account in one column and the total of all the credit entries in each account into another column. Finally, you would add up the two columns of figures and ensure they are equal. Using the worked example in Section 3.8, this trial balance would be:

Trial balance as at 31 May 2020		
	Dr	Cr
	£	£
Purchases	994	
Sales		490
Returns outwards		15
Returns inwards	16	
D. Small	220	220
A. Lyon & Son		624
D. Hughes	60	60
M. Spencer	45	16
Cash	445	355
	1,780	1,780

6.2 Total debit balances = Total credit balances

The method described in Section 6.1 is *not* the usual method of drawing up a trial balance, but it is the easiest to understand at first. The form of trial balance used by accountants is a list of account balances arranged according to whether they have debit balances or credit balances.

Let's balance-off the accounts you saw in Section 3.8. The new entries are in blue so that you can see the entries required to arrive at the closing balances that are used in the trial balance.

Go back to Section 3.8 and balance all the accounts before you read any further.

The balanced accounts are shown below:

Purchases

2020			£	2020			£
May	1	D. Small	220	May	31	Balance c/d	994
	2	A. Lyon & Son	410				
	12	Cash	150				
	31	A. Lyon & Son	214				
			994				994
June	1	Balance b/d	994				

Sales

2020			£	2020			£
May	31	Balance c/d	490	May	5	D. Hughes	60
					6	M. Spencer	45
					11	Cash	210
					21	Cash	175
			490				490
				June	11	Balance b/d	490

Returns outwards

2020			£	2020			£
May	31	Balance c/d	15	May	10	D. Small	15
				June	1	Balance b/d	15

Returns inwards

2020			£	2020			£
May	19	M. Spencer	16	May	31	Balance c/d	16
June	1	Balance b/d	16				

D. Small

2020			£	2020			£
May	10	Returns outwards	15	May	1	Purchases	220
	22	Cash	205				
			220				220

A. Lyon & Son

2020			£	2020			£
May	31	Balance c/d	624	May	2	Purchases	410
					31	Purchases	214
			624				624
				June	1	Balance b/d	624

D. Hughes

2020			£	2020			£
May	5	Sales	60	May	30	Cash	60

M. Spencer

2020			£	2020			£
May	6	Sales	45	May	19	Returns inwards	16
					31	Balance c/d	29
			45				45
June	1	Balance b/d	29				

Cash

2020			£	2020			£
May	11	Sales	210	May	12	Purchases	150
	21	Sales	175		22	D. Small	205
	30	D. Hughes	60		31	Balance c/d	90
			445				445
June	1	Balance b/d	90				

If you attempted this before looking at the answer, be sure you understand any mistakes you made before going on.

If the trial balance was drawn up using these closing account balances, it would appear as follows:

Trial balance as at 31 May 2020		
	Dr	*Cr*
	£	£
Purchases	994	
Sales		490
Returns outwards		15
Returns inwards	16	
A. Lyon & Son		624
M. Spencer	29	
Cash	90	
	1,129	1,129

This is the usual way in which a trial balance is presented.

The trial balance always has the date of the *last* day of the accounting period to which it relates. It is a *snapshot* of the balances on the ledger accounts at that date.

Just like the trial balance you saw in Section 6.1, the two sides of this one also 'balance'. However, the totals are lower. This is because the £220 in D. Small's account, £60 in D. Hughes' account, £16 in M. Spencer's account and £355 in the cash account have been cancelled out from each side of these accounts by taking only the *balances* instead of the *totals*. As equal amounts have been cancelled from each side, £651 in all, the new totals should still equal one another, as in fact they do at £1,129. (You can verify this if you subtract the new total of £1,129 from the previous one of £1,780. The difference is £651 which is the amount cancelled out from both sides.)

This form of trial balance is the easiest to extract when there are more than a few transactions during the period and it is the one accountants use.

Note that a trial balance can be drawn up at any time. However, it is normal practice to prepare one at the end of an accounting period before preparing an 'income statement' and a 'balance sheet'. The income statement shows what profit has been earned in a period. (You will be looking at income statements in the next chapter.) The balance sheet shows what the assets and liabilities of a business are at the end of a period.

Go back to Chapter 1 to refresh your understanding of the balance sheet.

Activity 6.3
What advantages are there in preparing a trial balance when you are about to prepare an income statement and balance sheet?

As you've just learnt from Activity 6.3, trial balances are not just done to find errors.

6.3 Trial balances and errors

Many students new to accounting assume that when the trial balance 'balances', the entries in the accounts must be correct. **This assumption is incorrect.** While it means that certain types of error have not been made (such as forgetting to enter the credit side of a transaction), there are several types of error that will not affect the balancing of a trial balance – omitting a transaction altogether, for example.

Examples of the errors which would be revealed, provided there are no compensating errors which cancel them out, are addition errors, using one figure for the debit entry and another figure for the credit entry, and entering only one side of a transaction.

We shall consider addition errors in greater detail in Chapter 27.

Activity 6.4
If a trial balance fails to agree, what steps would you take in order to find the cause of the difference?

6.4 Multiple choice self-test questions

A common practice of examining boards is to set multiple choice questions in accounting. In fact, this has become so popular with examiners that all the largest professional accounting bodies now use them, particularly in their first-level examinations.

Multiple choice questions give an examiner the opportunity to cover large parts of the syllabus briefly, but in detail. Students who omit to study areas of the syllabus will be caught out by an examiner's use of multiple choice questions. It is no longer possible to say that it is highly probable a certain topic will not be tested – the examiner can easily cover it with a multiple choice question.

We have deliberately included sets of 20 multiple choice questions at given places in this textbook, rather than a few at the end of each chapter. Such questions are relatively easy to answer a few minutes after reading the chapter. Asking the questions later is a far better test of your powers of recall and understanding. It also gives you practice at answering questions covering a range of topics in one block, as in an examination.

Each multiple choice question has a 'stem' (a part which poses the problem), a 'key' (which is the one correct answer), and a number of 'distractors', i.e. incorrect answers. The key plus the distractors are known as the 'options'.

If you do not know the answer, you should guess. You may be right by chance, or you may remember something subconsciously. In any event, unless the examiner warns otherwise, you will be expected to guess if you don't know the answer.

Read through the Learning Outcomes for this chapter and then attempt Multiple Choice Set 1.

Answers to all the multiple choice questions are given in Appendix 2 at the end of this book.

6.5 Closing inventory

Inventory at the end of a period is not usually to be found in an account in the ledger. It has to be found from inventory records and physical stocktaking. As it is typically not to be found in the ledger, it does not generally appear among the balances in a trial balance. However, the value of inventory at the beginning of a reporting period (opening inventory) is recorded in a ledger account, in which case the inventory balance at the start of a period would be included in the trial balance prepared at the end of that period.

Memory aid

The following diagram may help you to remember which accounts to debit and credit when they *increase* in value:

Debit	Credit
Expenses	Revenues
Losses	Profits
Assets	Liabilities
	Capital

Learning outcomes

You should now have learnt:

1 How to prepare a trial balance.

2 That trial balances are one form of checking the accuracy of entries in the accounts.

3 That errors can be made in the entries to the accounts that will not be shown up by the trial balance.

4 That the trial balance is used as the basis for preparing income statements and balance sheets.

Answers to activities

6.1   (a)   *Dr*   Van account   £9,000
                 Cr Bank account   £9,000
     (b)   *Dr*   Drawings account   £40
                 Cr Purchases account   £40

6.2   The alternate form of the accounting equation is Assets = Capital + Liabilities. All the accounts with debit balances are assets and all the accounts with credit balances are either capital or liabilities. This means that so long as you enter a debit for every credit, the alternate accounting equation must always balance. If the alternate accounting equation does not balance, you've made an error somewhere, either in your double entries, or in your arithmetic within the individual accounts. Virtually all occurrences where the accounting equation does not balance that arise in practice are the result of double entry errors.

6.3   Firstly, you can verify whether the total of the debit balances equals the total of the credit balances. They need to be equal, or your income statement and balance sheet will be incorrect and your balance sheet will not balance. (That is, the accounting equation will not balance.) Secondly, you need to know what the balance is on every account so that you can enter the appropriate figures into the income statement and balance sheet. If you don't prepare a trial balance, you will find it much more difficult to prepare these two accounting statements.

6.4   You need to check each entry to verify whether or not it is correct but firstly, it is best to start by checking that the totals in the trial balance have been correctly summed. Then, check that no account has been omitted from the trial balance. Then, check each account in turn.

Review questions

6.1   Darron starts his business on 1 May. He plans to buy plain T-shirts, print them with his own designs, and sell them to small retailers. The following transactions take place in his first month of trading, and you are asked to post them to T-accounts, balance-off the accounts and prepare a trial balance at 31 May:

May	1	Opens a business bank account with £800 of his own money.
	3	Borrows £2,000 from HBSC, repayable in four years' time.
	5	Buys screen printing machine (which he will use to produce the finished T-shirts) paying by cheque £2,500.
	7	Pays for online advertising, £75 using debit card.
	9	Buys plain T-shirts for £200, paying by cheque.
	11	Buys more plain T-shirts on time from M. Ball, £700.
	13	Sells some printed T-shirts; customer pays by cheque £380.
	15	Sells some printed T-shirts to N. Chadwick on time, £470.
	17	Sells some printed T-shirts to J. Vaughan on time, £550.
	19	Darron takes £110 from the business bank account for his own personal use.
	21	J. Vaughan returns unsatisfactory T-shirts (original sale value £60).
	23	Pays £300 cheque to M. Ball on account.
	25	Receives £170 cheque from N. Chadwick on account.
	31	Pays electricity charges for May, £145 direct debit.

6.2   Nicola Burt started her own business on 1 August. The following is a list of her transactions in that month:

Aug	1	Started business with £3,850 of her own cash.
	2	Paid £3,500 of this opening cash into a business bank account.
	4	Bought goods for resale on time, £414 from D. Bellini.
	5	Bought machinery, paying by bank transfer £2,500.
	7	Bought goods for resale, paying cash £323.
	10	Sold goods on time, £595 to J. Adams.
	11	N. Burt took goods from inventory for her own use, cost £98.
	12	Returned goods (to the value of £70) to D. Bellini.
	19	Sold goods for cash, £328.
	22	Bought computer equipment on time from TVC Ltd, £1,450.
	24	Received loan from G. Plover, £2,000 cheque, repayable in 10 years.
	29	Made a payment to D. Bellini, £180 cheque.
	30	Paid wages £530 to employee by bank transfer.
	31	Paid TVC Ltd in full by cheque £1,450.

Required
(a)   Enter the transactions in T-accounts and balance-off your accounts as at 31 August.
(b)   Prepare a trial balance as at 31 August.

6.3A   Record the following details relating to a carpet wholesaler for the month of November and extract a trial balance as at 30 November.

Nov	1	Started in business with £15,000 in the bank.
	3	Bought goods on time from: J. Small £290; F. Brown £1,200; R. Charles £530; T. Rae £610.
	5	Cash sales £610.
	6	Paid rent by cheque £175.
	7	Paid business rates by cheque £130.
	11	Sold goods on time to: T. Potts £85; J. Field £48; T. Gray £1,640.
	17	Paid wages by cash £290.
	18	We returned goods to: J. Small £18; R. Charles £27.
	19	Bought goods on time from: R. Charles £110; T. Rae £320; F. Jack £165.
	20	Goods were returned to us by: J. Field £6; T. Potts £14.
	21	Bought van on time from Turnkey Motors £4,950.
	23	We paid the following by cheque: J. Small £272; F. Brown £1,200; T. Rae £500.
	25	Bought another van, paying by cheque immediately £6,200.
	26	Received a loan of £750 cash from B. Bennet.
	28	Received cheques from: T. Potts £71; J. Field £42.
	30	Proprietor brings a further £900 into the business, by a payment into the business bank account

6.4A   Record the following transactions for the month of January of a small finishing retailer, balance-off all the accounts, and then extract a trial balance as at 30 June.

June	1	Started in business with £10,500 cash.
	2	Put £9,000 of the cash into a bank account.
	3	Bought goods for cash £550.
	4	Bought goods on time from: T. Dry £800; F. Hood £930; M. Smith £160; G. Low £510.
	5	Bought stationery on time from Buttons Ltd £89.
	6	Sold goods on time to: R. Tong £170; L. Fish £240; M. Singh £326; A. Tom £204.
	8	Paid rent by cheque £220.
	10	Bought fixtures on time from Chiefs Ltd £610.
	11	Paid salaries in cash £790.
	14	Returned goods to: F. Hood £30; M. Smith £42.
	15	Bought van by cheque £6,500.
	16	Received loan from B. Barclay by cheque £2,000.
	18	Goods returned to us by: R. Tong £5; M. Singh £20.
	21	Cash sales £145.
	24	Sold goods on time to: L. Fish £130; A. Tom £410; R. Pleat £158.
	26	We paid the following by cheque: F. Hood £900; M. Smith £118.
	29	Received cheques from: R. Pleat £158; L. Fish £370.
	30	Received a further loan from B. Barclay by cash £500.
	30	Received £614 cash from A. Tom.

6.5   Write up the accounts to record the following transactions in the books of M. Donnelly's business. Balance-off the accounts and prepare a trial balance at 30 April.

April	1	Starts his business by investing £3,500 of his own money (£500 in cash and £3,000 in a business bank account).
	5	Bought goods for resale on time for £475 from P. Thomas.
	6	Bought machinery for £1,450, paying by cheque.
	7	Paid insurance, £120 by debit card.
	9	Bought goods for resale on time, £255 from M. Wilkinson.

12	Sold goods on time to E. Grant £700.
15	Sold goods for cash, £300.
20	Paid the £475 due to P. Thomas with a cheque.
22	Returned goods (original cost £50) to M. Wilkinson.
24	Sold goods on time to E. Williams, £325.
25	Paid wages to employee, £45 by bank transfer.
27	E. Grant returned goods to M. Donnelly to the value of £80.
30	M. Donnelly took business cash for his personal use, £80.

6.6 Note, this question should not be attempted until cash discounts and trade discounts have been covered (see Chapters 9 and 11). It should also be noted that this is an example of the exception to the rule that closing inventory does not generally appear in a trial balance.

On 1 October 2019, the owner of the *USS Enterprise*, Mr Kirk, decides that he will boldly go and keep his records on a double entry system. His assets and liabilities at that date were:

	£
Fixtures and equipment	20,000
Inventory including weapons	15,000
Balance at Universe Bank	17,500
Cash	375

	£
Accounts payable – Spock	3,175
– Scott	200
– McCoy	500

Kirk's transactions during October were as follows:

1 Sold faulty phasers, original cost £500, to Klingon Corp, for cash £5,000.
2 Bought Photon Torpedoes (weapons), on time from Central Council £2,500.
3 Sold goods to Aardvarks, original cost £250, on time, £1,500.
4 Bought Cloaking Device (Fixture and Fittings) from Klingon Corp £3,500.
5 Paid the balance owed to Spock at 1 October less a 5 per cent cash discount.
6 Paid Central Council full amount due by cheque.
7 Received full amount due from Aardvarks by cheque.
8 Paid Klingon Corp by cheque after deducting 20 per cent cash discount.
9 Paid, by bankers order, £10,000 for repairs to *Enterprise* following disagreement over amount owing to Klingon Corp and faulty phasers.

Required:
Open *Enterprise*'s ledger accounts at 1 October, record all transactions for the month, balance the ledger accounts, and prepare a trial balance as at 31 October.

Multiple choice questions: Set 1

Now attempt Set 1 of multiple choice questions. (Answers to all the multiple choice questions are given in Appendix 2 at the end of this book.)

Each of these multiple choice questions has four suggested answers, (A), (B), (C) and (D). You should read each question and then decide which choice is best, either (A) or (B) or (C) or (D). *Write down your answers on a separate piece of paper.* You will then be able to redo the set of questions later without having to try to ignore your answers.

MC1 Which of the following statements is **incorrect**?

(A) Assets − Capital = Liabilities
(B) Liabilities + Capital = Assets
(C) Liabilities + Assets = Capital
(D) Assets − Liabilities = Capital

MC2 Which of the following is **not** an asset?

(A) Buildings
(B) Cash balance
(C) Accounts receivable
(D) Loan from K. Harris

MC3 Which of the following is a liability?

(A) Machinery
(B) Accounts payable for goods
(C) Motor vehicles
(D) Cash at bank

MC4 Which of the following is **incorrect**?

	Assets	Liabilities	Capital
	£	£	£
(A)	7,850	1,250	6,600
(B)	8,200	2,800	5,400
(C)	9,550	1,150	8,200
(D)	6,540	1,120	5,420

MC5 Which of the following statements is correct?

		Effect upon	
		Assets	Liabilities
(A)	We paid a creditor by cheque	− Bank	− Accounts payable
(B)	A debtor paid us £90 in cash	+ Cash	+ Accounts receivable
(C)	J. Hall lends us £500 by cheque	+ Bank	− Loan from Hall
(D)	Bought goods on time	+ Inventory	+ Capital

MC6   Which of the following are correct?

	Accounts	To record	Entry in the account
(i)	Assets	an increase	Debit
		a decrease	Credit
(ii)	Capital	an increase	Debit
		a decrease	Credit
iii)	Liabilities	an increase	Credit
		a decrease	Debit

(A)   (i) and (ii)
(B)   (ii) and (iii)
(C)   (i) and (iii)
(D)   (i), (ii) and (iii)

MC7   Which of the following are correct?

		Account to be debited	Account to be credited
(i)	Bought office furniture for cash	Office furniture	Cash
(ii)	A debtor, P. Sangster, pays us by cheque	Bank	P. Sangster
(iii)	Introduced capital by cheque	Capital	Bank
(iv)	Paid a creditor, B. Lee, by cash	B. Lee	Cash

(A)   (i), (ii) and (iii) only
(B)   (ii), (iii) and (iv) only
(C)   (i), (ii) and (iv) only
(D)   (i) and (iv) only

MC8   Which of the following are **incorrect**?

		Account to be debited	Account to be credited
(i)	Sold van for cash	Cash	Van
(ii)	Returned some of Office Equipment to Suppliers Ltd	Office Equipment	Suppliers Ltd
(iii)	Repaid part of loan from C. Charles by cheque	Loan from C. Charles	Bank
(iv)	Bought machinery on time from Betterways Ltd	Betterways Ltd	Machinery

(A)   (ii) and (iv) only
(B)   (iii) and (iv) only
(C)   (ii) and (iii) only
(D)   (i) and (iii) only

MC9   Which of the following best describes the meaning of 'Purchases'?

(A)   Items bought
(B)   Goods bought on time
(C)   Goods bought for resale
(D)   Goods paid for

→

→

MC10   Which of the following should not be called 'Sales'?

(A)   Office fixtures sold
(B)   Goods sold on time
(C)   Goods sold for cash
(D)   Sale of item previously included in 'Purchases'

MC11   Of the following, which are correct?

		Account to be debited	Account to be credited
(i)	Goods sold on time to R. Williams	R. Williams	Sales
(ii)	S. Johnson returns goods to us	Returns inwards	S. Johnson
(iii)	Goods bought for cash	Cash	Purchases
(iv)	We returned goods to A. Henry	A. Henry	Returns inwards

(A)   (i) and (iii) only
(B)   (i) and (ii) only
(C)   (ii) and (iv) only
(D)   (iii) and (iv) only

MC12   Which of the following are **incorrect**?

		Account to be debited	Account to be credited
(i)	Goods sold for cash	Cash	Sales
(ii)	Goods bought on time from T. Carter	Purchases	T. Carter
(iii)	Goods returned by us to C. Barry	C. Barry	Returns outwards
(iv)	Van bought for cash	Purchases	Cash

(A)   (i) and (iii) only
(B)   (iii) only
(C)   (ii) and (iv) only
(D)   (iv) only

MC13   Given the following, what is the amount of Capital? Assets: Premises £20,000; Inventory £8,500; Cash £100. Liabilities: Accounts payable £3,000; Loan from A. Adams £4,000

(A)   £21,100
(B)   £21,600
(C)   £32,400
(D)   £21,400

MC14   Which of the following is correct?

(A)   Profit does not alter capital
(B)   Profit reduces capital
(C)   Capital can only come from profit
(D)   Profit increases capital

MC15   Which of the following are correct?

		Account to be debited	Account to be credited
(i)	Received commission by cheque	Bank	Commission received
(ii)	Paid rates by cash	Rates	Cash
(iii)	Paid motor expenses by cheque	Motor expenses	Bank
(iv)	Received refund of insurance by cheque	Insurance	Bank

(A) (i) and (ii) only
(B) (i), (ii) and (iii) only
(C) (ii), (iii) and (iv) only
(D) (i), (ii) and (iv) only

MC16 Of the following, which are **incorrect**?

		Account to be debited	Account to be credited
(i)	Sold van for cash	Cash	Sales
(ii)	Bought stationery by cheque	Stationery	Bank
(iii)	Took cash out of business for private use	Cash	Drawings
(iv)	Paid general expenses by cheque	General expenses	Bank

(A) (ii) and (iv) only
(B) (i) and (ii) only
(C) (i) and (iii) only
(D) (ii) and (iii) only

MC17 What is the balance on the following account on 31 May 2020?

C. De Freitas

2020		£	2020		£
May	1 Sales	205	May	17 Cash	300
	14 Sales	360		28 Returns	50
	30 Sales	180			

(A) A credit balance of £395
(B) A debit balance of £380
(C) A debit balance of £395
(D) There is a nil balance on the account

MC18 What would have been the balance on the account of C. De Freitas in MC17 on 19 May 2020?

(A) A debit balance of £265
(B) A credit balance of £95
(C) A credit balance of £445
(D) A credit balance of £265

MC19 Which of the following best describes a trial balance?

(A) It shows the financial position of a business
(B) It is a special account
(C) It shows all the entries in the books
(D) It is a list of balances on the books

MC20 Is it true that the trial balance totals should agree?

(A) No, there are sometimes good reasons why they differ
(B) Yes, except where the trial balance is extracted at the year end
(C) Yes, always
(D) No, because it is not a balance sheet

Accounting concepts and assumptions

Learning objectives

After you have studied this chapter, you should be able to:

- describe the assumptions which are made when recording accounting data
- explain why one set of financial statements has to serve many purposes
- explain the implications of objectivity and subjectivity in the context of accounting
- explain what accounting standards are and why they exist
- describe the history of accounting standards in the UK and the current accounting standard options for UK entities
- explain the underlying concepts of accounting
- explain how the concepts and assumptions of materiality, going concern, comparability through consistency, prudence, accruals, separate determination, substance over form and other concepts and assumptions affect the recording and adjustment of accounting data and the reporting of accounting information

Introduction

What you have been reading about so far has been concerned with the recording of transactions in the books and the subsequent preparation of trial balances, income statements, and balance sheets. Such recording has been based on certain assumptions. Quite deliberately, these assumptions were not discussed in detail earlier. This is because it is much easier to look at them with a greater understanding *after* basic double entry has been covered. These assumptions are known as the *concepts of accounting.*

Income statements and balance sheets are prepared for the owners of a business. As shown later in this book, businesses are often owned by more than just one person and these accounting statements are for the use of all the owners.

However, if financial statements were solely for the use of the owner(s), there would be no need to adopt a common framework for the preparation and presentation of the information contained within them. As you learnt at the start of this book, there are a lot of other people who may also be interested in seeing these financial statements, and they need to be able to understand them. It is for this reason that there has to be a commonly established practice concerning how the information in the financial statements is prepared and presented.

In this chapter, you will learn about some of the agreed practices that underpin the preparation of accounting information, and about some of the regulations that have been developed to ensure that they are adhered to.

7.1 Objective of financial statements

Financial statements should provide information about the financial position, performance and changes in the financial position of an entity that is primarily useful to existing and potential investors, lenders and other creditors *in making decisions about providing resources to the entity.* Those decisions involve buying, selling or holding equity and debt instruments, and providing or settling loans and other forms of credit.

These primary users need information about the resources of the entity to assess:

● its potential for future net cash inflows
● its stewardship, i.e. how effectively and efficiently management has used the entity's resources.

In order to achieve this objective, financial statements are prepared on the basis of a number of established concepts and assumptions and must adhere to the rules and procedures set down in regulations called, '*accounting standards*'.

7.2 One set of financial statements for all purposes

If it had always been the custom to draft different financial statements for different purposes, so that one version was given to a banker, another to someone wishing to buy the business, etc., then financial accounting would be very different from what it is today. However, this has not occurred. Identical copies of the financial statements are given to all the different external stakeholders, irrespective of why they wish to look at them.

This means that the banker, the prospective buyer of the business, shareholders, etc. all see the same income statement and balance sheet. This is not an ideal situation as the interests of each party are different and each party seeks different kinds of information from those wanted by the others. For instance, bank managers would really like to know how much the assets would sell for if the business ceased trading. They could then see what the possibility would be of the bank obtaining repayment of its loan or the overdraft. Other people would also like to see the information in the way that is most useful to them.

 Activity 7.1 This doesn't sound very ideal for anyone, does it? What benefits do you think there may be that outweigh these disadvantages of one set of financial statements for all?

Because everyone receives the same income statement and balance sheet, in order to be of any use all the various stakeholders have to believe that the assumptions upon which these financial statements are based are valid and appropriate. If they don't, they won't trust the financial statements.

Assume that you are in a class of students and that you have the problem of valuing your assets, which consist of four textbooks. The first value you decide is based upon how much you could sell them for. Your own guess is £60, but the other members of your class suggest they should be valued at anything from £30 to £80.

Suppose that you now decide to put a value on their use to you. You may well think that the use of these textbooks will enable you to pass your examinations and that you'll then be able to get a good job. Another person may have the opposite idea concerning the use of the textbooks. The use value placed on the textbooks by others in the class will be quite different. Your value may be higher than those of some of your colleagues and lower than others.

Finally, you decide to value them by reference to cost. You take out the receipts you were given when you purchased the textbooks, which show that you paid a total of £120 for them. If the rest of the class does not think that you have altered the receipts, then they will all agree with you that the value of the books, expressed at original cost, is £120. At last, you have found a way of valuing the textbooks where everyone agrees on the same figure. As this is the only valuation that you can all agree upon, each of you decides to use the idea of valuing the asset of textbooks at their cost price so that you can have a meaningful discussion about what you are worth (in terms of your assets, i.e. your textbooks) compared with everyone else in the class. It probably won't come as a surprise to you to learn that this is precisely the basis upon which the assets of a business are valued. Accountants call it the **historical cost concept**.

7.3 Objectivity and subjectivity

The use of a method which arrives at a value that everyone can agree to *because it is based upon a factual occurrence* is said to be **objective**. Valuing your textbooks at their cost is, therefore, objective – you are adhering to and accepting the facts. You are not placing your own interpretation on the facts. As a result, everyone else knows where the value came from and can see that there is very good evidence to support its adoption.

If, instead of being objective, you were **subjective**, you would use your own judgement to arrive at a cost. This often results in the value you arrive at being biased towards your own views and preferences – as in the example above when the usefulness of the textbooks to you for examinations was the basis of their valuation. Subjective valuations seem right to the person who makes them, but many other people would probably disagree with the value arrived at, because it won't appear to them to be objectively based.

The desire to provide the same set of financial statements for many different parties, and so provide a basis for measurement that is generally acceptable, means that objectivity is sought in financial accounting. If you are able to understand this desire for objectivity, then many of the apparent contradictions in accounting can be understood, because objectivity is at the heart of the financial accounting methods we all use.

Financial accounting, therefore, seeks objectivity and it seeks consistency in how information is prepared and presented. To achieve this, there must be a set of rules which lay down the way in which the transactions of the business are recorded. These rules have long been known as 'accounting concepts'. A group of these have become known as 'fundamental accounting concepts' or 'accounting principles' and have been enforced through their incorporation in accounting standards issued on behalf of the accountancy bodies by accounting standards boards, and by their inclusion in the relevant legislation governing companies.

7.4 Accounting standards and financial reporting standards in the UK

At one time, there used to be quite wide differences in the ways that accountants calculated profits. In the late 1960s a number of cases led to a widespread outcry against this lack of uniformity in accounting practice.

In response, the UK accounting bodies formed the Accounting Standards Committee (ASC). It issued a series of accounting standards, called *Statements of Standard Accounting Practice* (SSAPs). The ASC was replaced in 1990 by the Accounting Standards Board (ASB), which also issued accounting standards, this time called *Financial Reporting Standards* (FRSs). Both these forms of accounting standards were compulsory, enforced by company law.

From time to time, the ASB also issued *Urgent Issue Task Force Abstracts* (UITFs). These were generally intended to be in force only while a standard was being prepared or an existing standard amended to cover the topic dealt with in the UITF. Not surprisingly, some issues did not merit a full standard and so a few UITFs were never replaced by a new standard. UITFs carried the same weight as accounting standards and their application was compulsory for financial statements prepared under *UK GAAP* – the term for the set of regulations and legislation applicable to and created for UK financial statements.

SSAPs and FRSs were generally developed with the larger company in mind. In an effort to make adherence to standards more manageable for smaller companies, in 1997 the ASB issued a third category of standard – the *Financial Reporting Standard for Smaller Entities* (FRSSE). It was, in effect, a collection of some of the rules from virtually all the other accounting standards. Small entities could choose whether to apply it or continue to apply all the other accounting standards.

The authority, scope and application of each document issued by the ASB was announced when the document was issued. Thus, even though each accounting standard and UITF must be applied by anyone preparing financial statements under UK GAAP, in some cases certain classes of organisations were exempted from applying some or all of the rules contained within them.

> **Activity 7.2** What benefits do you think there are if all entities adopt the same set of accounting standards?

In 2005, most companies whose shares were quoted on the London Stock Exchange were required to switch to International Accounting Standards, and other entities could do so if they wished. By 2010, many had switched voluntarily to International GAAP. Among those that had not switched to International GAAP, many had changed from UK GAAP terminology in their financial statements (such as 'stock' and 'Profit and Loss Account') to International GAAP terminology (such as 'inventory' and 'Income Statement').

The usefulness of UK accounting standards was clearly reducing. Consequently, in 2010 the ASB published an exposure draft on the future of financial reporting in the UK and Republic of Ireland. It proposed a revised **Conceptual Framework** aimed at balancing the needs of preparers and users of financial statements; and sought to simplify UK standards into a concise, coherent and updated form.

In 2012 the Financial Reporting Council (FRC) took over the work of the ASB. It very quickly replaced almost all extant standards and they were all replaced by the end of 2015. Currently, six Financial Reporting Standards have been issued:

● FRS 100 *Application of Financial Reporting Requirements*
● FRS 101 *Reduced Disclosure Framework*
● FRS 102 *The Financial Reporting Standard applicable in the UK and Republic of Ireland*
● FRS 103 *Insurance Contracts*
● FRS 104 *Interim Financial Reporting*
● FRS 105 *The Financial Reporting Standard applicable to the Micro-entities Regime.*

You can find out more about the work of the FRC and the standards currently in issue at its website (www.frc.org.uk/Our-Work/Codes-Standards/Accounting-and-Reporting-Policy/Accounting-Standards-and-Statements-issued-by-the/Standards-in-Issue.aspx).

> **Activity 7.3** What do you think the benefits were of a change to a reduced set of accounting standards?

7.5 International Accounting Standards

The Financial Reporting Council deals with the United Kingdom and Ireland. Besides this and other national accounting boards, there is an international organisation concerned with accounting standards. The International Accounting Standards Committee (IASC) was established in 1973 and changed its name to the International Accounting Standards Board (IASB) in 2000.

The perceived need for the IASB was due to:

(a) The considerable growth in international investment. This means that it is desirable to have similar accounting methods the world over so that investment decisions are more compatible.

(b) The growth in the number of multinational organisations. These organisations have to produce financial statements covering a large number of countries. Standardisation between countries makes the accounting work that much easier, and reduces costs.

(c) As quite a few countries now have their own standard-setting bodies, it is desirable that their efforts be harmonised.

(d) The need for accounting standards in countries that could not afford a standard-setting body of their own.

The IASB has 14 members, four from Europe, four from the Americas, four from Asia/Oceania, one from Africa, and one from the rest of the world. Its members are appointed by IFRS Foundation Trustees and must reflect an appropriate balance of auditors, financial statement preparers, users of financial statements and academics.

The IASC issued International Accounting Standards (IASs) and the IASB issues International Financial Reporting Standards (IFRSs). When the IASC was founded, it had no formal authority and IASs were entirely voluntary and initially intended for use in countries that either did not have their own accounting standards or would have had considerable logistical difficulty in establishing and maintaining the infrastructure necessary to sustain a national accounting standards board.

While the ASB had strived to ensure that most of the provisions of the relevant international standards were incorporated in its SSAPs and FRSs, there remained some differences between the two sets of standards. However, with the consolidation of all extant UK accounting standards by the FRC it is anticipated this will no longer be the case. It is also anticipated that international standards will be adopted in future by all but the smallest UK entities.

This textbook describes and discusses the contents of International Accounting Standards, and the terminology used throughout the book is that typically used under those standards.

7.6 Accounting standards and the legal framework

Accounting standards are given legal status under the Companies Acts and comply with European Union Directives. This ensures that there is no conflict between the law and accounting standards. Anyone preparing financial statements which are intended to show a 'true and fair view' (i.e. truly reflect what has occurred and the financial position of the organisation) must observe the rules laid down in the accounting standards.

7.7 Underlying accounting concepts

A number of *accounting concepts* have been applied ever since financial statements were first produced for external reporting purposes. These have become second nature to accountants and are not generally reinforced, other than through custom and practice.

The historical cost concept

The need for this has already been described in the textbook valuation example. It means that assets are normally shown at cost price, and that this is the basis for valuation of the assets.

The money measurement concept

Accounting information has traditionally been concerned only with those facts covered by (*a*) and (*b*) which follow:

(*a*) it can be measured in monetary units; and
(*b*) most people will agree to the monetary value of the transaction.

This limitation is referred to as the **money measurement concept**, and it means that accounting can never tell you everything about a business. For example, accounting does not show the following:

(*c*) whether the business has good or bad managers;
(*d*) whether there are serious problems with the workforce;
(*e*) whether a rival product is about to take away many of the best customers;
(*f*) whether the government is about to pass a law which will cost the business a lot of extra expense in future.

The reason that (*c*) to (*f*) or similar items are not recorded is that it would be impossible to work out a monetary value for them which most people would agree to.

Some people think that accounting and financial statements tell you everything you want to know about a business. The above shows that this is not the case.

The business entity concept

The **business entity concept** implies that the affairs of a business are to be treated as being quite separate from the non-business activities of its owner(s).

The items recorded in the books of the business are, therefore, restricted to the transactions of the business. No matter what activities the proprietor(s) get up to outside the business, they are completely disregarded in the books kept by the business.

The only time that the personal resources of the proprietor(s) affect the accounting records of a business is when they introduce new capital into the business, or take drawings out of it.

The dual aspect concept

This states that there are two aspects of accounting, one represented by the assets of the business and the other by the claims against them. The concept states that these two aspects are always equal to each other. In other words, this is the alternate form of the accounting equation:

$$\boxed{\text{Assets} = \text{Capital} + \text{Liabilities}}$$

As you know, double entry is the name given to the method of recording transactions under the **dual aspect concept**.

The time interval concept

One of the underlying principles of accounting, the **time interval concept**, is that financial statements are prepared at regular intervals of one year. Companies which publish further financial statements between their annual ones describe the others as 'interim statements'. For internal management purposes, financial statements may be prepared far more frequently, possibly on a monthly basis or even more often.

7.8 Underlying assumptions

The IASB Conceptual Framework lists two assumptions that must be applied if financial statements are to meet their objectives: the **accrual basis** (also called the **accruals concept**) and the **going concern concept**.

Accrual basis

The effects of transactions and other events are recognised when they occur and they are recorded in the books and reported in the financial statements of the period to which they relate.

Net profit is the difference between revenues and the expenses incurred in generating those revenues, i.e

$$\text{Revenues} - \text{Expenses} = \text{Net Profit}$$

Determining the expenses used up to obtain the revenues is referred to as *matching* expenses against revenues. The key to the application of the concept is that all income and charges relating to the financial period to which the financial statements relate should be taken into account without regard to the date of receipt or payment.

This concept is particularly misunderstood by people who have not studied accounting. To many of them, actual payment of an item in a period is taken as being matched against the revenue of the period when the net profit is calculated. The fact that expenses consist of the assets used up in a particular period in obtaining the revenues of that period, and that cash paid in a period and expenses of a period are usually different, as you will see later, comes as a surprise to a great number of them.

This assumption requires that adjustments are made to some figures in the trial balance before the financial statements can be prepared. The process of doing so is covered in Chapter 22.

Going concern

It is assumed that the business will continue to operate for at least twelve months after the end of the reporting period.

Suppose, however, that a business is drawing up its financial statements at 31 December 2019. Normally, using the historical cost concept, the assets would be shown at a total value of £100,000. It is known, however, that the business will be forced to close down in February 2020, only two months later, and the assets are expected to be sold for only £15,000.

In this case it would not make sense to keep to the going concern concept, and so we can reject the historical cost concept for asset valuation purposes. In the balance sheet at 31 December 2019, the assets will be shown at the figure of £15,000. Rejection of the going concern concept is the exception rather than the rule.

Examples where the going concern assumption should be rejected are:

● if the business is going to close down in the near future;
● where shortage of cash makes it almost certain that the business will have to cease trading;
● where a large part of the business will almost certainly have to be closed down because of a shortage of cash.

7.9 Qualitative characteristics of financial statements

A useful diagram (Exhibit 7.1) illustrating the qualitative characteristics of accounting information was included by the ASB in an early draft of its equivalent of the IASB principles (upon which it was based).

Exhibit 7.1 The qualitative characteristics of accounting information

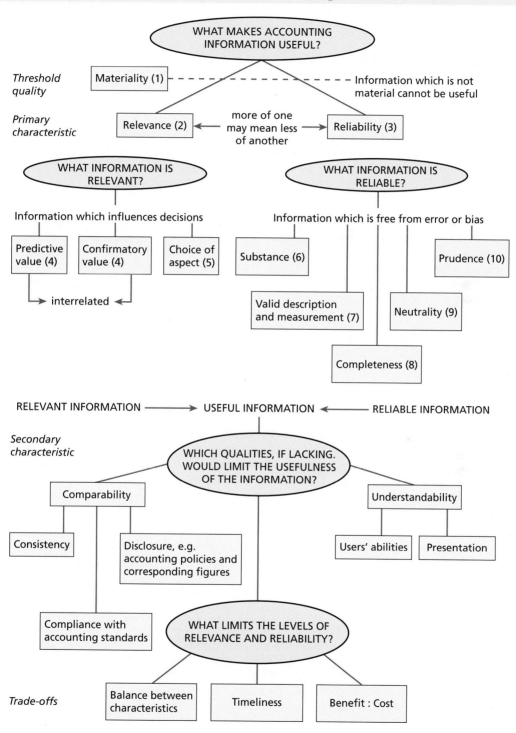

These are the attributes that make the information provided in financial statements useful to users. There are four principal qualitative characteristics: understandability, relevance, reliability and comparability.

Understandability

Information in financial statements should be readily understandable by users.

Relevance

Information in financial statements must be relevant to the decision-making needs of users. To be relevant, information must influence the economic decisions of users by helping them evaluate past, present or future events or confirming, or correcting, their past evaluation.

Materiality

Information is **material** if its omission or misstatement could influence the economic decisions of users. Materiality depends on the size of the item or error judged in the particular circumstances of its omission or misstatement.

Everything that appears in a financial accounting statement should be 'material'. That is, it should be of interest to the stakeholders, those people who make use of financial accounting statements – the present and potential future investors and creditors of the entity. It need not be material to every stakeholder, but it must be material to a stakeholder before it merits inclusion.

Accounting does not serve a useful purpose if the effort of recording a transaction in a certain way is not worthwhile. Thus, if a box of paper-clips was bought it would be used up over a period of time, and this cost is used up every time someone uses a paper-clip. It is possible to record this as an expense every time a paper-clip is used but, obviously, the price of a paper-clip is so small that it is not worth recording it in this fashion, nor is the entire box of paper-clips. The paper-clips are not a material item and, therefore, the box would be charged as an expense in the period when it was bought, irrespective of the fact that it could last for more than one accounting period. In other words, **do not waste your time in the elaborate recording of trivial items.**

Similarly, the purchase of a cheap metal ashtray would also be charged as an expense in the period when it was bought because it is not a material item, even though it may in fact last for twenty years. A lorry would, however, be deemed to be a material item in most businesses, and so, as will be seen in Chapter 21, an attempt is made to charge each period with the cost consumed in each period of its use.

 Activity 7.4 Which fundamental accounting concept is what is being described in the previous paragraph an example of?

Businesses fix all sorts of arbitrary rules to determine what is material and what is not. There is no law that lays down what these should be – the decision as to what is material and what is not is dependent upon judgement. A business may well decide that all items under £100 should be treated as expenses in the period in which they were bought, even though they may well be in use in the business for the following 10 years. Another business, especially a large one, may fix the limit at £1,000. Different limits may be set for different types of item.

It can be seen that the size and the type of business will affect the decisions as to which items are material. With individuals, an amount of £1,000 may well be more than you, as a student, possess. For a multi-millionaire, what is a material item and what is not will almost certainly not be comparable. Just as individuals vary, then, so do businesses. Some businesses have a great deal of machinery and may well treat all items of machinery costing less than £1,000 as not being material, whereas another business which makes about the same amount of profit, but has very little machinery, may well treat a £600 machine as being a material item as they have fixed their materiality limit at £250.

Reliability

To be useful, information must also be reliable. To be reliable, information must be free from material error and bias and able to be depended upon by users to represent faithfully what it claims to represent.

Faithful representation

A balance sheet should represent faithfully the transactions and other events that result in assets, liabilities and equity of the entity at the reporting date.

Substance over form

Transactions and other events must be accounted for and presented in accordance with their substance and economic reality and not merely their legal form. This is referred to as **substance over form**.

The legal form of a transaction can differ from its real substance. Where this happens, accounting should show the transaction in accordance with its real substance which is, basically, how the transaction affects the economic situation of the business. This means that accounting in this instance will not reflect the exact legal position concerning that transaction.

You have not yet come across the best and easiest illustration of this concept. Later in your studies you may have to learn about accounting for non-current assets being bought through a leasing agreement. We will take a car as an example. Imagine it was being bought in this way.

● From a legal point of view, the car does not belong to the business until (i) all the instalments on the lease have been paid *and* (ii) an option has been taken up whereby the business takes over legal possession of the car.
● From an economic point of view, you have used the car for business purposes, just as any other car owned by the business which was paid for immediately has been used. In this case, the business will show the car being bought under a leasing agreement in its ledger accounts and balance sheet as though it were legally owned by the business. It will also include an account in its ledger for the amount still to be paid and include it among the liabilities at the period end.

In this way, therefore, the substance of the transaction has taken precedence over the legal form of the transaction.

Neutrality

Information in financial statements must be free of bias.

Prudence

This is the inclusion of a degree of caution in the exercise of the judgement needed in making the estimates required under conditions of uncertainty (e.g. decisions relating to bad debts and allowances for doubtful debts), such that assets and income are not overstated and liabilities and expenses are not understated.

Very often accountants have to use their judgement to decide which figure to take for an item. Suppose a debt has been owing for quite a long time, and no one knows whether it will ever be paid. Should the accountant be optimistic and think that it will be paid, or be more pessimistic?

It is the accountant's duty to see that people get the proper facts about a business. The accountant should make certain that assets are not valued too highly. Similarly, liabilities should not be shown at values that are too low. Otherwise, people might inadvisedly lend money to a business, which they would not do if they had been provided with the proper facts.

The accountant should always exercise caution when dealing with uncertainty while, at the same time, ensuring that the financial statements are neutral – that gains and losses are neither overstated nor understated – and this is known as **prudence**.

It is true that, in applying the prudence concept, an accountant will normally make sure that all losses are recorded in the books, but that profits and gains will not be anticipated by recording them before they should be recorded. Although it emphasises neutrality, many people feel that the prudence concept means that accountants will normally take the figure relating to unrealised profits and gains which will understate rather than overstate the profit for a period. That is, they believe that accountants tend to choose figures that will cause the capital of the business to be shown at a lower amount rather than at a higher amount.

Activity 7.5

Do you agree with this view that the prudence concept results in accountants producing financial statements that understate profits and gains and therefore present a value for capital that is lower than it should be? Justify your answer.

Recognition of profits and gains

The recognition of profits at an appropriate time has long been recognised as being in need of guidelines and these have long been enshrined in what is known as the **realisation concept**. This is not so much a separate concept as a part of the broader concept of prudence.

The realisation concept holds to the view that profit and gains can only be taken into account when realisation has occurred and that realisation occurs only when the ultimate cash realised is capable of being assessed (i.e. determined) with reasonable certainty. Several criteria have to be observed before realisation can occur:

- goods or services are provided for the buyer;
- the buyer accepts liability to pay for the goods or services;
- the monetary value of the goods or services has been established;
- the buyer will be in a situation to be able to pay for the goods or services.

Notice that it is not the time

- when the order is received; or
- when the customer pays for the goods.

However, it is only when you can be reasonably certain as to how much will be received that you can recognise profits or gains.

Of course, recognising profits and gains now that will only be 100 per cent known in future periods is unlikely to ever mean that the correct amount has been recognised. Misjudgements can arise when, for example, profit is recognised in one period, and later it is discovered that this was incorrect because the goods involved have been returned in a later period because of some deficiency. Also, where services are involved rather than goods, the services might turn out to be subject to an allowance being given in a later period owing to poor performance.

Activity 7.6

What do you think the accountant should do about these possibilities when applying the realisation concept?

The accountant needs to take every possibility into account yet, at the same time, the prudence concept requires that the financial statements are 'neutral', that is, that neither gains nor losses should be overstated or understated.

As you will see if you take your studies to a more advanced stage, there are times other than on completion of a sale when profit may be recognised. These could include profits on long-term contracts spanning several years, such as the building of a hotel or a very large bridge. In this case, profit might be calculated for each year of the contract, even though the work is not finished at that date.

Completeness

To be reliable, information in financial statements must be complete within the bounds of materiality and cost.

Comparability

Comparability requires **consistency**. The measurement and display of the financial effect of similar transactions and other events must be done in a consistent way throughout an entity and over time for that entity, and in a consistent way for different entities. Users must be informed of the accounting policies used in the preparation of the financial statements. They must be informed of any changes in those policies and of the effects of such changes. Financial statements must include corresponding information for the preceding periods.

7.10 Constraints on relevant and reliable information

Timeliness

Information must be reported in a timely manner.

Balance between benefit and cost

The benefits of information should exceed the costs of obtaining it.

Balance between qualitative characteristics

The aim should be to achieve a balance among the characteristics that best meets the objective of financial statements – see Section 7.1.

7.11 Other assumptions

Separate determination

In determining the aggregate amount of each asset or liability, the amount of each individual asset or liability should be determined separately from all other assets and liabilities. This is called **separate determination**. For example, if you have three machines, the amount at which machinery is shown in the balance sheet should be the sum of the values calculated individually for each of the three machines. Only when individual values have been derived should a total be calculated.

Stability of currency

Accounting follows the historical cost concept, so assets are normally shown at their original cost. This has the effect of distorting the financial statements if inflation has caused the value of money to change over time – assets purchased 20 years ago for £50,000 would cost considerably more today, yet they would appear at that cost, not at the equivalent cost today. Users of financial statements need to be aware of this. There are techniques for eliminating these distortions, and they are covered in *Frank Wood's Business Accounting 2*.

7.12 Accounting concepts and assumptions in action

This is too early a stage in your studies for you to be able to appreciate more fully how these concepts and assumptions work in practice. It is far better left towards the end of this book. We consider this topic further in Chapter 41.

Learning outcomes

You should now have learnt:

1 Why one set of financial statements has to serve many purposes.

2 Why the need for general agreement has given rise to the concepts and conventions that govern accounting.

3 The implications of objectivity and subjectivity in the context of accounting.

4 What accounting standards are and why they exist.

5 That while most UK entities have adopted IFRS, those that have not apply the accounting standards issued by the Financial Reporting Council (FRC).

6 The assumptions which are made when recording accounting data.

7 The underlying concepts of accounting.

8 How the concepts and assumptions of materiality, going concern, comparability through consistency, prudence, accruals, separate determination, substance over form, and other concepts and assumptions affect the recording and adjustment of accounting data and the reporting of accounting information.

9 That an assumption is made that monetary measures remain stable, i.e. that accounts are not normally adjusted for inflation or deflation.

Answers to activities

7.1 Although this is hardly ideal, at least everyone receives the same basic financial information concerning an organisation and, because all financial statements are prepared in the same way, comparison between them is reasonably straightforward. Also, some of the users of these financial statements have other sources of information, financial and otherwise, about a business – the banker, for example, will also have access to the financial statements produced for use by the managers of the business. These 'management accounts' are considerably more detailed than the financial statements and most bankers insist upon access to them when large sums of money are involved. (The financial statements produced for internal use are dealt with in Chapter 36.) The banker will also have information about other businesses in the same industry and about the state of the market in which the business operates, and will thus be able to compare the performance of the business against that of its competitors.

7.2 The use of accounting standards does *not* mean that two identical businesses will show exactly the same revenue, expenditure and profits year by year in their financial statements. However, it does considerably reduce the possibilities of very large variations in financial reporting, facilitates comparison between entities, and encourages consistency in the preparation of financial statements.

7.3 Previously, there were 40 UK accounting standards which companies that had not adopted international financial reporting standards (IFRS) were required to observe – 11 SSAPs and 29 FRSs. Now, there are six, and most of what was covered by the 40 standards are now included in FRS 102. This makes preparing financial statements a lot less complex and far more efficient, with no possibility of any inconsistencies that may have existed under the previous set of standards which were released across a considerable period of time.

7.4 The accruals assumption (which is also sometimes referred to as the 'accruals concept').

7.5 Although accountants do include all the losses that have been identified in the financial statements, they also include all the gains that can be identified with reasonable certainty. In effect, by doing so, an accountant is being neutral and so, in practice, the amount of capital shown in the balance sheet should be a true reflection of the position as known when the financial statements were produced.

7.6 When applying the realisation concept, the accountant will endeavour to estimate as accurately as possible the returns or allowances that are reasonably likely to arise and will build that information into the calculation of the profit and gains to be recognised in the period for which financial statements are being prepared.

Review questions

7.1 What is meant by the 'money measurement concept'?

7.2 Explain the concept of prudence in relation to the recognition of profits and losses.

7.3 Explain the term 'materiality' as it is used in accounting.

7.4 'The historical cost convention looks backwards but the going concern convention looks forwards.'

Required:
(a) Explain clearly what is meant by:
   (i) the historical cost convention;
   (ii) the going concern convention.
(b) Does traditional financial accounting, using the historical cost convention, make the going concern convention unnecessary? Explain your answer fully.
(c) Which do you think a shareholder is likely to find more useful – a report on the past or an estimate of the future? Why?

(Association of Chartered Certified Accountants)

BOOKS AND TRANSACTIONS

Introduction

This part is concerned with the books into which transactions are first entered. It also includes a chapter on VAT. One important thing to realise is that most of what you will learn about in these chapters is now done using a computer. By learning how to make these entries yourself, you will be able to understand what has been done on a computer and use it effectively, just as if it had been done manually.

chapter

8

Books of original entry and ledgers

Learning objectives

After you have studied this chapter, you should be able to:

- justify the need for books of original entry
- explain what each book of original entry is used for
- describe the process of recording transactions in a book of original entry and then recording a summary of the transactions involving similar items in a ledger
- distinguish between personal and impersonal accounts
- list the ledgers most commonly used and distinguish between those that are used for personal accounts and those that are used for impersonal accounts
- explain the broader role of an accountant, the communicator role that lies beyond the recording and processing of data about transactions

Introduction

In this chapter, you will learn about the books in which details of accounting transactions are recorded. You will learn that Day Books are used to record all unpaid transactions made on credit and that the Cash Book is used to record all cash and bank transactions. Then, you will learn that these entries are transferred from the books of original entry to a set of books called Ledgers and that each Ledger is for a particular type of item and that, by having a set of Ledgers, entries in accounts of items of a similar nature are recorded in the same place.

8.1 The growth of the business

When a business is very small, all the double entry accounts can be kept in one book, which we would call a 'ledger'. As the business grows it would be impossible just to use one book, as the large number of pages needed for a lot of transactions would mean that the book would be too big to handle. Also, suppose we have several bookkeepers. They could not all do their work properly if there were only one ledger.

The answer to this problem was to use more books, with a book for each type of transaction. Sales will be entered in one book, purchases in another book, cash in another book, and so on.

8.2 Books of original entry

When a transaction takes place, we need to record as much as possible of the details of the transaction. For example, if we sold four computers on time to a Mr De Souza for £1,000 per computer, we would want to record that we sold four computers for £1,000 each to Mr De Souza on time. We would also want to record the address and contact information of Mr De Souza and the date of the transaction. Some businesses would also record information like the identity of the person who sold them to Mr De Souza and the time of the sale.

Books of original entry are the books in which we first record transactions, such as the sale of the four computers. When we enter transactions in these books, we record:

● the date on which each transaction took place – the transactions should be shown in date order; and
● details relating to the sale (as listed in the computer example above), which are entered in a 'details' column.

Also,

● a folio column entry is made cross-referencing back to the original 'source document', e.g. the invoice; and
● the monetary amounts are entered in columns included in the books of original entry for that purpose.

8.3 Types of books of original entry

Books of original entry are known as either 'journals' or '**day books**'. However, in the case of the last book of original entry shown below, it is always a '**journal**' and the second last is always known as the '**cash book**'. The term 'day book' is used for the others, as it more clearly indicates the nature of these books of original entry – entries are made to them every day. These commonly used books of original entry are:

● **Sales day book** (or *Sales journal*) – for credit sales.
● **Purchases day book** (or *Purchases journal*) – for credit purchases.
● **Returns inwards day book** (or *Returns inwards journal*) – for returns inwards.
● **Returns outwards day book** (or *Returns outwards journal*) – for returns outwards.
● **Cash book** – for receipts and payments of cash and cheques.
● General journal (or **Journal** if the term 'day book' is used for the other books of original entry) – for other items.

Note: Some entities use the word 'journal' instead of 'day book'. Be sure to remember this. Examiners may use either term in the name of the first four books listed above.

8.4 Using more than one ledger

Entries are made in the books of original entry. The entries are then summarised and the summary information is entered, using double entry, to accounts kept in the various ledgers of the business. One reason why a set of ledgers is used rather than just one big ledger is that this makes it easier to divide the work of recording all the entries between different bookkeepers.

Activity 8.1   Why else do you think we have more than one ledger?

8.5   Types of ledgers

The different types of ledgers most businesses use are:

- **Sales ledger.** This is for customers' personal accounts – the accounts receivable.
- **Purchases ledger.** This is for suppliers' personal accounts – the accounts payable.
- **General ledger.** This contains the remaining double entry accounts, such as those relating to expenses, non-current assets, and capital.

8.6   A diagram of the books commonly used

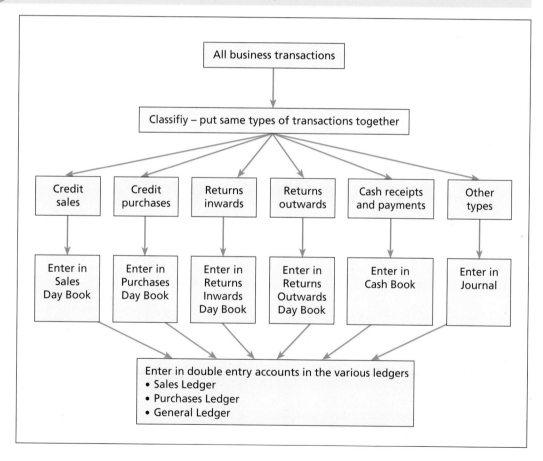

8.7   Description of books used

In the next few chapters we will look at the books used in more detail.

8.8 Types of accounts

Some people describe all accounts as personal accounts or as impersonal accounts.

● **Personal accounts** – these are for debtors and creditors (i.e. customers and suppliers).
● **Impersonal accounts** – divided between 'real' accounts and 'nominal' accounts:

  – **Real accounts** – accounts in which possessions are recorded. Examples are buildings, machinery, fixtures and inventory.
  – **Nominal accounts** – accounts in which expenses, income and capital are recorded.

A diagram may enable you to follow this better:

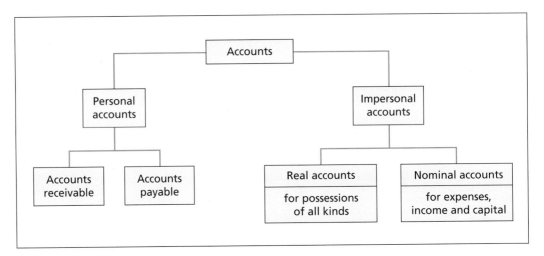

8.9 Nominal and private ledgers

The ledger in which the impersonal accounts are kept is known as the **Nominal** (or 'General') **Ledger**. In order to ensure privacy for the proprietor(s), the capital, drawings and other similar accounts are sometimes kept in a **Private Ledger**. This prevents office staff from seeing details of items which the proprietors want to keep secret.

Activity 8.2 Why bother with *books of original entry*? Why don't we just enter transactions straight into the ledgers?

8.10 The accountant as a communicator

The impression is often given that all that an accountant does is produce figures arranged in various ways. This has led to a perception that accountants are boring, pragmatic people with no sense of humour. While it is true that such work does take up quite a lot of an accountant's time, it does not account for all of a typical accountant's work. **Accountants also need to be good communicators**, not just in the way they present accounting information on paper, but also in how they verbally communicate the significance of the information they prepare.

An accountant can obviously arrange the financial figures so as to present the information in as meaningful a way as possible for the people who are going to use that information. That is, after all, what accountants are trained to do. If the financial figures are to be given to several people, all of whom are very knowledgeable about accounting, an accountant will simply apply all the conventions and regulations of accounting in order to present the information in the 'normal' accounting way, knowing full well that the recipients of the information will understand it.

On the other hand, accounting figures may well be needed by people who have absolutely no knowledge at all of accounting. In such a case, a typical accounting statement would be of little or no use to them. They would not understand it. In this case, an accountant might set out the figures in a completely different way to try to make it easy for them to grasp. For instance, instead of preparing a 'normal' income statement, the accountant might show the information as follows:

	£	£
In the year ended 31 December 2019 you sold goods for		100,000
Now, how much had those goods cost you to buy?		
At the start of the year you had inventory costing	12,000	
+ You bought some more goods in the year costing	56,000	
So altogether you had goods available to sell that cost	68,000	
− At the end of the year, you had inventory of goods unsold that cost	(6,000)	
So, the goods you had sold in the year had cost you	62,000	
Let us deduct this from what you had sold the goods for		(62,000)
This means that you had made a profit on buying and selling goods, before any other expenses had been paid, amounting to		38,000
(We call this type of profit the **gross** profit)		
But, during the year, you suffered other expenses such as wages, rent and electricity. The amount of these expenses, not including anything you took for yourself, amounted to		(18,000)
So, in this year your sales value exceeded all the costs involved in running the business (so that the sales could be made) by		20,000
(We call this type of profit the **net** profit)		

An accountant is failing to perform his or her role appropriately and effectively if the figures are not arranged so as to make them meaningful to the recipient. The accountant's job is not just to produce figures for the accountant's own consumption, it is to communicate the results to other people, many of whom know nothing about accounting.

Activity 8.3

Reconcile this observation with the standardisation of the presentation of financial accounting information as contained in accounting standards and the Companies Acts.

Nowadays, communication skills are a very important part of the accountant's role. Very often, the accountant will have to talk to people in order to explain the figures, or send a letter or write a report about them. The accountant will also have to talk or write to people to find out exactly what sort of accounting information is needed by them, or to explain to them what sort of information could be provided.

If accounting examinations contained only computational questions, they would not test the ability of candidates to communicate in any way other than writing down accounting figures and, as a result, the examinations would fail to examine these other important aspects of the job.

In recent years much more attention has been paid by examining boards to these other aspects of an accountant's work.

Learning outcomes

You should now have learnt:

1 That transactions are classified and details about them are entered in the appropriate book of original entry.

2 That the books of original entry are used as a basis for posting the transactions in summary form to the double entry accounts in the various ledgers.

3 That there is a set of books of original entry, each of which serves a specific purpose.

4 That there is a set of ledgers, each of which serves a specific purpose.

5 That accountants need to be good communicators.

Answers to activities

8.1 The most important reason is to aid analysis by keeping similar items together.

8.2 Books of original entry contain all the important information relating to a transaction. Ledgers just contain a summary. In fact, some of the entries in the ledgers are often just one-line entries covering an entire month of transactions.

8.3 There really is no conflict so far as financial information prepared for internal use is concerned. Financial statements produced for consumption by users outside the business do have to conform to the conventions relating to content and layout. However, those prepared for internal use do not. There is no reason why they could not be prepared along the lines of the unconventionally laid-out income statement shown on p. 111. External stakeholders will never receive their financial statements in this highly user-friendly form. It is simply too much work to customise the financial statement for every class of stakeholder.

Cash books

Learning objectives

After you have studied this chapter, you should be able to:

- explain the format of two-column and three-column cash books
- enter up and balance-off cash books
- use folio columns for cross-referencing purposes
- make the entries for discounts allowed and discounts received both in the cash book and, at the end of a period, in the discount accounts in the general ledger
- make similar entries in separate columns in the cash book for other recurring items

Introduction

In this chapter, you'll learn how businesses record cash and cheque transactions in the cash book. You'll learn that a memorandum column, called the 'folio column', is included in the cash book; and you'll learn the reasons why this is done. You will learn how to make the necessary entries in the cash book and how to include entries for discounts received from creditors and allowed to debtors, both in the cash book and in the general ledger.

9.1 Drawing up a cash book

The cash book consists of the cash account and the bank account put together in one book. We used to show these two accounts on different pages of the ledger. Now it is easier to put the two sets of account columns together. This means that we can record all money received and paid out on a particular date on the same page.

In the cash book, the debit column for cash is put next to the debit column for bank. The credit column for cash is put next to the credit column for bank.

Exhibit 9.1 shows how a cash account and a bank account would appear if they had been kept separately. In Exhibit 9.2, they are shown as if the transactions had, instead, been kept in a cash book.

The bank column contains details of the payments made by cheque and direct transfer from the bank account and of the money received and paid into the bank account. The bank will have a copy of the account in its own books.

Periodically, or on request from the business, the bank sends a copy of the account in its books to the business. This document is known as the **bank statement**. When the business receives the bank statement, it checks it against the bank columns in its cash book to ensure that there are no errors.

Exhibit 9.1

Cash

2019			£	2019			£
Aug	2	T. Moore	33	Aug	8	Printing	20
	5	K. Charles	25		12	C. Potts	19
	15	F. Hughes	37		28	Office stationery	25
	30	H. Howe	18		31	Balance c/d	49
			113				113
Sept	1	Balance b/d	49				

Bank

2019			£	2019			£
Aug	1	Capital	10,000	Aug	7	Rent	205
	3	W. P. Ltd	244		12	F. Small Ltd	95
	16	K. Noone	408		26	K. French	268
	30	H. Sanders	20		31	Balance c/d	10,104
			10,672				10,672
Sept	1	Balance b/d	10,104				

Exhibit 9.2

Cash book

2019			Cash £	Bank £	2019			Cash £	Bank £
Aug	1	Capital		10,000	Aug	7	Rent		205
	2	T. Moore	33			8	Printing	20	
	3	W. P. Ltd		244		12	C. Potts	19	
	5	K. Charles	25			12	F. Small Ltd		95
	15	F. Hughes	37			26	K. French		268
	16	K. Noone		408		28	Office stationery	25	
	30	H. Sanders		20		31	Balances c/d	49	10,104
	30	H. Howe	18						
			113	10,672				113	10,672
Sept	1	Balances b/d	49	10,104					

9.2 Cash paid into the bank

In Exhibit 9.2, the payments into the bank were cheques received by the business. They have been banked immediately upon receipt. We must now consider cash being paid into the bank.

1 Let's look at the position when customers pay their account in cash and, later, a part of this cash is paid into the bank. The receipt of the cash is debited to the cash column on the date

received, the credit entry being in the customer's personal account. The cash banked has the following effect needing action:

Effect	Action
1 Asset of cash is decreased	Credit the asset account, i.e. the cash account which is represented by the cash column in the cash book.
2 Asset of bank is increased	Debit the asset account, i.e. the bank account which is represented by the bank column in the cash book.

A cash receipt of £100 from M. Davies on 1 August 2019 which was followed by the banking on 3 August of £80 of this amount would appear in the cash book as follows:

Cash book							
		Cash	Bank			Cash	Bank
2019		£	£	2019		£	£
Aug 1	M. Davies	100		Aug 3	Bank	80	
3	Cash		80				

The details column shows entries against each item stating the name of the account in which the completion of double entry has taken place. Against the cash payment of £80 appears the word 'bank', meaning that the debit of £80 is to be found in the bank column, and the opposite applies.

2 Where the whole of the cash received is banked immediately the receipt can be treated in exactly the same manner as a cheque received, i.e. it can be entered directly into the bank column.

3 If the business requires cash, it may withdraw cash from the bank. Assuming this is done by use of a cheque, the business would write out a cheque to pay itself a certain amount in cash. The bank will give cash in exchange for the cheque over the counter. It could also be done using a cash card. The effect on the accounts is the same.

The twofold effect and the action required is:

Effect	Action
1 Asset of bank is decreased	Credit the asset account, i.e. the bank column in the cash book.
2 Asset of cash is increased	Debit the asset account, i.e. the cash column in the cash book.

A withdrawal of £75 cash on 1 June 2019 from the bank would appear in the cash book as:

Cash book							
		Cash	Bank			Cash	Bank
2019		£	£	2019		£	£
June 1	Bank	75		June 1	Cash		75

Both the debit and credit entries for this item are in the same book. When this happens it is known as a **contra** item.

9.3 The use of folio columns

As you have already seen, the details column in an account contains the name of the account in which the other part of the double entry has been entered. Anyone looking through the books should, therefore, be able to find the other half of the double entry in the ledgers.

However, when many books are being used, just to mention the name of the other account may not be enough information to find the other account quickly. More information is needed, and this is given by using **folio columns**.

In each account and in each book being used, a folio column is added, always shown on the left of the money columns. In this column, the name of the other book and the number of the page in the other book where the other part of the double entry was made is stated against each and every entry.

So as to ensure that the double entry is completed, the folio column should only be filled in when the double entry has been completed.

An entry for receipt of cash from C. Kelly whose account was on page 45 of the sales ledger, and the cash recorded on page 37 of the cash book, would have the following folio column entries:

● in the cash book, the folio column entry would be SL 45
● in the sales ledger, the folio column entry would be CB 37

Note how each of the titles of the books is abbreviated so that it can fit into the space available in the folio column. Each of any contra items (transfers between bank and cash) being shown on the same page of the cash book would use the letter '¢' (for 'contra') in the folio column. There is no need to also include a page number in this case.

The act of using one book as a means of entering transactions into the accounts, so as to perform or complete the double entry, is known as **posting**. For example, you 'post' items from the sales day book to the appropriate accounts in the sales ledger and to the sales account and you 'post' items from the cash book to the appropriate accounts in the sales ledger.

Activity 9.1 Why do you think only one account is posted to from the cash book rather than two, which is what happens with postings from the other day books (i.e. the other books of original entry)?

9.4 Advantages of folio columns

As described in Section 9.3, folio entries speed up the process of finding the other side of the double entry in the ledgers.

Activity 9.2 What other advantage can you think of for using a folio column?

9.5 Example of a cash book with folio columns

The following transactions are written up in the form of a cash book. The folio columns are filled in as though all the double entries had been completed to other accounts.

2019				£
Sept	1	Proprietor puts capital into a bank account for the business.		10,940
	2	Received cheque from M. Boon.		315
	4	Cash sales.		802
	6	Paid rent by cash.		135
	7	Banked £50 of the cash held by the business.		50
	15	Cash sales paid direct into the bank.		490
	23	Paid cheque to S. Wills.		277
	29	Withdrew cash from bank for business use.		120
	30	Paid wages in cash.		518

			Folio	Cash £	Bank £				Folio	Cash £	Bank £
Cash book											**(page 1)**
2019						2019					
Sept	1	Capital	GL1		10,940	Sept	6	Rent	GL65	135	
	2	M. Boon	SL98		315		7	Bank	¢	50	
	4	Sales	GL87	802			23	S. Wills	PL23		277
	7	Cash	¢		50		29	Cash	¢		120
	15	Sales	GL87		490		30	Wages	GL39	518	
	29	Bank	¢	120			30	Balances	c/d	219	11,398
				922	11,795					922	11,795
Oct	1	Balances	b/d	219	11,398						

The abbreviations used in the folio column are:

GL = general ledger   SL = sales ledger   ¢ = contra   PL = purchases ledger

9.6 Cash discounts

Businesses prefer it if their customers pay their accounts quickly. A business may accept a smaller sum in full settlement if payment is made within a certain period of time. The amount of the reduction of the sum to be paid is known as a 'cash discount'. The term 'cash discount' thus refers to the allowance given for quick payment. It is still called cash discount, even if the account is paid by cheque or by direct transfer into the bank account.

The rate of cash discount is usually stated as a percentage. Full details of the percentage allowed, and the period within which payment is to be made, are quoted on all sales documents by the seller. A typical period during which discount may be allowed is one month from the date of the original transaction.

Note: Cash discounts *always* appear in the profit and loss section of the income statement. They are not part of the cost of goods sold. Nor are they a deduction from selling price. Students often get this wrong in examinations – be careful!

9.7 Discounts allowed and discounts received

A business may have two types of cash discounts in its books. These are:

1 **Discounts allowed**: cash discounts allowed by a business to its customers when they pay their accounts quickly.

2 **Discounts received**: cash discounts received by a business from its suppliers when it pays what it owes them quickly.

We can now see the effect of discounts by looking at two examples.

Example 1

W. Clarke owed us £100. He pays us in cash on 2 September 2019, which is within the time limit applicable for a 5 per cent cash discount. He pays £100 − £5 = £95 in full settlement of his account.

Effect	Action

1 Of cash:
  Cash is increased by £95.
 	
  Asset of accounts receivable is decreased by £95.
	Debit cash account, i.e. enter £95 in debit column of cash book.
	Credit W. Clarke £95.

2 Of discounts:
  Asset of accounts receivable is decreased by £5.
  (After the cash was paid there remained a balance of £5. As the account has been paid, this asset must now be cancelled.)
  Expense of discounts allowed increased by £5.
	Credit W. Clarke £5.
	
	Debit discounts allowed account £5.

Example 2

The business owed S. Small £400. It pays him by cheque on 3 September 2019, which is within the time limit laid down by him for a 2½ per cent cash discount. The business will pay £400 − £10 = £390 in full settlement of the account.

Effect	Action

1 Of cheque:
  Asset of bank is reduced by £390.
 	
  Liability of accounts payable is reduced by £390.
	Credit bank, i.e. entry in the credit bank column for £390.
	Debit S. Small's account £390.

2 Of discounts:
  Liability of accounts payable is reduced by £10.
  (After the cheque was paid, a balance of £10 remained. As the account has been paid the wliability must now be cancelled.)
  Revenue of discounts received increased by £10.
	Debit S. Small's account £10.
	
	Credit discounts received account £10.

The entries made in the business's books would be:

Cash book								(page 32)
	Folio	Cash	Bank			Folio	Cash	Bank
		£	£				£	£
2019		95		2019				390
Sept 2 W. Clarke	SL12			Sept 3 S. Small	PL75			

				Discounts received			(General Ledger *page 18*)			*Folio*	£
						2019					
						Sept	2	S. Small		PL75	10

				Folio	£	Discounts allowed			(General Ledger *page 17*)		
2019											
Sept	2	W. Clarke		SL12	5						

W. Clarke (Sales Ledger *page 12*)

2019				*Folio*	£	2019				*Folio*	£
Sept	1	Balance		b/d	100	Sept	2	Cash		CB32	95
					___		2	Discount		GL17	5
					100						100

S. Small (Purchases Ledger *page 75*)

2019				*Folio*	£	2019				*Folio*	£
Sept	3	Bank		CB32	390	Sept	1	Balance		b/d	400
	3	Discount		GL18	10						___
					400						400

It is the accounting custom to enter the word 'Discount' in the personal accounts without stating whether it is a discount received or a discount allowed.

Activity 9.3 Why do you think it is accounting custom only to enter the word 'Discount' in the personal accounts?

9.8 Discounts columns in cash book

The *discounts allowed account* and the *discounts received account* are in the general ledger along with all the other revenue and expense accounts. It has already been stated that every effort should be made to avoid too many entries in the general ledger. To avoid this, we add two columns for discount in the cash book.

An extra column is added on each side of the cash book in which the amounts of discounts are entered. Discounts received are entered in the discounts column on the credit side of the cash book, and discounts allowed in the discounts column on the debit side of the cash book.

The cash book entries for the two examples so far dealt with would be:

Cash book									(page 32)		
	Folio	*Discount*	*Cash*	*Bank*			*Folio*	*Discount*	*Cash*	*Bank*	
2019		£	£	£	2019			£	£	£	
Sept 2 W. Clarke	SL12	5	95		Sept 3 S. Small	PL75		10		390	

There is no alteration to the method of showing discounts in the personal accounts.

To make entries in the discounts accounts in the general ledger

At the end of the period:

Total of discounts column on receipts side of cash book } Enter on **debit** side of discounts allowed account.

Total of discounts column on payments side of cash book } Enter on **credit** side of discounts received account.

9.9 A worked example

2019			£
May	1	Balances brought down from April:	
		Cash balance	29
		Bank balance	654
		Accounts receivable accounts:	
		B. King	120
		N. Campbell	280
		D. Shand	40
		Accounts payable accounts:	
		U. Barrow	60
		A. Allen	440
		R. Long	100
	2	B. King pays us by cheque, having deducted $2\frac{1}{2}$ per cent cash discount £3.	117
	8	We pay R. Long his account by cheque, deducting 5 per cent cash discount £5.	95
	11	We withdrew £100 cash from the bank for business use.	100
	16	N. Campbell pays us his account by cheque, deducting $2\frac{1}{2}$ per cent discount £7.	273
	25	We paid office expenses in cash.	92
	28	D. Shand pays us in cash after having deducted 5 per cent cash discount.	38
	29	We pay U. Barrow by cheque less 5 per cent cash discount £3.	57
	30	We pay A. Allen by cheque less $2\frac{1}{2}$ per cent cash discount £11.	429

Folio numbers have been included in the solution to make the example more realistic.

Cash book										(page 64)
		Folio	Discount	Cash	Bank			Folio	Discount	Cash	Bank
2019			£	£	£	2019			£	£	£
May 1	Balance	b/d		29	654	May 8	R. Long	PL58	5		95
2	B. King	SL13	3		117	11	Cash	¢			100
11	Bank	¢		100		25	Office	GL77		92	
16	N. Campbell	SL84	7		273		expenses				
28	D. Shand	SL91	2	38		29	U. Barrow	PL15	3		57
						30	A. Allen	PL98	11		429
						31	Balances	c/d		75	363
			12	167	1,044				19	167	1,044
Jun 1	Balances	b/d		75	363						

Sales ledger
B. King
(page 13)

2019			Folio	£	2019				Folio	£
May	1	Balance	b/d	120	May	2		Bank	CB64	117
				___		2		Discount	CB64	3
				120						120

N. Campbell
(page 84)

2019			Folio	£	2019				Folio	£
May	1	Balance	b/d	280	May	16		Bank	CB64	273
				___		16		Discount	CB64	7
				280						280

D. Shand
(page 91)

2019			Folio	£	2019				Folio	£
May	1	Balance	b/d	40	May	28		Cash	CB64	38
				___		28		Discount	CB64	2
				40						40

Purchases ledger
U. Barrow
(page 15)

2019			Folio	£	2019				Folio	£
May	29	Bank	CB64	57	May	1		Balance	b/d	60
	29	Discount	CB64	3						
				60						60

R. Long
(page 58)

2019			Folio	£	2019				Folio	£
May	8	Bank	CB64	95	May	1		Balance	b/d	100
	8	Discount	CB64	5						
				100						100

A. Allen
(page 98)

2019			Folio	£	2019				Folio	£
May	30	Bank	CB64	429	May	1		Balance	b/d	440
	30	Discount	CB64	11						
				440						440

General ledger
Office expenses
(page 77)

2019			Folio	£
May	25	Cash	CB64	92

Discounts received
(page 88)

					2019			Folio	£
					May	31 Total for the month		CB64	19

Discounts allowed
(page 89)

2019			Folio	£
May	31	Total for the month	CB64	12

Is the above method of entering discounts shown in the last two accounts correct?
You can easily check:

Discounts in ledger accounts	Debits		Credits	
		£		
Discounts received	U. Barrow	3	Discounts received	£19
	R. Long	5		
	A. Allen	11		
		19		
				£
Discounts allowed	Discounts allowed £12		B. King	3
			N. Campbell	7
			D. Shand	2
				12

You can see that proper double entry has been carried out. Equal amounts, in total, have been entered on each side of the two discount accounts.

9.10 Bank overdrafts

A business may borrow money from a bank by means of a bank **overdraft.** This means that the business is allowed to pay more out of its bank account than the total amount it has deposited in the account.

Up to this point, the bank balances have all been money at the bank, so they have all been assets, i.e. debit balances. When the bank account is overdrawn, the business owes money to the bank, so the account is a liability and the balance becomes a credit one.

Taking the cash book last shown, suppose that the amount payable to A. Allen was £1,429 instead of £429. The amount in the bank account, £1,044, is exceeded by the amount withdrawn. We will take the discount for Allen as being £11. The cash book would appear as follows:

			Cash book						(page 64)	
		Discount	Cash	Bank			Discount	Cash	Bank	
2019		£	£	£	2019		£	£	£	
May	1 Balances b/d		29	654	May	8 R. Long	5		95	
	2 B. King	3		117		11 Cash			100	
	11 Bank		100			25 Office				
	16 N. Campbell	7		273		expenses		92		
	28 D. Shand	2	38			29 U. Barrow	3		57	
	31 Balance c/d					30 A. Allen	11		1,429	
				637		31 Balance c/d		75		
		12	167	1,681			19	167	1,681	
Jun	1 Balance b/d		75		Jun	1 Balance b/d			637	

On a balance sheet, a bank overdraft is included under the heading 'current liabilities'.

9.11 Bank cash books

In the United Kingdom, except for very small organisations, three-column cash books are not usually used. All receipts, whether of cash or cheques, will be banked daily. A 'petty cash book' will be used for payments of cash. As a result, there will be no need for cash columns in the cash book itself.

This move towards only recording bank transactions in the cash book is not yet evident in countries where banking systems are not as developed or as efficient as in the UK.

9.12 Multiple column cash book

In Chapter 10, you will learn how to prepare an analytical (or multiple column) petty cash book. Cash books are often prepared with multiple columns where additional columns are added for each ledger account to which many entries may be made in a period. As with columns for discount, this has the advantage of reducing the number of entries made in the accounts in the general ledger.

Learning outcomes

You should now have learnt:

1 That a cash book consists of a cash account and a bank account put together into one book.

2 How to enter up and balance a two-column cash book, i.e. one containing a debit and a credit column for the bank account, and a debit and a credit column for the cash account.

3 That the bank columns in the cash book are for cheques and any other transfers of funds that have been made into or out of the bank account.

4 That a folio column is included in the cash book so as to help trace entries made into accounts in the ledgers and so as to provide assurance that the double entries have been made.

5 That cash discounts are given to encourage people to pay their accounts within a stated time limit.

6 That 'cash discount' is the name given for discount for quick payment even where the payment was made by cheque or by direct transfer into the bank account, rather than by payment in cash.

7 That cash discounts appear in the profit and loss part of the income statement.

8 How to enter up and balance a three-column cash book, i.e. one containing a debit and a credit column for the bank account, a debit and a credit column for the cash account, and a debit and a credit column for discount.

9 That the discounts columns in the cash book make it easier to enter up the books. They act as a collection point for discounts allowed and discounts received, for which double entry into the general ledger is completed when the totals are transferred to the discount accounts in the general ledger, usually at the end of the month.

→

10 That a multiple column cash book is often used in order to further reduce the number of entries made in the general ledger.

11 How to add additional columns to the cash book for frequently recurring items and make the appropriate entries in them and in the general ledger.

Answers to activities

9.1 Although the cash book is a book of original entry, it is also where the cash account and bank account are recorded. In effect, it is both a book of original entry and a ledger dedicated to those two accounts. As a result, each transaction in the cash book is only posted once to another account, the first part of the entry having been made when the transaction was recorded in the cash book.

9.2 If an entry has not been filled in, i.e. if the folio column is blank against an entry, the double entry has not yet been made. As a result, looking through the entry lines in the folio columns to ensure they have all been filled in helps detect such errors quickly.

9.3 It should be quite obvious whether discount is received or allowed. And, more importantly, the double entry is with the cash book columns for discount, not with either the discount allowed account or the discount received account in the general ledger. At the end of the period (usually a month) the totals of the two discount columns in the cash book are posted to the discount allowed and discount received accounts in the general ledger.

Review questions

9.1 Write up a two-column cash book for a bedroom furniture shop from the following details, and balance it off as at the end of the month:

2019
July
1 Started in business with capital in cash £10,000.
2 Paid rent by cash £1,000.
3 G. Broad lent us £12,000, paid by cheque.
4 We paid J. Fine by cheque £1,800.
5 Cash sales £800.
7 F. Love paid us by cheque £200.
9 We paid A. Moore in cash £300.
11 Cash sales paid direct into the bank £600.
15 P. Hood paid us in cash £700.
16 We took £4,000 out of the cash till and paid it into the bank account.
19 We repaid R. Onions £2,000 by cheque.
22 Cash sales paid direct into the bank £1,200.
26 Paid motor expenses by cheque £460.
30 Withdrew £320 cash from the bank for business use.
31 Paid wages in cash £1,200.

9.2A Write up a two-column cash book for a second-hand bookshop from the following:

2019
Nov
1 Balance brought forward from last month: Cash £295; Bank £4,240.
2 Cash sales £310.
3 Took £200 out of the cash till and paid it into the bank.
4 F. Bell paid us by cheque £194.
5 We paid for postage stamps in cash £80.

6 Bought office equipment by cheque £310.
7 We paid L. Root by cheque £94.
9 Received business rates refund by cheque £115.
11 Withdrew £150 from the bank for business use.
12 Paid wages in cash £400.
13 Cash sales £430.
14 Paid motor expenses by cheque £81.
16 J. Bull lent us £1,500 in cash.
20 K. Brown paid us by cheque £174.
28 We paid general expenses in cash £35.
30 Paid insurance by cheque £320.

9.3 A three-column cash book for a wine wholesaler is to be written up from the following details, balanced-off, and the relevant discount accounts in the general ledger shown.

2019
Mar 1 Balances brought forward: Cash £620; Bank £7,142.
2 The following paid their accounts by cheque, in each case deducting 5 per cent cash discounts: G. Slick £260; P. Fish £320; T. Old £420 (all amounts are pre-discount).
4 Paid rent by cheque £430.
6 F. Black lent us £5,000 paying by cheque.
8 We paid the following accounts by cheque in each case deducting a $2\frac{1}{2}$ per cent cash discount: R. White £720; G. Green £960; L. Flip £1,600 (all amounts are pre-discount).
10 Paid motor expenses in cash £81.
12 J. Pie pays his account of £90, by cheque £88, deducting £2 cash discount.
15 Paid wages in cash £580.
18 The following paid their accounts by cheque, in each case deducting 5 per cent cash discount: A. Pony £540; B. Line & Son £700; T. Owen £520 (all amounts are pre-discount).
21 Cash withdrawn from the bank £400 for business use.
24 Cash drawings £200.
25 Paid W. Peat his account of £160, by cash £155, having deducted £5 cash discount.
29 Bought fixtures paying by cheque £720.
31 Received commission by cheque £120.

9.4A Enter the following in the three-column cash book of an office supply shop. Balance-off the cash book at the end of the month and show the discount accounts in the general ledger.

June 1 Balances brought forward: Cash £420; Bank £4,940.
2 The following paid us by cheque, in each case deducting a 5 per cent cash discount: S. Braga £820; L. Pine £320; G. Hodd £440; M. Rae £1,040.
3 Cash sales paid direct into the bank £740.
5 Paid rent by cash £340.
6 We paid the following accounts by cheque, in each case deducting $2\frac{1}{2}$ per cent cash discount: M. Peters £360; G. Graham £960; F. Bell £400.
8 Withdrew cash from the bank for business use £400.
10 Cash sales £1,260.
12 B. Age paid us their account of £280 less £4 cash discount, by cheque.
14 Paid wages by cash £540.
16 We paid the following accounts by cheque: R. Todd £310 less cash discount £15; F. Dury £412 less cash discount £12.
20 Bought fixtures by cheque £4,320.

→

24 Bought lorry paying by cheque £14,300.
29 Received £324 cheque from A. Line.
30 Cash sales £980.
30 Bought stationery paying by cash £56.

9.5 On 1 September, R. Macve, a club manager and entrepreneur, has the following financial position relating to her activities as a corporate function organiser:

	£
Balance at bank	40,000
Accounts receivable – K. Hoskin	20,000
– G. Volmers	8,000
– G. Carnegie	4,000
Inventory	38,000
Accounts payable – Real Fine Ales	32,800
– R. Goldthwaite	1,000

During September the following events occur:

1 K. Hoskin settles his account after taking a cash discount of 10 per cent.
2 G. Volmers is declared bankrupt and no payments are anticipated in respect of the debt.
3 G. Carnegie pays in full.
4 Both accounts payable are paid. Real Fine Ales had indicated that, because of the speed of payment, a 5 per cent quick settlement discount may be deducted from the payment.

Required:

(a) Use T-accounts to open a bank account and the accounts for the accounts receivable and accounts payable at 1 September.
(b) Record the above transactions for September.
(c) Balance-off the accounts at the end of the month.

9.6A At 1 September the financial position of Sara Young's business was:

	£
Cash in hand	80
Balance at bank	900
Accounts receivable: AB	200
CD	500
EF	300
Inventory	1,000
Accounts payable: GH	600
IJ	1,400

During September:

1 The three debtors settled their accounts by cheque subject to a cash discount of 4 per cent.
2 A cheque for £100 was cashed for office use.
3 The amount owing to GH was paid by cheque less 7.5 per cent cash discount.
4 IJ's account was settled, subject to a discount of 5 percent, by cheque.
5 Wages of £130 were paid in cash.

Required:

(a) Open a three-column cash book and the accounts for the accounts receivable and accounts payable at 1 September.
(b) Record the above transactions for September in the accounts you opened in (a).

The analytical petty cash book and the imprest system

Learning objectives

After you have studied this chapter, you should be able to:

- explain why many organisations use a petty cash book
- make entries in a petty cash book
- transfer the appropriate amounts from the petty cash book to the ledgers at the end of each period
- explain and operate the imprest system for petty cash

Introduction

You may remember that you learnt in Chapter 9 that there is a second type of cash book, called the **petty cash book**, which many businesses use to record small amounts paid for in cash. In this chapter, you'll learn of the type of items that are recorded in the petty cash book, and how to make the entries to it. You'll also learn how to transfer financial data from the petty cash book into the ledgers. Finally, you will learn about bank cash books and how they differ from the cash books you learnt about in Chapter 9.

10.1 Division of the cash book

As businesses continue to grow, some have a commercial value in excess of that of many smaller countries. For many, it has become necessary to have several books instead of just one ledger. In fact, nowadays all but the very smallest organisations have multiple ledgers and day books.

Activity 10.1   Why do we have day books? Why don't we just enter every transaction directly into the appropriate ledger accounts?

The cash book became a book of original entry so that all cash and bank transactions could be separated from the rest of the accounts in the general ledger. It is for much the same reason that many organisations use a petty cash book. Every business has a number of transactions of very small value. If they were all recorded in the cash book, it would only make it more difficult to identify the important transactions in that book that businesses need to keep a close eye on. **Just like the cash book, the petty cash book is both a book of original entry and a ledger account.**

To create a trail of evidence, when a payment is made from petty cash, the recipient completes a voucher describing what the payment was for, attaches receipts, e.g. for petrol, to the voucher, and signs the voucher to confirm receipt of the cash.

The advantages of using a petty cash book are:

1 The cashier (the person responsible for recording entries in the cash book) can delegate these entries to a junior member of staff whose lower salary is less costly to the business.
2 If small cash payments were entered into the main cash book, these items would then need posting one by one to the ledgers. For example, if travelling expenses were paid to staff on a daily basis, this could mean approximately 250 postings to the staff travelling expenses account during the year, i.e. 5 days per week × 50 working weeks per year. If a petty cash book is used, it would only be the entries for the 12 monthly totals that would be posted to the general ledger.

10.2 The imprest system

It is all very well having a petty cash book, but where does the money paid out from it come from? The **imprest system** is one where the cashier provides enough cash to meet the petty cash needs for the following period. At the end of the period, the cashier tops up the amount remaining in petty cash to bring it back up to the level it was at when the period started. This process is the imprest system and this topped-up amount is known as the petty cash **float**.

Exhibit 10.1 shows an example of this method.

Exhibit 10.1

		£
Period 1	The cashier gives the petty cashier	100
	The petty cashier pays out in the period	(78)
	Petty cash now in hand	22
	The cashier now gives the petty cashier the amount spent	78
	Petty cash in hand at the end of Period 1	100
Period 2	The petty cashier pays out in the period	(84)
	Petty cash now in hand	16
	The cashier now gives the petty cashier the amount spent	84
	Petty cash in hand at the end of Period 2	100

Over time, the float may need to be increased. For instance, if at the end of the second period above we wanted to increase the float to £120, an extra £20 would have been given added to the float, i.e. £84 + £20 = £104.

Sometimes no petty cash book is kept. Instead, at the end of each period, the amount left in petty cash is reconciled (i.e. checked and verified as correct) with the receipts held by the petty cashier. The amount spent is then given to the petty cashier in order to restore the float to its agreed level. However, this is not an ideal method to adopt. Businesses need to control the uses of all their resources, including petty cash, and so virtually every organisation that operates a petty cash float maintains a petty cash book. The most common format adopted is the 'analytical petty cash book'.

Illustration of an analytical petty cash book

An analytical petty cash book is shown in Exhibit 10.2. This example shows one for a nursery school.

Exhibit 10.2

Petty Cash Book											(page 31)
Receipts	Folio	Date	Details	Voucher No.	Total	Motor Expenses	Staff Travelling Expenses	Postage	Cleaning	Ledger Folio	Ledger Accounts
£				£	£	£	£	£		£	
300	CB 19	Sept 1	Cash								
		2	Petrol	1	16	16					
		3	J. Green	2	23		23				
		3	Postage	3	12			12			
		4	D. Davies	4	32		32				
		7	Cleaning	5	11				11		
		9	Petrol	6	21	21					
		12	K. Jones	7	13		13				
		14	Petrol	8	23	23					
		15	L. Black	9	5		5				
		16	Cleaning	10	11				11		
		18	Petrol	11	22	22					
		20	Postage	12	12			12			
		22	Cleaning	13	11				11		
		24	G. Wood	14	7		7				
		27	C. Brown	15	13					PL18	13
		29	Postage	16	12			12			
					244	82	80	36	33		13
						GL	GL	GL	GL		
244	CB 22	30	Cash			17	29	44	64		
		30	Balance	c/d	300						
544					544						
300		Oct 1	Balance	b/d							

The receipts column is the debit side of the petty cash book. On giving £300 to the petty cashier on 1 September, the credit entry is made in the cash book while the debit entry is made in the petty cash book. A similar entry is made on 30 September for the £244 paid by the headteacher to the petty cashier. As this amount covers all the expenses paid by the petty cashier, the float is now restored to its earlier level of £300. The credit side is used to record all the payments made by the petty cashier.

The transactions that were recorded in the petty cash book were:

2019	Voucher number		£
Sept	1 –	The head teacher gives £300 as float to the petty cashier	
		Payments out of petty cash during September:	
	2 1	Petrol: School bus	16
	3 2	J. Green – travelling expenses of staff	23
	3 3	Postage	12
	4 4	D. Davies – travelling expenses of staff	32
	7 5	Cleaning expenses	11
	9 6	Petrol: School bus	21
	12 7	K. Jones – travelling expenses of staff	13
	14 8	Petrol: School bus	23
	15 9	L. Black – travelling expenses of staff	5
	16 10	Cleaning expenses	11
	18 11	Petrol: School bus	22
	20 12	Postage	12
	22 13	Cleaning expenses	11
	24 14	G. Wood – travelling expenses of staff	7
	27 15	Settlement of C. Brown's account in the Purchases Ledger	13
	29 16	Postage	12
	30 –	The headteacher reimburses the petty cashier the amount spent in the month.	

The process followed during the period that led to these entries appearing in the petty cash book as shown in Exhibit 10.2 is:

1 Enter the date and details of each payment. Put the amount paid in the Total column.
2 Put the same amount in the column for that type of expense.
3 At the end of each period, add up the Total column.
4 Add up each of the expense columns. The total found in step 3 should equal the total of all the expense columns. In Exhibit 10.2 this is £244.
5 Enter the amount reimbursed to make up the float in the Receipts column.
6 Balance-off the petty cash book, carrying down the petty cash in hand balance to the next period.

To make the double entries in the ledger:

1 The total of each expense column is debited to the appropriate expense account.
2 The folio number of each expense account in the general ledger is entered under the appropriate expense column in the petty cash book. (This signifies that the double entry to the ledger account has been made.)
3 The last column in the petty cash book is a Ledger column. It contains entries for items paid out of petty cash that need posting to a ledger other than the general ledger. (This might arise, for example, if a purchases ledger account was settled out of petty cash.)

Activity 10.2 Where is the other side of the double entry for all these expense postings to the ledgers recorded?

The account entries in the cash book for the two additions to the float in Exhibit 10.2 are shown in Exhibit 10.3.

Exhibit 10.3

Cash Book
(Bank and Folio columns only) *(page 19)*

			Folio	£
2019				
Sept	1	Petty cash	PCB 31	300
	30	Petty cash	PCB 31	244

Learning outcomes

You should now have learnt:

1 That the petty cash book saves (*a*) the cash book and (*b*) the ledger accounts from containing a lot of trivial detail.

2 That the use of the petty cash book enables the cashier or a senior member of staff to delegate this type of work to a more junior member of staff.

3 That the cashier should periodically check the work performed by the petty cashier.

4 That all payments made by the petty cashier should have petty cash vouchers as evidence of proof of expense.

5 How to enter petty cash transactions into the petty cash book.

6 How to transfer the totals for each expense recorded in the petty cash book to the appropriate ledger accounts.

7 How to operate a float system for petty cash.

Answers to activities

10.1 One reason why we have day books is to avoid too much detail being entered in the ledgers.

10.2 In the petty cash book. Like the cash book, the petty cash book is not only a book of original entry, it is also an account that would otherwise appear in the general ledger.

Review questions

10.1 The following is a summary of the petty cash transactions of Jockfield Ltd for May 2019:

			£
May	1	Received from Cashier £300 as petty cash float	
	2	Postage	18
	3	Travelling	12
	4	Cleaning	15
	7	Petrol for delivery van	22
	8	Travelling	25
	9	Stationery	17
	11	Cleaning	18
	14	Postage	5
	15	Travelling	8
	18	Stationery	9
	18	Cleaning	23
	20	Postage	13
	24	Delivery van 5,000 mile service	43
	26	Petrol	18
	27	Cleaning	21
	29	Postage	5
	30	Petrol	14

You are required to:
(a) Rule up a suitable petty cash book with analysis columns for expenditure on cleaning, motor expenses, postage, stationery, travelling.
(b) Enter the month's transactions.
(c) Enter the receipt of the amount necessary to restore the imprest and carry down the balance for the commencement of the following month.
(d) State how the double entry for the expenditure is completed.

(Association of Accounting Technicians)

10.2 Martin Battle runs a business and maintains a petty cash book using the imprest system. The cash float is £150. For June 2020 his petty cash transactions were as below:

			£
June	1	Petty cash balance	32.17
	2	Petty cashier presented vouchers for May 2020 to the cashier, receiving cash to restore the imprest	?
	5	Paid for postage stamps	17.57
	9	Paid for office coffee and biscuits	11.48
	13	Paid for taxi fares	18.00
	18	Paid for minor items of stationery	22.16
	22	Paid for cleaning materials	14.38
	23	Paid for herbal teabags for the office	9.95
	28	Paid for train fares	38.75
	30	Petty cashier presented vouchers for June 2020 to the cashier, receiving cash to restore the imprest	?

Required:
(a) Write up the petty cash book for June 2020, showing the balance carried down at the end of the month.
(b) Explain why most businesses maintain a petty cash book as well as a cash book.

(c) Compared to the value of its other assets, the amount of petty cash held by a business is usually very small. However, the system for controlling petty cash is given a degree of care and attention that is out of proportion to the financial amounts involved. Why is this?

(d) Explain the advantages of using the *imprest system* to control petty cash.

10.3A Rule up a petty cash book with analysis columns for office expenses, motor expenses, cleaning expenses and casual labour. The cash float is £450 and the amount spent is reimbursed on 30 November.

2020			£
November	1	T. Wise – casual labour	36
	2	Staples and tape dispenser	19
	2	Black Motors – motor repairs	42
	3	Cleaning materials	3
	6	Envelopes	10
	8	Petrol	18
	11	I. Dodds – casual labour	12
	12	J. Marsh – cleaner	7
	12	Paper clips	2
	14	Petrol	16
	16	Adhesive tape	1
	16	Petrol	24
	21	Car tyre	63
	22	T. Randall – casual labour	15
	23	J. Marsh – cleaner	16
	24	I. Gray – casual labour	21
	25	Paper	7
	26	Monday Cars – car puncture repairs	74
	29	Petrol	19
	30	T. Pointer – casual labour	20

10.4 Fine Teas operates its petty cash account on the imprest system. It is maintained at a figure of £140, with the balance being restored to that amount on the first day of each month. At 30 April the petty cash box held £24.37 in cash.

During May the following petty cash transactions arose:

			£
May	1	Cash received to restore imprest (to be derived)	?
	1	Bus fares	0.41
	2	Stationery	2.35
	4	Bus fares	0.30
	7	Postage stamps	6.50
	7	Trade journal	0.95
	8	Bus fares	0.64
	11	Highlighter pens	1.29
	12	Lightbulbs	5.42
	14	Parcel postage	3.45
	15	Paper-clips	0.42
	15	Newspapers	2.00
	16	Photocopier repair	16.80
	19	Postage stamps	1.50
	20	Drawing pins	0.38
	21	Train fare	5.40

→

	22	Photocopier paper	5.63
	23	Display decorations	3.07
	23	Pencil sharpener	1.14
	25	Wrapping paper	0.78
	27	String	0.61
	27	Sellotape	0.75
	27	Biro pens	0.46
	28	Replacement part for printer	13.66
	31	Bus fares	2.09
June	1	Cash received to restore imprest (to be derived)	?

Required:
(a) Open and post the company's analysed petty cash book for the period 1 May to 1 June inclusive.
(b) Balance the account at 31 May.
(c) Show the imprest reimbursement entry on June 1.

11

Accounting for sales, purchases and returns

Learning objectives

After you have studied this chapter, you should be able to:

- distinguish between a cash sale and a sale 'on time' (otherwise known as a 'credit' sale) and between the way they are recorded in the accounting books
- explain why, when credit card payments are received at the time of sale, details of the customer are not recorded even though a debtor is created at the same time
- draw up a sales invoice
- explain why multiple copies are often made of each sales invoice
- make the appropriate entries relating to sales 'on time' in a sales day book
- make the correct postings from the sales day book to the sales ledger and general ledger
- explain how trade discounts differ from cash discounts, both in nature and in the way they are treated in the accounting books
- describe measures that may be taken to exercise credit control over debtors
- make the appropriate entries relating to credit purchases in a purchases day book
- make the correct postings from the purchases day book to the purchases ledger and general ledger
- explain the differences between the process of recording credit sales and credit purchases in the books
- make the appropriate entries relating to returns outwards and returns inwards in the appropriate day book and ledger
- explain the differences between a credit note and a debit note
- describe how a debtor should use statements received from suppliers
- enter up the accounts for credit card transactions
- explain the need for internal checks on all sales and purchases invoices and credit notes
- describe what use may be made of factoring

Introduction

In Chapter 8, you learnt that, rather than having only one book of original entry and only one ledger, some businesses use a set of day books and a set of ledgers. In this chapter, you'll learn more about the sales and purchases day book and the sales and purchases ledgers. You'll also learn how cash and credit sales and purchases are entered in these books, about trade discounts and how to record them, and how sales returns and purchases returns are recorded.

Part One Sales

11.1 Cash sales

As you have already learnt, when goods are paid for immediately they are described as 'cash sales', even where the payment has been made by debit card, credit card, cheque, or transfer of funds from the customer's bank account into the seller's bank account. For accounting purposes, in such cases we do not need to know the names and addresses of customers nor what has been sold to them and, as a result, there is no need to enter such sales in the sales day book. **The sales day book (and all the other day books) are** *only* **used for transactions that are to be paid for at some future date, i.e. 'credit' transactions.**

 Activity 11.1 Other than for accounting purposes, can you think of anything a business might want to record somewhere outside the accounting records concerning these transactions?

Credit card payments

When customers pay immediately by credit card, so far as recording details of the customer is concerned, this is treated as if it were a payment made by cash. No record is required for accounting purposes concerning the contact details of the customer. However, it is a credit transaction and so does result in a debtor being created – the credit card company. The double entry would be a debit to the credit card company's account in the sales ledger and a credit to the sales account.

11.2 Sales 'on time': credit sales

In all but the smallest business, most sales will be made 'on time'. That is, they are not paid at the time of the sale, but at some future date. So far, I have referred to this form of settlement as an IOU. Sales of this type are usually called 'credit sales' and 'sales on credit'. These terms will be used throughout the rest of this book. The sales of many businesses will consist entirely of credit sales. The only major exceptions to this are Internet businesses (such as Amazon) and retailers (e.g. corner shops and supermarkets), where all sales are paid for at the time of sale.

For each credit sale, the selling business will give or send a document to the buyer showing full details of the goods sold and the prices of the goods. This document is an 'invoice'. It is known to the buyer as a 'purchase invoice' and to the seller as a **sales invoice**. The seller will keep one or more copies of each sales invoice for his or her own use.

 Activity 11.2 What uses would the seller have for these copies of the sales invoice?

Exhibit 11.1 is an example of an invoice:

Exhibit 11.1

Your Purchase Order: 10/A/980		J. Blake
INVOICE No. 16554		7 Over Warehouse
		Leicester LE1 2AP
		1 September 2020

To: D. Poole & Co
    45 Charles Street
    Manchester M1 5ZN

	Per unit	Total
	£	£
21 cases McBrand Pears	20	420
5 cartons Kay's Flour	4	20
6 cases Joy's Vinegar	20	120
		560

Terms $1\frac{1}{4}$% cash discount if paid within one month

You must not think that all invoices will look exactly like the one shown in Exhibit 11.1. Each business will have its own design. All invoices will be uniquely numbered, usually sequentially, and they will contain the names and addresses of both the supplier and the customer. In this case, the supplier is J. Blake and the customer is D. Poole. (A 'purchase order' – there's one referred to in the top left-hand corner of this sales invoice – is the record or document drawn up by the customer that the customer referred to or gave the seller when the order was placed with the seller. It is used by the buyer to check the details of the order against the invoice and against the goods delivered.)

11.3 Copies of sales invoices

As soon as the sales invoices for the goods being sold have been prepared, they are given or sent to the customer. The copies kept by the seller are created at the same time as the original.

11.4 Making entries in the sales day book

From the copy of the sales invoice, the seller enters up the transaction in the sales day book. This book is merely a list of details relating to each credit sale:

- date
- name of customer
- invoice number
- folio column
- final amount of invoice.

There is no need to show details of the goods sold in the sales day book. This can be found by looking at copy invoices.

We can now look at Exhibit 11.2, which shows page 26 of a sales day book, starting with the record of the sales invoice already shown in Exhibit 11.1. (These could have been on any page. In this example, we are assuming they have been entered on page 26 as pages 1–25 have been filled with details of earlier transactions.)

Exhibit 11.2

Sales Day Book		Invoice No.	Folio	Amount
				£
2020				
Sept	1 D. Poole	16554		560
	8 T. Cockburn	16555		1,640
	28 C. Carter	16556		220
	30 D. Stevens & Co	16557		1,100
				3,520

(page 26)

11.5 Posting credit sales to the sales ledger

Instead of having one ledger for all accounts, we now have a separate sales ledger for credit sale transactions. This was described in Chapter 8.

1 The credit sales are now posted, one by one, to the debit side of each customer's account in the sales ledger.
2 At the end of each period the total of the credit sales is posted to the credit of the sales account in the general ledger.

This is now illustrated in Exhibit 11.3.

Exhibit 11.3 Posting credit sales

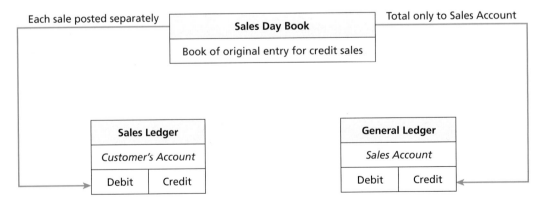

138

11.6 An example of posting credit sales

The sales day book in Exhibit 11.2 is now shown again. This time, posting is made to the sales ledger and the general ledger. Notice the completion of the folio columns with the reference numbers.

Sales Day Book			(page 26)
	Invoice No.	Folio	Amount
2020			£
Sept 1 D. Poole	16554	SL 12	560
8 T. Cockburn	16555	SL 39	1,640
28 C. Carter	16556	SL 125	220
30 D. Stevens & Co	16557	SL 249	1,100
Transferred to Sales Account		GL 44	3,520

Sales Ledger
D. Poole *(page 12)*

2020		Folio	£	
Sept 1 Sales		SB 26	560	

T. Cockburn *(page 39)*

2020		Folio	£	
Sept 8 Sales		SB 26	1,640	

C. Carter *(page 125)*

2020		Folio	£	
Sept 28 Sales		SB 26	220	

D. Stevens & Co *(page 249)*

2020		Folio	£	
Sept 30 Sales		SB 26	1,100	

General Ledger
Sales *(page 44)*

		2020		Folio	£
		Sept 30 Credit sales for the month		SB 26	3,520

Before you continue you should attempt Review Question 11.1

11.7 Trade discounts

Suppose you are the proprietor of a business. You are selling to three different kinds of customer:

1 traders who buy a lot of goods from you;
2 traders who buy only a few items from you;
3 the general public (direct).

The traders themselves have to sell the goods to the general public in their own areas. They have to make a profit to help finance their businesses, so they will want to pay you less than the retail price (i.e. the price at which the goods are sold to the general public). Traders who buy in larger quantities will want to pay less than you charge traders who buy in small quantities. As a result, you would normally sell at a different price to each of these three groups of customers.

 Activity 11.3 Why would you be willing to sell goods at a lower price to these traders?

Let's use an example to illustrate this. You sell a food mixing machine. The basic price is £200. The traders who buy in large quantities are given 25 per cent trade discount. The other traders are given 20 per cent, and the general public get no trade discount. The price paid by each type of customer would be:

		Trader 1		Trader 2	General Public
		£		£	£
Basic price		200		200	200
Less Trade discount	(25%)	(50)	(20%)	(40)	nil
Price to be paid by customer		150		160	200

You could deal with this by having three price lists, and many businesses do. However, some use trade discounts instead. This involves having only one price list but giving a **trade discount** to traders so that they are invoiced for the correct price.

Exhibit 11.4 is an example of an invoice for a food manufacturer and retailer that shows how trade discount is presented clearly and the trade discounted price easily identified. It is for the same items as were shown in Exhibit 11.1 as having been sold to D. Poole. In that example, the seller operated a different price list for each category of customer. This time the seller is R. Grant and trade discount is used to adjust the selling price to match the category of customer.

Exhibit 11.4

Your Purchase Order: 11/A/G80		R. Grant Higher Side Preston PR1 2NL 2 September 2020
INVOICE No. 30756		
To: D. Poole & Co 　45 Charles Street 　Manchester M1 5ZN		Tel (01703) 33122 Fax (01703) 22331

	Per unit	Total
	£	£
21 cases McBrand Pears	25	525
5 cartons Kay's Flour	5	25
6 cases Joy's Vinegar	25	150
		700
Less 20% trade discount		(140)
		560

By comparing Exhibits 11.1 and 11.4, you can see that the amount paid by D. Poole was the same. It is simply the method of calculating it and presenting it in the exhibit that is different.

11.8 No double entry for trade discounts

As trade discount is simply a way of calculating sales prices, no entry for trade discount should be made in the double entry records, nor in the sales day book. The recording of Exhibit 11.4 in R. Grant's sales day book and D. Poole's personal account will be:

Sales Day Book			*(page 87)*
	Invoice No.	*Folio*	*Amount*
2020			£
Sept　2　D. Poole	30756	SL 32	560

Sales Ledger
D. Poole　　　　　　　　　　　　　　　　　　　　　　　*(page 32)*

2020		*Folio*	£	
Sept　2　Sales		SB 87	560	

To compare with cash discounts:

● Trade discounts: *never* shown in double entry accounts, nor in the income statement.
● Cash discounts: *always* shown in double entry accounts and in the profit and loss part of the income statement.

Be very careful about this topic. Students often get confused between the treatment of trade discount and the treatment of cash discount. Remember, it is trade discount that is not entered anywhere in either the ledger accounts or the financial statements. Cash discount appears in the cash book and is always shown in the financial statements.

11.9 Manufacturer's recommended retail price

Looking at an item displayed in a shop window, you will frequently see something like the following:

50 inch 4K ultra HD TV	
Manufacturer's Recommended Retail Price	£1,200
Less discount of 20 per cent	(240)
You pay only	£ 960

Very often the manufacturer's recommended retail price is a figure above what the manufacturer would expect the public to pay for its product. In the case of the TV, the manufacturer would probably have expected the public to pay around £960 for the TV.

The inflated figure used for the 'manufacturer's recommended retail price' is simply a sales gimmick. Most people like to believe they are getting a bargain. They feel happier about making a purchase like this if they are told they are getting '20 per cent discount' and pay £960 rather than being told that the price is £960 and that they cannot get any discount.

11.10 Credit control

Any organisation that has credit sales (i.e. 'sales on credit') should keep a close check to ensure that debtors pay their accounts on time. If this is not done properly, the amount of accounts receivables can grow to a level that will make the business short of cash. Businesses that grow too short of cash will fail, no matter how profitable they may be.

The following procedures should be carried out:

1 A credit limit should be set for each debtor. Debtors should not be allowed to owe more than their credit limit. The amount of the limit will depend on the circumstances. Such things as the size of the customer's business and the amount of business done with it, as well as its past record of payments, will help guide the choice of credit limit. Credit rating agencies may be used to assess the credit worthiness of customers before credit is granted.
2 As soon as the payment date set by the seller has been reached, a check should be made to verify whether the debtor has paid the amount due. Failure to pay on time may trigger a refusal to supply any more goods to the customer until payment is received, even if the customer's credit limit has not been reached.
3 Where payment is not forthcoming, after investigation it may be necessary to take legal action to sue the customer for the debt. This will depend on the circumstances.
4 It is important that the customer is aware of what will happen if the amount due is not paid by the deadline set by the seller.

Part Two **Purchases**

11.11 Purchases invoices and the purchases day book

When an invoice is entered in the books of the buyer, it is called a '**purchases invoice**'. For example, in Exhibit 11.1, the first invoice you looked at,

● in the books of J. Blake, the seller, it is a sales invoice; and
● in the books of D. Poole, the buyer, it is a purchases invoice.

As you know, transactions – sales or purchases – may be for cash or they may be 'on time'. Just as we call sales made 'on time' 'credit sales' or 'sales on credit', so we call purchases made 'on time' '**credit purchases**' or '**purchases on credit**'. The details of credit purchases are entered in a purchases day book from purchases invoices in the same way as entries are made for sales in the sales day book.

Activity 11.4 Think back to what you learnt about the list of items contained in the sales day book. What do you think is the list of items recorded in the purchases day book?

There is no need to show details of the goods bought in the purchases day book. This can be found by looking at the invoices themselves. Exhibit 11.5 is an example of a purchases day book.

Exhibit 11.5

Purchases Day Book			(page 49)
	Invoice No.	Folio	Amount
2020			£
Sept 1 J. Blake	9/101		560
8 B. Hamilton	9/102		1,380
19 C. Brown	9/103		230
30 K. Gabriel	9/104		510
			2,680

Activity 11.5 Note the entry for 1 September and compare it to the entry on the same date shown in the sales day book of J. Blake in Exhibit 11.2. What differences are there between the entries in the two day books? Why do you think these differences arise?

11.12 Posting credit purchases to the purchases ledger

We also have a separate purchases ledger. The double entry is as follows:

1 The credit purchases are posted one by one, to the credit of each supplier's account in the purchases ledger.
2 At the end of each period the total of the credit purchases is posted to the debit of the purchases account in the general ledger. This is now illustrated in Exhibit 11.6.

Exhibit 11.6   Posting credit purchases

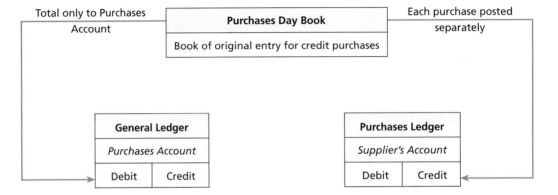

Part Three   Returns

11.13 Returns inwards and credit notes

You know that businesses allow customers to return goods they've bought. You've probably done so yourself at some time or other. Some retail businesses give every customer the right to do so within a few days of the sale and won't ask why they are being returned. It is a means of assuring the customer that the seller believes that the goods are of good quality and will do what the customer wants. Whatever the rights of return granted by the seller, in the UK there are also legal rights of return that permit retail customers to return goods for a refund should the goods prove to have been unfit for the purpose that was intended.

Businesses that deal with trade customers may operate a similar policy, but that would be more unusual and would normally include a proviso that the customer had a justifiable and reasonable reason for returning the goods.

Activity 11.6   List as many reasons as you can think of why (a) retail customers and (b) trade customers may return goods to the seller.

Sometimes sellers may agree to keep the goods returned, even when they don't normally do so, but won't provide a full refund. Sometimes buyers will agree to keep goods they had wanted to return if the seller offers to refund some of the price they paid.

When the seller agrees to take back goods and refund the amount paid, or agrees to refund part or all of the amount the buyer paid, a document known as a **credit note** will be sent to the customer, showing the amount of the allowance given by the seller.

It is called a credit note because the customer's account will be credited with the amount of the allowance, to show the reduction in the amount owed.

Referring back to Exhibit 11.4, if D. Poole returns two of the cases of McBrand Pears, a credit note like the one shown in Exhibit 11.7 would be issued by R. Grant, the seller.

Exhibit 11.7

To: D. Poole & Co
   45 Charles Street
   Manchester M1 5ZN
		R. Grant
		Higher Side
		Preston PR1 2NL
		8 September 2020	

	CREDIT NOTE No. 9/37	Tel (01703) 33122 Fax (01703) 22331	
		Per unit	Total
		£	£
2 cases McBrand Pears		25	50
Less 20% trade discount			(10)
			40

To stop them being mistaken for invoices, credit notes are often printed in red.

11.14 Returns inwards day book

The credit notes are listed in a returns inwards day book (or returns inwards journal). This is then used for posting the items, as follows:

1 Sales ledger: credit the amount of credit notes, one by one, to the accounts of the customers in the ledger.
2 General ledger: at the end of the period the total of the returns inwards day book is posted to the debit of the returns inwards account.

11.15 Example of a returns inwards day book

Exhibit 11.8 presents an example of a returns inwards day book showing the items to be posted to the sales ledger and the general ledger followed by the entries in the ledger accounts.

Exhibit 11.8

Returns Inwards Day Book				(page 10)
	Note No.	Folio		Amount
2020				£
Sept 8 D. Poole	9/37	SL 12		40
17 A. Brewster	9/38	SL 58		120
19 C. Vickers	9/39	SL 99		290
29 M. Nelson	9/40	SL 112		160
Transferred to Returns Inwards Account		GL 114		610

Sales Ledger

D. Poole (page 12)

	2020	Folio	£
	Sept 8 Returns inwards	RI 10	40

A. Brewster (page 58)

	2020	Folio	£
	Sept 17 Returns inwards	RI 10	120

C. Vickers (page 99)

	2020	Folio	£
	Sept 19 Returns inwards	RI 10	290

M. Nelson (page 112)

	2020	Folio	£
	Sept 29 Returns inwards	RI 10	160

General Ledger

Returns Inwards (page 114)

2020	Folio	£	
Sept 30 Returns for the month	RI 10	610	

The returns inwards day book is sometimes known as the sales returns day book, because it is goods that were sold that are being returned.

11.16 Returns outwards and debit notes

If the supplier agrees, goods bought previously may be returned. When this happens a **debit note** is sent by the customer to the supplier giving details of the goods and the reason for their return.

The credit note received from the supplier will simply be evidence of the supplier's agreement, and the amounts involved.

Also, an allowance might be given by the supplier for any faults in the goods. Here also, a debit note should be sent to the supplier. Referring back to Exhibit 11.7, Exhibit 11.9 shows an example of the debit note that Poole, the buyer, may have sent to Grant, the seller.

Exhibit 11.9

To: R. Grant Higher Side Preston PR1 2NL		D. Poole & Co 45 Charles Street Manchester M1 5ZN 7 September 2017
DEBIT NOTE No. 9.22		Tel (0161) 488 2142 Fax (0161) 488 2143
	Per unit	Total
	£	£
2 cases McBrand Pears damaged in transit	25	50
Less 20% trade discount		(10)
		40

Note the differences between this debit note and the credit note in Exhibit 11.7: the names and addresses have swapped places and the document is described as 'Debit Note No. 9.22' rather than 'Credit Note No. 9/37', because Poole uses its own debit note numbering sequence. Also, the dates are different. In this case, it is assumed that Poole raised the debit note on 7 September and sent it and the goods to Grant. Grant received the goods on 8 September and raised the credit note on that date. Finally, the reason for the return of the goods is given.

11.17 Returns outwards day book

The debit notes are listed in a returns outwards day book. This is then used for posting the items, as follows:

1 Purchases ledger: debit the amounts of debit notes, one by one, to the personal accounts of the suppliers in the ledger.
2 General ledger: at the end of the period, the total of the returns outwards day book is posted to the credit of the returns outwards account.

The entries made in the returns outwards day book are made in the same way as in the returns inwards day book.

11.18 Example of a returns outwards day book

Exhibit 11.10 presents an example of a returns outwards day book showing the items to be posted to the purchases ledger and the general ledger. Those entries in the ledgers are on the opposite side to those for returns inwards.

Exhibit 11.10

Returns Outwards Day Book			(page 7)
	Note No.	Folio	Amount
2020			£
Sept 7 R. Grant	9.22	PL 29	40
16 B. Rose	9.23	PL 46	240
28 C. Blake	9.24	PL 55	30
30 S. Saunders	9.25	PL 87	360
Transferred to Returns Outwards Account		GL 116	670

The returns outwards day book is sometimes known as the purchases returns day book, because it is goods that were purchased that are being returned.

11.19 Double entry and returns

Exhibit 11.11 shows how the entries are made for returns inwards and returns outwards.

Exhibit 11.11   Posting returns inwards and returns outwards

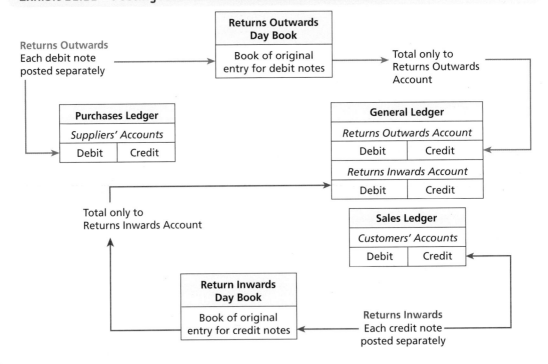

11.20 Statements

At the end of each month, a statement of account or, '**statement**', should be sent to each debtor who owes money on the last day of the month. It is really a copy of the debtor's account in the seller's books. It should show:

1 the amount owing at the start of the month;
2 the amount of each sales invoice sent to the debtor during the month;
3 credit notes sent to the debtor in the month;
4 cash and cheques received from the debtor during the month; and, finally,
5 the amount due from the debtor at the end of the month.

Exhibit 11.12 shows an example of a statement.

   Debtors will check to see if the account in their accounting records agrees with the statement. If the statement shows that they owe £520, but their records show a different amount due, they will investigate the difference in order to see whether either the statement or their records is incorrect. If they discover that there has been an error in their books, they will correct it. If they find that there is an error in the statement, they will contact the seller.

Activity 11.7 What sort of things could result in the statement and the account held in the books of the debtor showing different balances?

Exhibit 11.12

STATEMENT OF ACCOUNT
R. GRANT
Higher Side
Preston PR1 2NL
Tel (01703) 33122
Fax (01703) 22331

Accounts Dept
D. Poole & Co
45 Charles Street
Manchester M1 5ZN

Date	Details	Debit	Credit	Balance
2020		£	£	£
Sept 1	Balance b/d			880
2	Invoice 30756	560		1,440
8	Returns 9/37		40	1,400
25	Bank		880	520
Sept 30	Balance owing c/d			520

All accounts due and payable within 1 month

Apart from enabling debtors to check the amount due, the statement also acts as a reminder to debtors that they owe the seller money, and shows the date by which they should make payment. Sellers who are contacted by a debtor querying a statement will benefit from having any errors identified in their records.

11.21 Sales and purchases via credit cards

Various banks, building societies and other financial institutions issue credit cards to their customers. The most common examples are Visa and MasterCard. The holder of the credit card purchases goods or services without giving cash or cheques, but simply signs a credit card voucher. The customer is given a copy and the other copy is filed by the seller. Such sales are very rarely sales to anyone other than the general public.

The seller is paid later by the credit card company for all the credit card transactions in the period since the last payment made to the seller. This payment is subject to a deduction of commission by the credit card company.

Once a month, the customer pays the credit card company for all of the payments charged to the credit card during the previous month.

As far as the purchaser is concerned, he has seen goods and has received them (or received the service he requested). In the eyes of the customer, they were paid for at the time of purchase and a loan has been granted by the credit card company in order to do so.

Once the customer has the goods, or has received the appropriate services, the customer does not become a debtor needing an entry in a sales ledger and so, similarly to a cash sale, no ledger account is maintained for the customer. All the selling company is then interested in, from a recording point of view, is collecting the money from the credit card company.

The double entry needed is:

Sale of items via credit cards:	Dr: Credit card company
	Cr: Sales
Receipt of money from credit card company:	Dr: Bank
	Cr: Credit card company
Commission charged by credit card company:	Dr: Selling expenses
	Cr: Credit card company

Note: The commission is not a deduction from the selling price. It is treated in the same way as cash discounts. That is, it is a selling expense and is entered in the profit and loss account section of the income statement.

11.22 Internal check

When sales invoices are prepared, they should be very carefully checked. A system is usually set up so that each stage of the preparation of an invoice is checked by someone other than the person whose job is to send out the invoice.

 Activity 11.8 What sort of things could occur that make checking of all invoices, both those for sales and those for purchases, something that all businesses should do?

A system should, therefore, be set up whereby invoices are checked at each stage by someone other than the person who sends out the invoices or is responsible for paying them.

For purchase invoices, checks should be established, such as using a rubber stamp to stamp each incoming invoice with a mini form with spaces for ticks as each stage of the check on them is completed. The spaces in the stamp will be filled in by the people responsible for making each of the checks on the purchase invoices received, e.g.:

● one person certifying that the goods were actually received;
● a second person certifying that the goods were ordered;
● a third person certifying that the prices and calculations on the invoice are correct, and in accordance with the order originally placed and agreed;
● a fourth person certifying that the goods are in good condition and suitable for the purpose for which ordered.

Naturally, in a small business, simply because the office staff might be quite small, this cross-check may be in the hands of only one person other than the person who will pay the invoice.

A similar sort of check will be made in respect of sales invoices being sent out and on credit notes, both those being sent out and those being received.

11.23 Factoring

You've already learnt that one of the problems that many businesses face is the time taken by debtors to pay their accounts. Few businesses have so much cash available to them that they do not mind how long debtors take to pay. It is a rather surprising fact that a lot of businesses which fail do so not because the business is not making a profit, but because it has run out of cash funds. Once that happens, confidence in the business evaporates, and the business then finds that very few people will supply it with goods. It also cannot pay its employees. Closure of the business then happens fairly quickly in many cases.

In the case of accounts receivable, the cash flow problem may be alleviated by using the services of a financial intermediary called a factor.

Factoring is a financial service designed to improve the cash flow of healthy, growing companies, enabling them to make better use of management time and the money tied up in trade credit to customers.

In essence, factors provide their clients with three closely integrated services covering sales accounting and collection; credit management, which can include protection against bad debts; and the availability of finance against sales invoices.

11.24 Errors and Omissions Excepted (E&OE)

On some invoices and other documents you will see 'E&OE' printed at the bottom. This abbreviation stands for 'Errors and Omissions Excepted'. Basically, this is a warning that there may possibly be errors or omissions which could mean that the figures shown could be incorrect, and that the recipient should check carefully the figures before taking any action concerning them.

Learning outcomes

You should now have learnt:

1 That cash sales are not entered in the sales day book.

2 That when credit card payments are received at the time of sale, details of the customer are not recorded even though a debtor is created at the same time.

3 That sales made 'on time' are usually referred to as 'credit sales' or 'sales on credit'.

4 That the sales day book contains information relating to each credit sale made in each period.

5 That the sales day book is used for posting credit sales to the sales ledger.

6 That the total of the sales day book for the period is posted to the credit of the sales account in the general ledger.

7 How to make the appropriate entries relating to credit sales in a sales day book and make the correct postings from it to the sales ledger and general ledger.

8 How to prepare a sales invoice.

9 Why multiple copies are often made of each sales invoice.

10 That no entry is made for trade discounts in the double entry accounts.

11 That all businesses should operate a sound system of credit control over their debtors.

12 Some measures that may be taken to exercise credit control over debtors.

13 That cash purchases are not entered in the purchases day book.

14 That purchases made 'on time' are usually referred to as 'credit purchases' or 'purchases on credit'.

15 That the purchases day book is a list of all credit purchases.

16 That the purchases day book is used to post the items to the personal accounts in the purchases ledger.

17 That the total of credit purchases for the period is posted from the purchases day book to the debit of the purchases account in the general ledger.

18 How to make the appropriate entries relating to credit purchases in a purchases day book and make the correct postings from it to the purchases ledger and general ledger.

19 That the process of making entries in the books of the purchaser is very similar to that of making those in the books of the seller.

20 That 'returns inwards day book', 'returns inwards journal', 'sales returns journal' and 'sales returns day book' are different names for the same book.

21 That 'returns outwards day book' and 'purchases returns day book' are different names for the same book.

22 That goods returned by customers are all entered in a returns inwards day book.

23 That the returns inwards day book is used to post each item to the credit of the personal account of the customer in the sales ledger.

24 That the total of the returns inwards day book is debited at the end of the period to the returns inwards account in the general ledger.

25 That goods returned to suppliers are all entered in a returns outwards day book.

26 What the difference is between a credit note and a debit note.

27 That the returns outwards day book is used to debit the personal account of each supplier in the purchases ledger.

28 That the total of the returns outwards day book is credited at the end of the period to the returns outwards account in the general ledger.

29 How to make the appropriate entries relating to returns in the returns inwards and returns outwards day books and make the correct postings from them to the purchases ledger, sales ledger and general ledger.

30 That the process of making entries for returns in the books of purchasers and sellers is the mirror image of those made in their books for purchases and sales.

31 That statements are used by debtors to check the entries made in their books.

32 Of a range of causes for differences that can arise between statements and the seller's account in the debtor's purchases ledger and that such differences may not all be the result of an error.

33 How credit card transactions are recorded in the books and how commission charged to sellers by the credit card companies is treated in the income statement.

34 Why an effective system of invoice checking should be used by all businesses.

35 Why factoring is an attractive option for some businesses.

Answers to activities

11.1 A business may want to know the contact details of cash customers for marketing purposes. In fact, most businesses of any size would like to keep records in a database of all their cash customers for this reason. Businesses may also want to encourage cash customers to open credit accounts with the business so that they may be more likely to buy from the business in future. Also, where the goods sold are to be delivered to the customer, the customer's contact details will need to be recorded, but this will be in a record held elsewhere than in the accounting books.

11.2 Sellers keep copies of sales invoices for a number of reasons including: to prove that a sale took place; to enable the entries in the books to be correctly recorded and checked; to pass to the inventory department so that the correct goods can be selected for shipping to the customer; to pass to the delivery department, so that the correct goods will be shipped to the customer and to the correct address, and to enable the goods to be shipped accompanied by a copy of the sales invoice so that the customer can acknowledge receipt of the correct goods.

11.3 You want to attract large customers like these, so you are happy to sell to these traders at a lower price than the price you charge your other customers.

11.4 Similarly to the sales day book, the purchases day book is merely a list of details relating to each credit purchase. The list of items is virtually identical to those recorded in the sales day book, the only differences being that it is the name of the supplier that is recorded, not the purchaser, and that the invoice number is replaced with the buyer's own internally generated reference number:

● date
● name of supplier
● the reference number of the invoice
● folio column
● final amount of invoice.

11.5   Apart from the name of the day books, there are two differences. Firstly, the description of the entry in each case contains the name of the other party to the transaction. This is the personal account in the respective ledger (sales or purchases) where details of the transaction will be entered. The second difference is in the entry in the Invoice Number column. In the case of the seller, Blake, the number entered was the number of the invoice that Blake gave to the invoice and is the invoice number shown on the invoice in Exhibit 11.1. In the case of the buyer, Poole, the invoice number is one Poole gave the invoice when it was received from the seller, Blake. As with the number assigned to it by the seller, the buyer also gives each purchase invoice a unique number relating to its place in the sequence of purchase invoices that the buyer has received so far in the period. '9/101' probably means 'month nine' (9), 'purchase invoice' (1) 'number one' (01).

11.6   In either case, the reasons why goods may be returned include:

- they were of the wrong type (e.g. the wrong model number of replacement remote control for a TV);
- the item purchased was one that was already owned by the customer (e.g. a CD);
- they were the wrong colour (e.g. paint doesn't match the existing colour);
- they were the wrong size (e.g. a pair of trousers was too tight);
- they were faulty (e.g. a computer kept crashing);
- a customer bought more than was needed (newsagents returning unsold newspapers);
- a customer changed her mind (e.g. They were no longer needed because someone else had bought them for her);
- a customer saw the same goods elsewhere at a cheaper price;
- a customer found the goods too difficult to use (e.g. the instructions for setting up and operating a video recorder were too complicated);
- (for trade customers) a customer had returned a faulty item to them and they were now returning it to their supplier;
- items had been received in a damaged condition by the customer (e.g. fruit delivered to a supermarket);
- the seller had asked all customers to return a specific item (e.g. when an electrical good or a child's toy was found to be dangerous).

11.7   Differences could be due to a number of things having occurred, including the following:

- a purchase had been omitted from the books of either the seller or the debtor;
- a purchase had been incorrectly entered in the books of either the seller or the debtor;
- a purchase had been made at the end of the month but only entered in the books of either the seller or the debtor in the following month;
- goods returned had been entered in the books of the seller but not in the books of the debtor;
- goods returned had been incorrectly entered in the books of either the seller or the debtor;
- the debtor had entered goods as having been returned in the books when, in fact, the goods were not returned to the seller;
- a purchase had been recorded in the books of the seller in the debtor's account when it should have been entered in the account of another customer;
- a purchase had been recorded in the books of the debtor in the seller's account when it should have been entered in the account of another seller;
- a payment made to the supplier and entered in the books of the debtor had not yet been received by the seller;
- goods had been despatched by the seller and entered in the books of the seller but had not yet been received by the debtor.

11.8   If this were not done, it would be possible for someone inside a business to send out an invoice at a price less than the true price. Any difference could then be split between that person and the outside business. For example, if an invoice was sent to Ivor Twister & Co for £2,000 but the invoice clerk made it out deliberately for £200 then, if there was no cross-check, the difference of £1,800 could be split between the invoice clerk and Ivor Twister & Company.

    Similarly, outside businesses could send invoices for goods which were never received by the business. This might be in collaboration with an employee within the business, but there are businesses sending false invoices which rely on the businesses receiving them being inefficient and paying for items never received. There have been cases of businesses sending invoices for such items as advertisements which have never been published. The cashier of the business receiving the invoice, if the business is an inefficient one, might possibly think that someone in the business had authorised the advertisements and would pay the bill. Besides these there are, of course, genuine errors that an invoice checking system helps to avoid.

Review questions

11.1   You are to enter up the Sales Day Book from the following details. Post the items to the relevant accounts in the Sales Ledger and then show the transfer to the sales account in the General Ledger.

2019			£
Mar	1	Credit sales to P. Ryan	700
	3	Credit sales to T. Lee	320
	6	Credit sales to B. Cox	50
	10	Credit sales to P. Ryan	220
	17	Credit sales to J. Lock	960
	19	Credit sales to M. Gore	220
	27	Credit sales to C. Chen	95
	31	Credit sales to G. West	365

11.2A   Enter up the Sales Day Book from the following details. Post the items to the relevant accounts in the Sales Ledger and then show the transfer to the sales account in the General Ledger.

2020			£
January	1	Credit sales to S. Fry	970
	3	Credit sales to J. Hall	560
	5	Credit sales to R. Dunn	120
	7	Credit sales to P. Kay	430
	16	Credit sales to A. Dale	390
	23	Credit sales to D. Fu	240
	30	Credit sales to A. Cook	650

11.3   F. Benjamin of 10 Lower Street, Plymouth, is selling the following items at the recommended retail prices as shown: white tape £10 per roll, green felt at £4 per metre, blue cotton at £6 per sheet, black silk at £20 per dress length. He makes the following sales:

2020
May   1   To F. Gray, 3 Keswick Road, Portsmouth: 3 rolls white tape, 5 sheets blue cotton,
                 1 dress length black silk. Less 25 per cent trade discount.
            4   To A. Gray, 1 Shilton Road, Preston: 6 rolls white tape, 30 metres green felt. Less
                 $33\frac{1}{3}$ per cent trade discount.
            8   To E. Hines, 1 High Road, Malton: 1 dress length black silk. No trade discount.
           20   To M. Allen, 1 Knott Road, Southport: 10 rolls white tape, 6 sheets blue cotton,
                 3 dress lengths black silk, 11 metres green felt. Less 25 per cent trade discount.
           31   To B. Cooper, 1 Tops Lane, St. Andrews: 12 rolls white tape, 14 sheets blue
                 cotton, 9 metres green felt. Less $33\frac{1}{3}$ per cent trade discount.

You are to (a) draw up a sales invoice for each of the above sales, (b) enter them up in the Sales Day Book and post to the personal accounts, and (c) transfer the total to the sales account in the General Ledger.

→

11.4A   J. Fisher, White House, Bolton, is selling the following items at the prices as shown: plastic tubing at £1 per metre, polythene sheeting at £2 per length, vinyl padding at £5 per box, foam rubber at £3 per sheet. She makes the following sales:

June 1   To A. Portsmouth, 5 Rockley Road, Worthing: 22 metres plastic tubing, 6 sheets foam rubber, 4 boxes vinyl padding. Less 25 per cent trade discount.

   5   To B. Butler, 1 Wembley Road, Colwyn Bay: 50 lengths polythene sheeting, 8 boxes vinyl padding, 20 sheets foam rubber. Less 20 per cent trade discount.

  11   To A. Gate, 1 Bristol Road, Hastings: 4 metres plastic tubing, 33 lengths of polythene sheeting, 30 sheets foam rubber. Less 25 per cent trade discount.

  21   To L. Mackeson, 5 Maine Road, Bath: 29 metres plastic tubing. No trade discount is given.

  30   To M. Alison, Daley Road, Box Hill: 32 metres plastic tubing, 24 lengths polythene sheeting, 20 boxes vinyl padding. Less $33^{1}/_{3}$ per cent trade discount.

Required:
(a)   Draw up a sales invoice for each of the above sales.
(b)   Enter them up in the Sales Day Book and post to the personal accounts.
(c)   Transfer the total to the sales account in the General Ledger.

11.5   A. Jack has the following purchases for the month of May:

May 1   From A. Bell: 4 DVD players at £30 each, 3 mini hi-fi units at £180 each. Less 25 per cent trade discount.

   3   From C. Gray: 2 washing machines at £310 each, 5 vacuum cleaners at £60 each, 2 dishwashers at £190 each. Less 20 per cent trade discount.

  15   From C. Donald: 1 home entertainment centre at £400, 2 washing machines at £310 each. Less 25 per cent trade discount.

  20   From F. Perry: 6 external 1TB drives at £45 each. Less $33^{1}/_{3}$ per cent trade discount.

  30   From S. Turner: 4 dishwashers at £215 each Less 20 per cent trade discount.

Required:
(a)   Draw up a purchases invoice for each of the above purchases.
(b)   Enter up the purchases day book for the month.
(c)   Post the transactions to the suppliers' accounts in the purchases ledger.
(d)   Transfer the total to the purchases account in the general ledger.

11.6A   J. Glen has the following purchases for the month of June:

June 2   From J. Ring: 3 sets golf clubs at £900 each, 6 footballs at £36 each. Less 25 per cent trade discount.

  11   From F. Clark: 6 cricket bats at £70 each, 8 ice skates at £40 each, 5 rugby balls at £34 each. Less 20 per cent trade discount.

  18   From A. Lane: 6 sets golf trophies at £55 each, 4 sets golf clubs at £720. Less $33^{1}/_{3}$ per cent trade discount.

  25   From J. Jack: 5 cricket bats at £48 each. Less 25 per cent trade discount.

  30   From J. Wood: 8 goal posts at £95 each. Less 40 per cent trade discount.

Required:
(a)   Enter up the purchases day book for the month.
(b)   Post the items to the suppliers' accounts in the purchases ledger.
(c)   Transfer the total to the purchases account in the general ledger.

11.7 C. Phillips, a sole trader specialising in material for Asian clothing, has the following purchases and sales for March 2020:

Mar 1 Bought from Smith Stores: silk £40, cotton £80. All less 25 per cent trade discount.
8 Sold to A. Grantley: lycra goods £28, woollen items £44. No trade discount.
15 Sold to A. Henry: silk £36, lycra £144, cotton goods £120. All less 20 per cent trade discount.
23 Bought from C. Kelly: cotton £88, lycra £52. All less 25 per cent trade discount.
24 Sold to D. Sangster: lycra goods £42, cotton £48. Less 10 per cent trade discount.
31 Bought from J. Hamilton: lycra goods £270. Less $33\frac{1}{3}$ per cent trade discount.

Required:
(a) Prepare the purchases and sales day books of C. Phillips from the above.
(b) Post the items to the personal accounts.
(c) Post the totals of the day books to the sales and purchases accounts.

11.8A A. Henriques has the following purchases and sales for May 2020:

2020
May 1 Sold to M. Marshall: brass goods £24, bronze items £36. Less 25 per cent trade discount.
7 Sold to R. Richards: tin goods £70, lead items £230. Less $33\frac{1}{3}$ per cent trade discount.
9 Bought from C. Clarke: tin goods £400. Less 40 per cent trade discount.
16 Bought from A. Charles: copper goods £320. Less 50 per cent trade discount.
23 Sold to T. Young: tin goods £50, brass items £70, lead figures £80. All less 20 per cent trade discount.
31 Bought from M. Nelson: brass figures £100. Less 50 per cent trade discount.

Required:
(a) Write up the sales and purchases day books.
(b) Post the items to the personal accounts.
(c) Post the totals of the day books to the sales and purchases accounts in the general ledger.

11.9 A. Jones has the following credit purchases and credit sales for May:

May 1 Sold to J. Swift: brass goods £72, bronze items £108. All less 20 per cent trade discount.
Sold to D. Brown: tin goods £80, lead items £560. All less 30 per cent trade discount.
9 Bought from L. Syme: tin goods £300 less 40 per cent trade discount.
16 Bought from J. Wood: copper goods £460 less 70 per cent trade discount.
23 Sold to M. Peat: tin goods £50, brass items £70, lead figures £170. All less 10 per cent trade discount.
31 Bought from R. Gold: brass figures £345 less $33\frac{1}{3}$ per cent trade discount.

Required:
(a) Write up sales and purchases day books.
(b) Post the items to the personal accounts.
(c) Post the totals of the day books to the sales and purchases accounts in the general ledger.
(d) What are the books of prime entry within a business and why are they so called? Illustrate your answer with suitable examples.

11.10   You are to enter up the Purchases Day Book and the Returns Outwards Day Book from the following details, then to post the items to the relevant accounts in the Purchases Ledger and to show the transfers to the General Ledger at the end of the month.

2020

May	1	Credit purchase from S. Dodd £216.
	4	Credit purchases from the following: B. Line £324; F. Town £322; R. Pace £64; T. Pang £130.
	7	Goods returned by us to the following: S. Dodd £58; B. Line £63.
	10	Credit purchase from F. Town £90.
	18	Credit purchases from the following: D. Ince £230; P. Tago £310; R. Scott £405; N. Auld £220.
	25	Goods returned by us to the following: P. Tago £140; F. Town £47.
	31	Credit purchases from: R. Pace £174; J. Marsh £170.

11.11A   Enter up the Sales Day Book and the returns inwards day book from the following details. Then post to the customers' accounts and show the transfers to the General Ledger.

2019

June	1	Credit sales to: B. Dock £240; M. Ryan £126; G. Soul £94; F. Trip £107.
	6	Credit sales to: P. Coates £182; L. Job £203; T. Mann £99.
	10	Goods returned to us by: B. Dock £19; F. Trip £32.
	20	Credit sales to B. Uphill £1,790.
	24	Goods returned to us by L. Job £16.
	30	Credit sales to T. Kane £302.

11.12   You are to enter up the sales, purchases, returns inwards and returns outwards day books from the following details, then to post the items to the relevant accounts in the sales and purchases ledgers. The totals from the day books are then to be transferred to the accounts in the General Ledger.

2020

May	1	Credit sales: T. Thompson £56; L. Rodriguez £148; K. Barton £145.
	3	Credit purchases: P. Potter £144; H. Harris £25; B. Spencer £76.
	7	Credit sales: K. Kelly £89; N. Mendes £78; N. Lee £257.
	9	Credit purchases: B. Perkins £24; H. Harris £58; H. Miles £123.
	11	Goods returned by us to: P. Potter £12; B. Spencer £22.
	14	Goods returned to us by: T. Thompson £5; K. Barton £11; K. Kelly £14.
	17	Credit purchases: H. Harris £54; B. Perkins £65; L. Nixon £75.
	20	Goods returned by us to B. Spencer £14.
	24	Credit sales: K. Mohammed £57; K. Kelly £65; O. Green £112.
	28	Goods returned to us by N. Mendes £24.
	31	Credit sales: N. Lee £55.

11.13A You are to enter the following items in the relevant day books, post to the personal accounts, and show the transfers to the General Ledger.

2020
July

1	Credit purchases from: K. Hill £380; M. Norman £500; N. Senior £106.
3	Credit sales to: E. Rigby £510; E. Phillips £246; F. Thompson £356.
5	Credit purchases from: R. Morton £200; J. Cook £180; D. Edwards £410; C. Davies £66.
8	Credit sales to: A. Green £307; H. George £250; J. Ferguson £185.
12	Returns outwards to: M. Norman £30; N. Senior £16.
14	Returns inwards from: E. Phillips £18; F. Thompson £22.
20	Credit sales to: E. Phillips £188; F. Powell £310; E. Lee £420.
24	Credit purchases from: C. Ferguson £550; K. Ennevor £900.
31	Returns inwards from: E. Phillips £27; E. Rigby £30.
31	Returns outwards to: J. Cook £13; C. Davies £11.

The journal

After you have studied this chapter, you should be able to:

- explain the purpose of having a journal
- enter up the journal
- post from the journal to the ledgers
- complete opening entries for a new set of accounting books in the journal and make the appropriate entries in the ledgers
- describe and explain the accounting cycle

Introduction

In this chapter, you will learn about the book of original entry that sweeps up all the transactions that have not been entered fully in the other five books of original entry – the journal. You'll learn about the sort of transactions that are entered in the journal and how to make those entries. You'll also learn how to transfer those entries to the accounts in the ledgers. Finally, you will learn what the accounting cycle consists of and see how it links all the material you have learnt so far in this book.

12.1 Main books of original entry

We have seen in earlier chapters that most transactions are entered in one of the following books of original entry:

- cash book
- sales day book
- purchases day book
- returns inwards day book
- returns outwards day book.

These books are each devoted to a particular form of transaction. For example, all credit sales are in the sales day book. To trace any of the transactions entered in these five books would be relatively easy, as we know exactly which book of original entry would contain the information we are looking for.

12.2 The journal: the other book of original entry

The other items which do not pass through these five books are much less common, and sometimes much more complicated. It would be easy for a bookkeeper to forget the details of these transactions if they were made directly into the ledger accounts from the source documents and, if the bookkeeper left the business, it could be impossible to understand such bookkeeping entries.

Activity 12.1

If these five books are used to record all cash and bank transactions, and all credit purchase and sales items, what are these other items that need to be recorded in a sixth book of original entry?

What is needed is a form of diary to record such transactions, before the entries are made in the double entry accounts. This book is called the **journal.** For each transaction it will contain:

● the date
● the name of the account(s) to be debited and the amount(s)
● the name of the account(s) to be credited and the amount(s)
● a description and explanation of the transaction (this is called a **narrative**)
● a folio reference to the source documents giving proof of the transaction.

The use of a journal makes fraud by bookkeepers more difficult. It also reduces the risk of entering the item once only instead of having double entry. Despite these advantages there are many businesses which do not have such a book.

12.3 Typical uses of the journal

Some of the main uses of the journal are listed below. It must not be thought that this is a complete list.

1 The purchase and sale of fixed assets on credit.
2 Writing-off bad debts.
3 The correction of errors in the ledger accounts.
4 Opening entries. These are the entries needed to open a new set of books.
5 Adjustments to any of the entries in the ledgers.

The layout of the journal is:

The Journal				
Date	Details	Folio	Dr	Cr
	The name of the account to be debited. 　The name of the account to be credited. The narrative.			

On the first line in the entry is the account to be debited. The second line gives the account to be credited. It is indented so as to make it obvious that it is the credit part of the double entry. The final line is a description of what is being done and provides a permanent record of the reason(s) for the entry.

You should remember that the journal is not a double entry account. It is a form of diary, just as are the day books you learnt about in Chapter 11. Entering an item in the journal is not the same as recording an item in an account. Once the journal entry is made, the entry in the double entry accounts can then be made.

Note for students: The vertical lines have been included above in order to illustrate how the paper within the journal may be printed. You may find it useful to rule your paper according to this layout when attempting examples and questions on this topic.

12.4 Journal entries in examination questions

If you were to ask examiners what type of bookkeeping and accounting questions are always answered badly by students they would certainly include 'questions involving journal entries'.

This is not because they are difficult, but because many students seem to suffer some sort of mental block when doing such questions. The authors, who have been examiners for a large number of accounting bodies around the world, believe that this occurs because students fail to view the journal as a document containing instructions, three per transaction:

1 The account(s) to be debited.
2 The account(s) to be credited.
3 A description of the transaction.

To help you avoid this sort of problem with journal entries, you'll first of all see what the entries are in the accounts, and then be shown how to write up the journal for each of these entries. Let's now look at a few examples.

In practice, the folio reference entered in the T-accounts is often that of the other account involved in the transaction, rather than that of a journal entry. However, this is done when no journal entry has been prepared. When a journal entry has been prepared, it is always the journal entry folio reference that appears in the T-accounts.

Purchase and sale on credit of non-current assets

1 A milling machine is bought on credit from Toolmakers Ltd for £10,550 on 1 July 2019.

The transaction involves the acquisition of an asset matched by a new liability. From what you have learnt in earlier chapters, you will know that the acquisition of an asset is represented by a debit entry in the asset account. You will also know that a new liability is recorded by crediting a liability account. The double entries would be:

Machinery					Folio	GL1
2019				£		
July 1 Toolmakers Ltd	J1	10,550				

Toolmakers Ltd				Folio	PL55
		2019			£
		July 1 Machinery	J1		10,550

 Activity 12.2 All the folio numbers have been entered in these ledger accounts. You do need to enter them at some time so that you can trace the other side of the entries, but why have they already been entered?

Now what we have to do is to record those entries in the journal. Remember, the journal is simply a kind of diary, not in account form but in ordinary written form. It says which account has to been debited, which account has been credited, and then gives the narrative which simply describes the nature of the transaction. For the transaction above, the journal entry will appear as follows:

The Journal					(page 1)
Date	Details		Folio	Dr	Cr
2019				£	£
July 1	Machinery		GL1	10,550	
	Toolmakers Ltd		PL55		10,550
	Purchase of milling machine on credit, Purchases invoice No 7/159				

2 Sale of van no longer required for £800 on credit to K. Lamb on 2 July 2019.

Here again it is not difficult to work out what entries are needed in the double entry accounts. They are as follows:

K. Lamb				Folio	SL79
2019			£		
July 2 Van		J2	800		

				Van		Folio	GL51
			2019				£
			July 2 K.Lamb		J2		800

The journal entry will appear as follows:

The Journal					(page 2)
Date	Details		Folio	Dr	Cr
2019 July 2	K. Lamb Van Sales of van no longer required. See letter ref. KL3X8g		SL79 GL51	£ 800	£ 800

Bad debts

A debt of £78 owing to us from H. Mander is written off as a bad debt on 31 August 2019.

As the debt is now of no value, we have to stop showing it as an asset. This means that we will credit H. Mander to cancel it out of his account. A bad debt is an expense, and so we will debit it to a bad debts account. The double entry for this is shown as:

Bad Debts				Folio	GL16
2019			£		
Aug 31 H. Mander		J3	78		

			H. Mander		Folio	SL99
			2019			£
			Aug 31 Bad debts	J3		78

The journal entry is:

The Journal					(page 3)
Date	Details		Folio	Dr	Cr
2019 Aug 31	Bad debts H. Mander Debt written-off as bad. See letter in file HM2X8		GL16 SL99	£ 78	£ 78

Correction of errors

> This is explained in detail in Chapters 26 and 27.

However, the same procedures are followed as in the case of these other types of journal entries.

Opening entries

J. Brew, after being in business for some years without keeping proper records, now decides to keep a double entry set of books. On 1 July 2019 he establishes that his assets and liabilities are as follows:

Assets: Van £3,700; Fixtures £1,800; Inventory £4,200;
           Accounts receivable – B. Young £95, D. Blake £45; Bank £860; Cash £65.
Liabilities: Accounts payable – M. Quinn £129, C. Walters £410.

   The Assets therefore total £3,700 + £1,800 + £4,200 + £95 + £45 + £860 + £65 = £10,765; and the Liabilities total £129 + £410 = £539.

   The Capital consists of Assets − Liabilities, i.e. £10,765 − £539 = £10,226.

1 July 2019 will be the first day of the accounting period, as that is the date on which all the asset and liability values were established.

   We start the writing up of the books on 1 July 2019. To do this we:

1 Open the journal and make the journal entries to record the opening assets, liabilities and capital.
2 Open asset accounts, one for each asset. Each opening asset is shown as a debit balance.
3 Open liability accounts, one for each liability. Each opening liability is shown as a credit balance.
4 Open an account for the capital. Show it as a credit balance.

The journal records what you are doing, and why. Exhibit 12.1 shows:

● the journal
● the opening entries in the double entry accounts.

Exhibit 12.1

The Journal					(page 5)
Date	*Details*		*Folio*	*Dr*	*Cr*
2019				£	£
July 1	Van		GL1	3,700	
	Fixtures		GL2	1,800	
	Inventory		GL3	4,200	
	Accounts receivable – B. Young		SL1	95	
		D. Blake	SL2	45	
	Bank		CB1	860	
	Cash		CB1	65	
	Accounts payable – M. Quinn		PL1		129
		C. Walters	PL2		410
	Capital		GL4		10,226
	Assets and liabilities at this date entered to open the books			10,765	10,765

General Ledger
Van
(page 1)

2019		Folio	£			
July	1 Balance	J 5	3,700			

Fixtures
(page 2)

2019		Folio	£			
July	1 Balance	J 5	1,800			

Inventory
(page 3)

2019		Folio	£			
July	1 Balance	J 5	4,200			

Capital
(page 4)

				2019		Folio	£
				July	1 Balance	J 5	10,226

Sales Ledger
B. Young
(page 1)

2019		Folio	£				
July	1 Balance	J 5	95				

D. Blake
(page 2)

2019		Folio	£	
July	1 Balance	J 5	45	

Purchases Ledger
M. Quinn
(page 1)

				2019		Folio	£
				July	1 Balance	J 5	129

C. Walters
(page 2)

				2019		Folio	£
				July	1 Balance	J 5	410

Cash Book
			Cash	Bank	
					(page 1)
2019		Folio	£	£	
July	1 Balances	J 5	65	860	

Once these opening balances have been recorded in the books, the day-to-day transactions can be entered in the normal manner.

At the elementary level of examinations in bookkeeping, questions are often asked which require you to open a set of books and record the day-by-day entries for the ensuing period.

Activity 12.3 Do you think you will ever need to do this again for this business? (Hint: think about the entries to be made at the start of the next accounting period.)

Adjustments to any of the entries in the ledgers

These can be of many types and it is impossible to write out a complete list. Several examples are now shown:

1 Young, a debtor, owed £2,000 on 1 July 2020. He was unable to pay his account in cash, but offers a five-year-old car in full settlement of the debt. The offer is accepted on 5 July 2020.

The personal account has now been settled and needs to be credited with the £2,000. On the other hand, the business now has an extra asset, a car, resulting in the car account needing to be debited with the £2,000 value that has been placed upon the new car.

The double entry recorded in the ledgers is:

			Car			GL171
2020			£			
July 5 K. Young	J6		2,000			

			K. Young			SL333
2020		£	2020			£
July 1 Balance b/d		2,000	July 5 Motor car	J6		2,000

The journal entry is:

The Journal						*(page 6)*
Date	Details			Folio	Dr	Cr
2020					£	£
July 5	Car			GL171	2,000	
	K. Young			SL333		2,000
	Accepted car in full settlement of debt per letter dated 5/7/2020					

2 T. Jones is a creditor. On 10 July 2020 his business is taken over by A. Lee to whom the debt of £150 is now to be paid.

Here one creditor is just being exchanged for another one. The action needed is to cancel the amount owing to T. Jones by debiting his account, and to show it owing to Lee by opening an account for Lee and crediting it.

The entries in the ledger accounts are:

			T. Jones		SL92
2020		£	2020		£
July 10 A. Lee	J7	150	July 1 Balance b/d		150

		A. Lee			SL244
		2020			£
		July 10 T. Jones	J7		150

The journal entry is:

The Journal					(page 7)
Date	Details		Folio	Dr	Cr
2020 July 10	T. Jones A. Lee Transfer of indebtedness as per letter ref G/1335		SL92 SL244	£ 150	£ 150

3 We had not yet paid for an office printer we bought on credit for £310 because it was not working properly when installed. On 12 July 2020 we returned it to the supplier, RS Ltd. An allowance of £310 was offered by the supplier and accepted. As a result, we no longer owe the supplier anything for the printer.

The double entry in the ledger accounts is:

RS Ltd PL124

2020			£	2020			£
July	12 Office machinery	J8	310	July	1 Balance b/d		310

Office Machinery GL288

2020			£	2020			£
July	1 Balance b/d		310	July	12 RS Ltd	J8	310

The journal entry is:

The Journal					(page 8)
Date	Details		Folio	Dr	Cr
2020 July 12	RS Ltd Office machinery Faulty printer returned to supplier. Full allowance given. See letter 10/7/2020.		PL124 GL288	£ 310	£ 310

12.5 Examination guidance

Later on in your studies, especially in *Frank Wood's Business Accounting* 2, you may find that some of the journal entries are more complicated than those you have seen so far. The best plan for you is to follow this advice:

1 On your examination answer paper write a heading 'Workings'. Then show the double entry accounts under that heading.

2 Now put a heading 'Answer', and show the answer in the form of the Journal, as shown in this chapter.

If the question asks for journal entries, you must *not* fall into the trap of just showing the double entry accounts, as you could get no marks at all *even though your double entry records are correct*. The examiner wants to see the journal entries, and you *must* show those in your answer.

12.6 The basic accounting cycle

Now that we have covered all aspects of bookkeeping entries, we can show the whole **accounting cycle** in the form of the diagram in Exhibit 12.2.

Note that the 'accounting cycle' refers to the sequence in which data is recorded and processed until it becomes part of the financial statements at the end of the period.

Exhibit 12.2   The accounting cycle for a profit-making organisation

Source documents	● Sales and purchases invoices
Where original information is to be found	● Debit and credit notes for returns
	● Bank pay-in slips and cheque counterfoils
	● Receipts for cash paid out and received
	● Correspondence containing other financial information

Original entry	Classified and then entered in books of original entry:
What happens to it	● The cash books[Note]
	● Sales and purchases day books
	● Returns inwards and outwards day books
	● The journal

| **Double entry** | **Double entry accounts** |
| How the dual aspect of each transaction is recorded | |

General ledger	Sales ledger	Purchases ledger	Cash books*
Real and nominal accounts	Accounts receivable	Accounts payable	Cash book and petty cash book

(*Note*: Cash books fulfil the roles both of books of original entry and double entry accounts)

| **Check arithmetic** | |
| Checking the arithmetical accuracy of double entry accounts | Trial balance |

| **Profit or loss** | |
| Calculation of profit or loss for the reporting period shown in a financial statement | Income statement |

| **Closing balance sheet** | |
| Financial statement showing liabilities, assets and capital at the end of the reporting period | Balance sheet |

Activity 12.4   What are the six books of original entry?

Learning outcomes

You should now have learnt:

1 What the journal is used for.

2 That the journal is the collection place for items that do not pass fully through the other five books of original entry.

3 That there is a range of possible types of transactions that must be entered in the journal.

4 That the opening double entries made on starting a set of books for the first time are done using the journal.

5 How to make the opening entries for a new set of books in the journal and in the ledger accounts.

6 That the main parts of the accounting cycle are as follows:

(*a*) Collect source documents.
(*b*) Enter transactions in the books of original entry.
(*c*) Post to ledgers.
(*d*) Extract trial balance.
(*e*) Prepare the income statement.
(*f*) Draw up the balance sheet.

Answers to activities

12.1 All transactions relating to non-current assets. Also, entries have to be recorded somewhere when errors in the books have to be corrected, or when any figures in the ledger accounts need to be changed. Also, any transfers involving the Capital Account, such as when funds are set aside from the Capital Account to provide resources should a building need to be repaired or replaced.

12.2 You are looking at the ledger accounts after the details have been entered in them from the journal and you always enter the folio number in the ledger account as you make each entry, not afterwards. The check that the entries has been completed is made by only entering the folio numbers *in the journal* as each entry is written in the appropriate ledger account. You could, therefore, see an entry in the journal that has no folio numbers entered against it. This would signify that the journal entry has not yet been fully recorded in the appropriate ledger accounts. As mentioned above, you should *never* see this in a ledger account as the folio number is always entered *at the same time* as the rest of the details from the journal are entered.

12.3 The need for opening entries will not occur very often. They will not be needed each year as the balances from the previous period will have been brought forward. They will only be required a second time if the business goes through a change in status, for example, if it becomes a limited company.

12.4 Cash book, sales day book, purchases day book, returns inwards day book, returns outwards day book, and the journal. The petty cash book is also considered to be a book of original entry.

Review questions

12.1 You are to show the journal entries necessary to record the following items which occured in May 2019:

(a) May 1 Bought a motor bike on credit from Lakeside Garage for £5,500.
(b) May 3 A debt of £347 owing from T. Reason was written off as a bad debt.
(c) May 8 Office chairs bought by us for £600 were returned to the supplier UL Furniture Ltd, as they were unsuitable. Full allowance will be given to us.
(d) May 12 We are owed £300 by J. Day. He is declared bankrupt and we received £190 in full settlement of the debt.
(e) May 14 We take goods costing £60 out of the business inventory without paying for them.
(f) May 28 Some time ago we paid an insurance bill thinking that it was all in respect of the business. We now discover that £40 of the amount paid was in fact insurance of our private house.
(g) May 28 Bought a trailer for £1,700 on credit from C-Land Ltd.

12.2A Show the journal entries necessary to record the following items:

2020
Apr   1 Bought office furniture on credit from Durham Brothers Ltd £1,400.
      4 We take goods costing £270 out of the business inventory without paying for them.
      9 £90 of the goods taken by us on 4 April are returned back into inventory by us. We do not take any money for the return of the goods.
     12 M. Sharp owes us £460. He is unable to pay his debt. We agree to take some display cabinets from him at that value and so cancel the debt.
     18 Some of the items of office furniture bought from Durham Brothers Ltd, £36 worth, are found to be unsuitable and are returned to them for full allowance.
     24 A debt owing to us by T. Lyle of £80 is written off as a bad debt.
     30 Computers bought on credit from OTF Ltd for £2,300.

12.3 You are to open the books of F. Polk, a trader, via the journal to record the assets and liabilities, and are then to record the daily transactions for the month of May. A trial balance is to be extracted as on 31 May 2020.

2020
May   1 *Assets*: Premises £34,000; Van £5,125; Fixtures £810; Inventory £6,390; Accounts receivable: P. Mullen £140, F. Lane £310; Cash at bank £6,240; Cash in hand £560.
         Liabilities: Accounts payable: S. Hood £215, J Brown £640.
      1 Paid storage costs by cheque £40.
      2 Goods bought on credit from: S. Hood £145; D. Main £206; W. Tone £96; R. Foot £66.
      3 Goods sold on credit to: J. Wilson £112; T. Cole £164; F. Syme £208; J. Allen £91; P. White £242; F. Lane £90.
      4 Paid for motor expenses in cash £60.
      7 Cash drawings by proprietor £150.
      9 Goods sold on credit to: T. Cole £68; J. Fox £131.
     11 Goods returned to Polk by: J. Wilson £32; F. Syme £48.
     14 Bought another van on credit from Abel Motors Ltd £4,850.
     16 The following paid Polk their accounts by cheque less 5 per cent cash discount: P. Mullen; F. Lane; J. Wilson; F. Syme.
     19 Goods returned by Polk to R. Foot £6.
     22 Goods bought on credit from: L. Mole £183; W. Wright £191.
     24 The following accounts were settled by Polk by cheque less 5 per cent cash discount: S. Hood; J. Brown; R. Foot.
     27 Salaries paid by cheque £740.
     30 Paid business rates by cheque £140.
     31 Paid Abel Motors Ltd a cheque for £4,850.

13

Value added tax (VAT)

Learning objectives

After you have studied this chapter you should be able to:

● describe the key principles of VAT and how it must be accounted for

● distinguish between VAT-registered businesses and unregistered businesses

● make entries for VAT in the necessary books and accounts

● create sales invoices including VAT

● explain the purpose of the VAT return form and what it shows

Introduction

Most countries have a 'sales tax' of some sort and in the UK it is called value added tax (VAT). VAT is a tax that is charged on the supply of most goods and services in the UK. The majority of businesses must therefore keep account of all the VAT they charge on their sales, as well as all the VAT they pay on the goods and services they buy. The detailed rules of VAT are remarkably complex but in this chapter you'll learn the key principles regarding which businesses must charge VAT on their sales, how VAT must be accounted for, and how businesses must ultimately pay the VAT they have collected to the government.

13.1 What is VAT?

Value added tax (VAT) is a tax charged on the supply of most goods and services in the UK. Some goods and services (such as insurance) are not taxable but most are. VAT is administered in the UK by HM Revenue & Customs (HMRC). HMRC is the government department responsible for collecting all UK taxes. The rules of VAT are highly detailed and complicated and so are beyond the scope of this book. This chapter covers the basic principles only.

13.2 The different rates of VAT

Goods and services essentially fall into one of four categories in relation to VAT in the UK:

1 **Standard rate:** this applies to the majority of goods and services and at the time of writing the standard rate is 20 per cent.

2 **Reduced rate:** there are a *small* number of goods and services that are subject to a reduced rate of 5 per cent. Examples include domestic fuel (not business fuel), children's car seats, and nicotine patches. Since most businesses will very rarely buy or sell reduced rate items we will not see any examples of the reduced rate in this chapter.

3 **Zero-rate**: certain items (such as most food, printed books, and young children's clothes) are subject to VAT at a rate of 0 per cent.

4 **Exempt items**: some specific types of goods and services are not subject to VAT at all. Examples include banking and insurance services, betting, gaming and lotteries, and most healthcare services.

Standard rate VAT applies to the majority of goods and services that businesses deal in, so most of the sales and purchases in this chapter will be subject to VAT at 20 per cent.

13.3 Do all businesses have to add VAT to their selling prices?

The answer is no, but most do. Most businesses must 'register for VAT' with HMRC which means they will have to add VAT to the prices of the goods and services they sell. There are two types of business that do not have to register and these are categorised under two headings:

1 Nature of business: some specific types of goods and services are 'exempt' and not subject to VAT at all. If a business only sells *exempt* items (such as banking and insurance services) then they will not be able to register for VAT. (Note that a business that only sells *zero-rated* items must still register for VAT unless it falls under the second heading below.)

2 Size of business: UK businesses only have to register for VAT if their annual sales exceed £85,000 (£85,000 is the 'registration limit' at the time of writing, although it changes each year). Very small businesses therefore do not have to add VAT to their prices (although they are allowed to register voluntarily).

> **Activity 13.1** You have just learnt that small businesses do not have to register for VAT until their sales exceed a certain limit. Why does the government have this rule?

13.4 VAT-registered businesses: accounting for VAT

Suppose that Business A is registered for VAT and sells goods priced at £200 to Business B. The sales invoice issued by Business A will essentially show:

	£
Goods price ('net')	200
VAT at 20%	40
Invoice total including VAT ('gross')	240

Business A will receive the total amount of £240 from Business B. £40 of this represents VAT that Business A is collecting on behalf of HMRC. Business A will therefore have to hand over this £40 to HMRC in due course.

Suppose that Business B is also VAT-registered. Business B takes the goods, modifies them in some way and sells them to a member of the general public (Jane Smith) for £300 plus VAT. The sales invoice issued by Business B will show:

	£
Goods price ('net')	300
VAT at 20%	60
Invoice total including VAT ('gross')	360

Business B therefore receives £360 from Jane Smith and owes the £60 VAT element of this to HMRC. However, because Business B is VAT-registered it is also able to claim a refund of the £40 VAT it paid to Business A. It will therefore pay only £20 to HMRC (i.e. the £60 VAT collected on its sales minus the £40 VAT reclaimed on its purchases).

In this example, we can see that HMRC will receive £40 from Business A and £20 from Business B. The total tax collected is therefore £60, which ultimately has all been borne by Jane Smith (who paid £300 + VAT £60 for her goods). The final consumer of the goods (normally a member of the general public) is not registered for VAT so cannot reclaim it. Businesses A and B have effectively acted as collectors of the tax, the entire burden of which ultimately falls on the final customer.

This is the fundamental principle underlying how VAT works. VAT is collected and reclaimed by each business at each stage in the supply chain and it is the final consumer at the end of the chain that ultimately bears the tax in full.

Activity 13.2

A forestry business (X) sells timber to a carpentry business (Y) for £1,000 plus VAT at 20 per cent. With this wood, the carpenter makes furniture which it sells to a retail business (Z) for £1,500 plus VAT at 20 per cent. The retail business sells the furniture to customers for £2,200 plus VAT at 20 per cent. How much VAT will be received by HMRC from this chain of transactions, and from whom will it be collected?

13.5 VAT invoices

If a VAT-registered business supplies goods or services to another VAT-registered business it must issue a 'VAT invoice'. (If the business is a retailer it must issue a VAT invoice if the customer asks for one.)

A VAT invoice is required by law to show certain information. The principal requirements are that it must show:

● name, address and VAT-registration number of the business supplying the goods or services *(when a business registers for VAT it will be given a unique VAT registration number by HMRC)*
● customer's name and address
● invoice number and invoice date
● description of the goods or services supplied
● price before VAT is added
● total cost before VAT
● rate of VAT and the total VAT charged
● invoice total including VAT.

Exhibit 13.1 shows an example of a VAT invoice. Note that if the value of the sale is below a certain amount (£250 at the time of writing) then a simplified VAT invoice can be issued.

13.6 VAT and discounts

VAT is added to the price of goods or services sold after deducting both:

● trade discount; and
● cash discount.

This principle applies even if the cash discount is subsequently not taken-up by the customer.

Exhibit 13.1 shows an example of a VAT invoice featuring both trade discount and cash discount.

Exhibit 13.1

<table>
<tr><td colspan="4" align="center">**P. Wilson & Co**</td></tr>
<tr><td colspan="4" align="center">**51 Church Street**</td></tr>
<tr><td colspan="4" align="center">**London WC4 2NA**</td></tr>
<tr><td colspan="4" align="center">VAT registration number: 741 852 963</td></tr>
<tr><td colspan="4" align="center">**INVOICE**</td></tr>
</table>

To:	D. Murray	Invoice date:	23 May 2018
	22 Green Lane	Invoice number:	15984
	Manchester M13 6BA		

Description	*Quantity*	*Unit price*	Total £
Paper dispensers	10	£100	1,000
Less Trade discount of 10%			(100)
			900
Add VAT at 20%			171
Invoice total including VAT			1,071
Terms: Cash discount of 5% available if paid within 14 days			

Note that the VAT has been calculated at 20% on the net price after deducting both trade discount *and* cash discount. If a trade discount but no cash discount had been offered then the VAT amount in Exhibit 13.1 would have been £900 × 20% = £180.

But a cash discount of 5% *is* offered so the VAT amount can be reduced by 5%: £180 × 5% = £9, so the VAT amount on the invoice is £171 instead of £180. Even if the customer fails to pay within 14 days this VAT amount will not change.

13.7 Accounting entries for VAT-registered businesses

VAT on sales

Suppose J. Cuttle & Co, a VAT-registered business, only made three credit sales during March 2018:

	Price of goods sold before VAT is added	VAT at 20%
2018	£	£
March 7 D. Knowles	100	20
13 B. Grimes	300	60
24 N. Parkes	170	34

Businesses record their sales in a sales day book (see Chapter 11). If a business is VAT-registered this day book will now require an extra column for VAT. The sales day book for March will therefore appear as follows:

	Invoice number	Folio	Gross	VAT	Net
Sales Day Book					**(page 862)**
2018			£	£	£
March 7 D. Knowles	8436	SL189	120	20	100
13 B. Grimes	8437	SL296	360	60	300
24 N. Parkes	8438	SL73	204	34	170
Transferred to General Ledger			684	114	570
				GL67	GL101

Each invoice must be entered in the individual customers' accounts in the sales ledger. The customers owe the total amount of the invoice including VAT, so it is the gross amounts that must be entered in the individual accounts, as shown below:

Sales Ledger
D. Knowles   *(page 189)*

2018	Folio	£	
March 7 Sales	SB862	120	

B. Grimes   *(page 296)*

2018	Folio	£	
March 13 Sales	SB862	360	

N. Parkes   *(page 73)*

2018	Folio	£	
March 24 Sales	SB862	204	

The personal accounts have been debited with a total of £684, being the sum of the amounts that the customers will have to pay. These are debit entries because they are recording an increase in the assets of the business (amounts due from customers).

The actual value of the goods sold before VAT is added was only £570, so it is this amount that must be credited to the sales account in the general ledger. The £114 VAT on these sales is known as 'Output VAT'. It is owed to HMRC so will be credited to the *Output VAT* account in the general ledger:

General Ledger
Sales   *(page 101)*

		2018	Folio	£
		March 31 Sales	SB862	570

Output VAT   *(page 67)*

		2018	Folio	£
		March 31 Sales	SB862	114

Let's assume that all J. Cuttle & Co's sales in March were made on credit. However, if it had also made cash sales then these would be recorded in the business's cash book. The net value of the sales and the output VAT on those sales would still need to be recorded in the general ledger in the same manner as the two entries shown above.

VAT on purchases

A VAT-registered business like J. Cuttle & Co has to add VAT to their sales prices but is able to reclaim the VAT it pays on the goods and services it buys. Periodically the business will submit a 'VAT return' (normally every three months) to HMRC which will show:

	£
VAT on sales invoices (Output VAT)	A
Less VAT on goods & services bought (Input VAT)	(B)
Amount to be paid to HMRC	C

Normally A will be greater than B so the business will pay amount C to HMRC. Very occasionally A will be less than B, in which case HMRC will refund C to the business.

Businesses must therefore record the input VAT on all goods and services that they buy. Let's look at the credit purchases of J. Cuttle & Co (the same business whose sales we dealt with earlier in this section). Suppose J. Cuttle & Co made only three credit purchases in March 2018:

	Price of goods purchased before VAT is added	VAT at 20%
2018	£	£
March 5 P. Surtees	50	10
17 L. Gower	160	32
29 J. Cropper	120	24

Credit purchases are recorded in a purchases day book (see Chapter 11). As with the sales day book, an extra column for VAT will be required. The purchases day book for March will therefore be completed as follows:

Purchases Day Book					(page 943)
	Invoice number	Folio	Gross	VAT	Net
2018			£	£	£
March 5 P. Surtees	3/301	PL169	60	10	50
17 L. Gower	3/302	PL94	192	32	160
29 J. Cropper	3/303	PL183	144	24	120
Transferred to General Ledger			396	66	330
				GL68	GL111

These transactions must be entered in the individual accounts in the purchases ledger. J. Cuttle & Co owes the total amounts including VAT to its suppliers so it is the gross amounts that are entered in the personal accounts, as shown below:

Purchases Ledger
P. Surtees (page 169)

	2018	Folio	£
	March 5 Purchases	PB943	60

L. Gower (page 94)

	2018	Folio	£
	March 17 Purchases	PB943	192

J. Cropper (page 183)

	2018	Folio	£
	March 29 Purchases	PB943	144

The personal accounts have been credited with a total of £396, being the sum of the three amounts that J. Cuttle & Co will have to pay its suppliers.

But the actual cost of the goods purchased in this example is only £330. Being an increase in the business's possessions, £330 will be debited to the purchases account. The VAT of £66 is an asset because it can be reclaimed from HMRC, so this implies a debit to the *Input VAT* account:

General Ledger
Purchases *(page 111)*

2018		Folio	£	
March 31	Purchases	PB943	330	

Input VAT *(page 68)*

2018		Folio	£	
March 31	Purchases	PB943	66	

Again we'll assume that all J. Cuttle & Co's purchases in March were made on credit. However, if it also made cash purchases then these would be recorded in the business's cash book. The net value of the purchases and the input VAT on those purchases would still need to be recorded in the general ledger in the same manner as the two entries shown above.

VAT in the financial statements

To conclude our example for J. Cuttle & Co, an Income Statement for this business for the month ended 31 March 2018 would show a sales figure of £570 and a purchases figure of £330. In other words, the income and expenses in the Income Statement of a VAT-registered business do NOT include VAT.

In the Balance Sheet of J. Cuttle & Co as at 31 March 2018 the total figure for accounts receivable will be the total amounts due from customers, which will include VAT. Likewise, the figure for accounts payable will be the total amounts due to suppliers, which will include VAT.

Additionally, in J. Cuttle & Co's Balance Sheet as at 31 March 2018 the amount of VAT owed to HMRC will be shown as a current liability. In this very simple example (assuming there were no opening balances on the Input VAT and Output VAT accounts brought down at 1 March 2018) the current liability will be £48:

	£
Output VAT account *(a credit balance)*	114
Input VAT account *(a debit balance)*	66
VAT owed to HMRC *(a current liability)*	48

13.8 Accounting entries for businesses that are not VAT-registered

Businesses that are not VAT-registered will not add VAT to their sales prices so there will be no entries in their books whatsoever in relation to Output VAT.

Neither can such businesses reclaim input VAT on the goods and services they buy. Any VAT on goods and services bought will simply be included as part of the cost of whatever has been bought.

For example, if a business that is not VAT-registered buys goods in March 2018 for £200 plus £40 VAT then this will lead to £240 being debited to the purchases account in the general ledger, and the Income Statement for March 2018 will show purchases of £240.

13.9 VAT on expenses and on the purchase of non-current assets

Input VAT is not just paid on purchases of raw materials and goods for resale. It is also payable on many expenses and on the purchase of most non-current assets.

VAT-registered businesses can reclaim the VAT paid on expenses and the purchase of non-current assets. They will therefore not include the VAT as part of the amount recorded in the ledger account for that expense or non-current asset.

Businesses that are not VAT-registered cannot reclaim any VAT paid on such items. They will therefore record the total amount *including VAT* as the figure in the ledger account for every expense or non-current asset.

In other words, two different businesses buying exactly the same items would make the following entries in their ledger accounts:

	Business X: vat-registered	*Business Y: not registered for VAT*
Buy machinery, paying £200 + VAT £40	Debit Machinery £200 Debit Input VAT £40 Credit Bank £240	Debit Machinery £240 Credit Bank £240
Buy advertising, paying £150 + VAT £30	Debit Advertising expense £150 Debit Input VAT £30 Credit Bank £180	Debit Advertising expense £180 Credit Bank £180

Business X has an advantage in that it will be able to reclaim, in due course, the total of £70 input VAT from HMRC whereas Business Y cannot. But remember that Business X will also have to add VAT at 20 per cent to its sales prices, which might hand a significant competitive advantage to Business Y.

> **Activity 13.3**
>
> In Section 13.3 of this chapter you learnt that small businesses (with annual sales below a certain limit) do not have to register for VAT. Now that you know how VAT works, can you suggest why a small business might wish to register for VAT voluntarily?

13.10 Calculating the VAT included in a gross amount

Sometimes you will only know the gross amount of a transaction that includes VAT and you may be required to calculate the VAT amount.

Suppose the gross amount of a sale is £420 including VAT. VAT is calculated as 20% of the net amount, meaning that the gross amount is 120% of the net amount.

Since £420 represents 120% of the net amount, the net amount can be calculated by multiplying the gross amount by 100%/120% (which is the same, mathematically, as multiplying by 5/6, or dividing by 1.2, whichever you prefer!).

> £420 × 100%/120% = £350, so £350 is the net amount of the sale.

Subtracting £350 from £420 gives us £70, which is the VAT amount. This makes sense, because a net amount of £350 × 20% = £70, which is the VAT amount.

Accountants tend to use the 'VAT fraction' of 1/6 as a shortcut to arrive at the VAT included in a gross amount. In the example above, £420 × 1/6 = £70 which is the VAT amount. The VAT fraction of 1/6 comes from a simplification of 20%/120%, so 1/6 will always work when the VAT rate is 20%.

If the rate of VAT changes then the VAT fraction will change. A 'formula' for the VAT fraction for any rate of VAT will be:

$$\frac{\% \text{ rate of VAT}}{100 + \% \text{ rate of VAT}}$$

So if the standard rate of VAT increased to 25% then the new VAT fraction would be 25%/125%. This would simplify to 1/5: in order to calculate the VAT element of a gross amount that included VAT at 25%, accountants would simply multiply the gross amount by 1/5.

13.11 VAT on bad debts

Most business-to-business sales are on credit and there is always the risk that a few customers will never pay what they owe. These are known as 'bad debts' and are covered in detail in Chapter 20. But bad debts present a particular problem from a VAT perspective, as illustrated by the following example:

Suppose Mrs Scoggins (a VAT-registered trader) makes a sale on credit to Mr Carker on 15 March for £400 + VAT £80 = £480. The sum of £80 will be recorded in the Output VAT account of Scoggins, and this will form part of the payment that she must make to HMRC at the end of her VAT quarter.

However, suppose Carker's business collapses and Scoggins never receives the £480. The situation is now quite unfair to Scoggins because she must hand over £80 VAT to HMRC but she never actually collected this money from the customer. In principle Scoggins should act merely as a tax collector for HMRC, but in this case she has had to pay £80 out of her business's own money!

Because of this problem, the VAT rules allow Scoggins to subsequently get her £80 back from HMRC if she can demonstrate that the debt due from Carker will almost certainly never be received (i.e. that it is a 'bad debt').

 Activity 13.4 Smaller businesses are actually allowed to account for VAT using an alternative method that means this problem would never arise. Do you have any ideas about what that alternative method might be?

13.12 Input VAT that cannot be reclaimed by any business

There are a few instances where input VAT cannot be reclaimed, regardless of whether the business is VAT-registered. The two most common examples are:

● Normally the VAT on cars purchased and used in the business is not reclaimable.
● The input VAT on business entertainment costs is not reclaimable (apart from VAT on the costs of entertaining staff).

13.13 The VAT return

At the end of each period (normally every three months), VAT-registered businesses must complete a 'VAT return' and submit it online to HMRC.

A VAT return essentially shows:

(a) the total output VAT charged on the business's sales for the period; minus
(b) the total input VAT incurred on goods and services bought by the business during the period.

If (a) is greater than (b) then the balance must be paid to HMRC. Businesses must submit the return and electronically pay any tax due within about a month of the end of the quarter.

Occasionally, for some businesses (b) may be greater than (a) so HMRC will refund the difference to the business.

Activity 13.5 Why do you think that it is rare for a business's Input VAT (i.e. VAT on goods and services bought) for the period to be greater than its Output VAT (i.e. VAT on goods and services sold)? Can you think of any circumstances where it might happen?

The figures entered on a business's VAT return must be checked very carefully because the potential penalties for any errors can be very severe.

Smaller businesses are allowed to submit their VAT returns annually rather than quarterly. This reduces the administrative burden on small businesses.

13.14 HM Revenue and Customs (HMRC) VAT Guides and Notices

The detailed rules surrounding VAT are exceptionally complex and are beyond the scope of this book. However, all the rules (as well as introductory guidance) are available online and (at the time of writing) can be found from www.gov.uk/topic/business-tax/vat. If you search 'HMRC VAT' online this site should be one of the top results.

Learning outcomes

You should now have learnt:

1 VAT is a tax charged on the supply of the majority of goods and services in the UK and the standard rate of VAT is 20 per cent.

2 Most businesses must 'register' for VAT, which means they must charge VAT on their sales and (in due course) pay this 'Output VAT' to HMRC.

3 VAT-registered businesses are also allowed to reclaim from HMRC the VAT they pay on the goods and services they buy.

4 Amounts excluding VAT are known as 'net' and those including VAT are referred to as 'gross'.

5 The VAT on every credit sale must be separately recorded in a separate column in the sales day book. The total amount due from each customer will be debited to the personal accounts; the net amount of the sales made will be credited to the sales account; and the VAT on these sales is credited to the Output VAT account.

6 A VAT-registered business must record the VAT on credit purchases in a separate column in the purchases day book. The total amount owed to each supplier will be credited to the personal accounts; the net amount of the purchases will be debited to the purchases account; and the VAT on the purchases made is debited to the Input VAT account.

7 At the end of each period (normally every three months) VAT-registered businesses must submit a VAT return to HMRC which states (a) the total Output VAT charged on sales for the period; and (b) the total Input VAT incurred on goods and services bought during the period. Usually (a) will exceed (b) and this excess must be paid to HMRC.

8 To calculate the VAT included in a gross amount you can simply multiply the gross amount by 1/6 (1/6 being the 'VAT fraction' when the rate of VAT is 20%).

Answers to activities

13.1 There are various reasons. Above all, it will ease the administrative burden on small firms. Many small businesses are 'sole traders' who have to perform virtually all business tasks on their own, and VAT record-keeping means a lot of extra work. Second, it will potentially give small businesses a competitive advantage because their prices will be 20 per cent lower than those of larger rivals who must add VAT. This is good for encouraging small businesses and is also beneficial for consumers. Finally, it makes life simpler for HMRC. HMRC's resources are not unlimited, so exempting small businesses means that HMRC can focus its efforts on checking that larger businesses are accounting for VAT correctly.

13.2 The simple answer is that the final consumers pay £2,200 × 20% = £440 in VAT for their furniture and this will be the total that is collected by HMRC. However, the actual chain of events can be quite confusing:

● X receives £1,200 (i.e. £1,000 + 20% VAT) from Y and X must hand over the **£200** VAT on this transaction to HMRC.
● Y receives £1,800 (i.e. £1,500 + 20% VAT) from Z and Y owes the £300 VAT on this transaction to HMRC. But Y can also reclaim the £200 VAT it paid on its purchase from X, so only actually hands over the difference (**£100**) to HMRC.
● Z receives £2,640 (i.e. £2,200 + 20% VAT) from its customers. Z therefore collects £440 in VAT on these sales which it owes to HMRC, but it can also reclaim the £300 VAT it paid to Y, so only hands over the difference (**£140**) to HMRC.

So the customers have paid a total of £440 in VAT and cannot reclaim it. But this VAT has actually been collected by HMRC by way of **£200** from X, **£100** from Y and **£140** from Z as described above!

13.3 The advantage of registration would be that all the input VAT paid on the goods and services that the business buys can be reclaimed from HMRC. In the early stages of a new business, this could be advantageous if it is investing a lot in inventory and non-current assets. Another possible advantage is that registering for VAT may help the business appear big and reputable. The final (and perhaps most important) factor is whether most of the small business's customers are themselves VAT-registered. If they are, they will be able to reclaim all the VAT that the small business charges on its sales. Such customers won't be affected by whether the small business adds 20 per cent VAT to its prices. In these circumstances voluntary registration would probably be a good idea.

13.4 Smaller businesses are allowed to account for VAT on a 'cash basis' rather than the standard method described in this chapter. The 'cash basis' means that the small business only has to pay the output VAT on its sales to HMRC after the money has been received from the customer. If a few credit customers don't pay their bills (i.e. there are 'bad debts') then the VAT on these sales will never have to be paid to HMRC. It is usually a good idea for eligible small businesses to adopt the 'cash basis' for VAT because this method will generally be better for the business's cash flow.

13.5 Businesses normally aim to make a profit, so the sales revenue of the business will normally exceed the cost of goods and services purchased in the period. The output VAT at 20 percent on sales will therefore be greater than the input VAT at 20 per cent on goods and services purchased. However, input VAT might exceed output VAT for a new business in its first few months of trading: a new business might buy large quantities of inventory, equipment and advertising but sales may be very low initially.

Another example might be a highly seasonal business. Some businesses may make the bulk of their annual sales in one particular quarter of the year. In preparation, such businesses may purchase large quantities of inventory in the preceding quarter. For such a business, input VAT could therefore exceed output VAT during that preceding quarter.

A third example would be a trader that only sold zero-rated goods (such as young children's clothes). The output VAT on sales would be zero but the business could still reclaim input VAT on many of its expenses.

Review questions

13.1   On 1 March 2020, A. Cook, 7 Down Road, Middlefield, sold the following goods on credit to B. Pitt, Ballano Golf Club, Ringlee, Yorkshire:

> Order No. B/162
> 5 sets golf clubs at £1,250 per set.
> 500 golf balls at £25 per 10 balls.
> 5 golf bags at £370 per bag.

Trade discount is given at the rate of 30%.
All goods are subject to VAT at 20%.

(a)   Prepare the sales invoice. The invoice number will be 4231.
(b)   Show the entries in the personal ledgers of A. Cook and B. Pitt.

13.2A   On 1 March 2020, B. Cox, Middle Road, Paisley, a VAT-registered business, sold the following goods on credit to T. Ross, 24 Peter Street, Loughborough, Order No. 9841:

20,000 Coils Sealing Tape	@ £6.70 per 1,000 coils
40,000 Sheets Bank A5	@ £5.20 per 1,000 sheets
24,000 Sheets Bank A4	@ £9.00 per 1,000 sheets

All goods are subject to VAT at 20%.

(a)   Prepare the sales invoice (the invoice number will be 4632).
(b)   Show the entries in the personal ledgers of B. Cox and T. Ross.

13.3   The following sales have been made by C. Rice during the month of March 2019. All the figures are shown net after deducting trade discount, but before adding VAT at the rate of 20%.

		£
March 2	to G. Bush	430
6	to A. Gray	290
14	to L. Rowe	560
31	to S. Pegg	320

You are required to enter up the Sales Day Book, Sales Ledger and General Ledger in respect of the above items for the month.

13.4   The following sales and purchases were made by C. West during the month of May 2019.

		Net	VAT added
		£	£
2019			
May 1	Sold goods on credit to J. Royce	290	58
4	Sold goods on credit to D. Player and Co	440	88
10	Bought goods on credit from:		
	B. Hunter	360	72
	R. Dixon Ltd	230	46

		Net	VAT added
14	Bought goods on credit from G. Melly	80	16
16	Sold goods on credit to D. Player and Co	170	34
23	Bought goods on credit from G. Gooch	120	24
31	Sold goods on credit to N. Foster	110	22

Enter up the Sales and Purchases Day Books, Sales and Purchases Ledgers and the General Ledger for the month of May 2019.

13.5 You are informed that T. Dawson is a VAT-registered retailer. Her total sales for the week just ended amounted to £11,860 excluding VAT. All the business's sales are subject to VAT at 20 per cent. Dawson deposited the entire week's takings in the business bank account. What will be the entries in the business's general ledger that record this information?

13.6 Ghadiali & Co is a VAT-registered business. In the three months ended 31 July the business sold goods with a net value of £117,900, all of which were subject to VAT at standard rate (20%). In the same quarter, the business bought goods and services (all of which were subject to VAT at standard rate) totalling £88,140 including VAT.
After preparing its VAT return for the quarter ending 31 July, how much VAT must Ghadiali & Co pay to HMRC?

13.7A Robles & Co is a VAT-registered business. During the quarter just ended, it bought goods and services to the value of £46,020 excluding VAT, and its sales were £61,548 including VAT. All of Robles & Co's sales are subject to VAT at 20 per cent. However, only two-thirds of the goods and services it buys are subject to VAT at 20 per cent. The other third are either zero-rated or exempt.
After preparing its VAT return for the quarter just ended, how much must Robles & Co pay to HMRC?

13.8 Up until December 2020, K. Heitinga sold T-shirts for £15 including VAT at 20 per cent.
Suppose that the government announces a reduction in the rate of VAT to 17.5 per cent, effective from 1 January 2021 onwards.
If K. Heitinga reduces her selling price to exactly reflect the change in VAT rate, what will the selling price of her T-shirts be in 2021?

13.9A G. Brown's sales including VAT were £130,000 in November 2020, then £150,000 in December 2020, and £110,000 during January 2021.
Suppose that the rate of VAT was 20 per cent until 31 December 2020 and 22.5 per cent from 1 January 2021. Exactly three-fifths of Brown's net sales are subject to VAT, the rest being zero-rated.
What is the correct total credit to Output VAT in Brown's general ledger for the quarter to 31 January 2021?

13.10 Louise Baldwin commenced business as a wholesaler on 1 March 2019.

Her sales on credit during March 2019 were:

March 9	Neville's Electrical
	4 computer monitors list price £180 each, less 20% trade discount
March 17	Maltby plc
	20 computer printers list price £200 each, less 25% trade discount
March 29	Neville's Electrical
	Assorted software list price £460, less 20% trade discount

All transactions are subject to Value Added Tax at 10%.

(a) Rule up a Sales Day Book and head the main columns as follows.

Date	Name and Details	List price less trade discount	VAT	Total	
		£–p		£–p	£–p

Enter the above information in the Sales Day Book, totalling and ruling off at the end of March 2019.

(b) Make the necessary postings from the Sales Day Book to the personal and nominal accounts in the ledger.

(c) Prepare a trial balance as at 31 March 2019.

(Edexcel Foundation, London Examinations: GCSE)

13.11A Mudgee Ltd issued the following invoices to customers in respect of credit sales made during the last week of May 2020. The amounts stated are all net of Value Added Tax. All sales made by Mudgee Ltd are subject to VAT at 15%.

Invoice No.	Date	Customer	Amount
			£
3045	25 May	Laira Brand	1,060.00
3046	27 May	Brown Bros	2,200.00
3047	28 May	Penfold's	170.00
3048	29 May	T. Tyrrell	460.00
3049	30 May	Laira Brand	1,450.00
			£5,340.00

On 29 May Laira Brand returned half the goods (in value) purchased on 25 May. An allowance was made the same day to this customer for the appropriate amount.

On 1 May 2020 Laira Brand owed Mudgee Ltd £2,100.47. Other than the purchases detailed above Laira Brand made credit purchases (including VAT) of £680.23 from Mudgee Ltd on 15 May. On 21 May, Mudgee Ltd received a cheque for £2,500 from Laira Brand.

Required:

(a) Show how the above transactions would be recorded in Mudgee Ltd's Sales Day Book for the week ended 30 May 2020.

(b) Describe how the information in the Sales Day Book would be incorporated into Mudgee Ltd's double entry system.

(c) Reconstruct the personal account of Laira Brand as it would appear in Mudgee Ltd's ledger for May 2020.

(Association of Accounting Technicians)

part 3

FINANCIAL STATEMENTS

Introduction

This part is concerned with preparing financial statements from double entry records.

Income statements

Learning objectives

After you have studied this chapter, you should be able to:

- explain why income statements are not part of the double entry system
- explain why profit is calculated
- calculate cost of goods sold, gross profit, and net profit
- explain the difference between gross profit and net profit
- explain the relationship between the trading account and the profit and loss account
- explain how the trading account and the profit and loss account fit together to create the income statement
- explain how to deal with closing inventory when preparing the trading account section of an income statement
- close down the appropriate accounts and transfer the balances to the trading account
- close down the appropriate accounts and transfer the balances to the profit and loss account
- prepare an income statement from information given in a trial balance
- make appropriate double entries to incorporate net profit and drawings in the capital account

Introduction

In this chapter, you will learn how to close down revenue and expenditure accounts in order to calculate profit and prepare an income statement. You will learn how to adjust purchases with inventory and arrive at the cost of goods sold, and will discover the difference between gross profit and net profit. You will learn how to prepare an income statement, and, finally, you will learn how to transfer net profit and drawings to the capital account at the end of a period.

14.1 Purpose of income statements

The main reason why people set up businesses is to make profits. Of course, if the business is not successful, it may well incur losses instead. The calculation of such profits and losses is probably the most important objective of the accounting function. The owners will want to know how the actual profits compare with the profits they had hoped to make. Knowing what profits are being made helps businesses to do many things, including:

● planning ahead
● obtaining loans from banks, from other businesses, or from private individuals
● telling prospective business partners how successful the business is
● telling someone who may be interested in buying the business how successful the business is
● calculating the tax due on the profits so that the correct amount of tax can be paid to the tax authorities.

Chapter 4 dealt with the grouping of revenue and expenses prior to bringing them together to compute profit. In the case of a trader (someone who is mainly concerned with buying and selling goods), the profits are calculated by drawing up an **income statement**.

When it is shown in detail rather than in summary form (as is the case for the published income statements of companies), it contains something called the **trading account**. The trading account is prepared in order to arrive at a figure for **gross profit**.

Below the trading account is shown a summary of another account – the **profit and loss account**. The profit and loss account is prepared so as to arrive at the figure for **net profit**.

It is these two accounts that together comprise the income statement. Both the trading account and the profit and loss account *are* part of the double entry system. At the end of a financial period, they are closed off. They are then summarised and the information they contain is then copied into an income statement. **Income statements are not part of the double entry system.**

14.2 Gross profit

One of the most important uses of income statements is that of comparing the results obtained with the results expected. In a trading organisation, a lot of attention is paid to how much profit is made, before deducting expenses, for every £1 of sales revenue. As mentioned in Section 14.1, so that this can easily be seen in the profit calculation, the statement in which profit is calculated is split into two sections – one in which the gross profit is found (**this is the trading account section of the statement**), and the next section in which the **net profit** is calculated (**this is the 'profit and loss account' section of the statement**).

Gross profit is the excess of sales revenue over the **cost of goods sold**. Where the cost of goods sold is greater than the sales revenue, the result is a **gross loss**. By taking the figure of sales revenue less the cost of goods sold to generate that sales revenue, it can be seen that the accounting custom is to calculate a trader's profits **only on goods that have been sold**.

> **Activity 14.1** What does this tell you about the costs and revenues that are included in the calculation of gross profit? (*Hint*: what do you not include in the calculation?)

To summarise:

Gross profit (calculated in the **trading account**)	is the excess of sales revenue over the cost of goods sold in the period.

Activity 14.2

Calculate the gross profit or gross loss of each of the following businesses:

	Cost of goods purchased £	Sales £	Gross profit/(Gross loss) £
A	9,820	10,676	_____
B	7,530	14,307	_____
C	10,500	19,370	_____
D	9,580	9,350	_____
E	8,760	17,200	_____

14.3 Net profit

Net profit, found in the profit and loss account section of the income statement, consists of the gross profit plus any revenue other than that from sales, such as rents received or commissions earned, less the total costs used up during the period other than those already included in the 'cost of goods sold'. Where the costs used up exceed the gross profit plus other revenue, the result is said to be a **net loss**. Thus:

Net profit (calculated in the **profit and loss account**)	is what is left of the gross profit after all other expenses have been deducted.

Activity 14.3

Using the answer to Activity 14.2, complete the following:

	Other revenues £	Expenses £	Net profit/(Net loss) £
A	–	2,622	
B	4,280	2,800	
C	500	2,500	
D	–	1,780	
E	3,260	2,440	

14.4 Information needed

Before drawing up an income statement you should prepare the trial balance. This contains nearly all the information needed. (Later on in this book you will see that certain adjustments have to be made, but we will ignore these at this stage.)

We can now look at the trial balance of B. Swift, drawn up as on 31 December 2019 after the completion of his first year in business.

Exhibit 14.1

B. Swift Trial balance as at 31 December 2019	Dr	Cr
	£	£
Sales		38,500
Purchases	29,000	
Rent	2,400	
Lighting expenses	1,500	
General expenses	600	
Fixtures and fittings	5,000	
Accounts receivable	6,800	
Accounts payable		9,100
Bank	15,100	
Cash	200	
Drawings	7,000	
Capital		20,000
	67,600	67,600

Note: To make this easier to follow, we shall assume that purchases consist of goods that are resold without needing any further work. You'll learn later that these are known as 'finished goods' but, for now, we'll simply refer to them as 'goods'.

We have already seen that gross profit is calculated as follows:

> **Sales − Cost of goods sold = Gross profit**

It would be easier if all purchases in a period were always sold by the end of the same period. In that case, cost of goods sold would always equal purchases. However, this is not normally the case and so we have to calculate the cost of goods sold as follows:

What we bought in the period:	Purchases
Less Goods bought but not sold in the period:	(Closing inventory)
	= Cost of goods sold

In Swift's case, there are goods unsold at the end of the period. However, there is no record in the accounting books of the value of this unsold inventory. The only way that Swift can find this figure is by checking his inventory at the close of business on 31 December 2019. To do this he would have to make a list of all the unsold goods and then find out their value. The value he would normally place on them would be the cost price of the goods, i.e. what he paid for them. Let's assume that this is £3,000.

The cost of goods sold figure will be:

	£
Purchases	29,000
Less Closing inventory	(3,000)
Cost of goods sold	26,000

Based on the sales revenue of £38,500 the gross profit can be calculated:

$$\text{Sales} - \text{Cost of goods sold} = \text{Gross profit}$$
$$£38,500 - £26,000 = £12,500$$

We now have the information we need to complete the trading account section of the income statement. Next, we need to close off the sales and purchases accounts at the end of the period so that they start the next period with no balance. To do so, we need to create a trading account (this is *not* the same as the trading part of the income statement, though it does produce the same gross profit figure) and then make the following entries:

(A) The balance of the sales account is transferred to the trading account by:

    1 Debiting the sales account (thus closing it).
    2 Crediting the trading account.

(B) The balance of the purchases account is transferred to the trading account by:

    1 Debiting the trading account.
    2 Crediting the purchases account (thus closing it).

(C) There is, as yet, no entry for the closing inventory in the double entry accounts. This is achieved as follows:

    1 Debit a closing inventory account with the value of the closing inventory.
    2 Credit the trading account (thus completing the double entry).

The trading account will look like this:

Trading

2019				£	2019				£
Dec	31	Purchases	(B)	29,000	Dec	31	Sales	(A)	38,500
						31	Closing inventory	(C)	3,000

We now close off the trading account in the normal way. In this case, revenues exceed costs so we describe the balance as 'gross profit'.

Trading

2019				£	2019				£
Dec	31	Purchases	(B)	29,000	Dec	31	Sales	(A)	38,500
	31	Gross profit		12,500		31	Closing inventory	(C)	3,000
				41,500					41,500

Note that the balance shown on the trading account is described as 'gross profit' rather than being described as a balance. Also, note that the balance (i.e. the gross profit) is not brought down to the next period. The other accounts used in these double entries appear as shown below. (Note that there is no detail of the entries prior to the end of the period as all the information we have been given is the closing balances. These closing balances are simply described here as 'balance'.)

Sales

2019			£	2019			£
Dec	31	Trading	38,500	Dec	31	Balance	38,500

Purchases

2019			£	2019			£
Dec	31	Balance	29,000	Dec	31	Trading	29,000

Closing Inventory

2019			£	2019			£
Dec	31	Trading	3,000	Dec	31	Balance	3,000

The entry of the closing inventory on the credit side of the trading account is, in effect, a deduction from the purchases on the debit side. As you will see when we look later at the trading account part of the income statement, the closing inventory is shown as a deduction from the purchases and the figure then disclosed is described as 'cost of goods sold'.

It must be remembered that we are concerned here with the very first year of trading when, for obvious reasons, there is no opening inventory. In Chapter 16, we will examine how to account for inventory in the later years of a business.

We can now draw up a profit and loss account (which is an 'account' opened so that the end-of-period double entries can be completed). Double entries are then prepared, firstly transferring the gross profit from the trading account to the credit of the profit and loss account. To do this, you would change the entry in the trading account to read 'Gross profit transferred to profit and loss':

Trading

2019			£	2019			£
Dec	31	Purchases	29,000	Dec	31	Sales	38,500
	31	Gross profit transferred			31	Closing inventory	3,000
		to Profit and loss	12,500				
			41,500				41,500

Then, any revenue account balances, other than sales (which have already been dealt with in the trading account), are transferred to the credit of the profit and loss account. Typical examples are commissions received and rent received. In the case of B. Swift, there are no such revenue accounts.

The costs used up in the year, in other words, the expenses of the year, are then transferred to the debit of the profit and loss account. (It may also be thought, quite rightly, that, as the fixtures and fittings have been used during the year and have deteriorated as a result, something should be charged for this use. This charge is known as 'depreciation'. The methods for calculating this are left until Chapter 21.)

The profit and loss account will now appear as follows:

Profit and Loss

2019			£	2019			£
Dec	31	Rent	2,400	Dec	31	Gross profit transferred	12,500
						from Trading	
	31	Lighting expenses	1,500				
	31	General expenses	600				
	31	Net profit	8,000				
			12,500				12,500

The expense accounts closed off will now appear as:

Rent

2019			£	2019			£
Dec	31	Balance	2,400	Dec	31	Profit and loss	2,400

Lighting expenses

2019				£	2019				£
Dec	31	Balance		1,500	Dec	31	Profit and loss		1,500

General expenses

2019				£	2019				£
Dec	31	Balance		600	Dec	31	Profit and loss		600

You now have all the information you need in order to prepare the income statement for the year ending 31 December 2019. It looks like this:

Exhibit 14.2

B. Swift
Income Statement for the year ending 31 December 2019

	£	£
Sales		38,500
Less Cost of goods sold:		
Purchases	29,000	
Less Closing inventory	(3,000)	
		(26,000)
Gross profit		12,500
Less Expenses		
Rent	2,400	
Lighting expenses	1,500	
General expenses	600	
		(4,500)
Net profit		8,000

Note: 'Revenue' is often used instead of 'Sales' in this statement.

14.5 Effect on the capital account

Although the net profit has been calculated at £8,000 and is shown as a balancing figure on the debit side of the profit and loss account (on the previous page), no credit entry has yet been made to complete the double entry. In other accounts, the credit entry would normally be the 'balance b/d' at the start of the next period. However, as net profit increases the capital of the owner, the credit entry must be made in the capital account by transferring the net profit from income statement. (You would change the entry in the income statement from 'net profit' to read 'net profit transferred to capital'.)

The trading account and the profit and loss account, and, indeed, all the revenue and expense accounts, can thus be seen to be devices whereby the capital account is saved from being concerned with unnecessary detail. Every sale made at a profit increases the capital of the proprietor, as does each item of revenue, such as rent received. On the other hand, each sale made at a loss, or each item of expense, decreases the capital of the proprietor.

Instead of altering the capital after each transaction, the respective bits of profit and loss, and of revenue and expense, are collected together using suitably described accounts. Then all the balances are brought together in one financial statement, the 'income statement', and the increase in the capital, i.e. the net profit, is determined. Alternatively, in the case of a net loss, the decrease in the capital is ascertained.

The fact that a separate drawings account has been in use can now also be seen to have been in keeping with the policy of avoiding unnecessary detail in the capital account. There will, therefore, only be one figure for drawings entered in the debit side of the capital account – the total of the drawings for the whole of the period.

The capital account, showing these transfers, and the drawings account now closed are as follows:

Capital

2019			£	2019				£
Dec	31	Drawings	7,000	Jan	1	Cash		20,000
	31	Balance c/d	21,000	Dec	31	Net profit		8,000
			28,000					28,000
				2019				
				Jan	1	Balance b/d		21,000

Drawings

2019			£	2019			£
Dec	31	Balance	7,000	Dec	31	Capital	7,000

> **Activity 14.4**
>
> Bertram Quigley opened a pet shop on 1 January 2019. He invested £10,000 in the business. The following information was obtained from his accounting records at the end of the year: Purchases of goods for resale £7,381; Sales £13,311; Expenses £1,172; Drawings £800; Inventory £410. What is the balance on Bertram Quigley's capital account at 31 December 2019?

14.6 The balances still in our books

It should be noticed that not all the items in the trial balance have been used in the income statement. The remaining balances are assets or liabilities or capital, they are not expenses or revenue. These will be used later when a balance sheet is drawn up. (You'll remember learning in Chapter 1 that assets, liabilities and capital are shown in balance sheets.)

> Go back to Chapter 1 to refresh your understanding of assets, liabilities and capital.

Exhibit 14.3 shows the trial balance after the entries to the trading account and the profit and loss account have been made and the income statement prepared. All the accounts that were closed off in that process have been removed, and drawings and net profit have been transferred to the capital account. Notice also that the inventory account, which was not originally in the trial balance, is in the redrafted trial balance, as the item was not created as a balance in the books until the trading account was prepared. We will be using this trial balance when we start to look at balance sheets in the next chapter.

Exhibit 14.3

B. Swift		

B. Swift
Trial balance as at 31 December 2019

(after the trading account and the profit and loss account have been completed and the income statement prepared and the capital account adjusted for net profit and drawings)

	Dr	Cr
	£	£
Fixtures and fittings	5,000	
Accounts receivable	6,800	
Accounts payable		9,100
Inventory	3,000	
Bank	15,100	
Cash	200	
Capital		21,000
	30,100	30,100

Note for students: Now that you have learnt how to prepare a T-account for the trading account and a T-account for the profit and loss account, we will only rarely ask you to prepare them again. You should remember how they are used to calculate gross profit and net profit and the typical entries they may contain. From now on, we will concentrate on producing the financial statement that combines these two accounts: the income statement.

Note also that under UK GAAP (i.e. UK accounting rules) the income statement was called the 'profit and loss account'. This confusing use of the same title for a financial statement and for an account in the ledger caused many problems. However, even though we now use the term 'income statement' for the financial statement you may sometimes see such a statement with the old title, or you may even be asked to prepare a financial statement using that title or 'profit or loss account'. If so, remember that it is the same as the one we call an 'income statement'.

Learning outcomes

You should now have learnt:

1 Why income statements are not part of the double entry system.

2 Why profit is calculated.

3 How to calculate cost of goods sold, gross profit and net profit.

4 The double entries required in order to close off the relevant expense and revenue accounts at the end of a period and post the entries to the trading account and to the profit and loss account.

5 How to deal with inventory at the end of a period.

6 How to prepare an income statement from a trial balance.

7 How to transfer the net profit and drawings to the capital account at the end of a period.

8 That balances on accounts not closed off in order to prepare the income statement are carried down to the following period, that these balances represent assets, liabilities and capital, and that they are entered in the balance sheet.

Answers to activities

14.1 You only include the costs that were incurred in creating those goods that were sold. These costs include the cost of buying those goods and any costs incurred in converting goods purchased into the goods that were sold – for example, the costs of converting raw materials into finished goods. The only costs you include are those that relate to the goods sold. The costs relating to goods that have not yet been sold are not included. You do not include other costs of the business, such as postage, motor expenses, office expenses, salaries of managers, and advertising costs. Nor do you include any costs relating to the purchase or use of any assets, such as motor vehicles, computers, machinery, fixtures and fittings, and buildings.

14.2

	Cost of goods purchased	Sales	Gross profit/(Gross loss)
	£	£	£
A	9,820	10,676	856
B	7,530	14,307	6,777
C	10,500	19,370	8,870
D	9,580	9,350	(230)
E	8,760	17,200	8,440

14.3

	Other revenues	Expenses	Net profit/(Net loss)
	£	£	£
A	–	2,622	(1,766)
B	4,280	2,800	8,257
C	500	2,500	6,870
D	–	1,780	(2,010)
E	3,260	2,440	9,260

14.4 £14,368. That is, £10,000 + £13,311 − (£7,381 − £410) − £1,172 − £800.

Review questions

14.1 From the following trial balance of I. Lamb, extracted after one year's trading, prepare an income statement for the year ending 31 October 2019. A balance sheet is not required.

Trial balance as at 31 October 2019

	Dr	Cr
	£	£
Sales		100,250
Purchases	60,400	
Salaries	29,300	
Motor expenses	1,200	
Rent	950	
Insurance	150	
General expenses	85	
Premises	47,800	
Motor vehicles	8,600	
Accounts receivable	13,400	
Accounts payable		8,800
Cash at bank	8,200	
Cash in hand	300	
Drawings	4,200	
Capital		65,535
	174,585	174,585

Inventory at 31 October 2019 was £15,600.

(Keep your answer; it will be used later in Review Question 15.1.)

14.2 From the following trial balance of G. Foot after his first year's trading, you are required to draw up an income statement for the year ending 30 June 2019. A balance sheet is not required.

Trial balance as at 30 June 2019

	Dr	Cr
	£	£
Sales		266,000
Purchases	154,000	
Rent	3,800	
Lighting and heating expenses	700	
Salaries and wages	52,000	
Insurance	3,000	
Buildings	84,800	
Fixtures	2,000	
Accounts receivable	31,200	
Sundry expenses	300	
Accounts payable		16,000
Cash at bank	15,000	
Drawings	28,600	
Vans	16,000	
Motor running expenses	4,600	
Capital		114,000
	396,000	396,000

Inventory at 30 June 2019 was £18,000.

(Keep your answer; it will be used later in Review Question 15.2.)

14.3A From the following trial balance of F. Dover drawn-up on conclusion of his first year in business, draw up an income statement for the year ending 31 May 2020. A balance sheet is not required.

Trial balance as at 31 May 2020

	Dr	Cr
	£	£
General expenses	610	
Business rates	4,800	
Motor expenses	1,820	
Salaries	79,120	
Insurance	2,480	
Purchases	242,080	
Sales		471,624
Car	8,600	
Accounts payable		22,400
Accounts receivable	42,160	
Premises	106,000	
Cash at bank	5,430	
Cash in hand	650	
Capital		46,526
Drawings	46,800	
	540,550	540,550

Inventory at 31 May 2020 was £28,972.

(Keep your answer; it will be used later in Review Question 15.3A.)

→

14.4A Extract an income statement for the year ending 30 June 2019 for G. Graham. The trial balance as at 30 June 2019 after his first year of trading was as follows:

	Dr	Cr
	£	£
Equipment rental	940	
Insurance	1,804	
Lighting and heating expenses	1,990	
Motor expenses	2,350	
Salaries and wages	48,580	
Sales		382,420
Purchases	245,950	
Sundry expenses	624	
Lorry	19,400	
Accounts payable		23,408
Accounts receivable	44,516	
Fixtures	4,600	
Shop	174,000	
Cash at bank	11,346	
Drawings	44,000	
Capital		194,272
	600,100	600,100

Inventory at 30 June 2019 was £29,304.

(Keep your answer; it will be used later in Review Question 15.4A.)

14.5 Royston starts his own business on 1 September, operating as a wholesaler of novelty goods. His transactions during September were as follows:

Sep 1	Transfers £750 of his savings into a business bank account.
3	Borrows £3,000 from LloydWest Bank, repayable in three years' time.
5	Pays £320 to hire a van for September, using debit card.
7	Buys essential IT equipment for the business, paying £2,200 by debit card.
9	Buys goods for resale, paying by cheque £760.
11	Buys goods for resale £570 on time from J. Collins.
13	Sells goods for £930; customer pays by cheque.
15	Returns unsatisfactory goods to J. Collins, original cost of which was £120.
17	Buys goods for resale on time from M. Pembridge, £890.
19	Sells goods on time £1,770 to E. Barrett.
21	Pays £450 cheque to J. Collins.
23	Receives £590 cheque from E. Barrett on account.
25	Takes £280 from business bank account to pay for personal living expenses.
27	Pays staff wages for September, £410 by cheque.

Required:
(a) Record all the transactions and balance-off the accounts.
(b) Prepare a Trial Balance as at the end of the month.
(c) Assuming that the closing inventory has been counted and valued at cost totalling £570, prepare an Income Statement for the month.
(Keep your answer; it will be used later in Review Question 15.7.)

Balance sheets

Learning objectives

After you have studied this chapter, you should be able to:

- explain why balance sheets are not part of the double entry system
- explain why it is important that account balances are shown under appropriate headings in the balance sheet
- explain the meanings of the terms non-current asset, current asset, current liability, and non-current liability
- describe the sequence in which each of the five main categories of items appear in the balance sheet
- describe the sequence in which each non-current asset is entered in the balance sheet
- describe the sequence in which each current asset is entered in the balance sheet
- draw up a balance sheet from information given in a trial balance

Introduction

In this chapter, you'll learn how to present asset, liability and capital balances in a balance sheet and of the importance of adopting a consistent and meaningful layout.

15.1 Contents of the balance sheet

In Chapter 1, you learnt that balance sheets contain details of assets, liabilities and capital. The items and amounts to be entered in the balance sheet are found in the accounting books. As shown in the previous chapter, they comprise those **accounts with balances** that were *not* included in the income statement. All these accounts that continue to have balances must be assets, capital or liabilities.

Because it is these balances that are entered, it is called the 'balance sheet'. You should be aware of the other name it may be called: a 'statement of financial position'. You may meet this term in an examination question or in a textbook.

Activity 15.1

Why have the accounts entered into the income statement been removed from the trial balance? (*Hint:* it is *not* because they were entered in that statement.)

15.2 Drawing up a balance sheet

Let's look again at the post-income statement trial balance of B. Swift (from Exhibit 14.3):

Exhibit 15.1

B. Swift
Trial balance as at 31 December 2019
(after the trading account and the profit and loss account have been completed and the income statement prepared and the capital account adjusted for net profit and drawings)

	Dr	Cr
	£	£
Fixtures and fittings	5,000	
Accounts receivable	6,800	
Accounts payable		9,100
Inventory	3,000	
Bank	15,100	
Cash	200	
Capital		21,000
	30,100	30,100

You'll probably remember seeing examples of balance sheets in Chapter 1. If not, this would be a good time to spend a few minutes reading that chapter again.

Based on what you learnt in Chapter 1, let's now draw up the balance sheet for B. Swift as at 31 December 2019.

Exhibit 15.2

B. Swift
Balance Sheet as at 31 December 2019

	£
Assets	
Fixtures and fittings	5,000
Inventory	3,000
Accounts receivable	6,800
Bank	15,100
Cash	200
Total assets	30,100
Liabilities	
Accounts payable	(9,100)
Net assets	21,000
Capital	21,000

15.3 No double entry in balance sheets

After the way we used the double entry system in the previous chapter to prepare the information we needed in order to draw up the income statement, it should not surprise you to learn that balance sheets are also not part of the double entry system.

Activity 15.2   Why do you think it is that the balance sheet is not part of the double entry system?

When we draw up accounts such as a cash account, a rent account, a sales account, a trading account, or a profit and loss account, we are preparing them as part of the double entry system. We make entries on the debit side and on the credit side of these accounts.

As with income statements, when we draw up a balance sheet, we do not enter anything in the various accounts. We do not actually *transfer* the fixtures and fittings balance or the accounts payable balance, or any of the other balances, to the balance sheet.

All we do is to *list* the asset, capital and liabilities balances so as to form a balance sheet. This means that none of these accounts have been closed off. *Nothing is entered in the ledger accounts.*

When the next accounting period starts, these accounts are still open and they all contain balances. As a result of future transactions, entries are then made in these accounts that add to or deduct from these opening balances using double entry.

If you see the word 'account', you will know that what you are looking at is part of the double entry system and will include debit and credit entries. If the word 'account' is not used, it is not part of double entry. For instance, the following items are not 'accounts', and are therefore *not* part of the double entry:

Trial balance: this is a list of the debit and credit balances in the accounts.
Income statement: this is a list of revenues and expenditures arranged so as to produce figures for gross profit and net profit for a specific period of time.
Balance sheet: this is a list of balances arranged according to whether they are assets, capital or liabilities and so depict the financial situation on a specific date.

15.4 Layout of the balance sheet

Have you ever gone into a shop and found that the goods you were interested in were all mixed up and not laid out in a helpful or consistent way? You can see an example of this in most large shops specialising in selling CDs. They mix up some of their inventory, particularly anything on 'special offer', so that you need to search through everything in order to find what you want. In the process of doing so, the shop hopes that you will come across other things that you will buy that you would otherwise never have thought of. Some of Richard Branson's first Virgin music shops in the early 1970s used this technique and it seems to have developed from there as an effective way to sell music.

Unfortunately, this mix-up presentation technique would be of no benefit to the users of a balance sheet. They would never find anything they didn't set out to find, but they would still have to go through the hassle of sorting through all the information in order to produce a meaningful balance sheet for themselves. Because the balance sheet is intended to be helpful and informative, we take great care in ensuring that it portrays the information it contains in a consistent and meaningful way.

As a result, not only can a user who is only interested in looking at the balance sheet of one organisation find it easy to find information within it, other users who look at lots of different balance sheets, such as bank managers, accountants and investors, find it straightforward making comparisons between different balance sheets.

While the balance sheet layout used in Exhibit 15.2 could be considered useful, it can be improved. Let's look at how we can do this. Firstly, we'll look at how assets could be presented in a more helpful and more meaningful way.

Assets

We are going to show the assets under two headings, non-current assets and current assets.

Non-current assets

Non-current assets are assets that:

1 were not bought primarily to be sold; but
2 are to be used in the business; and
3 are expected to be of use to the business for a long time.

Examples: buildings, machinery, motor vehicles, fixtures and fittings.

Non-current assets are listed first in the balance sheet starting with those the business will keep the longest, down to those which will not be kept so long. For instance:

Non-current assets
1 Land and buildings
2 Fixtures and fittings
3 Machinery
4 Motor vehicles

Current assets

Current assets are assets that are likely to change in the short term and certainly within twelve months of the date of the balance sheet. They include items held for resale at a profit, accounts receivable, cash in the bank, and cash in hand.

These are listed in increasing order of liquidity – that is, starting with the asset furthest away from being turned into cash, and finishing with cash itself. For instance:

Current assets
1 Inventory
2 Accounts receivable
3 Cash at bank
4 Cash in hand

Some students feel that accounts receivable should appear before inventory because, at first sight, inventory would appear to be more easily realisable (i.e. convertible into cash) than accounts receivable. In fact, accounts receivable can normally be more quickly turned into cash – you can often **factor** them by selling the rights to the amounts owed by debtors to a finance company for an agreed amount.

As all retailers would confirm, it is not so easy to quickly turn inventory into cash. Another advantage of using this sequence is that it follows the order in which full realisation of the assets in a business takes place: before there is a sale, there must be an inventory of goods which, when sold on time, turns into accounts receivable and, when payment is made by the debtors, turns into cash.

Liabilities

There are two categories of liabilities, current liabilities and non-current liabilities.

Current liabilities: items that have to be paid within a year of the date of the balance sheet.

Examples: bank overdrafts, accounts payable resulting from the purchase on time of goods for resale.

Non-current liabilities: items that have to be paid more than a year after the date of the balance sheet.

Examples: bank loans, loans from other businesses.

15.5   A properly drawn up balance sheet

Exhibit 15.3 shows Exhibit 15.2 drawn up in a more appropriate way. You should also read the notes following the exhibit.

Exhibit 15.3

B. Swift
Balance Sheet as at 31 December 2019

	£	£
Non-current assets		
Fixtures and fittings		5,000
Current assets		
Inventory	3,000	
Accounts receivable	6,800	
Bank	15,100	
Cash	200	
	25,100	
Total assets		30,100
Current liabilities		
Accounts payable		(9,100)
Net assets		21,000
Capital		
Cash introduced		20,000
Add Net profit for the year		8,000
		28,000
Less Drawings		(7,000)
		21,000

Notes:

(a) There are four categories of entries shown in this balance sheet. In practice, the fifth, non-current liabilities, often appears. It is positioned after the current liabilities; and its total is added to the total of current liabilities to get the figure for total liabilities. Exhibit 15.4 shows where this would be if B. Swift had any non-current liabilities.

(b) The figure for each item within each category should be shown and a total for the category produced. An example of this is the £25,100 total of current assets. The figures for each asset are listed, and the total is shown below them.

(c) The total for non-current assets is added to the total for current assets and the total is labelled 'total assets'.

(d) The total for current liabilities is added to the total for non-current liabilities and the total is labelled 'total liabilities'.

(e) The total liabilities amount is subtracted from the total assets to get an amount labelled 'net assets'. This amount will be the same as the total capital (which, in company financial statements, is called 'total equity').

(f) You do not write the word 'account' after each item.

(g) The owners will be most interested in their capital and the reasons why it has changed during the period. To show only the final balance of £21,000 means that the owners will not know how it was calculated. So we show the full details of the capital account.

(h) Look at the date on the balance sheet. Now compare it with the dates put on the top of the income statement in the previous chapter. The balance sheet is a position statement – it is shown as being at one point in time, e.g. 'as at 31 December 2019'. The income statement is different. It is for a period of time, in this case for a whole year, and so it uses the phrase 'for the year ending'.

Note: The difference between current assets and total liabilities is known as 'net current assets' or 'working capital' and is the amount of resources the business has in a form that is readily convertible into cash. This figure is not shown in the balance sheet but is easy to produce from a completed balance sheet.

Exhibit 15.4

B. Swift
Balance Sheet as at 31 December 2019
(showing the position of non-current liabilities)

	£	£
Non-current assets		
Fixtures and fittings		5,000
Current assets		
Inventory	3,000	
Account receivable	6,800	
Bank	15,100	
Cash	200	
		25,100
Total assets		30,100
Current liabilities		
Accounts payable	9,100	
Non-current liabilities	–	
Total liabilities		(9,100)
Net assets		21,000
Capital		
Cash introduced		20,000
Add Net profit for the year		8,000
		28,000
Less Drawings		(7,000)
Total capital		21,000

Learning outcomes

You should now have learnt:

1 That all balances remaining on a trial balance after the income statement for a period has been drawn up are displayed in a balance sheet dated 'as at' the last day of the period.

2 That the balance sheet is *not* part of double entry.

3 That the balance sheet starts with non-current assets at the top, then current assets, then current liabilities, then non-current liabilities, then capital.

4 The meanings of the terms non-current asset, current asset, current liability, and non-current liability.

5 That you list non-current assets in descending order starting with those that will remain in use in the business for the longest time.

6 That you list current assets from top to bottom in increasing order of liquidity, with cash as the final item.

7 That current assets *less* current liabilities are known as 'net current assets' or 'working capital'.

8 Why the figure for net current assets is very important.

Answers to activities

15.1 All these accounts should have been closed-up when the trading account and the profit and loss account were completed and the income statement prepared. Only accounts with balances appear in a trial balance.

15.2 A balance sheet is a statement that summarises the financial position at the end of a period. It contains all the balances on the accounts held in the accounting books at that time. As it is prepared after the income statement, all the accounts have already been balanced-off. All we do with the balance sheet is copy the balances carried forward from the accounts and place them in an appropriate position in the statement.

Review questions

15.1 Return to Review Question 14.1 and prepare a balance sheet as at 31 October 2019.

15.2 Return to Review Question 14.2 and prepare a balance sheet as at 30 June 2019.

15.3A Return to Review Question 14.3A and prepare a balance sheet as at 31 May 2020.

15.4A Return to Review Question 14.4A and prepare a balance sheet as at 30 June 2019.

15.5 T. Smith started in business on 1 August 2019, with £60,000 capital in cash. During the first year he kept very few records of his transactions.
The assets and liabilities of the business at 30 July 2020 were:

	£
Freehold premises	160,000
Mortgage on the premises	120,000
Inventory	50,000
Accounts receivable	4,000
Cash and bank balances	8,300
Accounts payable	14,000

During the year, Smith withdrew £25,000 cash for his personal use but he also paid £8,000 received from the sale of his private car into the business bank account.

Required:
From the above information, prepare a balance sheet showing the financial position of the business at 30 June 2020 and indicating the net profit for the year.

15.6A The following information relates to A. Trader's business:

Assets and liabilities at	1 January 2019	31 December 2019
	£	£
Fixtures	18,000	16,200
Accounts receivable	4,800	5,800
Inventory	24,000	28,000
Accounts payable	8,000	11,000
Cash	760	240
Balance at bank	15,600	4,600
Loan from B. Burton	6,000	2,000
Motor vehicle	–	16,000

During the year, Trader had sold some of his personal investments for £4,000 which he paid into the business bank account, and he had drawn out £200 weekly for private use.

Required:
Prepare a balance sheet as at 31 December 2019 and give the net profit as at that date.

15.7 Return to your answer to Review Question 14.5 and prepare a balance sheet as at 30 September.

Income statements and balance sheets: further considerations

Learning objectives

After you have studied this chapter, you should be able to:

- explain the terms returns inwards, returns outwards, carriage inwards and carriage outwards
- record returns inwards and returns outwards in the income statement
- explain the difference between the treatment of carriage inwards and carriage outwards in the income statement
- explain why carriage inwards is treated as part of the cost of purchasing goods
- explain why carriage outwards is *not* treated as part of the cost of purchasing goods
- prepare an inventory account showing the entries for opening and closing inventory
- prepare an income statement and balance sheet containing the appropriate adjustments for returns, carriage and other items that affect the calculation of the cost of goods sold
- explain why the costs of putting goods into a saleable condition should be charged to the trading account

Introduction

This chapter contains material that *many* students get wrong in examinations. Take care as you work through it to understand and learn the points as they are presented to you.

In this chapter, you'll build on what you learnt in Chapter 3 and learn how to treat goods returned from customers and goods returned to suppliers in the trading account. You'll also learn how to deal with the costs of transporting goods into and out of a business. You will learn how to record inventory in an inventory account and then carry it forward in the account to the next period. You'll also learn how to enter opening inventory in the trading account. You'll learn that there are other costs that must be added to the cost of goods in the trading account. Finally, you'll learn how to prepare an income statement and balance sheet position when any of these items are included in the list of balances at the end of a period.

16.1 Returns inwards and returns outwards

In Chapter 3, the idea of different accounts for different movements of inventory was introduced. There are four accounts involved. The sales account and the **returns inwards account** deal with goods sold and goods returned by customers. The purchases account and the **returns outwards account** deal with goods purchased and goods returned to the supplier respectively. In our first look at the preparation of a trading account in Chapter 14, returns inwards and returns outwards were omitted. This was done deliberately, so that your first sight of income statements would be as straightforward as possible.

 Activity 16.1 Why do you think organisations bother with the two returns accounts? Why don't they just debit sales returned to the sales account and credit purchases returned to the purchases account?

Just as you may have done yourself, a large number of businesses return goods to their suppliers (**returns outwards**) and will have goods returned to them by their customers (**returns inwards**). When the gross profit is calculated, these returns will have to be included in the calculations.

Let's look at the first two lines of the trial balance you saw in Exhibit 14.1:

Exhibit 14.1 (extract)

		Dr	Cr
B. Swift **Trial balance as at 31 December 2019**			
		£	£
Sales			38,500
Purchases		29,000	

Now, suppose that in Exhibit 16.1 the trial balance of B. Swift, rather than simply containing a sales account balance of £38,500 and a purchases account balance of £29,000 the balances included those for returns inwards and outwards:

Exhibit 16.1

	Dr	Cr
B. Swift **Trial balance as at 31 December 2019 (extract)**		
	£	£
Sales		40,000
Purchases	31,200	
Returns inwards	1,500	
Returns outwards		2,200

Comparing these two exhibits reveals that they amount to the same thing so far as gross profit is concerned. Sales were £38,500 in the original example because returns inwards had already been deducted in arriving at the amount shown in Exhibit 14.1. In the amended version, returns inwards should be shown separately in the trial balance and then deducted on the face of the income statement to get the correct figure for goods sold to customers and *kept* by them, i.e. £40,000 − £1,500 = £38,500. Purchases were originally shown as being £29,000. In the new version, returns outwards should be deducted to get the correct figure of purchases *kept* by Swift. Both the returns accounts are included in the calculation of gross profit, which now becomes:

(Sales *less* Returns inwards) − (Cost of goods sold *less* Returns outwards) = Gross profit

---

The gross profit is therefore unaffected and is the same as in Chapter 14: £12,500.

The trading account section of the income statement will appear as in Exhibit 16.2:

Exhibit 16.2

B. Swift
Trading account section of the income statement for the year ending 31 December 2019

	£	£
Sales		40,000
Less Returns inwards		(1,500)
		38,500
Less Cost of goods sold:		
Purchases	31,200	
Less Returns outwards	(2,200)	
	29,000	
Less Closing Inventory	(3,000)	
		(26,000)
Gross profit		12,500

16.2 Carriage

If you have ever purchased anything over the Internet, you have probably been charged for 'postage and packing'. When goods are delivered by suppliers or sent to customers, the cost of transporting the goods is often an additional charge to the buyer. This charge is called 'carriage'. When it is charged for delivery of goods purchased, it is called **carriage inwards.** Carriage charged on goods sent out by a business to its customers is called **carriage outwards.**

When goods are purchased, the cost of carriage inwards may either be included as a hidden part of the purchase price, or be charged separately. For example, suppose your business was buying exactly the same goods from two suppliers. One supplier might sell them for £100 and not charge anything for carriage. Another supplier might sell the goods for £95, but you would have to pay £5 to a courier for carriage inwards, i.e. a total cost of £100. In both cases, the same goods cost you the same total amount. It would not be appropriate to leave out the cost of carriage inwards from the 'cheaper' supplier in the calculation of gross profit, as the real cost to you having the goods available for resale is £100.

As a result, in order to ensure that the true cost of buying goods for resale is *always* included in the calculation of gross profit, carriage inwards **is *always* added to the cost of purchases in the trading account.**

Carriage outwards is not part of the selling price of goods. Customers could come and collect the goods themselves, in which case there would be no carriage outwards expense for the seller to pay or to recharge customers. **Carriage outwards is *always* entered in the profit and loss account section of the income statement. It is *never* included in the calculation of gross profit.**

Suppose that in the illustration shown in this chapter, the goods had been bought for the same total figure of £31,200 but, in fact, £29,200 was the figure for purchases and £2,000 for carriage inwards. The trial balance extract would appear as in Exhibit 16.3.

Exhibit 16.3

	Dr	Cr
B. Swift		
Trial balance as at 31 December 2019 (extract)		
	£	£
Sales		40,000
Purchases	29,200	
Returns inwards	1,500	
Returns outwards		2,200
Carriage inwards	2,000	

The trading account section of the income statement would then be as shown in Exhibit 16.4:

Exhibit 16.4

B. Swift
Trading account section of the income statement for the year ending 31 December 2019

	£	£
Sales		40,000
Less Returns inwards		(1,500)
		38,500
Less Cost of goods sold:		
Purchases	29,200	
Less Returns outwards	(2,200)	
	27,000	
Carriage inwards	2,000	
	29,000	
Less Closing inventory	(3,000)	
		(26,000)
Gross profit		12,500

It can be seen that the three versions of B. Swift's trial balance have all been concerned with the same overall amount of goods bought and sold by the business, at the same overall prices. Therefore, in each case, the same gross profit of £12,500 has been found.

> **Before you proceed further, attempt Review Questions 16.1 and 16.2A.**

16.3 The second year of a business

At the end of his second year of trading, on 31 December 2020, B. Swift draws up another trial balance.

Exhibit 16.5

B. Swift
Trial balance as at 31 December 2020

	Dr	Cr
	£	£
Sales		67,000
Purchases	42,600	
Lighting and heating expenses	1,900	
Rent	2,400	
Wages: shop assistant	5,200	
General expenses	700	
Carriage outwards	1,100	
Buildings	20,000	
Fixtures and fittings	7,500	
Accounts receivable	12,000	
Accounts payable		9,000
Bank	1,200	
Cash	400	
Drawings	9,000	
Capital		31,000
Inventory (at 31 December 2019)	3,000	
	107,000	107,000

Adjustments needed for inventory

So far, we have been looking at new businesses only. When a business starts, it has no inventory brought forward. B. Swift started in business in 2019. Therefore, when we were preparing Swift's income statement for 2019, there was only closing inventory to worry about.

When we prepare the income statement for the second year we can see the difference. If you look back to the income statement in Exhibit 16.4, you can see that there was closing inventory of £3,000. This is, therefore, the opening inventory figure for 2020. We will need to incorporate in the trading account. It is also the figure for inventory that you can see in the trial balance at 31 December 2020.

The closing inventory for one period is *always* brought forward as the opening inventory for the next period.

Swift checked his inventory at 31 December 2020 and valued it at that date at £5,500.

We can summarise the opening and closing inventory account positions for Swift over the two years as follows:

Trading account for the period ⟶	Year ending 31 December 2019	Year ending 31 December 2020
Opening inventory 1.1.2019 Closing inventory 31.12.2019 Opening inventory 1.1.2020 Closing inventory 31.12.2020	None £3,000	£3,000 £5,500

Inventory account

Before going any further, let's look at the inventory account for both years:

Inventory

2019			£	2019			£
Dec	31	Trading	3,000	Dec	31	Balance c/d	3,000
2020				2020			
Jan	1	Balance b/d	3,000	Dec	31	Trading	3,000
Dec	31	Trading	5,500		31	Balance c/d	5,500
			8,500				8,500

You can see that in 2020 there is both a debit and a credit double entry made at the end of the period to the trading account. First, the inventory account is credited with the opening inventory amount of £3,000 and the trading account is debited with the same amount. Then, the inventory account is debited with the closing inventory amount of £5,500 and the trading account is credited with the same amount.

Thus, while the first year of trading only includes one inventory figure in the trading account, for the second year of trading both opening and closing inventory figures will be in the calculations.

Let's now calculate the cost of goods sold for 2020:

	£
Inventory of goods at start of year	3,000
Add Purchases	42,600
Total goods available for sale	45,600
Less What remains at the end of the year (i.e. closing inventory)	(5,500)
Therefore the cost of goods that have been sold is	40,100

We can look at a diagram to illustrate this:

Exhibit 16.6

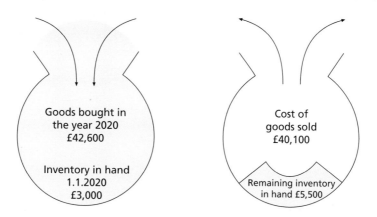

You can see that the left-hand container in the exhibit contains all the inventory available to be sold during the year. In the right-hand container, the closing inventory at the end of the year is now lying at the bottom and the empty space above it must, therefore, represent the inventory that has been sold.

The calculation of gross profit can now be done. You know from the trial balance that sales were £67,000 and from the calculation above that the cost of goods sold was £40,100. Gross profit is, therefore, £26,900.

Now the income statement and the balance sheet can be drawn up, as shown in Exhibits 16.7 and 16.8:

Exhibit 16.7

B. Swift
Income Statement for the year ending 31 December 2020

	£	£
Sales		67,000
Less Cost of goods sold:		
Opening inventory	3,000	
Add Purchases	42,600	
	45,600	
Less Closing inventory	(5,500)	
		(40,100)
Gross profit		26,900
Less Expenses:		
Wages	5,200	
Lighting and heating expenses	1,900	
Rent	2,400	
General expenses	700	
Carriage outwards	1,100	
		(11,300)
Net profit		15,600

Exhibit 16.8

B. Swift
Balance Sheet as at 31 December 2020

	£	£
Non-current assets		
Buildings		20,000
Fixtures and fittings		7,500
		27,500
Current assets		
Inventory	5,500	
Accounts receivable	12,000	
Bank	1,200	
Cash	400	
		19,100
Total assets		46,600
Current liabilities		
Accounts payable		(9,000)
Net assets		37,600
Capital		
Balance at 1 January 2020		31,000
Add Net profit for the year		15,600
		46,600
Less Drawings		(9,000)
Total capital		37,600

Financial statements

Financial statements is the term given to all the summary statements that accountants produce at the end of reporting periods. They are often called '**final accounts**', but this term is quite misleading (as none of the financial statements are 'accounts' in the accounting sense). Nevertheless, some people do still refer to them as the 'final accounts' or simply as **the accounts** of a business. You therefore, will, need to be aware of these terms, just in case you read something that uses these terms, or your teacher or lecturer, or an examiner, uses them at some time.

Other expenses in the trading account

You already know that carriage inwards is added to the cost of purchases in the trading account. You also need to add to the cost of goods in the trading account any costs incurred in converting purchases into goods for resale. In the case of a trader, it is very unusual for any additional costs to be incurred getting the goods ready for sale.

Activity 16.2 What costs do you think a trader may incur that would need to be added to the cost of the goods in the trading account?

For goods imported from abroad it is usual to find that the costs of import duty and insurance are treated as part of the cost of the goods, along with any costs incurred in repackaging the goods. Any such additional costs incurred in getting goods ready for sale are debited to the trading account.

Note: Students often find it difficult to remember how to treat returns and carriage when preparing the income statement. You need to be sure to learn and remember that all returns, inwards and outwards, and carriage inwards appear in the calculation of gross profit. Carriage outwards appears as an expense in the profit and loss account section of the income statement.

16.4 A warning

Students lose a lot of marks on the topics covered in this chapter because they assume that the topics are easy and unlikely to be things that they will forget. Unfortunately, they are fairly easy to understand, and that is why they are easily forgotten and confused. You would be wise to make sure that you have understood and learnt everything presented to you in this chapter before you go any further in the book.

16.5 Review questions: the best approach

Before you attempt the review questions at the end of this chapter, you should read the section on review questions in the Notes for Students (pp. xi–xx).

Learning outcomes

You should now have learnt:

1 That returns *inwards* should be deducted from sales in the *trading* account.

2 That returns *outwards* should be deducted from purchases in the *trading* account.

3 That carriage *inwards* is shown as an expense item in the *trading* account.

4 That carriage *outwards* is shown as an expense in the *profit and loss* account.

5 How to prepare the inventory account and carry forward the balance from one period to the next.

6 That in the second and later years of a business, both opening and closing inventory are brought into the trading account.

7 That it is normal practice to show cost of goods sold as a separate figure in the trading account.

8 How to prepare an income statement that includes the adjustments for carriage inwards and both opening and closing inventory in the trading section and carriage outwards as an expense in the profit and loss section.

9 That expense items concerned with getting goods into a saleable condition are charged in the trading account.

10 That where there is import duty or insurance charged on goods purchased, these costs are treated as part of the cost of goods sold.

Answers to activities

16.1 Organisations want to know how much they sold as a separate item from how much of those goods sold were returned. The same goes for purchases and the goods sent back to the supplier. It is useful to know what proportion of goods sold are returned and whether there is any pattern in which customers are returning them. On the purchases side, knowing how many times goods have been returned and the proportion of purchases from individual suppliers that are being returned helps with monitoring the quality of the goods being purchased. While this information could be gathered if returns accounts were not used, it would be a more complicated task obtaining it. Most of all, however, the sales account is a revenue account. Entering returns inwards amounts in the sales account is contrary to the nature of the sales account. The same holds for returns outwards and the purchases account, which is an expense account.

16.2 In the case of a trader, it is very unusual for any additional costs to be incurred getting the goods ready for sale. However, a trader who sells clocks packed in boxes might buy the clocks from one supplier, and the boxes from another. Both of these items would be charged in the trading account as purchases. In addition, if someone was paid to pack the clocks into the boxes, then the wages paid for that to be done would also be charged in the trading account as part of the cost of those goods. Be careful not to confuse this with the wages of shop assistants who sell the clocks. Those shop assistant wages *must* be charged in the profit and loss account because they are selling costs rather than extra costs incurred getting the goods ready for sale. The wages of the person packing the clocks would be the only wages in this case that were incurred while 'putting the goods into a saleable condition'.

Review questions

16.1 From the following information, draw up the trading account section of the income statement of B. Willis for the year ending 31 January 2019, which was her first year in business:

	£
Carriage inwards	3,470
Returns outwards	1,390
Returns inwards	7,470
Sales	249,000
Purchases	168,300
Inventory of goods: 31 January 2019	25,630

16.2A The following information is available for the year ending 31 December 2020. Draw up the trading account section of the income statement of A Higgins, who started trading in that year:

	£
Inventory: 31 December 2020	37,880
Returns inwards	23,010
Returns outwards	17,290
Purchases	353,690
Carriage inwards	5,420
Sales	575,430

16.3 From the following trial balance of G. Still, draw up an income statement for the year ending 30 September 2020, and a balance sheet as at that date.

	Dr	Cr
	£	£
Inventory: 1 October 2019	41,600	
Carriage outwards	2,100	
Carriage inwards	3,700	
Returns inwards	1,540	
Returns outwards		3,410
Purchases	188,430	
Sales		380,400
Salaries and wages	61,400	
Warehouse rent	3,700	
Insurance	1,356	
Motor expenses	1,910	
Office expenses	412	
Lighting and heating expenses	894	
General expenses	245	
Premises	92,000	
Motor vehicles	13,400	
Fixtures and fittings	1,900	
Accounts receivable	42,560	
Accounts payable		31,600
Cash at bank	5,106	
Drawings	22,000	
Capital		68,843
	484,253	484,253

Inventory at 30 September 2020 was £44,780.

16.4 The following trial balance was extracted from the books of F. Sorley on 30 April 2020. From it, and the note about inventory, prepare his income statement for the year ending 30 April 2020, and a balance sheet as at that date.

	Dr	Cr
	£	£
Sales		210,420
Purchases	108,680	
Inventory: 1 May 2019	9,410	
Carriage outwards	1,115	
Carriage inwards	840	
Returns inwards	4,900	
Returns outwards		3,720
Salaries and wages	41,800	
Motor expenses	912	
Rent	6,800	
Sundry expenses	318	
Motor vehicles	14,400	
Fixtures and fittings	912	
Accounts receivable	23,200	
Accounts payable		14,100
Cash at bank	4,100	
Cash in hand	240	
Drawings	29,440	
Capital		18,827
	247,067	247,067

Inventory at 30 April 2020 was £11,290.

16.5A   The following is the trial balance of T. Owen as at 31 March 2019. Draw up a set of financial statements for the year ended 31 March 2019.

	Dr	Cr
	£	£
Inventory at 1 April 2018	52,800	
Sales		276,400
Purchases	141,300	
Carriage inwards	1,350	
Carriage outwards	5,840	
Returns outwards		2,408
Wages and salaries	63,400	
Business rates	3,800	
Communication expenses	714	
Commissions paid	1,930	
Insurance	1,830	
Sundry expenses	208	
Buildings	125,000	
Accounts receivable	45,900	
Accounts payable		24,870
Fixtures	1,106	
Cash at bank	31,420	
Cash in hand	276	
Drawings	37,320	
Capital at 1 April 2018		210,516
	514,194	514,194

Inventory at 31 March 2019 was £58,440.

16.6A   F. Brown drew up the following trial balance as at 30 September 2020. You are to draft the income statement for the year ending 30 September 2020 and a balance sheet as at that date.

	Dr	Cr
	£	£
Capital as at 1 October 2019		49,675
Drawings	28,600	
Cash at bank	4,420	
Cash in hand	112	
Accounts receivable	38,100	
Accounts payable		26,300
Inventory: 30 September 2019	72,410	
Van	5,650	
Office equipment	7,470	
Sales		391,400
Purchases	254,810	
Returns inwards	2,110	
Carriage inwards	760	
Returns outwards		1,240
Carriage outwards	2,850	
Motor expenses	1,490	
Rent	8,200	
Telephone charges	680	
Wages and salaries	39,600	
Insurance	745	
Office expenses	392	
Sundry expenses	216	
	468,615	468,615

Inventory at 30 September 2020 was £89,404.

16.7   Andrew Joel is a market trader who started business on 1 August. The following is a list of his transactions in that month:

Aug	1	Started business with £1,000 of his own cash.
	2	Paid £900 of this opening cash into a business bank account.
	4	Bought goods for resale on time, £78 from S. Holmes.
	5	Bought a motor van by cheque, £500.
	7	Bought goods for resale, paying cash £55.
	10	Sold goods on time, £98 to D. Moore.
	11	A Joel took goods from inventory for his own use, cost £22.
	12	Returned goods (to the value of £18) to S. Holmes.
	19	Sold goods for cash, £28.
	22	Bought fixtures & fittings on time from Kingston Equip Co, £150.
	24	Received loan from D. Watson, £100 cheque, repayable in 5 years.
	29	Paid S. Holmes by cheque, £24 on account.
	30	Paid wages, £30 to employee, by bank transfer.
	31	Paid Kingston Equipment Co in full by cheque £150.

Required:
(a) Enter the transactions in T-accounts and balance-off your T-accounts as at 31 August.
(b) Prepare a Trial Balance as at 31 August.
(c) Assume that the closing inventory has been counted and valued at cost totalling £28. Prepare an Income Statement for the month ended 31 August.
(d) Prepare a Balance Sheet as at 31 August.

16.8A   Ms Porter's business position at 1 July was as follows:

	£
Inventory	5,000
Equipment	3,700
Creditor (OK Ltd)	500
Debtor (AB Ltd)	300
Money in business bank account	1,200

During July, she:

	£
Sold goods for cash – paid in to bank	3,200
Sold goods to AB Limited on time	600
Bought goods from OK Ltd on time	3,900
Paid OK Ltd by cheque	3,000
Paid general expenses by cheque	500
Received cheque from AB Ltd	300

Inventory at 31 July was £6,200

Required:
(a) Open ledger accounts (including capital) at 1 July.
(b) Record all transactions.
(c) Prepare a trial balance.
(d) Prepare an income statement for the period.
(e) Prepare a balance sheet as at 31 July.

→

16.9 From the following trial balance of Mr Tangle, extracted after one year of operations, prepare an income statement for the year ending 30 April 2019, together with a balance sheet as at that date.

Inventory on 30 April 2019 was £8,000.

	£	£
Sales		71,600
Purchases	29,050	
Salaries	14,650	
Motor expenses	1,860	
Rent and business rates	2,500	
Insurances – building	1,500	
– vehicles	2,400	
Motor vehicles	20,000	
Fixtures	35,000	
Cash in hand	1,000	
Cash at bank		2,500
Drawings	24,000	
Long-term loan		30,000
Capital		31,810
Accounts receivable	23,450	
Accounts payable		19,500
	155,410	155,410

Multiple choice questions: Set 2

Now attempt Set 2 of multiple choice questions. (Answers to all the multiple choice questions are given in Appendix 2 at the end of this book.)

Each of these multiple choice questions has four suggested answers, (A), (B), (C) and (D). You should read each question and then decide which choice is best, either (A) or (B) or (C) or (D). *Write down your answers on a separate piece of paper.* You will then be able to redo the set of questions later without having to try to ignore your answers from previous attempts.

MC21   Gross profit is

(A)   Excess of sales over cost of goods sold
(B)   Sales less purchases
(C)   Cost of goods sold + opening inventory
(D)   Net profit less expenses of the period

MC22   Net profit is calculated in the

(A)   Trading account
(B)   Profit and loss account
(C)   Trial balance
(D)   Balance sheet

MC23   To find the value of closing inventory at the end of a period we

(A)   Do this by physically counting the inventory (i.e. stocktaking)
(B)   Look in the inventory account
(C)   Deduct opening inventory from cost of goods sold
(D)   Deduct cost of goods sold from sales

MC24   The credit entry for net profit is on the credit side of

(A)   The trading account
(B)   The profit and loss account
(C)   The drawings account
(D)   The capital account

MC25   Which of these best describes a balance sheet?

(A)   An account proving the books balance
(B)   A record of closing entries
(C)   A listing of balances
(D)   A statement of assets

MC26   The descending order in which current assets should be shown in the balance sheet is

(A)   Inventory, Accounts receivable, Bank, Cash
(B)   Cash, Bank, Accounts receivable, Inventory
(C)   Accounts receivable, Inventory, Bank, Cash
(D)   Inventory, Accounts receivable, Cash, Bank

MC27   Which of these best describes non-current assets?

(A)   Items bought to be used in the business
(B)   Items which will not wear out quickly
(C)   Expensive items bought for the business
(D)   Items having a long life and not bought specifically for resale

MC28   Carriage inwards is charged to the trading account because

(A)   It is an expense connected with buying goods
(B)   It should not go in the balance sheet
(C)   It is not part of motor expenses
(D)   Carriage outwards goes in the profit and loss account

MC29   Given figures showing: Sales £8,200, Opening inventory £1,300, Closing inventory £900, Purchases £6,400, Carriage inwards £200, the cost of goods sold figure is

(A)   £6,800
(B)   £6,200
(C)   £7,000
(D)   Another figure

MC30   The costs of putting goods into a saleable condition should be charged to

(A)   The trading account
(B)   The profit and loss account
(C)   The balance sheet
(D)   None of these

MC31   Suppliers' personal accounts are found in the

(A)   Nominal ledger
(B)   General ledger
(C)   Purchases ledger
(D)   Sales ledger

MC32   The sales day book is best described as

(A)   Part of the double entry system
(B)   Containing customers' accounts
(C)   Containing real accounts
(D)   A list of credit sales

MC33   Which of the following are personal accounts?

(i)   Buildings
(ii)   Wages
(iii)   Accounts receivable
(iv)   Accounts payable

(A)   (i) and (iv) only
(B)   (ii) and (iii) only
(C)   (iii) and (iv) only
(D)   (ii) and (iv) only

MC34   If you sell a book to J. Flood on eBay and the buyer pays using Paypal, what are the accounts to debit and credit?

(A)   Dr Bank Cr Sales
(B)   Dr J. Flood Cr Sales
(C)   Dr Paypal Cr Sales
(D)   Dr Cash Cr Sales

MC35   Transactions involve two elements. Which one guides you to identify the accounts to debit and credit?

(A)   The item exchanged
(B)   The buyer
(C)   The seller
(D)   The form of settlement

MC36   What are the journal entries if you exchange a van for a car from a second-hand motor dealer called R. Main?

(A)   Dr R. Main Cr Van
(B)   Dr Car Cr Van
(C)   Dr Car Cr R Main
(D)   Dr Van Cr Car

MC37   A debit balance of £100 in a cash account shows that

(A)   There was £100 cash in hand
(B)   Cash has been overspent by £100
(C)   £100 was the total of cash paid out
(D)   The total of cash received was less than £100

MC38   £50 cash taken from the cash till and banked is entered

(A)   Debit cash column £50: Credit bank column £50
(B)   Debit bank column £50: Credit cash column £50
(C)   Debit cash column £50: Credit cash column £50
(D)   Debit bank column £50: Credit bank column £50

MC39   A credit balance of £200 on the cash columns of the cash book would mean

(A)   We have spent £200 more than we have received
(B)   We have £200 cash in hand
(C)   The bookkeeper has made a mistake
(D)   Someone has stolen £200 cash

MC40   'Posting' the transactions in bookkeeping means

(A)   Making the first entry of a double entry transaction
(B)   Entering items in a cash book
(C)   Making the second entry of a double entry transaction
(D)   Something other than the above

Capital expenditure and revenue expenditure

Introduction

In this chapter, you'll learn about the difference between capital expenditure and revenue expenditure. You will learn how to split expenditure that is a mixture of both capital and revenue expenditure and to make the appropriate entries in the ledgers and in the financial statements. You will also learn why organisations generally prefer to treat as much expenditure as possible as capital expenditure, how to deal with loan interest relating to acquisition of a non-current asset, and how to classify and deal with the income generated when a non-current asset is sold.

17.1 Capital expenditure

Before you start this topic, you need to be aware that 'capital expenditure' has nothing to do with the owner's Capital Account. The two terms happen to include the same first word, and they are both things that are likely to be around the business for quite a long time. While both are, in a sense, long-term investments, one made by the business, the other made by the owner, they are, by definition, two very different things.

Capital expenditure is incurred when a business spends money either to:

● buy non-current assets; or

● add to the value of an existing non-current asset.

Included in such amounts should be spending on:

● acquiring non-current assets

● bringing them into the business

● legal costs of buying buildings

● carriage inwards on machinery bought

● any other cost needed to get a non-current asset ready for use.

17.2 Revenue expenditure

Expenditure which is not spent on increasing the value of non-current assets, but is incurred in running the business on a day-to-day basis, is known as **revenue expenditure**.

The difference between revenue expenditure and capital expenditure can be seen clearly with the total cost of using a van for a business. Buying a van is an example of capital expenditure. The van will be in use for several years and is, therefore, a non-current asset.

Paying for petrol to use in the van is revenue expenditure. This is because the expenditure is used up in a short time and does not add to the value of non-current assets.

Activity 17.1

Why do you think a business might want to treat an item of expenditure as capital rather than as revenue? (*Hint*: where does an item of capital expenditure *not* appear in the financial statements?)

17.3 Differences between capital and revenue expenditure

The examples listed in Exhibit 17.1 demonstrate the difference in classification.

Exhibit 17.1

Expenditure	*Type of Expenditure*
1 Buying van	Capital
2 Petrol costs for van	Revenue
3 Repairs to van	Revenue
4 Putting extra headlights on van	Capital
5 Buying machinery	Capital
6 Electricity costs of using machinery	Revenue
7 We spent £1,500 on machinery: £1,000 was for an item (improvement) added to the machine; and £500 was for repairs	Capital £1,000 Revenue £500
8 Painting outside of new building	Capital
9 Three years later – repainting outside of the building in (8)	Revenue

You already know that revenue expenditure is chargeable to the income statement, while capital expenditure will result in increased figures for non-current assets in the balance sheet. Getting the classification wrong affects the profits reported and the capital account and asset values in the financial statements. It is, therefore, important that this classification is correctly done.

17.4 Capital expenditure: further analysis

As mentioned earlier, capital expenditure not only consists of the cost of purchasing a non-current asset, but also includes other costs necessary to get the non-current asset operational.

> **Activity 17.2**
> Spend a minute listing some examples of these other costs like the ones you've already learnt about.

17.5 Joint expenditure

Sometimes one item of expenditure will need to be divided between capital and revenue expenditure – there was an example in Exhibit 17.1 when £1,500 spent on machinery was split between capital and revenue.

Exhibit 17.2

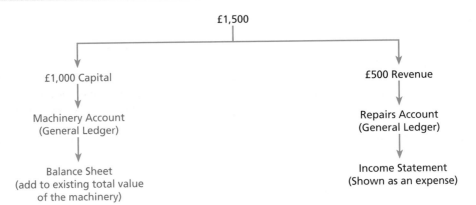

> **Activity 17.3**
> A builder was engaged to tackle some work on your premises, the total bill being for £3,000. If one-third of this was for repair work and two-thirds for improvements, where should the two parts be entered in the accounting books and where would they appear in the financial statements?

17.6 Incorrect treatment of expenditure

If one of the following occurs:

1 capital expenditure is incorrectly treated as revenue expenditure; or
2 revenue expenditure is incorrectly treated as capital expenditure;

then both the balance sheet figures and the income statement figures will be incorrect.

This means that the net profit figure will be incorrect and, if the expenditure affects items in the trading account part of the income statement, the gross profit figure will also be incorrect.

Activity 17.4

Can you think of an example where an item may have been treated wrongly as revenue expenditure and charged in the trading account when it should have been treated as capital expenditure?

17.7 Treatment of loan interest

If money is borrowed to finance the purchase of a non-current asset, interest will have to be paid on the loan. Most accountants would argue that the loan interest is *not* a cost of acquiring the asset, but is simply a cost of *financing* its acquisition. This meant that loan interest was revenue expenditure and *not* capital expenditure. In 1993, this changed and it because compulsory to capitalise interest incurred in *constructing* a non-current asset.

Activity 17.5

Why shouldn't the interest on the funds borrowed to finance *acquisition* of a non-current asset be included in its cost?

17.8 Capital and revenue receipts

When an item of capital expenditure is sold, the receipt is called a 'capital receipt'. Suppose a van is bought for £5,000 and sold five years later for £750. The £5,000 was treated as capital expenditure. The £750 received is treated as a capital receipt and credited to the non-current asset account in the General Ledger. (You will learn later in your studies that it is a bit more complicated than this, but this treatment is technically correct.)

'Revenue receipts' are sales and other revenue items that are added to gross profit, such as rent receivable and commissions receivable.

17.9 Finally

Students generally find this topic very difficult to grasp. Trying to remember when something should be treated as capital expenditure and when something should be treated as revenue expenditure seems just too difficult to remember correctly.

In fact, the rules are *very* simple:

1 If expenditure is *directly* incurred in bringing a non-current asset into use for the first time, it is capital expenditure.
2 If expenditure improves a non-current asset (by making it superior to what it was when it was first owned by the organisation, e.g. building an extension to a warehouse), it is capital expenditure.
3 All other expenditures are revenue expenditure.

So, faced with having to decide, ask if (1) is true. If it isn't, ask if (2) is true. If it isn't, it is revenue expenditure. If either (1) or (2) is true, it is capital expenditure. Try it on the items in Exhibit 17.1 – it works!

Learning outcomes
. . . .

You should now have learnt:

1 How to distinguish between capital expenditure and revenue expenditure.

2 That some items are a mixture of capital expenditure and revenue expenditure, and the total outlay need to be apportioned accordingly.

3 That if capital expenditure or revenue expenditure is mistaken one for the other, then gross profit and/or net profit will be incorrectly stated, as will the capital account and non-current assets in the balance sheet.

4 That if capital receipts or revenue receipts are mistaken one for the other, then gross profit and/or net profit will be incorrectly stated, as will the capital account and non-current assets in the balance sheet.

Answers to activities

17.1 Capital expenditure appears in the balance sheet whereas revenue expenditure appears in the income statement. If expenditure is treated as revenue expenditure, it reduces profit immediately by the amount spent. If it is treated as capital expenditure, there is no immediate impact upon profit. Profit is only affected when a part of the expenditure is charged against income during the time the item purchased is in use, and those charges (called 'depreciation') spread the cost of the item over a number of years. As a result, profits in the period in which the expenditure took place are lower if an item of expenditure is treated as revenue expenditure. Businesses like to show that they are being as profitable as possible, so they tend to want to treat everything possible as a capital expense. Doing this also makes the business look more wealthy as the non-current assets are at a higher value than they would have been had the expenditure been treated as revenue. (You'll learn about depreciation in Chapter 21.)

17.2 Some of the other possible additional costs are: (a) installation costs; (b) inspection and testing the asset before use; (c) architects' fees for building plans and for supervising construction of buildings; (d) demolition costs to remove something before new building can begin.

17.3 The debit entries would be Repairs £1,000 and Premises £2,000. The credit entry would be Accounts Payable 'Builder' £3,000. The £1,000 will appear, therefore, in the income statement (in the profit and loss part) as revenue expenditure. The £2,000 identified as capital expenditure will appear in the balance sheet as part of the figure for Premises.

17.4 When goods are being manufactured from raw materials, employees will be being paid wages. Those wages will be part of the cost of the inventory of finished goods. It sometimes happens that employees do other work in periods when their normal work is not keeping them busy. Imagine some employees were moved temporarily to help build an extension to the premises – for example, by helping to build a small garage to hold the company chairman's car while he was working in his office. If their wages for that period were mistakenly included as usual in the cost of goods produced, that would be an example of capital expenditure being wrongly classified as revenue expenditure and would result in gross profit being understated.

17.5 Organisations have a number of sources of funds, only one of which is borrowing. The non-current asset could have been paid for using existing funds already held by the organisation. The funds borrowed to pay for it could just as easily have been used to buy raw materials while the funds already available for purchase of raw materials could have been used to finance the new non-current asset. How could anyone be sure that the funds borrowed were actually used to purchase it, and why should they be tied so strongly to it when other funds could have been used instead? It is a very circuitous argument but, in the end, the funds borrowed entered the pool of all the organisation's funds. Just because an amount equal to the amount borrowed was then used to pay for the non-current asset is not sufficient reason to include the interest costs in the cost of the non-current asset. The interest costs are simply part of the costs of financing all the assets of the organisation.

However, this changed in 1993 when an accounting standard was issued (IAS 23 *Borrowing costs*) that allows interest directly attributable to the construction of a tangible non-current asset to be capitalised as part of the cost of that asset. In 2007, the standard was amended making it compulsory to capitalise such borrowing costs. Note that it *does not* permit capitalisation of interest incurred on the funds used to purchase a non-current asset, only interest incurred *on the construction* of one.

Review questions

17.1
(a) What is meant by 'capital expenditure' and by 'revenue expenditure'?
(b) Some of the following items should be treated as capital and some as revenue. For each of them state which classification applies:

   (i) The purchase of machinery for use in the business.
   (ii) Carriage paid to bring the machinery in (i) above to the works.
   (iii) Complete redecoration of the premises at a cost of £1,500.
   (iv) A quarterly account for heating.
   (v) The purchase of a soft drinks vending machine for the canteen with a stock of soft drinks.
   (vi) Wages paid by a building contractor to his own workmen for the erection of an office in the builder's stockyard.

17.2A Indicate which of the following would be revenue items and which would be capital items in a wholesale bakery:

(a) Purchase of a new van.
(b) Purchase of replacement engine for existing van.
(c) Cost of altering interior of new van to increase carrying capacity.
(d) Cost of motor tax for new van.
(e) Cost of motor tax for existing van.
(f) Cost of painting business's name on new van.
(g) Repair and maintenance of existing van.

17.3 State the type of expenditure, capital or revenue, incurred in the following transactions:

(a) Breakdown van purchased by a garage.
(b) Repairs to a fruiterer's van.
(c) The cost of installing a new machine.
(d) Cost of hiring refrigeration plant in a butcher's shop.
(e) Twelve dozen sets of cutlery, purchased by a catering firm for a new dining-room.
(f) A motor vehicle bought for resale by a motor dealer.
(g) The cost of acquiring patent rights.

17.4A On what principles would you distinguish between capital and revenue expenditure? Illustrate your answer by reference to the following:

(a) The cost of repairs and an extension to the premises.
(b) Installation of a gas central heating boiler in place of an oil-fired central heating boiler.
(c) Small but expensive alterations to a cigarette manufacturing machine which increased the machine's output by 20 per cent.

17.5 State which of the following you would classify as capital expenditure:

(a) Cost of building extension to warehouse.
(b) Purchase of extra filing cabinets for accounts office.
(c) Cost of repairs to computer equipment.
(d) Cost of installing reconditioned engine in delivery truck.
(e) Legal fees paid in connection with warehouse extension.

→

17.6A The data which follows was extracted from the books of account of H. Kirk, an engineer, on 31 March 2019, his financial year end.

		£
(a)	Purchase of extra milling machine (includes £300 for repair of an old machine)	2,900
(b)	Rent	750
(c)	Electrical expenses (includes new wiring £600, part of premises improvement)	3,280
(d)	Carriage inwards (includes £150 carriage on new cement mixer)	1,260
(e)	Purchase of extra drilling machine	4,100

You are required to allocate each or part of the items above to either 'capital' or 'revenue' expenditure.

17.7 For the business of J. Charles, wholesale chemist, classify the following between 'capital' and 'revenue' expenditure:

(a) Purchase of an extra van.
(b) Cost of rebuilding warehouse wall which had fallen down.
(c) Building extension to the warehouse.
(d) Painting extension to warehouse when it is first built.
(e) Repainting extension to warehouse three years later than that done in (d).
(f) Carriage costs on bricks for new warehouse extension.
(g) Carriage costs on purchases.
(h) Carriage costs on sales.
(i) Legal costs of collecting debts.
(j) Legal charges on acquiring new premises for office.
(k) Fire insurance premium.
(l) Costs of erecting new machine.

17.8A For the business of H. Ward, a food merchant, classify the following between 'capital' and 'revenue' expenditure:

(a) Repairs to meat slicer.
(b) New tyre for van.
(c) Additional shop counter.
(d) Renewing signwriting on shop.
(e) Fitting partitions in shop.
(f) Roof repairs.
(g) Installing thief detection equipment.
(h) Wages of shop assistant.
(i) Carriage on returns outwards.
(j) New cash register.
(k) Repairs to office safe.
(l) Installing extra toilet.

17.9 During its year ended 31 December 2020, Landon's business acquired a new machine from China. The business incurred the following costs in relation to this machine in 2020:

	£
Purchase price	25,000
Costs of testing the machine before its first use	240
One-year licence to operate the machine	360
Assembly of the machine	430
Delivery costs	510
Cost of preparatory modifications necessary for the installation of the machine	670
Installation of the machine	750
One-year maintenance cover for the machine	890
Import duties	920

In Landon's Balance Sheet, what amount should appear for the cost of this machine as at 31 December 2020?

17.10A   Classify the following items as either revenue or capital expenditure:

(a)   An extension to an office building costing £24,000.
(b)   The cost of replacement valves on all the labelling machines in a canning factory.
(c)   Repairs to the warehouse roof.
(d)   Annual service costs for a courier firm's fleet of vans.
(e)   Replacement of rubber tread on a printing press with a plastic one that has resulted in the useful economic life of the printing press being extended by three years.
(f)   A new bicycle purchased by a newsagent for use by the newspaper delivery boy.
(g)   Repairs to a refrigeration system of a meat wholesaler.
(h)   Repainting of the interior of a bar/restaurant which has greatly improved the potential for finding a buyer for the bar/restaurant as a going concern.
(i)   Wages paid to employees who worked on the construction of their company's new office building.

17.11   A Bloggs, a building contractor, had a wooden store shed and a brick-built office which have balances b/d in the books of £850 and £179,500 respectively. During the year, the wooden shed was pulled down at a cost of £265, and replaced by a brick building. Some of the timber from the old store shed was sold for £180 and the remainder, valued at £100, was used in making door frames, etc., for the new store. The new brick-built store was constructed by the builder's own employees, the expenditure thereon being materials (excluding timber from the old store shed) £4,750; wages £3,510; and direct expenses of £85.

   At about the same time, certain repairs and alterations were carried out to the office, again using the builder's own materials, the cost of which was: wages £290 and materials £460. It was estimated that £218 of this expenditure, being mainly that incurred on providing additional windows, represented improvements, 50% of this being wages, 50% materials.

Required:
Prepare the following four ledger accounts as they would appear after giving effect to all the above matters:

(a)   Wooden store shed account
(b)   Office buildings account
(c)   New brick-built store account
(d)   Office buildings repairs account

17.12A   Sema plc, a company in the heavy engineering industry, carried out an expansion programme in the 2019 financial year, in order to meet a permanent increase in contracts.

   The company selected a suitable site and commissioned a survey and valuation report, for which the fee was £1,500. On the basis of the report the site was acquired for £90,000.

   Solicitors' fees for drawing up the contract and conveyancing were £3,000.

Fees of £8,700 were paid to the architects for preparing the building plans and overseeing the building work. This was carried out partly by the company's own workforce (at a wages cost of £11,600), using company building materials (cost £76,800), and partly by subcontractors who charged £69,400, of which £4,700 related to the demolition of an existing building on the same site.

   The completed building housed two hydraulic presses.

   The cost of press A was £97,000 (ex-works), payable in a single lump sum two months after installation. Sema was given a trade discount of 10% and a cash discount for prompt payment of 2%. Hire of a transporter to collect the press and to convey it to the new building was £2,900. Installation costs were £2,310, including hire of lifting gear, £1,400.

   Press B would have cost £105,800 (delivered) if it had been paid in one lump sum. However, Sema opted to pay three equal annual instalments of £40,000, starting on the date of acquisition. Installation costs were £2,550, including hire of lifting gear, £1,750.

   The whole of the above expenditure was financed by the issue of £500,000 7% Loan notes (on which the annual interest payable was £35,000).

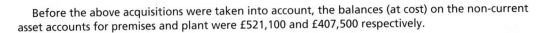

Before the above acquisitions were taken into account, the balances (at cost) on the non-current asset accounts for premises and plant were £521,100 and £407,500 respectively.

Required:
(a) Using such of the above information as is relevant, post and balance the premises and plant accounts for the 2019 financial year.
(b) State, with reasons, which of the given information you have not used in your answer to (a) above.

(*Association of Chartered Certified Accountants*)

17.13 Why is the distinction between classifying something as capital expenditure and classifying it as revenue expenditure so important to the users of financial statements?

17.14A On 18 August 2020 J. Barton purchased a new machine from DeFalco Ltd. Barton paid the following amounts in relation to this acquisition:

	£
List price of machine	195,000
Costs of preparing the site for installation	8,700
Delivery charges	3,000
Installation costs	4,400
Three-year maintenance contract with DeFalco Ltd	6,000
One year's insurance on the machine	2,450
Pre-production testing	5,800

Barton was able to negotiate a trade discount of 15% on the list price of the machine as well as a cash discount of 2.5% if payment was received within 21 days of purchase. Barton paid for the machine on 4 September 2020.

Required:
(a) How will the above information be treated in the financial statements of J. Barton?
(b) 'Materiality' is a concept that sometimes has an impact on the capitalisation of amounts in the balance sheet. Explain why this is the case and illustrate your answer with an example.

18

Inventory valuation

Learning objectives

After you have studied this chapter, you should be able to:

- calculate the value of inventory using three different methods
- explain why using the most appropriate method to value inventory is important
- explain what effect changing prices has on inventory valuation under each of three different methods
- explain why net realisable value is sometimes used instead of cost for inventory valuation
- adjust inventory valuations, where necessary, by a reduction to net realisable value
- explain how subjective factors influence the choice of inventory valuation method
- explain why goods purchased on 'sale or return' are not included in the buyer's inventory

Introduction

In this chapter, you will learn how to calculate the monetary value of inventory using a variety of methods. You will learn why choosing the most appropriate method of inventory valuation is important; and that a range of subjective factors can influence the choice of method, including the need to reflect how the inventory is physically used. Finally, you'll learn how to treat goods sold on 'sale or return' and about the need to adjust inventory levels identified in a stocktake (i.e. physical count of the inventory) to the level they would have been at the date of the balance sheet.

18.1 Different valuations of inventory

Inventory is the name given to the goods for resale, work-in-progress and raw materials that are held at a point in time. The rules to follow in valuing inventory are contained in IAS 2 (*Inventories*). This is dealt with in detail in *Frank Wood's Business Accounting 2*.

Most people assume that when a value is placed upon inventory, it is the only figure possible. This is not true.

Assume that a business has just completed its first financial year and is about to value inventory at cost price. It has dealt in only one item. A record of the transactions is now shown in Exhibit 18.1:

Exhibit 18.1

Bought			Sold		
2018		£	2018		£
January	10 at £30 each	300	May	8 for £50 each	400
April	10 at £34 each	340	November	24 for £60 each	1,440
October	20 at £40 each	800			
	40	1,440		32	1,840

A quick check by the storeman showed that there were still eight units in inventory at 31 December, which confirms what the records show above.

 Activity 18.1 What valuation do you think should be placed on the eight units of inventory? Why?

The total figure of purchases is £1,440 and sales revenue during the year was £1,840. The trading account for the first year of trading can now be completed using the closing inventory in the calculations.

Let's now look at the three most commonly used methods of valuing inventory.

18.2 First in, first out method (FIFO)

This is usually referred to as **FIFO**, from the first letters of each word. This method says that the first items to be received are the first to be issued. Using the figures in Exhibit 18.1 we can now calculate the cost of closing inventory on a FIFO basis as follows:

Date	Received	Issued	Inventory after each transaction		
				£	£
2018 January	10 at £30 each		10 at £30 each		300
April	10 at £34 each		10 at £30 each 10 at £34 each	300 340	640
May		8 at £30 each	2 at £30 each 10 at £34 each	60 340	400
October	20 at £40 each		2 at £30 each 10 at £34 each 20 at £40 each	60 340 800	1,200
November		2 at £30 each 10 at £34 each 12 at £40 each 24	8 at £40 each		320

Thus, the closing inventory at 31 December 2018 at cost is valued under FIFO at £320.

 Activity 18.2 Can you see another, simpler way of arriving at the same valuation under FIFO?

18.3 **Last in, first out method (LIFO)**

This is usually referred to as **LIFO**. As each issue of items is made they are assumed to be from the last batch received before that date. Where there is not enough left of the last batch, then the balance needed is assumed to come from the previous batch still unsold.

From the information shown in Exhibit 18.1 the calculation can now be shown.

Date	Received	Issued	Inventory after each transaction		
2018				£	£
January	10 at £30 each		10 at £30 each		300
April	10 at £34 each		10 at £30 each	300	
			10 at £34 each	340	640
May		8 at £34 each	10 at £30 each	300	
			2 at £34 each	68	368
October	20 at £40 each		10 at £30 each	300	
			2 at £34 each	68	
			20 at £40 each	800	1,168
November		20 at £40 each			
		2 at £34 each			
		2 at £30 each			
		24	8 at £30 each		240

Thus, the closing inventory at 31 December 2018 at cost is valued under LIFO at £240.

Activity 18.3 Can you see another, simpler way of arriving at the same valuation under LIFO?

18.4 **Average cost method (AVCO)**

Using the **AVCO** method, with each receipt of goods the average cost for each item is recalculated. Further issues of goods are then at that figure, until another receipt of goods means that another recalculation is needed. From the information in Exhibit 18.1 the calculation can be shown:

Date	Received	Issued	Average cost per unit of inventory held	Number of units in inventory	Total value of inventory
2018			£		£
January	10 at £30		30	10	300
April	10 at £34		32*	20	640
May		8 at £32	32	12	384
October	20 at £40		37**	32	1,184
November		24 at £37	37	8	296

The closing inventory at 31 December 2018 is therefore valued at £296.

*In April, this is calculated as follows: inventory 10 × £30 = £300 + inventory received (10 × £34) = £340 = total £640. You then divide the 20 units in inventory into the total cost of that inventory, i.e. £640 ÷ 20 = £32.
**In October, this is calculated as follows: inventory 12 × £32 = £384 + inventory received (20 × £40) = £800 = £1,184. There are 32 units in inventory, so the average is £1,184 ÷ 32 = £37.

Note, using this approach you recalculate the average after every receipt of a batch of new inventory and then use it as the cost of the next batch sold.

Activity 18.4 If two units had been sold in December, at what cost would they have been sold?

18.5 Inventory valuation and the calculation of profits

Using the figures from Exhibit 18.1 with inventory valuations shown by the three methods of FIFO, LIFO and AVCO, the trading account entries under each method would be:

Trading Account for the year ending 31 December 2018							
	FIFO	*LIFO*	*AVCO*		*FIFO*	*LIFO*	*AVCO*
	£	£	£		£	£	£
Purchases	1,440	1,440	1,440	Sales	1,840	1,840	1,840
less Closing inventory	(320)	(240)	(296)				
Cost of goods sold	1,120	1,200	1,144				
Gross profit	720	640	696				
	1,840	1,840	1,840		1,840	1,840	1,840

Activity 18.5 Which method has produced (a) the highest, (b) the middle and (c) the lowest value for closing inventory? Why do you think this has occurred?

As you can see, different methods of inventory valuation result in different profits. It is, therefore, important that the method chosen is the one that is closest in its assumptions to the nature of the business.

18.6 Reduction to net realisable value

Having selected the most appropriate method to apply when determining the cost of closing inventory, you next need to consider whether that value is realistic – that is, whether it is what the inventory is *actually* worth at the end of the period. This is an example of application of the prudence concept that you learnt about in Chapter 7. Following the prudence concept, inventory should never be undervalued or overvalued.

Activity 18.6 (a) What happens to gross profit if closing inventory is undervalued? Why?
(b) What happens to gross profit if closing inventory is overvalued? Why?

To check that inventory is not overvalued, accountants calculate its **net realisable value**. This is done according to the formula:

Saleable value (i.e. what it can be sold for) − Expenses needed before completion of sale (such as costs of delivery to the seller's shops) = Net realisable value.

If the net realisable value of inventory is less than the cost of the inventory, then the figure to be used in the financial statements is net realisable value *not* cost.

The following example illustrates why this is done. Assume that an art dealer has bought only two paintings during the financial year ended 31 December 2018. She starts off the year without any inventory, and then buys a genuine masterpiece for £6,000 and sells it later in the year for £11,500. The other is a fake, but she does not realise this when she buys it for £5,100. During the year she discovers that she made a terrible mistake and that its net realisable value is only £100. The fake remains unsold at the end of the year. The trading account part of the income statement, shown in Exhibit 18.2, would appear as (a) if inventory is valued at cost, and as (b) if inventory is valued at net realisable value.

Exhibit 18.2

Trading Account section of the Income Statement for the year ending 31 December 2018

	(a)		(b)
	£		£
Sales	11,500		11,500
Purchases	11,100	11,100	
Less: Closing inventory	(5,100)	(100)	
	(6,000)	(11,000)	
Gross profit	5,500	500	

Method (a) ignores the fact that the dealer had a bad trading year owing to her mistake. If this method was used, then the loss on the fake would reveal itself in the following year's trading account. Method (b) recognises that the loss really occurred at the date of purchase rather than at the date of sale. Following the concept of prudence, accounting practice is to use method (b).

18.7 Inventory groups and valuation

If there is only one sort of item in inventory, calculating the lower of cost or net realisable value is easy. If we have several or many types of item in inventory, we can use one of two ways of making the calculation – by category and by item.

Exhibit 18.3

Inventory at 31 December 2018			
Item	Different categories	Cost	Net realisable value
		£	£
1	A	100	80
2	A	120	150
3	A	300	400
4	B	180	170
5	B	150	130
6	B	260	210
7	C	410	540
8	C	360	410
9	C	420	310
		2,300	2,400

In Exhibit 18.3, Items 1, 2 and 3 are televisions; 4, 5 and 6 are DVD recorders; and 7, 8 and 9 are games consoles. From the information given in the exhibit, we will calculate the value of the inventory using both these approaches.

1 The category method

The same sorts of items are put together in categories. Thus, televisions are in Category A, DVDs are in Category B, and Category C is games consoles.

A calculation showing a comparison of cost valuation and net realisable value for each category is now shown.

Category	Cost	Net realisable value
A	£100 + £120 + £300 = £520	£80 + £150 + £400 = £630
B	£180 + £150 + £260 = £590	£170 + £130 + £210 = £510
C	£410 + £360 + £420 = £1,190	£540 + £410 + £310 = £1,260

The lower of cost and net realisable value is, therefore:

	£
Category A: lower of £520 or £630	= 520
Category B: lower of £590 or £510	= 510
Category C: lower of £1,190 or £1,260	= 1,190
Inventory is valued for financial statements at	2,220

2 The item method

By this method, the lower of cost or net realisable value for each item is compared and the lowest figure taken. From Exhibit 18.3 this gives us the following valuation:

Item	Valuation
	£
1	80
2	120
3	300
4	170
5	130
6	210
7	410
8	360
9	310
	£2,090

Of these two methods, it is Method 2, the item method, that should be used. It provides a more realistic overall value for the inventory.

18.8 Some other inventory valuation bases in use

Retail businesses often estimate the cost of inventory by calculating it in the first place at selling price, and then deducting the normal margin of gross profit on such inventory. Adjustment is made for items which are to be sold at other than normal selling prices.

Another approach is to use **standard cost**. Standard cost is, effectively, what you would expect something to cost. When standard costing is in use, a 'standard cost' will have been determined for purchases and it is that standard cost that would be used to value closing inventory.

'Base inventory' (often referred to as 'base stock') is another method. It is used in industries where a minimum level of inventory is always maintained. Power station fuel supplies, for example, may fall within this classification. The base inventory is assumed to never deteriorate or be replaced and is valued at its original cost. Any other inventory is valued using a 'normal' method, such as FIFO, LIFO or AVCO.

18.9 Periodic inventory valuation

Some businesses do not keep detailed inventory records like those shown in Exhibit 18.1. Instead, they wait until the end of a period before calculating the value of their closing inventory. In this case, AVCO is based upon the total cost of inventory available for sale in the period divided by the number of units of inventory available for sale in the period. You then multiply the closing inventory by the overall average cost of the inventory to get the value of that inventory.

If you did this for the data in Exhibit 18.1 the closing inventory value at cost would be (£1,440 ÷ 40 =) £36 × 8 = £288 (rather than £296, as calculated in Section 18.4). This method is also known as the 'weighted average cost method'.

If you used FIFO or LIFO in these circumstances, FIFO gives the same answer as under the method presented earlier. LIFO, on the other hand, would become the opposite of FIFO, with all closing inventory assumed to have come from the earliest batches of purchases.

Activity 18.7
If you have no detailed inventory records, how could you use AVCO, FIFO or LIFO?

Unless an examiner asks you to calculate them using a periodic inventory valuation basis, you should assume that you are to calculate AVCO, FIFO and LIFO in the way they were presented earlier in this chapter (i.e. on a perpetual valuation basis).

18.10 Factors affecting the inventory valuation decision

The overriding consideration applicable in all circumstances when valuing inventory is the need to give a 'true and fair view' of the state of affairs of the undertaking as at the date of the statement of financial position and of the trend of the business's trading results. There is, however, no precise definition of what constitutes a 'true and fair view' and it rests on the judgement of the persons concerned. Unfortunately, the judgement of any two persons will not always be the same in the differing circumstances of various businesses.

In fact, the only certain thing about inventory valuation is that the concept of consistency (which you learnt about in Chapter 7) should be applied, i.e. once adopted, the same basis should be used in the financial statements until some good reason occurs to change it. A reference should then be made in the notes that accompany the financial statements as to the effect of the change on the reported profits, if the amount involved is material.

Let's look briefly at some of the factors which cause a particular basis to be chosen. The list is intended to be indicative rather than comprehensive, and is merely intended as a first brief look at matters which will have to be studied in depth by those intending to make a career in accountancy.

1 **Ignorance.** The people involved may not appreciate the fact that there is more than one possible way of valuing inventory.
2 **Convenience.** The basis chosen may not be the best for the purposes of profit calculation but it may be the easiest to calculate. It must always be borne in mind that the benefits which flow from possessing information should be greater than the costs of obtaining it. The only difficulty with this is actually establishing when the benefits do exceed the cost but, in some circumstances, the decision not to adopt a given basis will be obvious.
3 **Custom.** It may be the particular method used in a certain trade or industry.
4 **Taxation.** The whole idea may be to defer the payment of tax for as long as possible. Because the inventory figures affect the calculation of profits on which the tax is based the lowest possible inventory figures may be taken to show the lowest profits up to the balance sheet date. (But doing this will result in a higher profit in the following period when the inventory is sold!)
5 **The capacity to borrow money or to sell the business at the highest possible price.** The higher the inventory value, the higher will be the profits calculated and, therefore, at first sight the business looks more attractive to a buyer or lender. Either of these considerations may be more important to the owners than anything else. It may be thought that those in business are not so gullible, but all business people are not necessarily well acquainted with accounting customs. In fact, many small businesses are bought, or money is lent to them, without the expert advice of someone well versed in accounting.
6 **Remuneration purposes.** Where someone managing a business is paid in whole or in part by reference to the profits earned, then one basis may suit them better than others. They may therefore strive to have that basis used to suit their own ends. The owner, however, may try to follow another course to minimise the remuneration that he/she will have to pay out.
7 **Lack of information.** If proper inventory records have not been kept, then such bases as the average cost method or the LIFO method may not be calculable using the approaches you learnt at the start of this chapter. Of course, a lack of proper inventory records makes it very difficult to detect theft or losses of inventory. If for no other reason than to enable these factors to be controlled, proper inventory records should be kept by all trading businesses. As a result, this barrier to adopting AVCO and LIFO should not arise very often.
8 **Advice of the auditors.** Auditors are accountants who review the accounting records and the financial statements in order to report whether or not the financial statements present a true and fair view of the financial performance and financial position of a business. Many businesses use a particular basis because the auditors advised its use in the first instance. A different auditor may well advise that a different basis be used.

18.11 The conflict of aims

The list given in the previous section of some of the factors which affect decisions concerning the valuation of inventory is certainly not exhaustive, but it does illustrate the fact that valuation is usually a compromise. There is not usually only one figure which is true and fair; there may be a variety of possibilities. The desire to borrow money and, in so doing, to paint a good picture by being reasonably optimistic in valuing inventory will be tempered by the fact that this may increase the tax bill. Inventory valuation is, therefore, a compromise between the various ends which it serves.

18.12 Work-in-progress

The valuation of work-in-progress is subject to all the various criteria and methods used in valuing inventory of finished goods. Probably the cost element is more strongly pronounced than in inventory valuation, as it is very often impossible or irrelevant to say what net realisable value or replacement price would be applicable to partly finished goods. Businesses operating in industries such as those which have contracts covering several years have evolved their own methods.

The valuation of long-term contract work-in-progress is regulated by IAS 11 (*Construction contracts*) and is dealt with in *Frank Wood's Business Accounting 2*.

18.13 Goods on sale or return

Goods received on sale or return

Sometimes goods may be received from a supplier on a **sale or return** basis. This is, for example, typically what happens when newsagents purchase newspapers. What this means is that the goods do not have to be paid for if they are not sold. If they cannot be sold, they are returned to the supplier. This means that until the goods are sold they belong to the seller, *not* the buyer.

The effect of an arrangement of this type is that there isn't a liability to pay the seller until the goods have been sold on to a customer of the buyer. If there is no liability, the buyer cannot recognise the existence of the goods held on this basis when the buyer's financial statements are being prepared at the end of the reporting period. As a result, if goods on sale or return are held by the buyer at the stocktaking date (i.e. the date when inventory is counted), they should not be included in the buyer's inventory valuation, nor in the figure for purchases.

Goods sent to customers on sale or return

If a seller sends goods to a customer on a sale or return basis, the goods will continue to belong to the seller until they are sold on by the buyer. At the end of the supplier's reporting period, any goods held on this basis by its customers should be included in the seller's inventory valuation, not in the figure for sales.

18.14 Stocktaking and the date of the balance sheet

All but the very smallest of trading businesses need to physically check that the inventory their records tell them they have actually exists. The process of doing so is called **stocktaking**. Students often think that all the counting and valuing of inventory is done on the last day of the accounting period. This might be true in a small business, but it is often impossible in larger businesses. There may be too many items of inventory to do it that quickly.

This means that stocktaking may take place over a period of days. To convert the physical stocktake inventory levels to their actual levels at the balance sheet date, adjustments must be made to the inventory levels found during the stocktake. Exhibit 18.4 gives an example of such adjustments.

Exhibit 18.4 Adjustments to inventory following stocktake

Lee Ltd has a financial year which ends on 31 December 2017. The stocktaking is not done until 8 January 2018; the items in the inventory on that date are valued at their cost of £28,850. The following information is available about transactions between 31 December 2017 and 8 January 2018:

1 Purchases since 31 December 2017 amounted to £2,370 at cost.
2 Returns inwards since 31 December 2017 were £350 at selling price.
3 Sales since 31 December 2017 amounted to £3,800 at selling price.
4 The selling price is always cost price + 25 per cent.

Lee Ltd
Computation of inventory on 31 December 2017

			£
Inventory (at cost)			28,850
Add Items now sold which were in inventory on 31 December 2017 (at cost)			
		£	
Sales		3,800	
Less Profit content (20 per cent of selling price)^{Note}		(760)	
			3,040
Less Items which were not in inventory on 31 December 2017 (at cost)			31,890
	£		
Returns inwards	350		
Less Profit content (20 per cent of selling price)^{Note}	(70)		
		280	
Purchases (at cost)		2,370	
			(2,650)
Inventory in hand as on 31 December 2017			29,240

Note: Inventory is valued at cost (or net realisable value), and not at selling price. As this calculation has a sales figure in it which includes profit, we must deduct the profit part to get to the cost price. This is true also for returns inwards.

The professional accountancy bodies encourage the auditors of companies to be present as observers at stocktaking in order to verify that procedures were correctly followed.

18.15 Inventory levels

One of the most common mistakes found in the running of a business is that too high a level of inventory is maintained.

A considerable number of businesses that have problems with a shortage of funds will find that they can help matters by having a look at the amount of inventory they hold. It would be a very rare business indeed which, if it had not investigated the matter previously, could not manage to let parts of its inventory run down. This would stop the investment of funds in items – the unneeded inventory – that are not required.

Learning outcomes

You should now have learnt:

1 That methods of valuing inventory, such as FIFO, LIFO and AVCO, are only that – methods of *valuing* inventory. It does not mean that goods are actually sold on a FIFO or LIFO basis.

2 That because different methods of valuing inventory result in different closing inventory valuations, the amount of profit reported for a particular accounting period is affected by the method of inventory valuation adopted.

3 That using net realisable when this is lower than cost, so that profits are not overstated, is an example of the application of the prudence concept in accounting.

4 That many subjective factors may affect the choice of inventory valuation method adopted.

5 That without inventory records of quantities of items, it would be very difficult to track down theft or losses or to detect wastage of goods.

6 That without proper inventory records, it is unlikely that AVCO and LIFO can be applied in the way described at the start of this chapter.

7 That goods sold on sale or return should be included in the inventory of the seller until the buyer has sold them.

8 That stocktaking is usually done over a period of time around the end of the accounting period.

9 That the inventory levels identified at a stocktake need to be adjusted to the level they would have been at had the stocktake taken place on the balance sheet date.

Answers to activities

18.1 This is not as easy a question to answer as it first appears, especially if you have never studied this topic before. Firstly, applying the historic cost convention you learnt about in Chapter 10, we should value the inventory at the cost of having it available for sale. That is, it should be valued at cost. If all purchases during the year cost the same per unit, arriving at the value to place on inventory would be trivially easy. For example, if all of the units cost £30 each, the closing value would be $8 \times £30 = £240$.

However, the goods in this example have been purchased at different prices. To cope with this, we look at it from the perspective of which of the goods purchased have been sold. Knowing which of them has been sold allows us to know which ones remain unsold, which will make valuing the inventory very straightforward. In this case, purchases were made at £30, £34 and £40. If all the £34 and £40 purchases have been sold, we know to use £30 as the unit cost of the stock.

Unfortunately, many businesses do not know whether they have sold all the older units before they sell the newer units. For instance, a business selling spanners may not know if the older spanners had been sold before the newer ones were sold. A petrol station doesn't know whether all the fuel it has was from one delivery or whether it is a mixture of all the deliveries received from the supplier. Accounting deals with this by selecting the method of valuation that is most likely to fairly represent the cost of the goods sold and, hence, the value of the remaining inventory.

To answer the question, you don't have enough information to decide what value to place on the eight units of inventory, but it should be based upon the best estimate you can make of the cost of those eight units.

18.2 As at least eight units were received in the last batch purchased, you can simply take the unit cost of that batch and multiply it by the units in inventory. If you are asked to show your workings for calculation of closing inventory under FIFO, this is a perfectly acceptable approach to adopt.

18.3 It's not so simple under LIFO. If you receive three batches of purchases of ten, four and six units respectively and you have ten left in inventory, there is no guarantee that they will all be from the first batch. You may have sold all ten of the first batch before the second batch was received. Alternatively, you may have sold three before the second batch of four was delivered and then sold six before the last batch of six was received and then sold one before the year end. You do have ten in inventory, but five are from the first batch received and five from the last one. There is no shortcut available for ascertaining in which batch the remaining inventory was received.

18.4 There have been no further deliveries of new inventory received so the average value of inventory is still £37.

18.5 The AVCO inventory valuation is between the values of FIFO and LIFO. FIFO has the highest value because the cost of purchases has been rising. Had they been falling, it would have been LIFO that had the greatest closing inventory value. AVCO will lie between the other two whichever way prices are moving.

18.6 (a) Gross profit will be understated if closing inventory is undervalued because the lower the value of closing inventory, the higher the cost of goods sold.
(b) Gross profit will be overstated if closing inventory is overvalued because the higher the value of closing inventory, the lower the cost of goods sold.

18.7 It may be impossible. However, whatever the quality of your inventory records, all businesses must retain evidence of their transactions. As a result, you could have a record of what was purchased, when, from whom and for how much, but you may well have no record at all of what was sold, when, to whom or for how much – if all sales are for cash, your only record may be the till receipt for each transaction, and that frequently shows no more than the date and value of the sale.

Review questions

18.1 From the following figures calculate the closing inventory-in-trade that would be shown using (*i*) FIFO, (*ii*) LIFO, (*iii*) AVCO methods.

Bought		Sold	
March	400 at £30 each	December	420 for £40 each
September	300 at £32 each		

18.2 For Review Question 18.1 draw up the trading account part of the income statement for the year showing the gross profits that would have been reported using (*i*) FIFO, (*ii*) LIFO, (*iii*) AVCO methods.

18.3A From the following figures calculate the closing inventory-in-trade that would be shown using (*i*) FIFO, (*ii*) LIFO, (*iii*) AVCO methods on a perpetual inventory basis.

Bought		Sold	
January	120 at £16 each	June	125 at £22 each
April	80 at £18 each	November	210 at £25 each
October	150 at £19 each		

18.4A Draw up trading account parts of the income statement using each of the three methods from the details in Review Question 18.3A.

18.5 The sixth formers at the Broadway School run a tuck shop business. They began trading on 1 December 2019 and sell two types of chocolate bar, 'Break' and 'Brunch'.

Their starting capital was a £200 loan from the School Fund.
Transactions are for cash only.
Each Break costs the sixth form 16p and each Brunch costs 12p.
25% is added to the cost to determine the selling price.
Transactions during December are summarised as follows:

December 6   Bought 5 boxes, each containing 48 bars, of Break; and 3 boxes, each containing 36 bars of Brunch.
December 20   The month's sales amounted to 200 Breaks and 90 Brunches.

(a) Record the above transactions in the cash, purchases and sales accounts. All calculations must be shown.
(b) On 20 December (the final day of term) a physical stocktaking showed 34 Break and 15 Brunch in inventory. Using these figures calculate the value of the closing inventory, and enter the amount in the inventory account.
(c) Prepare a trading account for the tuck shop, calculating the gross profit/loss for the month of December 2019.^{Author's Note}
(d) Calculate the number of each item that should have been in inventory. Explain why this information should be a cause for concern.

(*Edexcel, London Examinations: GCSE*)

Author's Note: Examiners typically only ask for 'a trading account' in questions rather than 'the trading account section of the income statement'. If you get a question asking for 'a trading account', assume you are being asked to prepare the trading account section of the income statement unless it is obvious that the examiner wants the trading account in the ledger rather than the financial statement.

18.6 Thomas Brown and Partners, a business of practising accountants, have several clients who are retail distributors of the Allgush Paint Spray guns.

The current price list of Gushing Sprayers Limited, manufacturers, quotes the following wholesale prices for the Allgush Paint Spray guns:

Grade A distributors   £500 each
Grade B distributors   £560 each
Grade C distributors   £600 each

The current normal retail price of the Allgush Paint Spray gun is £750.

Thomas Brown and Partners are currently advising some of their clients concerning the valuation of stock in trade of Allgush Paint Spray guns.

1 Charles Gray – Grade B distributor
On 30 April 2019, 15 Allgush Paint Spray guns were in inventory, including one gun which was slightly damaged and expected to sell at half the normal retail price. Charles Gray considers that this gun should remain in inventory at cost price until it is sold.

K. Peacock, a customer of Charles Gray, was expected to purchase a spray gun on 30 April 2019, but no agreement was reached owing to the customer being involved in a road accident and expected to remain in hospital until late May 2019.

Charles Gray argues that he is entitled to regard this as a sale during the year ended 30 April 2019.

→

2   Jean Kim – Grade C distributor

On 31 May 2019, 22 Allgush Paint Spray guns were in inventory. Unfortunately Jean Kim's business is suffering a serious cash flow crisis. It is very doubtful that the business will survive and therefore a public auction of the inventory-in-trade is likely. Reliable sources suggest that the spray guns may be auctioned for £510 each; auction fees and expenses are expected to total £300.

Jean Kim has requested advice as to the basis upon which her inventory should be valued at 31 May 2019.

3   Peter Fox – Grade A distributor

Peter Fox now considers that inventory valuations should be related to selling prices because of the growing uncertainties of the market for spray guns.

Alternatively, Peter Fox has suggested that he uses the cost prices applicable to Grade C distributors as the basis for inventory valuations – 'after all this will establish consistency with Grade C distributors'.

Required:

A brief report to each of Charles Gray, Jean Kim and Peter Fox concerning the valuation of their inventories-in-trade.

Note: Answers should include references to appropriate accounting concepts.

(*Association of Accounting Technicians*)

18.7A   Mary Smith commenced trading on 1 September 2019 as a distributor of the Straight Cut garden lawn mower, a relatively new product which is now becoming increasingly popular.

Upon commencing trading, Mary Smith transferred £7,000 from her personal savings to open a business bank account.

Mary Smith's purchases and sales of the Straight Cut garden lawn mower during the three months ended 30 November 2019 are as follows:

2019	Bought	Sold
September	12 machines at £384 each	–
October	8 machines at £450 each	4 machines at £560 each
November	16 machines at £489 each	20 machines at £680 each

Assume all purchases are made in the first half of the month and all sales are in the second half of the month.

At the end of October 2019, Mary Smith decided to take one Straight Cut garden lawn mower out of inventory for cutting the lawn outside her showroom. It is estimated that this lawn mower will be used in Mary Smith's business for eight years and have a nil estimated residual value. Mary Smith wishes to use the straight line basis of depreciation.

Additional information:

1   Overhead expenses paid during the three months ended 30 November 2019 amounted to £1,520.
2   There were no amounts prepaid on 30 November 2019, but sales commissions payable of 2½ of the gross profit on sales were accrued due on 30 November 2019.
3   Upon commencing trading, Mary Smith resigned a business appointment with a salary of £15,000 per annum.
4   Mary Smith is able to obtain interest of 10% per annum on her personal savings.
5   One of the lawn mowers not sold on 30 November 2019 has been damaged in the showroom and is to be repaired in December 2019 at a cost of £50 before being sold for an expected £400.

Note: Ignore taxation.

Required:

(a) Prepare, in as much detail as possible, Mary Smith's income statement for the quarter ending 30 November 2019 using:

(i) the first in first out basis of inventory valuation, and

(ii) the last in first out basis of inventory valuation.

(b) Using the results in (a) (i) above, prepare a statement comparing Mary Smith's income for the quarter ended 30 November 2019 with that for the quarter ended 31 August 2019.

(c) Give one advantage and one disadvantage of each of the bases of inventory valuations used in (a) above.

(*Association of Accounting Technicians*)

18.8 'The idea that inventory should be included in accounts at the lower of historical cost and net realisable value follows the prudence convention but not the consistency convention.'

Required:

(a) Do you agree with the quotation?

(b) Explain, with reasons, whether you think this idea (that inventory should be included in accounts at the lower of historical cost and net realisable value) is a useful one. Refer to at least two classes of user of financial accounting reports in your answer.

(*Associaation of Chartered Certified Accountants*)

18.9 After stocktaking for the year ended 31 May 2019 had taken place, the closing inventory of Cobden Ltd was aggregated to a figure of £87,612.

During the course of the audit which followed, the undernoted facts were discovered:

(a) Some goods stored outside had been included at their normal cost price of £570. They had, however, deteriorated and would require an estimated £120 to be spent to restore them to their original condition, after which they could be sold for £800.

(b) Some goods had been damaged and were now unsaleable. They could, however, be sold for £110 as spares after repairs estimated at £40 had been carried out. They had originally cost £200.

(c) One inventory sheet had been over-added by £126 and another under-added by £72.

(d) Cobden Ltd had received goods costing £2,010 during the last week of May 2019 but, because the invoices did not arrive until June 2019, they have not been included in inventory.

(e) An inventory sheet total of £1,234 had been transferred to the summary sheet as £1,243.

(f) Invoices totalling £638 arrived during the last week of May 2019 (and were included in purchases and in accounts payable) but, because of transport delays, the goods did not arrive until late June 2019 and were not included in closing inventory.

(g) Portable generators on hire from another company at a charge of £347 were included, at this figure, in inventory.

(h) Free samples sent to Cobden Ltd by various suppliers had been included in inventory at the catalogue price of £63.

(i) Goods costing £418 sent to customers on a sale or return basis had been included in inventory by Cobden Ltd at their selling price, £602.

(j) Goods sent on a sale or return basis to Cobden Ltd had been included in inventory at the amount payable (£267) if retained. No decision to retain had been made.

Required:

Using such of the above information as is relevant, prepare a schedule amending the inventory figure as at 31 May 2019. State your reason for each amendment or for not making an amendment.

(*Association of Chartered Certified Accountants*)

→

18.10A Yuan Ltd has an accounting year ended 28 February 2018. Due to staff shortages, the stocktaking had not been undertaken until 9 March 2018 and the inventory valued at this date is £100,600. This value was also used in the company draft accounts for the year ended 28 February 2018 which showed a net profit of £249,600 and a current asset total of £300,000. The selling price of goods is based on cost plus 25%.

During the company audit, the following errors were discovered:

1 Sales invoices for goods dispatched to customers during the period 1–9 March 2018 amounted to £43,838 which include carriage on sales of 5%.
2 Goods costing £14,000 were delivered to the company during the period 1–9 March 2018.
3 During the period 1–9 March 2018, returns from customers at selling price were £4,170, and returns to suppliers amounted to £850.
4 The inventory valuation of 9 March 2018 included the inventory of the company's office cleaning materials. These materials had all been bought during February 2018 at a cost of £600.
5 Inventory with a selling price of £1,650 had been borrowed by the marketing department on 27 February 2018 to be displayed at an exhibition from 28 February to 16 March. This had helped to attract orders of £27,400 for delivery in April 2018.
6 Inventory with a selling price of £800 was sent to a customer on sale or return basis on 14 February 2018. On 23 February 2018, the customer sold half of the consignment. This credit sale had not yet been recorded in Yuan Ltd's accounts for the year ended 28 February 2018. On 9 March 2018, the remaining half of the consignment had not been returned to Yuan Ltd, and the customer had not signified its acceptance.
7 On 3 March 2018, Yuan Ltd received a batch of free samples which had been included in the inventory valuation at the list price of £20.

Required:
(a) Prepare a schedule amending the inventory figure as at 28 February 2018.
(b) Calculate the revised net profit for the year ending 28 February 2018 and the correct value of current assets at that date.

ACCOUNTING TODAY

Introduction
This part presents an overview of accounting in the modern world, the accounting profession and the practice of accounting.

Accounting today

Learning objectives

After you have studied this chapter you should be able to:

- outline in general some of the principal attractions of working as an accountant today
- discuss some common preconceptions about careers in accountancy and assess how accurate they might be
- explain the range of skills required to be a successful accountant
- describe the different pathways to becoming a qualified professional accountant in the UK
- outline what it's actually like to work in accounting today (for some of the common job roles available to qualified accountants)
- describe some of the issues which might affect the work of the accountants of tomorrow

Introduction

You may be considering a career as a professional accountant in the future. In this chapter, you'll learn about some of the potential attractions of working as an accountant. We'll also look at three negative preconceptions concerning the career, and assess how accurate they might be. Next you'll learn that the best accountants possess a range of skills and attributes that extends way beyond just technical expertise: if you wish to build a successful career in accountancy you would be wise to start thinking about developing some of these skills now.

We'll go on to examine the various routes you can take to become a qualified accountant in the UK, and get a feel for what it's actually like to work as an accountant today. Finally, this chapter will consider a sample of the developments that may have an impact on the accountants of tomorrow.

19.1 Is accountancy a good career choice for you?

Whether accounting is a suitable profession for you depends very much on your attributes and personality, and the priorities you have for your life. However, we can make some general observations about the benefits of a career as an accountant that might help you begin to consider whether it may be a good choice.

The earning potential is excellent

This is probably the most well-known advantage. It is, of course, very easy to search on the internet for the average salary of an accountant, but your results will probably indicate a range of different 'average' figures. Different sources evidently have alternative ways of calculating the average. In any case, the 'average' can be quite misleading because there is such a wide range.

In the UK there will be a fair number of qualified accountants earning six-figure salaries, but many others in the £40,000–£60,000 bracket. However, what is clear is that qualified accountants command very decent salaries, significantly more than national average earnings. In Section 19.11 we'll start looking a bit closer at some of the different job roles in accountancy and Exhibit 19.1 shows the range of 2017 UK salaries for those jobs.

There are accounting jobs everywhere

All sizes and types of organisation require accounting services of some kind. This means that there are opportunities for accountants to find work everywhere, in large cities or small towns throughout the country. This gives accountants flexibility in choosing where they want to work. It also holds true internationally: organisations all over the world require accounting services and professional accounting qualifications are recognised internationally, so there may be scope to live and work overseas in your career too.

Demand for accountants is growing

Accountants have been needed for centuries and there is no indication that this demand is diminishing. All types of organisations require some sort of accounting services so the demand for accountants typically increases in line with economic growth. One implication of this is that there will always be more job opportunities for accountants in more prosperous areas of a country compared to struggling regions. But all over the country, there is always likely to be a reasonable number of job opportunities for qualified accountants.

You can aim to work in an industry that interests you

Again, because organisations of all types require accountants this means you can seek to work in an industry in which you have a real interest. The fashion, music, media, film, sport and automotive industries, as well as the charitable sector, might be areas that could interest you.

David Gill (former CEO of Manchester United), Barry Hearn (the snooker and boxing promoter), David Ross (co-founder of Carphone Warehouse), and David Bernstein (former chairman of the English Football Association) are just a few examples of chartered accountants who have built successful careers in sectors they have a real passion for.

There is great potential for career development

The professional accounting qualification is an outstanding business qualification that can form the platform for a variety of lucrative career paths. The most senior accounting roles (such as the chief financial officer of a company, or partner in an accounting firm) are very well-paid. Another option is to start your own accounting firm and work for yourself, which has its own attractions.

The qualification can also form the basis for branching out into a career in the city: companies like Goldman Sachs and JP Morgan commonly recruit newly qualified accountants for roles in finance and investment analysis. Finally, if your aim is the top job in a company (the chief executive officer, or CEO) then, of all business backgrounds, an accountancy qualification gives you the best chance of achieving this: the UK recruitment firm Robert Half reported in 2015 that nearly a quarter of CEOs of FTSE100 companies were chartered accountants, and over half came from a finance background.

19.2 Negative preconceptions about careers in accountancy

It's possible that you might have one or more of the following three reservations about a career in accounting. We'll consider all three, and consider how accurate they might be:

'Accountancy is boring'

There is a fairly widely held view, particularly in the UK, that accounting is a dull profession. A single sketch by Monty Python (the popular British comedy group) in 1969 is partially credited for creating the popular stereotype of accountants being boring (search YouTube for 'Monty Python Vocational Guidance Counsellor'). It is a reputation that has endured for decades.

However, the stereotype is not necessarily realistic: a day in the life of an accountant tends to consist of meetings, phone calls, paperwork and emails, which may not be particularly glamorous but neither is it very different from the vast majority of other office-based careers. Certainly the image of an accountant as a lonely 'number cruncher' tapping figures into his or her calculator for hours on end is completely outdated. Modern technology has meant that most basic book-keeping tasks are completely automated, and the role of today's accountant is more about analys-ing, interpreting, communicating and acting upon the information that the computer systems provide.

Accountants have therefore become integral to the management team of the business, working alongside colleagues from marketing, purchasing and production with the aim of driving the busi-ness forward. They typically have an overview of the entire organisation, which is one of the reasons why it isn't unusual for the CEO of a company to be an accountant.

Accordingly, the image of accountants is definitely changing: ICAEW magazine *Economia* reported a 2017 UK survey that found accountants were the fourth most desirable professionals that people would most like to date (after doctors, emergency service workers and artists)! If you watch the original Monty Python sketch it will quickly become apparent that the business world has changed dramatically since 1969, and so has accountancy.

'Accountancy is a stressful profession'

Accountants are typically responsible for large sums of money, need to be constantly vigilant that no significant mistakes are going undetected, and can sometimes feel that they are on a treadmill of meeting a series of monthly deadlines. At face value, the advance of technology might be assumed to have made accountants' jobs easier, but in reality technology tends to increase the requirements to produce and communicate results quicker and more accurately than ever before.

Additionally, the majority of working accountants find themselves in middle-management, needing to meet their bosses' demands at the same time as supervising a team of staff beneath them. In 2015 the Chartered Accountants Benevolent Association in the UK reported research that 32 per cent of accountants feel stressed by their work. However, to put that statistic in con-text, two points seem relevant:

1 Stress is a fairly subjective concept that is not easy to measure, but there is little evidence that accountancy is one of the most stressful careers today. Surveys suggest that soldiers, firefighters and airline pilots have the most stressful jobs by far. This is understandable: people in such roles face the risk of personal injury (or even death) to themselves or others. These are not hazards typically faced by accountants, so it's important to keep the stress experienced by accountants in perspective.

2 To a certain extent, the level of stress that an employee experiences can depend on their personality type as well as the actual job itself. In the face of busy schedules, multiple deadlines and high expectations from bosses or clients, some accountants unfortunately struggle with stress while others might thrive under the pressure. In other words, it can be the response of the individual, as well as the job itself, that determines how much stress someone experiences. Those who are able to adopt a positive, resilient and optimistic mindset may suffer less from stress, while others might unfortunately be susceptible to it whatever career they choose to pursue.

'Accountants work very long hours'

It is difficult to report 'typical' working hours because of the many different types of accountancy jobs. A 2014 survey by recruitment firm Robert Walters reported that the 'average' working week of a UK accountant was just over 44 hours, but that 30 per cent of accountants worked more than 50 hours a week. There will also be peaks and troughs over the course of the year: for example, some financial accountants might work weekends around their company's year-end date; tax accountants will be extremely busy around the time of annual tax return deadlines, and so on.

So some accountants do sometimes work long hours, but it is important to note that this is a trend in all professional occupations. The world is becoming more competitive and this pressure affects all professions. The same Robert Walters survey indicated that professionals in financial services, sales and legal all work a longer average working week than accountants. When it comes to working long hours, accountancy does not seem to be worse than many other professions.

19.3 The skills required to be a successful professional accountant

Having considered some of the potential pros and cons of careers in accountancy it would now be appropriate to consider whether you possess (or at least have the potential to acquire) the qualities required to build a successful career in the profession. It is impossible to specify the exact mix of skills you'll need because of the wide range of different roles, specialisms, organisations and industries. But the following is a list of ten qualities that the majority of successful accountants should possess to some degree:

1 *Technical expertise*: this is the knowledge of a range of accounting methods and regulations and the ability to apply that knowledge appropriately in any given scenario. Acquiring and applying this expertise will require a high degree of 'academic' intelligence; the judgement to apply it appropriately will also develop as you gain experience as an accountant.

All accountants are expected to master the fundamental technical elements of accounting (such as the material covered in this book). But it is understood that no single accountant can know everything: the range and complexity of modern accounting work means that specialisation is essential.

A high degree of technical expertise will be essential in your chosen area. Furthermore, qualified accountants are required to undertake continuing professional development (CPD) activity on an annual basis to ensure that their technical expertise remains up to date.

2 *Numeracy skills*: many students study accounting because they feel they are good at maths and believe that accounting is 'all about numbers'. It is absolutely true that accountants must be good with numbers and it is certainly important that they avoid arithmetical mistakes. They also need to be able to analyse data, detect errors and anomalies, spot trends in the numbers, and explain accounting information to people who have little understanding of finance. Simply being able to use a calculator or a spreadsheet is not enough. Chapter 36, *Maths for accounting*, focuses on some of the key mathematical concepts and tools you will need.

3 *Attention to detail*: it has traditionally been important that accountants are dedicated to checking and reconciling figures precisely so that no mistakes go undetected. After all, the most minor discrepancy in the accounts could be the result of two huge errors (in opposite directions) so it is vital that accountants are meticulous in balancing figures to the penny.

Some observers suggest that the importance of *attention to detail* will diminish as more and more basic accounting tasks become completely automated. To give just one example: the bank reconciliation statement (Chapter 24) will often be produced automatically, because the company's accounting software is able to import the business's bank statements and automatically match them against the payments and receipts recorded in the company's books.

Nevertheless, computerisation cannot eliminate absolutely all errors so a need for attention to detail will surely remain.

4 *Problem-solving skills*: in studying for accounting exams you learn a set of rules, techniques and practices that form an essential foundation of knowledge of the subject. But you will quickly learn that in the real world situations continually arise that you have not encountered before. These problems will have to be solved by thinking and reasoning with intelligence and imagination.

Your own levels of intelligence and creativity will be key drivers of your problem-solving potential, but it's also a skill that will develop as you gain experience as an accountant. A 2015 survey by financial recruitment firm Robert Half indicated that *solving problems* was the most popular answer given by accountants when asked what part of their job they most enjoyed.

5 *Communication skills*: the most important skill of an accountant is the ability to communicate. Survey after survey over the past 40 years has ranked this skill at the top. Yet accountants have an image of being shy and introverted, so many who embark on an accounting career get a shock when they discover that they must talk frequently with clients, managers and colleagues, and even make public presentations, particularly if they work for large firms or multinational companies.

6 *Interpersonal skills*: these are of immense importance to accountants. All accountants need to work effectively with colleagues as part of a team. For those that work for firms of accountants, the ability to build good relationships with clients is crucial. And as an accountant's career progresses, the capacity to lead and motivate their team of staff will become increasingly necessary.

7 *Writing skills*: accountants should be able to write well. They will often be called upon to write-up analyses and reports as well as emails and letters. Trainee auditors, for example, will need to write accurate reports of their audit findings almost every day. The writing must be clear, coherent and professional. Some students consider a career in accountancy because they are 'good with numbers' and prefer to avoid writing. This is a mistake: a successful accountant needs to be strong in both departments.

8 *IT skills*: all but the very smallest organisations will use computer software to maintain their accounts. Most modern accounting software is very user-friendly, so bookkeeping and accounting knowledge tends to be more important than IT skills in order to make effective use of it. Computerised accounting systems simply mimic manual accounting systems, which is why the basics of manual accounting (such as those covered in this book) remain a universal requirement.

However, the advance of technology means that accountants have to get to grips with developments beyond just their accounting software. Cloud computing, digital currencies, online payment mechanisms, new methods of investment (e.g. crowdfunding), and the use of graphics and video tools to produce effective, user-friendly reports are some current examples. The accountant of today must be flexible and receptive to new technologies and be ready to learn how they can be used most effectively.

In addition, some 'old-school' IT competencies are still highly valued by employers. The most obvious of these is spreadsheet skills. Spreadsheets remain widely used by accountants today. A common complaint of employers who take on business undergraduates for work placements is that their spreadsheet skills (usually Microsoft Excel) are not great. **There is no doubt that improving your spreadsheet skills remains an excellent investment for an accounting career.**

If your school, college or university offers any Excel courses you would be wise to take advantage of them. Alternatively, you can find a range of training resources online. Many accomplished Excel users are largely self-taught. If you are logical and numerate you will probably get the hang of the basics quite quickly. But Excel is a large, powerful package with a huge number of functions and you will need to use it repeatedly in order to develop more advanced skills.

9 *Emotional intelligence*: the concept of emotional intelligence was first popularised by Daniel Goleman in his 1995 book of the same name. The book became an international bestseller and the concept soon became recognised as essential to success in any profession. Goleman explains that emotional intelligence includes abilities such as *'being able to motivate oneself and persist in the face of frustrations; to control impulse and delay gratification; to regulate one's moods and keep distress from swamping the ability to think.'*

It certainly seems intuitively true that these sorts of qualities will be necessary to succeed in any modern career. Goleman presents the case that emotional intelligence is actually more important than both academic record and traditional measures of intelligence (IQ) as a predictor of how well a person will perform in their working life, and his arguments have a strong statistical and scientific basis.

10 *Ethics and integrity*: more than ever, accountants are expected to behave (and be seen to behave) with honesty, objectivity and fidelity. The 2007–8 financial crisis, as well as high-profile accounting scandals in recent years (involving companies such as Enron in the US, Satyam in India, or Tesco in the UK), have tended to contribute to the public's perception that many finance professionals are greedy, unethical and out of control.

As a result, professional accountancy bodies have worked hard to raise the profile of the principles and codes of conduct that accountants are expected to abide by. Modern professional training seeks to implant these principles and guidelines within accountants, but clearly it is preferable if those entering the profession are by nature inclined to behave with honesty and integrity in the first place.

 Activity 19.1 You could encounter ethical dilemmas in your capacity as a student of accounting. Can you suggest any?

Assuming you have read some of this book already it will be apparent to you that of the ten attributes listed above *technical expertise* is emphasised more than the other nine. Your numeracy skills will certainly be developed, and the need for attention to detail is implicit in much of the material, but some of the other skills aren't covered at all. Competencies like 'interpersonal skills' and 'emotional intelligence' are entirely absent from this (and virtually all) accounting textbooks. This is arguably a shortcoming of accounting education in general. Many schools, colleges and universities have tended to emphasise teaching traditional, academic knowledge, and the 'soft skills' receive less coverage.

In fairness, many schools and universities now run courses in 'personal development' and 'skills for accountants' but they usually make up only a small percentage of the curriculum. Moreover, things like 'interpersonal skills' and 'emotional intelligence' include a broad range of qualities that are not so easy to teach and develop. And some of these 'soft skills' are genetically predetermined to a certain extent, which means developing them may take a lot of practice.

Whatever your future career you would be wise to invest in developing your soft skills as much as possible. Suggestions could include getting as much as you can out of any 'personal development' or 'skills' courses that are available wherever you are studying; gaining work experience, especially working in teams; getting involved in a range of clubs and societies; competing in team sports; and cultivating your network of real, face-to-face friends.

Some employers fear that millennials are in danger of being a 'socially awkward generation' who prefer to communicate using SMS and social media and can be uncomfortable communicating and collaborating face-to-face. If this fear is justified then those who invest in developing their soft skills will have an even greater advantage in their future careers than ever before.

19.4 The scope of the accounting profession

You may be considering a career in accounting in the future. Before looking at the different pathways into the profession we need to clarify that accountants essentially work in one of three areas. Broadly speaking, accountants work:

1 *'In practice'*: Those 'in practice' work for professional firms of accountants that provide accounting, taxation and other services to their clients, who will be a range of different individuals and businesses. You may have heard of the 'Big Four' accounting firms (PwC, Deloitte, EY and KPMG). These are large, multinational firms that hire significant numbers of trainees every year around the world. But there are many other small- and medium-sized accounting firms that also recruit annually.

2 *'In industry'*: Accountants 'in industry' work for businesses across all sectors of the economy: retail, manufacturing, construction, financial services, and so on. All businesses above a certain size will usually employ at least one professional accountant. Larger businesses will have a team of accountants, each with different specialisms, roles and levels of seniority. Many of these larger businesses recruit trainee accountants each year.

3 *'In the public sector'*: Accountants in the public sector work for organisations such as the National Health Service (NHS), the government or the armed forces. The primary objectives of organisations in the public and private sectors differ: in the private sector the main objective of most businesses is to make a profit, whereas public sector organisations principally exist to provide services to the public. This fundamental difference means that the financial statements of public sector organisations are somewhat different to those in the private sector.

Many public sector organisations recruit accounting trainees every year, and there are plenty of opportunities for career development in that sector. However, be aware that it can be difficult to transfer to the private sector later in your career because of the differences. You can read more about public sector accounting in *Frank Wood's Business Accounting 2*.

19.5 The pathways to becoming a qualified professional accountant

Professional accountants (whether they work in practice, in industry or in the public sector) usually possess a professional accounting qualification. The majority (but certainly not all) will also have a university degree (although the degree does not have to be in accounting: it can be in any reputable subject).

Activity 19.2 To become a doctor you must study a degree in medicine, but to become an accountant your degree does not have to be in accounting. What is the point, therefore, of studying a degree in accounting?

To become qualified as a professional accountant you must pass a set of professional exams and also gain 3–4 years' work experience. This involves obtaining a job as a trainee and working as a junior accountant while at the same time sitting the exams. The exams are notoriously difficult and not all trainees will manage to pass them. Once a trainee has passed all the exams and has gained sufficient work experience they will become a qualified member of their professional body. At this point their salary will typically rise quite sharply.

The majority of trainee vacancies are aimed at graduates, but some organisations also recruit non-graduates to work in accounting. Non-graduate routes include first qualifying as an 'accounting technician'. The 'Association of Accounting Technicians' (AAT) qualification, for example, is widely respected and internationally recognised. Moreover, professional accountancy bodies typically offer a generous level of exemptions from several of their exams to those who are already AAT-qualified.

19.6 The different professional accountancy bodies in the UK

Rather confusingly there are six major professional accountancy bodies in the UK and each has its own set of exams:

1 ICAEW: the Institute of Chartered Accountants in England and Wales (members have the letters ACA or FCA after their names).
2 ICAS: the Institute of Chartered Accountants of Scotland (members have the letters CA after their names).
3 CAI: now known simply as 'Chartered Accountants Ireland' (members have the letters ACA or FCA after their names).
4 ACCA: the Association of Chartered Certified Accountants (members have the letters ACCA or FCCA after their names).
5 CIMA: the Chartered Institute of Management Accountants (members have the letters ACMA or FCMA after their names).
6 CIPFA: the Chartered Institute of Public Finance and Accountancy (members have the letters CPFA after their names).

All six are internationally recognised and highly respected qualifications. Which body you qualify with generally depends on what type of organisation you work for and the preferences of your employer:

● If you are training 'in practice' with a firm of accountants you will typically study for either the ICAEW, ICAS, CAI or ACCA qualification.
● If you are employed 'in industry' by a company you will normally work towards either CIMA or ACCA.
● Trainees in the public sector will commonly study either the CIPFA or CIMA exams.

Once qualified, many members of ICAEW, ICAS, CAI and ACCA who have trained with an accountancy firm subsequently move into careers 'in industry'.

19.7 Obtaining a position as a graduate trainee in accountancy

Regardless of which body you train with, there are some important general points in relation to what is necessary to obtain a position as an accountancy graduate trainee:

1 For the most desirable graduate trainee positions in the UK, organisations will sometimes look for a high number of UCAS points as well as a good degree. **Competition for places can be stiff and the selection process rigorous.** If you are studying at university you should definitely take

advantage of the support that your careers service can offer in relation to selection tests, assessment centres and interview practice.

2 Many positions are first advertised in the autumn, so undergraduates should start applying at the beginning of their final year in order to maximise their chances. **Every year, a surprisingly large proportion of final year undergraduates fail to apply for jobs until far later than this, which usually proves to be a costly error.**

3 It is highly advantageous to have relevant work experience such as shadowing, vacation work or a formal work placement. **A year's work placement is perhaps the single best thing that undergraduates can do to their CV in order to enhance their employability.** If you are an undergraduate and your university runs a 'placement' year scheme you would be wise to consider undertaking one.

4 Your starting salary as a trainee accountant may be a little lower than (say) some graduate roles in general management. This is because your employer will instead invest several thousands of pounds in your professional training and exams. Once you qualify, rest assured that your salary will more than catch up.

19.8 The differences between training with the different professional accountancy bodies

The professional accountancy exams will develop extensive understanding across a wide range of accountancy, finance and business areas. But the exact syllabus you study will differ depending on which body you qualify with. The CIMA exams, for example, will place greater emphasis on *management accounting* than the others. All six bodies update their syllabuses regularly. The websites of each will, of course, give full details of exactly what you would study.

19.9 Career options after qualifying with one of the professional accountancy bodies

Once qualified with a professional body there are a wide range of career options, but some general points can be made:

1 Those who train in an accountancy firm can remain employed in that sector (with career progression to the level of manager or even partner). Alternatively, they might set up their own accounting practice and work for themselves. A third option would be to move into 'industry', where becoming the chief financial officer (CFO) of a company might be their ultimate aim. Finally, there is also the option of using the qualification to move into a field like banking, finance or consultancy.

2 Those who train in industry will typically stay in industry, with potential to progress to the level of CFO or even chief executive officer (CEO). There also may be opportunities to move into areas such as business analysis, project management or management consultancy.

3 The careers of those who train in the public sector will often remain connected to the public sector because of the specialist nature of their experience and qualifications.

19.10 What is it like to work as a trainee accountant?

Owing to the varying specialisms of trainees, different sizes of organisations, and other factors, it is impossible to describe the 'typical' working life of a trainee accountant. However, the following three general comments can be made:

1 Those who train with a firm of accountants will work in one of the firm's departments: audit, tax or one of various others. The majority of vacancies are usually in audit (which is also

sometimes known as 'assurance'). An 'audit' essentially involves reviewing the annual financial statements (and the underlying financial records) of a company. On the basis of that review, the auditors give an opinion on whether the financial statements provide a true and fair view of that company's financial position and performance.

As a trainee auditor the majority of your time will be spent at clients' premises. This will entail quite a bit of travelling, and overnight stays will sometimes be necessary. Following instructions from more senior members of the audit team, you will carry out 'audit tests' to check the accuracy of the client's financial records and the reliability of their systems and controls. You will also be expected to identify any weaknesses in their procedures and suggest solutions.

2 If you train 'in industry' you will be employed full-time by one company so will normally commute to the same place of work each day. It is possible that there could be some travel if your organisation is based across various sites; overseas travel or secondment could be possible if you work for a multinational company. Your time will typically involve a combination of analytical work at your desk, formal and informal meetings with colleagues, and emails and phone calls. With the help of guidance and advice from senior colleagues, you will be involved in a range of accounting work that could include:

- assisting with the preparation of monthly financial statements for use by management within the company
- analysing financial reports to identify where actual performance is deviating from the plan, and determine trends or detect anomalies that need to be investigated
- analysing financial data and summarising it in report form
- working on projects to improve the company's financial systems or processes.

3 Regardless of whether they are working in practice or in industry, trainees will need to balance their workload with studying for the professional exams. The best employers will pay for all your tuition, and give you time off to attend classes as well as some additional study leave to revise. Tuition modes vary and can include day-release, block-release or evening classes.

Before accepting a job it is advisable to find out what the training and study package is: it is extremely difficult to pass the professional exams without good support. And regardless of the level of support, you will also need to undertake your own regular private study in evenings and at weekends if you wish to be successful.

19.11 What's it like to work in accounting once you are qualified?

If you search 'accountancy jobs' online your results will include a huge range of different job titles. This reflects the fact that there are many different types of accountant, with different levels of seniority for each type. There are so many different roles that it is impossible to describe the typical working day of a modern accountant. Instead, we'll look at just six of the many different job titles in accountancy and present a brief outline of what each might generally involve doing. The six roles are:

1 Audit manager
2 Audit partner
3 Tax adviser
4 Management accountant
5 Financial controller
6 Chief Financial Officer (CFO or 'Finance Director')

Before we begin, three general points about these six may be useful:

1 The first three jobs on the list involve working 'in practice' (for a firm of accountants), while the other three represent 'accountants in industry' (working for a company in any sector of the economy). In general, those in practice will travel more because client visits will be necessary.

In contrast, accountants 'in industry' will generally commute to and from the same place of work every day, although some travel may be necessary if the company operates from different sites. Regardless, an accountant working in industry will generally not be confined to their desk all day: there will be regular formal and informal meetings throughout the organisation.

2 It is difficult to be specific about the working hours of each of the six jobs. The actual hours worked in any accounting job will largely depend on the demands of that particular role and the culture in the organisation.

3 You may be interested to know the salaries earned by professional accountants. Exhibit 19.1 shows the results of a 2017 UK salary survey in relation to some of the jobs we look at in this chapter. The wide ranges indicated exist because the actual salary earned within each range shown will depend on the size, location and business sector of the organisation, and the seniority and responsibilities of the specific role.

Note that the ranges also appear to exclude some of those at the very top end: for example, a senior audit partner at a Big Four firm or the CFO of a FTSE 100 company would typically earn a seven-figure income.

Exhibit 19.1   Results of a 2017 UK salary survey

Job title	UK salary range 2017
Audit trainee	£18,250–£27,250
Audit manager	£33,500–£98,750
Audit partner	£100,000–£447,500
Assistant accountant (i.e. trainee in industry)	£18,750–£33,500
Management accountant	£36,000–£72,000
Financial controller	£49,000–£93,000
Chief Financial Officer (or 'Finance Director')	£64,500–£163,000

Source: figures extracted from the Robert Half 2017 UK Salary Guide, available at www.roberthalf.co.uk/salary-guide

19.12   What does an 'audit manager' do?

For those who train as auditors with an accounting firm then 2–4 years after qualifying they can expect to be promoted to 'audit manager'. Their role will be to plan and manage the audits of a set of clients, and they may act as line manager to a group of audit staff. Managers will typically spend some time out on site visiting clients and audit teams. This is necessary both to review the work the audit teams have done and to meet with the client.

When not on-site, audit managers will be based in the accounting firm's office and will be occupied with a variety of activities such as liaising with their on-site audit teams over the phone, planning upcoming audits, reviewing audit budgets, drafting reports to clients, and liaising with partners and other managers to deal with queries and resolve issues.

19.13   What does an 'audit partner' do?

After around 10–20 years as an auditor for an accounting firm there may be the possibility of being promoted to partner. Partnership is the pinnacle of the profession for those who work 'in practice'. A partner in a reasonably sized firm in the UK may expect to earn a six-figure income; the most senior partners in a 'Big Four' firm will receive a seven-figure income.

Each partner will look after a set of audit clients and they may be line manager to a number of audit managers. Activities will vary from day to day but will typically involve a mixture of:

● Meeting clients to discuss the issues that arose during the audit, and agree the client's final financial statements.
● Offering general business guidance to clients. In addition to audit skills, partners will be expected to fulfil the role of 'trusted business adviser' to their clients.
● Meeting with audit managers and fellow partners to discuss technical and operational issues that need to be resolved.
● Networking in business circles to help maintain and raise the profile of the firm.

Achieving promotion to partner is not easy. Accounting firms will have plenty of staff with outstanding technical expertise: what makes them stand out is the ability to build the trust and confidence of existing clients as well as being able to generate new fee income for the firm. The potential to win new clients and grow the firm is key to becoming partner. This means interpersonal, communication and networking skills are perhaps the most important in determining who will succeed.

19.14 What does a 'tax adviser' do?

Tax advisers work for firms of accountants and provide tax 'compliance' and 'consultancy' services to their clients. Clients may include companies, partnerships and wealthy individuals. 'Compliance' involves ensuring that the client has calculated their tax correctly and submitted their tax returns. 'Consultancy' involves advising clients on how to legally minimise the tax they pay.

There are several different types of tax in the UK and tax legislation is enormously complicated. It is therefore impossible for one person to master all aspects of tax. The larger accountancy firms are able to deal with this by employing specialists in particular areas, but in smaller firms the advisers may be expected to cover the range of different taxes.

The daily tasks of a tax adviser might typically include:

● communicating with clients to gather information and resolve queries
● completing and submitting tax returns on behalf of clients
● communicating and negotiating with the tax authorities (HM Revenue & Customs in the UK)
● studying and interpreting tax legislation
● working on tax planning schemes that will minimise the tax liabilities of clients within the bounds of current legislation

Tax advisers in the UK must pass a series of exams that culminate in them becoming a Chartered Tax Adviser (CTA). As with the audit profession, qualified advisers can expect to progress to manager within a few years. After that there is the potential to become a tax partner in the firm.

19.15 What does a 'management accountant' do?

As you learnt in Chapter 1, the main two branches of accounting are *financial accounting* and *management accounting*. The distinction between the two is convenient for textbooks and accounting courses, but in the workplace it is often far less clear. Companies above a certain size might employ both a 'financial accountant' and a 'management accountant': the 'financial accountant' will sometimes perform bits of 'management accounting' (such as being involved with preparing the annual budget) while the 'management accountant' will occasionally do some 'financial accounting' (such as posting the accruals and prepayments each month).

However, generally the role of a 'management accountant' is to produce and analyse financial information to help the business's managers plan, make better decisions, and monitor whether its spending and finances are under control. The management accountant will have various responsibilities but daily activities might include:

● preparing monthly financial statements, with a focus on monitoring how actual performance compares against the same month last year and with the budget
● liaising with non-financial managers across the organisation on various matters including the investigation of why actual performance may be worse than budget and what corrective action can be taken
● compiling the annual budget on the basis of information received from managers throughout the company
● providing an essential support service by supplying whatever financial information may be needed to assist management in making decisions

There will be variations in the management accountant's role depending on the size of the business and the way that it has decided to organise itself. For example, in a large company there may be several management accountants, each with a particular focus. In a smaller organisation there may be only one qualified accountant and that person will see to all the management and financial accounting needs of the company.

19.16 What does a 'financial controller' do?

The financial controller in a company is the person responsible for overseeing all operations in the accounting department. He or she may have been a more junior accountant in the business and been promoted to the position; alternatively, the post is sometimes filled by an accountant making the move from practice into industry.

The controller oversees the accounts department and will have a wide variety of tasks and responsibilities, which might include:

● managing the team of accounts staff
● maintaining and improving the system of checks and controls to minimise the risk of errors and fraud
● dealing with queries from members of the accounts team, and endeavouring to solve any problems that arise
● preparing the annual financial statements and liaising with the auditors.

There will be a lot of communication between the financial controller and members of the accounting department as well as with other managers in the company. Typically, the controller will report directly to the company's chief financial officer (CFO, also known as the 'Finance Director' in the UK) and this will be a particularly important relationship. The financial controller will often have their eye on becoming a CFO themselves in the future.

19.17 What does the Chief Financial Officer do? (Also known as the CFO, or 'Finance Director' or 'FD' in the UK)

For an accountant working in industry, after several years of post-qualification experience, the role of CFO may be the ultimate goal. The CFO will sit on the company's Board of Directors and they will typically:

● play a key role in formulating the company's strategy and making major business decisions
● regularly report the company's recent financial performance to the Board, and provide it with the latest financial forecasts and projections

● negotiate with lenders when raising funds for the organisation, and deal with the financial aspects of major business deals
● work closely with the financial controller, keeping informed of any significant issues or problems in the accounts department and helping to identify solutions.

A successful CFO needs outstanding technical expertise, intelligence and experience. They need to be able to think strategically and understand the implications of business decisions on every aspect of their organisation. Leadership, interpersonal and communication skills are also key, as are energy and sound judgement. To possess this combination of skills is rare, which is one of the reasons that the CFOs at the UK's biggest companies will earn seven-figure salaries.

19.18 Some of the potential issues and developments faced by the accountants of tomorrow

Progress and change are constant features of modern life. In the last 50 years the world of accounting has changed immensely. For example, in 1967 there was virtually no accounting software, the electronic spreadsheet did not exist, and no accounting standards had been issued. The profession will continue to change in the coming years, but it is always difficult to predict exactly what those changes will be.

To give you a flavour of the developments that the accountants of tomorrow may have to deal with, we will look at just three examples. You are at the first stage in your studies of accounting so you don't require an *in-depth* understanding of these issues yet. However, a chapter on accounting today would not be complete without considering a sample of the changes that may impact upon the accountants of tomorrow:

An increased focus on reporting non-financial information

You will learn in Chapter 36 that companies must publish annual financial statements (supported by detailed notes) that summarise their financial position and performance for the past year. This financial information forms the core of a company's 'Annual Report'. This report also contains some narrative commentaries on the company's performance more generally, but the main emphasis tends to be the financial results.

In recent years this emphasis has been criticised for various reasons:

1 In order to properly assess a company's performance, shareholders need a broader picture of the company, ranging from the satisfaction levels of its customers to its social and environmental sustainability record. Investors need a holistic picture of the company in order to make fully informed investment decisions. Its financial performance over the last 12 months is only one piece of the jigsaw.
2 The disproportionate emphasis on last year's financial results reflects an excessive focus on the short-term. In contrast, long-term success requires qualities such as the ability to innovate new products, to build a good reputation, and to manage environmental risks. These sorts of issues are not reflected in the annual financial results. Requiring companies to report more fully on these long-term factors should focus the directors' attention towards the creation of long-term value.
3 The growing power of large multinational companies (as well as the chequered history of some companies in relation to their social or environmental impact) has led various pressure groups (and the public in general) to demand that companies be required to disclose more information about their activities, way beyond merely their financial performance.

There is therefore a growing movement advocating that companies produce an 'Integrated Report'. These are not yet compulsory, and there is no universally agreed standard format, but many observers believe that *Integrated Reporting* is likely to become a requirement for large companies in many countries over the coming decade. An 'Integrated Report' aims to provide a complete picture of a company's financial and non-financial performance, together with its strategy, governance and future prospects.

Within a company, the CFO tends to take the lead in producing the Annual Report, and professional firms of accountants are the experts in providing assurance that the information in Annual Reports is true and fair. Annual reporting, therefore, is primarily the field of accountants.

So *Integrated Reporting* is likely to present both challenges and opportunities for the accounting profession. The accountants of tomorrow may need to develop new expertise to be able to report on a diverse range of non-financial measures from greenhouse gas emissions to employee satisfaction rates. Professional firms of accountants will require new skills in checking such non-financial information to be able to provide independent assurance to users with regard to its accuracy. You can read more about *Integrated Reporting* in *Frank Wood's Business Accounting 2*.

A need for more advanced maths skills

Contrary to popular belief, most traditional accounting only required a relatively basic level of maths skills. Accountants certainly needed to be 'good with numbers' but largely in terms of being good at arithmetic and being adept at identifying what the numbers signify, spotting trends and identifying anomalies. However, for some accountants, things may be different in the future.

Large companies in many parts of the world (including the UK) must comply with international accounting rules (or 'standards'). These standards are known as IASs and IFRSs. There is a trend for some of the more recently issued standards to require some fairly complex maths. IFRS 9 *Financial Instruments* is an example. The detail of IFRS 9 is well beyond the scope of this book but many observers are worried that the existing levels of understanding of financial maths amongst some current accountants are insufficient for them to properly apply this and some other recent standards.

This is a deficiency that may have to be addressed in the next generation of accountants. It is also another reason for the inclusion in this book of Chapter 38, *Maths for accounting*.

The impact of cloud computing on accountancy

Another development that is impacting the business landscape quite significantly is cloud computing. For businesses, cloud computing refers to the already common practice of using computer resources that are not physically based on the company premises but essentially reside on the internet. Anyone with a computing device and internet access can access software and their data in the cloud from wherever they happen to be working. And instead of purchasing costly hardware and software, users pay a relatively small monthly subscription for this access.

This is particularly attractive for small- and medium-sized enterprises (SMEs) because they are now able to use powerful accounting systems that previously were only available to large organisations with extensive financial resources and large IT departments. Many SMEs have already adopted cloud computing for their accounting data and many more are likely to follow. The impact on the accounting profession could include:

1 Access to more sophisticated software means that even more basic accounting tasks will become automated than before. This will further reduce demand within SMEs for basic bookkeeping skills and the role of the accountant will become that of a financial expert, analysing and interpreting the data, and predicting what is going to happen.

2 In theory, any manager in the business can access the same accounting information, wherever they are. This could lead to faster, more collaborative decision-making. However, non-financial managers may access financial data that they don't fully understand. The role of the accountant in explaining and clarifying the information could become more important than ever.

3 Firms of accountants that provide services to SMEs may find that their roles will change. Firms will be able to access their clients' accounting data from the office rather than having to visit the client. Demand for basic accounting services will diminish, because the more sophisticated software will take care of them. Instead, firms should be able to offer valuable business advice on planning, strategy, controls and financial analysis.

For decades, accountants have liked to think of themselves as 'trusted business advisers' because of the role they play in understanding and assessing the financial performance of a business. More than ever, it may be time for them to start fully living up to this role as more and more basic accounting tasks become automated.

Learning outcomes

You should now have learnt that:

1 There are several attractions of a career in accounting.

2 Some of the reservations that you may have about careers in accounting are not necessarily entirely accurate.

3 Successful accountants require a range of attributes: technical expertise, numeracy skills, attention to detail, problem-solving skills, communication skills, interpersonal skills, writing skills, IT skills, emotional intelligence, and ethics and integrity.

4 Broadly speaking, accountants work in practice, in industry or in the public sector.

5 A university degree is not always needed to become a professional accountant, but many trainee positions are aimed at graduates.

6 There are six main professional accountancy bodies in the UK and which body you qualify with depends on what type of organisation you train with and the preferences of your employer.

7 The work of a trainee accountant is varied and depends on whether you train in practice, industry or the public sector.

8 Once you are qualified there are a wide range of different job roles and career paths that you can pursue.

9 The accounting profession has seen significant changes in the last 50 years and there will be more changes in the coming decades.

Answers to activities

19.1 You could become aware, for example, that one of your friends on your accounting course:

● bought their latest essay online and has been awarded a very high mark
● has hidden a library book (one that is particularly useful for an upcoming assignment) somewhere in the library
● plans to sneak revision notes into a forthcoming exam and refer to them.

In each case, the fact that your friend's behaviour is 'wrong' is clear. However, your relationship with your friend might make you hesitant to take action. There is also the practical problem of it likely to be 'your word against theirs' if you report it to those in authority.

19.2 There are several good reasons. Here are just three:

1 Exemptions from future professional exams: if you have a degree in accounting (commonly in 'accounting & finance') and you decide to become a professional accountant you will usually be exempt from several professional exams. For example, a graduate with a degree in chemistry might have to pass (say) 14 professional exams while an accounting graduate might be exempted from the first (say) nine and would only sit the final five.

Some UK accounting degrees have even higher levels of accreditation than this. The professional exams are notoriously challenging: passing them all at the first time of asking is tough. To be exempt from so many is therefore typically seen as a major advantage of getting an accounting degree.

2 Accounting is a reputable, rigorous academic degree subject that will be respected by employers. A good degree in accounting signifies that you are an intelligent all-rounder: you are good with numbers and can also write well.

3 Universities often offer the opportunity of a year in industry work placement on 'vocational' degree courses like accounting. Undertaking one of these will be major asset on your CV when it comes to getting a graduate job. With high numbers of students attending university, a degree alone is not enough to make you stand out. A year of relevant work experience is invaluable.

Review questions

Author's note: It is felt that these review questions might best be covered in the context of a tutorial/classroom discussion, so the suggested solutions can all be found in the Instructor's Manual.

19.1A Electronic spreadsheets (such as Microsoft Excel) are extensively used by accountants today and have been for decades. With reference to some of the various topics covered in this book, can you suggest some specific purposes for which accountants might use spreadsheets?

19.2A There have been several high-profile scandals in accounting in recent times, which have contributed to the raised profile of ethics and integrity in accounting. The details of many of these scandals might be difficult to understand at this stage in your studies. However, search online for 'WorldCom scandal 2002' and read about what happened in that case. Can you relate a key element of the WorldCom affair to one particular chapter in this book?

19.3A There is now growing disapproval from some sections of the public of the elaborate tax planning arrangements that tax advisers at some accounting firms have recommended to their clients. These arrangements may be entirely legal, but are often highly complex schemes that exploit loopholes in the legislation. Critics argue that they go against the spirit, if not the letter, of the law.

In response, successive governments have promised to crackdown on the more extreme tax planning schemes, with limited success to date. Recent public interest in the social acceptability of some of these tax planning schemes has increased debate about the ethics of the activity.

What do you think? Is it ethically acceptable for accounting firms to advise their wealthy clients to adopt complex tax planning schemes to massively reduce their tax bills, as long as those schemes are completely legal?

19.4A For simplicity and convenience, this chapter discusses accountants as working 'in practice', 'in industry' or 'in the public sector'. However, some organisations might not fall neatly into one of these three categories but will still require accounting services. Can you suggest any such organisations?

→

19.5A   In this chapter you've learnt about some specific roles and areas of accountancy, such as 'financial controller' or 'tax adviser'. Can you suggest any other particular areas of accounting in which you can specialise?

19.6A   Some students who want to train with an accountancy practice tend to focus exclusively on trying to get a job with one of the 'Big Four' (PwC, Deloitte, EY and KPMG) and ignore smaller accounting firms altogether.

Required:
(a)   What do you think are the advantages of training with a 'Big Four' firm?
(b)   Can you suggest any disadvantages of focusing exclusively on the 'Big Four'?
(c)   Are you able to identify any potential benefits of training with a smaller firm?

19.7A   You may have no plans to become an accountant in the future. Why is it still important for you to study the basics of accounting, such as those covered in this book?

19.8A   The rate of progress in technology is so rapid that it is very difficult to predict exactly how new technology will affect accounting in the future. Can you suggest any developments in technology that could have a significant impact on accounting in the future?

ADJUSTMENTS FOR FINANCIAL STATEMENTS

Introduction

This part is concerned with all the adjustments that have to be made before financial statements can be prepared.

Bad debts, allowances for doubtful debts and provisions for discounts on accounts receivable

Learning objectives

After you have studied this chapter, you should be able to:

- explain and show how bad debts are written-off
- explain why allowances for doubtful debts are made
- make the necessary entries to record an allowance for doubtful debts in the books
- calculate and make provisions for discounts on accounts receivable
- make all the entries in the income statement and balance sheet for bad debts, allowances for doubtful debts, and provisions for cash discount

Introduction

In this chapter, you'll learn how businesses deal with bad debts and how they provide for the possibility that other debts will not be paid. You'll learn how to record increases and decreases in the allowance for doubtful debts. Finally, you'll learn how to make and adjust provisions for cash discounts.

20.1 Bad debts

With many businesses a large proportion, if not all, of the sales are on credit. The business is therefore taking the risk that some of the customers may never pay for the goods sold to them on credit. This is a normal business risk and such **bad debts** are a normal business expense. They must be charged to the income statement as an expense when calculating the net profit or loss for the period. The other thing that needs to be done is to remove the bad debt from the asset account. Usually, this will mean closing the debtor's account.

When a debt is found to be 'bad', the asset represented by the debt in the debtor's account is worthless. It must be eliminated from the account. If doing so reduces the balance to zero, the debtor's account is closed.

To record a bad debt, you credit the debtor's account to cancel the asset and increase the expense account by debiting it to the bad debts account.

Activity 20.1 What circumstances might lead you to write-off a debt as bad and *not* close the debtor's account?

There is a range of possible scenarios that may exist concerning a bad debt. The first two were discussed in the answer to Activity 20.1:

- the debtor may be refusing to pay one of a number of invoices;
- the debtor may be refusing to pay part of an invoice;
- the debtor may owe payment on a number of invoices and have indicated that only a proportion of the total amount due will ever be paid because the debtor's business has failed;
- the debtor's business has failed and nothing is ever likely to be received.

Whatever the reason, once a debt has been declared 'bad', the journal entry is the same. You debit the bad debt account with the amount of the bad debt and credit the debtor's account in the sales ledger to complete the double entry.

At the end of the period, the total of the bad debts account is transferred to the income statement. An example of debts being written off as bad is shown in Exhibit 20.1:

Exhibit 20.1

C. Bloom

2018			£	2018			£
Jan	8	Sales	520	Dec	31	Bad debts	520

R. Shaw

2018			£	2018			£
Feb	16	Sales	375	Aug	17	Cash	125
				Dec	31	Bad debts	250
			375				375

Bad Debts

2018			£	2018			£
Dec	31	C Bloom	520	Dec	31	Profit and loss	770
		R Shaw	250				
			770				770

Income Statement (extract) for the year ending 31 December 2018

	£
Gross profit	xxx
Less Expenses:	
Bad debts	(770)

20.2 Allowance for doubtful debts

Why allowances are needed

When we are drawing up our financial statements, we want to achieve the following objectives:

- to charge as an expense in the income statement for that year an amount representing debts that will never be paid;
- to show in the balance sheet a figure for accounts receivable as close as possible to the true value of accounts receivable at the date of the balance sheet.

Debts declared bad are usually debts that have existed for some time, perhaps even from previous reporting periods.

But, how about other debts that have not been paid by the year end? These may not have been owing for so long, in which case it will be more difficult to determine which of them will be bad debts. Nevertheless, as all businesses experience bad debts at some time, it is likely that at least some of these other debts will ultimately prove to be bad. The prudence concept – you learnt about this in Chapter 7 – says that this possibility needs to be provided for in the current period, otherwise both the accounts receivable balance reported in the balance sheet and the profit reported in the income statement will almost certainly be overstated.

It is impossible to determine with absolute accuracy at the year end what the true amount is in respect of debtors who will never pay their accounts. So, how do you decide on the amount of a provision (i.e. an allowance) against the possibility of some of the remaining debts (after removing those which have been written off as bad) proving bad in a future period?

In order to arrive at a figure for doubtful debts, a business must first consider that some debtors will never pay any of the amount they owe, while others will pay a part of the amount owing only, leaving the remainder permanently unpaid. The estimated figure can be made either:

(a) by looking at each debt, and deciding to what extent it will be bad; or
(b) by estimating, on the basis of experience, what percentage of the total amount due from the remaining debtors will ultimately prove to be bad debts.

It is well known that the longer a debt is owing, the more likely it is that it will become a bad debt. Some businesses draw up an 'ageing schedule', showing how long debts have been owing. Older debtors need higher percentage estimates of bad debts than do newer debtors. The percentages chosen should reflect the actual pattern of bad debts experienced in the past. Exhibit 20.2 gives an example of an ageing schedule.

Exhibit 20.2

Ageing Schedule for Doubtful Debts			
Period debt owing	Amount	Estimated percentage doubtful	Allowance for doubtful debts
	£	%	£
Less than 1 month	5,000	1	50
1 month to 2 months	3,000	3	90
2 months to 3 months	800	4	32
3 months to 1 year	200	5	10
Over 1 year	160	20	32
	9,160		214

Most businesses don't go to this level of detail. Instead, they apply a percentage to the overall balance of accounts receivable (after deducting the bad debts). The percentage will be one the business has established over the years as being the most appropriate.

Now, let's look at how the allowance for doubtful debts is entered in the books.

Accounting entries for allowances for doubtful debts

The accounting entries needed for the **allowance for doubtful debts** are:
Year in which the allowance is *first* made:

1 Debit the profit and loss account with the amount of the allowance (i.e. deduct it from gross profit as an expense).
2 Credit the *Allowance for doubtful debts account.*

Exhibit 20.3 shows the entries needed for the initial allowance for doubtful debts.

Exhibit 20.3

At 31 December 2018, the accounts receivable figure after deducting bad debts was £10,000. It is estimated that 2 per cent of debts (i.e. £200) will eventually prove to be bad debts, and it is decided to make a provision for these. The accounts will appear as follows:

Profit and Loss

2018		£	
Dec 31 Allowance for doubtful debts		200	

Allowance for Doubtful Debts

	2018	£
	Dec 31 Profit and loss	200

In the financial statements, the allowance is shown as follows:

Income Statement (extract) for the year ending 31 December 2018

	£
Gross profit	XXX
Less Expenses:	
Allowance for doubtful debts	(200)

Balance Sheet (extract) as at 31 December 2018

Current assets	£	£
Accounts receivable	10,000	
Less Allowance for doubtful debts	(200)	
		9,800

As shown, in the balance sheet, the balance on the allowance for doubtful debts is deducted from the accounts receivable total.

You'll have noticed that we are using two different accounts to make the two different types of adjustments to accounts receivable. This is done in order to make it clear how much is (a) being written-off as bad debts, and how much is (b) being treated as an allowance for doubtful debts:

1 **Bad debts account:** This expense account is used when a debt is believed to be irrecoverable and is written-off.
2 **Allowance for doubtful debts account:** This account is used only for estimates of the amount of debt remaining at the year end *after the debts have been written off* that are likely to finish up as bad debts. (This account is also known as the 'allowance for *bad* debts account'.)

By charging both (1) and (2) in the income statement, we present the full picture of the amounts provided for in respect of both bad and doubtful debts. As you've already seen in Exhibits 20.1 and 20.3, these amounts are shown as deductions from the gross profit.

By showing (2) as a deduction from the figure of accounts receivable in the statement of financial position, we get a net figure, which represents a more accurate figure of the value of accounts receivable than the total of all the accounts receivable balances in the sales ledger. It may not be absolutely accurate – only time will tell which debts will turn out to be bad – but it is better than not attempting to make an estimate.

When you look at depreciation in Chapter 21, you will see that it bears similarities to the allowance for doubtful debts. Depreciation is charged as a debit to the profit and loss account and as a credit against non-current asset accounts in the ledger. It represents an estimate of how much of the overall economic usefulness of a non-current asset has been used up in each accounting period. Like the allowance for doubtful debts, it can never be completely accurate since only in several years' time, when the asset is put out of use, can it be determined whether or not the provisions made have been appropriate. Having to make estimates where absolute accuracy is impossible is a part of accounting.

Activity 20.2   Why do accountants have to make these allowances?

20.3 Increasing the allowance

Let us suppose that for the same business as in Exhibit 20.3, at the end of the following year, 31 December 2019, the allowance for doubtful debts needed to be increased. This was because the allowance was kept at 2 per cent, but the accounts receivable figure had risen to £12,000. An allowance of £200 had been brought forward from the *previous* year, but we now want a total allowance of £240 (i.e. 2 per cent of £12,000). All that is now needed is a provision for an extra £40. The double entry will be:

1 Debit the *Profit and Loss Account* with the increase in the allowance (i.e. deduct it from gross profit as an expense).
2 Credit the *Allowance for doubtful debts account*.

These entries are illustrated in Exhibit 20.4.

Exhibit 20.4

Profit and Loss

2019		£			
Dec 31 Allowance for doubtful debts		40			

Allowance for Doubtful Debts

2019			£	2019				£
Dec	31	Balance c/d	240	Jan	1	Balance b/d		200
				Dec	31	Profit and loss		40
			240					240
				2020				
				Jan	1	Balance b/d		240

Income Statement (extract) for the year ending 31 December 2019

	£
Gross profit	xxx
Less Expenses	
Allowance for doubtful debts (increase)	(40)

Balance Sheet (extract) as at 31 December 2019

Current assets	£	£
Accounts receivable	12,000	
Less Allowance for doubtful debts	(240)	
		11,760

Activity 20.3 Why do you only need to create an expense for the difference between the provisions of the two years?

20.4 Reducing the allowance

To reduce the allowance, you simply do the opposite to what you did to increase it. The allowance for doubtful debts has a credit balance. Therefore, to reduce it we would need a debit entry in the allowance account. The credit would be in the profit and loss account. Let's assume that at 31 December 2020, the figure for accounts receivable had fallen to £10,500 but the allowance remained at 2 per cent, i.e. £210 (2 per cent of £10,500).

As the allowance had previously been £240, it now needs to be reduced by £30. The double entry is:

1 Debit *Allowance for doubtful debts account.*
2 Credit *Profit and Loss Account* (i.e. add it as a gain to gross profit).

These entries are illustrated in Exhibit 20.5.

Exhibit 20.5

Allowance for Doubtful Debts

2020			£	2020			£
Dec	31	Profit and loss	30	Jan	1	Balance b/d	240
	31	Balance c/d	210				
			240				240
				2021			
				Jan	1	Balance b/d	210

Profit and Loss

				2020			£
				Dec	31	Allowance for doubtful debts	30

Income Statement (extract) for the year ending 31 December 2020

	£
	xxx
Gross profit	
Add Reduction in allowance for doubtful debts	30

Balance Sheet (extract) as at 31 December 2020

	£	£
Current assets		
Accounts receivable	10,500	
Less Allowance for doubtful debts	(210)	
		10,290

You will have noticed that increases in the allowance for doubtful debts increases the total for expenses and so reduce net profit. On the other hand, a reduction in the allowance for doubtful debts will increase the gross profit.

Activity 20.4 Without looking back in your textbook, write down the double entries for (a) an increase and (b) a decrease in the allowance for doubtful debts.

Let us now look at a comprehensive example in Exhibit 20.6:

Exhibit 20.6

A business starts on 1 January 2017 and its financial year end is 31 December annually. A table of the accounts receivable, the bad debts written off and the estimated bad debts at the rate of 2 per cent of accounts receivable at the end of each year is now given. The double entry accounts and the extracts from the financial statements follow.

Year to 31 December	Bad debts written off during year	Accounts receivable at end of year (after bad debts written off)	Debts thought at end of year to be impossible to collect: 2% of accounts receivable
	£	£	£
2017	423	6,000	120 (2% of £6,000)
2018	510	7,000	140 (2% of £7,000)
2019	604	7,750	155 (2% of £7,750)
2020	610	6,500	130 (2% of £6,500)

Bad Debts

			£				£
2017				2017			
Dec	31	Various accounts receivable	423	Dec	31	Profit and loss	423
2018				2018			
Dec	31	Various accounts receivable	510	Dec	31	Profit and loss	510
2019				2019			
Dec	31	Various accounts receivable	604	Dec	31	Profit and loss	604
2020				2020			
Dec	31	Various accounts receivable	610	Dec	31	Profit and loss	610

Allowance for Doubtful Debts

			£				£
2017				2017			
Dec	31	Balance c/d	120	Dec	31	Profit and loss	120
2018				2018			
Dec	31	Balance c/d	140	Jan	1	Balance b/d	120
				Dec	31	Profit and loss	20
			140				140
2019				2019			
Dec	31	Balance c/d	155	Jan	1	Balance b/d	140
				Dec	31	Profit and loss	15
			155				155
2020				2020			
Dec	31	Profit and loss	25	Jan	1	Balance b/d	155
		Balance c/d	130				
			155				
				2021			155
				Jan	1	Balance b/d	130

→

Income Statements (extracts) for the years ending 31 December

		£	£
Gross profit for 2017, 2018, 2019, 2020			xxx
2017	*Less* Expenses:		
	Bad debts	423	
	Allowance for doubtful debts (increase)	120	
			(543)
2018	*Less* Expenses:		
	Bad debts	510	
	Allowance for doubtful debts (increase)	20	
			(530)
2019	*Less* Expenses:		
	Bad debts	604	
	Allowance for doubtful debts (increase)	15	
			(619)
2020	*Add* Reduction in allowance for doubtful debts	25	
	Less Expenses:		
	Bad debts	(610)	
			(585)

Balance Sheets (extracts) as at 31 December

		£	£
2017	Accounts receivable	6,000	
	Less Allowance for doubtful debts	(120)	
			5,880
2018	Accounts receivable	7,000	
	Less Allowance for doubtful debts	(140)	
			6,860
2019	Accounts receivable	7,750	
	Less Allowance for doubtful debts	(155)	
			7,595
2020	Accounts receivable	6,500	
	Less Allowance for doubtful debts	(130)	
			6,370

20.5 Bad debts recovered

Sometimes, a debt written-off in previous years is recovered. When this happens, you:

1 Reinstate the debt by making the following entries:
   Dr Debtor's account
      Cr Bad debts recovered account

2 When payment is received from the debtor in settlement of all or part of the debt:
   Dr Cash/bank
      Cr Debtor's account
   with the amount received.

At the end of the financial year, the credit balance in the bad debts recovered account is transferred either to the bad debts account or direct to the credit side of the profit and loss account. The effect is the same, since the bad debts account will, in itself, be transferred to the profit and loss account at the end of the financial year.

Activity 20.5 Why do you think we reinstate the debt just to cancel it out again? Why don't we simply debit the bank account and credit the bad debts recovered account?

20.6 Provisions for cash discounts on accounts receivable

Some businesses create provisions for cash discounts to be allowed on the accounts receivable outstanding at the balance sheet date. This, they maintain, is quite legitimate, as the amount of accounts receivable less any allowance for doubtful debts is not the best estimate of collectable debts, owing to cash discounts which will be given to debtors if they pay within a given time. The cost of discounts, it is argued, should be charged in the period when the sales were made. While this practice is of dubious merit (as cash discount is treated as a finance charge, not as an adjustment to sales revenue), it is one used in practice by some businesses.

The procedure for dealing with this is similar to the allowance for doubtful debts. It must be borne in mind that the estimate of discounts to be allowed should be based on the net figure of accounts receivable less the allowance for doubtful debts, as it is obvious that cash discounts are not allowed on bad debts! Let's look at an example in Exhibit 20.7:

Exhibit 20.7

Year ended 31 December	Accounts receivable	Allowance for doubtful debts	Provision for cash discounts allowed
	£	£	%
2017	4,000	200	2
2018	5,000	350	2
2019	4,750	250	2

Provision for Cash Discounts on Accounts Receivable

			£				£
2017				2017			
Dec	31	Balance c/d	76	Dec	31	Profit and loss	76
2018				2018			
Dec	31	Balance c/d	93	Jan	1	Balance b/d	76
				Dec	31	Profit and loss	17
			93				93
2019				2019			
Dec	31	Profit and loss	3	Jan	1	Balance b/d	93
		Balance c/d	90				
			93				93
				2020			
				Jan	1	Balance b/d	90

Income Statements (extracts) for the years ending 31 December

	£
Gross profits (2017, 2018 and 2019)	xxx
Less Expenses:	
(2017) Provision for cash discounts on accounts receivable	(76)
(2018) Increase in provision for cash discounts on accounts receivable	(17)
Add (2019) Reduction in provision for cash discounts on accounts receivable	3

Balance Sheets (extracts) as at 31 December

		£	£	£
2017	Accounts receivable		4,000	
	Less Allowance for doubtful debts	200		
	Provision for cash discounts on accounts receivable	76		
			(276)	
				3,724
2018	Accounts receivable		5,000	
	Less Allowance for doubtful debts	350		
	Provision for cash discounts on accounts receivable	93		
			(443)	
				4,557
2019	Accounts receivable		4,750	
	Less Allowance for doubtful debts	250		
	Provision for cash discounts on accounts receivable	90		
			(340)	
				4,410

Activity 20.6

Which one of the following would result from a decrease in the allowance for doubtful debts?

(a) An increase in gross profit
(b) A reduction in gross profit
(c) An increase in net profit
(d) A reduction in net profit

20.7 Finally

As with distinguishing between capital expenditure and revenue expenditure, students generally find this topic very difficult to grasp. It seems to be too difficult for some students to remember the difference between the treatment of bad debts and the treatment of allowances for doubtful debts. They also often struggle to make the correct adjustments when the allowance changes, with the most common error being that they charge all the allowance, instead of only the change, to profit and loss.

There is no shortcut to getting this right. You need to keep the difference between bad debts and allowances for doubtful debts very clearly in your mind. Learning them as two separate topics seems to help. So far as the treatment of the change in the allowance is concerned, don't try calling it 'change in the allowance for doubtful debts', you'll only get confused when you make the entry in the balance sheet. And there is where the difficulty lies: *In the balance sheet the entire allowance is deducted from the figure for accounts receivable but, in the income statement, you only include the change.* Try to memorise this last sentence. It may make all the difference.

Learning outcomes

You should now have learnt:

1 That debts we are unable to collect are called bad debts.

2 That bad debts are credited to the customer's account (to cancel them) and debited to a bad debts account.

3 That allowances for doubtful debts are needed, otherwise the value of the accounts receivable in the balance sheet will show too high a value, and could mislead anyone looking at the balance sheet. Also, making a provision of this type allows for more accurate calculation of profits and losses.

4 That the allowance for doubtful debts is calculated *after* bad debts have been deducted from the debtor balances.

5 That the amount of the allowance for doubtful debts is based on the best estimate that can be made taking all the facts into account.

6 That an increase in the allowance for doubtful debts will create a debit entry in the profit and loss account.

7 That a reduction in the allowance for doubtful debts will create a credit entry in the profit and loss account.

8 That the allowance for doubtful debts is shown as a deduction from accounts receivable in the balance sheet.

9 That provisions for cash discount are made in the same way as provisions for doubtful debts.

10 How to record bad debts, allowances for doubtful debts, and provisions for cash discounts in the accounting books and in the income statement and balance sheet.

Answers to activities

20.1 Sometimes a debtor will contest an invoice and refuse to pay it while continuing to pay all other invoices. This may happen, for example, when the debtor claims that the goods were delivered damaged and you have refused to issue a credit note because you believe the goods were delivered intact. Another example occurs when the debtor is refusing to pay part of an invoice. This may happen, for example, when the customer claims not to have received all the items on the invoice. In both those circumstances, many businesses will eventually write off the debt on the disputed invoice and continue to trade with the customer.

20.2 The prudence concept which you learnt about in Chapter 7 requires it.

20.3 During the year, some debts will have been written off as bad. They will include debts from the previous year which last year's allowance for doubtful debts was intended to cover. If last year's estimate was correct, you could add this year's bad debts to the change in the allowance and the total would be the same as the total allowance you want to make this year, not just the difference between the two years' provisions. So, in effect, you've converted last year's allowance into this year's bad debts. All you need do now is adjust the balance on the allowance for doubtful debts account to make it equal to the provision you want to make against this year's closing accounts receivable balance.

20.4   (a) *Dr* Profit and loss account   *Cr* Allowance for doubtful debts account
        (b) *Dr* Allowance for doubtful debts account   *Cr* Profit and loss account

       Note how they are the opposite of each other.

20.5 The reason for reinstating the debt in the ledger account of the debtor is to have a detailed history of the debtor's account as a guide for granting credit in future. When a debt is written-off as bad, it is recorded in the debtor's ledger account. Therefore, when a bad debt is recovered, it should also be shown in the debtor's ledger account, so as to provide the full picture.

20.6 (c) An increase in net profit.

Review questions

20.1   In a new business during the year ended 31 December 2020 the following debts are found to be bad, and are written-off on the dates shown:

31 May	T. Fox	£840
30 September	G. Pegg	£930
30 November	G. Swan	£720

On 31 December 2020 the schedule of remaining accounts receivable totalling £47,350 is examined and it is decided to make an allowance for doubtful debts of £947.

You are required to show:
(a)   The Bad Debts Account, and the Allowance for Doubtful Debts Account.
(b)   The charge to the Income Statement.
(c)   The relevant extracts from the Balance Sheet as at 31 December 2020.

20.2   A business had always made an allowance for doubtful debts at the rate of 4 per cent of accounts receivable. On 1 January 2018 the amount for this, brought forward from the previous year, was £1,300.
    During the year to 31 December 2018 the bad debts written-off amounted to £6,380.
    On 31 December 2018 the accounts receivable balance was £37,000 and the usual allowance for doubtful debts is to be made.

You are to show:
(a)   The Bad Debts Account for the year ended 31 December 2018.
(b)   The Allowance for Doubtful Debts Account for the year.
(c)   Extract from the Income Statement for the year.
(d)   The relevant extract from the Balance Sheet as at 31 December 2018.

20.3   A business started trading on 1 January 2017. During the two years ended 31 December 2017 and 2018 the following debts were written off to the Bad Debts Account on the dates stated:

31 May 2017	S. Gill	£500
31 October 2017	H. Black	£400
31 January 2018	A. Tims	£200
30 June 2018	F. Dale	£900
31 October 2018	J. Park	£100

On 31 December 2017 the total accounts receivable was £104,000. It was decided to make an allowance for doubtful debts of £3,120.
    On 31 December 2018 the total accounts receivable was £116,000. It was decided to make an allowance for doubtful debts of £3,480.

You are required to show:
(i)   The Bad Debts Account and the Allowance for Doubtful Debts Account for each of the two years.
(ii)   The relevant extracts from the Balance Sheets as at 31 December 2017 and 2018.

20.4A A business, which started trading on 1 January 2017, adjusted its allowance for doubtful debt at the end of each year on a percentage basis, but each year the percentage rate is adjusted in accordance with the current 'economic climate'. The following details are available for the three years ended 31 December 2017, 2018 and 2019.

	Bad debts written-off year to 31 December	Accounts receivable at 31 December after bad debts written-off	Percentage allowance for doubtful debts
	£	£	
2017	2,480	84,000	5
2018	5,216	154,000	4
2019	10,620	172,000	3

You are required to show:
(a)   Bad Debts Accounts for each of the three years.
(b)   Allowance for Doubtful Debts Accounts for each of the three years.
(c)   Balance Sheet extracts as at 31 December 2017, 2018 and 2019.

20.5 A business which prepares its financial statements annually to 31 December suffered bad debts which were written-off:

2017   £3,320
2018   £2,150
2019   £3,490

The business had a balance of £650 on the Allowance for Doubtful Debts Account on 1 January 2017.
    At the end of each year, the business considered which of its debtors appeared doubtful and carried forward an allowance of:

2017   £770
2018   £980
2019   £650

Prepare the Allowance for Doubtful Debts Account and relevant extracts from the income statements for each of the three years.

20.6A

(a)   As at 31 October 2018, a balance of £12,900 on the allowance for doubtful debts account of Abigail's business had been brought forward from the previous year-end. It was then decided that specific debts totalling £14,300 were to be written-off as the cash was considered to be irrecoverable, and that the allowance for doubtful debts was to be adjusted to £13,800.
        On the basis of this information, what is the net total expense in connection with bad and doubtful debts that should appear in the Income Statement of Abigail's business for her financial year ended 31 October 2018?

(b)   At 30 April 2020 Becky's business had an allowance for doubtful debts of £22,700. During her year ended 30 April 2021 debts totalling £29,400 were written off. Becky then decided to adjust the allowance for doubtful debts to £21,000 as at 30 April 2021.
        Given this information, what is the net total impact of bad and doubtful debts to be reflected in Becky's Income Statement for her year ended 30 April 2021?

(c)   As at 31 December 2018 Charlotte's business had an allowance for doubtful debts of £2,250. During the year to 31 December 2019 the following occurred:
        (i)   Irrecoverable debts of £3,960 were written off.
        (ii)   Charlotte received £261 in respect of a debt that had been written off completely during 2017.
        At 31 December 2019 the total of Charlotte's accounts receivable was £94,000. Charlotte has reviewed these carefully and determined that an allowance for doubtful debts of £2,100 is required.
        What is the impact of all this information on Charlotte's Income Statement for 2019 in relation to bad and doubtful debts?

(d)   On the morning of 31 December 2020 the total accounts receivable balances of Daisy's business amount to £97,000. However, in the afternoon the following events transpire:

(i) Daisy discovers that a credit customer (D Lucas) has ceased trading and it becomes apparent that the £1,375 owed by Lucas is virtually certain to be irrecoverable.

(ii) Daisy also learns that another customer (Adrian Webb) may be experiencing some financial difficulties and she now believes that an allowance should be set-up for the £1,268 owed by Webb.

(iii) A cheque for £1,523 is received from S Miller, a debt against which a specific allowance had been created in October 2020.

(iv) A cheque for £1,472 is received from T Cook. This amount had been written-off in November 2019.

What is the revised total of Daisy's accounts receivable balances after dealing with the four items above?

20.7 The balance sheet as at 31 May 2017 of Pondlake Limited included an allowance for doubtful debts of £4,600. The company's accounts for the year ended 31 May 2018 are now being prepared. The company's policy now is to relate the allowance for doubtful debts to the age of debts outstanding. The debts outstanding at 31 May 2018 and the required allowances for doubtful debts are as follows:

Debts outstanding	Amount	Allowance for doubtful debts
	£	%
Up to 1 month	60,000	0.5
More than 1 month and up to 2 months	42,000	1
More than 2 months and up to 3 months	34,000	2
More than 3 months	20,000	3

Customers are allowed a cash discount of 2% for settlement of debts within one month. It is now proposed to make a provision for discounts to be allowed in the company's accounts for the year ended 31 May 2018.

Required:
Prepare the following accounts for the year ended 31 May 2018 in the books of Pondlake Limited to record the above transactions:

(a) Allowance for doubtful debts;
(b) Provision for discounts to be allowed on debtors.

20.8A D. Noakes makes an allowance for doubtful debts of 4% of accounts receivable, also a provision of 1% for discount on accounts receivable.

On 1 January 2018 the balances brought forward on the relevant accounts were allowance for doubtful debts £2,166 and provision for discounts on accounts receivable £526.

(a) Enter the balances in the appropriate accounts, using a separate Allowance for Doubtful Debts Account.

During 2018 Noakes incurred bad debts of £16,349 and allowed discounts of £3,857. On 31 December 2018 accounts receivable amounted to £67,500.

(b) Show the entries in the appropriate accounts for the year 2018, assuming that the business's accounting year ends on 31 December 2018, also Income Statement extracts at 31 December 2018.

20.9 J. Blane commenced business on 1 January 2016 and prepares her financial statements to 31 December every year. For the year ended 31 December 2016, bad debts written-off amounted to £1,400. It was also found necessary to create an allowance for doubtful debts of £2,600.

In 2017, debts amounting to £2,200 proved bad and were written-off. J. Sweeny, whose debt of £210 was written-off as bad in 2016, settled her account in full on 30 November 2017. As at 31

December 2017 total debts outstanding were £92,000. It was decided to bring the allowance up to 4% of this figure on that date.

In 2018, £3,800 of debts were written-off during the year, and another recovery of £320 was made in respect of debts written-off in 2016. As at 31 December 2018, total debts outstanding were £72,000. The allowance for doubtful debts is to be changed to 5% of this figure.

Required:
Show for the years 2016, 2017 and 2018, the:
(a) Bad Debts Account
(b) Bad Debts Recovered Account
(c) Allowance for Doubtful Debts Account
(d) Extract from the Income statement.

20.10

(A) Explain why an allowance may be made for doubtful debts.
(B) Explain the procedure to be followed when a customer whose debt has been written-off as bad subsequently pays the amount originally owing.
(C) On 1 January 2017 D. Watson had debtors of £25,000 on which he had made an allowance for doubtful debts of 3%.
During 2017,
(i)   A. Stewart, who owed D. Watson £1,200, was declared bankrupt and a settlement of 25p in the £ was made, the balance being treated as a bad debt.
(ii) Other bad debts written-off during the year amounted to £2,300.

On 31 December 2017 total accounts receivable amounted to £24,300 but this requires to be adjusted as follows:

(a) J. Smith, a debtor owing £600, was known to be unable to pay and this amount was to be written-off.
(b) A cheque for £200 from S. McIntosh was returned from the bank unpaid.

D. Watson maintained his allowance for doubtful debts at 3% of accounts receivable.

Required:
(1) For the financial year ended 31 December 2017, show the entries in the following accounts:
(i) Allowance for doubtful debts
(ii) Bad debts
(2) What is the effect on net profit of the change in the allowance for doubtful debts?

(*Scottish Qualifications Authority*)

20.11A The following balances appeared in the trial balance of J. McGovern's business as at 30 June 2020:

	£
Accounts receivable	145,000
Bad debt expense	23,200
Bad debts recovered	830
Allowance for doubtful debts at 1 July 2019	4,500

After this trial balance had been constructed, McGovern decided to write-off further debts amounting to £6,000 which were deemed to be irrecoverable.

He also decided to carry forward at 30 June 2020 a general allowance equal to (based on an analysis of his business's recent experience and history) 4% of remaining accounts receivable.

What is the impact of all this information on the net profit of McGovern's business for the year ended 30 June 2020?

Depreciation

Learning objectives

After you have studied this chapter, you should be able to:

● define depreciation

● explain why depreciation is provided

● calculate depreciation using both the straight line and the reducing balance methods

● explain how to calculate depreciation using five other methods

● calculate depreciation on assets bought or sold within an accounting period

● incorporate depreciation calculations into the accounting records

● record the entries relating to disposal of non-current assets

● make depreciation entries using either a one-stage or a two-stage approach to recording depreciation

Introduction

In this chapter, you'll learn why depreciation must be provided and how to calculate it using the two most widely used methods, in the year of acquisition, year of disposal, and all the years in between. You will also learn how to use five other depreciation methods and make appropriate entries in the accounting books and in the financial statements.

21.1 Nature of non-current assets

Before going any further, you need to be sure that you know what a non-current asset is.

 Activity 21.1 Write down the three characteristics that distinguish non-current assets from current assets.

If you don't or didn't know how to define non-current assets, be sure that you do before going on to look at the topic of depreciation.

21.2 Depreciation of tangible non-current assets

Tangible non-current assets (i.e. long-term assets which can be touched, such as machinery, motor vehicles, fixtures and even buildings) do not last for ever. If the amount received (if any) on the disposal of a non-current asset is deducted from the cost of buying it, the value of the non-current asset can be said to have 'depreciated in value' by that amount over its period of usefulness to the business. For example, if a van was bought for £10,000 and sold five years later for £2,000 then its value has depreciated over the period of its use by £8,000.

This is the only time that depreciation can be calculated accurately. That is, you can only *estimate* what it should be each year while the non-current asset continues to be used.

21.3 Depreciation is an expense

Depreciation is that part of the original cost of a non-current asset that is consumed during its period of use by the business. It needs to be charged to the profit and loss account every year. The amount charged in a year for depreciation is based upon an estimate of how much of the overall economic usefulness of non-current assets has been used up in that accounting period. It is an expense for services consumed in the same way as expenses are incurred for items such as wages, rent or electricity. Because it is charged as an expense to the profit and loss account, depreciation reduces net profit.

For example, if a PC cost £1,200 and was expected to be used for three years, it might be estimated at the end of the first year that a third of its overall usefulness had been consumed. Depreciation would then be charged at an amount equal to one-third of the cost of the PC, i.e. £400. Profit would be reduced by £400 and the value of the PC in the balance sheet would be reduced from £1,200 to £800.

Using an example of a van and the petrol it consumes, you can see that the only real difference between the expense of depreciation for the van and the expense of petrol incurred in order to use the van is that the petrol expense is used up in a short time, whereas the expense for use of the van is spread over several years. Both the petrol and the cost of the van are expenses of the business.

Activity 21.2
If depreciation reduces profits and reduces the value of assets and so reduces the capital account of the owner, why do businesses bother providing for depreciation?

21.4 Causes of depreciation

Physical deterioration, economic factors, time and depletion all give rise to a reduction in the value of a tangible non-current asset. Let's look at these in more detail.

Physical deterioration

1 **Wear and tear.** When a motor vehicle or machinery or fixtures and fittings are used they eventually wear out. Some last many years, others last only a few years. This is also true of buildings, although some may last for a long time.
2 **Erosion, rust, rot and decay.** Land may be eroded or wasted away by the action of wind, rain, sun and other elements of nature. Similarly, the metals in motor vehicles or machinery will rust away. Wood will rot eventually. Decay is a process which will also be present due to the elements of nature and the lack of proper attention.

Economic factors

These may be said to be the reasons for an asset being put out of use even though it is in good physical condition. The two main factors are usually **obsolescence** and **inadequacy**.

1 **Obsolescence.** This is the process of becoming out of date. For instance, over the years there has been great progress in the development of synthesisers and other electronic devices used by leading commercial musicians. The old equipment will therefore have become obsolete, and much of it will have been taken out of use by such musicians.

This does not mean that the equipment is worn out. Other people may well buy the old equipment and use it, possibly because they cannot afford to buy new up-to-date equipment.

2 **Inadequacy.** This arises when an asset is no longer used because of the growth and changes in the size of the business. For instance, a small ferryboat that is operated by a business at a coastal resort will become entirely inadequate when the resort becomes more popular. Then it will be found that it would be more efficient and economical to operate a large ferryboat, and so the smaller boat will be put out of use by the business.

In this case also it does not mean that the ferryboat is no longer in good working order, nor that it is obsolete. It may, for example, be sold to a business at a smaller resort.

Time

Obviously, time is needed for wear and tear, erosion, etc., and for obsolescence and inadequacy to take place. However, there are non-current assets to which the time factor is connected in a different way. These are assets which have a legal life fixed in terms of years.

For instance, you may agree to rent some buildings for 10 years. This is normally called a lease. When the years have passed, the lease is worth nothing to you, as it has finished. Whatever you paid for the lease is now of no value.

A similar case arises when you buy a patent so that only you are able to produce something. When the patent's time has finished it then has no value. The usual length of life of a patent is sixteen years.

Instead of using the term depreciation, the term **amortisation** is often used for these assets.

Depletion

Other assets are of wasting character, perhaps due to the extraction of raw materials from them. These materials are then either used by the business to make something else, or are sold in their raw state to other businesses. Natural resources such as mines, quarries and oil wells come under this heading. To provide for the consumption of an asset of a wasting character is called provision for **depletion**.

21.5 Land and buildings

Prior to the issue in 1977 of a UK accounting standard (SSAP 12) which focused on this topic, freehold and long-term leasehold properties were very rarely subject to a charge for depreciation. It was contended that, as property values tended to rise rather than fall, it was inappropriate to charge depreciation.

The accounting standard changed that by requiring that depreciation be written off over the property's useful life, with the exception that freehold land does not normally require a provision for depreciation. This is because land normally has an unlimited useful life. Buildings do, however, eventually fall into disrepair or become obsolete and must be subject to a charge for depreciation each year.

When FRS 15 replaced SSAP 12 in 1999, it repeated these requirements. It also dealt with the problem of the distinction between the cost of freehold land and the cost of the buildings upon it, by insisting that the two elements of the cost be separated.

IASs 16 (*Property, plant and equipment*), 23 (*Borrowing costs*) and 36 (*Impairment of assets*) are the relevant international standards and they also insist that the two elements of the cost be separated.

21.6 Appreciation

At this stage, you may be wondering what happens when non-current assets increase (appreciate) in value. The answer is that normal accounting procedure would be to ignore any such appreciation, as to bring appreciation into account would be to contravene both the historical cost concept and the prudence concept you learnt about in Chapter 7.

> **Go back to Chapter 7 to refresh your understanding of the historical cost concept and the prudence concept.**

However, one of the problems when SSAP 12 was introduced was that the UK was in the middle of a boom in property prices which had been going on for some time and didn't end until the early 1990s. Businesses could see that the market value of their properties was rising. At the same time, they were being instructed (by the accounting standard) to charge their profit and loss account with depreciation that represented a fall in the value of the property over the period. Not surprisingly, this didn't seem to make any sense. To address this, IAS 16 allows non-current assets to be revalued at fair value (which is determined from market-based evidence) for land and buildings or market value (= open market value, i.e. the amount for which it could currently be sold) for plant and equipment. Depreciation is then calculated on the basis of the new value.

21.7 Provision for depreciation as an allocation of cost

Depreciation in total over the life of a non-current asset can be calculated quite simply as cost less the amount receivable when the non-current asset is put out of use by the business. This amount receivable is normally referred to as the **residual value** (or 'scrap value') of an asset. IAS 16 states that residual value should be based on prices current at the balance sheet date, not at the date of original purchase. If the item is bought and sold for a lower amount within the same accounting period, then the difference in value is charged as depreciation in arriving at that period's net profit.

The difficulties start when the asset is used for more than one accounting period: an attempt has to be made to charge each period with an appropriate amount of depreciation.

Although depreciation provisions are intended to allocate the cost of a non-current asset to each accounting period in which it is in use, it does not follow that there is any truly accurate method of performing this task. All that can be said is that the cost should be allocated over the life of the non-current asset in such a way as to charge it as equitably as possible to the periods in which it is used. The difficulties involved are considerable and include:

1 Apart from a few assets, such as leases, how accurately can a business assess an asset's useful life? Even a lease may be put out of use if the leased asset has become inadequate or inappropriate (e.g. after a change in the product being sold or unexpected growth in the size of the business).
2 How is 'use' measured? A car owned by a business for two years may have been driven one year by a very careful driver and another year by a reckless driver. The standard of driving will affect the condition of the car and also the amount of cash receivable on its disposal. How should a business apportion the car's depreciation costs?
3 There are other expenses besides depreciation, such as repairs and maintenance of the non-current asset. As both of these affect the rate and amount of depreciation, should they not also affect the depreciation provision calculations?
4 How can a business possibly know the amount receivable in x years' time when an asset is put out of use?

These are only some of the difficulties. Accounting has developed some methods that can be used to calculate depreciation. However, you will see that none of them really manages to address all these issues. Nevertheless, just as with doubtful debts, making some allowance for depreciation is better than making none at all.

21.8   Non-current assets held for sale

When non-current assets are reclassified as being held for sale, they become inventory and must not be depreciated.

21.9   Methods of calculating depreciation charges

The two main methods in use are the **straight line method** and the **reducing balance method.** Other methods may be used in certain cases, and some are discussed briefly in Section 21.12. Most accountants think that the straight line method is the one that is generally most suitable.

Straight line method

In this method, the number of years of use is estimated. The cost is then divided by the number of years. This gives the depreciation charge for each year.

For instance, if a van was bought for £22,000 and we thought we would keep it for four years and then sell it for £2,000 the depreciation to be charged each year would be:

$$\frac{\text{Cost } (£22,000) - \text{Estimated disposal value } (£2,000)}{\text{Number of expected years of use } (4)} = \frac{£20,000}{4}$$

$$= £5,000 \text{ depreciation each year for four years.}$$

On the other hand, if we thought that after four years the van would have no disposal value, the charge for depreciation would be:

$$\frac{\text{Cost } (£22,000)}{\text{Number of expected years of use } (4)} = \frac{£22,000}{4}$$

$$= £5,500 \text{ depreciation each year for four years.}$$

Reducing balance method

In this method, a fixed percentage for depreciation is deducted from the cost in the first year. In the second and later years the same percentage is taken of the reduced balance (i.e. cost *less* depreciation already charged). This method is also known as the *diminishing balance method* or the *diminishing debit balance method*.

If a machine is bought for £10,000 and depreciation is to be charged at 20 per cent, the calculations for the first three years would be as follows:

	£
Cost	10,000
First year: depreciation (20%)	(2,000)
	8,000
Second year: depreciation (20% of £8,000)	(1,600)
	6,400
Third year: depreciation (20% of £6,400)	(1,280)
Cost not yet apportioned, end of Year 3	5,120

The formula used to find the percentage to apply with this method is:

$$r = 1 - \sqrt[n]{\frac{s}{c}}$$

where n = the number of years

s = the net residual value (this must be a significant amount or the answers will be absurd, since the depreciation rate would amount to nearly one)

c = the cost of the asset

r = the rate of depreciation to be applied.

Using as an example the figures

n = 4 years

s = residual value £256

c = cost £10,000

the calculations would appear as:

$$r = 1 - \sqrt[4]{\frac{256}{£10,000}} = 1 - \frac{4}{10} = 0.6 \text{ or } 60 \text{ per cent}$$

The depreciation calculation applied to each of the four years of use would be:

	£
Cost	10,000
Year 1: Depreciation provision 60% of £10,000	(6,000)
Cost not yet apportioned, end of Year 1	4,000
Year 2: Depreciation provision 60% of £4,000	(2,400)
Cost not yet apportioned, end of Year 2	1,600
Year 3: Depreciation provision 60% of £1,600	(960)
Cost not yet apportioned, end of Year 3	640
Year 4: Depreciation provision 60% of £640	(384)
Cost not yet apportioned, end of Year 4	256

In this case, the percentage to be applied worked out conveniently to an easy to calculate figure of 60 per cent. However, the answer will often come out to several decimal places, e.g. 59.846512. When it does, normal practice is to take the nearest whole figure as a percentage to be applied. However, nowadays, this calculation is usually performed using a spreadsheet. Doing so means you don't need to worry any more about the difficulties of performing calculations using numbers with lots of decimal places. You simply build the formula into the calculation and don't need to worry about how many decimal places the depreciation rate may have. The spreadsheet will then produce the depreciation amount for each year.

Activity 21.3 What do you think you do when the *amount* of depreciation to be charged in a period is not a whole number?

The depreciation rate percentage to be applied under this method, assuming a significant amount for residual value, is usually between two and three times greater than under the straight line method.

The advocates of the reducing balance method usually argue that it helps to even out the total amount charged as expenses for the use of the asset each year. Provisions for depreciation are not the only costs charged. There are also the running costs. The repairs and maintenance element of running costs usually increases with age. Therefore, in order to equate total usage costs for each year of use, the depreciation provisions should fall over time, while the repairs and maintenance element increases. However, as can be seen from the figures in the example already given, the repairs and maintenance element would have to be comparatively large after the first year to bring about an equal total charge for each year of use.

To summarise, the people who favour this method say that:

In the early years A higher charge for depreciation + A lower charge for repairs and upkeep	will tend to be close to the sum of	In the later years A lower charge for depreciation + A higher charge for repairs and upkeep

21.10 Choice of method

The purpose of depreciation is to spread the total cost of a non-current asset over the periods in which it is to be used. The method chosen should be that which allocates cost to each period in accordance with the proportion of the overall economic benefit from using the non-current asset that was expended during that period.

If, therefore, the main value is to be obtained from the asset in its earliest years, it may be appropriate to use the reducing balance method, which charges more in the early years. If, on the other hand, the benefits are to be gained evenly over the years, then the straight line method would be more appropriate.

The repairs and maintenance factor also has to be taken into account. One argument supporting this was mentioned in the last section.

Exhibit 21.1 gives a comparison of the calculations using the two methods.

Exhibit 21.1

A business has just bought a machine for £8,000. It will be kept in use for four years, when it will be disposed of for an estimated amount of £500. The accountant has asked you to prepare a comparison of the amounts charged as depreciation using both methods.

For the straight line method, a figure of (£8,000 − £500) ÷ 4 = £7,500 ÷ 4 = £1,875 per annum is to be used. For the reducing balance method, a percentage figure of 50 per cent will be used.

	Method 1 Straight Line		Method 2 Reducing Balance
	£		£
Cost	8,000		8,000
Depreciation: Year 1	(1,875)	(50% of £8,000)	(4,000)
	6,125		4,000
Depreciation: Year 2	(1,875)	(50% of £4,000)	(2,000)
	4,250		2,000
Depreciation: Year 3	(1,875)	(50% of £2,000)	(1,000)
	2,375		1,000
Depreciation: Year 4	(1,875)	(50% of £1,000)	(500)
Disposal value	500		500

This example illustrates the fact that using the reducing balance method has a much higher charge for depreciation in the early years, and lower charges in the later years.

21.11 Depreciation provisions and assets bought or sold

There are two main methods of calculating depreciation provisions for assets bought or sold during an accounting period.

1 Ignore the dates during the accounting period that the assets were bought or sold, and simply calculate a full period's depreciation on the assets in use at the end of the period. Thus, assets sold during the accounting period will have had no provision for depreciation made for that last period irrespective of how many months they were in use. Conversely, assets bought during the period will have a full period of depreciation provision calculated even though they may not have been owned throughout the whole of the period.
2 Provide for depreciation on the basis of 'one month's ownership = one month's provision for depreciation'. Fractions of months are usually ignored. This is obviously a more precise method than Method 1.

The first method is the one normally used in practice. However, for examination purposes, where the dates on which assets are bought and sold are shown, you should use Method 2. If no such dates are given then, obviously, Method 1 is the one to use, but you should indicate that you are assuming this is the method to be adopted.

21.12 Other methods of calculating depreciation

There are many more methods of calculating depreciation, some of which are used in particular industries, such as the hotel and catering industry. We'll now look briefly at five of these other methods so that you are aware of how and why they may be used.

There is no information easily available to show how many organisations are using each method. It is possible to devise one's own special method. If it brings about an equitable charge for depreciation for the organisation, then the method will be suitable.

The revaluation method

When there are a few expensive non-current assets, it is not difficult to draw up the necessary accounts for depreciation. For each item we:

(a) Find its cost.
(b) Estimate its years of use to the business.
(c) Calculate and provide depreciation.
(d) Make the adjustments when the asset is disposed of.
(e) Calculate profit or loss on disposal.

This is worth doing for expensive items. There are, however, many examples of non-current assets for which the calculation would not be worth doing and, in fact, may be impossible. Some businesses will have many low-cost non-current assets. Garages or engineering works will have a lot of spanners, screwdrivers and other small tools; brewers will have kegs and casks; laboratories will have many small, low-cost glass instruments.

It would be impossible to follow procedures (a) to (e) above for every screwdriver or test tube. Instead the revaluation method is used.

The method is not difficult to use. An example is shown in Exhibit 21.2:

Exhibit 21.2

A business has a lot of steel containers. These are not for sale but are used by the business.

	£
On 1 January 2016 the containers were valued at	3,500
During the year to 31 December containers were purchased costing	1,300
On 31 December 2016 the containers were valued at	3,800

The depreciation is calculated:

	£
Value at start of period	3,500
Add Cost of items bought during period	1,300
	4,800
Less Value at close of period	(3,800)
Depreciation for year to 31 December 2016	1,000

The depreciation figure of £1,000 will be charged as an expense. Using this approach, we can look at Exhibit 21.3, where depreciation is entered in the books for the first three years of a new business.

Exhibit 21.3

The business starts in business on 1 January 2016.

	£
In its first year it buys casks costing	800
Their estimated value at 31 December 2016	540
Casks bought in the year ended 31 December 2017	320
Estimated value of all casks in hand on 31 December 2017	530
Casks bought in the year ended 31 December 2018	590
Estimated value of all casks in hand on 31 December 2018	700

Casks

2016			£	2016				£
Dec	31	Cash (during the year)	800	Dec	31	Profit and loss	260
					31	Inventory c/d	540
			800				800
2017				2017			
Jan	1	Inventory b/d	540	Dec	31	Profit and loss	330
Dec	31	Cash (during the year)	320		31	Inventory c/d	530
			860				860
2018				2018			
Jan	1	Inventory b/d	530	Dec	31	Profit and loss	420
Dec	31	Cash (during the year)	590		31	Inventory c/d	700
			1,120				1,120
2019							
Jan	1	Inventory b/d	700				

Profit and Loss for the year ending 31 December

			£
2016			
Dec	31	Use of casks	260
2017			
Dec	31	Use of casks	330
2018			
Dec	31	Use of casks	420

The balance of the casks account at the end of each year is shown as a non-current asset in the balance sheet.

Sometimes the business may make its own items such as tools or boxes. In these instances the tools account or boxes account should be debited with labour costs and material costs.

Revaluation is also used, for instance, by farmers for their cattle. As with other non-current assets depreciation should be provided for, but during the early life of an animal it will be appreciating in value, only to depreciate later. The task of calculating the cost of an animal becomes virtually impossible if it has been born on the farm, and reared on the farm by grazing on the pasture land and being fed on other foodstuffs, some grown on the farm and others bought by the farmer.

To get over this problem the revaluation method is used. Because of the difficulty of calculating the cost of the animals, they are valued at the price which they would fetch if sold at market. This is an exception to the general rule of assets being shown at cost price.

Depletion unit method

With non-current assets such as a quarry from which raw materials are dug out to be sold to the building industry, a different method is needed: the depletion unit method.

If a quarry was bought for £5,000 and it was expected to contain 1,000 tonnes of saleable materials, then for each tonne taken out we would depreciate it by £5, since £5,000 ÷ 1,000 = £5.

This can be shown as:

$$\frac{\text{Cost of asset}}{\text{Expected total contents in units}} \times \text{Number of units taken in period}$$

$$= \text{Depreciation for that period.}$$

Machine hour method

With a machine the depreciation provision may be based on the number of hours that the machine was operated during the period compared with the total expected running hours during the machine's life with the business. A business which bought a machine costing £2,000 having an expected running life of 1,000 hours, and no scrap value, could provide for depreciation of the machine at the rate of £2 for every hour it was operated during a particular accounting period.

Sum of the years' digits method

This method is popular in the USA but not common in the UK. It provides for higher depreciation to be charged early in the life of an asset with lower depreciation in later years.

Given an asset costing £3,000 which will be in use for five years, the calculations will be:

From purchase the asset will last for	5 years
From the second year the asset will last for	4 years
From the third year the asset will last for	3 years
From the fourth year the asset will last for	2 years
From the fifth year the asset will last for	1 year
Sum of these digits	15

	£
1st year 5/15 of £3,000 is charged =	1,000
2nd year 4/15 of £3,000 is charged =	800
3rd year 3/15 of £3,000 is charged =	600
4th year 2/15 of £3,000 is charged =	400
5th year 1/15 of £3,000 is charged =	200
	3,000

Units of output method

This method establishes the total expected units of output expected from the asset. Depreciation, based on cost less salvage value, is then calculated for the period by taking that period's units of output as a proportion of the total expected output over the life of the asset.

An instance of this could be a machine which is expected to be able to produce 10,000 widgets over its useful life. It has cost £6,000 and has an expected salvage value of £1,000. In year 1 a total of 1,500 widgets are produced, and in year 2 the production is 2,500 widgets.

The depreciation per period is calculated:

$$(\text{Cost} - \text{salvage value}) \times \left(\frac{\text{period's production}}{\text{total expected production}} \right)$$

$$\text{Year 1:} \quad £5,000 \times \frac{1,500}{10,000} = £750 \text{ depreciation}$$

$$\text{Year 2:} \quad £5,000 \times \frac{2,500}{10,000} = £1,250 \text{ depreciation}$$

21.13 Recording depreciation

Because depreciation is an expense that reflects the decrease in the economic value of a non-current asset over a period of time, it is charged at the end of each reporting period. Imagine you have a machine with a five-year economic life that you bought on the first day of your reporting period, which is a year. You believe that it will lose its value to you at an equal rate throughout the five years. You do not believe it will be worth anything at the end of that time. The depreciation you would charge at the end of each year is one-fifth of what it cost.

From your knowledge of double entry, you know that an increase in a possession is a debit. You also know that a decrease is the opposite, i.e. a credit. But, accounting regulations forbid you from making the entry for depreciation in the account for the possession (asset) that is being depreciated.

 Activity 21.4 In the past you were allowed to credit depreciation to the account of the non-current asset. Why do you think this is now no longer allowed?

Instead, you must make it in an 'accumulated provision for depreciation account', often shortened to the **accumulated depreciation account** (or sometimes, confusingly, known as the 'provision for depreciation account').

 Activity 21.5 Why do you think it would be confusing to call the accumulated provision for depreciation account the 'provision for depreciation account'?

The form of settlement is depreciation, it is an expense, so it is debit. The item exchanged is part of a specific non-current asset, which is a credit (to the accumulated provision for depreciation account for that non-current asset). We can either create an account for depreciation, or we simply debit the expense directly to the profit and loss account. When we do the latter, the double entry is:

Debit the profit and loss account
Credit the accumulated provision for depreciation account

Let's look at how this is done in an example, shown in Exhibit 21.4.

Exhibit 21.4

A business has a financial year end of 31 December. A computer is bought for £2,000 on 1 January 2015. It is to be depreciated at the rate of 20 per cent using the reducing balance method. The records for the first three years are:

Computer

2015			£	
Jan	1	Cash	2,000	

Accumulated Provision for Depreciation: Computer

2015			£	2015				£
Dec	31	Balance c/d	400	Dec	31	Profit and loss		400
2016				2016				
Dec	31	Balance c/d	720	Jan	1	Balance b/d		400
				Dec	31	Profit and loss		320
			720					720
2017				2017				
Dec	31	Balance c/d	976	Jan	1	Balance b/d		720
				Dec	31	Profit and loss		256
			976					976
				2018				
				Jan	1	Balance b/d		976

Profit and Loss

2015			£	
Dec	31	Acc Provn for Depn: Computer	400	
2016				
Dec	31	Acc Provn for Depn: Computer	320	
2017				
Dec	31	Acc Provn for Depn: Computer	256	

Income Statement (extracts) for the years ending 31 December

		£
2015	Depreciation	400
2016	Depreciation	320
2017	Depreciation	256

Note: In this case, the depreciation for the period being entered in the income statement is being described as 'depreciation' and *not* by the name of the account it originated from (the accumulated provision for depreciation account).

Activity 21.6

What advantages are there in making this exception to the rule by using 'depreciation' rather than 'accumulated provision for depreciation' in the entry in the income statement?

Now the balance on the *Computer Account* is shown on the balance sheet at the end of each year less the balance on the *Accumulated Provision for Depreciation Account*.

Balance Sheets (extracts)

	£	£
As at 31 December 2015		
Computer at cost	2,000	
Less Accumulated depreciation	(400)	
		1,600
As at 31 December 2016		
Computer at cost	2,000	
Less Accumulated depreciation	(720)	
		1,280
As at 31 December 2017		
Computer at cost	2,000	
Less Accumulated depreciation	(976)	
		1,024

21.14 The disposal of a non-current asset

Reason for accounting entries

Upon the sale of a non-current asset, we will want to remove it from our ledger accounts. This means that the cost of that asset needs to be taken out of the asset account. In addition, the accumulated depreciation on the asset which has been sold will have to be taken out of the accumulated provision. Finally, the profit and loss on sale, if any, will have to be calculated and posted to the profit and loss account.

When we charge depreciation on a non-current asset we are having to make an informed guess. We will not often guess correctly. This means that, when we dispose of an asset, the amount received for it is usually different from our estimate.

Activity 21.7 List as many things as you can think of in one minute that could cause the amount charged for depreciation to have been incorrect.

Accounting entries needed

On the sale of a non-current asset, in this example a computer, the following entries are needed:

(A) Transfer the cost price of the asset sold to an assets disposal account (in this case a computer disposals account):

> *Debit* computer disposals account
> *Credit* computer account

(B) Transfer the depreciation already charged to the assets disposal account:

> *Debit* accumulated provision for depreciation: computer
> *Credit* computer disposals account

(C) For the amount received on disposal:

> *Debit* cash book
> *Credit* computer disposals account

(D) Transfer the difference (i.e. the amount needed to balance the computer disposals account) to the profit and loss account.

(*i*) If the computer disposals account shows a difference on the debit side (i.e. if more has been credited to the account than has been debited to it), there is a profit on the sale:

> Debit computer disposals account
> Credit profit and loss account

(*ii*) If the computer disposals account shows a difference on the credit side, there is a loss on sale:

> Debit profit and loss account
> Credit computer disposals account

These entries can be illustrated by looking at those needed if the computer in Exhibit 21.4 was sold on 2 January 2018. At 31 December 2017, the cost was £2,000 and a total of £976 had been written off as depreciation leaving a net book value of £2,000 − £976 = £1,024. If the computer is sold in 2018 for *more* than £1,024 a profit on sale will be made. If, on the other hand, the computer is sold for *less* than £1,024 then a loss will be incurred.

Exhibit 21.5 shows the entries needed when the computer has been sold for £1,070 and a profit of £46 on sale has, therefore, been made. Exhibit 21.6 shows the entries where the computer has been sold for £950, thus incurring a loss on sale of £74. In both cases, the sale is on 2 January 2018 and no depreciation is to be charged for the two days' ownership in 2018. (The letters in brackets refer to the accounting double entries, A–D, above.)

Exhibit 21.5   Non-current asset sold at a profit

Computer

2015		£	2018			£
Jan 1 Cash		2,000	Jan 2 Computer disposals	(A)	2,000

Accumulated Provision for Depreciation: Computer

2018			£	2018		£
Jan 2 Computer disposals	(B)	976	Jan 1 Balance b/d		976

Computer Disposals

2018			£	2018			£
Jan 2 Computer	(A)	2,000	Jan 2 Accumulated provision		
Dec 31 Profit and loss	(D)	46		for depreciation	(B)	976
				2 Cash	(C)	1,070
		2,046				2,046

Profit and Loss

	2018		£
	Dec 31 Computer disposal (gain)	(D)	46

Income Statement (extract) for the year ending 31 December 2018

	£
Gross profit	XXX
Add Gain on sale of computer	46

Exhibit 21.6 Non-current asset sold at a loss

Computer

2015		£	2018			£
Jan 1 Cash		2,000	Jan 2 Computer disposals		(A)	2,000

Accumulated Provision for Depreciation: Computer

2018		£	2018		£
Jan 2 Computer disposals	(B)	976	Jan 1 Balance b/d		976

Computer Disposals

2018		£	2018				£
Jan 2 Computer	(A)	2,000	Jan 2 Accumulated provision for depreciation		(B)	976
			2 Cash		(C)	950
			Dec 31 Profit and loss		(D)	74
		2,000					2,000

Profit and Loss

2018		£	
Dec 31 Computer disposal (loss)	(D)	74	

Income Statement (extract) for the year ending 31 December 2018

	£
Gross profit	xxx
Less Loss on sale of computer	(74)

In many cases, the disposal of an asset will mean that we have sold it. This will not always be the case. For example, a car may be given up in part payment for a new car. Here the disposal value is the exchange value. If a new car costing £10,000 was to be paid for with £6,000 in cash and an allowance of £4,000 for the old car, then the disposal value of the old car is £4,000.

Similarly, a car may have been in an accident and is now worthless. If a payment is received from an insurance company, the amount of that payment will be the disposal value. If an asset is scrapped, the disposal value is that received from the sale of the scrap, which may be nil.

21.15 Change of depreciation method

It is possible to make a change in the method of calculating depreciation. This should not be done frequently, and it should only be undertaken after a thorough review. Where a change is made, if material (see Chapter 7 on materiality), the effect of the change on the figures reported should be shown as a note to the financial statements in the year of change.

Further examples

So far, the examples have deliberately been kept simple. Only one non-current asset has been shown in each case. Exhibits 21.7 and 21.8 give examples of more complicated cases.

Exhibit 21.7

A machine is bought on 1 January 2015 for £1,000 and another one on 1 October 2016 for £1,200. The first machine is sold on 30 June 2017 for £720. The business's financial year ends on 31 December. The machinery is to be depreciated at 10 per cent, using the straight line method. Machinery in existence at the end of each year is to be depreciated for a full year. No depreciation is to be charged on any machinery disposed of during the year.

Machinery

2015			£	2015			£
Jan	1	Cash	1,000	Dec	31	Balance c/d	1,000
2016				2016			
Jan	1	Balance b/d	1,000	Dec	31	Balance c/d	2,200
Oct	1	Cash	1,200				
			2,200				
							2,200
2017				2017			
Jan	1	Balance b/d	2,200	Jun	30	Machinery disposals	1,000
				Dec	31	Balance c/d	1,200
			2,200				2,200
2018							
Jan	1	Balance b/d	1,200				

Accumulated Provision for Depreciation: Machinery

2015			£	2015			£
Dec	31	Balance c/d	100	Dec	31	Profit and loss	100
2016				2016			
Dec	31	Balance c/d	320	Jan	1	Balance b/d	100
				Dec	31	Profit and loss	220
			320				320
2017				2017			
Jun	30	Disposals of machinery	200	Jan	1	Balance b/d	320
		(2 years × 10% × £1,000)		Dec	31	Profit and loss	120
Dec	31	Balance c/d	240				440
			440	2018			
				Jan	1	Balance b/d	240

Machinery Disposals

2017			£	2017			£
Jun	30	Machinery	1,000	Jun	30	Cash	720
					30	Accumulated provision for depreciation	200
				Dec	31	Profit and loss	80
			1,000				1,000

Profit and Loss (extracts)

2015			£	
Dec	31	Acc Provn for Depn: Machinery	100	
2016				
Dec	31	Acc Provn for Depn: Machinery	220	
2017				
Dec	31	Acc Provn for Depn: Machinery	120	
	31	Machinery disposals (loss)	80	

Income Statement (extracts) for the years ending 31 December

		£
Gross profit		xxx
Less Expenses:		
2015 Provision for depreciation: Machinery		(100)
2016 Provision for depreciation: Machinery		(220)
2017 Provision for depreciation: Machinery		(120)
Loss on machinery sold		(80)

Balance Sheet (extracts) as at 31 December

	£	£
2015 Machinery at cost	1,000	
Less Accumulated depreciation	(100)	
		900
2016 Machinery at cost	2,200	
Less Accumulated depreciation	(320)	
		1,880
2017 Machinery at cost	1,200	
Less Accumulated depreciation	(240)	
		960

A more complex example can now be given. It involves a greater number of items; and the depreciation provisions are calculated on a proportionate basis, i.e. one month's depreciation for one month's ownership.

Exhibit 21.8

A business with its financial year end on 31 December buys two vans on 1 January 2015, No. 1 for £8,000 and No. 2 for £5,000. It also buys another van, No. 3, on 1 July 2017 for £9,000 and another, No. 4, on 1 October 2017 for £7,200. The first two vans are sold, No. 1 for £2,290 on 30 September 2018, and No. 2 for scrap for £50 on 30 June 2019.

Depreciation is on the straight line basis, 20 per cent per annum, ignoring scrap value in this particular case when calculating depreciation per annum. Shown below are extracts from the assets account, provision for depreciation account, disposal account, profit and loss account, and income statements for the years ending 31 December 2015, 2016, 2017, 2018 and 2019 and the balance sheets as at those dates.

Vans

			£					£
2015				2015				
Jan	1	Cash	13,000	Dec	31	Balance c/d		13,000
2016				2016				
Jan	1	Balance b/d	13,000	Dec	31	Balance c/d		13,000
2017				2017				
Jan	1	Balance b/d	13,000	Dec	31	Balance c/d		29,200
July	1	Cash	9,000					
Oct	1	Cash	7,200					
			29,200					29,200
2018				2018				
Jan	1	Balance b/d	29,200	Sept	30	Disposals		8,000
				Dec	31	Balance c/d		21,200
			29,200					29,200
2019				2019				
Jan	1	Balance b/d	21,200	June	30	Disposals		5,000
				Dec	31	Balance c/d		16,200
			21,200					21,200
2020								
Jan	1	Balance b/d	16,200					

Accumulated Provision for Depreciation: Vans

2015		£	2015			£
Dec 31	Balance c/d	2,600	Dec 31	Profit and loss		2,600
2016			2016			
Dec 31	Balance c/d	5,200	Jan 1	Balance b/d		2,600
			Dec 31	Profit and loss		2,600
		5,200				5,200
2017			2017			
Dec 31	Balance c/d	9,060	Jan 1	Balance b/d		5,200
			Dec 31	Profit and loss		3,860
		9,060				9,060
2018			2018			
Sept 30	Disposals	6,000	Jan 1	Balance b/d		9,060
Dec 31	Balance c/d	8,500	Dec 31	Profit and loss		5,440
		14,500				14,500
2019			2019			
June 30	Disposals	4,500	Jan 1	Balance b/d		8,500
Dec 31	Balance c/d	7,740	Dec 31	Profit and loss		3,740
		12,240				12,240
			2020			
			Jan 1	Balance b/d		7,740

Workings – depreciation provisions		£	£
2015	20% of £13,000		2,600
2016	20% of £13,000		2,600
2017	20% of £13,000 × 12 months	2,600	
	20% of £9,000 × 6 months	900	
	20% of £7,200 × 3 months	360	
			3,860
2018	20% of £21,100 × 12 months	4,240	
	20% of £8,000 × 9 months	1,200	
			5,440
2019	20% of £16,200 × 12 months	3,240	
	20% of £5,000 × 6 months	500	
			3,740

Workings – transfers of depreciation provisions to disposal accounts

Van 1 Bought Jan 1 2015 Cost £8,000
       Sold Sept 30 2018
       Period of ownership 3¾ years
       Depreciation provisions 3¾ × 20% × £8,000 = £6,000

Van 2 Bought Jan 1 2015 Cost £5,000
       Sold June 30 2019
       Period of ownership 4½ years
       Depreciation provisions 4½ × 20% × £5,000 = £4,500

Disposals of Vans

2018		£	2018		£
Sept 30	van	8,000	Sept 30	Accumulated provision	6,000
Dec 31	Profit and loss	290		for depreciation	
				Cash	2,290
		8,290			8,290

→

→

Disposals of Vans (Continued)

2019			£	2019				£
Jun	30	Van	5,000	Jun	30	Accumulated provision for depreciation		4,500
						Cash		50
				Dec	31	Profit and loss		450
			5,000					5,000

Profit and Loss (extracts)

2015			£				£
Dec	31	Acc Provn for Depn: Vans	2,600				
2016							
Dec	31	Acc Provn for Depn: Vans	2,600				
2017							
Dec	31	Acc Provn for Depn: Vans	3,860				
2018				2018			
Dec	31	Acc Provn for Depn: Vans	5,440	Dec	31	Disposal of Vans (Gain)	290
2019							
Dec	31	Acc Provn for Depn: Vans	3,740				
		Disposal of Vans (loss)	450				

Income Statement (extracts) for the years ending 31 December

		£	£
Gross profit (each year 2015, 2016, 2017)			xxx
	Less Expenses:		
2015	Provision for depreciation: vans		(2,600)
2016	Provision for depreciation: vans		(2,600)
2017	Provision for depreciation: vans		(3,860)
2018	Gross profit		x,xxx
	Add Profit on van sold		290
			x,xxx
	Less Expenses:		
	Provision for depreciation: vans		(5,440)
			x,xxx
2019	Gross profit		x,xxx
	Less Expenses:		
	Provision for depreciation: vans	3,740	
	Loss on van sold	450	
			(4,190)

Balance Sheet (extracts) as at 31 December

2015	Vans at cost	13,000	
	Less Accumulated depreciation	(2,600)	
			10,400
2016	Vans at cost	13,000	
	Less Accumulated depreciation	(5,200)	
			7,800

Balance Sheet (extracts) as at 31 December *(Continued)*

		£	£
2017	Vans at cost	29,200	
	Less Accumulated depreciation	(9,060)	
			20,140
2018	Vans at cost	21,200	
	Less Accumulated depreciation	(8,500)	
			12,700
2019	Vans at cost	16,200	
	Less Accumulated depreciation	(7,740)	
			8,460

21.16 Depreciation provisions and the replacement of assets

Making a provision for depreciation does not mean that money is invested somewhere to finance the replacement of the asset when it is put out of use. It is simply a bookkeeping entry, and the end result is that lower net profits are shown because the provisions have been charged to profit and loss.

It is not surprising to find that many people – especially students – who have not studied accounting misunderstand the situation. They often think that a provision is the same as money kept somewhere with which to replace the asset eventually. Never make that mistake. It may cost you a lot of marks in an exam!

A cautious owner may take out less drawings if the net profit is lower, but that is no justification for arguing that depreciation results in funds being available to replace the asset later!

21.17 Another approach

The approach you've learnt to record the periodic change for depreciation is known as the 'one-stage approach'. It was based upon the use of one double entry, a credit to the accumulated provision for depreciation account and a debit to the profit and loss account.

There is another approach which is widely used in practice. It involves using a '**provision for depreciation account**', often shortened to '**depreciation account**', as well as the 'accumulated provision for depreciation account'. At the end of the period, you calculate the depreciation for the period and make the following double entries:

1 *Debit* the depreciation account
   Credit the accumulated provision for depreciation account
2 *Debit* the profit and loss account
   Credit the depreciation account

Compare this two-stage approach to the one-stage approach you learnt earlier:

> *Debit* the profit and loss account
>   *Credit* the accumulated provision for depreciation account

Note how the double entry you learnt earlier combines the two entries used in the two-stage approach by cancelling out the debit and credit to the depreciation account. This makes it much simpler to record the entries required, but adopting the two-stage approach has the advantage that it actually shows what has happened rather than compressing the two double entries, that theory says should be used, into one.

However, some accountants still prefer to keep recording the entries as simple as possible and so use only the 'accumulated provision for depreciation account' (i.e. the 'one-stage approach').

Nevertheless, you need to be aware of and able to use the two-stage approach described above, just in case you should be asked to do so by an examiner. If you are *not* asked for two accounts (a depreciation account *plus* an accumulated provision for depreciation account) you should assume that the one-stage approach is the one you are expected to use.

> *Note:* As in Review Questions 21.17A, 21.18 and 21.19A, examiners sometimes ask for a 'depreciation' account to be shown in an answer and they do not mention an 'accumulated provision for depreciation' account. When this happens, it is usually the 'accumulated provision for depreciation' account they are looking for. That is, they expect the balance on it to be carried forward to the next period, as in the case of the one-stage method. It is the one-stage method they want you to use but they have given the account the 'wrong' name. Use the name they used ('depreciation') but treat it as if it were an 'accumulated provision for depreciation' account. When examiners want you to prepare both a 'depreciation' account and an 'accumulated provision for depreciation' account, it will be obvious from the wording of the question.

21.18 Finally

This chapter has covered all the principles involved. Obviously examiners can present their questions in their own way. In fact, in order to better test your understanding, examiners do tend to vary the way questions involving depreciation are presented. Practise all the questions in this book, including those in the exhibits, and compare them with the answers shown in full. Doing so will demonstrate the truth of this statement and prepare you better for your examination when you can be virtually guaranteed that you will need to be able to calculate and make appropriate entries for depreciation.

Learning outcomes

You should now have learnt:

1 That depreciation is an expense of the business and has to be charged against any period during which a non-current asset has been in use.

2 That the main causes of depreciation are: physical deterioration, economic factors, the time factor and depletion.

3 How to calculate depreciation using the straight line method.

4 How to calculate depreciation using the reducing balance method.

5 How to calculate depreciation on assets bought or sold within an accounting period.

6 That there are other methods of calculating depreciation in addition to the straight line and reducing balance methods.

7 That the method of showing depreciation in the asset account is now used only by some small organisations, and should be avoided.

8 That non-current asset accounts should show only the cost. Depreciation is credited to an accumulated provision for depreciation account.

9 That when we sell a non-current asset, we must transfer both the cost and the accumulated depreciation to a separate disposal account.

10 That it is very rare for the depreciation provided to have been accurate.

11 That a profit on the disposal of a non-current asset is transferred to the credit of the profit and loss account.

12 That a loss on the disposal of a non-current asset is transferred to the debit of the profit and loss account.

13 That there are two approaches which may be adopted when entering depreciation into the accounting books.

14 That the approach you have learnt does so in one double entry and uses one ledger account for the accumulated provision for depreciation.

15 That the other, 'two-stage', approach uses two journal entries and two ledger accounts, one for the depreciation expense and the other to record the accumulated provision for depreciation.

16 That there are a number of alternatives for the names of the depreciation accounts involved under these two approaches.

17 That the name 'provision for depreciation' is often used in place of 'accumulated provision for depreciation' in the balance sheet account that shows the depreciation accumulated to date.

Answers to activities

21.1 Non-current assets are those assets of material value which are:

- of long life; and
- to be used in the business; and
- not bought with the main purpose of resale.

21.2 Firstly, financial statements must show a true and fair view of the financial performance and position of the business. If depreciation was not provided for, both non-current assets and profits would be stated in the financial statements at inflated amounts. This would only mislead the users of those financial statements and so depreciation must be charged. Secondly, IAS 16 requires that non-current assets are depreciated.

21.3 Just as with the depreciation percentage, you round it to the nearest whole number.

21.4 It has the effect of reducing the balance shown in the ledger for the non-current asset so that, over time, it may be very much less than the original cost. This makes it difficult to identify the original cost of non-current assets and means that, in the balance sheet the only information that can be given is the value to which each non-current asset has been written-down. Anyone looking at this information will have no way of assessing whether a non-current asset was originally very expensive (which may be relevant, for example, if it is a building) and so cannot arrive at a realistic view of what the non-current assets really comprise. Nor, especially in the case of smaller businesses, is it immediately obvious how long a non-current asset is likely to continue to be used or, in fact, whether there is actually an asset in current use – if the value has been written down to zero, it wouldn't have a balance, may have been written out of the ledger, and certainly wouldn't be included in the balance sheet.

21.5 Use of the term 'provision for depreciation account' can be very confusing as the name of the account used to record provisions for doubtful debts is the 'allowance for doubtful debts account' and, as you know, that account is closed off at the end of the accounting period and the balance transferred to the debit side of the profit and loss account. In contrast, the balance on the 'accumulated provision for depreciation account' is shown in the balance sheet at the year end and carried forward to the next accounting period. The two treatments could hardly be more different. It is, therefore, asking for mistakes to be made if you use the same stem, 'provision for . . .', for them both. It must be said, however, that many people do, including some examiners. So, you need to be aware that when you see an account called the 'provision for depreciation account', it is referring to the account we shall call in this book the 'accumulated provision for depreciation account'. To help you get used to this, some of the multiple choice questions and review questions at the end of this chapter use the term 'provision for depreciation account'.

21.6 Doing so makes it clear that just one period's depreciation is involved and *not* the entire accumulated depreciation to date.

21.7 We cannot be absolutely certain how long we will keep the asset in use, nor can we be certain how much the asset will be sold for when we dispose of it, or even that it will be possible to sell it at that time. We may also have chosen the wrong depreciation method causing the net book value of the asset (i.e. cost less accumulated depreciation) to have been reduced too quickly (reducing balance) or too slowly (straight line) in the event that it is disposed of earlier than expected.

Review questions

21.1 D. Bell purchased a laptop for £480. It has an estimated life of three years and a scrap value of £60.

She is not certain whether she should use the straight line or the reducing balance basis for the purpose of calculating depreciation on the computer.

You are required to calculate the depreciation (to the nearest £) using both methods, showing clearly the balance of cost minus accumulated depreciation at the end of each year under each method. (Assume that 50 per cent per annum is to be used for the reducing balance method.)

21.2 A machine costs £26,660. It will be kept for four years, and then sold for an estimated figure of £6,400. Show the calculations of the figures for depreciation (to nearest £) for each year using (a) the straight line method, (b) the reducing balance method, for this method using a depreciation rate of 30 per cent.

21.3 A car costs £24,000. It will be kept for three years, and then sold for £6,000. Calculate the depreciation for each year using (a) the reducing balance method, using a depreciation rate of 35 per cent, (b) the straight line method.

21.4A A photocopier costs £23,000. It will be kept for four years, and then traded in for £4,000. Show the calculations of the figures for depreciation for each year using (a) the straight line method, (b) the reducing balance method, for this method using a depreciation rate of 35 per cent.

21.5A A printer costs £800. It will be kept for five years and then scrapped. Show your calculations of the amount of depreciation each year if (a) the reducing balance method at a rate of 60 per cent was used, (b) the straight line method was used.

21.6A A bus is bought for £56,000. It will be used for four years, and then sold back to the supplier for £18,000. Show the depreciation calculations for each year using (a) the reducing balance method with a rate of 25 per cent, (b) the straight line method.

21.7 A company which makes up its financial statements annually to 31 December, charges depreciation on its machinery at the rate of 12 per cent per annum using the reducing balance method.

On 31 December 2018, the machinery consisted of three items purchased as shown:

	£
On 1 January 2016 Machine A	Cost 4,000
On 1 September 2017 Machine B	Cost 7,000
On 1 May 2018 Machine C	Cost 2,000

Required:
Your calculations showing the depreciation expense for the year 2018.

21.8 A motor vehicle which cost £12,000 was bought on credit from Trucks Ltd on 1 January 2016. Financial statements are prepared annually to 31 December and depreciation of vehicles is provided at 25 per cent per annum under the reducing balance method.

Required:
Prepare the motor vehicle account and the accumulated provision for depreciation on motor vehicles account for the first two years of the motor vehicle's working life.

21.9 Ivor Innes has supplied you with the following information:

	1 April 2017	31 March 2018
	£	£
Cash	840	700
Fixtures	7,600	7,600
Balance at bank	5,500	8,320
Inventory	17,800	19,000
Accounts receivable	8,360	4,640
Accounts payable	5,200	8,800

During the year to 31 March 2018, Ivor withdrew £11,400 from the business for private purposes. In November 2017, Ivor received a legacy of £18,000 which he paid into the business bank account.

Ivor agrees that £600 should be provided for depreciation of fixtures and £200 for doubtful debts.

Required:
Prepare a balance sheet as at 31 March 2018 which clearly indicates the net profit or loss for the year.

21.10A Vinny purchased some new equipment on 28 February 2016 for £240,000. Vinny's policy is to depreciate equipment at 30 per cent using the reducing balance method. He calculates a full year's charge in the year of acquisition and none in the year of disposal.

(a) What will be the depreciation expense in respect of this equipment in Vinny's financial year ended 31 August 2020?
(b) Suggest why it might be more appropriate to use the reducing balance method of depreciation for certain assets.

21.11A C. Harvey, a sole trader, purchased a delivery van on 1 March 2020 for £11,360 and some new equipment on 1 September 2020 for £7,000.

He expects that the van will have a useful life of four years, after which it should have a trade-in value of £2,000. The scrap value of the equipment after ten years' use is estimated to be £1,000. Harvey charges depreciation using the straight-line method.

Required:
What should the depreciation expense be in relation to these two items for Harvey's financial year ended 30 November 2020 assuming that:

(a) He charges a full year's depreciation in the year of purchase and none in the year of sale.
(b) He charges depreciation on a monthly basis.

21.12   State which depreciation method will be the most appropriate in the case of each of the following assets and why. Also, indicate to what extent obsolescence will affect each of the assets.

(a)   A delivery van used by a baker.
(b)   A filing cabinet.
(c)   A shop held on a twenty-year lease.
(d)   A plastic moulding machine to manufacture a new novelty – plastic fireguards. It is expected that these will be very popular next Christmas and that sales will continue for a year or two thereafter but at a very much lower level.
(e)   Machine X. This machine is used as a standby when the normal machines are being maintained. Occasionally it is used to increase capacity when there is a glut of orders. Machine X is of an old type and is inefficient compared with new machines. When used on a full-time basis, the machine should last for approximately four years.

21.13A   At the beginning of the financial year on 1 April 2020, a company had a balance on plant account of £372,000 and on provision for depreciation of plant account of £205,400.

The company's policy is to provide depreciation using the reducing balance method applied to the non-current assets held at the end of the financial year at the rate of 20% per annum.

On 1 September 2020 the company sold for £13,700 some plant which it had acquired on 31 October 2016 at a cost of £36,000. Additionally, installation costs totalled £4,000. During 2018 major repairs costing £6,300 had been carried out on this plant and, in order to increase the capacity of the plant, a new motor had been fitted in December 2018 at a cost of £4,400. A further overhaul costing £2,700 had been carried out during 2019.

The company acquired new replacement plant on 30 November 2020 at a cost of £96,000, inclusive of installation charges of £7,000.

Required:
Calculate:

(a)   the balance of plant at cost at 31 March 2021
(b)   the provision for depreciation of plant at 31 March 2021
(c)   the profit or loss on disposal of the plant.

(*Association of Chartered Certified Accountants*)

21.14   A company starts in business on 1 January 2018. You are to write up the vans account and the accumulated depreciation account for the year ended 31 December 2018 from the information given below. Depreciation is at the rate of 25 per cent per annum, using the basis that one complete month's ownership needs one month's depreciation.

2018   Bought one van for £69,000 on 1 January
       Bought two vans for £72,000 each on 1 August

21.15   A company starts in business on 1 January 2017, the financial year end being 31 December. You are to show:

(a)   The equipment account.
(b)   The accumulated depreciation account.
(c)   The balance sheet extracts for each of the years 2017, 2018, 2019, 2020.

The equipment bought was:

2017	1 January	1 machine costing £800
2018	1 July	2 machines costing £1,200 each
	1 October	1 machine costing £600
2020	1 April	1 machine costing £1,400

Depreciation is over 10 years, using the straight line method, machines being depreciated for the proportion of the year that they are owned.

21.16A A company maintains its non-current assets at cost. An accumulated provision for depreciation account is used for each type of asset. Machinery is to be depreciated at the rate of 15 per cent per annum, and fixtures at the rate of 5 per cent per annum, using the reducing balance method. Depreciation is to be calculated on assets in existence at the end of each year, giving a full year's depreciation even though the asset was bought part of the way through the year. The following transactions in assets have taken place:

2019	1 January	Bought machinery £2,800, fixtures £290
	1 July	Bought fixtures £620
2020	1 October	Bought machinery £3,500
	1 December	Bought fixtures £130

The financial year end of the business is 31 December.

You are to show:
(a) The machinery account.
(b) The fixtures account.
(c) The two separate accumulated provision for depreciation accounts.
(d) The non-current assets section of the balance sheet at the end of each year, for the years ended 31 December 2019 and 2020.

21.17 A company depreciates its plant at the rate of 25 per cent per annum, straight line method, for each month of ownership. From the following details draw up the plant account and the accumulated depreciation account for each of the years 2017, 2018, 2019 and 2020.

2017	Bought plant costing £2,600 on 1 January.
	Bought plant costing £2,100 on 1 October.
2019	Bought plant costing £2,800 on 1 September.
2020	Sold plant which had been bought for £2,600 on 1 January 2017 for the sum of £810 on 31 August 2020.

You are also required to draw up the plant disposal account and the extracts from the balance sheet as at the end of each year.

21.18 A company maintains its non-current assets at cost. Accumulated depreciation accounts for each asset are kept.

At 31 December 2018 the position was as follows:

	Total cost to date	Total depreciation to date
	£	£
Machinery	94,500	28,350
Office furniture	3,200	1,280

The following additions were made during the financial year ended 31 December 2019:
Machinery £16,000, office furniture £460.
A machine bought in 2015 for £1,600 was sold for £360 during the year.
The rates of depreciation are:
Machinery 20 per cent, office furniture 10 per cent, using the straight line basis, calculated on the assets in existence at the end of each financial year irrespective of the date of purchase.

You are required to show the asset, accumulated depreciation and disposal accounts for the year ended 31 December 2019 and the balance sheet extracts at that date.

21.19A   Distance Limited owned three lorries at 1 April 2019:

> Lorry A: purchased on 21 May 2015 for £31,200
> Lorry B: purchased on 20 June 2017 for £19,600
> Lorry C: purchased on 1 January 2019 for £48,800

Depreciation is charged annually at 20 per cent on cost on all vehicles in use at the end of the year.

During the year ended 31 March 2020, the following transactions occurred:

(i)   1 June 2019: Lorry B was involved in an accident and considered to be a write-off by the insurance company which paid £10,500 in settlement.

(ii)   7 June 2019: Lorry D was purchased for £32,800.

(iii)   21 August 2019: Lorry A was sold for £7,000.

(iv)   30 October 2019: Lorry E was purchased for £39,000.

(v)   6 March 2020: Lorry E was considered not to be suitable for carrying the type of goods required and was exchanged for lorry F. The value of lorry F was deemed to be £37,600.

Required:

Prepare the ledger T-accounts recording these transactions for the year ending 31 March 2020 and bring down the balances at 1 April.

21.20

(a)   Identify the four factors which cause non-current assets to depreciate.

(b)   Which one of these factors is the most important for each of the following assets?

   (i)   a gold mine;

   (ii)   a van;

   (iii)   a fifty-year lease on a building;

   (iv)   land;

   (v)   a ship used to ferry passengers and vehicles across a river following the building of a bridge across the river;

   (vi)   a franchise to market a new computer software package in a certain country.

(c)   The financial year of Ochre Ltd will end on 31 December 2018. At 1 January 2018 the company had in use equipment with a total accumulated cost of £135,620 which had been depreciated by a total of £81,374. During the year ended 31 December 2018 Ochre Ltd purchased new equipment costing £47,800 and sold off equipment which had originally cost £36,000, and which had been depreciated by £28,224, for £5,700. No further purchases or sales of equipment are planned for December. The policy of the company is to depreciate equipment at 40% using the diminishing balance method. A full year's depreciation is provided for on all equipment in use by the company at the end of each year.

Required:

Show the following ledger accounts for the year ended 31 December 2018:

(i)   the Equipment Account;

(ii)   the Provision for Depreciation on Equipment Account;[Author's Note]

(iii)   the Assets Disposals Account.

(Association of Accounting Technicians)

Author's Note: this is the accumulated provision for depreciation account.

21.21A Mavron plc owned the following motor vehicles as at 1 April 2017:

Motor Vehicle	Date Acquired	Cost £	Estimated Residual Value £	Estimated Life (years)
AAT 101	1 October 2014	8,500	2,500	5
DJH 202	1 April 2015	12,000	2,000	8

Mavron plc's policy is to provide at the end of each financial year depreciation using the straight line method applied on a month-by-month basis on all motor vehicles used during the year.

During the financial year ended 31 March 2018 the following occurred:

(i) On 30 June 2017 AAT 101 was traded in and replaced by KGC 303. The trade-in allowance was £5,000. KGC 303 cost £15,000 and the balance due (after deducting the trade-in allowance) was paid partly in cash and partly by a loan of £6,000 from Pinot Finance. KGC 303 is expected to have a residual value of £4,000 after an estimated economic life of five years.

(ii) The estimated remaining economic life of DJH 202 was reduced from six years to four years with no change in the estimated residual value.

Required:

(a) Show any Journal entries necessary to give effect to the above.

(b) Show the Journal entry necessary to record depreciation on Motor Vehicles for the year ended 31 March 2018.

(c) Reconstruct the Motor Vehicles Account and the Provision for Depreciation Account for the year ended 31 March 2018. Author's Note

Show the necessary calculations clearly.

(*Association of Accounting Technicians*)

Author's Note: this is the accumulated provision for depreciation account.

21.22 A business buys a non-current asset for £10,000. The business estimates that the asset will be used for five years. After exactly two and a half years, however, the asset is suddenly sold for £5,000. The business always provides a full year's depreciation in the year of purchase and no depreciation in the year of disposal.

Required:

(a) Write up the relevant accounts (including disposal account but not profit and loss account) for each of Years 1, 2 and 3:

(i) Using the straight line depreciation method (assume 20% pa);

(ii) Using the reducing balance depreciation method (assume 40% pa).

(b) (i) What is the purpose of depreciation? In what circumstances would each of the two methods you have used be preferable?

(ii) What is the meaning of the net figure for the non-current asset in the balance sheet at the end of Year 2?

(c) If the asset was bought at the beginning of Year 1, but was not used at all until Year 2 (and it is confidently anticipated to last until Year 6), state under each method the appropriate depreciation charge in Year 1, and briefly justify your answer.

(*Association of Chartered Certified Accountants*)

21.23A Contractors Ltd was formed on 1 January 2019 and the following purchases and sales of machinery were made during the first 3 years of operations.

Date	Asset	Transaction	Price
1 January 2019	Machines 1 and 2	purchase	£40,000 each
1 October 2019	Machines 3 and 4	purchase	£15,200 each
30 June 2021	Machine 3	sale	£12,640
1 July 2021	Machine 5	purchase	£20,000

Each machine was estimated to last 10 years and to have a residual value of 5 per cent of its cost price. Depreciation was by equal instalments, and it is company policy to charge depreciation for every month an asset is owned.

Required:

(*a*) Calculate
   (*i*) the total depreciation on Machinery for each of the years 2019, 2020 and 2021;
   (*ii*) the profit or loss on the sale of Machine 3 in 2021.

(*b*) Contractors Ltd depreciates its vehicles by 30 per cent per annum using the diminishing balance method. What difference would it have made to annual reported profits over the life of a vehicle if it had decided instead to depreciate this asset by 20 per cent straight line?

(*Scottish Qualifications Authority*)

21.24   A friend of the family believes that depreciation provides him with a reserve to purchase new assets. His secretary has blown up his computer, but he knows he has the funds to replace it in the accumulated depreciation account. You know he is wrong and have grown tired of listening to him going on about it, but he won't listen to what you have to say. You decide to put him out of his misery by writing a letter to him about it that he may actually read before he realises that it is telling him things he does not want to hear.

Write him a letter, using fictitious names and addresses, which defines depreciation and explains why his view is incorrect.

21.25A   On 31 March 2019 Dixie's business traded-in a machine (a Z-15 model) which it had originally purchased on 1 April 2016 for £19,000. Dixie had depreciated the Z-15 at 10 per cent per annum using the straight-line method.

Dixie part-exchanged the Z-15 for a newer model (the Z-18). The vendor's list price for the Z-18 was £32,000 but Dixie only paid £20,000 plus the trade-in in full settlement.

Required:

What was the profit or loss on the disposal of the Z-15 in Dixie's Income Statement for the financial year to 31 March 2019?

21.26   XY Ltd provides for depreciation of its machinery at 20 per cent per annum on cost; it charges for a full year in the year of purchase but no provision is made in the year of sale/disposal.

Financial statements are prepared annually to 31 December.

2018

| January 1 | Bought machine 'A' £10,000 |
| July 1 | Bought machine 'B' £6,000. |

2019

| March 31 | Bought machine 'C' £8,000 |

2020

| October 7 | Sold machine 'A' – proceeds £5,500 |
| November 5 | Bought machine 'D' £12,000 |

2021

February 4	Sold machine 'B' – proceeds £3,000
February 6	Bought machine 'E' £9,000
October 11	Exchanged machine 'D' for machinery valued at £7,000

Prepare

(*a*) The machinery account for the period 1 January 2018 to 31 December 2021.

(*b*) The accumulated provision for depreciation on machinery account, for the period 1 January 2018 to 31 December 2021.

(c)   The disposal of machinery accounts showing the profit/loss on sale for each year.
(d)   The balance sheet extract for machinery at (i) 31 December 2020 and (ii) 31 December 2021.

21.27A   A company maintains its non-current assets at cost. Accumulated provision for depreciation accounts are kept for each class of asset.

At 31 December 2018 the position was as follows:

	Total cost to date £	Total depreciation to date £
Machinery	52,950	25,670
Office furniture	2,860	1,490

The following transactions were made in the year ended 31 December 2019:

(a)   Purchased – machinery £2,480 and office furniture £320
(b)   Sold machinery which had cost £2,800 in 2015 for £800

Depreciation is charged, on a straight line basis, at 10 per cent on machinery and at 5 per cent on office furniture on the basis of assets in use at the end of the year irrespective of the date of purchase.

Required:
Show the asset and accumulated provision for depreciation accounts for the year to 31 December 2019 and the relevant balance sheet extracts at that date.

21.28A

(a)   The following trial balance was extracted from the books of Peter Mackie on 30 April 2020. From it, and the note below it, prepare his income statement for the year ending 30 April 2020, and a balance sheet as at that date.

	Dr £	Cr £
Sales		26,200
Purchases	16,450	
Inventory 1 May 2019	2,266	
Carriage outwards	534	
Carriage inwards	295	
Motor Vehicles: accumulated depreciation		3,800
Fixtures and Fittings: accumulated depreciation		240
Returns inwards	670	
Returns outwards		392
Salaries and wages	2,692	
Motor expenses	729	
Rent	843	
Sundry expenses	1,390	
Motor vehicles	7,600	
Fixtures and fittings	800	
Accounts receivable	4,965	
Accounts payable		3,277
Cash at bank	1,648	
Cash in hand	150	
Drawings	8,400	
Capital		15,523
	49,432	49,432

Note:
Closing inventory amounted to £2,860. Depreciation is to be charged at rates of 10 per cent on cost for fixtures and fittings and 25 per cent on cost for motor vehicles. Bad debts of £365 are to be written off.

(b) Peter has indicated that he thinks that the accounts receivable amounts that have been written off will be paid eventually. He is also querying why adjustments are made in the financial statements for bad debts and depreciation. Write a short note to him, making appropriate references to accounting concepts, outlining why these adjustments are made.

21.29 On 1 April 2016 a business purchased a machine costing £112,000. The machine can be used for a total of 20,000 hours over an estimated life of 48 months. At the end of that time the machine is expected to have a trade-in value of £12,000.

The financial year of the business ends on 31 December each year. It is expected that the machine will be used for:

4,000 hours during the financial year ending 31 December 2016
5,000 hours during the financial year ending 31 December 2017
5,000 hours during the financial year ending 31 December 2018
5,000 hours during the financial year ending 31 December 2019
1,000 hours during the financial year ending 31 December 2020

Required:
(a) Calculate the annual depreciation charges on the machine on each of the following bases for each of the financial years ending on 31 December 2016, 2017, 2018, 2019 and 2020:
   (i) the straight line method applied on a month for month basis,
   (ii) the diminishing balance method at 40% per annum applied on a full year basis, and
   (iii) the units of output method.
(b) Suppose that during the financial year ended 31 December 2017 the machine was used for only 1,500 hours before being sold for £80,000 on 30 June.
   Assuming that the business has chosen to apply the straight line method on a month for month basis, show the following accounts for 2017 only:
   (i) the Machine account,
   (ii) the Provision for Depreciation – Machine account, and
   (iii) the Assets Disposals account.

(*Association of Accounting Technicians*)

21.30A On 1 January 2018 a business purchased a laser printer costing £1,800. The printer has an estimated life of four years after which it will have no residual value.

It is expected that the output from the printer will be:

Year	Sheets printed
2018	35,000
2019	45,000
2020	45,000
2021	55,000
	180,000

Required:
(a) Calculate the annual depreciation charges for 2018, 2019, 2020 and 2021 on the laser printer on the following bases:
   (i) the straight line basis,
   (ii) the diminishing balance method at 60 per cent per annum, and
   (iii) the units of output method.

Note: Your workings should be to the nearest £.

(*b*)   Suppose that in 2021 the laser printer were to be sold on 1 July for £200 and that the business had chosen to depreciate it at 60 per cent per annum using the diminishing balance method applied on a month for month basis.

　　Reconstruct the following accounts for 2021 only:

(*i*)   the Laser Printer account,

(*ii*) the Provision for Depreciation – Laser Printer account, and

(*iii*) the Assets Disposals account.

(*Association of Accounting Technicians*)

Accruals and prepayments

22

Learning objectives

After you have studied this chapter, you should be able to:

● adjust expense accounts for accruals and prepayments

● adjust revenue accounts for amounts owing

● show accruals, prepayments and revenue accounts receivable in the balance sheet

● ascertain the amounts of expense and revenue items to be shown in the income statement after making adjustments for accruals and prepayments

● make the necessary end-of-period adjustments relating to drawings that have not yet been entered in the books

● explain what an extended trial balance is and describe what it looks like

● prepare accrual and prepayment entries to the accounts using two different methods

Introduction

In this chapter, you'll continue to learn about adjustments made to the ledger accounts at the end of a period. You'll learn how to make the appropriate entries in the accounts for outstanding balances on expense and income accounts and make the appropriate entries in the income statement and the balance sheet.

22.1 Financial statements so far

The statements of profit or loss you have looked at so far have taken the sales for a period and deducted all the expenses for that period, the result being a net profit or a net loss.

Up to this part of the book it has always been assumed that the expenses incurred belong to the period of the income statement when they took place. If the income statement for the year ending 31 December 2019 was being prepared, then the rent paid as shown in the trial balance was all treated as relating to 2019. There was no rent owing at the beginning of 2019 nor any owing at the end of 2019, nor had any rent been paid in advance relating to 2020.

This was done to make your first encounter with financial statements as straightforward as possible.

22.2 Adjustments needed

Let's look at two businesses which pay rent for buildings in Oxford. The rent for each building is £6,000 a year.

1 Business A pays £5,000 in the year. At the year end it owes £1,000 for rent.

$$\text{Rent expense used up} = £6,000$$
$$\text{Rent paid for} \quad = £5,000$$

2 Business B pays £6,500 in the year. This figure includes £500 paid in advance for the following year.

$$\text{Rent expense used up} = £6,000$$
$$\text{Rent paid for} \quad = £6,500$$

An income statement for 12 months needs 12 months' rent as an expense = £6,000. This means that in both 1 and 2 the double entry accounts will have to be adjusted.

 Activity 22.1 From your knowledge of double entry, you should be able to work out what the double entry required is in these two cases. What do you think it is? If you don't know what names to give the accounts, have a guess. (Hint: in the first case, there will be a credit balance in the balance sheet and in the other, it will be a debit balance.)

In all the examples in this chapter the income statements are for the year ending 31 December 2018. Unless otherwise indicated, all entries in the income statement are in the profit and loss section of the statement. All mentions of 'profit and loss' refer to the ledger account of that name which is summarised in the income statement.

22.3 Accrued expenses

Assume that rent of £4,000 per year is payable at the end of every three months. The rent was paid on time in March, but this is not always the case.

Amount	Rent due	Rent paid
£1,000	31 March 2018	31 March 2018
£1,000	30 June 2018	2 July 2018
£1,000	30 September 2018	4 October 2018
£1,000	31 December 2018	5 January 2019

Rent

2018			£	
Mar	31	Cash	1,000	
Jul	2	Cash	1,000	
Oct	4	Cash	1,000	

The rent for the last quarter was paid on 5 January 2019 and so will appear in the books of the year 2019 as the result of a double entry made on that date.

The expense for 2018 is obviously £4,000 as that is the year's rent, and this is the amount needed to be transferred to the profit and loss account. But, if £4,000 was put on the credit side of the rent account (the debit being in the profit and loss account) the account would be out of balance by £1,000 because the payment due on 31 December 2018 was not made until 5 January 2019. That is, if we posted £4,000 to profit and loss on 31 December, we would have £4,000 on the credit side of the account and only £3,000 on the debit side:

Rent

2018			£	2018		£
Mar	31	Cash	1,000	Dec 31 Profit and loss		4,000
Jul	2	Cash	1,000			
Oct	4	Cash	1,000			

This cannot be right.

To make the account balance the £1,000 rent owing for 2018, but paid in 2019, must be carried down to 2019 as a credit balance because it is a liability on 31 December 2018. Instead of rent owing it could be called rent accrued or just simply an 'accrual'.

The completed account can now be shown:

Rent

2018			£	2018		£
Mar	31	Cash	1,000	Dec 31 Profit and loss		4,000
Jul	2	Cash	1,000			
Oct	4	Cash	1,000			
Dec	31	Accrued c/d	1,000			
			4,000			4,000
				2019		
				Jan 1 Accrued b/d		1,000

The balance c/d has been described as 'accrued c/d', rather than as 'balance c/d'. This is to explain what the balance is for. It is for an **accrued expense**.

22.4 Prepaid expenses

Insurance for a business is at the rate of £840 a year, starting from 1 January 2015. The business has agreed to pay this at the rate of £210 every three months. However, payments were not made at the correct times. Details were:

Amount	Insurance due	Insurance paid
£210	31 March 2018	£210 28 February 2018
£210 £210	30 June 2018 30 September 2018	£420 31 August 2018
£210	31 December 2018	£420 18 November 2018

The insurance account in the ledger for the year ended 31 December 2018 is:

Insurance

2018			£	2018		£
Feb	28	Bank	210	Dec 31 Profit and loss		840
Aug	31	Bank	420			
Nov	18	Bank	420			

The last payment of £420 is not just for 2018. It can be split as £210 for the three months to 31 December 2018 and £210 for the three months ended 31 March 2019. For a period of 12 months the cost of insurance is £840 and this is, therefore, the figure needing to be transferred to the income statement.

If £840 is posted to the debit of profit and loss at 31 December 2018, the insurance account will still have a debit balance of £210. This is a benefit paid for but not used up at the end of the period. It is an asset and needs carrying forward as such to 2019, i.e. as a debit balance. Items like this are called **prepaid expenses**, 'prepayments' or 'amounts paid in advance'.

The account can now be completed:

Insurance

2018			£	2018			£
Feb	28	Bank	210	Dec	31	Profit and loss	840
Aug	31	Bank	420		31	Prepaid c/d	210
Nov	18	Bank	420				
			1,050				1,050
2019							
Jan	1	Prepaid b/d	210				

Prepayment happens when items other than purchases are bought for use in the business, but are not fully used up in the period.

For instance, packing materials are normally not entirely used up over the period in which they are bought. There is usually an inventory of packing materials in hand at the end of the period. This is a form of prepayment and needs carrying down to the period in which it will be used.

This can be seen in the following example:

Year ended 31 December 2018:
Packing materials bought in the year = £2,200.
Inventory of packing materials in hand as at 31 December 2018 = £400.

Looking at the example, it can be seen that in 2018 the packing materials used up will have been £2,200 − £400 = £1,800. (We are assuming that there was no inventory of packing materials at the start of 2018.) We have an inventory of £400 packing materials at 31 December 2018 to be carried forward to 2019. The £400 inventory of packing materials will be carried forward as an asset balance (i.e. a debit balance) to 2019:

Packing Materials

2018			£	2018			£
Dec	31	Bank	2,200	Dec	31	Profit and loss	1,800
					31	Inventory c/d	400
			2,200				2,200
2019							
Jan	1	Inventory b/d	400				

The inventory of packing materials is *not* added to the inventory of unsold goods in hand in the balance sheet, but is added to the other prepaid expenses in that statement.

22.5 Revenue owing at the end of period

The revenue owing for sales is already shown in the books as the debit balances on customers' accounts, i.e. accounts receivable. There may be other kinds of revenue, all of which has not been received by the end of the period, e.g. rent receivable. An example now follows.

Example

Our warehouse is larger than we need. We rent part of it to another business for £1,800 per annum. Details for the year ended 31 December were as follows:

Amount	Rent due	Rent received
£450	31 March 2018	4 April 2018
£450	30 June 2018	6 July 2018
£450	30 September 2018	9 October 2018
£450	31 December 2018	7 January 2019

The *Rent Receivable Account* entries for 2018 will appear as:

Rent Receivable

	2018			£
	Apr	4	Bank	450
	Jul	6	Bank	450
	Oct	9	Bank	450

The rent received of £450 on 7 January 2019 will be entered in the accounting records in 2019.

Any rent paid by the business would be charged as a debit to the profit and loss account. Any rent received, being the opposite, is transferred to the credit of the profit and loss account, as it is a revenue.

The amount to be transferred for 2018 is that earned for the 12 months, i.e. £1,800. The rent received account is completed by carrying down the balance owing as a debit balance to 2019. The £450 owing is an asset on 31 December 2018.

The rent receivable account can now be completed:

Rent Receivable

2018				£	2018				£
Dec	31	Profit and loss		1,800	Apr	4	Bank		450
					Jul	6	Bank		450
					Oct	9	Bank		450
					Dec	31	Accrued c/d		450
				1,800					1,800
2019									
Jan	1	Accrued b/d		450					

22.6 Expenses and revenue account balances and the balance sheet

In all cases dealing with adjustments in the financial statements, there will still be a balance on each account after the preparation of the income statement. All such balances remaining should appear in the balance sheet. The only question left is where and how they should be shown.

The amounts owing for expenses could be called expenses payable, expenses owing or accrued expenses. However, we'll use the term 'accruals'. They represent *very* current liabilities – they will have to be paid in the very near future.

The items prepaid could be called prepaid expenses or payments in advance, but we'll call them 'prepayments'. Similarly to accruals, they represent *very* current assets as they should be received very soon.

 Activity 22.2 From your knowledge of accounting, how should all accruals and all the prepayments appear in the balance sheet – as one debit entry and one credit entry or as a separate entry for each item? Why?

 Activity 22.3
(a) Where in the current asset sequence do you place prepayments?
(b) Where in the current liability sequence do you place accruals?
(c) Why?

Amounts owing for rents receivable or other revenue owing are a special case. If you look back at the T-account in Section 22.5, you'll see that they are described as 'accrued'. However, they are not accrued expenses, as they represent amounts receivable. They are, therefore, **accrued income**.

 Activity 22.4 Where do you think these items of accrued income go in the balance sheet?

The part of the balance sheet in respect of the accounts so far seen in this chapter is therefore:

Balance Sheet as at 31 December 2018 (extract)

	£	£
Current assets		
Inventory	xxx	
Accounts receivable	450	
Prepayments (400 + 210)	610	
Bank	xxx	
Cash	xxx	
		x,xxx
Current liabilities		
Trade accounts payable	xxx	
Accrued expenses	1,000	
		(x,xxx)

22.7 Expenses and revenue accounts covering more than one period

So far we've only looked at accounts where there were closing accruals or prepayments. In real life, you will also expect to see some opening accruals and prepayments, such as that shown in the final version of the *Rent Receivable Account* in Section 22.5. This is something that students are often asked to deal with in examinations as it tests their knowledge and ability to distinguish the treatment of these items at the beginning and end of a period. Typically, they may be asked to draw up an expense or revenue account for a full year which has amounts owing or prepaid at both the beginning and end of the year. We can now see how this is done.

Example A

The following details are available:

(A) On 31 December 2017, three months' rent amounting to a total of £3,000 was owing.
(B) The rent chargeable per year was £12,000.
(C) The following rent payments were made in the year 2018: 6 January £3,000; 4 April £3,000; 7 July £3,000; 18 October £3,000.
(D) The final three months' rent for 2018 is still owing.

Now we can look at the completed rent account. The letters (A) to (D) give reference to the details above.

Rent

2018				£	2018				£
Jan	6	Bank	(C)	3,000	Jan	1	Accrued b/d	(A)	3,000
Apr	4	Bank	(C)	3,000	Dec	31	Profit and loss	(B)	12,000
Jul	7	Bank	(C)	3,000					
Oct	18	Bank	(C)	3,000					
Dec	31	Accrued c/d	(D)	3,000					
				15,000					15,000
					2019				
					Jan	1	Accrued b/d		3,000

Example B

The following details are available:

(A) On 31 December 2017, packing materials in hand amounted to £1,850.
(B) During the year to 31 December 2018, we paid £27,480 for packing materials.
(C) There was no inventory of packing materials on 31 December 2018.
(D) On 31 December 2018, we still owed £2,750 for packing materials already received and used.

The packing materials account will appear as:

Packing Materials

2018				£	2018			£
Jan	1	Inventory b/d	(A)	1,850	Dec	31	Profit and loss	32,080
Dec	31	Bank	(B)	27,480				
	31	Owing c/d	(D)	2,750				
				32,080				32,080
					2019			
					Jan	1	Owing b/d	2,750

The figure of £32,080 is the difference on the account, and is transferred to the profit and loss account.

We can prove it is correct:

	£	£
Inventory at start of year		1,850
Add Bought and used:		
Paid for	27,480	
Still owed for	2,750	
Cost of packing materials bought and used in the year		30,230
Cost of packing materials used in the year		32,080

Example C

Where different expenses are put together in one account, it can get even more confusing. Let us look at where rent and rates are joined together. Here are the details for the year ended 31 December 2018:

(A) Rent is payable of £6,000 per annum.
(B) Rates of £4,000 per annum are payable by instalments.
(C) At 1 January 2018, rent of £1,000 had been prepaid in 2017.
(D) On 1 January 2018, rates of £400 were owed.
(E) During 2018, rent of £4,500 was paid.
(F) During 2018, rates of £5,000 were paid.
(G) On 31 December 2018, rent of £500 was owing.
(H) On 31 December 2018, rates of £600 had been prepaid.

A combined rent and rates account is to be drawn up for the year 2018 showing the transfer to profit and loss, and the balances to be carried down to 2019.

Rent and Rates

2018				£	2018				£
Jan	1	Rent prepaid b/d	(C)	1,000	Jan	1	Rates owing b/d	(D)	400
Dec	31	Bank: rent	(E)	4,500	Dec	31	Profit and loss	A + B	10,000
	31	Bank: rates	(F)	5,000					
	31	Rent accrued c/d	(G)	500		31	Rates prepaid c/d	(H)	600
				11,000					11,000
2019					2019				
Jan	1	Rates prepaid b/d	(H)	600	Jan	1	Rent accrued b/d	(G)	500

To enter the correct figures, you need to keep the two items separate in your own mind. This is easiest if you produce a schedule like the one we produced above for packing materials inventory. The one for rent would look like this:

	£	£
Rent due during the year		6,000
Less:		
Rent prepaid at start of year	1,000	
Rent paid during the year	4,500	
		(5,500)
Rent accrued at the end of the year		500

Activity 22.5

Prepare a similar schedule for rates.

22.8 Goods for own use

Traders will often take inventory out of their business for their own use without paying for them. There is nothing wrong about their doing this, but an entry should be made to record that this has happened. This is done by:

1 Debit drawings account, to show that the owner has taken the goods for private use.
2 Credit purchases account, to reduce cost of goods available for sale.

In the United Kingdom, an adjustment may be needed for Value Added Tax. If goods supplied to a trader's customers have VAT added to their price, then any such goods taken for own use will need such an adjustment. This is because the VAT regulations state that VAT should be added to the cost of goods taken. The double entry for the VAT content would be:

1 Debit drawings account.
2 Credit VAT account.

Adjustments may also be needed for other private items. For instance, if a trader's private insurance (e.g. insurance premiums for the contents of the trader's home) had been incorrectly charged to the business insurance account, then the correction would be:

1 Debit drawings account.
2 Credit insurance account.

22.9 Distinctions between various kinds of capital

The capital account represents the claim the owner has against the assets of the business at a point in time. That is, the amount of the business that belongs to the owner. The word **capital** is, however, often used in a specific sense. The main meanings are listed below.

Capital invested

This means the total monetary value of everything brought into the business by the owners from their outside interests. The amount of capital invested is not disturbed by the amount of profits made by the business or losses incurred.

Capital employed

Students at an early stage in their studies are often asked to define this term. In fact, for those who progress to a more advanced stage, it will be seen in *Frank Wood's Business Accounting 2* that capital employed could have several meanings as the term is often used quite loosely. At its simplest, it is taken to mean the monetary value of the resources that are being used in the business. Thus, if all the assets were added together and the liabilities of the business deducted, the answer would be that the difference is the amount of money employed in the business. You will by now realise that this is the same as the closing balance of the capital account. It is also sometimes called 'net assets' or 'net worth'.

Working capital

This is a term for the excess of the current assets over the current liabilities of a business and is the same as '**net current assets**'.

22.10 Financial statements in the services sector

So far we have only looked at financial statements for businesses trading in some sort of goods. We drew up a trading account for some of these businesses because we wanted to identify the gross profit on goods sold.

There are, however, many businesses which do not deal in 'goods' but instead supply 'services'. This will include professional businesses such as accountants, solicitors, doctors, dentists, vets, management consultants, advertising agencies, estate agents and Internet service providers. Other examples include businesses specialising in computer repairs, window cleaning, gardening, hairdressing, chimney sweeping, piano tuning, and banks, football clubs, health clubs, gyms and leisure centres.

As they do not deal in 'goods' there is no point in their attempting to draw up trading accounts. While it is quite possible for, say, a dentist to treat depreciation on equipment, the costs of materials consumed, and the dental assistant's salary as deductions from income in order to arrive at a figure for gross profit, such information is likely to be of little benefit in terms of decision-making. They will, however, prepare an income statement (containing only the profit and loss items) and a balance sheet.

The first item in the income statement will be the revenue. It might be called 'work done', 'fees', 'charges', 'accounts rendered', 'takings', etc., depending on the nature of the organisation. Any other items of income will be added, e.g. rent receivable, and then the expenses will be listed and deducted to arrive at a net profit or net loss.

An example of the income statement of a solicitor might be as per Exhibit 22.1:

Exhibit 22.1

J. Plunkett, Solicitor
Income Statement for the year ending 31 December 2018

	£	£
Revenue:		
Fees charged		87,500
Insurance commissions		1,300
		88,800
Less Expenses:		
Wages and salaries	29,470	
Rent and rates	11,290	
Office expenses	3,140	
Motor expenses	2,115	
General expenses	1,975	
Depreciation	2,720	
		(50,710)
Net profit		38,090

Other than for the descriptions given in the revenue section, it doesn't look very different from the ones you've prepared for traders. In effect, if you can prepare an income statement for a trader, you can do so for a service organisation. You just need to remember that it will contain no trading account items and that the income will need to be appropriately described.

22.11 Extended trial balances

Instead of drafting a set of financial statements in the way shown so far in this textbook, you could prepare an 'extended trial balance', or 'worksheet'. It can be very useful when there are a large number of adjustments to be made. Professional accountants use them a lot for that very reason.

Extended trial balances are usually drawn up on specially preprinted types of stationery with suitable vertical columns printed across the page. You start with the trial balance extracted from the ledgers and then enter adjustments in the columns to the right. Columns for the trading account, income statement, and the balance sheet then follow.

Exhibit 22.2 shows an example of the extended trial balance that could have been drawn up as an answer to Review Question 22.11. Once you have attempted the question yourself, compare your answer to the one shown in Exhibit 22.2. The gross profits and net profits are the same; it is simply the method of displaying the information that is different.

If you look carefully, you will notice that all the journal entries are dealt with in one double column. That column has been split vertically in two. On the left is a sub-column for debit entries and, on the right, is a sub-column for credit entries. The reference number of each journal entry is placed to the right of each debit entry and each credit entry.

This makes it easy to detect errors in each entry, such as where a debit entry is for a different total amount than that shown in the relevant credit entry.

Activity 22.6

Why is identifying errors of this type easier when using an extended trial balance than when using a conventional manual approach to preparing the financial statements?

Sometimes, students confuse their debits and their credits and switch the entries to the accounts, the one that should have been debited being credited, and vice versa. If this happens, the trial balance and the balance sheet will still balance, but the information contained in the balance sheet will be incorrect. This is no different from what may occur with journal entries being processed in 'the books', rather than in an extended trial balance. However, if the extended trial balance is prepared using a spreadsheet, correcting the entries and producing correct financial statements may be done considerably faster, which is one reason why it is wise to use a spreadsheet rather than paper to prepare an extended trial balance.

Another advantage of the use of a spreadsheet relates to how easy it is to amend adjustments. If profit is too high or too low, some businessmen will seek ways of using journal entries to adjust it down or up. If their accountant has an extended trial balance on a spreadsheet, this makes such sensitivity analysis very easy. Thankfully for everyone else, there are rules and regulations governing the adjustments that can be made (Chapter 7). However, there are times when for genuinely honest reasons, tinkering with the figures in this way may be appropriate.

Activity 22.7

List three examples of situations where this may be appropriate.

If you were an accountant, the financial statements you prepare and give to the owner and to anyone else who was an interested party, such as the Inspector of Taxes or a bank, would not be in the style of an extended trial balance. Instead, having completed the extended trial balance, the figures for the trading account, profit and loss, and balance sheet would be transferred to financial statements prepared using the conventional style of presentation.

To provide such special stationery in an examination is unusual, although it has been known to happen. For students to draw-up an extended trial balance from scratch could be very time-consuming. Therefore, it is very rare for examiners to ask for one to be prepared. However, the examiner may ask you something about extended trial balances (or worksheets) or provide a partially completed one to work on, if this topic is included in the syllabus. You should note, however, that nowadays spreadsheets are often used to produce financial statements in this way. If your course includes use of spreadsheets to prepare financial statements, you are more likely to be asked to prepare an extended trial balance in your examination or as part of your assessed coursework.

Exhibit 22.2

JOHN BROWN WORKSHEET	Trial Balance 1 Dr	Trial Balance 2 Cr	Adjustments 3 Dr	Adjustments 4 Cr	Trading Account 5 Dr	Trading Account 6 Cr	Profit and Loss Account 7 Dr	Profit and Loss Account 8 Cr	Balance Sheet 9 Dr	Balance Sheet 10 Cr
See Review Question 22.11										
Sales		400,000				400,000				
Purchases	350,000				350,000					
Sales returns	5,000				5,000					
Purchases returns		6,200				6,200				
Inventory 1.1.2020	100,000				100,000					
Allowance for doubtful debts		800		180 (*iv*)						980
Wages and salaries	30,000		5,000 (*ii*)				35,000			
Rates	6,000			500 (*iii*)			5,500			
Telephone	1,000		220 (*v*)				1,220			
Shop fittings	40,000			4,000 (*vi*)					36,000	
Van	30,000			6,000 (*vi*)					24,000	
Accounts receivable	9,800								9,800	
Accounts payable		7,000								7,000
Bad debts	200						200			
Capital		179,000								179,000
Bank	3,000								3,000	
Drawings	18,000								18,000	
	593,000	593,000								
Inventory 31.12.2020 – Asset			120,000 (*i*)						120,000	
Inventory 31.12.2020 – Cost of goods sold				120,000 (*i*)		120,000				
Accrued expenses				5,000 (*ii*) / 220 (*v*)						5,000 / 220
Allowance for doubtful debts			180 (*iv*)				180			
Prepaid expenses			500 (*iii*)						500	
Depreciation shop fittings			4,000 (*vi*)				4,000			
Depreciation van			6,000 (*vi*)				6,000			
			135,900	135,900						
Gross profit (balancing figure)					71,200			71,200		
Net profit (balancing figure)							19,100			19,100
					526,200	526,200	71,200	71,200	211,300	211,300

22.12 Definition of accounting

In Chapter 1, you were given a definition of bookkeeping as being concerned with the work of entering information into accounting records and afterwards maintaining such records properly. This definition does not need to be amended.

However, **accounting** was not fully defined in Chapter 1. It would probably not have meant much to you at that stage in your studies. The following is a commonly used definition: '*The process of identifying, measuring, and communicating economic information to permit informed judgements and decisions by users of the information.*'

22.13 An alternative way to record accruals and prepayments

After learning in Chapter 21 that there was a second commonly used way to record provisions for depreciation, it will come as no surprise to you to learn that there is a second commonly used way to record accruals and prepayments. Just as with the two-stage method of recording depreciation provisions, the alternative way to record accruals and prepayments requires that you create additional ledger accounts. You open an accruals account and a prepayments account and post any balances on expense accounts at the period end to the appropriate one of the two new accounts.

The balance carried down in an expense account under the method you learnt earlier in this chapter is described as either 'accrued c/d' or 'prepaid c/d'. Under the alternative method, there would be no balance in the expense account after the double entry to the accruals account or prepayments account. Instead, there will be a balance on these two accounts which is then entered in the balance sheet in exactly the same way as you did under the other method.

At the start of the next period, you reverse the entry by crediting the prepayments account and debiting each of the expense accounts that had debit balances. Similarly, the accruals account is debited and the expense accounts that had credit balances are credited with the appropriate amounts.

For example, in the insurance account from Section 22.4, the entries in the insurance account were:

Insurance

2018			£	2018			£
Feb	28	Bank	210	Dec	31	Profit and loss	840
Aug	31	Bank	420				
Nov	18	Bank	420		31	Prepaid c/d	210
			1,050				1,050
2019							
Jan	1	Prepaid b/d	210				

The same information if a prepayments account were used would be entered:

Insurance

2018			£	2018			£
Feb	28	Bank	210	Dec	31	Profit and loss	840
Aug	31	Bank	420				
Nov	18	Bank	420		31	Prepayments	210
			1,050				1,050
2019							
Jan	1	Prepayments	210				

Prepayments

2018			£	2018			£
Dec	31	Insurance	210	Dec	31	Balance c/d	210
2019				2019			
Jan	1	Balance b/d	210	Jan	1	Insurance	210

In reality, it doesn't matter which of these two methods you use. Examiners will accept them both unless they specifically ask for one of them to be used. Your teacher or lecturer will know whether this is likely to happen. Follow the guidance of your teacher or lecturer and use whichever method he or she indicates is more appropriate.

In order not to confuse things by switching back and forth between the two methods, all examples of accruals and prepayments and all questions involving accruals and prepayments in the rest of this textbook will use the first method that has been covered in detail in this chapter. Should you be using the second method, as you will have seen above, it is very obvious what the equivalent entries would be when you look at examples prepared using the method adopted in this textbook.

Mnemonic

The following acronyms may help you to remember the treatment of accruals and prepayments in the balance sheet:

PAPA and **ALLA**

		Treated as current
Prepaid		Asset
Accured	Expense	Liability
Prepaid	Revenue	Liability
Accured		Asset

Learning outcomes

You should now have learnt:

1 That adjustments are needed so that the expenses and income shown in the financial statements equal the expenses incurred in the period and the revenue that has arisen in the period.

2 That the balances relating to the adjustments will be shown on the balance sheet at the end of the period as current assets and current liabilities.

3 That goods taken for the owner's own use without anything being recorded in the books will necessitate a transfer from purchases to the drawings account, plus an adjustment for VAT if appropriate.

4 How to record appropriate entries in the accounts and financial statements at the end of a period for accrued expenses, prepaid expenses, accrued income, and drawings.

5 That private expenses should not be charged as an expense in the income statement, but should be charged to the drawings account.

6 That an extended trial balance is an alternative way of arriving at the figures to be included in the financial statements.

7 That there are two common ways to prepare accruals and prepayments.

Answers to activities

22.1 Don't worry if you didn't know what names to give the accounts other than the rent account. What is important is that you thought about it and that you knew which side the entries should be in the rent account.

(a) *Dr* Rent account £1,000   *Cr* Accruals account £1,000
(b) *Dr* Prepayments account £500   *Cr* Rent account £500

Note how the two entries in the rent account are on opposite sides. The £200 rent owing at the end of the year is an expense that has not yet been entered in the books, but it must be as it relates to the current year. The £100 paid in advance for next year is not an expense of the current year, so you need to reduce the amount you have currently in the rent account so that the correct expense will be included in the income statement. The accruals account is similar to a creditor's account, but it is used for expenses unpaid at the year end. Similarly, the prepayments account is like a debtor's account, but it is used to record amounts paid for expenses in advance of the accounting period in which the benefit (i.e. what was paid for) is received.

22.2 All the debit entries should be added together and shown as one entry called 'prepayments' within current assets. Similarly, all the credit entries should be added together and shown as one entry called 'accruals' under current liabilities. This is done so as to minimise the clutter in the balance sheet while providing enough information for anyone looking at the financial statement to be able to identify the figure for accruals and the figure for prepayments.

22.3 (a) Between accounts receivable and bank.
(b) Between accounts payable and bank overdraft.
(c) Their degree of liquidity.

22.4 They are usually added to accounts receivable. This is because these represent a regular source of income and, even though the income has nothing to do with the goods or services that form the main activity of the business, they are in every other sense another form of customer account. It makes sense, therefore, to include them in the accounts receivable balance shown in the balance sheet.

22.5

	£
Rates due during the year	4,000
Add: Rates accrued at the start of the year	400
	4,400
Less: Rates paid during the year	(5,000)
Rates prepaid at the end of the year	(600)

22.6 Under a conventional manual approach, the journal entries will be made in the accounts in the ledger, so changing the balances as shown in that book. If the amount debited is different from the amount credited, the ledger accounts used for these entries will need to be inspected in order to discover what the error was. Looking at the note of the journal entry in the Journal is not likely to be of help. It will almost certainly show the same amounts in the debit and the credit parts of the entry. Errors in posting journal entries are usually made at the point of completion rather than at the point of origin.

With an extended trial balance, you take the balance on the ledger account before it was changed by the journal entry. You know that the balance on the ledger account is likely to be correct because your trial balance has balanced. In producing your financial statements, you do not first enter the adjustments in your ledger. First, you complete your extended trial balance. You can then make the appropriate entries in the ledger and check the resulting balances against the figures shown in the extended trial balance.

Of course, you can take a similar approach using a conventional approach and make the adjustments to your trial balance on a piece of paper before entering numbers in your financial statements. However, it will lack the neatness and internal checks that are built into the matrix of the extended trial balance.

22.7 You could list a number of situations where this may be appropriate. For example, if a businessman was unhappy with the amount set aside as an allowance for doubtful debts, he could suggest a more appropriate figure and see if it was worth making the change. Another example would be where an error was found in the accounts that required changes to be made to some of the adjustments, such as depreciation or bad debts. Despite what many people believe, businessmen do not generally adjust their accounting numbers simply to look better but they do adjust them when it is believed to be appropriate to do so. Sometimes, things come to light after an extended trial balance has been prepared that should have been included in it.

Review questions

22.1 The financial year of S. Smith ended on 31 December 2016. Show the ledger accounts for the following items including the balance transferred to the necessary part of the financial statements, also the balances carried down to the next year:

(a) Motor expenses: Paid in 2016 £1,400; Owing at 31 December 2016 £200.

(b) Insurance: Paid in 2016 £1,700; Prepaid as at 31 December 2016 £130.

(c) Computer supplies: Paid during 2016 £900; Owing as at 31 December 2015 £300; Owing as at 31 December 2016 £400.

(d) Business rates: Paid during 2016 £5,600; Prepaid as at 31 December 2015 £580; Prepaid as at 31 December 2016 £560.

(e) Smith sublets part of the premises. He receives £3,800 during the year ended 31 December 2016. West, the tenant, owed Smith £380 on 31 December 2015 and £420 on 31 December 2016.

22.2A W. Hope's year ended on 30 June 2020. Write up the ledger accounts, showing the transfers to the financial statements and the balances carried down to the next year for the following:

(a) Stationery: Paid in the year to 30 June 2020 £240; Inventory of stationery at 30 June 2019 £60; at 30 June 2020 £95.

(b) General expenses: Paid in the year to 30 June 2020 £470; Owing at 30 June 2019 £32; Owing at 30 June 2020 £60.

(c) Rent and business rates (combined account): Paid in the year to 30 June 2020 £5,410; Rent owing at 30 June 2019 £220; Rent paid in advance at 30 June 2020 £370; Business rates owing 30 June 2019 £191; Business rates owing 30 June 2020 £393.

(d) Motor expenses: Paid in the year to 30 June 2020 £1,410; Owing as at 30 June 2019 £92; Owing as at 30 June 2020 £67.

(e) Hope earns commission from the sales of one item. Received in the year to 30 June 2020 £1,100; Owing at 30 June 2019 £50; Owing at 30 June 2020 £82.

22.3 On 1 January 2018 the following balances, among others, stood in the books of A. Cook, a sole proprietor:

(a) Business rates, £600 (Dr);

(b) Packing materials, £1,400 (Dr).

During the year ended 31 December 2018 the information related to these two accounts is as follows:

(i) Business rates of £6,200 were paid to cover the period 1 April 2018 to 31 March 2019;

(ii) £4,000 was paid for packing materials bought;

(iii) £900 was owing on 31 December 2018 in respect of packing materials bought on credit;

(iv) Old materials amounting to £300 were sold as scrap for £300 cash;

(v) Closing inventory of packing materials was valued at £2,400.

You are required to write up the two accounts showing the appropriate amounts transferred to the income statement at 31 December 2018, the end of the financial year of the trader.

Note: Individual accounts are not opened for accounts payable for packing materials bought on credit.

22.4A On 1 January 2019 the following balances, among others, stood in the books of B. Baxter:

(a) Lighting and heating, (Dr) £192.

(b) Insurance, (Dr) £1,410.

During the year ended 31 December 2019 the information related to these two accounts is as follows:

(i) Fire insurance, £1,164 covering the year ended 31 May 2020 was paid.

(ii) General insurance, £1,464 covering the year ended 31 July 2020 was paid.

(*iii*) An insurance rebate of £82 was received on 30 June 2019.
(*iv*) Electricity bills of £1,300 were paid.
(*v*) An electricity bill of £162 for December 2019 was unpaid as on 31 December 2019.
(*vi*) Oil bills of £810 were paid.
(*vii*) Inventory of oil as on 31 December 2019 was £205.

You are required to write up the accounts for lighting and heating, and for insurance, for the year to 31 December 2019. Carry forward necessary balances to 2020.

22.5 Three of the accounts in the ledger of Charlotte Williams indicated the following balances at 1 January 2020:

Insurance paid in advance £562;
Wages outstanding £306;
Rent receivable, received in advance £36.

During 2020 Charlotte:

Paid for insurance £1,019, by bank standing order;
Paid £15,000 wages, in cash;
Received £2,600 rent, by cheque, from the tenant.

At 31 December 2020, insurance prepaid was £345. On the same day rent receivable in arrears was £105 and wages accrued amounted to £419.

(*a*) Prepare the insurance, wages and rent receivable accounts for the year ended 31 December 2020, showing the year end transfers and the balances brought down.
(*b*) Prepare the income statement extract showing clearly the amounts transferred from each of the above accounts for the year ending 31 December 2020.
(*c*) Explain the effects on the financial statements of accounting for (*i*) expenses accrued and (*ii*) income received in advance at year end.
(*d*) What are the purposes of accounting for (*i*) expenses accrued and (*ii*) income received in advance at year end?

(Edexcel Foundation, London Examinations: GCSE)

22.6A

(*a*) Angela's business pays for its lighting and heating usage in arrears. The business's books showed an accrual in connection with lighting & heating expenses of £840 as at 1 January 2020 and an accrual of £910 as at 31 December 2020. The cash book revealed that the business made payments totalling £2,930 for lighting & heating during 2020. What figure should appear for 'lighting & heating expense' in Angela's Income Statement for the year ended 31 December 2020?
(*b*) Belinda is a sole trader. Her business's financial year ends on 31 July each year. Machine maintenance costs accrued of £325 as at 31 July 2019 were treated as prepaid in her Income Statement for the year ended 31 July 2019. Was her net profit for the year understated or overstated as a result, and by how much?
(*c*) The annual insurance premium for Claire's business premises (covering the period 1 September 2018 to 31 August 2019) is £7,200, which is exactly 20% more than her previous year's premium. Claire paid the £7,200 in full on 15 August 2018. What will be the expense reported for premises insurance in Claire's Income Statement for her financial year ended 31 March 2019?
(*d*) Denise's business pays £1,440 rent on 15 April 2018 in respect of the quarter ended 30 June 2018. She also pays an electricity bill of £864 covering energy used in the three months to 31 May 2018. The electricity bill was received on 10 June 2018, and Denise paid it on 20 June. Her financial year ends on 30 April 2018. What is the correct figure for accruals in Denise's Balance Sheet as at that date?
(*e*) Erica's business produces its financial statements for the year to 31 August. The business pays its rent quarterly in advance on 1 January, 1 April, 1 July and 1 October each year. The annual rent was increased from £45,600 to £51,600 per year with effect from 1 April 2020. In Erica's

business's financial statements for the year ended 31 August 2020, what figures should appear in the Income Statement and Balance Sheet in relation to rent?

(f) Fiona runs a business which owns three delivery vans. As at 1 April, there were five months' van insurance prepaid totalling £565 and diesel costs accrued of £367. During April, the outstanding diesel costs were paid as well as additional bills of £886. At 30 April there are further outstanding unpaid diesel costs of £291. What is the total amount to be disclosed in Fiona's Income Statement for April in connection with van expenses?

22.7A The owner of a small business selling and repairing cars which you patronise has just received a copy of his accounts for the current year.

He is rather baffled by some of the items and as he regards you as a financial expert, he has asked you to explain certain points of difficulty to him. This you have readily agreed to do. His questions are as follows:

(a) 'What is meant by the term "assets"? My mechanical knowledge and skill is an asset to the business but it does not seem to have been included.'

(b) 'The house I live in cost £130,000 five years ago and is now worth £360,000, but that is not included either.'

(c) 'What is the difference between "non-current assets" and "current assets"?'

(d) 'Why do amounts for "vehicles" appear under both non-current asset and current asset headings?'

(e) 'Why is the "bank and cash" figure in the balance sheet different from the profit for the year shown in the income statement?'

(f) 'I see the income statement has been charged with depreciation on equipment, etc. I bought all these things several years ago and paid for them in cash. Does this mean that I am being charged for them again?'

Required:
Answer each of his questions in terms which he will be able to understand.

(*Association of Chartered Certified Accountants*)

22.8 D. Staunton is a sole trader and you are given the following information relating to her business:

Trial balance as at 30 September 2020

	Dr £	Cr £
Accounts receivable	73,200	
Business rates	19,978	
Accounts payable		62,165
Returns outwards		2,064
Drawings	34,792	
Inventory as at 1 October 2019	25,967	
Utilities	18,603	
Wages & salaries	136,163	
Sales		592,013
Equipment: at cost	188,760	
Delivery vans: at cost	92,220	
Equipment: accumulated depreciation at 1 Oct 2019		74,100
Delivery vans: accumulated depreciation at 1 Oct 2019		60,720
Purchases	307,847	
Bank	1,337	
Bad debt expense	13,192	
Allowance for doubtful debts at 1 October 2019		2,240
Capital		118,757
	912,059	912,059

Additional information:
1 The inventory was counted at 30 September 2020 and was valued at £26,424.
2 Depreciation is to be applied at the following rates:

Equipment:	(reducing balance)	30%
Delivery vans:	(straight-line)	20%

3 The amount shown for business rates on the trial balance includes a payment of £11,760, which represents twelve months' business rates to 31 January 2021.
4 Utilities charges incurred for which no invoices have yet been received amount to a total of £4,167.
5 The allowance for doubtful debts is to be set at 4% of accounts receivable.

Required:
Prepare the following financial statements for D. Staunton's business:
(a) An Income Statement for the year ended 30 September 2020.
(b) A Balance Sheet as at 30 September 2020.

22.9 The trial balance for a small business at 31 August 2018 is as follows:

	£	£
Inventory 1 September 2017	8,200	
Purchases and sales	26,000	40,900
Rent	4,400	
Business rates	1,600	
Sundry expenses	340	
Motor vehicle at cost	9,000	
Accounts receivable and accounts payable	1,160	2,100
Bank	1,500	
Accumulated depreciation on motor vehicle at 1 September 2017		1,200
Capital at 1 September 2017		19,700
Drawings	11,700	
	63,900	63,900

At 31 August 2018 there was:

● Inventory valued at cost prices £9,100
● Accrued rent of £400
● Prepaid business rates of £300
● The motor vehicle is to be depreciated at 20 per cent of cost

Required:
1 The adjustments to the ledger accounts for rent and business rates for the year to 31 August 2018.
2 An income statement for the year ending 31 August 2018, together with a balance sheet as at that date.

22.10A J. Wright, a sole trader, extracted the following trial balance from his books at the close of business on 31 March 2019:

	Dr £	Cr £
Purchases and sales	61,420	127,245
Inventory 1 April 2018	7,940	
Capital 1 April 2018		23,930
Bank overdraft		2,490
Cash	140	
Discounts	2,480	62
Returns inwards	3,486	
Returns outwards		1,356

	Dr £	Cr £
Carriage outwards	3,210	
Rent and insurance	8,870	
Allowance for doubtful debts		630
Fixtures and fittings at cost	1,900	
Van at cost	5,600	
Fixtures and fittings: accumulated depreciation at 1.4.18		570
Van: accumulated depreciation at 1.4.18		700
Accounts receivable and accounts payable	12,418	11,400
Drawings	21,400	
Wages and salaries	39,200	
General office expenses	319	
	168,383	168,383

Notes:
(a) Inventory 31 March 2019 £6,805.
(b) Wages and salaries accrued at 31 March 2019 £3,500; Office expenses owing £16.
(c) Rent prepaid 31 March 2019 £600.
(d) Increase the allowance for doubtful debts by £110 to £740.
(e) Provide for depreciation as follows: Fixtures and fittings £190; Van £1,400.

Required:
Prepare the income statement for the year ending 31 March 2019 together with a balance sheet as at that date.

22.11   Mr Khan is a sole trader and you are given the following information relating to his business:

Trial balance as at 30 September 2020

		Dr £	Cr £
Inventory as at 1 October 2019		19,134	
Wages & salaries		106,483	
Sales			462,970
Carriage inwards		2,229	
Rent		18,465	
Gas		20,005	
Purchases		226,855	
Accounts receivable		74,400	
Accounts payable			53,749
Machinery:	at cost	232,140	
Computers:	at cost	97,080	
Machinery:	accumulated depreciation at 1 Oct 2019		77,580
Computers:	accumulated depreciation at 1 Oct 2019		54,600
Drawings		34,102	
Bank			1,807
Bad debt expense		13,408	
Allowance for doubtful debts at 1 October 2019			2,276
Capital			191,319
		844,301	844,301

Additional information:
1 The inventory was counted at 30 September 2020 and was valued at £19,491.
2 Depreciation is to be applied at the following rates:
       Machinery: (reducing balance) 15%
       Computers: (straight-line) 25%
3 The amount shown for rent on the trial balance includes a payment of £10,500, which represents twelve months' rent to 31 May 2021.

→

4 Gas charges incurred for which no invoices have yet been received amount to a total of £4,786.
5 The allowance for doubtful debts is to be set at 4 per cent of accounts receivable.

Required:
Prepare the following financial statements for Mr Khan's business:
(a) An income statement for the year ended 30 September 2020.
(b) A balance sheet as at 30 September 2020.

22.12A The following trial balance has been extracted from the ledger of Mr Yousef, a sole trader.

Trial Balance as at 31 May 2019

	Dr £	Cr £
Sales		138,078
Purchases	82,350	
Carriage	5,144	
Drawings	7,800	
Rent, rates and insurance	6,622	
Postage and stationery	3,001	
Advertising	1,330	
Salaries and wages	26,420	
Bad debts	877	
Allowance for doubtful debts		130
Accounts receivable	12,120	
Accounts payable		6,471
Cash in hand	177	
Cash at bank	1,002	
Inventory as at 1 June 2018	11,927	
Equipment		
at cost	58,000	
accumulated depreciation as at 1 June 2018		19,000
Capital		53,091
	216,770	216,770

The following additional information as at 31 May 2019 is available:

(a) Rent is accrued by £210.
(b) Rates have been prepaid by £880.
(c) £2,211 of carriage represents carriage inwards on purchases.
(d) Equipment is to be depreciated at 15% per annum using the straight line method.
(e) The allowance for doubtful debts to be increased by £40.
(f) Inventory at the close of business has been valued at £13,551.

Required:
Prepare an income statement for the year ending 31 May 2019 and a balance sheet as at that date.

(*Association of Accounting Technicians*)

Multiple choice questions: Set 3

Now attempt Set 3 of multiple choice questions. (Answers to all the multiple choice questions are given in Appendix 2 at the end of this book.)

Each of these multiple choice questions has four suggested answers, (A), (B), (C) and (D). You should read each question and then decide which choice is best, either (A) or (B) or (C) or (D). *Write down your answers on a separate piece of paper.* You will then be able to redo the set of questions later without having to try to ignore your answers.

MC41 A cash discount is best described as a reduction in the sum to be paid

(A) If payment is made within a previously agreed period
(B) If payment is made by cash, not cheque
(C) If payment is made either by cash or cheque
(D) If purchases are made for cash, not on credit

MC42 Discounts received are

(A) Deducted when we receive cash
(B) Given by us when we sell goods on credit
(C) Deducted by us when we pay our accounts
(D) None of these

MC43 The total of the 'Discounts Allowed' column in the Cash Book is posted to

(A) The debit of the Discounts Allowed account
(B) The debit of the Discounts Received account
(C) The credit of the Discounts Allowed account
(D) The credit of the Discounts Received account

MC44 Sales invoices are first entered in

(A) The Cash Book
(B) The Purchases Journal
(C) The Sales Account
(D) The Sales Day Book

MC45 The total of the Sales Day Book is entered on

(A) The credit side of the Sales Account in the General Ledger
(B) The credit side of the General Account in the Sales Ledger
(C) The debit side of the Sales Account in the General Ledger
(D) The debit side of the Sales Journal

MC46 Given a purchases invoice showing five items of £80 each, less trade discount of 25 per cent and cash discount of 5 per cent, if paid within the credit period, your would pay

(A) £285
(B) £280
(C) £260
(D) None of these

MC47   An alternative name for a Sales Day Book is

(A)   Sales Invoice
(B)   Sales Journal
(C)   Daily Sales
(D)   Sales Ledger

MC48   Entered in the Purchases Day Book are

(A)   Payments to suppliers
(B)   Trade discounts
(C)   Purchases invoices
(D)   Discounts received

MC49   The total of the Purchases Day Book is transferred to the

(A)   Credit side of the Purchases Account
(B)   Debit side of the Purchases Journal
(C)   Credit side of the Purchases Book
(D)   Debit side of the Purchases Account

MC50   Credit notes issued by us will be entered in our

(A)   Sales Account
(B)   Returns Inwards Account
(C)   Returns Inwards Book
(D)   Returns Outwards Book

MC51   The total of the Returns Outwards Book is transferred to

(A)   The credit side of the Returns Outwards Account
(B)   The debit side of the Returns Outwards Account
(C)   The credit side of the Returns Outwards Book
(D)   The debit side of the Purchases Returns Journal

MC52   We originally sold 25 items at £12 each, less $33\frac{1}{3}$ per cent trade discount. Our customer now returns 4 of them to us. What is the amount of credit note to be issued?

(A)   £48
(B)   £36
(C)   £30
(D)   £32

MC53   Depreciation is

(A)   The amount spent to buy a non-current asset
(B)   The salvage value of a non-current asset
(C)   The part of the cost of the non-current asset consumed during its period of use by the firm
(D)   The amount of money spent replacing non-current assets

MC54   A firm bought a machine for £3,200. It is to be depreciated at a rate of 25 per cent using the reducing balance method. What would be the remaining book value after two years?

(A)   £1,600
(B)   £2,400
(C)   £1,800
(D)   Some other figure

MC55 A firm bought a machine for £16,000. It is expected to be used for five years then sold for £1,000. What is the annual amount of depreciation if the straight line method is used?

(A) £3,200
(B) £3,100
(C) £3,750
(D) £3,000

MC56 At the balance sheet date the balance on the Accumulated Provision for Depreciation Account is

(A) Transferred to the Depreciation account
(B) Transferred to Profit and Loss
(C) Simply deducted from the asset in the Balance Sheet
(D) Transferred to the Asset account

MC57 In the trial balance the balance on the Provision for Depreciation Account is

(A) Shown as a credit item
(B) Not shown, as it is part of depreciation
(C) Shown as a debit item
(D) Sometimes shown as a credit, sometimes as a debit

MC58 If an accumulated provision for depreciation account is in use then the entries for the year's depreciation would be

(A) Credit Provision for Depreciation Account, debit Profit and Loss Account
(B) Debit Asset Account, credit Profit and Loss Account
(C) Credit Asset Account, debit Provision for Depreciation Account
(D) Credit Profit and Loss Account, debit Provision for Depreciation Account

MC59 When the financial statements are prepared, the Bad Debts Account is closed by a transfer to the

(A) Balance Sheet
(B) Profit and Loss Account
(C) Trading Account
(D) Allowance for Doubtful Debts Account

MC60 An Allowance for Doubtful Debts is created

(A) When debtors become bankrupt
(B) When debtors cease to be in business
(C) To provide for possible bad debts
(D) To write-off bad debts

CHECKS AND ERRORS

Introduction

This part presents an overview of the devices used to check for and correct errors, including a third financial statement – the *Statement of cash flows* – that can be used to confirm the change in the total of each equivalents over the reporting period.

The Scenario Questions take the knowledge you have acquired in Parts 1 to 5 and apply it to what you have learnt in Part 6.

23

Control accounts

Learning objectives

After you have studied this chapter, you should be able to:

● explain why control accounts can be useful
● draw up sales ledger control accounts
● draw up purchases ledger control accounts
● reconcile the purchases ledger and the sales ledger with their respective control accounts

Introduction

In this chapter, you'll learn about the benefits of using control accounts in manual accounting systems and the process involved in both preparing control accounts and reconciling them to the ledgers.

23.1 The benefits of accounting controls

In any but the smallest business, the accounting information system is set up so as to include controls that help ensure that errors are minimised and that nothing occurs that shouldn't, such as the cashier embezzling funds. One of the tasks undertaken by auditors is to check the various controls that are in place to ensure they are working satisfactorily and one of the things they will look out for is segregation of duties. So, for example, the same person will not both invoice customers and act as cashier when payment is received and, if someone claims reimbursement of an expense, it will be authorised for payment by someone else. Another form of control you've already learnt about involves whether or not customers are allowed to purchase goods on credit.

All these controls are 'organisational'. That is, they do not directly impose controls over the accounting data, nor do they ensure that accounting entries are correct. One control measure that does these things will be covered in Chapter 24 – the process of bank reconciliation. In this chapter, we'll look at another type of accounting control which is used mainly in manual accounting systems, **control accounts**.

When all the accounts were kept in one ledger, a trial balance could be drawn up as a test of the arithmetical accuracy of the accounts. If the trial balance totals disagree, the books of a small business could easily and quickly be checked so as to find the errors. Of course, as you know, even when the totals do agree, certain types of error may still have occurred, the nature of which makes it impossible for them to be detected in this way. Nevertheless, using a trial balance ensures that all the double entries appear, at least, to have been recorded correctly.

Acitivity 23.1 How do you find errors of the types that a trial balance cannot detect?

When a business has grown and the accounting work has been so divided up that there are several ledgers, any errors could be very difficult to find if a trial balance was the only device used to try to detect errors. Every item in every ledger may need to be checked just to find one error that caused the trial balance not to balance. What is required is a type of trial balance for each ledger, and this requirement is met by control accounts. A control account is a summary account that enables you to see at a glance whether the general ledger balance for the ledger to which that control account belongs agrees with the total of all the individual accounts held within that ledger.

If you use control accounts, only the ledgers where the control accounts do not balance need detailed checking to find errors.

23.2 Principle of control accounts

The principle on which the control account is based is simple and is as follows: if the opening balance of an account is known, together with information of the additions and deductions entered in the account, the closing balance can be calculated.

Applying this to a complete ledger, the total of opening balances together with the additions and deductions during the period should give the total of closing balances. This can be illustrated by reference to a sales ledger for entries for a month:

	£
Total of opening balances, 1 January 2019	3,000
Add Total of entries which have increased the balances	9,500
	12,500
Less Total of entries which have reduced the balances	(8,000)
Total of closing balances should be	4,500

Because totals are used, control accounts are sometimes known as 'total accounts'. Thus, a control account for a sales ledger could be known as either a '**sales ledger control account**' or as a '**total accounts receivable account**'.

Similarly, a control account for a purchases ledger could be known either as a '**purchases ledger control account**' or as a '**total accounts payable account**'.

A control account is a memorandum account. It is not part of the double entry system. It will be prepared either in the general ledger or in the ledger to which it relates, i.e. the purchases ledger or the sales ledger.

A control account looks like any other T-account:

Sales Ledger Control

2019			£	2019			£
Jan	1	Balances b/d	x,xxx	Jan	31	Returns Inwards Day Book (total of all goods returned from debtors in the period)	xxx
	31	Sales day book (total of sales invoiced in the period)	| xx,xxx		31	Cash book (total of all cash received from debtors in the period)	x,xxx
					31	Cash book (total of all cheques received from debtors in the period)	xx,xxx
					31	Balances c/d	x,xxx
			xx,xxx				xx,xxx

23.3 Information for control accounts

Exhibits 23.1 and 23.2 list the sources of information used to draw up control accounts.

Exhibit 23.1

Sales Ledger Control	Source
1 Opening accounts receivable	List of debtor balances drawn up at the end of the previous period
2 Credit sales	Total from the Sales Day Book
3 Returns inwards	Total of the Returns Inwards Day Book
4 Cheques received	Cash Book: bank column on received side. List extracted or the total of a special column for cheques which has been included in the Cash Book
5 Cash received	Cash Book: cash column on received side. List extracted or the total of a special column for cash which has been included in the Cash Book
6 Discounts allowed	Total of discounts allowed column in the Cash Book
7 Closing accounts receivable	List of debtor balances drawn up at the end of the period

Exhibit 23.2

Purchases Ledger Control	Source
1 Opening accounts payable	List of creditor balances drawn up at the end of the previous period
2 Credit purchases	Total from Purchases Day Book
3 Returns outwards	Total of Returns Outwards Day Book
4 Cheques paid	Cash Book: bank column on payments side. List extracted or total of a special column for cheques which has been included in the Cash Book
5 Cash paid	Cash Book: cash column on payments side. List extracted or total of a special column for cash which has been included in the Cash Book
6 Discounts received	Total of discounts received column in the Cash Book
7 Closing accounts payable	List of creditor balances drawn up at the end of the period

23.4 Form of control accounts

As shown in Section 23.2, control accounts kept in the general ledger are normally prepared in the same form as an account, with the totals of the debit entries in the ledger on the left-hand side of the control account, and the totals of the various credit entries in the ledger on the right-hand side.

The process is very straightforward. Take the sales ledger as an example. The first two steps are identical to those you learnt in Chapters 9 and 11.

1 Individual amounts received from debtors are transferred from the cash book into the personal accounts in the sales ledger. (The double entry is completed automatically in the normal way, because the cash book is, in itself, a ledger account.)
2 Individual invoice amounts are transferred from the sales day book into the personal accounts in the sales ledger. (You would complete the double entry in the normal way, by crediting the sales account.)
3 The sales ledger control account would open each period with the total of the accounts receivable balances at the start of the period.
4 Then, post the total of the returns inwards day book to the credit side of the sales ledger control account. (This is new.)
5 At the end of the period, you post the totals of all the payments from debtors received during the period from the cash book to the credit side of the sales ledger control account. (This is new.)
6 This is followed by posting to the debit side of the sales ledger control account the totals of all new sales during the period shown in the sales day book. (This is new.)
7 Balance-off the control account.
8 Check whether the balance on the control account is equal to the total of all the accounts receivable balances in the sales ledger.

If the balance is not the same as the total of all the balances in the sales ledger, there is an error either in the totals entered in the control account from the books of original entry or, more likely, somewhere in the sales ledger.

Note: You do not enter the total of the balances from the sales ledger in the control account. Instead, you balance-off the control account and check whether the balance c/d is the same as the total of all the individual balances in the sales ledger.

> **Activity 23.2**
>
> If you look at these eight steps, you can see that the first three are those you learnt to do earlier in the book, so you know that the other part of the double entry has been completed in the normal way. However, what about the double entries for (4), (5) and (6)? What is the other side of the double entry in each case?

Exhibit 23.3 shows an example of a sales ledger control account for a sales ledger in which all the entries are arithmetically correct and the totals transferred from the books of original entry are correct.

Exhibit 23.3

Sales Ledger Control Account data:	£
Accounts receivable balances on 1 January 2019	1,894
Total credit sales for the month	10,290
Cheques received from customers in the month	7,284
Cash received from customers in the month	1,236
Returns inwards from customers during the month	296
Accounts receivable balances on 31 January as extracted from the Sales Ledger	3,368

Sales Ledger Control

2019			£	2019			£
Jan	1	Balances b/d	1,894	Jan	31	Bank	7,284
	31	Sales	10,290		31	Cash	1,236
					31	Returns inwards	296
					31	Balances c/d	3,368
			12,184				12,184

We have proved the ledger to be arithmetically correct, because the control account balances with the amount equalling the total of the balances extracted from the sales ledger.

Like a trial balance, if the totals of a control account are not equal and the entries made to it were correct (i.e. the amounts transferred to it from the books of original entry have been corrrectly summed), this shows that there is an error somewhere in the ledger.

Exhibit 23.4 shows an example where an error is found to exist in a purchases ledger. The ledger will have to be checked in detail, the error found, and the control account then corrected.

Exhibit 23.4

Purchases Ledger Control Account data:	£
Accounts payable balances on 1 January 2019	3,890
Cheques paid to suppliers during the month	3,620
Returns outwards to suppliers in the month	95
Bought from suppliers in the month	4,936
Accounts payable balances on 31 January as extracted from the Purchases Ledger	5,151

Purchases Ledger Control

2019			£	2019			£
Jan	31	Bank	3,620	Jan	1	Balances b/d	3,890
	31	Returns outwards	95		31	Purchases	4,936
	31	Balances c/d	5,151				
			8,866 (Note)				8,826 (Note)

Note: Providing all the totals transferred into the Purchases Ledger Control Account from the books of original entry were correct, there is a £40 difference between the debit and credit entries in the Purchases Ledger.

We will have to check the purchases ledger in detail to find the error. A double line has not yet been drawn under the totals. We will do this (known as 'ruling off the account') when the error has been found and the totals corrected.

Note: You need to be sure that the totals transferred from the books of original entry were correct before assuming that an out-of-balance control account means that the ledger is incorrect.

23.5 Other advantages of control accounts in a manual accounting system

Control accounts are usually only maintained in a manual accounting system. They are not normally maintained in a computerised accounting system.

Control accounts have merits other than that of locating errors. When used, control accounts are normally under the charge of a responsible official, and fraud is made more difficult because transfers made (in an effort) to disguise frauds will have to pass the scrutiny of this person.

The balances on the control account can always be taken to equal accounts receivable and accounts payable without waiting for an extraction of individual balances. Management control is thereby aided, for the speed at which information is obtained is one of the prerequisites of efficient control.

23.6 Other sources of information for control accounts

With a large organisation there may well be more than one sales ledger or purchases ledger. The accounts in the sales ledgers may be divided up in ways such as:

● alphabetically: thus we may have three sales sub-ledgers split A–F, G–O and P–Z;
● geographically: this could be split: Europe, Far East, Africa, Asia, Australia, North America and South America.

For each of these sub-ledgers we must have a separate control account. An example of a columnar sales day book is shown as Exhibit 23.5:

Exhibit 23.5

Date		Details	Total	A–F	G–O	P–Z
			Columnar Sales Day Book		*Ledgers*	
2019			£	£	£	£
Feb	1	J. Archer	58	58		
	3	G. Gaunt	103		103	
	4	T. Brown	116	116		
	8	C. Dunn	205	205		
	10	A. Smith	16			16
	12	P. Smith	114			114
	15	D. Owen	88		88	
	18	B. Blake	17	17		
	22	T. Green	1,396		1,396	
	27	C. Males	48		48	
			2,161	396	1,635	130

The total of the A–F column will be the total sales figures for the Sales Ledger A–F control account, the total of the G–O column for the G–O control account, and so on.

A similar form of analysis can be used in the purchases day book, the returns inwards day book, the returns outwards day book and the cash book. The *totals* necessary for each of the control accounts can be obtained from the appropriate columns in these books.

Other items, such as bad debts written off or transfers from one ledger to another, will be recorded in the Journal.

23.7 Other transfers

Transfers to bad debt accounts will have to be recorded in the sales ledger control account as they involve entries in the sales ledger.

Similarly, a contra account, whereby the same entity is both a supplier and a customer, and inter-indebtedness is set off, will also need to be entered in the control accounts. An example of this follows:

(A) The business has sold A. Hughes £600 goods.
(B) Hughes has supplied the business with £880 goods.
(C) The £600 owing by Hughes is set off against £880 owing to him.
(D) This leaves £280 owing to Hughes.

Sales Ledger
A. Hughes

		£			
Sales	(A)	600			

Purchases Ledger
A. Hughes

					£
			Purchases	(B)	880

The set-off now takes place following the preparation of a journal entry in the Journal:

Sales Ledger
A. Hughes

		£			£
Sales	(A)	600	Set-off: Purchases ledger	(C)	600

Purchases Ledger
A. Hughes

		£			£
Set-off: Sales ledger	(C)	600	Purchases	(B)	880
Balance c/d	(D)	280			
		880			880
			Balance b/d	(D)	280

The set-off will be posted from the Journal to the credit side of the sales ledger control account and to the debit side of the purchases ledger control account.

23.8 A more complicated example

Exhibit 23.6 shows a worked example of a more complicated control account.

You will see that there are sometimes credit balances in the sales ledger as well as debit balances. Suppose for instance we sold £500 goods to W. Young, he then paid in full for them, and then afterwards he returned £40 goods to us. This would leave a credit balance of £40 on the account, whereas usually the balances in the sales ledger are debit balances.

Exhibit 23.6

2019			£
Aug	1	Sales ledger – debit balances	3,816
	1	Sales ledger – credit balances	22
	31	Transactions for the month:	
		Cash received	104
		Cheques received	6,239
		Sales	7,090
		Bad debts written off	306
		Discounts allowed	298
		Returns inwards	664
		Cash refunded to a customer who had overpaid his account	37
		Dishonoured cheques	29
		Interest charged by us on overdue debt	50
		At the end of the month:	
		Sales ledger – debit balances	3,429
		Sales ledger – credit balances	40

Sales Ledger Control Account

2019			£	2019			£
Aug	1	Balances b/d	3,816	Aug	1	Balances b/d	22
	31	Sales	7,090		31	Cash	104
		Cash refunded	37			Bank	6,239
		Bank: dishonoured cheques	29			Bad debts	306
		Interest on debt	50			Discounts allowed	298
		Balances c/d	40			Returns inwards	664
						Balances c/d	3,429
			11,062				11,062

Note that you do *not* set off the debit and credit balances in the Sales Ledger.

23.9 Control accounts as part of a double entry system

Many students find control accounts confusing. This is because, as shown in Section 23.4, the existence of a control account requires extra entries to be made in the accounts over and above those that would be made were a control account not being used.

What you need to realise is that the double entry belongs to the original entries in the accounts. For example, if a debtor pays the amount due on his account, you credit the account of the debtor and debit the bank account. No entry is made in the sales ledger control account at this stage. As a result, the double entry is the same irrespective of whether or not there is a control account.

When an entry is made to the control account, it includes all movements on the personal accounts, not just the amount in the single debtor example above. There may be payments from 5 debtors or 50 or 500 included in the amount posted to the control account. And, the posting is from the Cash Book for payments received from debtors; and from the Sales Day Book for sales to debtors. It is not from the individual debtor accounts.

It is at this point that confusion sets in – where is the second part of this 'double entry'? The answer is: there isn't one. **The posting to the control account is not part of a double entry.** Think of it as equivalent of posting each receipt from each debtor to the debtor's account and then writing the total cash received from all the debtors on a piece of paper. The control account is that 'piece of paper'. It is a note, a helpful piece of information.

If the control account is kept in the subsidiary ledger – the Sales Ledger in this example – all it shows is the total of all the amounts received from debtors, the total of all credit sales to debtors, plus the opening balance. You can then take these three numbers and discover the closing balance on your Sales Ledger:

Opening Balance + Credit Sales to Debtors — Amounts received from Debtors

When preparing a trial balance, you can include that balance rather than all the individual debtor account balances.

If the control account is kept in the General Ledger, it is considered to be part of the double entry system **because the General Ledger will balance without any need to include balances on accounts held in subsidiary ledgers.**

**Activity
23.3**
Why may some people consider this to be incorrect? That is, why is the fact that the control account is kept in the General Ledger *not* enough to justify saying that the control account is part of the double entry system?

This is not strictly correct. Yet, organisations that operate control accounts for their subsidiary ledgers often keep them in the General Ledger and view them as an integral part of the double entry system. When a trial balance is extracted, it is always the balances on the control accounts that are used rather than the balances on all the individual personal accounts.

When this is the case, the Sales Ledger and the Purchases Ledger are described as 'memorandum books' lying outside the double entry system.

This is technically incorrect but, when control accounts are kept in the General Ledger, it is 'normal' practice to describe the subsidiary ledgers in this way. **You need to be aware of this and to use the terminology in this way because it is what your examiners expect.**

In organisations **where the control accounts are kept in the subsidiary ledgers, the control accounts are *not* considered to be part of the double entry system.** In this case, the control account is normally described as a 'memorandum entry' in the individual subsidiary ledgers. The individual personal accounts in those subsidiary entries *are* considered to be part of the double entry system; and the subsidiary ledgers *are not* considered to be memorandum books.

Despite this difference in terminology, the same entries are made to control accounts kept in a General Ledger as are made to control accounts kept in subsidiary ledgers. In addition, it is the balance on the control account that is used in a trial balance, irrespective of whether it is kept in the General Ledger or in a subsidiary ledger.

In brief, it does not matter where a control account is kept. It is compiled in the same way and it is used in the same way. The artificial distinction concerning its place inside or outside the double entry system attributed to it depending upon the ledger in which it appears developed through custom and practice over many centuries. Control accounts are not part of a double entry system because the entries within them are not made using double entry principles. If you remember this point, you should find it relatively easy to understand the principles of control accounts.

Finally, do not confuse control accounts, which are used in order to operate subsidiary ledgers more efficiently, with wage control accounts which are used to maintain an element of control over the amounts paid relating to wages and salaries. Control accounts relate to subsidiary ledgers. Wages control accounts relate solely to wages and salaries. The two items both contain the word, 'control' in their title, but that is the only thing they have in common.

23.10 Self-balancing ledgers and adjustment accounts

Because ledgers which have a control account system are proved to be correct as far as the double entry is concerned they used to be called 'self-balancing ledgers'. The control accounts were often called 'adjustment accounts'. These terms are very rarely used nowadays, but you should remember them in case an examiner uses them.

23.11 Reconciliation of control accounts

Errors and omissions can occur when entering information into the accounting records. You will see in Chapter 24 how these are identified and used to reconcile differences between the bank account and the bank statement balances. When a ledger control account is not in balance, it indicates that something has gone wrong with the entries made to the accounting records. This leads to an investigation which (hopefully) reveals the cause(s). Then, in order to verify whether the identified item(s) caused the failure to balance the control account, a reconciliation is carried out.

Exhibit 23.7 shows an example of a **purchases ledger control account reconciliation**. It takes the original control account balance and adjusts it to arrive at an amended balance which should equal the revised total of the source amounts that, together, equal the control account balance.

It can be seen that the general approach is similar to that adopted for bank reconciliation statements. However, as each control account may be constructed using information from a number of sources (see Section 23.3) the extent of the investigation to identify the cause of the control account imbalance is likely to be far greater than that undertaken when performing a bank reconciliation.

Exhibit 23.7

An example of a Purchases Ledger Control Account Reconciliation

		£
Original purchases ledger control account balance		xxx
Add	Invoice omitted from control account, but entered in Purchases Ledger	xxx
	Supplier balance excluded from Purchases Ledger total because the account had been included in the Sales Ledger by mistake	xxx
	Credit sale posted in error to the debit of a Purchases Ledger account instead of the debit of an account in the Sales Ledger	xxx
	Undercasting error in calculation of total end of period creditors' balances	xxx
		xxx

Less	Customer account with a credit balance included in the Purchases Ledger that should have been included in the Sales Ledger	(xxx)
	Return inwards posted in error to the credit of a Purchases Ledger account instead of the credit of an account in the Sales Ledger	(xxx)
	Credit note entered in error in the Returns Outwards Day Book as £223 instead of £332	(xxx)
Revised purchases ledger control account balance obtained from revised source amounts		xxx

23.12 A cautionary note

Students often get the following wrong: only credit purchases are recorded in a Purchases Ledger control account. Also, in Sales Ledger control accounts, do not include cash sales or allowances for doubtful debts.

23.13 Finally

Control accounts are used in manual accounting systems. Most computerised accounting systems automatically provide all the benefits of using control accounts without the necessity of actually maintaining them. This is because computerised accounting systems automatically ensure that all double entries are completed, so ensuring that all the ledgers balance. Of course, errors can still arise, such as a posting made to the wrong ledger account, but not of the type that control accounts can detect.

Learning outcomes

You should now have learnt:

1 How to prepare control accounts.

2 How to prepare a control account reconciliation.

3 That control accounts enable errors to be traced down to the ledger that does not balance. Thus there will be no need to check all the books in full to find an error.

4 That transfers between sales and purchases ledgers should be prepared in the journal and shown in the control accounts.

5 That control accounts for most businesses are outside the double entry system and are kept as memorandum accounts in the general ledger or in the individual ledgers.

6 That control accounts of large organisations may be part of the double entry system, which means that the sales ledger and purchases ledger are treated as memorandum books outside the double entry system. The entries to such control accounts are the same as for control accounts that lie outside the double entry system.

7 That control accounts are normally only used in manual accounting systems.

Answers to activities

23.1 These errors tend to be detected either as the result of someone drawing attention to an entry that appears to be incorrect or as the result of sample checking of the entries that have been made in the accounting books. A debtor may, for example, question whether the amount on an invoice is correctly summed or suggest that one of the invoices listed in the debtor's monthly statement had nothing to do with the debtor. One of the tasks that auditors carry out involves checking a sample of the transactions during a period so as to determine the level of errors within the entries made relating to them. If the level of error detected is considered material, a more extensive check will be carried out.

23.2 (4) The other side of this double entry was to the debit of the returns inwards account.

(5) The other side of the double entry was done earlier at the time when the individual amounts received from debtors were posted as credits to the individual debtor accounts in the sales ledger. That is, *the other side of this double entry was all the debit entries to the cash book* (see Chapter 9). The posting of each receipt as a credit to the individual debtor accounts done in step (1) is actually a memorandum entry and does not form part of the double entry system. So, in effect, the sales ledger has been taken out of the double entry system and is now a memorandum book. *To summarise, step (5) is actually the credit side of the double entry whose debit side is all the debit entries in the cash book.*

(6) The other side of the double entry was done earlier at the time when each sale was posted from the sales day book to the individual accounts receivable accounts in the sales ledger. That is, *the other side of this double entry was the credit entry made when the total of the sales shown in the sales day book was posted to the sales account in the general ledger* (see Chapter 11). The posting of each sale as a debit to the individual accounts receivable accounts done in step (2) is actually a memorandum entry and does not form part of the double entry system. *To summarise, step (6) is actually the debit side of the double entry whose credit side is all the credit entries in the sales account.*

23.3 The double entry system involves the entry of financial transactions into accounts using the principle of at least one debit entry for every credit entry, and vice versa. Entries into control accounts are supplementary one-sided entries for which there is no debit to match the credit or credit to match the debit. They are simply summary statements constructed in the form of an account.

The balance they produce does reflect the balance on the subsidiary ledger to which they relate, but only because the totals of all the entries into the subsidiary ledgers have been calculated and inserted into the control accounts. They are not, and never could be, 'part of the double entry system'. However, for simplicity, when control accounts are kept in the General Ledger, they are referred to in this (incorrect) way.

Review questions

23.1 You are required to prepare a sales ledger control account from the following information for the month of September:

			£
Sep	1	Sales ledger balances	45,000
		Totals for September:	
		Sales day book	32,000
		Returns inwards day book	1,900
		Cheques and cash received from customers	29,800
		Discounts allowed	3,000
	30	Sales ledger balances	42,300

23.2A You are required to prepare a purchases ledger control account from the following information for the month of April. The balance of the account is to be taken as the amount of accounts payable as on 30 April.

			£
April	1	Purchases ledger balances	23,700
		Totals for April:	
		Purchases day book	14,200
		Returns outwards day book	950
		Cheques paid to suppliers	16,695
		Discounts received from suppliers	845
	30	Purchases ledger balances	?

23.3 Prepare a sales ledger control account from the following information:

2019			£
March	1	Debit balances	18,000
		Totals for March:	
		Sales day book	14,000
		Cash and cheques received from debtors	16,000
		Discounts allowed	1,400
		Debit balances in the sales ledger set off against credit balances in the purchases ledger	120
	31	Debit balances	?
		Credit balances	60

23.4A Prepare a sales ledger control account from the following information for October 2019, carrying down the balance at 31 October:

			£
Oct	1	Sales ledger balances	36,210
	31	Sales day book	31,470
		Bad debts written off	536
		Cheques received from debtors	26,306
		Discounts allowed	668
		Cheques dishonoured	260
		Returns inwards	1,878
		Set-offs against balances in purchases ledger	404

23.5 The trial balance of Outsize Books Ltd revealed a difference in the books. In order that the error(s) could be located it was decided to prepare purchases and sales ledger control accounts.

From the following information prepare the control accounts and show where an error may have been made:

2018			£
Jan	1	Purchases ledger balances	19,420
		Sales ledger balances	28,227
		Totals for the year 2018	
		Purchases journal	210,416
		Sales journal	305,824
		Returns outwards journal	1,452
		Returns inwards journal	3,618
		Cheques paid to suppliers	205,419
		Petty cash paid to suppliers	62
		Cheques and cash received from customers	287,317
		Discounts allowed	4,102
		Discounts received	1,721
		Balances on the sales ledger set off against balances in the purchases ledger	640
Dec	31	The list of balances from the purchases ledger shows a total of £20,210 and that from the sales ledger a total of £38,374	

23.6 The following information relates to the business of Romelu for the year ended 31 December 2020:

	£
Doubtful debts to be allowed for (in addition to those written-off)	660
Discounts received	1,310
Cash sales	1,490
Returns outwards (of goods previously bought on credit)	2,330
Discounts allowed	3,160
Bad debts written-off during 2020	4,770
Returns inwards (of goods previously sold on credit)	8,150
Total payables at 1.1.2020	16,400
Total receivables at 1.1.2020	23,220
Amounts paid to credit suppliers	109,040
Credit purchases	114,800
Cash from credit customers (including £370 from a customer whose debt was written off in 2019)	146,980
Credit sales	162,540

Required:
Prepare the sales ledger control account and purchases ledger control account for 2020.

23.7A The following information relates to the business of Amit Juneja for the year ended 31 December 2019:

	£
Amounts paid to credit suppliers	223,990
Bad debts written-off	7,220
Cheques and bank transfers received from credit customers	213,420
Contras (set-offs) between accounts receivable and payable	3,230
Credit purchases	243,920
Credit sales	240,740
Discounts allowed	4,860
Discounts received	4,870
Dishonoured cheques received from credit customers	810
Interest charged to customers for late payment	1,340
Refunds of credit balances paid to customers	2,150
Refunds of debit balances received from suppliers	610
Returns inwards	12,280
Returns outwards	9,780
Total payables at 1.1.2019	30,490
Total receivables at 1.1.2019	40,290

Required:
Prepare the sales ledger control account and purchases ledger control account for 2019.

23.8A The details below have been taken from the books of Sue Sprung's business in connection with the quarter ended 30 June 2020:

	£
Trade payables as at 1/4/2020	48,261
Trade receivables as at 1/4/2020	80,436
Credit purchases	96,255
Discounts allowed	3,441
Interest charged to customers in respect of overdue debts	1,895
Total of cheques and bank transfers received from trade receivables	147,593
Returns inwards (all from credit customers)	8,606
Allowance for doubtful debts as at 1/4/2020	2,415
Credit sales	172,139
Contras (set-offs) between trade receivables and trade payables	479
Refunds of credit balances paid to customers	797
Dishonoured cheques received from credit customers	488
Cash purchases	9,011
Returns outwards (all to credit suppliers)	3,850
Refunds of debit balances received from suppliers	242
Discounts received	1,925
Allowance for doubtful debts as at 30/6/2020	2,779
Payments to trade payables	95,242
Bad debts written-off	5,164
Cash sales	17,213

Required:
(a) Construct Sue's sales ledger control account and purchases ledger control account for the quarter ended 30 June 2020.
(b) State the source documents which will have been used for making entries in the:
   (i) Sales day book
   (ii) Returns inwards day book.
(c) Explain three benefits of maintaining a purchases ledger control account.

23.9 The financial year of The Better Trading Company ended on 30 November 2019. You have been asked to prepare a Total Accounts Receivable Account and a Total Accounts Payable Account in order to produce end-of-year figures for Accounts Receivable and Accounts Payable for the draft final accounts.

You are able to ovv the following information for the financial year from the books of original entry:

	£
Sales – cash	344,890
– credit	268,187
Purchases – cash	14,440
– credit	496,600
Total receipts from customers	600,570
Total payments to suppliers	503,970
Discounts allowed (all to credit customers)	5,520
Discounts received (all from credit suppliers)	3,510
Refunds given to cash customers	5,070
Balance in the sales ledger set off against balance in the purchases ledger	70
Bad debts written off	780
Increase in the allowance for doubtful debts	90
Credit notes issued to credit customers	4,140
Credit notes received from credit suppliers	1,480

According to the audited financial statements for the previous year accounts receivable and accounts payable as at 1 December 2018 were £26,555 and £43,450 respectively.

Required:
Draw up the relevant Total Accounts entering end-of-year totals for accounts receivable and accounts payable.

(*Association of Accounting Technicians*)

23.10

(a) Why are many accounting systems designed with a purchases ledger (accounts payable ledger) control account, as well as with a purchases ledger (accounts payable ledger)?

(b) The following errors have been discovered:
  (i) An invoice for £654 has been entered in the purchases day book as £456;
  (ii) A prompt payment discount of £100 from a creditor had been completely omitted from the accounting records;
  (iii) Purchases of £250 had been entered on the wrong side of a supplier's account in the purchases ledger;
  (iv) No entry had been made to record an agreement to contra an amount owed to X of £600 against an amount owed by X of £400;
  (v) A credit note for £60 had been entered as if it was an invoice.
  State the numerical effect on the purchases ledger control account balance of correcting each of these items (treating each item separately).

(c) Information technology and computerised systems are rapidly increasing in importance in data recording. Do you consider that this trend will eventually remove the need for control accounts to be incorporated in the design of accounting systems? Explain your answer briefly.

(*Association of Chartered Certified Accountants*)

23.11 Control Accounts are used mainly for accounts receivable and accounts payable. Explain:

(a) why it may be appropriate to use control accounts;
(b) the advantages of using them.

24

Bank reconciliations

Learning objectives

After you have studied this chapter, you should be able to:

- explain why bank reconciliations are prepared
- reconcile ledger accounts to suppliers' statements
- make the necessary entries in the accounts for dishonoured cheques

Introduction

In this chapter, you'll learn how to prepare a bank reconciliation statement and why you need to do this when a bank statement is received from the bank. You will also learn how to deal with dishonoured cheques in the ledger accounts.

24.1 Completing entries in the cash book

In the books of a business, funds paid into and out of the bank are entered into the bank columns of the cash book. At the same time, the bank will also be recording the flows of funds into and out of the business bank account.

If all the items entered in the cash book were the same as those entered in the records held by the bank, the balance on the business bank account as shown in the cash book and the balance on the account as shown by the bank's records would be the same.

Unfortunately, it isn't usually that simple, particularly in the case of a current account. There may be items paid into or out of the business bank account which have not been recorded in the cash book. And there may be items entered in the cash book that have not yet been entered in the bank's records of the account. To see if any of these things have happened, the cash book entries need to be compared to the record of the account held by the bank. Banks usually send a copy of that record, called a **bank statement**, to their customers on a regular basis, but a bank statement can be requested by a customer of the bank at any time.

Bank statements should *always* be checked against the cash book entries! (And you would be wise to do so yourself with your own bank account.)

Activity 24.1 What might cause the two balances to be different? Spend two minutes making a list.

Let's look at an example of a cash book and a bank statement in Exhibit 24.1:

Exhibit 24.1

Cash Book (bank columns only: *before* balancing on 31.12.2018)

2018				£	2018				£
Dec	1	Balance b/d	✔	250	Dec	5	J. Gordon	✔	65
	20	P. Thomas	✔	100		27	K. Hughes	✔	175
	28	D. Jones	✔	190					

Bank Statement

2018				Withdrawals £	Deposits £	Balance £
Dec	1	Balance b/d	✔			250
	8	10625^Note	✔	65		185
	21	Deposit	✔		100	285
	28	Deposit	✔		190	475
	29	10626^Note	✔	175		300
	30	Bank Giro credit: P. Smith			70	370
	31	Bank charges		50		320

Note: **10625** and **10626** refer to the serial numbers on the cheques paid out.

It is now clear that the two items not shown in our cash book are:

Bank Giro credit: P. Smith	£70
Bank charges	£50

P. Smith had paid £70 but, instead of sending a cheque, he paid the money by bank giro credit transfer direct into the business bank account. The business did not know of this until it received the bank statement.

The other item was in respect of bank charges. The bank has charged £50 for keeping the bank account and all the work connected with it. Instead of sending an invoice, the bank has simply taken the money out of the bank account.

 Activity 24.2 What sensible rule does this give you relating to when you should balance-off the bank account in the cash book at the end of the accounting period?

As we have now identified the items missing from the cash book, we can now complete writing it up by entering the two items we have identified:

Cash Book (bank columns only: *after* balancing on 31.12.2018)

2018			£	2018			£
Dec	1	Balance b/d	250	Dec	5	J. Gordon	65
	20	P. Thomas	100		27	K. Hughes	175
	28	D. Jones	190		31	Bank charges	50
	30	P. Smith	70		31	Balance c/d	320
			610				610
2019							
Jan	1	Balance b/d	320				

Both the bank statement and cash book closing balances are now shown as being £320.

24.2 Where closing balances differ

Although a cash book may be kept up to date by a business, it obviously cannot alter the bank's own records. Even after writing up entries in the cash book, there may still be a difference between the cash book balance and the balance on the bank statement. Exhibit 24.2 shows such a case.

Exhibit 24.2

Cash Book (after being completed to date)

2019			£	2019			£
Jan	1	Balance b/d	320	Jan	10	C. Morgan	110
	16	R. Lomas	160		20	M. McCarthy	90
	24	V. Verity	140		28	Cheshire CC rates	180
	31	J. Soames	470		30	M. Peck	200
	31	R. Johnson	90		31	Balance c/d	600
			1,180				1,180
Feb	1	Balance b/d	600				

Bank Statement

2019			Withdrawals £	Deposits £	Balance £
Jan	1	Balance b/d			320
	12	10627	110		210
	16	Deposit		160	370
	23	10628	90		280
	24	Deposit		140	420
	28	Direct debit: Cheshire CC	180		240
	31	Bank Giro credit: R. Johnson		90	330

Activity 24.3 Try to identify which items are causing the two balances to be different even after the bank statement has been checked against the cash book and the necessary additional entries have been made in the cash book. (*Hint*: there are two items involved.)

You can see that two items are in the cash book but are not shown on the bank statement. These are:

(i) A cheque had been paid to M. Peck on January 30. He deposited it in his bank on January 31 but his bank didn't collect the money from the business's bank until February 2. This is known as an **unpresented cheque**.

(ii) Although a cheque for £470 was received from J. Soames on January 31 and the business deposited it with the bank on that date, the bank did not receive the funds from Soames' bank until February. This is known as a 'bank lodgement not yet credited' to the business bank account.

The cash book balance on January 31 was £600, whereas the bank statement shows a balance of £330. To prove that although the balances are different they can be 'reconciled' (i.e. made to agree) with each other, a **bank reconciliation statement** is prepared. It will either start with the bank statement balance and then reconcile it to the cash book balance, or it will start with the cash book balance and then reconcile it to the bank statement balance. If the second approach is adopted, it would appear as:

Bank Reconciliation Statement as at 31 December 2018

		£
Balance as per cash book		600
Add Unpresented cheque	(i)	200
		800
Less Bank lodgement not on statement	(ii)	(470)
Balance per bank statement		330

If the two balances cannot be reconciled then there will be an error somewhere. This will have to be located and then corrected.

This reconciliation technique is also used when dealing with other statements drawn up outside the firm: for example, when reconciling purchase ledger accounts to suppliers' statements.

24.3 The bank balance in the balance sheet

The balance to be shown in the balance sheet is that per the cash book after it has been written up to date. In Exhibit 24.2, the balance sheet figure would be £600.

This is an important point, and one that students often get wrong! The bank reconciliation shown in the last section is simply verifying that you know why there is a difference between the two balances. It is *not* calculating what the bank account figure in the balance sheet should be because it starts with the balance in the cash book *after* adjusting it for items revealed in the bank statement.

24.4 An alternative approach to bank reconciliations

In order to avoid the confusion that may arise concerning what figure to include in the balance sheet, many accountants use a slightly different form of bank reconciliation. In this approach, you take the balance as shown on the bank statement and the balance in the cash book *before* making any adjustments that are identified when it is compared to the bank statement. You then reconcile each of them in turn to arrive at the balance that should appear in the balance sheet.

Having completed the reconciliation, you then update the cash book so that it balances at the correct amount, i.e. the amount that will be shown in the balance sheet. An example is shown in Exhibit 24.3.

Exhibit 24.3

Cash Book (bank columns only: *before* balancing on 31.12.2018)

2018				£	2018				£
Dec	1	Balance b/d	✔	160	Dec	8	V. O'Connor	✔	115
	12	D. Tyrrall	✔	80		21	G. Francis	✔	35
	23	P. McCarthy	✔	130		31	D. Barnes		25
	31	S. Aisbitt		72					

Bank Statement

2018				Withdrawals £	Deposits £	Balance £
Dec	1	Balance b/d	✔			160
	11	24621	✔	115		45
	14	Deposit	✔		80	125
	23	24622	✔	35		90
	29	Deposit	✔		130	220
	30	Bank Giro credit: A Parkinson			24	244
	31	Bank charges		40		204

You can see that the following are missing from the cash book:

(*a*) A bank giro credit of £24 made on December 30 by A. Parkinson.
(*b*) Bank charges of £40.

And you can see that the following are missing from the bank statement:

(*c*) A cheque paid to D. Barnes for £25 on December 31 has not yet been presented.
(*d*) A bank lodgement has not yet been credited – the cheque for £72 received from S. Aisbitt on 31 December.

The bank reconciliation statement would be:

Bank Reconciliation Statement as at 31 December 2018

		£
Balance as per cash book		267
Add Bank giro credit not yet entered	(a)	24
		291
Less Bank lodgement not on balance sheet	(b)	(40)
Balance in balance sheet		251
Add Cheque not yet presented	(c)	25
		276
Less Bank lodgement not on statement	(d)	(72)
Balance per bank statement		204

When you have adjustments to make to both the cash book and the bank account balances in order to reconcile them, this form of bank reconciliation statement is more useful than one that simply shows that you know why their balances are different (which is all the bank reconciliation statement in Section 24.2 shows).

An alternative approach that is often used in practice is to start with the balance as per the cash book and adjust it to arrive at the balance per the balance sheet (i.e. the same as in the first half of the bank reconciliation statement shown above). You then have a second section that starts with the balance as per the bank statement and adjust it to once again arrive at the balance per the balance sheet. Either of these two approaches is perfectly acceptable and both provide the same information.

24.5 Other terms used in banking

1 **Standing Orders.** A firm can instruct its bank to pay regular amounts of money at stated dates to persons or firms. For instance, you may ask your bank to pay £200 a month to a building society to repay a mortgage.

2 **Direct Debits.** These are payments which have to be made, such as gas bills, electricity bills, telephone bills, rates and insurance premiums. Instead of asking the bank to pay the money, as with standing orders, you give permission to the creditor to obtain the money directly from your bank account. This is particularly useful if the amounts payable may vary from time to time, as it is the creditor who changes the payments, not you. With standing orders, if the amount is ever to be changed, *you* have to inform the bank. With direct debits it is *the creditor* who informs the bank.

Just as with anything else omitted from the cash book, items of these types need to be included in the reconciliation and entered in the cash book before balancing it off at the end of the period.

24.6 Bank overdrafts

The adjustment needed to reconcile a bank overdraft according to the firm's books (shown by a credit balance in the cash book) with that shown in the bank's records are the same as those needed when the account is not overdrawn.

Exhibit 24.4 is of a cash book and a bank statement both showing an overdraft. Only the cheque for G. Cumberbatch (A) £106 and the cheque paid to J. Kelly (B) £63 need adjusting. Work through the reconciliation statement and then read the note after it. Because the balance shown by the cash book is correct (and, therefore, the balance that will appear in the balance sheet), you can use the form of bank reconciliation statement shown in Section 24.2.

Exhibit 24.4

Cash Book

2018				£	2018					£
Dec	5	I. Howe		308	Dec	1	Balance b/d		709
	24	L. Mason		120		9	P. Davies		140
	29	K. King		124		27	J. Kelly	(B)	63
	31	G. Cumberbatch	(A)	106		29	United Trust		77
	31	Balance c/d		380		31	Bank charges		49
				1,038					1,038

Bank Statement

			Dr	Cr	Balance
			£	£	£
2018					
Dec	1	Balance b/d			709 O/D
	5	Cheque		308	401 O/D
	14	P. Davies	140		541 O/D
	24	Cheque		120	421 O/D
	29	K. King: Credit transfer		124	297 O/D
	29	United Trust: Standing order	77		374 O/D
	31	Bank charges	49		423 O/D

Note: An overdraft is often shown with the letters 'O/D' following the amount. Alternatively, some banks use 'Dr' and 'Cr' after every balance entry to indicate whether the account is overdrawn.

Activity 24.4 Will the bank statement show 'Dr' or 'Cr' if an account is overdrawn?

Bank Reconciliation Statement as at 31 December 2018

	£
Overdraft as per cash book	(380)
Add Unpresented cheque	63
	(317)
Less Bank lodgement not on bank statement	(106)
Overdraft per bank statement	(423)

Note: You may find it confusing looking at this bank reconciliation statement because the opening entry is an overdraft, i.e. a negative number. However, the adjusting entries are the same as those you make when it is positive:

	£
Balance/overdraft per cash book	xxxx
Adjustments	
Unpresented cheque	Plus
Bank lodgement not on bank statement	Less
Balance/overdraft per bank statement	xxxx

24.7 Dishonoured cheques

When a cheque is received from a customer and paid into the bank, it is recorded on the debit side of the cash book. It is also shown on the bank statement as a deposit increasing the balance on the account. However, at a later date it may be found that the customer's bank will not pay the amount due on the cheque. The customer's bank has failed to 'honour' the cheque. The cheque is described as a **dishonoured cheque**.

There are several possible reasons for this. Imagine that K. King paid a business with a cheque for £5,000 on 20 May 2019. The business deposits it at the bank but, a few days later, the bank contacts the business and informs it that the cheque has been dishonoured. Typical reasons are:

1 King had put £5,000 in figures on the cheque, but had written it in words as 'five thousand *five hundred* pounds'. A new cheque correctly completed will need to be provided by King.
2 Normally cheques are considered *stale* six months after the date on the cheque. In other words, banks will not honour cheques that are more than six months old. If King had put the year 2015 on the cheque instead of 2019, then King's bank would dishonour the cheque and King would need to be asked for a correctly dated replacement.
3 King simply did not have sufficient funds in her bank account. Suppose she had previously a balance of only £2,000 and yet she has made out a cheque for £5,000. Her bank has not allowed her an overdraft in order to honour the cheque. As a result, the cheque has been dishonoured. The bank inform the business that this has happened and the business would have to contact King, explain what has happened and ask for valid payment of the account.

In all of these cases, the bank would record the original entry in its records as being reversed.

This is shown on the bank statement, for example, by the entry 'dishonoured cheque £5,000'. The business then makes the equivalent credit entry in the cash book while, at the same time, debiting King's account by the same amount.

When King originally paid the £5,000 the accounts in the ledger and cash book would have appeared as:

K. King

2019			£	2019			£
May	1	Balance b/d	5,000	May		20 Bank	5,000

Bank Account

2019			£		
May	20	K. King	5,000		

After recording the dishonoured cheque, the accounts would be:

K. King

2019			£	2019			£
May	1	Balance b/d	5,000	May	20	Bank	5,000
May	25	Bank: cheque dishonoured	5,000				

Bank Account

2019			£	2019			£
May	20	K. King	5,000	May	25	K. King: cheque dishonoured	5,000

In other words, King is once again shown as owing the business £5,000.

Learning outcomes

You should now have learnt:

1 Why it is important to perform a bank reconciliation when a bank statement is received.

2 That a bank reconciliation statement should show whether or not errors have been made either in the bank columns of the cash book or on the bank statement.

3 That a bank reconciliation statement can be prepared either before or after updating the cash book with items omitted from it that are shown on the bank statement.

4 That a bank reconciliation statement prepared after updating the cash book with items omitted from it that are shown on the bank statement shows that you know why the bank statement balance is different from that shown in the cash book and the balance sheet.

5 That a bank reconciliation statement prepared before updating the cash book with items omitted from it that are shown on the bank statement is reconciled from cash book to the balance sheet amount and then to the bank statement. It shows the amount to be entered in the balance sheet and also shows that you know why the bank statement balance is different from the balances shown in the cash book and in the balance sheet.

6 That in the case of bank overdrafts, the reconciliation statement adjustments are the same as those shown when there is a positive bank balance, but the opening and closing balances are negative.

7 How to prepare a bank reconciliation statement after updating the cash book with items omitted from it that are shown on the bank statement.

8 How to prepare a bank reconciliation statement before updating the cash book with items omitted from it that are shown on the bank statement.

9 Why cheques may be dishonoured and what the effect is upon the bank balance.

10 How to make the appropriate entries to the accounts when a cheque is dishonoured.

Answers to activities

24.1 There is quite a long list of possible causes, including:

- a business may take a day or two to deposit some cheques that it has already entered in the cash book;
- a cheque may take a few days to be entered in the account of the business held at the bank after it is deposited (because the bank won't recognise the amount received until a few days later, in case there is a problem with it);
- bank interest paid and bank charges often aren't known by a business until a bank statement is received;
- bank interest received won't be known by a business until it receives a bank statement;
- standing orders may not be written up in the cash book of the business until they are identified on the bank statement;
- the amount of a direct debit is sometimes not known and so should not be entered in the cash book until it is confirmed how much was paid out of the bank account;
- customers may pay their accounts by direct transfer from their bank account or by paying cash directly into the business bank account and the business may only learn of their having done so some time later;
- there may have been an error made in the cash book entries;
- the bank may have made an error in operating the account, such as adding funds to it instead of to the account of the person depositing the funds;
- a cheque paid into the bank may have 'bounced' (i.e. there were insufficient funds in the writer of the cheque's bank account to make the payment).

24.2 It is wise to wait until receiving the bank statement before balancing-off the bank account in the cash book at the end of the accounting period. In a manual accounting system, if a cash book is balanced on a regular basis, balancing-off is usually done at the end of the time period selected and any additional entries are recorded along with the other entries made in the following day, week, month or quarter. However, at the end of the accounting year, the balancing-off is often done in pencil (so that financial statements can be drafted) and then done in ink after any missing entries and corrections of errors have been entered following receipt of the bank statement.

24.3 M. Peck £200 and J. Soames £470.

24.4 'Dr' indicates an overdraft. The customer is a debtor of the bank. In the customer's balance sheet, the overdraft is included in the current liabilities, indicating that the bank is a creditor. Always remember that a bank is looking at the relationship from the opposite side to the view seen by the customer.

Review questions

24.1 From the following, draw up a bank reconciliation statement from details as on 31 December 2019 for T. Higgins:

	£
Cash at bank as per bank column of the cash book	5,300
Unpresented cheques	1,640
Cheques received and paid into the bank, but not yet appeared on the bank statement	970
Credit transfers received according to the bank statement but not yet entered in the cash book	245
Cash at bank as per bank statement	6,215

24.2A Draw up a bank reconciliation statement, after writing the cash book up to date, ascertaining the balance on the bank statement, from the following as on 31 March 2019:

	£
Cash at bank as per bank column of the cash book (Dr)	8,340
Bankings made but not yet appeared on bank statement	420
Bank charges on bank statement but not yet in cash book	25
Unpresented cheques	277
Standing order to DMC Ltd on bank statement, but not in cash book	99
Credit transfer received from P. Fox on bank statement, but not yet in cash book	435

24.3 The following are extracts from the cash book and the bank statement of P. Wilson's business.

You are required to:
(a) Write the cash book up to date, showing the new balance as on 31 December 2019, and
(b) Draw up a bank reconciliation statement as on 31 December 2019.

Cash Book

2019		Dr	£	2019		Cr	£
Dec	1	Balance b/d	1,234	Dec	8	S. Fry	678
	7	M. Fox	236		15	S. Mall	99
	22	L. Shaw	189		28	A. Cole	125
	31	L. King	366		31	Balance c/d	1,535
	31	L. Ross	412				
			2,437				2,437

Bank Statement

2019			Dr	Cr	Balance
			£	£	£
Dec	1	Balance b/d			1,234
	7	Deposit		236	1,470
	11	Cheque payment	678		792
	20	Cheque payment	99		693
	22	Deposit		189	882
	31	Credit transfer: J. Watt		251	1,133
	31	Bank charges	49		1,084

24.4A The bank columns in the cash book for June 2019 and the bank statement for that month for D. Hogan are as follows:

Cash Book

2019		Dr	£	2019		Cr	£
Jun	1	Balance b/d	1,410	Jun	5	L. Holmes	180
	7	J. May	62		12	J. Rebus	519
	16	T. Wilson	75		16	T. Silver	41
	28	F. Slack	224		29	Blister Disco	22
	30	G. Baker	582		30	Balance c/d	1,591
			2,353				2,353

Bank Statement

2019			Dr	Cr	Balance
			£	£	£
Jun	1	Balance b/d			1,410
	7	Cheque		62	1,472
	8	L. Holmes	180		1,292
	16	Cheque		75	1,367
	17	J. Rebus	519		848
	18	T. Silver	41		807
	28	Cheque		224	1,031
	29	SLM standing order	52		979
	30	Flynn: trader's credit		64	1,043
	30	Bank charges	43		1,000

You are required to:
(a) Write the cash book up to date to take the above into account, and then
(b) Draw up a bank reconciliation statement as on 30 June 2019.

24.5 Read the following and answer the questions below.

On 31 December 2018 the bank column of C. Tench's cash book showed a debit balance of £1,500.

The monthly bank statement written up to 31 December 2018 showed a credit balance of £2,950.

On checking the cash book with the bank statement it was discovered that the following transactions had not been entered in the cash book:

Dividends of £240 had been paid directly to the bank.
A credit transfer – HM Revenue & Customs VAT refund of £260 – had been collected by the bank.
Bank charges £24.
A direct debit of £70 for the RAC subscription had been paid by the bank.
A standing order of £200 for C. Tench's loan repayment had been paid by the bank.
Tench's deposit account balance of £1,400 was transferred into his bank current account.

A further check revealed the following items:

Two cheques drawn in favour of T. Cod £250 and F. Haddock £290 had been entered in the cash book but had not been presented for payment.
Cash and cheques amounting to £690 had been paid into the bank on 31 December 2018 but were not credited by the bank until 2 January 2019.

(a) Starting with the debit balance of £1,500, bring the cash book (bank columns) up to date and then balance the bank account.
(b) Prepare a bank reconciliation statement as at 31 December 2018.

(Midland Examining Group: GCSE)

→ **24.6A** In the draft accounts for the year ended 31 October 2019 of Thomas P. Lee, garage proprietor, the balance at bank according to the cash book was £894.68 in hand.

Subsequently the following discoveries were made:

(1) Cheque number 176276 dated 3 September 2019 for £310.84 in favour of G. Lowe Limited has been correctly recorded in the bank statement, but included in the cash book payments as £301.84.

(2) Bank commission charged of £169.56 and bank interest charged of £109.10 have been entered in the bank statement on 23 October 2019, but not included in the cash book.

(3) The recently received bank statement shows that a cheque for £29.31 received from T. Andrews and credited in the bank statements on 9 October 2019 has now been dishonoured and debited in the bank statement on 26 October 2019. The only entry in the cash book for this cheque records its receipt on 8 October 2019.

(4) Cheque number 177145 for £15.10 has been recorded twice as a credit in the cash book.

(5) Amounts received in the last few days of October 2019 totalling £1,895.60 and recorded in the cash book have not been included in the bank statements until 2 November 2019.

(6) Cheques paid according to the cash book during October 2019 and totalling £395.80 were not presented for payment to the bank until November 2019.

(7) Traders' credits totalling £210.10 have been credited in the bank statement on 26 October 2019, but not yet recorded in the cash book.

(8) A standing order payment of £15.00 on 17 October 2019 to Countryside Publications has been recorded in the bank statement but is not mentioned in the cash book.

Required:

(a) Prepare a computation of the balance at bank to be included in Thomas P. Lee's balance sheet as at 31 October 2019.

(b) Prepare a bank reconciliation statement as at 31 October 2019 for Thomas P. Lee.

(c) Briefly explain why it is necessary to prepare bank reconciliation statements at accounting year ends.

(*Association of Accounting Technicians*)

24.7 The bank statement for R. Hood for the month of March 2019 is:

2019			Dr £	Cr £	Balance £
Mar	1	Balance			4,200 O/D
	8	T. MacLeod	184		4,384 O/D
	16	Cheque		292	4,092 O/D
	20	W. Milne	160		4,252 O/D
	21	Cheque		369	3,883 O/D
	31	G. Frank: trader's credit		88	3,795 O/D
	31	TYF: standing order	32		3,827 O/D
	31	Bank charges	19		3,846 O/D

The cash book for March 2019 is:

2019		Dr	£	2019		Cr	£
Mar	16	G. Philip	292	Mar	1	Balance b/d	4,200
	21	J. Forker	369		6	T. MacLeod	184
	31	S. O'Hare	192		30	W. Milne	160
	31	Balance c/d	4,195		30	S. Porter	504
			5,048				5,048

You are required to:
(a) Write the cash book up to date, and
(b) Draw up a bank reconciliation statement as on 31 March 2019.

24.8A The following is the cash book (bank columns) of F. King for December 2020:

2020		Dr	£	2020		Cr	£
Dec	6	P. Pan	230	Dec	1	Balance b/d	1,900
	20	C. Hook	265		10	J. Lamb	304
	31	W. Britten	325		19	P. Wilson	261
	31	Balance c/d	1,682		29	K. Coull	37
			2,502				2,502

The bank statement for the month is:

2020			Dr £	Cr £	Balance £
Dec	1	Balance			1,900 O/D
	6	Cheque		230	1,670 O/D
	13	J. Lamb	304		1,974 O/D
	20	Cheque		265	1,709 O/D
	22	P. Wilson	261		1,970 O/D
	30	Tox: standing order	94		2,064 O/D
	31	F. Ray: trader's credit		102	1,962 O/D
	31	Bank charges	72		2,034 O/D

You are required to:
(a) Write the cash book up to date to take the necessary items into account, and
(b) Draw up a bank reconciliation statement as on 31 December 2020.

24.9 The following is a summary of a cash book as presented by George Ltd for the month of October:

	£		£
Receipts	1,469	Balance b/d	761
Balance c/d	554	Payments	1,262
	2,023		2,023

All receipts are banked and all payments are made by cheque.

On investigation you discover:

(1) Bank charges of £136 entered on the bank statement have not been entered in the cash book.
(2) Cheques drawn amounting to £267 had not been presented to the bank for payment.
(3) Cheques received totalling £762 had been entered in the cash book and paid into the bank, but had not been credited by the bank until 3 November.
(4) A cheque for £22 for sundries had been entered in the cash book as a receipt instead of as a payment.
(5) A cheque received from K. Jones for £80 had been returned by the bank and marked 'No funds available'. No adjustment has been made in the cash book.
(6) A standing order for a business rates instalment of £150 on 30 October had not been entered in the cash book.

→ (7) All dividends received are credited directly to the bank account. During October amounts total-ling £62 were credited by the bank but no entries were made in the cash book.

(8) A cheque drawn for £66 for stationery had been incorrectly entered in the cash book as £60.

(9) The balance brought forward in the cash book should have been £711, not £761.

Required:

(a) Show the adjustments required to the cash book balance.

(b) Prepare a bank reconciliation statement as at 31 October.

Statements of cash flows

After you have studied this chapter, you should be able to:

- draw up a statement of cash flows for any type of organisation
- explain how statements of cash flows can give a different view of a business to that simply concerned with profits
- describe the contents of International Accounting Standard 7 (IAS 7) and the format to be used when preparing statements of cash flows using IAS 7
- describe some of the uses that can be made of statements of cash flows

Introduction
·············

In this chapter, you'll learn about statements of cash flows, how to prepare them, and the requirements of IAS 7 (*Statement of cash flows*), the accounting standard that regulates their preparation.

25.1 The importance of cash

Imagine that you were the sole proprietor of a small newsagent shop and you were asked which would you prefer:

(a) your shop makes a net profit of £30,000 this year and, at the year end, all your £10,000 of assets are invested in inventory and you owe your suppliers £10,000;

(b) your shop makes a net profit of £8,000 this year but you have £5,000 in cash, £2,000 in inventory, no debtors and no liabilities at the year end.

What would you reply?

It sounds like a stupid question. Here's another: Imagine that you were the sole proprietor of an advertising agency and that you have no employees. Which would you prefer:

(c) your business makes a net profit of £30,000 this year and, at the year end, all your £10,000 of assets are amounts owed by clients and you owe £10,000 to your trade creditors;

(d) you make a net profit of £8,000 this year but you have £5,000 in cash, £2,000 is owed to you by clients, and you have no liabilities.

You are in business because you want to make a profit, aren't you? But, is (a) the sensible answer to the first question, or (c) a sensible answer to the second? Probably not. If you have no cash, how will you pay your creditors?

This is a problem faced by many small businesses and is the main cause of between 20 and 30 per cent failing in their first 12 months of trading. It does not improve very much for those that survive their first year. While two-thirds survive for two years, under half survive for four years. On average, more than 10 per cent of small businesses fail every year in the UK.

More than half of all small business failures are due to a shortage of cash, yet, a recent study of UK small businesses found that:

● 29 per cent of owners were too busy to find the time to keep a close eye on their financial position;
● checks on the credit worthiness of new customers (something that is very easy and cheap to do) are not done by two-thirds and three-quarters undertake no credit check when existing customers ask for an increase in the level of their credit.

The importance of cash for any business cannot be understated. In almost all cases, the appropriate answer to select to the questions at the start of this section are (*b*) and (*d*). It is better to have enough cash to pay your creditors, particularly in the early years of a business. As businesses mature, they can relax their need for cash to some extent, but they must always be vigilant and must always have the means to raise cash when required.

If all your assets are in inventory, you may find it very difficult to raise sufficient cash to meet the needs of your creditors. Selling inventory at cost is not good for profits. Selling inventory at below cost is disastrous if done excessively. All businesses do it occasionally, none that survive do it other than in order to get rid of unsalable goods. Similarly, getting money from your debtors is not something that tends to occur quickly, especially if they think you may be having problems raising cash.

 Activity 25.1 Why might the fact you are having difficulty raising cash make some debtors take longer to pay you what they owe?

This book deals mainly with how to enter transactions in the accounting records of a business; and in how to determine the financial position of a business at a point in time (balance sheet) and the profit of a business over a period of time (income statement). It does not focus upon cash. However, it would be wrong to learn how to record everything and produce financial statements of this type in ignorance of the importance of cash.

As cash flows through an entity, the impact of the timing of its injections and withdrawals changes the levels of debtors, creditors, funds in the bank, and many other assets and liabilities. For example, if you reduce the number of days you wait to pay your accounts payable (i.e. your creditors), you reduce what is in your bank account. Alternatively, if you instead increase the days you take to pay them, you increase what is in your bank account. If you have too little cash in your bank account, you may need to borrow to raise the cash to pay for inventory. That may be expensive, so instead you delay paying your creditors. That risks their refusing to continue to sell inventory to you on credit, so inventory reduces, possibly to the point where orders cannot be met and sales are lost. Alternatively, you may reduce the period of credit you allow your accounts receivable (i.e. your debtors), which risks their going elsewhere in future; or you may simply not order any inventory, which reduces it to possibly dangerously low levels, and so on. Entities that do not understand these cashflow connections can find themselves running out of cash, and many find eventually that they cannot continue in business. It is of vital importance that this is understood.

It is for this reason that the **statement of cash flows**, the subject of this chapter, is considered an essential component of a business's set of financial statements.

In the rest of this chapter, we shall concentrate upon reporting how cash has been used which, in the absence of any other information, may indicate how it will be used in future. At the very least, when used in conjunction with an income statement and a balance sheet, a statement of cash flows may highlight issues relating to use of cash that may merit attention or of the need for changes to the cash management policy of the business.

Firstly, we shall look at why it is considered necessary to prepare statements of cash flows.

25.2 Need for statements of cash flows

For any business it is important to ensure that:

● sufficient profits are made to finance the business activities; and that
● sufficient cash funds are available as and when needed.

> **Activity 25.2**
>
> What do you think is meant by 'cash' in this context? (*Hint*: which are the truly liquid assets?)

We ascertain the amount of profits in an income statement. We also show what the assets, capital and liabilities are at a given date by drawing up a balance sheet. Although the balance sheet shows the cash balance (see the definition in the solution to Activity 25.1) at a given date, it does not show us how we have used our cash funds during the accounting period.

What we really need, to help throw some light on to the cash situation, is some form of statement which shows us exactly where the cash has come from during the year, and exactly what we have done with it. The statement that fulfils these needs is called a statement of cash flows.

It is also sometimes called a 'cash flow statement' but IAS 1 recommends use of 'statement of cash flows' so this is the term we will use in this book. You need to be aware of the alternative title in case your examiner uses it.

25.3 International Accounting Standard 7: Statement of Cash Flows

This standard, as its title suggests, concerns the preparation of statements of cash flows.

The International Accounting Standards Board requires all companies to include a statement of cash flows with their published financial statements.

25.4 Businesses other than companies

Although partnerships and sole traders do not have to prepare them, statements of cash flows can be of considerable use to all organisations.

IAS 7 prescribes a format for statements of cash flows. An example is shown later in Exhibit 25.6. This is suitable for a company but, obviously, there are factors concerning partnerships and sole traders which do not occur in companies. It will be of help to students if the statements of cash flows for sole traders and partnerships are fashioned to be as similar to those for companies as is possible. Consequently, the layouts for statements of cash flows of sole traders and partnerships in this book will follow the style of layout presented in IAS 7.

25.5 Profit and liquidity are *not* directly related

Many people think that if we are making profits then there should be no shortage of cash. As you have learnt earlier in this book, this is not necessarily so. Let's look at a few instances where, although reasonable profits are being made by each of the following businesses, they could find themselves short of cash, maybe not now, but at some time in the future.

● A sole trader is making £40,000 a year profits. However, his drawings have been over £60,000 a year for some time.
● A company has been over-generous with credit terms to debtors, and last year extended the time in which debtors could pay from one month to three months. In addition it has taken on quite a few extra customers who are not creditworthy and such sales may result in bad debts in the future.
● A partnership whose products will not be on the market for quite a long time has invested in some very expensive machinery. A lot of money has been spent now, but no income will result in the near future.

In all of these cases, each of the businesses could easily run out of cash. In fact many businesses fail and are wound up because of cash shortages, despite adequate profits being made. Statements of cash flows can help to signal the development of such problems.

> **Activity 25.3**
>
> Can you think of any more examples? Spend a minute thinking about this and then write down any you come up with.

25.6 Where from: where to

Basically a statement of cash flows shows where the cash resources came from, and where they have gone to. Exhibit 25.1 shows details of such cash flows.

Exhibit 25.1

Cash comes from	Cash resources		Cash goes to
	In	Out	
1 Sales of goods and services	→	→	1 Purchases of goods and services for resale
2 Sales of Non-current Assets	→	→	2 Purchase of Non-current Assets
3 Decrease in Inventory	→	→	3 Increase in Inventory
4 Decrease in Accounts receivable	→	→	4 Increase in Accounts receivable
5 Capital Introduced	→	→	5 Drawings/Dividends
6 Loans Received	→	→	6 Loans Repaid
7 Increase in Account payable	→	→	7 Decrease in Account payable

These can be explained as follows:

1 Sales of goods and services bring a flow of cash into the business. Purchases take cash out of it.
2 The cash received from sales of non-current assets comes into the business. A purchase of non-current assets takes it out.
3 Reducing inventory in the normal course of business means turning it into cash. An increase in inventory ties up cash funds.
4 A reduction in accounts receivable means that the extra amount paid comes into the business as cash. Letting accounts receivable increase stops that extra amount of cash coming in.
5 An increase in a sole proprietor's capital, or issues of shares in a company, brings cash in. Drawings or dividends take it out.
6 Loans received bring in cash, while their repayment reduces cash.
7 An increase in accounts payable keeps the extra cash in the business. A decrease in accounts payable means that the extra payments take cash out.

If, therefore, we take the cash (and bank) balances at the start of a financial period, and adjust it for cash flows in and out during the financial period, then we should arrive at the cash (and bank) balances at the end of the period. This can be shown as:

Cash[Note] per balance sheet at the end of the previous period	+	Changes – which must be the result of cash flows during the current period	=	Cash per balance sheet at the end of the current period

Note: 'Cash' in this context includes amounts held in bank accounts. We don't usually refer to 'cash and bank', but simply to 'cash'.

25.7 Construction of a statement of cash flows

We will first of all look at a couple of examples of statements of cash flows drawn up for sole trader businesses, as this will make it easier to understand the process of preparing one before we go on to look at a more complicated example of a limited company's statement of cash flows in Exhibit 25.7.

First, we will start with Exhibit 25.2 and use it to construct Exhibit 25.3, a statement of cash flows using the (indirect method) format prescribed by IAS 7. (We'll explain what is meant by 'indirect method' in Section 25.12.)

Exhibit 25.2

The following are the balance sheets of T. Holmes as at 31 December 2019 and 31 December 2020:

	31.12.2019		31.12.2020	
	£	£	£	£
Non-current assets				
Premises at cost		25,000		28,800
Current assets				
Inventory	12,500		12,850	
Accounts receivable	21,650		23,140	
Cash and bank balances	4,300		5,620	
		38,450		41,610
Total assets		63,450		70,410
Current liabilities				
Accounts payable		(11,350)		(11,120)
		52,100		59,290
Net assets				
Capital				
Opening balances b/d		52,660		52,100
Add Net profit for year		16,550		25,440
		69,210		77,540
Less Drawings		(17,110)		(18,250)
Total capital		52,100		59,290

Note: For simplicity, no depreciation has been charged.

Exhibit 25.3

T. Holmes
Statement of Cash Flows for the year ending 31 December 2020

	£
Net cash flow from operating activities (see Note 1)	23,370
Investing activities	
Payment to acquire extra premises	(3,800)
Financing activities	
Drawings	(18,250)
Increase in cash	1,320

Notes:

1 Reconciliation of net profit to net cash inflow:

	£	£
Net profit		25,440
Less cash used for:		
Increase in inventory	350	
Increase in accounts receivable	1,490	
Decrease in accounts payable	230	
		(2,070)
Net cash flow from operating activities		23,370

2 Analysis of changes in cash during the year:

	£
Balance at 1 January 2020	4,300
Net cash inflow	1,320
Balance at 31 December 2020	5,620

25.8 Note on the use of brackets

As you know, in accounting it is customary to show a figure in brackets if it is a minus figure. This would be deducted from the other figures to arrive at the total of the column. These are seen very frequently in statements of cash flows. For example, instead of bringing out a sub-total of the deductions, Note 1 accompanying Exhibit 25.3 would normally be shown as:

	£
Net profit	25,440
Increase in inventory	(350)
Increase in accounts receivable	(1,490)
Decrease in accounts payable	(230)
Net cash flow from operating activities	23,370

25.9 Adjustments needed to net profit

You saw in the statement of cash flows in Exhibit 25.3 that when net profit is included as a source of cash funds, the net profit figure has to be adjusted to take account of items included which do not involve a movement of cash *in the period covered by the statement of cash flows*. The most common examples are depreciation, allowances for doubtful debts, and book profits and losses on the sale or disposal of non-current assets.

Depreciation

For example, suppose we bought equipment costing £3,000 in the year ended 31 December 2019. It is depreciated at £1,000 per annum for three years and then scrapped, disposal value being nil. This would result in the following:

		Years to 31 December		
		2019	2020	2021
		£	£	£
(i)	Item involving flow of cash: Cost of equipment (as this is purchase of an asset this is not part of the net profit calculation)	3,000		
(ii)	Net profit before depreciation	12,000	13,000	15,000
(iii)	Items not involving flow of cash: Depreciation	(1,000)	(1,000)	(1,000)
(iv)	Net profit after depreciation	11,000	13,000	14,000

Now the question arises as to which of figures (*i*) to (*iv*) are the ones to be used in statements of cash flows. Let's consider items (*i*) to (*iv*):

(i) A payment of £3,000 is made to buy equipment. This *does* involve a flow of cash and should therefore be included in the statement of cash flows for 2019.

(ii) Net profit before depreciation. This brings cash flowing into the business and therefore *should* be shown in statements of cash flows.

(*iii*) Depreciation does not involve a flow of cash. It is represented by a bookkeeping entry:
Debit profit and loss: Credit provision for depreciation.
As this does not involve any outflow of cash, it *should not* be shown in a statement of cash flows.

(*iv*) Net profit after depreciation. Depreciation does not involve cash flow, and therefore (*ii*) is the net profit we need to include in the statement of cash flows.

In most examination questions (*ii*) will not be shown. As we will show you, the figure for net profit before depreciation is calculated in the statement of cash flows itself.

Allowances for doubtful debts

An allowance for doubtful debts is similar to a provision for depreciation. The cash flow occurs when a debt is paid, *not* when provisions are made in case there may be bad debts in the future. As a result, when preparing the statement of cash flows, you need to add back to net profit any increase in the allowance for doubtful debts or deduct from net profit any decrease in the allowance for doubtful debts.

If an examination question gives you the net profits *after* an allowance for doubtful debts, then the allowance has to be added back to exclude it from the profit calculations.

 Activity 25.4 What about bad debts? Should you make similar adjustments in the cash flow statement for them? Why/why not?

Book profit/loss on sales of non-current assets

If a non-current asset with a book value (after depreciation) of £5,000 is sold for £6,400 cash, the flow of cash is £6,400. The fact that there has been a book profit of £1,400 does not provide any more cash above the figure of £6,400. Similarly, the sale of an asset with a book value of £3,000 for £2,200 cash produces a flow of cash of £2,200. Book profits and losses of this type need to be eliminated by adjusting the net profit when preparing the statement of cash flows.

25.10 Example of adjustments

As the net profit figure in accounts is:

(*i*)   *after* adjustments for depreciation;
(*ii*) *after* adjustment to allowances for doubtful debts; and
(*iii*) *after* book profits/losses on sales of non-current assets;

net profit needs to be adjusted in statements of cash flows for these three events. However, the adjustments are only for depreciation in *that period*, and for non-current asset book profits/losses for *that period*. No adjustments are needed with reference to previous periods. Exhibit 25.4 shows examples of three businesses.

Exhibit 25.4

	Business A	Business B	Business C
	£	£	£
Depreciation for the year	2,690	4,120	6,640
Increase in allowance for doubtful debts	540	360	
Decrease in allowance for doubtful debts			200
Book loss on sale of non-current assets	1,200		490
Book profit on sale of non-current assets		750	
Net profit after the above items are included	16,270	21,390	32,410
Reconciliation of net profit to net cash inflow	£	£	£
Net profit	16,270	21,390	32,410
Adjustment for items not involving the movement of cash:			
Depreciation	2,690	4,120	6,640
Book profit on sale of non-current assets		(750)	
Book loss on sale of non-current assets	1,200		490
Increase in allowance for doubtful debts	540	360	
Decrease in allowance for doubtful debts			(200)
Net cash flow from operating activities	20,700	25,120	39,340

You will notice that the items in brackets, i.e. (750) and (200), had been credits in the income statements and need to be deducted, while the other items were debits and need to be added back.

25.11 A comprehensive example

Exhibit 25.5

The balance sheets of R. Lester are as follows:

	31.12.2020				31.12.2021	
	£	£	£	£	£	£
Non-current assets						
Equipment at cost			28,500			26,100
Less Depreciation to date			(11,450)			(13,010)
			17,050			13,090
Current assets						
Inventory		18,570			16,250	
Accounts receivable	8,470			14,190		
Less Allowance for doubtful debts	(420)			(800)		
		8,050			13,390	
Cash and bank balances		4,060			3,700	
			30,680			33,340
Total assets			47,730			46,430
Current liabilities						
Accounts payable		4,140			5,730	
Non-current liability						
Loan from J. Gorsey		10,000			4,000	
Total liabilities			(14,140)			(9,730)
Net assets			33,590			36,700

→

→
Capital		
Opening balances b/d	35,760	33,590
Add Net profit	10,240	11,070
Add Cash introduced	–	600
	46,000	45,260
Less Drawings	(12,410)	(8,560)
Total capital	33,590	36,700

Note: Equipment with a book value of £1,350 was sold for £900. Depreciation of equipment during the year was £2,610.

The (indirect method) cash flow statement will be as follows:

Exhibit 25.6

R. Lester
Statement of Cash Flows for the year ending 31 December 2021

	£	£
Net cash flow from operating activities (see Note 1)		12,700
Investing activities		
Receipts from sale of non-current assets		900
Financing activities		
Capital introduced	600	
Loan repaid to J. Gorsey	(6,000)	
Drawings	(8,560)	
		(13,960)
Decrease in cash		360)

Notes:

1 Reconciliation of net profit to net cash inflow:

	£
Net profit	11,070
Depreciation	2,610
Loss on sale of non-current assets	450
Increase in allowance for doubtful debts	380
Decrease in inventory	2,320
Increase in accounts payable	1,590
Increase in accounts receivable	(5,720)
Net cash flow from operating activities	12,700

2 Analysis of changes in cash during the year:

	£
Balance at 1 January 2021	4,060
Net cash inflow	(360)
Balance at 31 December 2021	3,700

25.12 Companies and statements of cash flows

We have already stated that companies must publish a statement of cash flows for each accounting period. Students whose level of studies terminates with the conclusion of *Frank Wood's Business Accounting 1* will not normally need to know more than has already been explained in this chapter. However, some will need to know the basic layout given in IAS 7.

There are two approaches available under the standard: the 'direct' method, which shows the operating cash receipts and payments summing to the net cash flow from operating activities – in effect, it summarises the cash book; and the 'indirect' method, which (as you've seen already) identifies the net cash flow via a reconciliation to operating profit. As the reconciliation has also to be shown when the direct method is used, it is hardly surprising that the indirect method is the more commonly adopted one. Although the IASB recommend use of the direct method, the indirect method is permitted because the cost of producing the data required for the direct method is likely to be greater than the benefit of doing so, in most cases. The direct method is too advanced for this book and is dealt with in *Frank Wood's Business Accounting 2*.

As you've already seen, IAS 7 requires that cash flows be shown under only three categories of activity: operating; investing; and financing. (This is how it was presented in Exhibits 25.3 and 25.6.)

IAS 7 defines cash flows to include cash equivalents: 'short-term, highly liquid investments that are readily convertible to known amounts of cash and which are subject to an insignificant risk of changes in values'.

You have already been introduced to the basic layout of the indirect method in Exhibits 25.3 and 25.6. Exhibit 25.6 shows another example using the indirect method, this time for a company.

Exhibit 25.7 Format for an IAS 7 Statement of Cash Flows (indirect method)

X Limited
Statement of Cash Flows for the year ending 31 December 2020

	£000	£000
Cash flows from operating activities		
Operating profit before taxation	XXX	
Adjustments for:		
Depreciation	XXX	
(Profit)/Loss on sale of tangible non-current assets	XXX	
Operating cash flows before movements in working capital		XXX
(Increase)/Decrease in inventory	XXX	
(Increase)/Decrease in accounts receivable	XXX	
Increase/(Decrease) in accounts payable	XXX	
		XXX
Cash generated by operations		XXX
Tax paid	(XXX)	
Interest paid	(XXX)	
		(XXX)
Net cash from/(used in) operating activities		XXX
Cash flows from investing activities		
Dividends from joint ventures	XXX	
Dividends from associates	XXX	
Interest received	XXX	
Payments to acquire intangible non-current assets	(XXX)	
Payments to acquire tangible non-current assets	(XXX)	
Receipts from sales of tangible non-current assets	XXX	
Purchase of subsidiary undertaking	(XXX)	
Sale of business	XXX	
Net cash from/(used in) investing activities		(XXX)

→

→ Cash flows from financing activities
    Ordinary dividends paid   (XXX)
    Preference dividends paid   (XXX)
    Issue of ordinary share capital   XXX
    Repurchase of loan note   (XXX)
    Expenses paid in connection with share issues   (XXX)

Net cash from/(used in) financing activities	XXX
Net Increase/(decrease) in cash and cash equivalents	XXX
Cash and cash equivalents at beginning of year	XXX
Cash and cash equivalents at end of year	XXX

Note: The inclusion of the reconciliation of operating profit to net cash from/(used in) operating activities at the start of the statement of cash flows in Exhibit 25.7 rather than as a note follows the approach given in the Appendix to IAS 7.

25.13   Uses of statements of cash flows

Statements of cash flows have many uses other than the legal need for some companies to prepare them.

Cases where a business might find them useful in helping to answer their queries include:

(*a*) A small businessman wants to know why he now has an overdraft. He started off the year with money in the bank, he has made profits, and yet he now has a bank overdraft.

(*b*) Another businessman wants to know why the bank balance has risen even though the business is losing money.

(*c*) The partners in a business have put in additional capital during the year. Even so, the bank balance has fallen dramatically. They want an explanation as to how this has happened.

A study of the other financial statements themselves would not provide the information they needed. However, a study of the statement of cash flows in each case will reveal the answers to their questions.

Besides the answers to such specific queries, statements of cash flows should also help businesses to assess the following:

● the cash flows which the business may be able to generate in the future;
● how far the business will be able to meet future commitments, e.g. tax due, loan repayments, interest payments, contracts that could possibly lose quite a lot of money;
● how far future share issues may be needed, or additional capital in the case of sole traders or partnerships;
● a valuation of the business.

Learning outcomes

You should now have learnt:

1 Why statements of cash flows provide useful information for decision-making.

2 A range of sources and applications of cash.

3 How to adjust net profit for non-cash items to find the net cash flow from operating activities.

4 How to prepare a statement of cash flows as defined by IAS 7.

5 How to present the net cash flow from operating activities using the indirect method.

6 Some of the uses that can be made of statements of cash flows.

Answers to activities

25.1 When people believe that a business is trying to raise cash quickly, they may assume that the business is finding it difficult to pay its creditors. If so, this is a sign that the business may fail. Some debtors may believe that they will not have to pay their debt to the business if that happens. As a result, they will delay paying their debts to the business for as long as possible.

25.2 Liquidity is the key. Nowadays, something is generally considered as sufficiently liquid to be described as 'cash' in this context if it can definitely be turned into cash within three months. Not only does **cash** in this sense include the obvious – cash balances and bank balances – it also includes funds invested in **cash equivalents**. These cash equivalents consist of the temporary investments of cash not required at present by the business, such as funds put on short-term deposit with a bank. Such investments must be readily convertible into cash, or available as cash.

This is an important definition and is one you should memorise if cash flow statements are examinable under the syllabus of your course.

25.3 Other examples include:

● The bank overdraft has been growing steadily and is now greater than the amount owed by debtors.
● A major supplier is experiencing cash flow problems and is threatening not to provide any further goods unless all bills are paid within five working days. Your business has no other sources of supply for these goods and the bank has indicated that it will not advance any further loans or increase the overdraft facility.
● A seriously dangerous defect has been identified in the sole product manufactured by the business. This could lead to all items sold in the last year having to be replaced with newly produced replacements. The faulty items cannot be repaired. The business has already borrowed as much as it is allowed by the bank.

25.4 A bad debt that is written-off represents an expense that *does not* involve a flow of cash during the period. A debt becomes cash when paid, and only does so at the time payment is received. In writing-off the debt, you are saying that cash will not be received and have written off the debt to the profit and loss account. In theory, you need to adjust both the profit (by adding it back) and the change in the debtor balance. *However, these adjustments cancel each other out, so you need do nothing when preparing the statement of cash flows.*

Review questions

25.1 Amanda Hartford is preparing her statement of cash flows for the 12 months to 30 September 2020, and you determine the following facts in relation to that financial year:

	£000
Net profit for the year	227
Depreciation expense	58
Increase in inventory	29
Decrease in accounts receivable	45
Decrease in accounts payable	36

On the basis of the above information, what net cash will have been generated from operating activities according to the statement of cash flows?

25.2A Lee Cairns is in the process of preparing a statement of cash flows for his business for the year to 30 April 2019. You establish the following facts in connection with that financial year:

	£000
Net profit for the year	347
Depreciation expense	86
Profit on disposal of non-current assets	19
Decrease in inventory	31
Increase in accounts receivable	44
Decrease in accounts payable	25

On the basis of the above information, what net cash will have been generated from operating activities according to the statement of cash flows?

25.3 You establish the following details in connection with the non-current assets of P. Akpan for the year ended 31 December 2020:

	£000
1 January 2020, non-current assets at cost less accumulated depreciation	460
Proceeds from the sale of non-current assets during the year	59
Depreciation expense for the year	68
Profit on the disposal of non-current assets during the year	12
31 December 2020, non-current assets at cost less accumulated depreciation	417

What figure for *acquisition of non-current assets* will appear in the *investing activities* section of the statement of cash flows for Akpan's business for the year ended 31 December 2020?

25.4A You establish the following details in connection with the non-current assets of Brian Finlay for the year ended 31 July 2019:

	£000
1 August 2018, non-current assets at cost minus accumulated depreciation	580
Acquisitions of non-current assets during the year	170
Depreciation expense for the year	95
Loss on the disposal of non-current assets during the year	18
31 July 2019, non-current assets at cost minus accumulated depreciation	610

What figure for *proceeds from the disposal of non-current assets* will appear in the *investing activities* section of the statement of cash flows for Finlay's business for the year ended 31 July 2019?

25.5A

Pat Bond
Balance Sheets as at 31 December

	2019		2020	
	£	£	£	£
Non-current assets				
Buildings		100,000		100,000
Fixtures *less* accumulated depreciation		3,600		4,000
Van *less* accumulated depreciation		7,840		14,800
		111,440		118,800
Current assets				
Inventory	11,200		24,800	
Trade accounts receivable	12,800		16,400	
Bank	1,800		–	
Cash	440		400	
		26,240		41,600
Total assets		137,680		160,400
Accounts payable	12,600		6,012	
Bank overdraft	–		188	
	12,600		6,200	
Non-current liabilities				
Loan (repayable in 10 years time)	20,000		30,000	
Total liabilities		(32,600)		(36,200)
Net assets		105,080		124,200
Capital account:				
Balance at 1 January		74,080		105,080
Add Net profit for the year		70,400		42,320
Cash introduced		–		20,000
		144,480		167,400
Less Drawings		(39,400)		(43,200)
Total capital		105,080		124,200

Draw up a statement of cash flows for the year ending 31 December 2020 using the IAS 7 layout. You are told that fixtures bought in 2020 cost £800, whilst a van was also bought for £11,000. There were no disposals of non-current assets during the year.

25.6 Malcolm Phillips is a sole trader who prepares his financial statements annually to 30 April. His summarised balance sheets for the last two years are shown below.

Balance Sheets as at 30 April

	2018 £	2018 £	2019 £	2019 £
Non-current assets		15,500		18,500
Less Accumulated depreciation		(1,500)		(1,700)
		14,000		16,800
Current assets				
Inventory	3,100		5,900	
Trade accounts receivable	3,900		3,400	
Bank	1,500		—	
		8,500		9,300
Total assets		22,500		26,100
Current liabilities				
Trade accounts payable	2,000		2,200	
Bank overdraft	—		900	
Total liabilities		(2,000)		(3,100)
Net assets		20,500		23,000
Capital account:				
Balance at 1 May		20,000		20,500
Add Net profit for the year		7,000		8,500
Additional capital introduced		—		2,000
		27,000		31,000
Less Drawings		(6,500)		(8,000)
Total capital		20,500		23,000

Malcolm is surprised to see that he now has an overdraft, in spite of making a profit and bringing in additional capital during the year.

Questions:

(a) Draw up a suitable financial statement which will explain to Malcolm how his overdraft has arisen.

(b) The following further information relates to the year ended 30 April 2019.

	£
Sales (all on credit)	30,000
Cost of sales	22,500

Calculate Malcolm's

(i)   gross profit margin
(ii) rate of inventory turnover.

(*Midland Examining Group: GCSE*)

25.7 From the following details you are to draft a statement of cash flows for D. Duncan for the year ending 31 December 2020, using the IAS 7 layout.

D. Duncan
Income Statement for the year ending 31 December 2020

	£	£
Gross profit		44,700
Add Discounts received	410	
Profit on sale of van	620	1,030
		45,730
Less Expenses		
Motor expenses	1,940	
Wages	17,200	
General expenses	830	
Bad debts	520	
Increase in allowance for doubtful debts	200	
Depreciation: Van	1,800	22,490
		23,240

Balance Sheets as at 31 December

	2019		2020	
	£	£	£	£
Non-current assets				
Vans at cost		15,400		8,200
Less Depreciation to date		(5,300)		(3,100)
		10,100		5,100
Current assets				
Inventory	18,600		24,000	
Accounts receivable *less* allowance*	8,200		6,900	
Bank	410		720	
		27,210		31,620
Total assets		37,310		36,720
Current liabilities				
Accounts payable	5,900		7,200	
Non-current liability				
Loan from J. Fry	10,000		7,500	
Total liabilities		(15,900)		(14,700)
Net assets		21,410		22,020
Capital				
Opening balance b/d		17,210		21,410
Add Net profit		21,200		23,240
		38,410		44,650
Less Drawings		(17,000)		(22,630)
Total capital		21,410		22,020

*Accounts receivable 2019 £8,800 – allowance £600.
Accounts receivable 2020 £7,700 – allowance £800.
Note: A van was sold for £3,820 during 2020. No new vans were purchased during the year.

25.8A You are required to draw up a statement of cash flows for K. Rock for the year ending 30 June 2020 from the following information using the IAS 7 layout.

K. Rock

Income Statement for the year ending 30 June 2020

	£	£
Gross profit		155,030
Add Reduction in allowance for doubtful debts		200
		155,230
Less Expenses:		
Wages and salaries	61,400	
General trading expenses	15,200	
Equipment running costs	8,140	
Motor vehicle expenses	6,390	
Depreciation: Motor vehicles	5,200	
Equipment	6,300	
Loss on sale of equipment	1,600	
		(104,230)
Net profit		51,000

Balance Sheets as at 30 June

	2019		2020	
	£	£	£	£
Non-current assets				
Equipment at cost	40,400		30,800	
Less Depreciation to date	(24,600)		(20,600)	
		15,800		10,200
Motor vehicles at cost	28,300		28,300	
Less Depreciation to date	(9,200)		(14,400)	
		19,100		13,900
		34,900		24,100
Current assets				
Inventory	41,700		44,600	
Accounts receivable *less* allowance*	21,200		19,800	
Bank	12,600		28,100	
		75,500		92,500
Total assets		110,400		116,600
Current liabilities				
Accounts payable	14,300		17,500	
Non-current liability				
Loan from T Pine	20,000		10,000	
Total liabilities		(34,300)		(27,500)
Net assets		76,100		89,100
Capital				
Opening balance		65,600		76,100
Add Net profit		42,500		51,000
		108,100		127,100
Less Drawings		(32,000)		(38,000)
Total capital		76,100		89,100

*Accounts receivable 2019 £22,100 – allowance £900.

 Accounts receivable 2020 £20,500 – allowance £700.

Note: Equipment was sold for £15,800. Equipment costing £18,100 was purchased during the year.

Errors not affecting the balancing of the trial balance

Learning objectives

After you have studied this chapter, you should be able to:

● correct errors which are not revealed by a trial balance
● distinguish between the different kinds of errors that may arise

Introduction

In this chapter, you'll learn how to identify and correct a range of errors that can arise when financial transactions are entered in the ledger accounts.

26.1 Types of error

In Chapter 6 it was seen that if we followed the rules:

● every debit entry needs a corresponding credit entry;
● every credit entry needs a corresponding debit entry;

and entered transactions in our ledgers on this basis then, when we extracted the trial balance, the totals of the two columns would be the same, i.e. it would 'balance'.

Suppose we correctly entered cash sales £70 to the debit of the Cash Book, but did not enter the £70 to the credit of the sales account. If this were the only error in the books, the trial balance totals would differ by £70. However, there are certain kinds of error which would not affect the agreement of the trial balance totals, and we will now consider these:

1 **Errors of omission** – where a transaction is completely omitted from the books. If we sold £90 goods to J. Brewer, but did not enter it in either the sales account or Brewer's personal account, the trial balance would still 'balance'.

2 **Errors of commission** – this type of error occurs when the correct amount is entered but in the wrong account, e.g. where a sale of £11 to C. Green is entered in the account of K. Green.

3 **Errors of principle** – where an item is entered in the wrong class of account, e.g. if purchase of a fixed asset, such as a van, is debited to an expenses account, such as motor expenses account.

4 **Compensating errors** – where errors cancel each other out. If the sales account was added up to be £10 too much and the purchases account was also added up to be £10 too much, then these two errors would cancel out in the trial balance. This is because the totals of both the debit side and the credit side of the trial balance will be overstated by £10.

5 **Errors of original entry** – where the original figure is incorrect, yet double entry is correctly done using the incorrect figure. For example, where a sale should have totalled £150 but an error is made in calculating the total on the sales invoice. If it were calculated as £130, and £130 were credited as sales and £130 were debited to the personal account of the customer, the trial balance would still balance.

6 **Complete reversal of entries** – where the correct accounts are used but each item is shown on the wrong side of the account. Suppose we had paid a cheque to D. Williams for £200, the double entry of which should be debit D. Williams £200, credit Bank £200. In error it is entered as debit Bank £200, credit D. Williams £200. The trial balance totals will still agree.

7 **Transposition errors** – where the wrong sequence of the individual characters within a number was entered (for example, £142 entered instead of £124). This is a common type of error and is very difficult to spot when the error has occurred in both the debit and the credit entries, as the trial balance would still balance. It is, however, more common for this error to occur on one side of the double entry only. When it does, it is easier to find.

26.2 Correction of errors

Most errors are found after the date on which they are made. When we correct errors, we should not do so by crossing out items, tearing out accounts and throwing them away, or using chemicals to make the writing disappear.

 Activity 26.1 In which book should all the correcting double entries first be entered?

We make corrections to double entry accounts by preparing journal entries. We should:

1 prepare the corrections by means of journal entries; then
2 post the journal entries to the appropriate ledger accounts.

1 Error of omission

A sale of £59 worth of goods to E. George has been completely omitted from the books. We must correct this by entering the sale in the books. The journal entry for the correction is:[Note]

The Journal

	Dr	Cr
	£	£
E. George	59	
Sales		59

Correction of omission of Sales Invoice Number . . . from sales day book

Note: in all these examples, the folio column has been omitted so as to make the example clearer.

2 Error of commission

A purchase £44 worth of goods from C. Simons on 4 September was entered in error in C. Simpson's account. The error was found on 30 September. To correct this, it must be cancelled out of C. Simpson's account and entered where it should be (in C. Simons' account). The journal entry will be:

The Journal

	Dr	Cr
	£	£
C. Simpson	44	
C. Simons		44
Purchase Invoice Number . . . entered in wrong personal account, now corrected		

The entries in the ledger accounts would be:

C. Simpson

			£					£
Sept	30	C. Simons (error corrected)	44	Sept	4	Purchases		44

C. Simons

			£
Sept	30	Purchases (error corrected)	44

3 Error of principle

The purchase of a machine for £200 is debited to the purchases account instead of being debited to a machinery account. We therefore cancel the item out of the purchases account by crediting that account. It is then entered where it should be by debiting the machinery account.

The Journal

	Dr	Cr
	£	£
Machinery	200	
Purchases		200
Correction of error: purchase of fixed asset debited to purchases account		

4 Compensating error

In the cash book, the amount of cash sales transferred to the sales account was overstated by £20 and the amount transferred to the wages account was also overstated by £20. The trial balance therefore still balances.

The Journal

	Dr	Cr
	£	£
Sales	20	
Wages		20
Correction of two overcasts of £20 posted from the cash book to the sales account and to the wages account which compensated for each other		

5 Error of original entry

A sale of £38 to A. Smailes was entered in the books as £28. The other £10 must be entered:

The Journal

	Dr	Cr
	£	£
A. Smailes	10	
Sales		10
Correction of error whereby sales were understated by £10		

6 Complete reversal of entries

A payment of cash of £16 to M. Dickson was entered on the receipts side of the Cash Book in error and credited to M. Dickson's account. This is somewhat more difficult to adjust. First must come the amount needed to cancel the error, then comes the actual entry itself. Because of this, the correcting entry is double the actual amount first recorded. We can now look at why this is so.

We should have had:

Cash

			£
		M. Dickson	16

M. Dickson

	£		
Cash	16		

This was entered wrongly as:

Cash

	£		
M. Dickson	16		

M. Dickson

			£
		Cash	16

We can now see that we have to enter double the original amount to correct the error.

Cash

	£		£
M. Dickson	16	M. Dickson (error corrected)	32

M. Dickson

	£		£
Cash (error corrected)	32	M. Dickson	16

Overall, when corrected, the £16 debit and £32 credit in the cash account means there is a net credit of £16. Similarly, Dickson's account shows £32 debit and £16 credit, a net debit of £16. As the final (net) answer is the same as what should have been entered originally, the error is now corrected.

The Journal entry appears:

The Journal

	Dr	Cr
	£	£
M. Dickson	32	
Cash		32
Payment of cash £16 debited to cash and credited to M. Dickson in error on . . . Error now corrected		

7 Transposition error

A credit purchase from P. Maclaran costing £56 was entered in the books as £65. The £9 error needs to be removed.

The Journal

	Dr	Cr
	£	£
P. Maclaran	9	
Purchases		9
Correction of error whereby purchases were overstated by £9		

26.3   Casting

You will sometimes notice the use of the term **casting**, which means adding up. **Overcasting** means incorrectly adding up a column of figures to give an answer which is greater than it should be. **Undercasting** means incorrectly adding up a column of figures to give an answer which is less than it should be.

Mnemonic

The following acronym may help you to remember which types of errors do not affect the balancing of a trial balance:

POOR CC
P – Principle
O – Omission
O – Original entry
R – Reversal

C – Compensating
C – Commission

Learning outcomes

You should now have learnt:

1 How to describe each of a range of possible errors that can be made when recording financial transactions in the accounts that will not be detected by producing a trial balance.

2 How to identify and correct each of these types of errors.

3 That when errors are found, they should be amended by using proper double entry procedures.

4 That all corrections of errors should take place via the Journal, where entries are first recorded before being posted to the appropriate ledger accounts.

Answer to activity

26.1 The Journal.

Review questions

26.1 Give an example of each of the different types of error which are *not* revealed by a trial balance.

26.2 Show the journal entries necessary to correct the following errors:

(a) A sale of goods for £630 to J. Trees had been entered in J. Tees's account.
(b) The purchase of a printer on credit from D. Hogg for £846 had been completely omitted from our books.
(c) The purchase of a laptop for £389 had been entered in error in the Office Expenses account.
(d) A sale of £260 to G. Lee had been entered in the books, both debit and credit, as £206.
(e) Commission received £340 had been entered in error in the Sales account.
(f) A receipt of cash from A. Salmond £130 had been entered on the credit side of the cash book and the debit side of A. Salmond's account.
(g) A purchase of goods for £410 had been entered in error on the debit side of the Drawings account.
(h) Discounts Allowed £46 had been entered in error on the debit side of the Discounts Received account.

26.3A Show the journal entries needed to correct the following errors:

(a) Purchases £1,410 on credit from A. Ray had been entered in B. Roy's account.
(b) A cheque of £94 paid for printing had been entered in the cash column of the cash book instead of in the bank column.
(c) Sale of goods £734 on credit to D. Rolls had been entered in error in D. Rollo's account.
(d) Purchase of goods on credit L. Hand £819 entered in the correct accounts in error as £891.
(e) Cash paid to G. Boyd £64 entered on the debit side of the cash book and the credit side of G. Boyd's account.
(f) A sale of fittings £320 had been entered in the Sales account.
(g) Cash withdrawn from bank £200 had been entered in the cash column on the credit side of the cash book, and in the bank column on the debit side.
(h) Purchase of goods £1,182 has been entered in error in the Furnishings account.

26.4   After preparing its draft final accounts for the year ended 31 March 2019 and its draft balance sheet as at 31 March 2019 a business discovered that the inventory lists used to compute the value of inventory as at 31 March 2019 contained the following entry:

Inventory item	Number	Cost per unit	Total cost
K604	200	£2.62	£5,240

Required:
(a)   What is wrong with this particular entry?
(b)   What would the effect of the error have been on
    (i)   the value of inventory as at 31 March 2019?
    (ii)   the cost of goods sold for the year ended 31 March 2019?
    (iii)   the net profit for the year ended 31 March 2019?
    (iv)   the total for Current Assets as at 31 March 2019?
    (v)   the Owner's Capital as at 31 March 2019?

26.5   Give the journal entries needed to record the corrections of the following. Narratives are not required.

(a)   Extra capital of £12,000 paid into the bank had been credited to Sales account.
(b)   Goods taken for own use £140 had been debited to Sundry Expenses.
(c)   Private rent £740 had been debited to the Rent account.
(d)   A purchase of goods from F. Smith £530 had been entered in the books as £350.
(e)   Cash banked £620 had been credited to the bank column and debited to the cash column in the cash book.
(f)   Cash drawings of £270 had been credited to the bank column of the cash book.
(g)   Returns inwards £205 from N. Sturgeon had been entered in error in G. Milne's account.
(h)   A sale of an old printer for £70 had been credited to Office Expenses.

26.6A   Journal entries to correct the following are required, but the narratives can be omitted.

(a)   Rent Received £430 has been credited to the Commissions Received account.
(b)   Bank charges £34 have been debited to the Business Rates account.
(c)   Completely omitted from the books is a payment of Motor Expenses by cheque £37.
(d)   A purchase of a fax machine £242 has been entered in the Purchases account.
(e)   Returns inwards £216 have been entered on the debit side of the Returns Outwards account.
(f)   A loan from G. Bain £2,000 has been entered on the credit side of the Capital account.
(g)   Loan interest of £400 has been debited to the Van account.
(h)   Goods taken for own use £84 have been debited to the Purchases account and credited to Drawings.

26.7A   Thomas Smith, a retail trader, has very limited accounting knowledge. In the absence of his accounting technician, he extracted the following trial balance as at 31 March 2018 from his business's accounting records:

	£	£
Inventory-in-trade at 1 April 2017		10,700
Inventory-in-trade at 31 March 2018	7,800	
Discounts allowed		310
Discounts received	450	
Allowance for doubtful debts	960	
Purchases	94,000	
Purchases returns	1,400	
Sales		132,100
Sales returns	1,100	
Freehold property: at cost	70,000	
Provision for depreciation	3,500	
Motor vehicles: at cost	15,000	
Provision for depreciation	4,500	
Capital – Thomas Smith		84,600
Balance at bank	7,100	
Trade accounts receivable		11,300
Trade accounts payable	7,600	
Establishment and administrative expenditure	16,600	
Drawings	9,000	
	£239,010	£239,010

Required:

(a) Prepare a corrected trial balance as at 31 March 2018.

After the preparation of the above trial balance, but before the completion of the final accounts for the year ended 31 March 2018, the following discoveries were made:

(i) The correct valuation of the inventory-in-trade at 1 April 2017 is £12,000; apparently some inventory lists had been mislaid.

(ii) A credit note for £210 has now been received from J. Hardwell Limited; this relates to goods returned in December 2017 by Thomas Smith. However, up to now J. Hardwell Limited had not accepted that the goods were not of merchantable quality and Thomas Smith's accounting records did not record the return of the goods.

(iii) Trade sample goods were sent to John Grey in February 2018. These were free samples, but were charged wrongly at £1,000 to John Grey. A credit note is now being prepared to rectify the error.

(iv) In March 2018, Thomas Smith painted the inside walls of his stockroom using materials costing £150 which were included in the purchases figure in the above trial balance. Thomas Smith estimates that he saved £800 by doing all the painting himself.

(b) Prepare the journal entries necessary to amend the accounts for the above discoveries. *Note*: narratives are required.

(*Association of Accounting Technicians*)

Suspense accounts and errors

Learning objectives

After you have studied this chapter, you should be able to:

- explain why a suspense account may be used
- create a suspense account in order to balance the trial balance
- correct errors using a suspense account
- recalculate profits after errors have been corrected
- explain why using a suspense account is generally inappropriate

Introduction

In this chapter, you'll learn how to use suspense accounts to temporarily balance an out-of-balance trial balance. You'll also learn that it is usually not a wise thing to do, even temporarily.

27.1 Errors and the trial balance

In the previous chapter, we looked at errors that do not affect the trial balance. However, many errors will mean that trial balance totals will not be equal. These include:

- incorrect additions in any account;
- making an entry on only one side of the accounts, e.g. a debit but no credit; a credit but no debit;
- entering a different amount on the debit side from the amount on the credit side.

27.2 Suspense account

We should try very hard to find errors when the trial balance totals are not equal. When such errors cannot be found, the trial balance totals can be made to agree with each other by inserting the amount of the difference between the two totals in a **suspense account**. This is shown in Exhibit 27.1 where there is a £40 difference.

Exhibit 27.1

Trial Balance as at 31 December 2018

	Dr	Cr
	£	£
Totals after all the accounts have been listed	100,000	99,960
Suspense		40
	100,000	100,000

To make the two totals the same, a figure of £40 for the suspense account has been shown on the credit side of the trial balance. A suspense account is opened and the £40 difference is also shown there on the credit side:

Suspense

				£
2018				
Dec	31	Difference per trial balance		40

Activity 27.1 Where is the debit side of this entry made?

27.3 Suspense accounts and the balance sheet

If the errors are not found before the financial statements are prepared, the suspense account balance will be included in the balance sheet. The balance should be included shown after the figure for net current assets, either as a negative amount (credit balance) or a positive amount (debit balance) (see Exhibit 27.5).

Activity 27.2 Does the use of a suspense account in financial statements affect the true and fair view that they are meant to portray?

27.4 Correction of errors

When errors are found they must be corrected using double entry. Each correction must first have an entry in the journal describing it, and then be posted to the accounts concerned.

One error only

Let's look at two examples:

Example 1

Assume that the cause of the error of £40 in Exhibit 27.1 is found on 31 March 2019. The error was that the sales account was undercast by £40. The action taken to correct this is:

Debit suspense account to close it: £40.
    Credit sales account to show item where it should have been: £40.

The accounts now appear as Exhibit 27.2:

Exhibit 27.2

Suspense

2019			£	2019				£
Mar	31	Sales	40	Jan	1		Balance b/d	40

Sales

				2019			£
				Mar	31	Suspense	40

This can be shown in journal form as:

The Journal

				Dr	Cr
2019				£	£
Mar	31	Suspense		40	
		Sales			40
		Correction of undercasting of sales by £40 last year			

Here's another example.

Example 2

The trial balance on 31 December 2019 had a difference of £168. It was a shortage on the debit side.

A suspense account is opened, and the difference of £168 is entered on the debit side in the account. On 31 May 2020 the error was found. We had made a payment of £168 to K. Leek to close his account. It was correctly entered in the cash book, but was not entered in K. Leek's account.

First of all, the account of K. Leek is debited with £168, as it should have been in 2019. Second, the suspense account is credited with £168 so that the account can be closed.

Exhibit 27.3

K. Leek

2020			£	2020			£
May	31	Bank	168	Jan	1	Balance b/d	168

The account of K. Leek is now correct.

Suspense

2020			£	2020			£
Jan	1	Balance b/d	168	May	31	K. Leek	168

→

→

The Journal entry is:

The Journal

				Dr	Cr
				£	£
2020					
May	31	K. Leek		168	
		Suspense			168
		Correction of non-entry of payment last year in K. Leek's account			

More than one error

Let's now look at Example 3 where the suspense account difference was caused by more than one error.

Example 3

The trial balance at 31 December 2017 showed a difference of £77, being a shortage on the debit side. A suspense account is opened, and the difference of £77 is entered on the debit side of the account. On 28 February 2018 all the errors from the previous year were found.

(A) A cheque of £150 paid to L. Kent had been correctly entered in the cash book, but had not been entered in Kent's account.
(B) The purchases account had been undercast by £20.
(C) A cheque of £93 received from K. Sand had been correctly entered in the cash book, but had not been entered in Sand's account.

These three errors resulted in a net error of £77, shown by a debit of £77 on the debit side of the suspense account. These are corrected as follows:

(a) Make correcting entries in accounts for (A), (B) and (C).
(b) Record double entry for these items in the suspense account.

Exhibit 27.4

L. Kent

2018				£	
Feb	28	Suspense	(A)	150	

Purchases

2018				£	
Feb	28	Suspense	(B)	20	

K. Sand

					2018				£
					Feb	28	Suspense	(C)	93

Suspense

2018				£	2018				£
Jan	1	Balance b/d		77	Feb	28	L. Kent	(A)	150
Feb	28	K. Sand	(C)	93		28	Purchases	(B)	20
				170					170

The Journal

			Dr	Cr
2018			£	£
Feb	28	L. Kent	150	
		Suspense		150
		Cheque paid omitted from Kent's account		
	28	Purchases	20	
		Suspense		20
		Undercasting of purchases by £20 in last year's accounts		
	28	Suspense	93	
		K. Sand		93
		Cheque received omitted from Sand's account		

Note: Only errors which make the trial balance totals different from each other can be corrected using a suspense account.

27.5 The effect of errors on profits

Some of the errors will have meant that original profits calculated will be wrong. Other errors will have no effect upon profits. We will use Exhibit 27.5 to illustrate the different kinds of errors. Exhibit 27.5 shows a set of financial statements in which errors have been made.

Exhibit 27.5

K. Davis
Income Statement for the year ending 31 December 2018

		£	£
Sales			180,000
Less	Cost of goods sold:		
	Opening inventory	15,000	
	Add Purchases	92,000	
		107,000	
	Less Closing inventory	(18,000)	
			(89,000)
Gross profit			91,000
Add Discounts received			1,400
			92,400

→

→

Less Expenses:		
Rent	8,400	
Insurance	1,850	
Lighting	1,920	
Depreciation	28,200	
		(40,370)
Net profit		52,030

Balance Sheet as at 31 December 2018

	£	£
Non-current assets		
Equipment at cost		62,000
Less Depreciation to date		(41,500)
		20,500
Current assets		
Inventory	18,000	
Accounts receivable	23,000	
Bank	19,000	
	60,000	
Less Current liabilities		
Accounts payable	(14,000)	
		46,000
Suspense account		80
		66,580
Capital		
Balance as at 1.1.2018		46,250
Add Net profit		52,030
		98,280
Less Drawings		(31,700)
		66,580

The errors that have been made may be of three types.

1 Errors which do not affect profit calculations

If an error affects items only in the balance sheet, then the original calculated profit will not need to be changed. Example 4 shows this.

Example 4

Assume that in Exhibit 27.5 the £80 debit balance on the suspense account was because of the following error:

On 1 November 2018 we paid £80 to a creditor T. Monk. It was correctly entered in the cash book. It was not entered anywhere else. The error was identified on 1 June 2019.

The journal entries to correct it will be:

The Journal

				Dr	Cr
2019				£	£
June	1	T. Monk		80	
		Suspense			80
		Payment to T. Monk on 1 November 2018 not entered in his account. Correction now made.			

Both of these accounts appeared in the balance sheet only with T. Monk as part of accounts payable. The net profit of £52,030 does not have to be changed.

2 Errors which do affect profit calculations

If the error is in one of the figures shown in the income statement, then the original profit will need to be amended. Example 5 shows this.

Example 5

Assume that in Exhibit 27.5 the £80 debit balance was because the rent account was added up incorrectly. It should be shown as £8,480 instead of £8,400. The error was identified on 1 June 2019. The journal entries to correct it are:

The Journal

				Dr	Cr
2019				£	£
Jun	1	Rent		80	
		Suspense			80
		Correction of rent undercast last year			

Rent last year should have been increased by £80. This would have reduced net profit by £80. A statement of corrected profit for the year is now shown.

K. Davis
Statement of Corrected Net Profit for the year ending 31 December 2018

	£
Net profit per the financial statements	52,030
Less Rent understated	(80)
Corrected net profit for the year	51,950

3 Where there have been several errors

Let's assume that in Exhibit 27.5 there had been four errors in the ledger accounts of K. Davis that were all identified on 31 March 2019:

(A)	Sales overcast by	£90
(B)	Insurance undercast by	£40
(C)	Cash received from a debtor, E. Silva, entered in the Cash Book only	£50
(D)	A purchase of £59 is entered in the books, debit and credit entries as	£95

Note: Error (D) is known as an 'error of transposition', as the correct numbers have been included but in the wrong order, i.e. they have been 'transposed'. It did not affect the trial balance, so it is not included in the £80 adjustment made by opening the suspense account.

The entries in the suspense account and the journal entries will be as follows:

Suspense Account

2019				£	2019					£
Jan	1	Balance b/d		80	Mar	31	Sales	(A)		90
Mar	31	E. Silva	(C)	50		31	Insurance	(B)		40
				130						130

The Journal

			Dr	Cr
			£	£
2019				
1	Mar 31	Sales	90	
		Suspense		90
		Sales overcast of £90 in 2018		
2	Mar 31	Insurance	40	
		Suspense		40
		Insurance expense undercast by £40 in 2018		
3	Mar 31	Suspense	50	
		E. Silva		50
		Cash received omitted from accounts receivable account in 2018		
4	Mar 31	Creditor's account	36	
		Purchases		36
		Credit purchase of £59 entered both as debit and credit as £95 in 2018		

Note: Remember that in (D), the correction of the overstatement of purchases does *not* pass through the suspense account because it did not affect the balancing of the trial balance.

Now we can calculate the corrected net profit for the year 2018. Only items (A), (B) and (D) affect figures in the income statement. These are the only adjustments to be made to profit.

K. Davis
Statement of Corrected Net Profit for the year ending 31 December 2018

			£
Net profit per the financial statements			52,030
Add Purchases overstated	(D)		36
			52,066
Less Sales overcast	(A)	90	
Insurance undercast	(B)	40	
			(130)
Corrected net profit for the year			51,936

Error (C), the cash not posted to an accounts receivable account, did not affect profit calculations.

27.6 Suspense accounts: businesses and examinations

Businesses

Every attempt should be made to find errors. A suspense account should be opened only if all other efforts have failed, and they *never* should!

Examinations

Unless it is part of a question, *do not* make your balance sheet totals agree by using a suspense account. The same applies to trial balances. Examiners are very likely to penalise you for showing a suspense account when it should not be required.

Overall

Suspense accounts have probably been used ever since people first started keeping accounts and using them to produce financial statements. However, just because suspense accounts have been used for a very long time does not mean that they should still be used today.

Long ago, accounting records were very poorly maintained. The people maintaining them were frequently untrained. Errors were fairly common, and no one was very concerned when it proved difficult to find out what had caused a trial balance not to balance, if they even went to the extent of preparing one.

Businesses were largely owned by one person who would often also prepare the financial statements, more out of interest than in order to make much use of what they showed which, before there was some regulation concerning what they presented, was frequently little more than the excess or shortfall of revenue over expenditure.

Nowadays, accounting is far more sophisticated and the people maintaining the accounting records are much better trained. Many organisations use computerised accounting systems and very few organisations of any complexity continue to do everything manually. When they do, their records will be good enough to make tracing an error reasonably straightforward.

Errors of the types that cause trial balances not to balance are, therefore, much less common and much easier to detect. As a result, it is inconceivable that a suspense account will ever be needed in practice when an accountant is involved in preparing or auditing the financial statements.

Nevertheless, circumstances may make it impossible for a sole trader's financial statements to be ready in time, for example, to show the bank manager when asking for a loan. It is probably only in circumstances of this type that you may find suspense accounts still in use, albeit rarely. An example may be when money is received by post or credited in to the business's bank account with no explanation and no information. It needs to be put somewhere in the ledger accounts, so a suspense account is used while the reason it was sent to the business is identified.

Learning outcomes

You should now have learnt:

1 How to make the appropriate entries in setting up a suspense account.

2 How to make the correcting entries involving the suspense account when the cause of an error is identified.

3 That some errors may cause the profits originally calculated to have been incorrect.

4 That errors that do not affect profit calculations will have an effect only on items in the balance sheet.

5 That nowadays suspense accounts very rarely need to be used, if at all.

Answers to activities

27.1 This is a major problem in the use of suspense accounts. There is no double entry and, therefore, no debit to match the credit of £40! The justification for this is that there is either a £40 hidden credit somewhere in the accounts that has been omitted when the balances were extracted for the trial balance, or that an extra £40 has been added by mistake to the debit entries in the trial balance. As a result, making this single entry is only completing the existing double entry, the other side being the mistake. Many accountants believe that it is bad practice to open a suspense account as it contravenes the basic principles of double entry. You would be wise to follow that advice and only open a suspense account if an examiner requires you to do so.

27.2 If it is material, definitely. If it is not material, it could be argued that no one will be concerned. However, the appearance of a suspense account in the balance sheet is, by definition, material – you don't include anything in the financial statements as a separate entry that is not of interest to the users of the financial statements. There has been *at least* one error made in the accounting entries and the fact that it cannot be found may indicate a much more serious problem with the accounting system. This is of concern to anyone with a knowledge of accounting for, nowadays, when all complex accounting systems are computerised, *no* error should be that difficult to find, no matter how large or complicated the financial system or the organisation.

Review questions

27.1 A trial balance was extracted from the books of Vinod Gowda, and it was found that the debit side exceeded the credit side by £71. This amount was entered in the suspense account. The following errors were later discovered and corrected:

(*i*) Purchases were over-summed by £90.
(*ii*) The balance on the drawings account of £73 has been omitted from the trial balance.
(*iii*) Sales were under-summed by £54.

Required:
Write up and rule off the suspense account as it would appear in the ledger.

27.2 Your bookkeeper extracted a trial balance on 31 December 2019 which failed to agree by £860, a shortage on the credit side of the trial balance. A suspense account was opened for the difference.

In January 2020 the following errors made in 2019 were found:

(*i*)   Sales day book had been undercast by £1,205.
(*ii*) Sales of £980 to I. Blane had been debited in error to I. Blank's account.
(*iii*) Rent account had been undercast by £404.
(*iv*) Discounts allowed account had been overcast by £59.
(*v*)   The sale of a computer at net book value had been credited in error to the Sales account £200.

Required:
(*a*)   Show the journal entries necessary to correct the errors.
(*b*)   Draw up the suspense account after the errors described have been corrected.
(*c*)   If the net profit had previously been calculated at £58,600 for the year ending 31 December 2019, show the calculations of the corrected net profit.

27.3A   You have extracted a trial balance and drawn up accounts for the year ended 31 December 2017. There was a shortage of £78 on the credit side of the trial balance, a suspense account being opened for that amount.

During 2018 the following errors made in 2017 were found:

(*i*)   £125 received from sales of old office equipment has been entered in the sales account.
(*ii*) Purchases day book had been overcast by £10.
(*iii*) A private purchase of £140 had been included in the business purchases.
(*iv*) Bank charges £22 entered in the cash book have not been posted to the bank charges account.
(*v*)   A sale of goods to K. Lamb £230 was correctly entered in the sales book but entered in the personal account as £320.

Required:
(*a*)   Show the requisite journal entries to correct the errors.
(*b*)   Write up the suspense account showing the correction of the errors.
(*c*)   The net profit originally calculated for 2017 was £28,400. Show your calculation of the correct figure.

27.4   Show how each of the following errors would affect trial balance agreement:

(*i*)   Computer repairs £184 was debited to the computer account.
(*ii*)   £918 discounts received credited to discounts allowed account.
(*iii*) Inventory at close undervalued by £2,050.
(*iv*)   £260 commission received was debited to the sales account.
(*v*)   Drawings £106 credited to the capital account.
(*vi*)   Cheque paying £380 to M. Wilson entered in the cash book but not in the personal account.
(*vii*) Cheque £264 from T. Pane credited to T. Pain.

Use the following format for your answer:

Item	If no effect state 'No'	Debit side exceeds credit side by amount shown	Credit side exceeds debit side by amount shown
(*i*)			
(*ii*)			
(*iii*)			
(*iv*)			
(*v*)			
(*vi*)			
(*vii*)			

27.5 The following is a trial balance which has been incorrectly drawn up:

Trial Balance at 31 January 2019

	£	£
Capital 1 February 2018	7,845	
Drawings	19,500	
Inventory 1 February 2018		8,410
Trade accounts receivable		34,517
Furniture and fittings	2,400	
Cash in hand	836	
Trade accounts payable		6,890
Sales		127,510
Returns inwards		2,438
Discount received	1,419	
Business expenses	3,204	
Purchases	72,100	
	107,304	179,765

In addition to the mistakes evident above, the following errors were also discovered:

1 A payment of £315 made to a creditor had not been posted from the cash book into the purchases ledger.
2 A cheque for £188 received from a customer had been correctly entered in the cash book but posted to the customer's account as £180.
3 A purchase of fittings £407 had been included in the purchases account.
4 The total of the discounts allowed column in the cash book of £42 had not been posted into the general ledger.
5 A page of the sales day book was correctly totalled as £765 but carried forward as £675.

Show the trial balance as it would appear after all the errors had been corrected. Show all your workings.

27.6 Study the following and answer the questions below.

The trial balance of Mary Harris (Gowns) as at 31 December 2018 showed a difference which was posted to a suspense account. Draft final accounts for the year ended 31 December 2018 were prepared showing a net profit of £47,240. The following errors were subsequently discovered:

● Sales of £450 to C. Thomas had been debited to Thomasson Manufacturing Ltd.
● A payment of £275 for telephone charges had been entered on the debit side of the Telephone account as £375.
● The sales journal had been undercast by £2,000.
● Repairs to a machine, amounting to £390, had been charged to Machinery account.
● A cheque for £1,500, being rent received from Atlas Ltd, had only been entered in the cash book.
● Purchases from P. Brooks, amounting to £765, had been received on 31 December 2018 and included in the closing inventory at that date, but the invoice had not been entered in the purchases journal.

Questions:
(a) (i) Give the journal entries, without narratives, necessary to correct the above errors.
      (ii) Show the effect of each of these adjustments on the net profit in the draft financial statements and the correct profit for the year ended 31 December 2018.
(b) (i) State briefly the purpose of the journal, giving a suitable example of its use.
      (ii) State why it is necessary to distinguish between capital and revenue expenditure.

(Midland Examining Group: GCSE)

27.7A Lee Crosby has just completed his first year of trading selling cookery equipment. He attempted to prepare a balance sheet from his trial balance before seeking expert help as he was having difficulty getting the balance sheet totals to agree. The trial balance included a suspense account balance of £10,000. This amount has not been entered on the balance sheet.

Balance sheet for Lee Crosby for the year ended 31 March 2018

Capital at 1 April 2017			136,175
Shop fittings			38,000
Drawings			71,201
Current liabilities			
Loan payable 2023	52,000		
Trade receivables	3,740		
Accrual of expenses	160		
Cash at bank	2,140		
		58,040	
Current assets			
Property	108,000		
Trade payables	4,220		
Prepayment of expenses	225	112,445	
			56,405
			190,971
Closing inventories			31,517
Cash in hand			155
Profit for the year			52,423
			84,095

Additional information at 31 March 2018

1 During the year cookery equipment purchased for resale, that had cost £3,500 has been entered in error into the shop fittings account.
2 Lee believes the shop fittings will have an economic life of 5 years and have an estimated residual value of £2,000.
3 The property should be depreciated by 5% using the straight-line method.
4 Lee had withdrawn £75 in cash from the business for his own personal use. This transaction has not yet been accounted for.
5 A credit customer has ceased trading owing Lee £1,040 that will never be received.
6 The wages account has been overstated by £10,000.
7 A credit supplier has issued a credit note of £55 for goods that have been damaged and this has not been entered into the books of account.

Required
Prepare a corrected balance sheet at 31 March 2018 taking into account the additional information in points 1–7.

(AQA AS Level)

27.8 The trial balance as at 30 April 2019 of Timber Products Limited was balanced by the inclusion of the following debit balance:

Difference on trial balance suspense account £2,513.

Subsequent investigations revealed the following errors:

(i)   Discounts received of £324 in January 2019 have been posted to the debit of the discounts allowed account.

(ii)   Wages of £2,963 paid in February 2019 have not been posted from the cash book.

(iii)   A remittance of £940 received from K. Mitcham in November 2018 has been posted to the credit of B. Mansell Limited.

(iv)   In December 2018, the company took advantage of an opportunity to purchase a large quantity of stationery at a bargain price of £2,000. No adjustments have been made in the accounts for the fact that three-quarters, in value, of this stationery was in the inventory on 30 April 2019.

(v)   A payment of £341 to J. Winters in January 2019 has been posted in the personal account as £143.

(vi)   A remittance of £3,000 received from D. North, a credit customer, in April 2019 has been credited to sales.

The draft accounts for the year ended 30 April 2019 of Timber Products Limited show a net profit of £24,760.

Timber Products Limited has very few personal accounts and therefore does not maintain either a purchases ledger control account or a sales ledger control account.

Required:
(a)   Prepare the difference on trial balance suspense account showing, where appropriate, the entries necessary to correct the accounting errors.
(b)   Prepare a computation of the corrected net profit for the year ended 30 April 2019 following corrections for the above accounting errors.
(c)   Outline the principal uses of trial balances.

(*Association of Accounting Technicians*)

27.9A Chi Knitwear Ltd is an old-fashioned business with a handwritten set of books. A trial balance is extracted at the end of each month, and an income statement and a balance sheet are computed. This month, however, the trial balance will not balance, the credits exceeding debits by £1,536.

You are asked to help and after inspection of the ledgers discover the following errors.

(i)   A balance of £87 on a debtor's account has been omitted from the schedule of debtors, the total of which was entered as accounts receivable in the trial balance.

(ii)   A small piece of machinery purchased for £1,200 had been written off to repairs.

(iii)   The receipts side of the cash book had been undercast by £720.

(iv)   The total of one page of the sales day book had been carried forward as £8,154, whereas the correct amount was £8,514.

(v)   A credit note for £179 received from a supplier had been posted to the wrong side of his account.

(vi)   An electricity bill in the sum of £152, not yet accrued for, is discovered in a filing tray.

(vii)   Mr Smith, whose past debts to the company had been the subject of a provision, at last paid £731 to clear his account. His personal account has been credited but the cheque has not yet passed through the cash book.

Required:
(a)   Write up the suspense account to clear the difference, and
(b)   State the effect on the accounts of correcting each error.

(*Association of Chartered Certified Accountants*)

27.10A   The trial balance of Happy Bookkeeper Ltd, as produced by its bookkeeper, includes the following items:

Sales ledger control account	£110,172
Purchases ledger control account	£78,266
Suspense account (debit balance)	£2,315

You have been given the following information:

(*i*)   The sales ledger debit balances total £111,111 and the credit balances total £1,234.

(*ii*)   The purchases ledger credit balances total £77,777 and the debit balances total £1,111.

(*iii*)   The sales ledger includes a debit balance of £700 for business X, and the purchases ledger includes a credit balance of £800 relating to the same business X. Only the net amount will eventually be paid.

(*iv*)   Included in the credit balance on the sales ledger is a balance of £600 in the name of H. Smith. This arose because a sales invoice for £600 had earlier been posted in error from the sales day book to the debit of the account of M. Smith in the purchases ledger.

(*v*)   An allowance of £300 against some damaged goods had been omitted from the appropriate account in the sales ledger. This allowance had been included in the control account.

(*vi*)   An invoice for £456 had been entered in the purchases day book as £654.

(*vii*)   A cash receipt from a credit customer for £345 had been entered in the cash book as £245.

(*viii*) The purchases day book had been overcast by £1,000.

(*ix*)   The bank balance of £1,200 had been included in the trial balance, in error, as an overdraft.

(*x*)   The bookkeeper had been instructed to write off £500 from customer Y's account as a bad debt, and to reduce the provision for doubtful debts by £700. By mistake, however, he had written off £700 from customer Y's account and *increased* the allowance for doubtful debts by £500.

(*xi*)   The debit balance on the insurance account in the nominal ledger of £3,456 had been included in the trial balance as £3,546.

Required:
Record corrections in the control and suspense accounts. Attempt to reconcile the sales ledger control account with the sales ledger balances, and the purchases ledger control account with the purchases ledger balances. What further action do you recommend?

(*Association of Chartered Certified Accountants*)

27.11   The following points were discovered in the books of a small building business before the closing entries had been made. Draft financial statements had already been prepared and showed a net profit of £23,120.

(*i*)   The purchase of a new van for £6,000 was included in the motor vehicle expenses account.

(*ii*)   The drawings account included £250 for the purchase of fuel which was used to heat the business offices.

(*iii*)   £300 paid by a customer, B. Burton Ltd, had been credited to B. Struton's account in error.

(*iv*)   The water rates on the proprietor's home of £750 has been paid by the business and debited to the business rates account.

(*v*)   £720 included in the wages account was paid to workmen for building a greenhouse in the proprietor's garden.

(*vi*)   Building materials bought on credit from K. Jarman for £500, has been delivered to the business on the balance sheet date and had been included in the inventory figure at that date, but the invoice for these goods had not been entered in the purchases day book.

Required:
(*a*)   The journal entries to record the necessary adjustments arising from the above.

(*b*)   A statement showing the effect of these adjustments on the profit shown in the draft financial statements.

→ **27.12** At the end of a financial year, the trial balance of a small company failed to agree and the difference was entered in a suspense account. Subsequently, the following errors were discovered:

(*i*)   The sales day book had been undercast by £10.
(*ii*) A customer's personal account has been correctly credited with £2 discount, but no corresponding entry was made in the discount column of the cash book.
(*iii*) Discounts allowed for July amounting to £70 were credited instead of being debited to the discount account.
(*iv*) A debit balance on the account of D. Bird, a customer, was carried forward £10 short.
(*v*)   An old credit balance of £3 on a customer's account (J. Flyn) had been entirely overlooked when extracting the balances.

Required:
(*a*) Prepare, where necessary, the journal entries to correct the errors.
(*b*) Draw up a statement showing the impact of these errors upon the trial balance.

27.13A Journalise the matters arising from the following items in the books of B. Danby, including the narrative in each case. Note that for this purpose cash and bank items may be journalised.

In the case of those items which gave rise to a difference in the trial balance you are to assume that the difference was previously recorded in a suspense account.

(*a*) Discounts allowed during March amounting to £62 were posted to the credit of the discounts received account.
(*b*) The sales day book was overcast by £100.
(*c*) The motor van standing in the ledger at £1,800 was exchanged for fittings valued at £1,400 plus a cheque for £700.
(*d*) £470 has been included in the wages account and £340 in the purchases account. These amounts represent expenditure on an extension to the business premises.
(*e*) A cheque for £86 received from C. Blimp and discount of £4 allowed to him were correctly recorded but, when the cheque was subsequently dishonoured, no further entries were recorded.
(*f*) A cheque for £76 paid to D. Hood was correctly recorded in the cash book but was posted in error to D. I. Hoade's account as £67.

27.14 The bookkeeper of a firm failed to agree the trial balance at 30 June, the end of the financial year. She opened a suspense account into which she entered the amount she was out of balance and carried this amount to a draft balance sheet that she prepared.

The following errors were subsequently discovered in the books:

(*i*)   The purchase day book had been undercast by £10.
(*ii*)   Goods bought on credit from A. Supplier for £5 had been posted to his account as £50.
(*iii*) A new machine costing £70 had been posted to the debit of the repairs to machinery account.
(*iv*)   S. Kane, a customer, returned goods valued at £10. This had been entered in the sales returns day book and posted to the debit of the customer's account.
(*v*)   The sale on credit of various items of plant and machinery at their book value of £300 had been recorded in the sales day book.
(*vi*)   £60 owed by D. Clarke, a customer, had been overlooked when drawing up a schedule of accounts receivable from the ledger.
(*vii*) An item of cash discount allowed £2 had been correctly entered in the cash book but had not been posted to the account of B. Luckwood, the customer.
(*viii*) Business rates, treated as having been paid in advance in the previous accounting period, amounting to £45 had not been brought down as a balance on the business rates account at the start of the accounting period. Instead it was included in the prepayments account.

As a result of posting these errors to the suspense account, the balance on the suspense account was reduced to zero.

Required:

(a) Prepare the suspense account, including the initial opening entry made by the bookkeeper, along with all the necessary adjusting entries identified above.

(b) Explain clearly the effect of correcting the above errors:
  (i) on the net profit shown in the draft income statement
  (ii) on any of the items in the draft balance sheet

Note: You will find this question easier if you prepare journal entries for each item before answering (a) and (b).

Scenario questions

The following questions are designed to reinforce learning of the adjustments covered in Part 5 and 6 through their application in the preparation of financial statements previously learnt in Parts 1–5.

The answers to these questions are to be found on pp. 723–6.

SQ1

Michael Angelo owns Picta Simpla, a company specialising in selling painting by numbers packs by mail order. The packs are purchased from a wholesaler and then resold. The public have no access to the wholesaler and so there is no competition.

During the year ended 30 June 2020 Michael sold 2,900 units at £89 each, having started the year with £19,250 of inventory (600 units). During the year, he purchased a total of 3,150 packs from the wholesaler at £59 each. Michael wants to value his inventory using the FIFO basis.

Staff have been paid wages totalling £14,500, which is only slightly less than the advertising bills paid of £15,000. Michael is upset since the advertising agency has yet to send a final bill, estimated to be £500. Postage per unit sent out was £2. The packing costs were £0.50 per unit.

Rent was £1,000 per month. Insurance of £3,500 has been paid but £650 of this relates to the year ending 30 June 2021. Electricity bills amounted to £2,900, but the bill for the final quarter is still outstanding and is expected to be approximately £500.

The business has a computer which was purchased about two years ago and which Michael reckons has about another three years of useful life left, at which point it will be worthless. It cost £4,000 and Michael uses the straight line method when calculating the depreciation charge. He also has a fax machine which he uses to communicate with his suppliers.

Stationery charges have amounted to £1,350 and he has had telephone bills of £3,500, of which £200 relates to July and August 2020. In the year ending 30 June 2019, he paid £150 for July and August 2019.

Michael has also paid £5,000 from the business bank account for a month-long holiday in Florida. He has asked you whether he can class this as business expenses since it has enabled him to recover from the stresses and strain of running his own business.

Required:
(a) Prepare an income statement for the year ending 30 June 2020.
(b) Write a brief letter to Michael explaining what drawings are in relation to a small business and answering his query concerning his holiday.

SQ2

The following balance sheet has been prepared by your client, Mr Conman, proprietor of the Sleasy Cars second hand car dealership:

Balance Sheet as at 31 December 2019

	£	£
Non-current Assets		
Freehold land, at valuation		10,000
Offices		1,000
Breakdown truck		5,000
		16,000
Current Assets		
Inventory	23,000	
Accounts receivable and prepayments	3,500	
Cash in hand	100	
		26,600
Total assets		42,600
Current Liabilities		
Account payable and accruals	8,200	
Bank Overdraft	6,400	
Total liabilities		(14,600)
Net assets		28,000
Capital		
Capital Introduced		15,500
Add Profit for the year		23,500
		39,000
Less Drawings		(11,000)
Total capital		28,000

This was the first year of trading for Sleasy Cars. Mr Conman acquired a field in Hull (which had previously been used for a rubbish tip and then filled in) for £5,000 on 1 January 2019 and erected a portacabin on the site to be used as an office at a cost of £500. He then bought ten second hand cars from a national dealership for £10,000. He has some accountancy training and has taken a lot of care in producing the balance sheet but confesses that he did not produce an income statement. Instead, as it must be the correct figure, the amount shown for profit in the balance sheet was the amount required to make it balance.

The following points have come to light in your discussion:

(*i*) The office was bought at a discount from a friend who had acquired it from a builder's yard and Conman has included it in the balance sheet at the proper price as he knows that accountants like original costs to be shown. The office should last for five years and Conman agrees that maybe that thing called depreciation should be included at straight line. The office will be worthless at the end of the five years.

(*ii*) The land was a bargain. Conman heard on the grapevine that the council were going to take the previous owners to court as it was an environmental hazard. The owners put it up for sale at £10,000 so he made an offer to the owners of £5,000 which was accepted. He is ignoring the court order to clean up the site since this would cost approximately £3,000. His reason for ignoring it is that although the order was made in December 2018 (i.e. before he bought the land), he did not receive the notice until January 2020 (i.e. after he had bought the land).

(*iii*) The breakdown truck is very old and was bought at the start of the year. It has been shown at cost although it is probably only going to last another year and will have no residual value.

(*iv*) Inventory has all been valued at cost although on one car there is a good chance that it will sell at a loss of £500. Another one was sold in January 2020 for £3,000 but the new owner has not picked it up yet – the profit was £1,500 so this has been included in the valuation of the car. As he has included the car, Conman has not included the debtor in the balance sheet.

(v) A customer has owed £2,000 for six months and Mr Conman is becoming slightly bothered. The customer has moved away from the address she gave Mr Conman and he thinks that this debt might not be recoverable.

(vi) After hearing the above, you have decided to check the figures and have found that the cash, overdraft and drawings figures are correct and also that there has been no adjustment for the fact that he has not paid his electricity bill of £250 nor his telephone bill of £150. The reason for this is that he is subletting part of the field and is owed £400 in rent and, therefore, the two cancel each other out.

Required

(a) A revised balance sheet after taking into account all of the above.

(b) A description of each of the adjustments that have been made and why each of them is necessary.

SQ3

The following represents the trial balance extracted from the books of Mr Jones, a small businessman based in Aboyne. The books are well-maintained and there is no reason to doubt the accuracy of the entries.

	£	£
Sales		430,000
Purchases	293,500	
Carriage in	2,100	
Drawings	31,000	
Rent	5,200	
Business rates	2,600	
Insurance	550	
Postage	250	
Stationery	986	
Advertising	250	
Wages	10,500	
Bad debts	400	
Allowance for doubtful debts	400	
Accounts receivable	5,120	
Accounts payable		3,600
Cash in hand	120	
Cash at bank	3,257	
Inventory	6,520	
Equipment at cost	150,000	
Accumulated depreciation – equipment		35,000
Capital		43,353
	512,353	512,353

Following a discussion with Mr Jones, the following points have come to light:

(a) Accruals are necessary for rent (£150), business rates (£200), and stationery (£16).

(b) Insurance has been prepaid by £150, advertising by £50.

(c) Inventory at the year end is £7,000.

(d) Depreciation is to be charged on the equipment at a rate of 10 per cent on cost.

(e) The allowance for doubtful debts is to be increased to 10 per cent of the year-end balance.

(f) Purchase invoices to the value of £12,000 were found in a desk drawer the day before the meeting with Mr Jones. Half of them have been paid by cheque (but no record made in the cash book) and the rest are outstanding.

Required

(a) Prepare an income statement for the year ending on the date of extraction of the trial balance together with a balance sheet as at that date.

(b) Mr Jones has kept accurate records (with the exception of point (f)) and yet the accountant must still adjust the figures in the trial balance before preparing the financial statements. As the accountant, write a letter to Mr Jones outlining why the accountant must adjust the figures to convey meaningful information.

SQ4

The following balances were extracted from the books of Mr Try, a window cleaner. He has no knowledge of double entry bookkeeping but records everything correctly. His year end is 30 June and the following balances relate to the year ended 30 June 2020:

	£
Accounts to be paid	100
Cleaning income	17,644
Cash balance	35
Own wages	10,600
Ladders and equipment	750
Repairs to customers' houses due to damage	230
Miscellaneous expenses	110
Owed by customers	220
Insurances	350
Accountancy fees (relating to 2016 – paid in this year)	250
Postage and stationery	50
Bank	2,345
Cleaning materials and cloths	3,400

He has not included the following items as he is not sure how to record them:

(i) Bank charges of £45 are to be levied for the year – they are to be processed by the bank in September 2020.
(ii) Insurances have been prepaid by £50.
(iii) None of the amounts owed by customers can be realistically recovered but Mr Try wants to keep on trying and therefore wants a provision to be made of 50 per cent of the balances.
(iv) Accountancy charges for the current year ended 2020 are to be £275.
(v) The ladders, including the ones bought in the year, will only last until the end of 2021 and are to be depreciated using the straight line method with no residual value.

Required
(a) Prepare an income statement for the year ending 30 June 2020.
(b) Prepare a balance sheet at that date.
(c) Mr Try has heard about a treatment of non-current assets which he thinks is 'consumables'. He wonders if his ladders could be treated as consumables and not depreciated. Write a letter to Mr Try, using fictitious names and addresses, to answer his query.

SQ5

Michael Baldwin owns B's Casuals, a company specialising in low-quality, high-priced clothing. The material is purchased from Canada, made up into the finished garments in his own factory, and then sold in the local markets through stallholders.

During the year ended 30 June 2020 Michael had sales of £260,040.

Inventory levels have remained relatively consistent over the years, the starting inventory being £21,500 and the closing inventory £22,500.

Michael is not very generous to his staff. This is reflected in the wages paid during the year of only £24,500.

Business rates are a problem, since there is a dispute with the local council. He has paid a total of £7,500 but there is a good chance that he will have to pay a further £2,450.

Postage and advertising is another problem area. For the imports from Canada it is necessary to pay all of the flight costs. These amounted to £5,200 over the year.

He delivers all of his invoices to the stallholders in person and is paid promptly, with the exception of one debtor who owes £2,000 and who has been declared bankrupt. This amount is to be written off.

Advertising is minimal and is done in the local pub: £20 per week is paid to the landlord in return for permission to pin leaflets on the walls and an agreement that the landlord will place a leaflet every day on each table in the bar.

Insurance of £3,500 has been paid, but £650 of this relates to the year ending 30 June 2021.

Electricity bills amounted to £2,900, but the bill for the final quarter is still outstanding and is expected to be approximately £500. Purchases of cloth from Canada for the year are currently recorded as being £65,000, but there is an outstanding bill of £3,500 which is not yet included in that figure.

The factory and the machinery were bought at the same time and originally cost £400,000. Depreciation has accumulated to the sum of £100,000. The current year charge is 5 per cent on the reducing balance basis.

The business had a computer which was purchased about three years ago and which Michael reckons has about another two years of life left. It cost £4,000 and Michael uses the straight line method of calculating the depreciation charge. The computer will be worthless at the end of that time.

Stationery charges amounted to £1,350 and he had telephone bills of £3,500, £200 of which relates to July and August 2020. In the year ending 30 June 2020, he had paid £150 which related to telephone charges in the year ending 30 June 2020.

Michael has also paid £5,000 for a top-of-the-range digital home cinema system. He has enquired as to whether he can class this as a business expense as it has enabled him to unwind after long days at the office.

His salary for the year was £50,000.

Cash in hand at 30 June 2020 was £600 which he borrowed from his wife temporarily on 30 June when he realised that there was no cash available to pay any expenses.

Required

(a) Prepare an income statement for the year ending 30 June 2020.

(b) Prepare a balance sheet as at 30 June 2020 showing clearly Mr Baldwin's opening capital, net assets and the profit for the year.

(c) Michael has enquired why he should include the amounts owing to both the council and the Canadians in the current year's financial statements and also why he cannot include his own wages within expenses since they have been paid out from the business. Write a letter to Michael explaining these points and answering his query concerning the home cinema system.

SPECIAL ACCOUNTING PROCEDURES

Introduction

This part is concerned with the accounting procedures that are adopted for specific forms of organisations.

Receipts and payments accounts and income and expenditure accounts

Learning objectives

After you have studied this chapter, you should be able to:

● explain the main differences between the financial statements of non-profit-oriented organisations and those of profit-oriented organisations

● prepare receipts and payments accounts

● prepare income and expenditure accounts and balance sheets for non-profit-oriented organisations

● calculate profits and losses from special activities and incorporate them into the financial statements

● make appropriate entries relating to subscriptions, life membership, and donations

Introduction

In this chapter, you'll learn about the financial statements prepared by non-profit-oriented organisations, and about how they differ from those prepared for profit-oriented organisations.

28.1 Non-profit-oriented organisations

As their main purpose is not trading or profit-making, charities, clubs, associations and other non-profit-oriented organisations do not prepare income statements. They are run so that their members can do things such as play tennis, bridge, football, chess, role playing games, etc. Rather than producing income statements they prepare either 'receipts and payments accounts' or 'income and expenditure accounts'.

28.2 Receipts and payments accounts

Receipts and payments accounts are a summary of the cash book for the period. For an organisation with no assets (other than cash) and no liabilities, a summary of the cash book reveals everything about what has happened financially during a period.

Exhibit 28.1 is an example:

Exhibit 28.1

Haven Running Club
Receipts and Payments Account for the year ended 31 December 2018

Receipts	£	Payments	£
Bank balance at 1.1.2018	2,360	Groundsman's wages	7,280
Subscriptions received in 2018	11,480	Sports ground rental	2,960
Rent received	1,160	Committee expenses	580
		Printing and stationery	330
		Bank balance at 31.12.2018	3,850
	15,000		15,000

Activity 28.1 Why do you think non-profit-oriented organisations prepare receipts and payments accounts when they have all this information in the cash book already?

28.3 Income and expenditure accounts

When assets are owned and/or there are liabilities, the receipts and payments account is not sufficient. Other than the cash received and paid out, it shows only the cash balances. The other assets and liabilities are not shown at all. What is required is:

1 a balance sheet; and
2 a statement showing whether the association's capital has increased.

In a profit-oriented organisation, **2** would be an income statement. In a non-profit-oriented organisation, **2** would be an **income and expenditure account**.

An income and expenditure account follows the same rules as an income statement. The only differences are the terms used.

A comparison between the terminology of financial statements produced by profit-oriented and non-profit-oriented organisations now follows.

Terms used

Profit-oriented organisation	Non-profit-oriented organisation
1 Income Statement	1 Income and Expenditure Account
2 Net Profit	2 Surplus of Income over Expenditure
3 Net Loss	3 Deficit of Income over Expenditure

28.4 Profit or loss for a special purpose

Sometimes there are reasons why a non-profit-oriented organisation would want to prepare either a trading account or a full income statement.

This is where something is done by it in order to make a profit. The profit is not to be kept, but is used to pay for the main purpose of the organisation.

For instance, a football club may organise and run dances which people pay to go to. Any profit from these helps to pay football expenses. For these dances, either a trading account or a full income statement would be drawn up. Any profit (or loss) would be transferred to the income and expenditure account.

28.5 Accumulated fund

A sole proprietor has a capital account. A non-profit-oriented organisation has an **accumulated fund**. In effect, it is the same as a capital account, as it is the difference between the assets and liabilities.

For a sole proprietor:

$$\text{Capital} = \text{Assets} - \text{Liabilities}$$

For a non-profit-oriented organisation:

$$\text{Accumulated Fund} = \text{Assets} - \text{Liabilities}$$

28.6 Drawing up income and expenditure accounts

We can now look at the preparation of an income and expenditure account and a balance sheet of a club in Exhibit 28.2. A separate trading account is to be prepared for a bar, where refreshments are sold to make a profit.

The majority of clubs and associations keep their accounts using single entry methods. You will read more about single entry in Chapter 40. This example will therefore be from single entry records.

Exhibit 28.2

The treasurer of the Long Lane Football Club has prepared a receipts and payments account, but members have complained about the inadequacy of such an account. She therefore asks an accountant to prepare a trading account for the bar, and an income and expenditure account and a balance sheet. The treasurer gives the accountant a copy of the receipts and payments account together with information on assets and liabilities at the beginning and end of the year:

Long Lane Football Club
Receipts and Payments Account for the year ended 31 December 2019

Receipts	£	Payments	£
Bank balance at 1.1.2019	524	Payment for bar supplies	38,620
Subscriptions received for		Wages:	
2018 (arrears)	1,400	Groundsman and assistant	19,939
2019	14,350	Barman	8,624
2020 (in advance)	1,200	Bar expenses	234
Bar sales	61,280	Repairs to stands	740
Donations received	800	Ground upkeep	1,829
		Secretary's expenses	938
		Transport costs	2,420
		Bank balance at 31.12.2019	6,210
	79,554		79,554

→

➔ *Additional information:*

		31.12.2018	31.12.2019
		£	£
1	Inventory in the bar – at cost	4,496	5,558
	Owing for bar supplies	3,294	4,340
	Bar expenses owing	225	336
	Transport costs	–	265

2   The land and football stands were valued at 31 December 2018 at: land £40,000; football stands £20,000; the stands are to be depreciated by 10 per cent per annum.

3   The equipment at 31 December 2018 was valued at £2,500, and is to be depreciated at 20 per cent per annum.

4   Subscriptions owing by members amounted to £1,400 on 31 December 2018, and £1,750 on 31 December 2019.

From this information, in the following three stages, the accountant drew up the appropriate accounts and statements:

Stage 1

Draw up a Statement of Affairs at the end of the previous period in order to identify the balance on the Accumulated Fund brought forward to 2019.

Statement of Affairs as at 31 December 2018

	£	£
Non-current assets		
Land		40,000
Stands		20,000
Equipment		2,500
		62,500
Current assets		
Inventory in bar	4,496	
Accounts receivable for subscriptions	1,400	
Cash at bank	524	
		6,420
Total assets		71,920
Current liabilities		
Accounts payable	3,294	
Bar expenses owing	225	
Total liabilities		(3,519)
Net assets		65,401
Accumulated fund (difference)		65,401

Activity 28.2   Why do you think this statement was described as being a 'statement of affairs' rather than a 'balance sheet'?

Stage 2

Draw up a Bar Trading Account.

Long Lane Football Club
Bar Trading Account for the year ending 31 December 2019

	£	£
Sales		61,280
Less Cost of goods sold:		
Inventory 1.1.2019	4,496	
Add Purchases[Note 1]	39,666	
	44,162	
Less Inventory 31.12.2019	(5,558)	
		(38,604)
Gross profit		22,676
Less Bar expenses[Note 2]	345	
Barman's wages	8,624	
		(8,969)
Net profit to income and expenditure account		13,707

Notes:

1
Purchases Control

	£		£
Cash	38,620	Balances (creditors) b/d	3,294
Balances c/d	4,340	Trading account (difference)	39,666
	42,960		42,960

2
Bar Expenses

	£		£
Cash	234	Balance b/d	225
Balance c/d	336	Trading account (difference)	345
	570		570

Stage 3

Draw up the financial statements.

Long Lane Football Club
Income and Expenditure Account for the year ending 31 December 2019

Income	£	£	£
Subscriptions for 2019[Note 1]			16,100
Profit from the bar			13,707
Donations received			800
			30,607
Less Expenditure			
Wages – Groundsman and assistant		19,939	
Repairs to stands		740	
Ground upkeep		1,829	
Secretary's expenses		938	
Transport costs[Note 2]		2,685	
Depreciation			
Stands	2,000		
Equipment	500		
		2,500	
			(28,631)
Surplus of income over expenditure			1,976

Notes:

1

Subscriptions Received

	£		£
Balance (accounts receivable) b/d	1,400	Cash 2018	1,400
Income and expenditure (difference)	16,100	2019	14,350
		2020	1,200
Balance (in advance) c/d	1,200	Balance (accounts receivable) c/d	1,750
	18,700		18,700

2

Transport Costs

	£		£
Cash	2,420	Income and expenditure (difference)	2,685
Accrued c/d	265		
	2,685		2,685

Note that subscriptions received in advance are carried down as a credit balance to the following period.

Long Lane Football Club
Balance Sheet as at 31 December 2019

	£	£
Non-current assets		
Land at valuation		40,000
Football stands at valuation	20,000	
Less Depreciation	(2,000)	
		18,000
Equipment at valuation	2,500	
Less Depreciation	(500)	
		2,000
		60,000
Current assets		
Inventory of bar supplies	5,558	
Accounts receivable for subscriptions	1,750	
Cash at bank	6,210	
		13,518
Total assets		73,518
Current liabilities		
Accounts payable for bar supplies	4,340	
Bar expenses owing	336	
Transport costs owing	265	
Subscriptions received in advance	1,200	
Total liabilities		(6,141)
Net assets		67,377
Accumulated fund		
Balance as at 1.1.2019		65,401
Add Surplus of income over expenditure		1,976
		67,377

28.7 Outstanding subscriptions and the prudence concept

So far we have treated subscriptions owing as being an asset. However, as any treasurer of a club would tell you, most subscriptions that have been owing for a long time are never paid – members lose interest or simply go somewhere else. As a result, many clubs do not include unpaid subscriptions as an asset in the balance sheet.

Activity 28.3 Does this policy of ignoring subscriptions due when preparing the financial statements comply with the prudence concept? Why/Why not?

In an examination, you should assume that subscriptions owing are to be brought into the financial statements, unless instructions to the contrary are given.

Exhibit 28.3 shows an instance where subscriptions in arrears and in advance occur at the beginning and end of a period.

Exhibit 28.3

An amateur theatrical group charges its members an annual subscription of £20 per member. It accrues for subscriptions owing at the end of each year and also adjusts for subscriptions received in advance.

(A) On 1 January 2020, 18 members had not yet paid their subscriptions for the year 2019.
(B) In December 2019, 4 members paid £80 for the year 2020.
(C) During the year 2020 it received £7,420 in cash for subscriptions:

	£
For 2019	360
For 2020	6,920
For 2021	140
	7,420

(D) At 31 December 2020, 11 members had not paid their 2020 subscriptions.

Subscriptions

2020				£	2020				£
Jan	1	Owing b/d	(A)	360	Jan	1	Prepaid b/d	(B)	80
Dec	31	Income and expenditure*		7,220	Dec	31	Bank	(C)	7,420
	31	Prepaid c/d	(C)	140		31	Owing c/d	(D)	220
				7,720					7,720
2021					2021				
Jan	1	Owing b/d	(D)	220	Jan	1	Prepaid b/d	(C)	140

*This is the difference between the two sides of the account.

28.8 Life membership

In some clubs and societies, members can make a payment for life membership. This means that by paying a fairly large amount once, members can enjoy the facilities of the club for the rest of their lives.

Such a receipt should not be treated as income in the income and expenditure account solely in the year in which the member paid the money. It should be credited to a life membership account, and transfers should be made from that account to the credit of the income and expenditure account of an appropriate amount annually.

Exactly what is meant by 'an appropriate amount' to transfer each year is decided by the committee of the club or society. The usual basis is to establish, on average, how long members will continue to use the benefits of the club. To take an extreme case, if a club was in existence which could not be joined below the age of 70, then the expected number of years' use of the club on average per member would be relatively few. Another club, such as a golf club, where a fair proportion of the members joined when reasonably young, and where the game is capable of being played by members until and during old age, would expect a much higher average of years of use per member. In the end, the club has to decide for itself.

As a club has to provide amenities for life members without any further payment, the credit balance remaining on the account, after the transfer of the agreed amount has been made to the credit of the income and expenditure account, should be shown on the balance sheet as a liability.

In an examination, be sure to follow the instructions set by the examiner.

28.9 Donations

Any donations received are usually shown as income in the year that they are received.

28.10 Entrance fees

When they first join a club, in addition to the membership fee for that year, new members often have to pay an entrance fee. Entrance fees are normally included as income in the year that they are received. A club could, however, decide to treat them differently, perhaps by spreading the income over a number of years. It all depends on the circumstances.

Learning outcomes

You should now have learnt:

1 That a receipts and payments account does not show the full financial position of an organisation, except for one where the only asset is cash and there are no liabilities.

2 That an income and expenditure account is drawn up to show either the surplus of income over expenditure or the excess of expenditure over income. These are the same as 'profit' or 'loss' in a profit-oriented organisation.

3 That the accumulated fund is basically the same as a capital account.

4 That although the main object of the organisation is non-profit-oriented, certain activities may be run at a profit (or may lose money) in order to help finance the main objectives of the organisation.

5 That in an examination you should treat subscriptions owing at the end of a period in the same way as accounts receivable, unless told otherwise.

6 That donations are usually treated as income in the period in which they are received.

7 That entrance fees are usually treated as income in the year in which they are received.

8 That the treatment of life membership fees is purely at the discretion of the organisation, but that they are usually amortised over an appropriate period.

Answers to activities

28.1 Just as you would prepare a balance sheet for a profit-oriented organisation in order to summarise its financial position at a specific point in time, so non-profit-oriented organisations that deal only in cash, own no assets and have no liabilities, may prepare a receipts and payments account in order to show what happened over a period and the amount of funds left at the end. Non-profit-oriented organisations with assets and liabilities may also prepare them, but only normally in order to help prepare their main financial statements.

28.2 You could just as easily draw up a balance sheet but you're trying to summarise the financial statement even more than in a balance sheet. You would not, for example, show provision for doubtful debts being subtracted from debtors in a statement of affairs, but you might in the balance sheet of a sole trader. To avoid confusion, the title 'statement of affairs' is used when performing any preparatory work prior to preparing the balance sheet. (It must be said, however, that you would not be wrong if you called the statement of affairs a balance sheet.)

28.3 It does not comply with the prudence concept. You will remember from your coverage of the prudence concept in Chapter 7 that you should not overstate *or* understate income and expenditure. While this practice ensures the figure for subscriptions due is not overstated, it does understate them.

Review questions

28.1 A summary of the Balgreen Bowling Club's cash book is shown below. From it, and the additional information, you are to construct an income and expenditure account for the year ending 31 December 2019, and a balance sheet as at that date.

Cash Book Summary

	£		£
Balance at 1.1.2019	5,600	Purchase of equipment	1,200
Collections at matches	17,200	Rent for green	4,800
Profit on sale of refreshments	22,000	Printing and stationery	200
		Secretary's expenses	320
		Repairs to equipment	280
		Groundsman's wages	16,000
		Miscellaneous expenses	240
		Balance at 31.12.2019	21,760
	44,800		44,800

Further information:
(*i*)   At 1.1.2019 equipment was valued at £6,000.
(*ii*) Depreciate all equipment 10 per cent for the year 2019.
(*iii*) At 31.12.2019 rent paid in advance was £1,200.
(*iv*) At 31.12.2019 there was £80 owing for printing.

28.2A The following trial balance of the Grampian Golf Club was extracted from the books as on 31 December 2019:

	Dr	Cr
	£	£
Clubhouse	284,000	
Equipment	37,200	
Profits from raffles		13,016
Subscriptions received		366,800
Wages of bar staff	58,400	
Bar inventory 1 January 2019	18,800	
Bar purchases and sales	82,600	169,200
Greenkeepers' wages	43,000	
Golf professional's salary	74,000	
General expenses	1,820	
Cash at bank	7,848	
Accumulated fund at 1 January 2019		58,652
	607,668	607,668

Notes:

(*i*)   Bar purchases and sales were on a cash basis. Bar inventory at 31 December 2019 was valued at £12,820.

(*ii*)   Subscriptions paid in advance by members at 31 December 2019 amounted to £3,740.

(*iii*) Provide for depreciation of equipment £4,800.

Required:

(*a*)   Draw up the bar trading account for the year ending 31 December 2019.

(*b*)   Draw up the income and expenditure account for the year ending 31 December 2019, and a balance sheet as at 31 December 2019.

28.3   Read the following and answer the questions below.

On 1 January 2018 the Happy Haddock Angling Club had the following assets:

	£
Cash at bank	200
Snack bar inventory	800
Club house buildings	12,500

During the year to 31 December 2018 the Club received and paid the following amounts:

Receipts	£	*Payments*	£
Subscriptions 2018	3,500	Rent and rates	1,500
Subscriptions 2019	380	Extension to club house	8,000
Snack bar income	6,000	Snack bar purchases	3,750
Visitors' fees	650	Secretarial expenses	240
Loan from bank	5,500	Interest on loan	260
Competition fees	820	Snack bar expenses	600
		Games equipment	2,000

Notes: The snack bar inventory on 31 December 2018 was £900.
           The games equipment should be depreciated by 20%.

(*a*)   Prepare an income and expenditure account for the year ending 31 December 2018. Show, either in this account or separately, the snack bar profit or loss.

(*b*)   Prepare a balance sheet as at 31 December 2018.

(Midland Examining Group: GCSE)

28.4A   The treasurer of the Plumpton Leisure Centre has produced the following receipts and payments account for the year ended 31 December 2020:

Receipts	£	*Payments*	£
Balance at bank 1 January 2020	3,900	Refreshment supplies bought	4,320
Subscriptions received	45,060	Wages of attendants and cleaners	31,400
Profits from dances	4,116	Rent of building	8,700
Profit on exhibition	890	New equipment bought	18,200
Refreshment takings	16,290	Travelling expenses of teams	1,900
Sale of equipment	340	Balance at bank 31 December 2020	6,076
	70,596		70,596

Notes:

(*i*)   Refreshment inventory was valued: 31 December 2019 £680; 31 December 2020 £920. There was nothing owing for refreshment inventory on either of these dates.

(*ii*)   On 1 January 2020 the club's equipment was valued at £32,400. Included in this figure, valued at £420, was the equipment sold during the year for £340.

(*iii*) The amount to be charged for depreciation of equipment for the year is £5,200. This is in addition to the loss on equipment sold during the year.

(*iv*) Subscriptions owing by members at 31 December 2019 nil; at 31 December 2020 £860.

Required:

(*a*) Draw up the refreshment trading account for the year ending 31 December 2020. For this purpose £4,680 of the wages is to be charged to this account; the remainder is to be charged in the income and expenditure account.

(*b*) Calculate the accumulated fund as at 1 January 2020.

(*c*) Draw up the income and expenditure account for the year ending 31 December 2020, and a balance sheet as at 31 December 2020.

28.5 The following is a summary of the receipts and payments of the Miniville Rotary Club during the year ended 31 July 2019.

Miniville Rotary Club
Receipts and Payments Account for the year ended 31 July 2019

	£		£
Cash and bank balances b/d	210	Secretarial expenses	163
Sales of competition tickets	437	Rent	1,402
Members' subscriptions	1,987	Visiting speakers' expenses	1,275
Donations	177	Donations to charities	35
Refund of rent	500	Prizes for competitions	270
Balance c/d	13	Stationery and printing	179
	£3,324		£3,324

The following valuations are also available:

as at 31 July	2018	2019
	£	£
Equipment (original cost £1,420)	975	780
Subscriptions in arrears	65	85
Subscriptions in advance	10	37
Owing to suppliers of competition prizes	58	68
Inventory of competition prizes	38	46

Required:

(*a*) Calculate the value of the accumulated fund of the Miniville Rotary Club as at 1 August 2018.

(*b*) Reconstruct the following accounts for the year ended 31 July 2019:
  (*i*) the subscriptions account,
  (*ii*) the competition prizes account.

(*c*) Prepare an income and expenditure account for the Miniville Rotary Club for the year ending 31 July 2019 and a balance sheet as at that date.

(*Association of Accounting Technicians*)

28.6 The accounting records of the Happy Tickers Sports and Social Club are in a mess. You manage to find the following information to help you prepare the accounts for the year to 31 December 2018.

Summarised Balance Sheet as at 31 December 2017

	£
Half-share in motorised roller	600
New sports equipment unsold	1,000

→

Summarised Balance Sheet as at 31 December 2017

Used sports equipment at valuation	700
Rent prepaid (2 months)	200
Subscriptions 2017	60
Café inventory	800
Cash and bank	1,210
	4,570
Life subscriptions	1,400
Subscriptions 2018	120
Insurance accrued (3 months)	150
Accumulated fund	2,900
	4,570

Receipts in the year to 31 December 2018:	£
Subscriptions – 2017	40
– 2018	1,100
– 2019	80
– Life	200
From sales of new sports equipment	900
From sales of used sports equipment	14
Café takings	4,660
	6,994

Payments in the year to 31 December 2018:	
Rent (for 12 months)	1,200
Insurance (for 18 months)	900
To suppliers of sports equipment	1,000
To café suppliers	1,900
Wages of café manager	2,000
Total cost of repairing motorised roller	450
	7,450

Notes:
(i) Ownership and all expenses of the motorised roller are agreed to be shared equally with the Carefree Conveyancers Sports and Social Club which occupies a nearby site. The roller cost a total of £2,000 on 1 January 2014 and had an estimated life of 10 years.
(ii) Life subscriptions are brought into income equally over 10 years, in a scheme begun 5 years ago in 2014. Since the scheme began the cost of £200 per person has been constant. Prior to 31 December 2017 10 life subscriptions had been received.
(iii) Four more annual subscriptions of £20 each had been promised relating to 2018, but not yet received. Annual subscriptions promised but unpaid are carried forward for a maximum of 12 months.
(iv) New sports equipment is sold to members at cost plus 50%. Used equipment is sold off to members at book valuation. Half the sports equipment bought in the year (all from a cash and carry supplier) has been used within the club, and half made available for sale, new, to members. The 'used equipment at valuation' figure in the 31 December 2018 balance sheet is to remain at £700.
(v) Closing café inventory is £850, and £80 is owed to suppliers at 31 December 2018.

Required:
(a) Calculate the profit on café operations and the profit on sale of sports equipment.
(b) Prepare a statement of subscription income for 2018.
(c) Prepare an income and expenditure statement for the year ending 31 December 2018, and balance sheet as at 31 December 2018.
(d) Why do life subscriptions appear as a liability?

(Association of Chartered Certified Accountants)

Manufacturing accounts

Learning objectives

After you have studied this chapter, you should be able to:

● calculate prime cost and production cost of goods manufactured

● draw up a manufacturing account and income statement

● adjust the manufacturing account in respect of work-in-progress

Introduction

In this chapter, you'll learn how to prepare manufacturing accounts and the reasons for doing so.

29.1 Manufacturing: not retailing

We now have to deal with businesses which are manufacturers. For these businesses, a **manufacturing account** is prepared in addition to the income statement. **It is produced for internal use only.** People other than the owners and managers of the organisation concerned rarely see a manufacturing account.

If a business is using manufacturing accounts, instead of a figure for purchases (of finished goods) the trading account will contain the cost of manufacturing the goods that were manufactured during the period. The manufacturing account is used to calculate and show the cost of manufacturing those goods. The figure it produces that is used in the trading account is known as the **production cost**.

29.2 Divisions of costs

In a manufacturing business the costs are divided into different types. These may be summarised in chart form as in Exhibit 29.1:

Exhibit 29.1

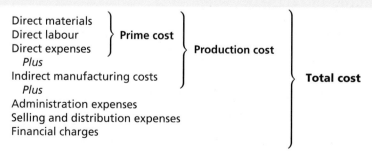

The prime cost items and the other production cost items are shown in the manufacturing account. The administration expenses, selling and distribution expenses and the financial charges appear in the income statement.

29.3 Direct and indirect costs

In Exhibit 29.1, when you see the word *direct* followed by a type of cost, you know that it has been possible to trace the costs to an item being manufactured.

As shown in the chart, the sum of all the **direct costs** is known as the **prime cost**. If a manufacturing-related cost cannot easily be traced to the item being manufactured, then it is an indirect cost and will be included under **indirect manufacturing costs** (which are also sometimes known as 'factory overhead expenses'). 'Production cost' is the sum of prime cost plus the indirect manufacturing costs.

For example, the wages of a machine operator making a particular item will be direct labour. The wages of a foreman in charge of many men on different jobs will be indirect labour, and will be part of the indirect manufacturing costs. Other examples of costs being direct costs would be:

1 Cost of raw materials including carriage inwards on those raw materials.
2 Hire of special machinery for a job.

> **Activity 29.1**
>
> Think about it for a minute and then list five costs you think are direct and five that you think are indirect.

29.4 Indirect manufacturing costs

'Indirect manufacturing costs' are all those costs which occur in the factory or other place where production is being done, but which cannot easily be traced to the items being manufactured. Examples are:

● wages of cleaners
● wages of crane drivers
● rent of a factory
● depreciation of plant and machinery
● costs of operating forklift trucks
● factory power
● factory lighting.

29.5 Administration expenses

'Administration expenses' consist of such items as managers' salaries, legal and accountancy charges, the depreciation of accounting machinery and secretarial salaries.

29.6 Selling and distribution expenses

'Selling and distribution expenses' are items such as sales staff's salaries and commission, carriage outwards, depreciation of delivery vans, advertising and display expenses.

29.7 Financial charges

'Financial charges' are expense items such as bank charges and discounts allowed.

Activity 29.2

Place a tick in the appropriate column for each of the following cost items:

	Direct materials	Direct labour	Direct expenses	Indirect manufacturing costs	Administration expenses	Selling and distribution expenses	Financial charges
(a) Purchases of raw materials							
(b) Direct wages							
(c) General factory expenses							
(d) Depreciation of machinery							
(e) Commission on sales							
(f) Factory rent							
(g) Carriage inwards of raw materials							
(h) Royalties paid							
(i) Inventory of raw materials							
(j) Administration salaries							
(k) Indirect labour							
(l) Bank charges							
(m) Carriage outwards							
(n) Discounts allowed							
(o) Factory lighting							

29.8 Format of financial statements

Manufacturing account section

This is debited with the production cost of goods completed during the accounting period. It contains costs of:

● direct materials;
● direct labour;
● direct expenses; and
● indirect manufacturing costs.

The manufacturing account includes all purchases of raw materials, including the inventory adjustments for raw materials. It also includes inventory adjustments for **work-in-progress** (goods that are partly completed at the end of a period). Let's put this into a series of steps:

1 Add opening inventory of raw materials to purchases and subtract the closing inventory of raw materials.
2 Add in all the direct costs to get the prime cost.
3 Add in all the indirect manufacturing costs.
4 Add the opening inventory of work-in-progress and subtract the closing inventory of work-in-progress to get the production cost of all goods completed in the period.

Thus, when completed, the manufacturing account shows the total of production cost that relates to those manufactured goods that have been available for sale during the period. This figure will then be transferred down to the income statement where it will replace the entry for purchases.

Trading account section of the income statement

This account includes:

● production cost brought down from the manufacturing account
● opening and closing inventory of finished goods
● sales.

When completed, this account shows the gross profit. This is then carried down to the profit and loss account part.

The manufacturing account and the trading account can be shown as in Exhibit 29.2.

Exhibit 29.2

Manufacturing Account

	£
Production costs for the period:	
Direct materials	xxx
Direct labour	xxx
Direct expenses	xxx
Prime cost	xxx
Indirect manufacturing costs	xxx
Production cost of goods completed c/d to trading account	xxx

Trading Account

		£	£
Sales			xxx
Less Production cost of goods sold:			
Opening inventory of finished goods	(A)	xxx	
Add Production costs of goods completed b/d		xxx	
		xxx	
Less Closing inventory of finished goods	(B)	(xxx)	
Gross profit			(xxx)
			xxx

(A) is production costs of goods unsold in previous period.
(B) is production costs of goods unsold at end of the current period.

Profit and loss section of the Income Statement

This is prepared in the way you learnt in earlier chapters in this book. You know, therefore, that it includes:

● gross profit brought down from the trading account
● all administration expenses
● all selling and distribution expenses
● all financial charges.

However, some of the items you would normally put in the profit and loss account part are already included in the manufacturing account, e.g. depreciation on machines, and canteen wages. When completed, this account will show the net profit.

Activity 29.3 Why do you think some expenses have been moved to the manufacturing account?

29.9 A worked example of a manufacturing account

Exhibit 29.3 shows the necessary details for a manufacturing account. It has been assumed that there were no partly completed units (work-in-progress) either at the beginning or end of the period.

Exhibit 29.3

Details of production costs for the year ended 31 December 2017:

	£
1 January 2017, inventory of raw materials	5,000
31 December 2017, inventory of raw materials	7,000
Raw materials purchased	80,000
Manufacturing (direct) wages	210,000
Royalties	1,500
Indirect wages	90,000
Rent of factory – excluding administration and selling and distribution blocks	4,400
Depreciation of plant and machinery in factory	4,000
General indirect expenses	3,100

Manufacturing Account for the year ending 31 December 2017

	£	£
Inventory of raw materials 1.1.2017		5,000
Add Purchases		80,000
		85,000
Less Inventory of raw materials 31.12.2017		(7,000)
Cost of raw materials consumed		78,000
Manufacturing wages		210,000
Royalties		1,500
Prime cost		289,500
Indirect manufacturing costs		
Rent	4,400	
Indirect wages	90,000	
General expenses	3,100	
Depreciation of plant and machinery	4,000	
		101,500
Production cost of goods completed c/d		391,000

Sometimes, if a business has produced less than the customers have demanded, it may buy in some finished goods. In this case, the trading account will have both a figure for purchases of finished goods and a figure for production cost of goods completed.

29.10 Work-in-progress

The production cost to be carried down to the trading account is that of production cost of goods completed during the period. If items have not been completed, they cannot be sold. Therefore, they should not appear in the trading account.

For instance, if we have the following information, we can calculate the transfer to the trading account:

	£
Total production costs expended during the year	50,000
Production costs last year on goods not completed last year, but completed in this year (work-in-progress)	3,000
Production costs this year on goods which were not completed by the year end (work-in-progress)	4,400

The calculation is:

	£
Total production costs expended this year	50,000
Add Costs from last year, in respect of goods completed in this year (work-in-progress)	3,000
	53,000
Less Costs in this year, for goods to be completed next year (work-in-progress)	(4,400)
Production costs expended on goods completed this year	48,600

29.11 Another worked example

Exhibit 29.4

	£
1 January 2017, Inventory of raw materials	8,000
31 December 2017, Inventory of raw materials	10,500
1 January 2017, Work-in-progress	3,500
31 December 2017, Work-in-progress	4,200
Year to 31 December 2017:	
Wages: Direct	39,600
Indirect	25,500
Purchase of raw materials	87,000
Fuel and power	9,900
Direct expenses	1,400
Lubricants	3,000
Carriage inwards on raw materials	2,000
Rent of factory	7,200
Depreciation of factory plant and machinery	4,200
Internal transport expenses	1,800
Insurance of factory buildings and plant	1,500
General factory expenses	3,300

This information produces the following manufacturing account:

Manufacturing Account for the year ending 31 December 2017

	£	£
Inventory of raw materials 1.1.2017		8,000
Add Purchases		87,000
Carriage inwards		2,000
		97,000
Less Inventory of raw materials 31.12.2017		(10,500)
Cost of raw materials consumed		86,500
Direct wages		39,600
Direct expenses		1,400
Prime cost		127,500
Indirect manufacturing costs:		
Fuel and power	9,900	
Indirect wages	25,500	
Lubricants	3,000	
Rent	7,200	
Depreciation of plant and machinery	4,200	
Internal transport expenses	1,800	
Insurance	1,500	
General factory expenses	3,300	
		56,400
		183,900
Add Work-in-progress 1.1.2017		3,500
		187,400
Less Work-in-progress 31.12.2017		(4,200)
Production cost of goods completed c/d		**183,200**

The trading account is concerned with finished goods. If in the above example there had been £3,500 inventory of finished goods at 1 January 2017 and £4,400 at 31 December 2017, and the sales of finished goods amounted to £250,000 then the trading account would be:

Trading Account for the year ending 31 December 2017

	£	£
Sales		250,000
Less Cost of goods sold:		
Inventory of finished goods 1.1.2017	3,500	
Add **Production cost of goods completed b/d**	183,200	
	186,700	
Less Inventory of finished goods 31.12.2017	(4,400)	
		182,300
Gross profit c/d		67,700

The profit and loss section is then constructed in the normal way.

29.12 Apportionment of expenses

Quite often expenses will have to be split between –

● Indirect manufacturing costs: to be charged in the manufacturing account section;
and
● Administration expenses:
● Selling and distribution expenses: } to be charged in the profit and loss section.
● Financial charges:

An example of this could be the rent expense. If the rent is paid separately for each part of the organisation, then it is easy to charge the rent to each sort of expense. However, only one figure of rent may be paid, without any indication as to how much is for the factory, how much is for the selling and distribution building and how much is for the administration building.

How the rent expense will be apportioned in the latter case will depend on the circumstances, using the most equitable way of doing it. A range of methods may be used. Common ones include apportionment on the basis of:

● floor area
● property valuations of each part of the buildings and land.

29.13 Full set of financial statements

A complete worked example is now given. Note that in the profit and loss account part the expenses have been separated so as to show whether they are administration expenses, selling and distribution expenses, or financial charges.

The trial balance in Exhibit 29.5 has been extracted from the books of J. Jarvis, Toy Manufacturer, as at 31 December 2017.

Exhibit 29.5

J. Jarvis
Trial Balance as at 31 December 2017

	Dr	Cr
	£	£
Inventory of raw materials 1.1.2017	21,000	
Inventory of finished goods 1.1.2017	38,900	
Work-in-progress 1.1.2017	13,500	
Wages (direct £180,000; factory indirect £145,000)	325,000	
Royalties	7,000	
Carriage inwards (on raw materials)	3,500	
Purchases of raw materials	370,000	
Productive machinery (cost £280,000)	230,000	
Administration computers (cost £20,000)	12,000	
General factory expenses	31,000	
Lighting	7,500	
Factory power	13,700	
Administration salaries	44,000	
Sales reps' salaries	30,000	
Commission on sales	11,500	
Rent	12,000	
Insurance	4,200	
General administration expenses	13,400	
Bank charges	2,300	
Discounts allowed	4,800	
Carriage outwards	5,900	
Sales		1,000,000
Accounts receivable and accounts payable	142,300	64,000
Bank	16,800	
Cash	1,500	
Drawings	60,000	
Capital as at 1.1.2017		357,800
	1,421,800	1,421,800

Notes at 31.12.2017:

1 Inventory of raw materials £24,000; inventory of finished goods £40,000; work-in-progress £15,000.
2 Lighting, rent and insurance are to be apportioned: factory $5/6$, administration $1/6$.
3 Depreciation on productive machinery and administration computers at 10 per cent per annum on cost.

J. Jarvis
Manufacturing Account and Income Statement for the year ending 31 December 2017

	£	£	£
Inventory of raw materials 1.1.2017			21,000
Add Purchases			370,000
Carriage inwards			3,500
			394,500
Less Inventory raw materials 31.12.2017			(24,000)
Cost of raw materials consumed			370,500
Direct labour			180,000
Royalties			7,000
Prime cost			557,500
Indirect manufacturing costs:			
General factory expenses		31,000	
Lighting $5/6$		6,250	
Power		13,700	
Rent $5/6$		10,000	
Insurance $5/6$		3,500	
Depreciation of productive machinery		28,000	
Indirect labour		145,000	
			237,450
			794,950
Add Work-in-progress 1.1.2017			13,500
			808,450
Less Work-in-progress 31.12.2017			(15,000)
Production cost of goods completed c/d			793,450
Sales			1,000,000
Less Cost of goods sold:			
Inventory of finished goods 1.1.2017		38,900	
Add Production cost of goods completed b/d		793,450	
		832,350	
Less Inventory of finished goods 31.12.2017		(40,000)	
			(792,350)
Gross profit			207,650
Administration expenses			
Administration salaries	44,000		
Rent $1/6$	2,000		
Insurance $1/6$	700		
General expenses	13,400		
Lighting $1/6$	1,250		
Depreciation of administration computers	2,000		
		63,350	
Selling and distribution expenses			
Sales reps' salaries	30,000		
Commission on sales	11,500		
Carriage outwards	5,900		
		47,400	
Financial charges			
Bank charges	2,300		
Discounts allowed	4,800		
		7,100	
			(117,850)
Net profit			89,800

→

J. Jarvis
Balance Sheet as at 31 December 2017

	£	£
Non-current assets		
Productive machinery at cost	280,000	
Less Depreciation to date	(78,000)	
		202,000
Administration computers at cost	20,000	
Less Depreciation to date	(10,000)	
		10,000
		212,000
Current assets		
Inventory		
Raw materials	24,000	
Finished goods	40,000	
Work-in-progress	15,000	
Accounts receivable	142,300	
Bank	16,800	
Cash	1,500	
		239,600
		451,600
Less Current liabilities		
Accounts payable		(64,000)
		387,600
Financed by		
Capital		
Balance as at 1.1.2017		357,800
Add Net profit		89,800
		447,600
Less Drawings		(60,000)
		387,600

29.14 Market value of goods manufactured

The financial statements of Jarvis are subject to the limitation that the respective amounts of the gross profit attributable to the manufacturing side or to the selling side of the business are not known. A technique is sometimes used to bring out this additional information. This method uses the cost that would have been involved if the goods had been bought in their finished state instead of being manufactured by the business. This figure is credited to the manufacturing account and debited to the trading account so as to throw up two figures of gross profit instead of one. It should be pointed out that the net profit will remain unaffected. All that will have happened will be that the gross profit will be shown as two figures instead of one. When added together, they will total £207,650.

Assume that the cost of buying the goods instead of manufacturing them had been £950,000. The relevant parts of the Manufacturing Account and Income Statement will then be:

Manufacturing Account and Income Statement extract for the year ending
31 December 2017

	£	£
Market value of goods completed		950,000
Less Production cost of goods completed (as before)		(793,450)
Gross profit on manufacture c/d		156,550
Sales		1,000,000
Inventory of finished goods 1.1.2017	38,900	
Add Market value of goods completed b/d	950,000	
	988,900	
Less Inventory of finished goods 31.12.2017	(40,000)	
		(948,900)
Gross profit on trading c/d		51,100
Gross profit		
On manufacturing	156,550	
On trading	51,100	
		207,650

Learning outcomes

You should now have learnt:

1 Why manufacturing accounts are used.

2 How to prepare a manufacturing account and income statement.

3 That the trading account section of the income statement is used for calculating the gross profit made by selling the goods manufactured.

4 That the profit and loss account section of the income statement shows as net profit what is left of gross profit after all administration, selling and distribution and finance costs incurred have been deducted.

5 That work-in-progress, both at the start and the close of a period, must be adjusted so as to identify the production costs of goods completed in the period.

Answers to activities

29.1 You may have included some of the following:

	Direct costs	*Indirect costs*
(1)	raw materials	canteen wages
(2)	machine operator's wages	business rates
(3)	packer's wages	rent
(4)	machine set-up costs	insurance
(5)	crane hire for building contract	storage of finished goods costs

However, you can only really do a split like this if you have a specific job or product in mind. You must first identify the 'cost object', that is, the item you are making or providing. Taking the example of a construction company building a hotel (it is engaged in other similar projects at the same time). The direct and indirect costs may include:

	Direct costs	*Indirect costs*
(1)	concrete	site canteen wages
(2)	forklift truck operator's wages	company lawyer's salary
(3)	bricklayer's wages	company architect's salary
(4)	steel girders	company headquarters insurance
(5)	windows	company warehousing costs

Now you should see that the indirect costs are not solely incurred in order to build the hotel. This is the key. Direct costs are those costs you can specifically link to a specific job. All the other costs of a job are indirect.

29.2   Direct materials (a) (g) (i)
Direct labour (b)
Direct expenses (h)
Indirect manufacturing costs (c) (d) (f) (k) (o)
Administration expenses (j)
Selling and distribution expenses (e) (m)
Financial charges (l) (n)

29.3   Because only administration expenses, selling and distribution expenses, and financial charges appear in the profit and loss account part when a manufacturing account is being used. The rest all arose because manufacturing was taking place and can be directly or indirectly attributed to the products being produced, so they appear in the manufacturing account.

Review questions

29.1   A business both buys loose tools and also makes some itself. The following data is available concerning the years ended 31 December 2018, 2019 and 2020.

2018		£
Jan 1	Inventory of loose tools	6,000
	During the year:	
	Bought loose tools from suppliers	8,000
	Made own loose tools: the cost of wages of employees being £1,300	
	and the materials cost £900	
Dec 31	Loose tools valued at	12,000
2019		
	During the year:	
	Loose tools bought from suppliers	4,000
	Made own loose tools: the cost of wages of employees being £1,600	
	and the materials cost £1,200	
Dec 31	Loose tools valued at	12,800
2020		
	During the year:	
	Loose tools bought from suppliers	7,200
	Made own loose tools: the cost of wages of employees being £1,000	
	and the materials cost £1,340.	
	Received £320 refund from a supplier for faulty tools returned to him	
Dec 31	Loose tools valued at	14,600

You are to draw up the Loose Tools Account for the three years, showing the amount transferred as an expense in each year to the Manufacturing Account.

29.2   Using whichever of the following figures are required, prepare a manufacturing account and trading account for 2020. The manufacturing account should show clearly the prime cost of manufacture and the production cost of finished goods produced.

	£
Inventory, 1 January 2020:	
Raw materials	24,600
Partly finished goods	20,200
Finished goods	18,600
Inventory, 31 December 2020:	
Raw materials	31,300
Partly finished goods	23,400
Finished goods	29,200
Purchases of raw materials	165,400
Carriage on raw materials	9,100
Salaries and wages: factory (including £44,500 for management and supervision)	151,400
Salaries and wages: general office	28,400
Rent and business rates (three-quarters works, one-quarter office)	3,000
Lighting and heating (seven-eighths works, one-eighth office)	5,600
Repairs to machinery	3,400
Depreciation of machinery	5,600
Factory direct expenses	730
Insurance of plant and machinery	860
Sales	406,120

Note: partly finished goods are valued at their production cost.

29.3A From the following information, prepare a manufacturing account and income statement for the year ending 31 December 2019 and a balance sheet as at 31 December 2019 for J Jones' business:

	£	£
Purchase of raw materials	258,000	
Fuel and light	21,000	
Administration salaries	17,000	
Factory wages	59,000	
Carriage outwards	4,000	
Rent and business rates	21,000	
Sales		482,000
Returns inward	7,000	
General office expenses	9,000	
Repairs to plant and machinery	9,000	
Inventory at 1 January 2019:		
Raw materials	21,000	
Work-in-progress	14,000	
Finished goods	23,000	
Sundry accounts payable		37,000
Capital account		457,000
Freehold premises	410,000	
Plant and machinery	80,000	
Accounts receivable	20,000	
Accumulated provision for depreciation on plant and machinery		8,000
Cash in hand	11,000	
	984,000	984,000

Make provision for the following:

(i) Inventory in hand at 31 December 2019:
Raw materials £25,000
Work-in-progress £11,000
Finished goods £26,000.

(*ii*) Depreciation of 10% on plant and machinery using the straight line method.
(*iii*) 80% of fuel and light and 75% of rent and rates to be charged to manufacturing.
(*iv*) Allowance for doubtful debts: 5% of accounts receivable.
(*v*) £4,000 outstanding for fuel and light.
(*vi*) Rent and business rates paid in advance: £5,000.

29.4 Prepare a manufacturing account and income statement from the following balances of Z. Varga for the year ending 31 December 2020.

	£
Inventory at 1 January 2020:	
Raw materials	50,800
Work-in-progress	62,200
Finished goods	46,520
Purchases: Raw materials	183,070
Carriage on raw materials	3,920
Direct labour	168,416
Office salaries	66,838
Rent	10,400
Office lighting and heating	8,840
Depreciation expense: Works machinery	20,400
Office equipment	4,600
Sales	637,244
Factory fuel and power	16,240

Rent is to be apportioned: Factory $^3/_4$; Office $^1/_4$. Inventory at 31 December 2020 was: Raw materials £57,800; Work-in-progress £49,200; Finished goods £57,692.

29.5 From the following information, draw up a manufacturing account and the trading account section of the income statement for the six months ending 30 September 2020. You should show clearly:

(*a*) Cost of raw materials consumed.
(*b*) Prime cost of production.
(*c*) Production cost of finished goods.
(*d*) Gross profit.

	£
Inventory, 1 April 2020:	
Raw materials	2,990
Work-in-progress	3,900
Finished goods	15,300
Inventory, 30 September 2020:	
Raw materials	4,200
Work-in-progress	3,600
Finished goods	17,700
Purchases of raw materials	15,630
Carriage on raw materials	126
Direct wages	48,648
Factory general expenses	7,048
Office salaries	22,200
Depreciation of office furniture	420
Carriage outwards	191
Advertising	1,472
Bad debts	200
Sales less returns	112,410
Sales of scrap	1,317
Discounts received	188
Depreciation of factory equipment	4,200
Rent and business rates (factory three-quarters, office one-quarter)	2,800

29.6A From the following figures prepare a manufacturing account and the trading account section of the income statement so as to show:

(a) Cost of raw materials used in production.
(b) Prime cost.
(c) Production cost of finished goods produced.
(d) Cost of goods sold.
(e) Gross profit.

	£
Inventory at 1 January 2020:	
Raw materials	10,500
Goods in course of manufacture (at factory cost)	2,400
Finished goods	14,300
Inventory at 31 March 2020:	
Raw materials	10,200
Goods in course of manufacture (at factory cost)	2,900
Finished goods	13,200
Expenditure during the quarter:	
Purchases of raw materials	27,200
Factory wages: direct	72,600
indirect	13,900
Carriage on purchases of raw materials	700
Rent and business rates of the factory	1,200
Power	2,000
Depreciation of machinery	3,900
Repairs to factory buildings	1,300
Sundry factory expenses	900
Sales during the quarter	160,400

29.7 E. Wilson is a manufacturer. His trial balance at 31 December 2020 is as follows:

	£	£
Delivery van expenses	1,760	
Lighting and heating: Factory	7,220	
Office	1,490	
Manufacturing wages	72,100	
General expenses: Factory	8,100	
Office	1,940	
Sales reps: commission	11,688	
Purchase of raw materials	57,210	
Rent: Factory	6,100	
Office	2,700	
Machinery (cost £40,000)	28,600	
Office equipment (cost £9,000)	8,200	
Office salaries	17,740	
Accounts receivable	34,200	
Accounts payable		9,400
Bank	16,142	
Sales		194,800
Van (cost £6,800)	6,200	
Inventory at 31 December 2019:		
Raw materials	13,260	
Finished goods	41,300	
Drawings	24,200	
Capital at 31 December 2019		155,950
	360,150	360,150

Prepare the manufacturing account and income statement for the year ending 31 December 2020 and a balance sheet as at that date. Give effect to the following adjustments:

1 Inventory at 31 December 2020: raw materials £14,510; finished goods £44,490. There is no work-in-progress.
2 Depreciate machinery £3,000; office equipment £600; van £1,200.
3 Manufacturing wages due but unpaid at 31 December 2020 £550; office rent prepaid £140.

29.8 The financial year end of Mendip Limited is 30 June. At 30 June 2020, the following balances are available:

	£
Freehold land and buildings at cost	143,000
Plant and machinery at cost	105,000
Accumulated depreciation on plant and machinery	23,000
Purchase of raw materials	130,100
Sales	317,500
Factory rates	3,000
Factory heat and light	6,500
Accounts receivable	37,200
Accounts payable	30,900
Wages (including £15,700 for supervision)	63,000
Direct factory expenses	9,100
Selling expenses	11,000
Office salaries and general expenses	43,000
Bank	24,500
General reserve	30,000
Retained profits	18,000
Inventory 1 July 2019: Raw materials	20,000
Finished goods	38,000
Dividends paid	840
Ordinary shares	20,000

(i) The inventory at 30 June 2020 was: raw materials £22,000; finished goods £35,600.
(ii) Salaries include £6,700 for directors' fees.
(iii) Depreciation is to be charged at 10% on cost of plant and machinery.

Required:
Prepare a manufacturing account and income statement for the year ending 30 June 2020.

Author's Note: if necessary, see Chapter 28 for guidance regarding the financial statements of limited companies.

29.9A Jean Marsh owns a small business making and selling children's toys. The following trial balance was extracted from her books on 31 December 2020.

	Dr £	Cr £
Capital		15,000
Drawings	2,000	
Sales		90,000
Inventory at 1 January 2020:		
Raw materials	3,400	
Finished goods	6,100	
Purchases of raw materials	18,000	
Carriage inwards	800	
Factory wages	18,500	
Office salaries	16,900	
J. Marsh: salary and expenses	10,400	
General expenses:		
Factory	1,200	
Office	750	
Lighting	2,500	
Rent	3,750	
Insurance	950	
Advertising	1,400	
Bad debts	650	
Discount received		1,600
Carriage outwards	375	
Plant and machinery, at cost less depreciation	9,100	
Car, at cost less depreciation	4,200	
Bank	3,600	
Cash in hand	325	
Accounts receivable and accounts payable	7,700	6,000
	112,600	112,600

You are given the following additional information.

1 Inventory at 31 December 2020:

Raw materials	£2,900
Finished goods	£8,200

There was no work-in-progress.

2 Depreciation for the year is to be charged as follows:

Plant and machinery	£1,500
Car	£500

3 At 31 December 2020 insurance paid in advance was £150 and office general expenses unpaid were £75.
4 Lighting and rent are to be apportioned: $^4/_5$ Factory, $^1/_5$ Office.
   Insurance is to be apportioned: $^3/_4$ Factory, $^1/_4$ Office.
5 Jean is the business's salesperson and her salary and expenses are to be treated as a selling expense. She has sole use of the business's car.

Questions:
For the year ended 31 December 2020 prepare:
(a) the manufacturing account showing prime cost and factory cost of production.
(b) the trading account section of the income statement.
(c) the profit and loss account section of the income statement, distinguishing between administrative and selling costs.
(d) a balance sheet as at 31 December 2020.Author's Note

(Midland Examining Group: GCSE)

Author's Note: Part (d) of the question was not in the original examination question. It has been added to give you further practice.

29.10   The following list of balances as at 31 July 2019 has been extracted from the books of Jane Seymour who commenced business on 1 August 2018 as a designer and manufacturer of kitchen furniture:

	£
Plant and machinery, at cost on 1 August 2018	60,000
Motor vehicles, at cost on 1 August 2018	30,000
Loose tools, at cost	9,000
Sales	170,000
Raw materials purchased	43,000
Direct factory wages	39,000
Light and power	5,000
Indirect factory wages	8,000
Machinery repairs	1,600
Motor vehicle running expenses	12,000
Rent and insurances	11,600
Administrative staff salaries	31,000
Administrative expenses	9,000
Sales and distribution staff salaries	13,000
Capital at 1 August 2018	122,000
Sundry accounts receivable	16,500
Sundry accounts payable	11,200
Balance at bank	8,500
Drawings	6,000

Additional information for the year ended 31 July 2019:

(*i*)   It is estimated that the plant and machinery will be used in the business for ten years and the motor vehicles used for four years: in both cases it is estimated that the residual value will be nil. The straight line method of providing for depreciation is to be used.

(*ii*)   Light and power charges accrued due at 31 July 2019 amounted to £1,000 and insurances prepaid at 31 July 2019 totalled £800.

(*iii*)   Inventory was valued at cost at 31 July 2019 as follows:

Raw materials	£7,000
Finished goods	£10,000

(*iv*)   The valuation of work-in-progress at 31 July 2019 included variable and fixed factory overheads and amounted to £12,300.

(*v*)   Two-thirds of the light and power and rent and insurances costs are to be allocated to the factory costs and one-third to general administration costs.

(*vi*)   Motor vehicle costs are to be allocated equally to factory costs and general administration costs.

(*vii*)   Goods manufactured during the year are to be transferred to the trading account at £95,000.

(*viii*) Loose tools in hand on 31 July 2019 were valued at £5,000.

Required:

(*a*)   Prepare a manufacturing account and income statement for the year ending 31 July 2019 of Jane Seymour.

(*b*)   An explanation of how each of the following accounting concepts have affected the preparation of the above accounts:
   ● conservatism
   ● matching
   ● going concern.

(*Association of Accounting Technicians*)

Departmental accounts

After you have studied this chapter, you should be able to:

● draw up departmental income statements on the gross profit basis
● draw up departmental income statements on the contribution basis
● calculate the contribution made by each section of a business
● explain why departmental accounts can be more meaningful to management than a single income statement
● apportion expenses between departments on an appropriate basis

In this chapter, you'll learn how to prepare departmental income statements and about how they can be used in order to inform decision-makers considering the closure of a department. You'll learn how to apportion indirect costs and, finally, you'll learn that basing departmental income statements on contribution is both more helpful and informative and less misleading than when they are prepared on the gross profit basis.

30.1 Use of departmental accounts

Some items of accounting information are more useful than others. For a retail store with five departments, it is better to know that the store has made £100,000 gross profit than not to know what the gross profit was. However, it would obviously be better if we knew how much gross profit was made in each department.

Assume that the gross profits and losses of a business's departments were as follows:

Department	Gross profit	Gross loss
	£	£
A	40,000	
B	30,000	
C	50,000	
D		80,000
E	60,000	
	180,000	80,000

Gross profit of the business, £100,000.

If we knew the above information, we could see how well, or how badly, each part of the business was doing. If we closed down Department D we could make a greater total gross profit of £180,000. Perhaps we could replace Department D with a department which would make a gross profit instead of a gross loss.

Activity 30.1   Why do you think we have only mentioned gross profit and haven't referred to net profit?

You would have to know more about the business before you could be certain what the figures in the account mean. For example, some stores deliberately allow parts of their business to lose money, so that customers come to the store to buy the cheap goods and then spend money in the other departments.

Accounting information seldom tells all the story. It serves as one measure, but there are other non-accounting factors to be considered before a relevant decision for action can be made.

The various pros and cons of the actions to be taken to increase the overall profitability of a business cannot therefore be properly considered until the departmental gross profits or gross losses are known. It must not be thought that departmental accounts refer only to department stores, such as Marks & Spencer or Debenhams. They can be prepared for the various departments or sections of any business.

The reputation of many a successful business person has been built up on an ability to utilise the departmental account principle to guide decision-making and so increase the profitability of a business. The lesson still has to be learnt by many medium-sized and small businesses. It is one of accounting's greatest and simplest aids to business efficiency.

To find out how profitable each part of the business is, we have to prepare departmental accounts to give us the facts for each department.

30.2 Allocation of expenses

The expenses of a business can be split between the various departments, and then the net profit for each department calculated. Each expense is divided between the departments on what is considered to be the most logical basis. This will differ considerably between businesses. An example of a departmental income statement drawn up in such a manner is shown in Exhibit 30.1:

Exhibit 30.1

Northern Stores has three departments:

	(a) Jewellery £	(b) Hairdressing £	(c) Clothing £
Inventory of goods or materials at 1 January 2018	20,000	15,000	30,000
Purchases	110,000	30,000	150,000
Inventory of goods or materials at 31 December 2018	30,000	25,000	40,000
Sales and work done	180,000	90,000	270,000
Wages of assistants in each department	28,000	50,000	60,000

The following expenses cannot be traced to any particular department:

	£
Rent	8,200
Administration expenses	48,000
Air conditioning and lighting	6,000
General expenses	2,400

It is decided to apportion (i.e. spread) the cost of rent together with air conditioning and lighting in accordance with the floor space occupied by each department. These were taken up in the ratios of (a) one-fifth, (b) half, (c) three-tenths. Administration expenses and general expenses are to be split in the ratio of sales and work done.

Northern Stores
Departmental Income Statement for the year ending 31 December 2018[Note]

	(a) Jewellery		(b) Hairdressing		(c) Clothing	
	£	£	£	£	£	£
Sales and work done		180,000		90,000		270,000
Less: Cost of goods or materials:						
Inventory 1.1.2018	20,000		15,000		30,000	
Add Purchases	110,000		30,000		150,000	
	130,000		45,000		180,000	
Less Inventory 31.12.2018	(30,000)		(25,000)		(40,000)	
		(100,000)		(20,000)		(140,000)
Gross profit		80,000		70,000		130,000
Less Expenses:						
Wages	28,000		55,000		60,000	
Rent	1,640		4,100		2,460	
Administration expenses	16,000		8,000		24,000	
Air conditioning and lighting	1,200		3,000		1,800	
General expenses	800		400		1,200	
		(47,640)		(70,500)		(89,460)
Net profit/(loss)		32,360		(500)		40,540

The overall net profit is, therefore, £32,360 − £500 + £40,540 = £72,400.

Note: This has been prepared on the gross profit basis.

This way of calculating net profits and losses seems to imply a precision that is, in fact, lacking. This can lead to the mistaken interpretation that the loss of £500 by the Hairdressing Department would be saved if the department were closed down. This is not what the loss of £500 implies. It has already been stated that different departments are very often dependent on one another, and the answer to Activity 30.1 explained why. Therefore, you should realise that this amount of loss would not necessarily be saved by closing the Hairdressing Department.

To explain this further, the calculation of departmental net profits and losses is dependent on the arbitrary division of indirect costs. It is by no means certain that the indirect costs of the Hairdressing Department would be avoided if it were closed down. Assuming that the sales staff of the department could be discharged without compensation, then £55,000 would be saved in wages. The other expenses shown under the Hairdressing Department would not, however, necessarily disappear.

The rent may still be payable in full even if the department were closed down. The administration expenses may turn out to be only slightly down, say from £48,000 to £46,100 – a saving of £1,900; air conditioning and lighting may fall by £300 to £5,700; general expenses may be reduced by £100 to £2,300. None of these reductions are obvious from the Departmental Income Statement.

Taking these cost reductions as what would actually happen were the Hairdressing Department to be closed, indicates that there would be a saving of £57,300:

	£
Administration expenses	1,900
Air conditioning and lighting	300
General expenses	100
Wages	55,000
	57,300

But when open, assuming this year is typical, the Hairdressing Department makes £70,000 gross profit. The business is therefore £12,700 a year better off (i.e. £70,000 minus £57,300) when the department is open than when it is closed, subject to certain assumptions, such as:

(a) That the remaining departments would not be profitably expanded into the space vacated to give greater proportionate benefits than the Hairdressing Department.
(b) That a new type of department which would be more profitable than hairdressing could not be set up.
(c) That the floor space could not be leased to another business at a more profitable figure than that shown by hairdressing – you can see examples of this in many large stores where a part of the store has been leased to a coffee house like Starbucks or Costa Coffee.

Activity 30.2 What other possible events that can only occur if the department is closed could make it profitable to close the Hairdressing Department?

There are also other factors which, though not easily seen in an accounting context, are still extremely pertinent. They are concerned with the possible loss of confidence in the business by customers generally – what appears to be an ailing business does not usually attract large numbers of customers.

Also, the effect on the remaining staff should not be ignored. The fear that the dismissal of the hairdressing staff may also happen to them may result in the loss of other staff, especially the most competent members who could easily find work elsewhere, and so the general quality of the staff may decline with serious consequences for the business.

30.3 Allocation of expenses: a better method

It is less misleading to show costs split as follows:

First section of income statement	Direct costs allocated entirely to the department (i.e. costs which would *not* be paid if the department closed down)
Second section of income statement	Costs not directly traceable to the department or which would still be payable even if the department closed down (i.e. indirect costs and fixed costs)

The *surpluses* brought down from the first of these two sections represent the **contribution** that each department has made to cover the remaining costs, the remainder being the net profit for the whole of the business. If direct costs of a department were greater than the sales figure then the result would be a **negative contribution**.

From the figures given in Exhibit 30.1 the departmental income statement prepared on the basis of contribution rather than gross profit would appear as in Exhibit 30.2:

Exhibit 30.2

Northern Stores
Departmental Income Statement for the year ending 31 December 2018
(Contribution basis)

	(a) Jewellery		(b) Hairdressing		(c) Clothing	
	£	£	£	£	£	£
Sales and work done		180,000		90,000		270,000
Less Cost of goods or materials:						
Inventory 1.1.2018	20,000		15,000		30,000	
Add Purchases	110,000		30,000		150,000	
	130,000		45,000		180,000	
Less Inventory 31.12.2018	(30,000)		(25,000)		(40,000)	
	100,000		20,000		140,000	
Wages	28,000		55,000		60,000	
		(128,000)		(75,000)		(200,000)
Contribution c/d		52,000		15,000		70,000

All Departments

	£	£
Contribution b/d:		
Jewellery	52,000	
Hairdressing	15,000	
Clothing	70,000	
		137,000
Less		
Rent	8,200	
Administration expenses	48,000	
Air conditioning and lighting	6,000	
General expenses	2,400	
		(64,600)
Net profit		72,400

As you can see, this is the same overall net profit as found in Exhibit 30.1, and now no department is seen as making a loss.

The contribution of a department is the result of activities which are under the control of a departmental manager. The efficiency of their control will affect the amount of the contribution. If a department's contribution is negative, it would be a strong candidate for closure, or for a change in its management. Similarly, if a department has a far lower contribution to revenue ratio than the others, it may be a candidate for closure if its closure would allow other departments to expand.

The costs in the second section, such as rent, insurance or lighting, cannot be affected by the departmental manager. It is therefore only fair if the departmental manager is judged by the *contribution* of his or her department rather than the net profit of the department.

In examinations, you must answer the questions as set, and not give your own interpretations of what the question should be. Therefore, if examiners give details of the methods of apportionment of expenses, then they are really looking for an answer in the same style as Exhibit 30.1. However, if you are then asked to comment on the performance of individual departments, it would be wise to indicate that, had a contribution approach been adopted, a different view of their performance may have been obtained which would have been more meaningful and useful than the one produced using the approach taken in Exhibit 30.1.

30.4 The balance sheet

The balance sheet does not usually show assets and liabilities split between different departments.

30.5 Inter-departmental transfers

Purchases made for one department may be subsequently sold in another department. In such a case, the items should be deducted from the figure for purchases of the original purchasing department, and added to the figure for purchases for the subsequent selling department.

Learning outcomes

You should now have learnt:

1 How to prepare departmental income statements on the gross profit basis.

2 How to prepare departmental income statements on the contribution basis.

3 That it is desirable for the contribution of each section of a business to be calculated to aid management decisions and that the contribution-based income statement is more appropriate for departmental closure decisions than the gross-profit-based statement.

4 That costs should be divided between those which can logically be allocated to departments and those which cannot.

5 That a negative contribution is only one guide as to whether a section of a business should be closed. There may be other factors which would go against such a closure, and others that would suggest that even departments with positive contributions should be closed.

Answers to activities

30.1 Indirect costs and fixed costs. Net profit includes them. Unlike a manufacturing company, in a trading company, the only costs that are included in the calculation of gross profit are the purchase costs of the items that were sold.

Indirect costs and direct wages and direct expenses appear in the income statement as deductions from gross profit. So far as the direct costs are concerned, it would be appropriate to include them in any comparison between departments because they were definitely incurred for and by the department to which their cost is charged. However, it is not appropriate to include the indirect costs because they have to be spread across all the departments on a basis that is subjective rather than objective. That is, you cannot be certain that they were incurred in respect of the department to which they are charged.

Fixed costs can be direct expenses (e.g. lease of a cash register) or indirect expenses (e.g. rates). They are period costs of the business. They cannot be changed in the timescale you are looking at. If you wanted to know the net profit of a department, you would need to spread the indirect fixed costs across all the departments. This results in charges that are, at best, a close approximation to the extent to which each department merits that level of indirect fixed cost.

Often it has very little to do with appropriateness of the charge made on each department. If you tried to use net profit to make comparisons, you would be basing any conclusion on figures that could easily have been very different had another, possibly, more appropriate method of spreading the indirect fixed costs been used. In addition to all this, there is also the question of what happens to the fixed costs, both direct and indirect, that you have charged to a department that you have decided to close because it is making a net loss. Perhaps the other departments are only profitable because the loss-making department is absorbing some of the fixed costs.

30.2 There is a large range of possibilities. You may have suggested some of the following:

● a restaurant could be opened by the store, attracting more shoppers and, therefore, boosting the sales of the remaining departments;
● the floor space could be used for a children's play area, thereby making the store more attractive to shoppers with young children;
● the floor space could be converted to contain chairs, tables, plants and sculptures so that shoppers can relax and chat to each other during the time they are in the store – you can see examples of this in many modern shopping centres.

Review questions

30.1 From the following you are to draw up a departmental trading account for SJD Sports Stores for the year ending 30 June 2019:

Inventory:	1.7.2018		30.6.2019
	£		£
Footwear Department	69,000		77,000
Clothing Department	56,000		48,000
Equipment Department	47,000		53,000

Sales for the year:	£
Footwear Department	621,000
Clothing Department	419,000
Equipment Department	328,000

Purchases for the year:	
Footwear Department	404,000
Clothing Department	287,000
Equipment Department	185,000

30.2 J. Horner is the proprietor of a shop selling paintings and ornaments. For the purposes of his financial statements he wishes the business to be divided into two departments:

Department A	Paintings
Department B	Ornaments

The following balances have been extracted from his nominal ledger at 31 August 2020:

	Dr	Cr
	£	£
Sales Department A		75,000
Sales Department B		50,000
Inventory Department A, 1 September 2019	1,250	
Inventory Department B, 1 September 2019	1,000	
Purchases Department A	51,000	
Purchases Department B	38,020	
Wages of sales assistants Department A	7,200	
Wages of sales assistants Department B	6,800	
Picture framing costs	300	
General office salaries	13,200	
Fire insurance – buildings	360	
Lighting and heating	620	
Repairs to premises	175	
Internal telephone	30	
Cleaning	180	
Accountancy charges	1,490	
General office expenses	510	

Inventory at 31 August 2020 was valued at:

Department A £1,410
Department B £912

The proportion of the total floor area occupied by each department was:

Department A two-fifths
Department B three-fifths

Prepare J. Horner's departmental income statement for the year ending 31 August 2020, apportioning the costs, where necessary, to show the net profit or loss of each department. The apportionment should be made by using the methods as shown:

Area – Fire insurance, Lighting and heating, Repairs, Telephone, Cleaning; Turnover – General office salaries, Accountancy, General office expenses.

30.3A From the following list of balances you are required to prepare a departmental income statement for the year ending 31 March 2018, in respect of the business carried on under the name of Jack's Superstores:

			£	£
Rent and business rates				9,300
Delivery expenses				3,600
Commission				10,000
Insurance				1,800
Purchases:	Dept.	A	101,300	
		B	81,200	
		C	62,900	
				245,400
Discounts received				2,454
Salaries and wages				91,200
Advertising				2,307
Sales:	Dept.	A	180,000	
		B	138,000	
		C	82,000	
				400,000
Depreciation expense				4,200
Opening inventory:	Dept.	A	27,100	
		B	21,410	
		C	17,060	
				65,570
Administration and general expenses				19,800
Closing inventory:	Dept.	A	23,590	
		B	15,360	
		C	18,200	
				57,150

Except as follows, expenses are to be apportioned equally between the departments.

Delivery expenses – proportionate to sales.
Commission –2 $\frac{1}{2}$ per cent of sales.
Salaries and wages; Insurance – in the proportion of 3:2:1.
Discounts received – 1 per cent of purchases.

Joint ventures

Learning objectives

After you have studied this chapter, you should be able to:

- explain what is meant by the term 'joint venture'
- explain why separate joint venture accounts are kept by each of the parties to a joint venture
- make the entries in the accounts for a joint venture
- calculate and enter the profits of the joint venture into the accounts of the parties to the joint venture
- identify the amount owing to or owed by each of the parties to the other parties in the joint venture and make the appropriate entries in the joint venture accounts when payment is made and received
- name two accounting standards relating to joint ventures

Introduction

Joint ventures have existed since Roman times but for the last 200–300 years they have tended to be used for small-scale activities. This has changed in recent times and they are becoming increasingly commonly used for larger-scale business projects. In this chapter, you'll learn how to record joint ventures in the books of the parties to a joint venture. You'll learn how to calculate profits and identify how much each of the parties must pay to the other parties at the end of the joint venture. Finally, you'll learn that accounting standards have been issued to regulate accounting for longer-term and larger joint ventures.

31.1 Nature of joint ventures

Sometimes a particular business venture can best be done by two or more businesses joining together to do it instead of doing it separately. The joining together is for that one venture only, it is not joining together to make a continuing business.

Such projects are known as **joint ventures**. For instance, a merchant might provide the capital, the transport to the markets and the selling skills. The farmer grows the produce. The profits or losses are then shared between them in agreed ratios. It is like a partnership, but only for this one venture. There may be several joint ventures between the same businesses, but each one is a separate venture. The agreements for each venture may be different from each other.

31.2 Accounting for large joint ventures

For large-scale or long-term joint ventures, a separate bank account and separate set of books are kept. In such cases the calculation of profit is not difficult. It is similar to preparing a set of financial statements for an ordinary business.

31.3 Accounting for smaller joint ventures

No separate set of books or separate bank accounts are kept for smaller joint ventures. Each of the parties will record in their own books only those transactions with which they have been concerned. Exhibit 31.1 gives an example of such a joint venture.

Exhibit 31.1

White of London and Green of Glasgow enter into a joint venture. White is to supply the goods and pay some of the expenses. Green is to sell the goods and receive the cash, and pay the remainder of the expenses. Profits are to be shared equally.

Details of the transactions are as follows:

	£
White supplied the goods costing	1,800
White paid wages	200
White paid for storage expenses	160
Green paid transport expenses	120
Green paid selling expenses	320
Green received cash from sales of all the goods	3,200

Stage 1

White and Green will each have entered up their own part of the transactions. White will have opened an account named 'Joint Venture with Green'. Similarly, Green will have opened a 'Joint Venture with White' account. The double entry to these joint venture accounts will be:

In White's books:

Payments by White:	Debit Joint venture with Green
	Credit Cash Book
Goods supplied to Green:	Debit Joint venture with Green
	Credit purchases

In Green's books:

Payments by Green:	Debit Joint venture with White
	Credit Cash Book
Cash received by Green:	Debit Cash Book
	Credit Joint venture with White

At this point the joint venture accounts in each of their books will appear as follows:

White's books (in London):

Joint Venture with Green

	£		
Purchases	1,800		
Cash: wages	200		
Cash: storage expenses	160		

Green's books (in Glasgow):

Joint Venture with White

	£		£
Cash: transport expenses	120	Cash: sales	3,200
Cash: selling expenses	320		

Stage 2

At this stage, White and Green know only the details in their own set of books. They do not yet know what the details are in the other person's books.

This means that they cannot yet calculate profits, or find out how much cash has to be paid or received to close the venture. To do this they must each send a copy of their joint venture accounts to the other person.

Each person will then draw up a **memorandum joint venture account**, to include all the details from each joint venture account. The memorandum joint venture account is not a double entry account. It is drawn up only (*a*) to find out the shares of net profit or loss of each party to the joint venture, and (*b*) to help calculate the amounts payable and receivable to close the venture. White and Green's memorandum joint venture account is now shown:

White and Green
Memorandum Joint Venture Account

	£	£		£
Purchases		1,800	Sales	3,200
Wages		200		
Storage expenses		160		
Transport expenses		120		
Selling expenses		320		
Net profit:				
White (one-half)	300			
Green (one-half)	300			
		600		
		3,200		3,200

Note: The profit is the difference between the two sides of the account. You find out what the balancing figure is; in this case, it is £600. Then you split it in the profit sharing ratio. In this case, profits are shared equally. White and Green, therefore, each receive half the profit, £300 each. Now you enter the figures, £300 to White, £300 to Green, and the total of £600, which balances and closes off the account.

 Activity 31.1

Look closely at the Memorandum Joint Venture account. Where does each entry in the Memorandum Joint Venture account appear in the Joint Venture with Green and Joint Venture with White T-accounts? Are they on the same side in each case, or the opposite side? What does this tell you about making entries in the Memorandum Joint Venture account?

Stage 3

The net profit shares for White and Green need to be brought into their own books. This is done as follows:

White's books:
Debit share of profit to Joint Venture with Green account
    Credit White's profit and loss account

The Joint Venture account in White's books now looks like this:

White's books (in London):

Joint Venture with Green

	£		
Purchases	1,800		
Cash: wages	200		
Cash: storage expenses	160		
Profit and loss: share of profit	300		

You then do the same in Green's books:

Green's books:

  Debit share of profit to Joint Venture with White account
    Credit Green's profit and loss account

Green's books (in Glasgow):

Joint Venture with White

	£		£
Cash: transport expenses	120	Cash: sales	3,200
Cash: selling expenses	320		
Profit and loss: share of profit	300		

It won't come as a surprise to see that you have now copied the profit share entries from the Memorandum Joint Venture account into the Joint Venture accounts held by White and Green. Now you need to balance-off the two Joint Venture accounts:

White's books (in London):

Joint Venture with Green

	£		£
Purchases	1,800	Balance c/d	2,460
Cash: wages	200		
Cash: storage expenses	160		
Profit and loss: share of profit	300		
	2,460		2,460
Balance b/d	2,460		

Green's books (in Glasgow):

Joint Venture with White

	£		£
Cash: transport expenses	120	Cash: sales	3,200
Cash: selling expenses	320		
Profit and loss: share of profit	300		
Balance c/d	2,460		
	3,200		3,200
		Balance b/d	2,460

Activity 31.2

Can you remember what is meant by a debit balance? Is it where the balance c/d is a debit or where the balance b/d is a debit?

Finally, the parties in the joint venture need to settle their debts to each other. They know whether they are to pay money or receive money when they look at the side of their copy of the joint venture account and see whether the balance is a debit or a credit:

(a) If the balance brought down is a credit balance, money is owing to the other party in the joint venture. In this case, Green owes White the amount shown by the credit balance, £2,460.

(b) If the balance brought down is a debit balance, money is due from the other party in the joint venture. In this case White is owed the amount of the balance, £2,460 by Green.

The payment is now made by Green to White and the final entry is made in each of the joint venture accounts, closing off the accounts.

White's books (in London):

Joint Venture with Green

	£		£
Purchases	1,800	Balance c/d	2,460
Cash: wages	200		
Cash: storage expenses	160		
Profit and loss: share of profit	300		
	2,460		2,460
Balance b/d	2,460	Cash: settlement from Green	2,460

Green's books (in Glasgow):

Joint Venture with White

	£		£
Cash: transport expenses	120	Cash: sales	3,200
Cash: selling expenses	320		
Profit and loss: share of profit	300		
Balance c/d	2,460		
	3,200		3,200
Cash: settlement to White	2,460	Balance b/d	2,460

31.4 Joint venture reporting: IFRS 11 and IAS 28

Currently, joint ventures are defined in IFRS 11 (*Joint arrangements*) and their treatment is described in IAS 28 (*Investments in associates and joint ventures*).

Learning outcomes

You should now have learnt:

1 That when two or more businesses join together for a particular business venture, and do not form a permanent business entity, they have entered into a joint venture.

2 That larger and long-term joint ventures operate a separate bank account and books dedicated to the project.

3 That the participants in smaller joint ventures rely on their own bank accounts and books to run and record their part of the project, using a *memorandum joint venture account* to pass the details of their part of the project to the other participant(s).

4 Why separate joint venture accounts are kept by each party to smaller and short-term joint ventures.

5 How to make the appropriate entries in the books of the parties to the joint venture, calculate the profit, share that profit among the parties to the joint ventures and close off the joint venture accounts at the end of the joint venture.

6 That IFRS 11 and IAS 28 regulate accounting for joint ventures.

Answers to activities

31.1 It's quite simple really, isn't it? You take each debit entry in the first of the T-accounts (Joint Venture with Green) and copy it as a debit entry into the Memorandum Joint Venture account. You then do the same with the debits in the second T-account (Joint Venture with White). Then you do exactly the same with the credit entries. The order you do this in doesn't matter. All you need to ensure is that you have replicated all the T-account entries from the individual joint venture accounts in the Memorandum Joint Venture account. You have to do this because the Memorandum Joint Venture account lies outside the double entry system.

31.2 An account with a debit balance has more value on the debit side. That is, it is the side on which the balance b/d figure lies that tells you whether the balance is a debit or a credit. In this case, the Joint Venture account in White's books has a debit balance. The one in Green's books has a credit balance. Therefore, Green owes White £2,460.

Review questions

31.1 Jack and Wellie enter a joint venture to share profits or losses equally resulting from dealings in second-hand TVs. Both parties take an active part in the business, each recording their own transactions. They have no joint banking account or separate set of books.

2020
July
1 Jack buys four TVs for a total of £3,000.
3 Jack pays for repairs £1,600.
4 Wellie pays office rent £900 and advertising expenses £300.
6 Wellie pays for packaging materials £90.
7 Wellie buys a TV in excellent condition for £1,600.
31 Jack sells the five TVs to various customers, the sales being completed on this date and totalling £8,300.

Show the relevant accounts in the books of both joint venturers.

31.2A   Frank entered into a joint venture with Graham for the purchase and sale of robot mowers. They agreed that profits and losses should be shared equally.

The following transactions took place:

(a)   Frank purchased mowers for £120,400 and paid carriage £320.
(b)   Graham purchased mowers for £14,860 and paid carriage £84.
(c)   Graham paid to Frank £70,000.
(d)   Frank sold mowers for £104,590 and sent a cheque for £50,000 to Graham.
(e)   Graham sold for £19,200 all the mowers he had purchased.
(f)   The unsold mowers in the possession of Frank were taken over by him at a valuation of £40,000.
(g)   The amount due from one venturer to the other was paid and the joint venture was dissolved.

You are required to prepare:
(i)   a statement to show the net profit or loss of the joint venture; and
(ii)   the accounts for the joint venture in the books of Frank and Graham.

31.3   Bull, Craig and Finch entered into a joint venture for dealing in strawberries. The transactions connected with this venture were:

2019

May	1	Bull rented land for two months for £600.
	2	Craig supplied plants cost £510.
	3	Bull employed labour for planting £260.
	16	Craig charged motor expenses £49.
	19	Bull employed labour for fertilising £180.
	29	Bull paid the following expenses: Sundries £19, Labour £210, Fertiliser £74.
June	11	Finch employed labour for lifting strawberries £416.
	24	Sale expenses paid by Finch £318.
	26	Finch received cash from sale proceeds £2,916.

Required:
Show the joint venture accounts in the books of Bull, Craig and Finch. Also show in full the method of arriving at the profit on the venture which is to be apportioned: Bull four-sevenths; Craig two-sevenths; Finch one-seventh.

Any outstanding balances between the parties are settled by cheque on 31 July.

31.4A Rock, Hill and Pine enter into a joint venture for dealing in paintings. The following transactions took place:

2020		
May	1	Rock rented a shop paying three months' rent £2,100.
	3	Hill bought a van for £2,200.
	5	Hill bought paintings for £8,000.
	17	Pine received cash from sale proceeds of paintings £31,410.
	23	Rock bought paintings for £17,000.
June	9	Van broke down. Pine agreed to use his own van for the job until cessation of the joint venture at an agreed charge of £600.
	14	Van bought on May 3 was sold for £1,700. Proceeds were kept by Rock.
	17	Sales of paintings, cash being received by Hill £4,220.
	25	Lighting bills paid for shop by Pine £86.
	29	Pine bought paintings for £1,700.
July	3	General expenses of shop paid for £1,090, Pine and Rock paying half each.
	16	Paintings sold by Pine £2,300, proceeds being kept by him.
	31	Joint venture ended. The paintings still in inventory were taken over at an agreed valuation of £6,200 by Hill.

Required:

Show the joint venture accounts in the books of the three parties. Show in full the workings needed to arrive at the profit on the venture. The profit or loss was to be split: Hill one-half; Rock $^3/_8$; Pine $^1/_8$. Any outstanding balances between the parties were settled on 31 July 2020.

Multiple choice questions: Set 4

Now attempt Set 4 of multiple choice questions. (Answers to all the multiple choice questions are given in Appendix 2 at the end of this book.)

Each of these multiple choice questions has four suggested answers, (A), (B), (C) and (D). You should read each question and then decide which choice is best, either (A) or (B) or (C) or (D). *Write down your answers on a separate piece of paper.* You will then be able to redo the set of questions later without having to try to ignore your answers.

MC61   Working Capital is a term meaning

(A)   The amount of capital invested by the proprietor
(B)   The excess of the current assets over the current liabilities
(C)   The capital less drawings
(D)   The total of Non-current Assets – Current Assets

MC62   A credit balance brought down on a Rent Account means

(A)   We owe that rent at that date
(B)   We have paid that rent in advance at that date
(C)   We have paid too much rent
(D)   We have paid too little in rent

MC63   A debit balance brought down on a Packing Materials Account means

(A)   We owe for packing materials
(B)   We are owed for packing materials
(C)   We have lost money on packing materials
(D)   We have an inventory of packing materials unused

MC64   If we take goods for own use we should

(A)   Debit Drawings Account: Credit Purchases Account
(B)   Debit Purchases Account: Credit Drawings Account
(C)   Debit Drawings Account: Credit Inventory Account
(D)   Debit Sales Account: Credit Inventory Account

MC65   Capital Expenditure is

(A)   The extra capital paid in by the proprietor
(B)   The costs of running the business on a day-to-day basis
(C)   Money spent on buying non-current assets or adding value to them
(D)   Money spent on selling non-current assets

MC66   In the business of C. Sangster, who owns a clothing store, which of the following are Capital Expenditure?

(*i*)   Shop fixtures bought
(*ii*)   Wages of assistants
(*iii*)   New van bought
(*iv*)   Petrol for van

(A)   (*i*) and (*iii*)
(B)   (*i*) and (*ii*)
(C)   (*ii*) and (*iii*)
(D)   (*ii*) and (*iv*)

MC67   If £500 was shown added to Purchases instead of being added to a non-current asset

(A)   Net profit only would be understated
(B)   Net profit only would be overstated
(C)   It would not affect net profit
(D)   Both gross profit and net profit would be understated

MC68   A cheque paid by you, but not yet passed through the banking system, is

(A)   A standing order
(B)   A dishonoured cheque
(C)   A credit transfer
(D)   An unpresented cheque

MC69   A Bank Reconciliation Statement is a statement

(A)   Sent by the bank when the account is overdrawn
(B)   Drawn up by us to verify our cash book balance with the bank statement balance
(C)   Drawn up by the bank to verify the cash book
(D)   Sent by the bank when we have made an error

MC70   Which of the following are not true? A Bank Reconciliation Statement is

(i)   Part of the double entry system
(ii)   Not part of the double entry system
(iii) Sent by the firm to the bank
(iv)   Posted to the ledger accounts

(A)   (i), (iii) and (iv)
(B)   (i) and (ii)
(C)   (i), (ii) and (iv)
(D)   (ii), (iii) and (iv)

MC71   Which of the following should be entered in the Journal?

(i)   Payment for cash purchases
(ii)   Fixtures bought on credit
(iii) Credit sale of goods
(iv)   Sale of surplus machinery

(A)   (i) and (iv)
(B)   (ii) and (iii)
(C)   (iii) and (iv)
(D)   (ii) and (iv)

MC72   The Journal is

(A)   Part of the double entry system
(B)   A supplement to the Cash Book
(C)   Not part of the double entry system
(D)   Used when other journals have been mislaid

MC73   Given a desired cash float of £200, if £146 is spent in the period, how much will be reimbursed at the end of the period?

(A)   £200
(B)   £54
(C)   £254
(D)   £146

→

MC74   When a petty cash book is kept there will be

(A)   More entries made in the general ledger
(B)   Fewer entries made in the general ledger
(C)   The same number of entries in the general ledger
(D)   No entries made at all in the general ledger for items paid by petty cash

MC75   Which of the following do *not* affect trial balance agreement?

(*i*)   Sales £105 to A. Henry entered in P. Henry's account
(*ii*)   Cheque payment of £134 for Motor expenses entered only in Cash Book
(*iii*)   Purchases £440 from C. Browne entered in both accounts as £404
(*iv*)   Wages account added up incorrectly, being totalled £10 too much

(A)   (*i*)and (iv)
(B)   (*i*) and (*iii*)
(C)   (*ii*) and (*iii*)
(D)   (*iii*) and (*iv*)

MC76   Which of the following are *not* errors of principle?

(*i*)   Motor expenses entered in Motor Vehicles account
(*ii*)   Purchases of machinery entered in Purchases account
(*iii*)   Sale of £250 to C. Phillips completely omitted from books
(*iv*)   Sale to A. Henriques entered in A. Henry's account

(A)   (*ii*) and (*iii*)
(B)   (*i*) and (*ii*)
(C)   (*iii*) and (*iv*)
(D)   (*i*) and (*iv*)

MC77   Errors are corrected via the Journal because

(A)   It saves the bookkeeper's time
(B)   It saves entering them in the ledger
(C)   It is much easier to do
(D)   It provides a good record explaining the double entry records

MC78   Which of these errors would be disclosed by the trial balance?

(A)   Cheque £95 from C. Smith entered in Smith's account as £59
(B)   Selling expenses had been debited to Sales Account
(C)   Credit sales of £300 entered in both double entry accounts as £30
(D)   A purchase of £250 was omitted entirely from the books

MC79   If the two totals of a trial balance do *not* agree, the difference must be entered in

(A)   The Income Statement
(B)   A Suspense Account
(C)   A Nominal Account
(D)   The Capital Account

MC80   What should happen if the balance on a Suspense Account is of a material amount?

(A)   Should be written off to the Balance Sheet
(B)   Carry forward the balance to the next period
(C)   Find the error(s) before publishing the final accounts
(D)   Write it off in the Income Statement

PARTNERSHIP ACCOUNTS
AND COMPANY ACCOUNTS

Introduction

This part is concerned with accounting procedures, particularly those affecting partnerships; it gives an introduction to goodwill in relation to partnerships and other business organisations, and introduces the accounts of limited liability companies.

Partnerships

Learning objectives

After you have studied this chapter, you should be able to:

- explain what a partnership is and how it differs from a joint venture
- explain the rules relating to the number of partners
- distinguish between limited partners and general partners
- describe the main features of a partnership agreement
- explain what will happen if no agreement exists on how to share profits or losses
- draw up the ledger accounts and financial statements for a partnership

Introduction

In this chapter, you'll learn about the nature of partnerships and the regulations governing them. You'll learn that there are two types of partner, limited and general, and about the difference between them, and about the difference between partnerships that are limited partnerships and those that are not. Finally, you'll learn how to prepare partnership ledger accounts and how to prepare partnership financial statements.

32.1 The need for partnerships

So far we have mainly considered businesses owned by only one person. We've also looked at joint ventures, which are temporary projects involving two or more parties where they work together to make a profit and then disband the venture. When a more permanent possibility exists, two or more people may form themselves into a **partnership**. This is a long-term commitment to operate in business together. The people who own a partnership are called **partners**. They do not have to be based or work in the same place, though they do in most cases. However, they maintain one set of accounting records and share the profits and losses.

Activity 32.1 From your general knowledge, can you think of any well-known partnerships where the partners are located, not just in different cities, but in different countries? What line of business are they in?

There are various reasons for multiple ownership of a business.

Activity 32.2   Think about this for a minute and then write down as many reasons as you can for people wanting to form a partnership.

In addition to the reasons suggested in the answer, there is also the fact that many business ventures carry financial risk should they fail. When a partnership is formed, the level of risk is reduced. Firstly, any loss can be shared by all the partners and, secondly, when more than one person's expertise is involved, the chances of failure are reduced.

There are two types of multiple ownership: partnerships and limited companies. This chapter deals only with partnerships. Limited companies are the subject of Chapter 36.

32.2   Nature of a partnership

A partnership has the following characteristics:

1   It is formed to make profits.
2   It must obey the law as given in the Partnership Act 1890. If there is a **limited partner** (as described in Section 32.3 below), it must also comply with the Limited Partnership Act of 1907.
3   Normally there can be a minimum of two partners and a maximum of twenty partners. Exceptions are banks, where there cannot be more than ten partners; and there is no maximum for firms of accountants, solicitors, stock exchange members, surveyors, auctioneers, valuers, estate agents, land agents, estate managers or insurance brokers.
4   Each partner (except for limited partners, described below) must pay their share of any debts that the partnership could not pay. If necessary, they could be forced to sell all their private possessions to pay their share of the debts. This can be said to be unlimited liability.
5   Partners who are not limited partners are known as **general partners.**

32.3   Limited partnerships

Limited partnerships are partnerships containing one or more **limited partners.** Limited partnerships must be registered with the Registrar of Companies. Limited partners are not liable for the debts as in Section 32.2 (4) above. Limited partners have the following characteristics and restrictions on their role in the partnership:

1   Their liability for the debts of the partnership is limited to the capital they have put in. They can lose that capital, but they cannot be asked for any more money to pay the debts unless they contravene the regulations relating to their involvement in the partnership (see 2 and 3 below).
2   They are not allowed to take out or receive back any part of their contribution to the partnership during its lifetime.
3   They are not allowed to take part in the management of the partnership or to have the power to make the partnership take a decision. If they do, they become liable for all the debts and obligations of the partnership up to the amount taken out or received back or incurred while they were taking part in the management of the partnership.
4   All the partners cannot be limited partners, so there must be at least one general partner with unlimited liability.

Activity 32.3   What advantages do you think there might be to general partners in having a limited partner?

478

32.4 Limited liability partnerships

This form of partnership was first introduced in 2000. They differ from limited partnerships (Section 32.3) in that partners are liable only to the extent of their capital invested. Also, all partners are permitted to take part in the management of the partnership.

32.5 Partnership agreements

Agreements in writing are not necessary. However, it is better if a written agreement is drawn up by a lawyer or an accountant. Where there is a proper written agreement there will be fewer problems between partners. A written agreement eliminates confusion about what has been agreed.

32.6 Contents of partnership agreements

The written agreement can contain as much, or as little, as the partners want. The law does not say what it must contain. The usual accounting contents are:

1 the capital to be contributed by each partner;
2 the ratio in which profits (or losses) are to be shared;
3 the rate of interest, if any, to be paid on capital before the profits are shared;
4 the rate of interest, if any, to be charged on partners' drawings;
5 salaries to be paid to partners;
6 arrangements for the admission of new partners;
7 procedures to be carried out when a partner retires or dies.

Activity 32.4

Some partnerships don't bother drawing up a partnership agreement. How do you think the partners in those partnerships know what rights and responsibilities they have? (You have not been told this yet, but it should be obvious if you think about it.)

Points **1** to **5** in the list above are considered below. Points **6** and **7** will be taken up in later chapters.

1 Capital contributions

Partners need not contribute equal amounts of capital. What matters is how much capital each partner *agrees* to contribute. It is not unusual for partners to increase the amount of capital they have invested in the partnership.

2 Profit (or loss) sharing ratios

Partners can agree to share profits/losses in any ratio or any way that they may wish. However, it is often thought by students that profits should be shared in the same ratio as that in which capital is contributed. For example, suppose the capitals were Allen £40,000 and Beet £20,000. Some would assume that the partners would share the profits in the ratio of two-thirds to one-third, even though the work to be done by each partner is similar. The division of the profits of the first few years on such a basis might be:

Years	1	2	3	4	5	Total
	£	£	£	£	£	£
Net profits	36,000	48,000	60,000	60,000	72,000	276,000
Shared:						
Allen ²⁄₃	24,000	32,000	40,000	40,000	48,000	184,000
Beet ¹⁄₃	12,000	16,000	20,000	20,000	24,000	92,000

Overall, Allen would receive £184,000, i.e. £92,000 more than Beet. As the duties of the partners are the same, in order to treat each partner fairly, the difference between the two shares of profit should be adequate to compensate Allen for putting extra capital into the firm. It should not be excessive. It is obvious that £92,000 extra profits is excessive, as Allen only put in an extra £20,000 as capital.

Consider too the position of capital ratio sharing of profits if one partner puts in £99,000 and the other puts in £1,000 as capital.

To overcome the difficulty of compensating fairly for the investment of extra capital, the concept of **interest on capital** was devised.

3 Interest on capital

If the work to be done by each partner is of equal value but the capital contributed is unequal, it is reasonable to pay interest on the partners' capitals out of partnership profits. This interest is treated as a deduction prior to the calculation of profits and their distribution among the partners according to the profit sharing ratio.

The rate of interest is a matter of agreement between the partners. Often it will be based upon the return which they would have received if they had invested the capital elsewhere.

Taking Allen and Beet's partnership again, but sharing the profits equally after charging 5 per cent per annum interest on capital, the division of profits would become:

Years	1	2	3	4	5		Total
	£	£	£	£	£		£
Net profit	36,000	48,000	60,000	60,000	72,000		276,000
Interest on capitals							
Allen	2,000	2,000	2,000	2,000	2,000	=	10,000
Beet	1,000	1,000	1,000	1,000	1,000	=	5,000
Remainder shared:							
Allen ¹⁄₂	16,500	22,500	28,500	28,500	34,500	=	130,500
Beet ¹⁄₂	16,500	22,500	28,500	28,500	34,500	=	130,500

Summary	Allen	Beet
	£	£
Interest on capital	10,000	5,000
Balance of profits	130,500	130,500
	140,500	135,500

Allen has thus received £5,000 more than Beet, this being adequate return (in the partners' estimation) for having invested an extra £20,000 in the partnership for five years.

4 Interest on drawings

It is obviously in the best interests of the partnership if cash is withdrawn from it by the partners in accordance with the two basic principles of (a) as little as possible, and (b) as late as possible. The more cash that is left in the partnership, the more expansion can be financed, the greater the economies of having ample cash to take advantage of bargains and of not missing cash discounts because cash is not available, and so on.

To deter the partners from taking out cash unnecessarily the concept can be used of charging the partners interest on each withdrawal, calculated from the date of withdrawal to the end of the financial year. The amount charged to them helps to swell the profits divisible between the partners. The rate of interest should be sufficient to achieve this without being too harsh.

Suppose that Allen and Beet have decided to charge **interest on drawings** at 5 per cent per annum, and that their year end was 31 December. The following drawings are made:

Allen

Drawings		Interest	
	£		£
1 January	2,000	£2,000 × 5% × 12 months	= 100
1 March	4,800	£4,800 × 5% × 10 months	= 200
1 May	2,400	£2,400 × 5% × 8 months	= 80
1 July	4,800	£4,800 × 5% × 6 months	= 120
1 October	1,600	£1,600 × 5% × 3 months	= 20
		Interest charged to Allen	= 520

Beet

Drawings		Interest	
	£		£
1 January	1,200	£1,200 × 5% × 12 months	= 60
1 August	9,600	£9,600 × 5% × 5 months	= 200
1 December	4,800	£4,800 × 5% × 1 months	= 20
		Interest charged to Beet	= 280

5 Partnership salaries

One partner may have more responsibility or tasks than the others. As a reward for this, rather than change the profit and loss sharing ratio, the partner may have a **partnership salary** which is deducted before sharing the balance of profits.

Performance-related payments to partners

Partners may agree that commission or performance-related bonuses be payable to some or all of the partners linked to their individual performance. As with salaries, these would be deducted before sharing the balance of profits.

32.7 An example of the distribution of profits

Taylor and Clarke have been in partnership for one year sharing profits and losses in the ratio of Taylor $^3/_5$, Clarke $^2/_5$. They are entitled to 5 per cent per annum interest on capitals, Taylor having £20,000 capital and Clarke £60,000. Clarke is to have a salary of £15,000. They charge interest on drawings, Taylor being charged £500 and Clarke £1,000. The net profit, before any distributions to the partners, amounted to £50,000 for the year ended 31 December 2020.

The way in which the net profit is distributed among the partners can be shown as:

	£	£	£
Net profit			50,000
Add Charged for interest on drawings:			
Taylor		500	
Clarke		1,000	
			1,500
			51,500
Less Salary: Clarke		15,000	
Interest on capital:			
Taylor	1,000		
Clarke	3,000		
		4,000	
			(19,000)
Balance of profits			32,500
Shared:			
Taylor $^3/_5$		19,500	
Clarke $^2/_5$		13,000	
			32,500

The £50,000 net profits have therefore been shared:

	Taylor £	Clarke £
Balance of profits	19,500	13,000
Interest on capital	1,000	3,000
Salary	–	15,000
	20,500	31,000
Less Interest on drawings	(500)	(1,000)
	20,000	30,000
	£50,000	

32.8 The financial statements

If the sales, inventory and expenses of a partnership were exactly the same as those of a sole trader, then the income statement would be identical with that prepared for the sole trader. However, a partnership would have an extra section at the end of the income statement. This section is called the **profit and loss appropriation account**, and it is in this account that the distribution of profits is shown. The heading to the income statement for a partnership does not normally include the words 'appropriation account'. It is purely an accounting custom not to include it in the heading. (**Sometimes examiners ask for it to be included in the heading, in which case, you need to do so!**)

The profit and loss appropriation account of Taylor and Clarke from the details given would be:

Taylor and Clarke
Income Statement for the year ending 31 December 2020

(Trading Account section – same as for sole proprietor)
(Profit and Loss Account section – same as for sole proprietor)
Profit and Loss Appropriation Account

	£	£	£
Net profit (*from the Profit and Loss Account section*)			50,000
Interest on drawings:			
Taylor		500	
Clarke		1,000	
			1,500
			51,500
Less: Salary: Clarke		15,000	
Interest on capitals			
Taylor	1,000		
Clarke	3,000		
		4,000	(19,000)
			32,500
Balance of profits shared:			
Taylor $^3/_5$		19,500	
Clarke $^2/_5$		13,000	
			32,500

32.9   Fixed and fluctuating capital accounts

There are two choices open to partnerships: **fixed capital accounts** plus current accounts, and **fluctuating capital accounts**.

1 Fixed capital accounts plus current accounts

The capital account for each partner remains year by year at the figure of capital put into the partnership by the partners. The profits, interest on capital and the salaries to which the partner may be entitled are then credited to a separate current account for the partner, and the drawings and the interest on drawings are debited to it. The balance of the current account at the end of each financial year will then represent the amount of undrawn (or withdrawn) profits. A credit balance will be undrawn profits, while a debit balance will be drawings in excess of the profits to which the partner was entitled.

For Taylor and Clarke, capital and current accounts, assuming drawings of £15,000 for Taylor and £26,000 for Clarke will be:

Taylor – *Capital*

	2020				£
	Jan	1	Bank		20,000

Clarke – *Capital*

	2020				£
	Jan	1	Bank		60,000

Taylor – *Current Account*

2020			£	2020			£
Dec	31	Cash: Drawings	15,000	Dec	31	Profit and loss	
	31	Profit and loss appro-				appropriation account:	
		priation account:				Interest on capital	1,000
		Interest on drawings	500			Share of profits	19,500
	31	Balance c/d	5,000				
			20,500				20,500
				2021			
				Jan	1	Balance b/d	5,000

Clarke – *Current Account*

2020			£	2020			£
Dec	31	Cash: Drawings	26,000	Dec	31	Profit and loss	
	31	Profit and loss				appropriation account:	
		appropriation account:				Salary	
		Interest on drawings	1,000			Interest on capital	3,000
	31	Balance c/d	4,000			Share of profits	13,000
			31,000				31,000
				2021			
				Jan	1	Balance b/d	4,000

Notice that the salary of Clarke was not paid to him, it was merely credited to his current account. If instead it was paid in addition to his drawings, the £15,000 cash paid would have been debited to the current account, changing the £4,000 credit balance into a £11,000 debit balance.

Note also that the drawings have been posted to the current accounts at the end of the year. The amounts withdrawn which add up to these amounts were initially recorded in the Cash Book. Only the totals for the year are posted to the current account, rather than each individual withdrawal.

Examiners often ask for the capital accounts and current accounts to be shown in columnar form rather than as T-accounts. For Taylor and Clarke, these would appear as follows:

Capital Accounts

		Taylor	Clarke					Taylor	Clarke
		£	£	2020				£	£
				Jan	1	Bank		20,000	60,000

Current Accounts

			Taylor	Clarke				Taylor	Clarke
2020			£	£	2020			£	£
Dec	31	Cash: Drawings	15,000	26,000	Dec	31	Salary	19,500	15,000
	31	Interest on drawings	500	1,000		31	Interest on capital	1,000	3,000
	31	Balances c/d	5,000	4,000		31	Share of profits		13,000
			20,500	31,000				20,500	31,000
					2021				
					Jan	1	Balances b/d	5,000	4,000

2 Fluctuating capital accounts

The distribution of profits would be credited to the capital account, and the drawings and interest on drawings debited. Therefore, the balance on the capital account will change each year, i.e. it will fluctuate.

If fluctuating capital accounts had been kept for Taylor and Clarke they would have appeared:

Taylor – *Capital*

2020			£	2020				£
Dec	31	Cash: Drawings	15,000	Jan	1	Bank		20,000
	31	Profit and loss		Dec	31	Profit and loss		
		appropriation account:				appropriation account:		
		Interest on drawings	500			Interest on capital		1,000
	31	Balance c/d	25,000			Share of profits		19,500
			40,500					40,500
				2021				
				Jan	1	Balance b/d		25,000

Clarke – *Capital*

2020			£	2020				£
Dec	31	Cash: Drawings	26,000	Jan	1	Bank		60,000
	31	Profit and loss appro-		Dec	31	Profit and loss appro-		
		priation account:				priation account:		
		Interest on	1,000			Salary		15,000
		drawings				Interest on capital		3,000
	31	Balance c/d	64,000			Share of profit		13,000
			91,000					91,000
				2021				
				Jan	1	Balance b/d		64,000

Fixed capital accounts preferred

The keeping of fixed capital accounts plus current accounts is considered preferable to fluctuating capital accounts. When partners are taking out greater amounts than the share of the profits that they are entitled to, this is shown up by a debit balance on the current account and so acts as a warning.

32.10 Where no partnership agreement exists

As mentioned in the answer to Activity 32.4, where no partnership agreement exists, express or implied, Section 24 of the Partnership Act 1890 governs the situation. The accounting content of this section states:

(*a*) Profits and losses are to be shared equally.
(*b*) There is to be no interest allowed on capital.
(*c*) No interest is to be charged on drawings.
(*d*) Salaries are not allowed.
(*e*) Partners who put a sum of money into a partnership in excess of the capital they have agreed to subscribe are entitled to interest at the rate of 5 per cent per annum on such an advance.

Section 24 applies where there is no agreement. There may be an agreement not by a partnership deed but in a letter, or it may be implied by conduct, for instance when a partner signs a balance sheet which shows profits shared in some other ratio than equally. Where a dispute arises as to whether an agreement exists or not, and this cannot be resolved by the partners, only the courts are competent to decide.

32.11 The balance sheet

For the partnership, the capital part of the balance sheet will appear in this form:

Taylor and Clarke
Balance Sheet as at 31 December 2020 (extract)

						£	£
Capital accounts	Taylor					20,000	
	Clarke					60,000	
							80,000

		Taylor		*Clarke*			
Current accounts		£	£	£	£		
Salary			–		15,000		
Interest on capital			1,000		3,000		
Share of profits			19,500		13,000		
			20,500		31,000		
Less Drawings		15,000		26,000			
Interest on drawings		500		1,000			
			(15,500)		(27,000)		
			5,000		4,000		
							9,000

If one of the current accounts had finished in debit, for instance if the current account of Clarke had finished up as £400 debit, the figure of £400 would appear in brackets and the balances would appear net in the totals column:

	Taylor	*Clarke*	
	£	£	£
Closing balance	5,000	(400)	4,600

If the net figure turned out to be a debit figure then this would be deducted from the total of the capital accounts.

Learning outcomes

You should now have learnt:

1 That there is no limited liability in partnerships except for 'limited partners'.

2 That limited partners cannot withdraw any of the capital they invested in the partnership or take part in the management of the partnership.

3 That apart from some professions, if more than twenty owners of an organisation are needed, a limited company would need to be formed, not a partnership.

4 That the contents of a partnership agreement will override anything written in this chapter. Partners can agree to anything they want to, in as much or as little detail as they wish.

5 That if there is no partnership agreement, then the provisions of the Partnership Act 1890 (details shown in Section 32.10) will apply.

6 That partners can agree to show their capital accounts using either the fixed capital or fluctuating capital methods.

7 How to prepare the ledger accounts and financial statements of partnerships.

Answers to activities

32.1 The best example is accounting partnerships. Some of them have offices all over the world.

32.2 Your answer could have included some of the following:

- The capital required is more than one person can provide.
- The experience or ability required to manage the business cannot be found in one person alone.
- Many people want to share management instead of doing everything on their own.
- Very often the partners will be members of the same family.

32.3 Limited partners contribute capital. They may also contribute expertise. Either of these is a benefit to the general partners – they have to contribute less capital and they can rely on the additional expertise when appropriate without needing to seek assistance from people outside the partnership. Also, because limited partners cannot be involved in the management of the partnership, general partners can take decisions without consulting a limited partner, thus saving time and effort when, in many instances, the limited partner will be busy doing other things that have nothing to do with the partnership business.

32.4 The Partnership Act 1890 imposes a standard partnership agreement upon partnerships that do not draw up a partnership agreement. See Section 32.10.

Review questions

32.1 Gow, Short and Hill are partners. They share profits and losses in the ratios of $^3/_{11}$, $^4/_{11}$ and $^4/_{11}$ respectively.

For the year ending 31 July 2019, their capital accounts remained fixed at the following amounts:

	£
Gow	120,000
Short	80,000
Hill	50,000

They have agreed to give each other 4 per cent interest per annum on their capital accounts.

In addition to the above, partnership salaries of £70,000 for Short and £40,000 for Hill are to be charged.

The net profit of the partnership, before taking any of the above into account was £230,000.

You are required to draw up the appropriation account of the partnership for the year ending 31 July 2019.

32.2A George, Henry and Lee are partners. They share profits and losses in the ratios of 5:3:2 respectively.

For the year ending 31 December 2019 their capital accounts remained fixed at the following amounts:

	£
George	120,000
Henry	80,000
Lee	60,000

They have agreed to give each other 4% interest per annum on their capital accounts.

In addition to the above, partnership salaries of £50,000 for Henry and £30,000 for Lee are to be charged.

The net profit of the partnership before taking any of the above into account was £215,400.

Required:
Draw up the appropriation account of the partnership for the year ending 31 December 2019.

32.3 Dunn and Outram sell toys. Their individual investments in the business on 1 January 2018 were: Dunn £160,000; Outram £70,000.

For the year to 31 December 2018, the net profit was £90,000 and the partners' drawings were: Dunn £26,000; Outram £32,000.

For 2018 (their first year), the partners agreed to share profits and losses equally, but they decided that from 1 January 2019:

(*i*) The partners should be entitled to annual salaries of: Dunn £20,000; Outram £30,000.
(*ii*) Interest should be allowed on capital at 5 per cent per annum.
(*iii*) The profit remaining should be shared equally (as should losses).

	Net trading profit before dealing with partners' items	Drawings	
		Dunn	Outram
	£	£	£
2019	110,000	24,000	28,000
2020	50,000	22,000	34,000

Required:
Prepare the profit and loss appropriation accounts and the partners' current accounts for the three years.

32.4 Draw up a profit and loss appropriation account for the year ending 31 December 2020 and balance sheet extract at that date, from the following:

(*i*) Net profits £111,100.
(*ii*) Interest to be charged on capitals: Blair £3,000; Short £2,000; Steel £1,500.
(*iii*) Interest to be charged on drawings: Blair £400; Short £300; Steel £200.

(*iv*) Salaries to be credited: Short £20,000; Steel £25,000.
(*v*) Profits to be shared: Blair 70%; Short 20%; Steel 10%.
(*vi*) Current accounts: balances b/d Blair £18,600; Short £9,460; Steel £8,200.
(*vii*) Capital accounts: balances b/d Blair £100,000; Short £50,000; Steel £25,000.
(*viii*) Drawings: Blair £39,000; Short £27,100; Steel £16,800.

32.5A   Draw up a profit and loss appropriation account for Cole, Knox and Lamb for the year ending 31 December 2020, and a balance sheet extract at that date, from the following:

(*i*)   Net profits £184,800.
(*ii*) Interest to be charged on capitals: Cole £3,600; Knox £2,700; Lamb £2,100.
(*iii*) Interest to be charged on drawings: Cole £1,200; Knox £900; Lamb £500.
(*iv*) Salaries to be credited: Knox £22,000; Lamb £28,000.
(*v*)   Profits to be shared: Cole 55 per cent; Knox 25 per cent; Lamb 20 per cent.
(*vi*) Current accounts: Cole £18,000; Knox £8,000; Lamb £6,000.
(*vii*) Capital accounts: Cole £60,000; Knox £45,000; Lamb £35,000.
(*viii*) Drawings: Cole £27,000; Knox £23,000; Lamb £17,000.

32.6A   Smith and Tolhurst are in partnership, sharing profits and losses in the ratio 5:3. The following information has been taken from the partnership records for the year ended 31 October 2019:

(i)   According to its Income Statement, the net profit of the partnership for the year ended 31 October 2019 was £79,600.
(ii) Interest to be charged on drawings taken by the partners has been correctly calculated as:

Smith	£1,360
Tolhurst	£1,520

(iii) Tolhurst is to be allowed a salary of £20,000 per year.
(iv) Interest is to be paid on capital account balances at the rate of 4% per year.
(v)   The partners' capital account balances throughout the year were:

Smith	£160,000
Tolhurst	£90,000

(vi) The balances as at 1 November 2018 on the partners' current accounts were:

Smith	£12,400 Cr
Tolhurst	£9,200 Dr

(vii) During the year ended 31 October 2019 Smith's and Tolhurst's drawings were £37,300 and £49,800 respectively.

Required
(a) Prepare the appropriation account for the year ended 31 October 2019.
(b) Calculate the balance on each partner's current account as at 31 October 2019.
(c) At 1 November 2018 there was a debit balance on Tolhurst's current account. What does this signify?
(d) Why do many partnerships take account of 'interest on capital' and 'interest on drawings'?

32.7A A and B are in partnership sharing profits and losses 3:2. Under the terms of the partnership agreement, the partners are entitled to interest on capital at 5 per cent per annum and B is entitled to a salary of £4,500. Interest is charged on drawings at 5 per cent per annum and the amounts of interest are given below. No interest is charged or allowed on current account balances.

The partners' capitals at 1 July 2019 were: A £30,000 and B £10,000.

The net trading profit of the firm before dealing with partners' interest or B's salary for the year ended 30 June 2020 was £25,800. Interest on drawings for the year amounted to A £400, B £300.

At 1 July 2019, there was a credit balance of £1,280 on B's current account, while A's current account balance was a debit of £500. Drawings for the year to 30 June 2020 amounted to £12,000 for A and £15,000 for B.

Required:
Prepare, for the year to 30 June 2020:

(a) The profit and loss appropriation account.
(b) The partners' current accounts.

32.8 Bee, Cee and Dee have been holding preliminary discussions with a view to forming a partnership to buy and sell antiques.

The position has now been reached where the prospective partners have agreed the basic arrangements under which the partnership will operate.

Bee will contribute £40,000 as capital, and up to £10,000 as a long-term loan to the partnership, if needed. He has extensive other business interests and will not therefore be taking an active part in the running of the business.

Cee is unable to bring in more than £2,000 as capital initially, but, because he has an expert knowledge of the antique trade, will act as the manager of the business on a full-time basis.

Dee is willing to contribute £10,000 as capital. He will also assist in running the business as the need arises. In particular, he is prepared to attend auctions anywhere within the United Kingdom in order to acquire trading inventory which he will transport back to the firm's premises in his van. On occasions he may also help Cee to restore the articles prior to sale to the public.

At the meeting, the three prospective partners intend to decide upon the financial arrangements for sharing out the profits (or losses) made by the firm, and have approached you for advice.

You are required to prepare a set of explanatory notes, under suitable headings, of the considerations which the prospective partners should take into account in arriving at their decisions at the next meeting.

(*Association of Chartered Certified Accountants*)

32.9 Frame and French are in partnership sharing profits and losses in the ratio 3:2. The following is their trial balance as at 30 September 2019:

	Dr £	Cr £
Buildings (cost £210,000)	210,000	
Accumulated depreciation: Buildings at 30.9.2018		50,000
Fixtures at cost	8,200	
Accumulated depreciation: Fixtures at 30.9.2018		4,200
Accounts receivable	61,400	
Accounts payable		26,590
Cash at bank	6,130	
Inventory at 30 September 2018	62,740	
Sales		363,111
Purchases	210,000	
Carriage outwards	3,410	
Discounts allowed	620	
Loan interest: P. Prince	3,900	
Office expenses	4,760	
Salaries and wages	57,809	
Bad debts	1,632	
Allowance for doubtful debts as at 30.9.2018		1,400
Loan from P. Prince		65,000
Capitals: Frame		100,000
French		75,000
Current accounts: Frame		4,100
French		1,200
Drawings: Frame	31,800	
French	28,200	
	690,601	690,601

(a) Inventory at the end of the year was £74,210.
(b) Expenses to be accrued: Office Expenses £215; Wages £720.
(c) Depreciate fixtures 15 per cent on reducing balance basis, buildings £5,000.
(d) Reduce allowance for doubtful debts to £1,250.
(e) Partnership salary: £30,000 to Frame. Not yet entered.
(f) Interest on drawings: Frame £900; French £600.
(g) Interest on capital account balances at 5 per cent.

Required:
Prepare an income statement and profit and loss appropriation account for the year ending 30 September 2019 and a balance sheet as at that date.

32.10A Scot and Joplin are in partnership. They share profits in the ratio: Scot 70 per cent; Joplin 30 per cent. The following trial balance was extracted as at 31 December 2020:

	Dr	Cr
	£	£
Office equipment at cost	9,200	
Motor vehicles at cost	21,400	
Accumulated depreciation at 31.12.2019:		
Motor vehicles		12,800
Office equipment		3,600
Inventory at 31 December 2019	38,410	
Accounts receivable and accounts payable	41,940	32,216
Cash at bank	2,118	
Cash in hand	317	
Sales		180,400
Purchases	136,680	
Salaries	27,400	
Office expenses	2,130	
Discounts allowed	312	
Current accounts at 31.12.2019		
Scot		7,382
Joplin		7,009
Capital accounts: Scot		50,000
Joplin		20,000
Drawings: Scot	17,500	
Joplin	16,000	
	313,407	313,407

The following notes are applicable at 31 December 2020:

(a) Inventory, 31 December 2020 £41,312.
(b) Office expenses owing £240.
(c) Provide for depreciation: motor 25 per cent of cost, office equipment 20 per cent of cost.
(d) Charge interest on capitals at 5 per cent.
(e) Charge interest on drawings: Scot £300; Joplin £200.

Required:
Draw up a set of financial statements for the year ending 31 December 2020 for the partnership.

32.11 Sage and Onion are trading in partnership, sharing profits and losses equally. Interest at 5% per annum is allowed or charged on both the capital account and the current account balances at the beginning of the year. Interest is charged on drawings at 5% per annum. The partners are entitled to annual salaries of: Sage £12,000; Onion £8,000.

Sage and Onion
Trial Balance as at 31 December 2020

	Dr £	Cr £
Capital accounts: Sage		100,000
Onion		50,000
Current accounts: Sage		2,000
Onion	600	
Cash drawings for the year: Sage	15,000	
Onion	10,000	
Freehold premises at cost	50,000	
Inventory at 1 January 2020	75,000	
Fixtures and fittings at cost	15,000	
Purchases and purchase returns	380,000	12,000
Bank	31,600	
Sales and sales returns	6,000	508,000
Accounts receivable and accounts payable	52,400	33,300
Carriage inwards	21,500	
Carriage outwards	3,000	
Staff salaries	42,000	
VAT		8,700
Office expenses	7,500	
Allowance for doubtful debts		2,000
Advertising	5,000	
Discounts received		1,000
Discounts allowed	1,200	
Bad debts	1,400	
Rent and business rates	2,800	
Accumulated depreciation of fixtures and fittings at 1.1.2020		3,000
	720,000	720,000

At 31 December 2020:
(a) Inventory was valued at £68,000.
(b) Purchase invoices amounting to £3,000 for goods included in the inventory valuation at (a) above had not been recorded.
(c) Staff salaries owing £900.
(d) Business rates paid in advance £200.
(e) Allowance for doubtful debts to be increased to £2,400.
(f) Goods withdrawn by partners for private use had not been recorded and were valued at: Sage £500, Onion £630. No interest is to be charged on these amounts.
(g) Provision is to be made for depreciation of fixtures and fittings at 10% on cost.
(h) Interest on drawings for the year is to be charged: Sage £360, Onion £280.

Required:
From the information given below, prepare the partnership income statement and profit and loss appropriation account for the year ending 31 December 2020, and the balance sheet as at that date.

32.12A Bush, Home and Wilson share profits and losses in the ratios 4:1:3 respectively. Their trial balance as at 30 April 2020 was as follows:

	Dr £	Cr £
Sales		334,618
Returns inwards	10,200	
Purchases	196,239	
Carriage inwards	3,100	
Inventory 30 April 2019	68,127	
Discounts allowed	190	
Salaries and wages	54,117	
Bad debts	1,620	
Allowance for doubtful debts 30 April 2019		950
General expenses	1,017	
Business rates	2,900	
Postage	845	
Computers at cost	8,400	
Office equipment at cost	5,700	
Accumulated depreciation at 30 April 2019:		
Computers		3,600
Office equipment		2,900
Accounts payable		36,480
Accounts receivable	51,320	
Cash at bank	5,214	
Drawings: Bush	39,000	
Home	16,000	
Wilson	28,000	
Current accounts: Bush		5,940
Home	2,117	
Wilson		9,618
Capital accounts: Bush		60,000
Home		10,000
Wilson		30,000
	494,106	494,106

Draw up a set of financial statements for the year ending 30 April 2020. The following notes are relevant at 30 April 2020:

(i) Inventory 30 April 2020, £74,223.
(ii) Business rates in advance £200; Inventory of postage stamps £68.
(iii) Increase Allowance for doubtful debts to £1,400.
(iv) Salaries: Home £18,000; Wilson £14,000. Not yet recorded.
(v) Interest on Drawings: Bush £300; Home £200; Wilson £240.
(vi) Interest on Capitals at 8 per cent.
(vii) Depreciate Computers £2,800; Office equipment £1,100.

32.13 Reid and Benson are in partnership as lecturers and tutors. Interest is to be allowed on capital and on the opening balances on the current accounts at a rate of 5% per annum and Reid is to be given a salary of £18,000 per annum. Interest is to be charged on drawings at 5% per annum (see notes below) and the profits and losses are to be shared Reid 60% and Benson 40%.

The following trial balance was extracted from the books of the partnership at 31 December 2021:

	£	£
Capital account – Benson		50,000
Capital account – Reid		75,000
Current account – Benson		4,000
Current account – Reid		5,000
Drawings – Reid	17,000	
Drawings – Benson	20,000	
Sales – goods and services		541,750
Purchases of textbooks for distribution	291,830	
Returns inwards and outwards	800	330
Carriage inwards	3,150	
Staff salaries	141,150	
Rent	2,500	
Insurance – general	1,000	
Insurance – public indemnity	1,500	
Compensation paid due to Benson error	10,000	
General expenses	9,500	
Bad debts written-off	1,150	
Fixtures and fittings – cost	74,000	
Fixtures and fittings – accumulated depreciation at 1 January 2021		12,000
Accounts receivable and accounts payable	137,500	23,400
Cash	400	
Total	711,480	711,480

- An allowance for doubtful debts is to be created of £1,500.
- Insurances paid in advance at 31 December 2021 were General £50; Professional Indemnity £100.
- Fixtures and fittings are to be depreciated at 10% on cost.
- Interest on drawings: Benson £550, Reid £1,050.
- Inventory of books at 31 December 2021 was £1,500.

Required:
Prepare an income statement together with an appropriation account at 31 December 2021 and a balance sheet as at that date.

33

Goodwill for sole proprietors and partnerships

Learning objectives

After you have studied this chapter, you should be able to:

- describe a range of methods for arriving at the selling price of a business
- explain and calculate super profits
- explain why goodwill exists
- explain why goodwill has a monetary value
- distinguish between purchased and non-purchased goodwill
- calculate purchased goodwill
- calculate the adjustments needed when there is some form of change in a partnership

Introduction

In this chapter, you'll learn about purchased goodwill and its treatment in the books and financial statements of sole proprietors and partnerships. You will also learn how to make adjustments to the partnership capital accounts when circumstances change.

33.1 Nature of goodwill

Suppose you have been running a business for some years and you want to sell it. How much would you ask as the total sale price of the business? You decide to list how much you could get for each asset if sold separately. This list might be as follows:

	£
	£
Buildings	225,000
Machinery	75,000
Accounts receivable	60,000
Inventory	40,000
	400,000

Note: if there are any liabilities, you would deduct them from the total value of the assets to arrive at the value of the net assets, which is the net amount you would have left if you sold all the assets and paid off all the creditors.

So, if you sold off everything separately, you would expect to receive £400,000.

Activity 33.1 If you were running a successful business, would you be willing to sell it for the value of its net assets? Why/why not?

As the business is successful, a prospective buyer has been found who is willing to pay more than the £400,000 net asset value. As a result, you sell the whole of the business as a going concern to Mr Lee for £450,000. He has, therefore, paid £50,000 more than the total value of all the assets. This extra payment of £50,000 is called **goodwill**. He has paid this because he wanted to take over the business as a going concern, and so benefit from the product and customer base that already exists. Thus:

> **Purchased Goodwill** = Total Price *less* value of net identifiable assets

Goodwill is an **intangible asset**. It can only exist if the business was purchased and the amount paid was greater than the value of the net assets. In many cases, goodwill represents the value of the reputation of the business at the time it was purchased.

33.2 Reasons for payment of goodwill

In buying an existing business which has been established for some time there may be quite a few possible advantages. Some of them are listed here:

● The business has a large number of regular customers who will continue to deal with the new owner.
● The business has a good reputation.
● It has experienced, efficient and reliable employees.
● The business is situated in a good location.
● It has good contacts with suppliers.
● It has well-known brand names that have not been valued and included as assets.

None of these advantages is available to completely new businesses. For this reason, many people are willing to pay an additional amount for goodwill when they buy an existing business.

33.3 Existence of goodwill

Goodwill does not necessarily exist in a business. If a business has a bad reputation, an inefficient labour force or other negative characteristics, it is unlikely that the owner would be paid for goodwill on selling the business.

Activity 33.2 In the example in Section 33.1, goodwill was a positive figure of £50,000. If, instead, it had been a negative figure of £100,000 (being the estimated cost of a marketing campaign that would be necessary to restore customers' faith in the business) at what price would the business be most likely to be sold? Why?

33.4 Methods of calculating goodwill

There is no single way of calculating goodwill on which everyone can agree. The seller will probably want more for the goodwill than the buyer will want to pay. All that is certain is that when agreement is reached between buyer and seller concerning how much is to be paid for a business, the amount by which the agreed price exceeds the value of the net assets represents the goodwill. Various methods are used to help buyer and seller come to an agreed figure for a business. The calculations give the buyer and the seller a figure with which to begin discussions of the value.

Very often an industry or occupation has its own customary way of calculating goodwill:

(a) In more than one type of retail business it has been the custom to value goodwill at the average weekly sales for the past year multiplied by a given figure. The given figure will, of course, differ between different types of businesses, and often changes gradually in the same type of business in the long term.

(b) With many professional firms, such as accountants in public practice, it is the custom to value goodwill as being the gross annual fees times a given number. For instance, what is termed a two years' purchase of a firm with gross fees of £300,000 means goodwill = 2 × £300,000 = £600,000.

(c) The average net annual profit for a specified past number of years multiplied by an agreed number. This is often said to be x years' purchase of the net profits.

(d) The super-profits method.

Let's consider the last of these, the super-profits method. It may be argued, as in the case of a sole trader for example, that the net profits are not 'true profits'. This is because the sole trader has not charged for the following expenses:

(a) Services of the proprietor. He has worked in the business, but he has not charged for such services. Any drawings he makes are charged to a capital account, not to the profit and loss account.

(b) The use of the money he has invested in the business. If he had invested his money elsewhere he would have earned interest or dividends on such investments.

Super profits are what an accountant would call what is left of the net profits after allowances have been made for (a) services of the proprietor and (b) the use of the capital.

They are usually calculated as:

		£	£
Annual net profits			80,000
Less	(i) Remuneration proprietor would have earned for similar work elsewhere	36,000	
	(ii) Interest that would have been earned if capital had been invested elsewhere	7,000	
			(43,000)
Annual super profits			37,000

The annual super profits are then multiplied by a number agreed by seller and purchaser of the business in order to arrive at the selling price.

33.5 Sole proprietor's books

Goodwill is only entered in a sole proprietor's accounts when it has been purchased. The existence of goodwill in the financial statements usually means that the business was purchased as a going concern by the owner. That is, the owner did not start the business from scratch.

Activity 33.3 There is another possible explanation for purchased goodwill appearing in a sole proprietor's balance sheet. What do you think it might be?

33.6 Partnership books

Although goodwill is not *normally* entered in the financial statements unless it has been purchased, sometimes it is necessary where partnerships are concerned.

Unless it has been agreed differently, partners own a share in the goodwill in the same ratio in which they share profits. For instance, if A receives one-quarter of the profits, A will be the owner of one-quarter of the goodwill. This is true even if there is no goodwill account.

This means that when something happens such as:

(a) existing partners deciding to change profit and loss sharing ratios; or
(b) a new partner being introduced; or
(c) a partner retiring or dying;

then the ownership of goodwill by partners changes in some way.

The change may involve cash passing from one partner to another, or an adjustment in the books, so that the changes in ownership do not lead to a partner (or partners) giving away their share of ownership for nothing.

33.7 Change in profit sharing ratios of existing partners

Sometimes the profit and loss sharing ratios have to be changed. Typical reasons are:

● A partner may now not work as much as in the past, possibly because of old age or ill-health.
● A partner's skills and ability may have changed, perhaps after attending a course or following an illness.
● A partner may now be doing much more for the business than in the past.

If the partners decide to change their profit sharing ratios, an adjustment will be needed.

To illustrate why this is so, let's look at the following example of a partnership in which goodwill is not already shown in a goodwill account at its correct value.

(a) A, B and C are in partnership, sharing profits and losses equally.
(b) On 31 December 2019 they decide to change this to A one-half, B one-quarter and C one-quarter.
(c) On 31 December 2019 the goodwill, which had never been shown in the books, was valued at £60,000. If, just before the change in the profit sharing ratio, the business had been sold and £60,000 received for goodwill, then each partner would have received £20,000 as they shared profits equally.
(d) At any time after 31 December 2019, once the profit sharing ratio has changed, their ownership of goodwill is worth A £30,000, B £15,000 and C £15,000. If goodwill is sold for that amount then those figures will be received by the partners for goodwill.
(e) If, when (b) above happened, there had been no change in activity or commitment to the business by A, B, or C, or no other form of adjustment, then B and C would each have given away a £5,000 share of the goodwill for nothing. This would not be sensible.

We can now look at how the adjustments can be made when a goodwill account with the correct valuation does not already exist.

Exhibit 33.1

E, F and G have been in business for 10 years. They have always shared profits equally. No goodwill account has ever existed in the books. On 31 December 2019 they agree that G will take only a one-fifth share of the profits as from 1 January 2020, because he will be devoting less of his time to the business in the future. E and F will each take two-fifths of the profits. The summarised balance sheet of the business on 31 December 2019 appears as follows:

Balance Sheet as at 31 December 2019

	£
Net Assets	70,000
Capital: E	30,000
F	18,000
G	22,000
	70,000

The partners agree that the goodwill should be valued at £30,000. Answer (1) shows the solution when a goodwill account is opened. Answer (2) is the solution when a goodwill account is not opened.

1 Goodwill account opened

Open a goodwill account. Then make the following entries: Debit goodwill account: total value of goodwill.

Credit partners' capital accounts: each one with his share of goodwill in old profit sharing ratio.

The goodwill account will appear as:

Goodwill

	£		£
Capitals: valuation shared		Balance c/d	30,000
E	10,000		
F	10,000		
G	10,000		
	30,000		30,000

The capital accounts may be shown in columnar fashion as:

Capital Accounts

	E £	F £	G £		E £	F £	G £
Balances c/d	40,000	28,000	32,000	Balances b/d	30,000	18,000	22,000
				Goodwill: old ratios	10,000	10,000	10,000
	40,000	28,000	32,000		40,000	28,000	32,000

The balance sheet items before and after the adjustments will appear as:

	Before £	After £		Before £	After £
Goodwill	–	30,000	Capitals: E	30,000	40,000
Other assets	70,000	70,000	F	18,000	28,000
			G	22,000	32,000
	70,000	100,000		70,000	100,000

2 Goodwill account not opened

The effect of the change of ownership of goodwill may be shown in the following form:

Before		After		Loss or Gain		Action Required
	£		£			
E One-third	10,000	Two-fifths	12,000	Gain	£2,000	Debit E's capital account £2,000
F One-third	10,000	Two-fifths	12,000	Gain	£2,000	Debit F's capital account £2,000
G One-third	10,000	One-fifth	6,000	Loss	£4,000	Credit G's capital account £4,000
	30,000		30,000			

The column headed 'Action Required' shows that a partner who has gained goodwill because of the change must be charged for it by having his capital account debited with the value of the gain. A partner who has lost goodwill must be compensated for it by having his capital account credited.

The capital accounts will appear as:

Capital Accounts

	E	F	G		E	F	G
	£	£	£		£	£	£
Goodwill adjustments	2,000	2,000		Balances b/d	30,000	18,000	22,000
Balances c/d	28,000	16,000	26,000	Goodwill adjustments			4,000
	30,000	18,000	26,000		30,000	18,000	26,000

As there is no goodwill account, the balance sheet items before and after the adjustments will therefore appear as:

	Before	After		Before	After
	£	£		£	£
Net assets	70,000	70,000	Capitals: E	30,000	28,000
			F	18,000	16,000
			G	22,000	26,000
	70,000	70,000		70,000	70,000

Comparison of methods 1 and 2

Let's compare the methods. Assume that shortly afterwards the assets in 1 and 2 are sold for £70,000 and the goodwill for £30,000. The total of £100,000 would be distributed

Method 1. The £100,000 is exactly the amount needed to pay the partners according to the balances on their capital accounts. The payments are therefore made of

		£
Capitals paid to	E	40,000
	F	28,000
	G	32,000
Total cash paid		100,000

Method 2. First of all the balances on capital accounts, totalling £70,000, are to be paid. Then the £30,000 received for goodwill will be split between the partners in their profit and loss ratios. This will result in payments as follows:

	Capitals		Goodwill Shared		Total Paid
	£		£		£
E	28,000	($^2/_5$)	12,000		40,000
F	16,000	($^2/_5$)	12,000		28,000
G	26,000	($^1/_5$)	6,000		32,000
	70,000		30,000		100,000

You can see that the final amounts paid to the partners are the same whether a goodwill account is opened or not.

33.8 Admission of new partners

New partners may be admitted, usually for one of two reasons:

1 As an extra partner, either because the firm has grown or because someone is needed with different skills.
2 To replace partners who are leaving the firm. This might be because of retirement or death of a partner.

33.9 Goodwill on admission of new partners

The new partner will be entitled to a share in the profits, and, normally, also to the same share of the value of goodwill. It is correct to charge the new partner for taking over that share of the goodwill.

33.10 Goodwill adjustments when new partners are admitted

This calculation is done in four stages:

1 Show value of goodwill divided between old partners in the old profit and loss sharing ratios.
2 Then show value of goodwill divided between partners (including new partner) in the new profit and loss sharing ratio.
3 Goodwill gain shown: charge these partners for the gain.
4 Goodwill loss shown: give these partners an allowance for their losses.

This is illustrated in Exhibits 33.2 and 33.3.

Exhibit 33.2

A and B are in partnership, sharing profits and losses equally. C is admitted as a new partner. The three partners will share profits and losses one-third each.

Total goodwill is valued at £60,000.

	Stage 1		Stage 2		Stage 3	
Partners	Old profit shares	Share of goodwill	New profit shares	Share of goodwill	Gain or loss	Adjustment needed
		£		£	£	
A	$\frac{1}{2}$	30,000	$\frac{1}{3}$	20,000	10,000 Loss	Cr A Capital
B	$\frac{1}{2}$	30,000	$\frac{1}{3}$	20,000	10,000 Loss	Cr B Capital
C	–		$\frac{1}{3}$	20,000	20,000 Gain	Dr C Capital
		60,000		60,000		

This means that A and B need to have their capitals increased by £10,000 each. C's capital needs to be reduced by £20,000.

Note that A and B have kept their profits in the same ratio to each other. While they used to have one-half each, now they have one-third each.

We will now see in Exhibit 33.3 that the method shown is the same even when existing partners take a different share of the profit to that before the change.

Exhibit 33.3

D and E are in partnership sharing profits one-half each. A new partner F is admitted. Profits will now be shared D one-fifth, and E and F two-fifths each. D and E, therefore, have not kept their shares equal to each other. Goodwill is valued at £60,000.

	Stage 1		Stage 2		Stage 3	
Partners	Old profit shares	Share of goodwill	New profit shares	Share of goodwill	Gain or loss	Adjustment needed
		£		£	£	
D	$\frac{1}{2}$	30,000	$\frac{1}{5}$	12,000	18,000 Loss	Cr D Capital
E	$\frac{1}{2}$	30,000	$\frac{2}{5}$	24,000	6,000 Loss	Cr E Capital
F	–		$\frac{2}{5}$	24,000	24,000 Gain	Dr F Capital
		60,000		60,000		

D needs his capital increased by £18,000. E's capital is to be increased by £6,000. F's capital needs to be reduced by £24,000.

33.11 Accounting entries for goodwill adjustments

These depend on how the partners wish to arrange the adjustment. Three methods are usually used:

1 Cash is paid by the new partner privately to the old partners for his/her share of the goodwill. No goodwill account is to be opened.

In Exhibit 33.3, F would therefore give £24,000 in cash, being £18,000 to D and £6,000 to E. They would bank these amounts in their private bank accounts. No entry is made for this in the accounts of the partnership.

2 Cash is paid by the new partner into the business bank account for his/her share of the goodwill. No goodwill account is to be opened. Assume that the capital balances before F was admitted were D £50,000, E £50,000, and F was to pay in £50,000 as capital plus £24,000 for goodwill.

The £24,000 payment is made in order to secure a share of the £60,000 existing goodwill. The £24,000 is shared between the two existing partners by increasing their capital accounts by the amounts shown in Stage 3 of Exhibit 33.3. The debit entry is to the bank account. The entries in the capital accounts are:

Capital Accounts

	D £	E £	F £		D £	E £	F £
Adjustments for goodwill			24,000	Balances b/d	50,000	50,000	
				Cash for capital			50,000
				Cash for goodwill			24,000
Balances c/d	68,000	56,000	50,000	Loss of goodwill	18,000	6,000	
	68,000	56,000	74,000		68,000	56,000	74,000

3 Goodwill account to be opened. No extra cash to be paid in by the new partner for goodwill.

In Exhibit 33.3, the opening capitals were D £50,000, E £50,000. F paid in £50,000 as capital.

Here, the situation is different from under the second method. The new partner is not paying anything in order to secure a share of the £60,000 of existing goodwill. As a result, it is shared now among the two original partners in their original profit sharing ratio (half each) and the new partner's capital account is credited only with the £50,000 he/she is investing. This is done because the new partner is not entitled to any of the previously established goodwill and the only way to prevent that permanently is to recognise all the goodwill now and credit it to the existing partners' capital accounts.

The action required is:

● Debit goodwill account: with total value of goodwill;
● Credit capitals of old partners: with their shares of goodwill in old profit sharing ratios.

No adjustments for goodwill gains and losses are required as the capital accounts of D and E have been increased by the full value of the goodwill at the time of F's admission to partnership.

For Exhibit 33.3, the entries would appear as:

Goodwill

	£		£
Value divided: D Capital	30,000	Balance c/d	60,000
E Capital	30,000		
	60,000		60,000

Capital Accounts

	D £	E £	F £		D £	E £	F £
				Balances b/d	50,000	50,000	
				Cash for capital			50,000
Balances c/d	80,000	80,000	50,000	Goodwill	30,000	30,000	
	80,000	80,000	50,000		80,000	80,000	50,000

As shown in Section 33.7, if the partnership was dissolved and realised the £210,000 it was valued at when F was admitted, this would first be used to repay the capital account balances. D and F would, therefore, be fully compensated for the value of the goodwill at the time of F's admission to partnership, and F would receive exactly the amount of his/her investment.

33.12 Where new partners pay for share of goodwill

The last section looked at how the partners' capital accounts are adjusted to account for goodwill when a new partner is admitted. In the second case, £24,000 was paid for goodwill by the new partner. Total goodwill at that time was £60,000. The profit share of the new partner is 2/5. If you divide £24,000 by 2/5 you get £60,000. Therefore, if you didn't know that the total goodwill was £60,000 you can calculate it by dividing the amount a new partner pays for goodwill by that new partner's profit sharing ratio.

Unless otherwise agreed, the assumption is that the total value of goodwill is directly proportionate to the amount paid by the new partner for the share of profit the new partner will receive in future. If a new partner pays £12,000 for a one-fifth share of future profits, goodwill is taken to be £60,000. A sum of £18,000 for a one-quarter share of future profits would, therefore, be taken to imply a total value of £72,000 for goodwill.

33.13 Goodwill on withdrawal or death of partners

This depends on whether or not a goodwill account exists.

If there was no goodwill account

If no goodwill account already existed the partnership goodwill should be valued because the outgoing partner is entitled to his/her share of its value. This value is entered in double entry accounts:

● Debit goodwill account with valuation.
● Credit each old partner's capital account in profit sharing ratios.

Exhibit 33.4

H, I and J have been in partnership for many years sharing profit and losses equally. No goodwill account has ever existed.

J is leaving the partnership. The other two partners are to take over his share of profits equally. Each partner's capital before entering goodwill was £50,000. The goodwill is valued at £45,000.

Goodwill

	£		£
Valuation: Capital H	15,000	Balance c/d	45,000
Capital I	15,000		
Capital J	15,000		
	45,000		
	45,000		45,000
Balance b/d	45,000		

Capital Accounts

	H £	I £	J £		H £	I £	J £
Balances c/d	65,000	65,000	65,000	Balances b/d	50,000	50,000	50,000
				Goodwill shares	15,000	15,000	15,000
	65,000	65,000	65,000		65,000	65,000	65,000
				Balances b/d	65,000	65,000	65,000

When J leaves the partnership, his capital balance of £65,000 will be paid to him.

If a goodwill account exists

1 If a goodwill account exists with the correct valuation of goodwill entered in it, no further action is needed.
2 If the valuation in the goodwill account needs to be changed, the following will apply:

Goodwill undervalued: Debit increase needed to goodwill account.
Credit increase to old partners' capital accounts in their old profit sharing ratios.

Goodwill overvalued: Debit reduction to old partners' capital accounts in their old profit sharing ratios.
Credit reduction needed to goodwill account.

Learning outcomes

You should now have learnt:

1 What is meant by the term 'goodwill'.

2 What is meant by the term 'purchased goodwill', and how to calculate it.

3 How to calculate super profits.

4 How to record goodwill in the accounts of a partnership.

5 That the true value of goodwill can be established only when the business is sold, but for various reasons of fairness between partners it is valued the best way possible when there is no imminent sale of a business.

6 That if the old partners agree, a new partner can be admitted without paying anything in as capital.

7 That goodwill is usually owned by the partners in the ratio in which they share profits.

8 That if there is a change in partnership without adjustments for goodwill, then some partners will make an unfair gain while others will quite unfairly lose money.

9 That if a new partner pays a specific amount for his or her share of the goodwill, then that payment is said to be a 'premium'.

Answers to activities

33.1 What if someone wanted to buy the business so that they could run it for themselves? Would they not be willing to pay a bit extra so as to benefit from the customer and product base you've built up? When a business is sold as a 'going concern', the owners can usually receive more than simply the value of the assets or, to be more accurate, the value of its net assets (i.e. all assets less all liabilities). This difference is known as 'goodwill'.

33.2 It is unlikely that a potential buyer would be willing to pay more than £300,000 for the business and so it would most likely be sold, asset by asset, for £400,000.

33.3 The business may have been founded by the present owner who, at some time after starting the business, bought another business and combined the two businesses into one. For example, a newsagent may take over another newsagent and run both shops as one business. The purchased goodwill included in the amount paid for the second business would appear in the balance sheet of the combined business.

Review questions

33.1 The partners have always shared their profits in the ratios of Vantuira 3: Aparecida 2: Fraga 5. They are to alter their profit ratios to Vantuira 4: Aparecida 1: Fraga 3. The last balance sheet before the change was:

Balance Sheet as at 31 March 2019

	£
Net Assets (not including goodwill)	100,000
	100,000
Capitals:	
Vantuira	30,000
Aparecida	20,000
Fraga	50,000
	100,000

The partners agree to bring in goodwill, being valued at £24,000 on the change.

Show the balance sheet on 1 April 2019 after goodwill has been taken into account if:

(a) Goodwill account was opened.
(b) Goodwill account was not opened.

33.2A The partners are to change their profit ratios as shown:

	Old ratio	New ratio
Abel	1	2
Burt	4	3
Cole	2	4
Dodds	3	1

They decide to bring in a goodwill amount of £72,000 on the change. The last balance sheet before any element of goodwill has been introduced was:

Balance Sheet as at 30 September 2019

	£
Net assets (not including goodwill)	330,000
	330,000
Capitals:	
Abel	55,000
Burt	120,000
Cole	65,000
Dodds	90,000
	330,000

Show the balance sheet on 1 October 2019 after necessary adjustments have been made if:

(a) Goodwill account was opened.
(b) Goodwill account was not opened.

33.3 Black and Smart are in partnership, sharing profits and losses equally. They decide to admit King. By agreement, goodwill valued at £40,000 is to be introduced into the business books. King is required to provide capital equal to that of Smart after she has been credited with her share of goodwill. The new profit sharing ratio is to be 8:3:5 respectively for Black, Smart and King.

The balance sheet before admission of King showed:

	£
Non-current and current assets (other than cash)	160,000
Cash	1,000
Total assets	161,000
Current liabilities	(41,000)
Net assets	120,000
Capital: Black	70,000
Capital: Smart	50,000
	120,000

Show:

(a) Journal entries for admission of Smart.
(b) Opening balance sheet of new business.
(c) Journal entries for writing off the goodwill which the new partners decided to do soon after the start of the new business.

33.4A Blunt, Dodds and Fuller are in partnership. They shared profits in the ratio 1:3:2. It is decided to admit Baxter. It is agreed that goodwill is worth £60,000, but that this is not to be brought into the business records. Baxter will bring £24,000 cash into the business for capital. The new profit sharing ratio is to be Blunt 4: Dodds 5: Fuller 2: Baxter 1.

The balance sheet before Baxter was introduced was as follows:

	£
Assets (other than in cash)	66,000
Cash	1,200
Total assets	67,200
Accounts payable	(8,400)
Net assets	58,800
Capitals: Blunt	14,000
Dodds	24,400
Fuller	20,400
	58,800

Show:

(a) The entries in the capital accounts of Blunt, Dodds, Fuller and Baxter, the accounts to be in columnar form.
(b) The balance sheet after Baxter has been introduced.

33.5 Wilson, Player and Sharp are in partnership. They shared profits in the ratio 2:4:3. It is decided to admit Titmus. It is agreed that goodwill is worth £72,000 and that it is to be brought into the business records. Titmus will bring £30,000 cash into the business for capital. The new profit sharing ratio is to be Wilson 5: Player 8: Sharp 4: Titmus 3.

The balance sheet before Titmus was introduced was as follows:

	£
Assets (other than in cash)	200,000
Cash	2,000
Total assets	202,000
Liabilities	(31,000)
Net assets	171,000
Capitals: Wilson	57,000
Player	76,000
Sharp	38,000
	171,000

→ **Show:**
(a) The entries in the capital accounts of Wilson, Player, Sharp and Titmus, the accounts to be in columnar form.
(b) The balance sheet after Titmus has been introduced.

33.6 A new partner has joined the business during the year and has paid in £10,000 for 'goodwill'. This £10,000 has been credited by the bookkeeper to the account of the new partner. The senior partner had objected to this, but the bookkeeper had replied: 'Why not credit the £10,000 to the account of the new partner? It is his money after all.'

Required:
Give your advice as to the proper treatment of this £10,000. Explain your reasons fully.

(*Association of Chartered Certified Accountants*)

33.7 Owing to staff illnesses, the draft final accounts for the year ended 31 March 2019 of Messrs Stone, Pebble and Brick, trading in partnership as the Bigtime Building Supply Company, have been prepared by an inexperienced, but keen, clerk. The draft summarised balance sheet as at 31 March 2019 is as follows:

	£
Tangible non-current assets: At cost less depreciation to date	45,400
Current assets	32,290
Total assets	77,690
Trade accounts payable	(6,390)
Net assets	71,300

Represented by:	Stone	Pebble	Brick	Total
	£	£	£	£
Capital accounts: at 1 April 2018	26,000	18,000	16,000	60,000
Current accounts:				
Share of net profit for the year ended 31 March 2019	12,100	12,100	12,100	
Drawings year ended 31 March 2019	(8,200)	(9,600)	(7,200)	
At 31 March 2019	3,900	2,500	4,900	11,300
				71,300

The partnership commenced on 1 April 2018 when each of the partners introduced, as their partnership capital, the net tangible non-current and current assets of their previously separate businesses. However, it has now been discovered that, contrary to what was agreed, no adjustments were made in the partnership books for the goodwill of the partners' former businesses now incorporated in the partnership. The agreed valuations of goodwill at 1 April 2018 are as follows:

	£
Stone's business	30,000
Pebble's business	20,000
Brick's business	16,000

It is agreed that a goodwill account should not be opened in the partnership's books.

It has now been discovered that effect has not been given in the accounts to the following provisions in the partnership agreement effective from 1 January 2019:

1 Stone's capital to be reduced to £20,000, the balance being transferred to a loan account upon which interest at the rate of 11% per annum will be paid on 31 December each year.
2 Partners to be credited with interest on their capital account balances at the rate of 5% per annum.

3 Brick to be credited with a partner's salary at the rate of £8,500 per annum.
4 The balance of the net profit or loss to be shared between Stone, Pebble and Brick in the ratio 5:3:2 respectively.

Notes:

1 It can be assumed that the net profit indicated in the draft accounts accrued uniformly throughout the year.
2 It has been agreed between the partners that no adjustments should be made for any partnership goodwill as at 1 January 2019.

Required:
(*a*) Prepare the profit and loss appropriation account for the year ended 31 March 2019.
(*b*) Prepare a corrected statement of the partners' capital and current accounts for inclusion in the partnership balance sheet as at 31 March 2019.

(*Association of Accounting Technicians*)

Revaluation of partnership assets

Learning objectives

After you have studied this chapter, you should be able to:

● explain why there may be a need for revaluation of assets in a partnership
● calculate the amount of asset revaluation gain or loss attributable to each partner
● make the necessary entries to the ledger accounts when assets are revalued

Introduction

In this chapter, you'll learn about the events that make it necessary to revalue the assets of a partnership. You'll learn the journal entries required to record asset revaluations in the ledger accounts of the partnership and how to apportion gains and losses on revaluation between the partners.

34.1 Need for revaluation

When a business is sold and the sale price of the assets differs from their book values, there will be a profit or loss on the sale. This profit or loss will be shared between the partners in their profit and loss sharing ratios.

This sharing of profits and losses that result from changing asset values doesn't just need to be done when a partnership is sold. It should also be done whenever any of the following happens:

● a new partner is admitted;
● a partner leaves the firm;
● the partners change profit and loss sharing ratios.

As no sale has taken place in any of these circumstances, the assets will have to be revalued to reflect what they are worth at the date when the change occurs. Once they are revalued, the gains and losses can be identified.

Activity 34.1

Why do the assets need to be revalued in these cases? The business has not been sold. (*Hint*: there is no legal requirement to do so; and consider this question in the light of what you learnt in Chapter 33 about goodwill when new partners are admitted.)

Once the assets have been revalued, you need to record the changes and gains and losses in the ledger accounts of the partnership.

34.2 Profit or loss on revaluation

If the revaluation shows no difference in asset values, no further action is needed. This will not happen very often, especially if assets include buildings. These are normally shown at cost less accumulated depreciation, but this is very rarely the actual value of buildings after they have been owned for a few years.

		£
If:	New total valuation of assets	90,000
Is *more* than:	Old total valuation of assets	(60,000)
The result is:	Gain on revaluation	30,000

		£
If:	New total valuation of assets	40,000
Is *less* than:	Old total valuation of assets	(50,000)
The result is:	Loss on revaluation	(10,000)

34.3 Accounting for revaluation

The first thing you do upon revaluing partnership assets is to open a **revaluation account** and make the appropriate entries:

1 *For each asset showing a gain on revaluation:*
    Debit asset account with gain.
        Credit revaluation account.

2 *For each asset showing a loss on revaluation:*
    Debit revaluation account.
        Credit asset account with loss.

3 *If there is an increase in total valuation of assets:*
    Debit profit to revaluation account.
        Credit **old** partners' capital accounts in **old** profit and loss sharing ratios.[Note]

4 *If there is a fall in total valuations of assets:*
    Debit **old** partners' capital accounts in **old** profit and loss sharing ratios.[Note]
        Credit loss to revaluation account.

Note: If current accounts are kept for the partners, the entries should be made in their current accounts.

Activity 34.2

When you were looking at goodwill in the previous chapter, you were interested in the difference between the amount received and the value of *net* assets. Why do we consider *only the assets* when there is a change in partners or a change in the profit sharing ratio?

Exhibit 34.1

Following is the balance sheet as at 31 December 2018 of W and Y, who shared profits and losses in the ratios: W two-thirds; Y one-third. From 1 January 2019 the profit and loss sharing ratio is to be altered to W one-half; Y one-half.

Balance Sheet as at 31 December 2018

	£	£
Premises (at cost)		65,000
Equipment (at cost less depreciation)		15,000
		80,000
Inventory	20,000	
Accounts receivable	12,000	
Bank	8,000	
		40,000
Total assets		120,000
Capitals: W		70,000
Y		50,000
		120,000

The assets were revalued on 1 January 2019 to be: Premises £90,000; Equipment £11,000. Other asset values were unchanged.

Accounts to show the assets at revalued amounts show:

Revaluation

	£	£		£
Assets reduced in value:			Assets increased in value:	
Equipment		4,000	Premises	25,000
Gain on revaluation carried				
to Capital accounts:				
W two-thirds	14,000			
Y one-third	7,000			
		21,000		
		25,000		25,000

Premises

	£		£
Balance b/d	65,000	Balance c/d	90,000
Revaluation: Increase	25,000		
	90,000		90,000
Balance b/d	90,000		

Equipment

	£		£
Balance b/d	15,000	Revaluation: Reduction	4,000
		Balance c/d	11,000
	15,000		15,000
Balance b/d	11,000		

Capital: W

	£		£
Balance c/d	84,000	Balance b/d	70,000
		Revaluation: Share of gain	14,000
	84,000		84,000
		Balance b/d	84,000

Capital: Y

	£		£
Balance c/d	57,000	Balance b/d	50,000
		Revaluation: Share of gain	7,000
	57,000		57,000
		Balance b/d	57,000

34.4 Revaluation of goodwill

This chapter deals with the revaluation of all assets other than goodwill. The revaluation of goodwill has already been dealt with in Chapter 33.

Learning outcomes

You should now have learnt:

1 How to make the entries arising from revaluations of partnership assets.

2 That when a new partner joins a firm, or a partner retires or dies, the partnership assets should be revalued.

3 That revaluation of assets should also occur when there is a change in the profit and loss sharing ratios of partners.

4 That profits on revaluation of assets are credited to the old partners' capital accounts in the old profit and loss sharing ratios.

5 That losses on revaluation of assets are debited to the old partners' capital accounts in the old profit and loss sharing ratios.

6 That the asset accounts also show the revalued amounts. Losses will have been credited to them and profits debited.

Answers to activities

34.1 When partners join or partners leave a partnership, there is, in effect, a new partnership. You learnt in Chapter 33 about goodwill that, when a new partner is admitted, the existing partners generally seek to ensure that they retain their share of the goodwill that has built up to that date. It should be fairly obvious, therefore, that the existing partners will also want to maintain the true value of their share of the business at that date in their capital accounts, rather than some historically-based figure.

　　If this were not done, new partners admitted would benefit from increases in value before they joined the business, without having to pay anything for them. Similarly, if the value of assets had fallen before they had joined the business, and no revaluation took place, they would share that loss of value without any adjustment being made for it. Partners who leave or change their profit and loss sharing ratios would also be affected if there were no payments or allowances for such gains or losses.

34.2   In this case, you are only concerned about whether the assets are stated at their true values. You assume that the liabilities are correctly stated and ignore them because they are already included in the calculation of capital. In other words, when considering goodwill, you are comparing the amount received with the total of the partners' account balances, i.e. the net worth of the business (assets less liabilities). In this case, you are only concerned in the first instance with what the true value is of *part* of the other side of the accounting equation, assets, and not with the true value of the net worth. When you make the entries in the ledger accounts, you effectively bring in the liabilities and calculate a new net worth, which is reflected in the new balances on the partners' account balances. The overall effect is the same, only you don't need to calculate net worth to know whether there has been a gain or loss on revaluation of the assets. You do need to do that in order to calculate goodwill.

Review questions

34.1

Cox, Fox and Lock
Balance Sheet as at 31 December 2018

	£	£
Buildings (at cost *less* accumulated depreciation)		175,000
Motor vehicles (at cost *less* accumulated depreciation)		43,000
Office fittings (at cost *less* accumulated depreciation)		4,700
		222,700
Inventory	15,900	
Accounts receivable	22,200	
Bank	3,600	
		41,700
Net assets		264,400
		£
Capitals:		
Cox		140,000
Fox		80,000
Lock		44,400
Total capital		264,400

The above partners have always shared profits and losses in the ratio: Cox 5: Fox 3: Lock 2.

From 1 January the assets were to be revalued as the profit sharing ratios are to be altered soon. The following assets are to be revalued to the figures shown: Buildings £250,000; Motor vehicles £30,000; Inventory £14,000; Office fittings £3,000.

Required:
(*a*)   You are required to show all the ledger accounts necessary to record the revaluation.
(*b*)   Draw up a balance sheet as at 1 January 2019.

34.2A   Fitch and Wall have been in partnership for many years sharing profits and losses in the ratio 5:3 respectively. The following was their balance sheet as at 31 December 2019:

	£	£
Goodwill		12,400
Plant and machinery		16,320
		28,720

Inventory	6,420	
Accounts receivable	4,100	
Cash at bank	626	
		11,146
Total assets		39,866
Sundry accounts payable		(5,928)
		33,938
Capital: Fitch		19,461
Wall		14,477
Total capital		33,938

On 1 January 2020, they decided to admit Home as a partner on the condition that she contributed £12,000 as her capital but that the plant and machinery and inventory should be revalued at £16,800 and £6,100 respectively, with the other assets, excepting goodwill, remaining at their book values. The goodwill was agreed to be valueless.

You are required to show:
(a) The ledger entries dealing with the above in the following accounts:
   (i) Goodwill account,
   (ii) Revaluation accounts,
   (iii) Capital accounts;
(b) The balance sheet of the partnership immediately after the admission of Home.

34.3 Alan, Bob and Charles are in partnership sharing profits and losses in the ratio 3:2:1 respectively. The balance sheet for the partnership as at 30 June 2019 is as follows:

	£	£
Non-current assets		
Premises		90,000
Plant		37,000
Vehicles		15,000
Fixtures		2,000
		144,000
Current assets		
Inventory	62,379	
Accounts receivable	34,980	
Cash	760	
		98,119
Total assets		242,119
Current liabilities		
Accounts payable	19,036	
Bank overdraft	4,200	
	23,236	
Loan – Charles	28,000	
Total liabilities		(51,236)
Net assets		190,883
Capital		
Alan		85,000
Bob		65,000
Charles		35,000
		185,000
Current account		
Alan	3,714	
Bob	(2,509)	
Charles	4,678	
		5,883
Total capital		190,883

Charles decides to retire from the business on 30 June 2019, and Don is admitted as a partner on that date. The following matters are agreed:

(a) Certain assets were revalued: Premises £120,000; Plant £35,000; Inventory £54,179.
(b) Provision is to be made for doubtful debts in the sum of £3,000.
(c) Goodwill is to be recorded in the books on the day Charles retires in the sum of £42,000. The partners in the new firm do not wish to maintain a goodwill account so that amount is to be written back against the new partners' capital accounts.
(d) Alan and Bob are to share profits in the same ratio as before, and Don is to have the same share of profits as Bob.
(e) Charles is to take his car at its book value of £3,900 in part payment, and the balance of all he is owed by the firm in cash except £20,000 which he is willing to leave as a loan account.
(f) The partners in the new firm are to start on an equal footing so far as capital and current accounts are concerned. Don is to contribute cash to bring his capital and current accounts to the same amount as the original partner from the old firm who has the lower investment in the business.

The original partner in the old firm who has the higher investment will draw out cash so that his capital and current account balances equal those of his new partners.

Required:
(a) Account for the above transactions, including goodwill and retiring partners' accounts.
(b) Draft a balance sheet for the partnership of Alan, Bob and Don as at 30 June 2019.

(*Association of Accounting Technicians*)

34.4A The balance sheet of A. Barnes and C. Darwin at 31 March 2018 is as follows:

	£	£
Non-current assets		
Building		51,000
Fittings		29,000
		80,000
Current assets		
Inventory	16,000	
Accounts receivable	5,000	
		21,000
Total assets		101,000
Current liabilities		
Bank	3,000	
Accounts payable	8,000	
Total liabilities		(11,000)
Net assets		90,000
Capital accounts		
Barnes		60,000
Darwin		30,000
Total capital		90,000

The partners share profits and losses: Barnes three-fifths and Darwin two-fifths. At the date of the above balance sheet, it was agreed to admit E. Fox who was to bring cash of £25,000 into the firm as capital. The new profit and loss ratio would be Barnes, one-half; Darwin, one-third; and Fox, one-sixth.

Barnes and Darwin agreed the following revaluation amounts prior to the admission of Fox. Any goodwill arising is to remain in the ledger.

	£
Buildings	55,000
Fittings	27,000
Inventory	15,500
Accounts receivable	4,800
Goodwill	12,000
Accrued expenses (previously omitted)	300

Required:
(a) Prepare the journal entries to record the above.
(b) Prepare the balance sheet of the new business.
(c) Show by journal entry how the necessary adjustment would be made if the partners agreed that goodwill should *not* remain in the ledger.

34.5 At 31 December 2020, the balance sheet of A, B and C, who are equal partners, was as follows:

	£	£
Non-current assets		
Freehold premises		16,000
Machinery and tools		15,100
Investment, at cost		4,000
		35,100
Current assets		
Inventory	16,000	
Accounts receivable	12,800	
Bank	12,100	
		40,900
Total assets		76,000
Current liabilities		
Accounts payable		(14,000)
Net assets		62,000
Capital accounts		
A		20,000
B		17,000
C		25,000
Total capital		62,000

A retired at that date. In order to determine the amount due to him the following revaluations were made: Freehold premises £18,000; machinery and tools £16,000; investments £5,100.

The value of the goodwill was agreed at £8,000. It was arranged that A should take over the investments in part payment of the amount due to him, the balance to be settled in cash. B and C would increase their capitals by paying in £10,000 and £6,000 respectively. These changes were all carried out.

Required:
(a) Prepare the revaluation account, bank account and capital accounts.
(b) Prepare the opening balance sheet of B and C.

35

Partnership dissolution

Learning objectives

After you have studied this chapter, you should be able to:

● explain what happens upon dissolution of a partnership

● record the entries relating to the dissolution of a partnership

● explain the differences between recording a partnership dissolution and making the entries when one partner leaves a partnership

● explain the Partnership Act 1890 rules relating to partnership dissolution

● explain the *Garner* v *Murray* rule

Introduction

In this chapter, you'll learn how to calculate and record the necessary entries when a partnership is dissolved. You'll learn that the process is laid down in the Partnership Act 1890 and what to do under the *Garner* v *Murray* rule when partners are unable to pay the amount they owe the partnership. Finally, you'll learn how to deal with a situation where the partnership assets are being disposed of over a long period of time.

35.1 Need for dissolution

You will recall from Chapter 31 that joint ventures are often short-term and that when the project they were formed to do has ended, the joint venture is terminated. You learnt in Chapter 32 that partnerships are long-term ventures that are formed with a long-term commitment on the part of the partners to operate in business together. In Chapter 33, you learnt that new partners are admitted from time to time; and, in Chapter 34, you learnt that partners can also leave partnerships. So, you'll have realised by now that partnerships really are not as permanent as they may at first appear.

Activity 35.1 Can you think of any partnership you know of where a partner left? How do you think the change in the partnership was treated in the ledgers?

In fact, so far as the UK tax authorities are concerned, every time a partner joins or leaves a partnership, a new partnership is brought into existence. Intuitively, this does make sense. Partnerships exist because of the desire to merge the skills, resources and expertise of the partners. Imagine a band whose lead singer leaves. The replacement is never quite the same. As another example, if two people are in a partnership running a restaurant and the one that does the cooking leaves, the replacement isn't going to want to prepare exactly the same meals.

Partnerships do change when a partner leaves. And they do change when a new partner joins. However, for accounting purposes, we only consider partnerships as changing sufficiently to merit treating them as ceasing to exist when the partners go their separate ways. When they do, this is known as partnership **dissolution** – the partnership has been dissolved.

Reasons for dissolution include:

(*a*) The partnership is no longer profitable, and there is no longer any reason to carry on trading.
(*b*) The partners cannot agree between themselves how to operate the partnership. They therefore decide to finish the partnership.
(*c*) Factors such as ill-health or old age may bring about the close of the partnership.

Activity 35.2   What is the difference between these events and partners simply leaving a partnership? For example, if there are three partners in a dental practice and two leave, why can't the third continue the business with new partners?

35.2   What happens upon dissolution

Upon **dissolution** the partnership firm stops trading or operating. Then, in accordance with the Partnership Act 1890:

(*a*) the assets are disposed of;
(*b*) the liabilities of the firm to everyone other than partners are paid;
(*c*) the partners are repaid their advances and current balances – advances are the amounts they have put in above and beyond the capital;
(*d*) the partners are paid the final amounts due to them on their capital accounts.

Any profit or loss on dissolution would be shared by all the partners in their profit and loss sharing ratios. Profits would increase capitals repayable to partners. Losses would reduce the capitals repayable.

If the final balance on a partner's capital and current accounts is in deficit, the partner will have to pay that amount into the partnership bank account.

35.3   Disposal of assets

The assets do not have to be sold to external parties. Quite often one or more existing partners will take assets at values agreed by all the partners. In such a case the partner may not pay in cash for such assets; instead they will be charged to that partner's capital account.

35.4   Accounting for partnership dissolution

The main account around which the dissolution entries are made is known as the **realisation account**. It is this account in which the profit or loss on the realisation of the assets is calculated.

Exhibit 35.1 shows the simplest of partnership dissolutions. We will then look at a more difficult example in Exhibit 35.2.

Exhibit 35.1

The last balance sheet of X and Y, who share profits X two-thirds: Y one-third is shown below. On this date they are to dissolve the partnership.

Balance Sheet at 31 December 2019

	£	£
Non-current assets		
Buildings		100,000
Motor vehicle		12,000
		112,000
Current assets		
Inventory	6,000	
Accounts receivable	8,000	
Bank	2,000	
		16,000
Total assets		128,000
Current liabilities		
Accounts payable		(5,000)
Net assets		123,000
Capitals: X		82,000
Y		41,000
Total capital		123,000

The buildings were sold for £105,000 and the inventory for £4,600. £6,800 was collected from debtors. The motor vehicle was taken over by X at an agreed value of £9,400, but he did not pay any cash for it. £5,000 was paid to settle the accounts payable. The £400 cost of the dissolution was paid.

The accounting entries needed are:

(A) Transfer book values of all assets to the realisation account:
  Debit realisation account
    Credit asset accounts

(B) Amounts received from disposal of assets:
  Debit bank
    Credit realisation account

(C) Values of assets taken over by partner without payment:
  Debit partner's capital account
    Credit realisation account

(D) Creditors paid:
  Debit accounts payable
    Credit bank

(E) Costs of dissolution:
  Debit realisation account
    Credit bank

(F) Profit or loss on realisation to be shared between partners in profit and loss sharing ratios:
  If a profit: Debit realisation account
        Credit partners' capital accounts

If a loss: Debit partners' capital accounts
                      Credit realisation account

(G) Pay to the partners their final balances on their capital accounts:
    Debit capital accounts
       Credit bank

The entries are now shown. The letters (A) to (G) as above are shown against each entry:

Buildings

		£			£
Balance b/d		100,000	Realisation	(A)	100,000

Motor Vehicle

		£			£
Balance b/d		12,000	Realisation	(A)	12,000

Inventory

		£			£
Balance b/d		6,000	Realisation	(A)	6,000

Accounts Receivable

		£			£
Balance b/d		8,000	Realisation	(A)	8,000

Realisation

		£				£
Assets to be realised:			Bank: Assets sold			
Buildings	(A)	100,000	Buildings	(B)		105,000
Motor vehicle	(A)	12,000	Inventory	(B)		4,600
Inventory	(A)	6,000	Accounts receivable	(B)		6,800
Accounts receivable	(A)	8,000	Taken over by partner A:			
Bank:			Motor vehicle	(C)		9,400
Dissolution costs	(E)	400	Loss on realisation		£	
			X $^2/_3$	(F)	400	
			Y $^1/_3$	(F)	200	
						600
		126,400				126,400

Accounts Payable

		£		£
Bank	(D)	5,000	Balance b/d	5,000

X: Capital

		£		£
Realisation: Motor	(C)	9,400	Balance b/d	82,000
Realisation: Share of loss	(F)	400		
Bank: to close	(G)	72,200		
		82,000		82,000

Y: Capital

		£			£
Realisation: Share of loss	(F)	200	Balance b/d		41,000
Bank: to close	(G)	40,800			
		41,000			41,000

Bank

		£			£
Balance b/d		2,000	Accounts payable	(D)	5,000
Realisation: Assets sold			Realisation: Costs	(E)	400
Buildings	(B)	105,000	Capitals: to close		
Inventory	(B)	4,600	X	(G)	72,200
Accounts receivable	(B)	6,800	Y	(G)	40,800
		118,400			118,400

The final balances on the partners' capital accounts should always equal the amount in the bank account from which they are to be paid. For instance, in the above exhibit there was £113,000 in the bank from which to pay X £72,200 and Y £40,800. You should always complete the capital account entries before you can complete the bank account entries. If the final bank balance does not pay out the partners' capital accounts exactly, you will have made a mistake somewhere.

35.5 A more detailed example

Exhibit 35.1 did not show the more difficult accounting entries. A more difficult example appears in Exhibit 35.2.

The extra complexities are:

(a) Any allowance such as doubtful debts or depreciation is to be transferred to the credit of the asset account: see entries (A) in Exhibit 35.2.
(b) Discounts on accounts payable – to balance the accounts payable, transfer the discounts on accounts payable to the credit of the realisation account: see entries (F) in the exhibit.
(c) Transfer the balances on the partners' current accounts to their capital accounts: see entries (I) of the exhibit.
(d) A partner who owes the partnership money because his capital account is in deficit must now pay the money owing: see entries (J) of the exhibit.

As a result, you will see that the list of accounting entries to be made is extended to run from A to K, compared with A to G.

Exhibit 35.2

On 31 December 2018, P, Q and R decided to dissolve their partnership. They had always shared profits in the ratio of P3 : Q2 : R1.

Their goodwill was sold for £30,000, the machinery for £24,000 and the inventory for £12,000. There were three cars, all taken over by the partners at agreed values, P taking one for £4,000, Q one for £6,000 and R one for £3,000. The premises were taken over by R at an agreed value of £162,000. The amounts collected from debtors amounted to £7,400 after bad debts and discounts had been deducted. The creditors were discharged for £6,280, the difference being due to discounts received. The costs of dissolution amounted to £700.

Their last balance sheet prior to dissolution of the partnership is summarised as:

Balance Sheet as at 31 December 2018

	£	£	£
Non-current assets			
Premises			150,000
Machinery			36,000
Motor vehicles			14,000
			200,000
Current assets			
Inventory		11,000	
Accounts receivable	8,000		
Less Allowance for doubtful debts	(400)		
		7,600	
Bank		1,200	
			19,800
Total assets			219,800
Current liabilities			
Accounts payable			(6,400)
Net assets			213,400
Capital accounts: P			70,000
Q			60,000
R			50,000
			180,000
Current accounts: P		9,700	
Q		7,500	
R		16,200	
			33,400
Total capital			213,400

Description of transactions:

(A) The provision accounts are transferred to the relevant asset accounts so that the net balance on the asset accounts may be transferred to the realisation account. Debit provision accounts. Credit asset accounts.

(B) The net book values of the assets are transferred to the realisation account. Debit realisation account. Credit asset accounts.

(C) Assets sold. Debit bank account. Credit realisation account.

(D) Assets taken over by partners. Debit partners' capital accounts. Credit realisation account.

(E) Liabilities discharged. Credit bank account. Debit liability accounts.

(F) Discounts on accounts payable. Debit accounts payable account. Credit realisation account.

(G) Costs of dissolution. Credit bank account. Debit realisation account.

(H) Profit or loss split in profit/loss sharing ratio. Profit – debit realisation account. Credit partners' capital accounts. The opposite if a loss.

(I) Transfer the balances on the partners' current accounts to their capital accounts.

(J) Any partner with a capital account in deficit, i.e. debits exceeding credits, must now pay in the amount needed to cancel his/her indebtedness to the partnership. Credit capital account. Debit bank account.

(K) The credit balances on the partners' capital accounts can now be paid to them. Debit partners' capital accounts. Credit bank account.

The payments made under (K) should complete the payment of all the balances in the partnership books.

The accounts recording the dissolution are shown below. The letters (A) to (K) against each entry indicate the relevant descriptions.

→

Premises

		£			£
Balance b/d		150,000	Realisation	(B)	150,000

Machinery

		£			£
Balance b/d		36,000	Realisation	(B)	36,000

Motor Vehicles

		£			£
Balance b/d		14,000	Realisation	(B)	14,000

Inventory

		£			£
Balance b/d		11,000	Realisation	(B)	11,000

Accounts Receivable

		£			£
Balance b/d		8,000	Allowance for doubtful debts	(A)	400
			Realisation	(B)	7,600
		8,000			8,000

Realisation

		£			£
Assets to be realised:			Bank: Assets sold		
Premises	(B)	150,000	Goodwill	(C)	30,000
Machinery	(B)	36,000	Machinery	(C)	24,000
Motor vehicles	(B)	14,000	Inventory	(C)	12,000
Inventory	(B)	11,000	Accounts receivable	(C)	7,400
Accounts receivable	(B)	7,600	Taken over by partners:		
Bank: Dissolution costs	(G)	700	P: Car	(D)	4,000
Profit on realisation:	(H)		Q: Car	(D)	6,000
	£		R: Car	(D)	3,000
P	14,610		R: Premises	(D)	162,000
Q	9,740		Accounts payable: Discounts	(F)	120
R	4,870				
	29,220				
	248,520				248,520

Accounts Payable

		£			£
Bank	(E)	6,280	Balance b/d		6,400
Realisation: Discounts	(F)	120			
		6,400			6,400

Allowance for Doubtful Debts

		£		£
Accounts receivable	(A)	400	Balance b/d	400

P Capital

		£			£
Realisation: Car	(D)	4,000	Balance b/d		70,000
Bank	(K)	90,310	Current account transferred	(I)	9,700
			Realisation: Share of profit	(H)	14,610
		94,310			94,310

P Current

		£		£
P: Capital	(I)	9,700	Balance b/d	9,700

Q Capital

		£			£
Realisation: Car	(D)	6,000	Balance b/d		60,000
Bank	(K)	71,240	Current account transferred	(I)	7,500
			Realisation: Share of profit	(H)	9,740
		77,240			77,240

Q Current

		£		£
Q: Capital	(I)	7,500	Balance b/d	7,500

R Capital

		£			£
Realisation: Car	(D)	3,000	Balance b/d		50,000
Realisation: Premises	(D)	162,000	Current account transferred	(I)	16,200
			Realisation: Share of profit	(H)	4,870
			Bank	(J)	93,930
		165,000			165,000

R Current

		£		£
R: Capital	(I)	16,200	Balance b/d	16,200

Bank

		£			£
Balance b/d		1,200	Accounts payable	(E)	6,280
Realisation: Assets sold			Realisation: Costs	(G)	700
Goodwill	(C)	30,000	P: Capital	(K)	90,310
Machinery	(C)	24,000	Q: Capital	(K)	71,240
Inventory	(C)	12,000			
Accounts receivable	(C)	7,400			
R: Capital	(J)	93,930			
		168,530			168,530

35.6 The *Garner* v *Murray* rule

It sometimes happens that a partner's capital account finishes up with a debit balance. Normally the partner will pay in an amount to clear his/her indebtedness to the firm. However, sometimes the partner will be unable to pay all, or part, of such a balance. In the case of ***Garner* v *Murray*** in 1904 (a case in England) the court ruled that, subject to any agreement to the contrary, such a deficiency was to be shared by the other partners *not* in their profit and loss sharing ratios but in the ratio of their 'last agreed capitals'. By 'their last agreed capitals' is meant the credit balances on their capital accounts in the normal balance sheet drawn up at the end of their last accounting period.

It must be borne in mind that the balances on their capital accounts after the assets have been realised may be far different from those on the last balance sheet. Where a partnership deed is drawn up it is commonly found that agreement is made to use normal profit and loss sharing ratios instead, thus rendering the *Garner* v *Murray* rule inoperative. **The *Garner* v *Murray* rule does not apply to partnerships in Scotland.**

Before reading further you should check whether or not this topic is in the requirements for your examinations.

Exhibit 35.3

After completing the realisation of all the assets, in respect of which a loss of £14,000 was incurred, but before making the final payments to the partners, the balance sheet shows:

Balance Sheet

	£	£
Cash at bank		91,000
Capitals: R	66,000	
S	18,000	
T	8,000	
	92,000	
Less Q (debit balance)	(1,000)	
		91,000

According to the last balance sheet drawn up before the dissolution, the partners' capital account credit balances were: Q £5,000; R £70,000; S £20,000; T £10,000; while the profits and losses were shared Q3 : R2 : S1 : T1.

Q is unable to meet any part of his deficiency. Under the *Garner* v *Murray* rule, each of the other partners suffers the deficiency as follows:

$$\frac{\text{Own capital per balance sheet before dissolution}}{\text{Total of all solvent partners' capitals per same balance sheet}} \times \text{Deficiency}$$

This can now be calculated.

$$R \quad \frac{£70,000}{£70,000 + £20,000 + £10,000} \times 1,000 = £700$$

$$S \quad \frac{£20,000}{£70,000 + £20,000 + £10,000} \times 1,000 = £200$$

$$T \quad \frac{£10,000}{£70,000 + £20,000 + £10,000} \times 1,000 = \underline{£100}$$

$$\underline{\underline{£1,000}}$$

When these amounts have been charged to the capital accounts, the balances remaining on them will equal the amount of the bank balance. Payments may therefore be made to clear their capital accounts.

	Credit balance b/d £		Share of deficiency now debited £		Final credit balances £
R	66,000	–	700	=	65,300
S	18,000	–	200	=	17,800
T	8,000	–	100	=	7,900
Equals the bank balance					91,000

35.7 Piecemeal realisation of assets

Frequently the assets may take a long time to be turned into cash (i.e. 'realised'). The partners will naturally want payments made to them on account as cash is received. They will not want to wait for payments until the dissolution is completed just for the convenience of the accountant. There is, however, a danger that if too much is paid to a partner, and he is unable to repay it, then the person handling the dissolution could be placed in a very awkward position.

To counteract this, the concept of prudence is brought into play. This is done as follows:

(a) Each receipt of sale money is treated as being the final receipt, even though more could be received.
(b) Any loss then calculated so far to be shared between partners in profit and loss sharing ratios.
(c) Should any partner's capital account after each receipt show a debit balance, then he is assumed to be unable to pay in the deficiency. This deficit will be shared (failing any other agreement) between the partners using the *Garner* v *Murray* rule.
(d) After payments of liabilities and the costs of dissolution the remainder of the cash is then paid to the partners.
(e) In this manner, even if no further money were received, or should a partner become insolvent, the division of the available cash would be strictly in accordance with the legal requirements. Exhibit 35.4 shows such a series of calculations.

Exhibit 35.4

The following is the summarised balance sheet of H, I, J and K as at 31 December 2018. The partners had shared profits in the ratios H6 : I4 : J1 : K1.

Balance Sheet as at 31 December 2018

	£
Assets	84,000
Accounts payable	(18,000)
	66,000
Capitals:	
H	6,000
I	30,000
J	20,000
K	10,000
	66,000

On 1 March 2019 some of the assets were sold for cash £50,000. Out of this the creditors' £18,000 and the cost of dissolution £800 are paid, leaving £31,200 distributable to the partners.

On 1 July 2019 some more assets are sold for £21,000. As all of the liabilities and the costs of dissolution have already been paid, the whole of the £21,000 is available for distribution between the partners.

→

On 1 October 2019 the final sale of the assets realised £12,000.

First distribution: 1 March 2019	H	I	J	K	Total
	£	£	£	£	£
Capital balances before dissolution	6,000	30,000	20,000	10,000	66,000
Loss if no further assets realised: Assets £84,000 − Sales £50,000 = £34,000 + Costs £800 = £34,800 loss					
Loss shared in profit/loss ratios	(17,400)	(11,600)	(2,900)	(2,900)	(34,800)
	11,400 *Dr*	18,400Cr	17,100Cr	7,100Cr	31,200
H's deficiency shared in *Garner* v *Murray* ratios		³⁄₆ (5,700)	²⁄₆ (3,800)	¹⁄₆ (1,900)	
Cash paid to partners		12,700	13,300	5,200	31,200

Second distribution: 1 July 2019	H	I	J	K	Total
	£	£	£	£	£
Capital balances before dissolution	6,000	30,000	20,000	10,000	66,000
Loss if no further assets realised: Assets £84,000 − Sales (£50,000 + £21,000) = £13,000 + Costs £800 = £13,800 loss					
Loss shared in profit/loss ratios	(6,900)	(4,600)	(1,150)	(1,150)	(13,800)
	900 *Dr*	25,400Cr	18,850Cr	8,850Cr	52,200
H's deficiency shared in *Garner* v *Murray* ratios		³⁄₆ (450)	²⁄₆ (300)	¹⁄₆ (150)	
		24,950	18,550	8,700	
Less First distribution already paid		(12,700)	(13,300)	(5,200)	31,200
Cash now paid to partners		12,250	5,250	3,500	21,000
					52,200

Third and final distribution: 1 October 2019	H	I	J	K	Total
	£	£	£	£	£
Capital balances before dissolution	6,000	30,000	20,000	10,000	66,000
Loss finally ascertained: Assets £84,000 − Sales (£50,000 + £21,000 + £12,000) = £1,000 + Costs £800 = £1,800 loss					
Loss shared in profit/loss ratios	(900)	(600)	(150)	(150)	(1,800)
	5,100Cr	29,400Cr	19,850Cr	9,850Cr	64,200
(No deficiency now exists on any capital account)					
Less First and second distributions	–	(24,950)	(18,550)	(8,700)	52,200
Cash now paid to partners	5,100	4,450	1,300	1,150	12,000
					64,200

In any subsequent distribution following that in which all the partners have shared (i.e. no partners could then have had a deficiency left on their capital accounts) all receipts of cash are divided between the partners in their profit and loss sharing ratios. Following the above method would give the same answer for these subsequent distributions but obviously an immediate division in the profit and loss sharing ratios would be quicker. Try it for yourself and you'll see that the same answer would result.

35.8 A final word

The partnership income and profit and loss appropriation account which you have headed-up using that rather long-winded heading is often simply referred to and headed-up as 'Income statement'. You will see an example of this shorter heading when you look at the solution to Review Question 35.7.

Learning outcomes

You should now have learnt:

1 How to calculate the amounts due to and from each partner when a partnership is dissolved.

2 How to record partnership dissolution in the ledger accounts.

3 That upon dissolution, a partnership stops trading or operating, any profit or loss on dissolution being shared by the partners in their profit sharing ratio.

4 That the *Garner* v *Murray* rule does not apply to partnerships in Scotland.

Answers to activities

35.1 There is obviously no 'right' answer to this question. You may have noticed partnership changes at your local doctor's or dental practice. They can have quite an impact upon some of the patients. Similarly, there have been famous partnerships in ice skating, the theatre, music, and in sport, especially tennis, where switching partners creates a very different visual effect and level of satisfaction for the audience.

Many of these examples are really short-term joint ventures rather than partnerships. The doctors and dentists are most definitely partnerships. In many cases where one of *these* examples of joint ventures or partnerships change, a new one tends to develop in its place. In the case of partnerships where the business is continuing with new partners, you can apply the techniques you've already learnt to apply when a partner leaves a partnership and when a partner joins and make the necessary entries in the partnership ledger accounts.

35.2 That may happen, in which case it could be argued that it should be treated as simply a change of membership of the partnership. There's nothing wrong with doing so if the business is continuing as before but, even in those cases, you will probably find it easier to treat it as a partnership dissolution, close off all the books and start afresh with the new partnership. This is because if only one partner is left in the business, you would need to remove each of the partners who have left from the accounts anyway before adding in the new one(s).

Review questions

35.1 Adrian and Thomas, who share profits and losses equally, decide to dissolve their partnership as at 30 June 2020. Their balance sheet on that date was as follows:

	£	£
Buildings		150,000
Tools and fixtures		11,600
		161,600
Accounts receivable	22,300	
Cash	1,800	
		24,100
		185,700
Sundry accounts payable		18,400
		167,300
Capital account: Adrian		108,000
Thomas		59,300
		167,300

The accounts receivable realised £20,900, the buildings £139,000 and the tools and fixtures £5,000. The expenses of dissolution were £1,950 and discounts totalling £700 were received from creditors.

Required:
Prepare the accounts necessary to show the results of the realisation and of the disposal of the cash.

35.2 Mears, Pugh and Stafford were in partnership sharing profits and losses in the ratio 5:3:2 respectively.

The partners had agreed that the partnership would be dissolved on 1 April 2019.

The partnership balance sheet at 31 March 2019 was as follows:

Mears, Pugh and Stafford
Balance sheet at 31 March 2019

	£	£
Non-current assets		185,000
Current assets		
Inventory	31,600	
Trade receivables	14,850	46,450
		231,450
Current liabilities		
Bank overdraft	9,210	
Trade payables	8,900	18,110
		213,340
Capital accounts		
Mears	25,000	
Pugh	84,000	
Stafford	56,000	165,000
Current accounts		
Mears	(19,500)	
Pugh	31,704	
Stafford	36,136	48,340
		213,340

Additional information

1 A vehicle could have been sold for £18,800. However, because this would have generated a loss of £3,200, it was decided instead that Pugh would take the vehicle at the net book value as part of his settlement.

2 All other non-current assets were found to be impaired. They could only be disposed of for the recoverable amount. The fair value of these assets was £150,000 and the value in use was £125,000.

3 Inventory would usually be sold at a mark-up of 25% on cost price. However, because the inventory was damaged, it was actually sold for £14,220 less than this amount.

4 A bankrupt customer owed £2,350. All other trade receivables paid in full after being given a 5% settlement discount.

5 The partnership is owed a refund of £100 from a supplier and this has not been accounted for. All other trade payables were settled in full after receiving a 2% discount.

6 The costs of dissolving the partnership of £1,951 were paid by cheque.

Mears was bankrupt and so was unable to repay any amounts owing to the partnership from her own personal finance.

Required:
(a) Prepare the realisation account for the partnership at 1 April 2019.
(b) Prepare the partnership capital accounts for Mears, Pugh and Stafford at 1 April 2019.
(c) Prepare the partnership bank account at 1 April 2019 to show all transactions relating to the dissolution of the partnership.

(AQA A Level)

35.3A The following trial balance has been extracted from the books of Gain and Main as at 31 March 2018; Gain and Main are in partnership sharing profits and losses in the ratio 3 to 2:

	£	£
Capital accounts:		
Gain		10,000
Main		5,000
Cash at bank	1,550	
Accounts payable		500
Current accounts:		
Gain		1,000
Main	2,000	
Accounts receivable	2,000	
Depreciation: Fixtures and fittings		1,000
Motor vehicles		1,300
Fixtures and fittings	2,000	
Land and buildings	30,000	
Motor vehicles	4,500	
Net profit (for the year to 31 March 2018)		26,250
Inventory, at cost	3,000	
	£45,050	£45,050

In appropriating the net profit for the year, it has been agreed that Main should be entitled to a salary of £9,750. Each partner is also entitled to interest on his opening capital account balance at the rate of 10 per cent per annum.

Gain and Main have decided to convert the partnership into a limited company, Plain Limited, as from 1 April 2018. The company is to take over all the assets and liabilities of the partnership, except that Gain is to retain for his personal use one of the motor vehicles at an agreed transfer price of £1,000.

The purchase consideration will consist of 40,000 ordinary shares of £1 each in Plain Limited, to be divided between the partners in profit-sharing ratio. Any balance on the partners' current accounts is to be settled in cash.

Required:
Prepare the main ledger accounts of the partnership in order to close off the books as at 31 March 2018.

(Association of Accounting Technicians)

35.4A A, B and C are partners sharing profits and losses in the ratio 2 : 2 : 1. The balance sheet of the partnership as at 30 September 2020 was as follows:

	£	£
Freehold premises		18,000
Equipment and machinery		12,000
Cars		3,000
		33,000
Inventory	11,000	
Accounts receivable	14,000	
Bank	9,000	
		34,000
		67,000
Accounts payable	10,000	
Loan account – A	7,000	
Total liabilities		(17,000)
Net assets		50,000
Capital accounts		
A		22,000
B		18,000
C		10,000
		50,000

The partners agreed to dispose of the business to CNO Limited with effect from 1 October 2020 under the following conditions and terms:

(i) CNO Limited will acquire the goodwill, all non-current assets and the inventory for the purchase consideration of £58,000. This consideration will include a payment of £10,000 in cash and the issue of 12,000 10 per cent preference shares of £1 each at par, and the balance by the issue of £1 ordinary shares at £1.25 per share.
(ii) The partnership business will settle amounts owing to creditors.
(iii) CNO Limited will collect the debts on behalf of the vendors.

Purchase consideration payments and allotments of shares were made on 1 October 2020.

The partnership accounts payable were paid off by 31 October 2020 after the taking of cash discounts of £190.

CNO Limited collected and paid over all partnership debts by 30 November 2020 except for bad debts amounting to £800. Discounts allowed to debtors amounted to £400.

Required:
(a) Journal entries (including those relating to cash) necessary to close the books of the partnership, and
(b) Set out the basis on which the shares in CNO Limited are allotted to partners. Ignore interest.

(Institute of Chartered Secretaries and Administrators)

35.5   Amis, Lodge and Pym were in partnership sharing profits and losses in the ratio 5 : 3 : 2. The following trial balance has been extracted from their books of account as at 31 March 2020:

	£	£
Bank interest received		750
Capital accounts (as at 1 April 2019):		
Amis		80,000
Lodge		15,000
Pym		5,000
Carriage inwards	4,000	
Carriage outwards	12,000	
Cash at bank	4,900	
Current accounts:		
Amis	1,000	
Lodge	500	
Pym	400	
Discounts allowed	10,000	
Discounts received		4,530
Drawings:		
Amis	25,000	
Lodge	22,000	
Pym	15,000	
Motor vehicles:		
at cost	80,000	
accumulated depreciation (at 1 April 2019)		20,000
Office expenses	30,400	
Plant and machinery:		
at cost	100,000	
accumulated depreciation (at 1 April 2019)		36,600
Allowance for doubtful debts (at 1 April 2019)		420
Purchases	225,000	
Rent, rates, heat and light	8,800	
Sales		404,500
Inventory (at 1 April 2019)	30,000	
Trade accounts payable		16,500
Trade accounts receivable	14,300	
	£583,300	£583,300

Additional information:

(*a*)   Inventory at 31 March 2020 was valued at £35,000.

(*b*)   Depreciation on the non-current assets is to be charged as follows:
   Motor vehicles – 25 per cent on the reduced balance.
   Plant and machinery – 20 per cent on the original cost.
   There were no purchases or sales of non-current assets during the year to 31 March 2020.

(*c*)   The allowance for doubtful debts is to be maintained at a level equivalent to 5 per cent of the total trade accounts receivable as at 31 March 2020.

(*d*)   An office expense of £405 was owing at 31 March 2020, and some rent amounting to £1,500 had been paid in advance as at that date. These items had not been included in the list of balances shown in the trial balance.

(*e*)   Interest on drawings and on the debit balance on each partner's current account is to be charged as follows:

	£
Amis	1,000
Lodge	900
Pym	720

(f) According to the partnership agreement, Pym is allowed a salary of £13,000 per annum. This amount was owing to Pym for the year to 31 March 2020, and needs to be accounted for.

(g) The partnership agreement also allows each partner interest on his capital account at a rate of 10 per cent per annum. There were no movements on the respective partners' capital accounts during the year to 31 March 2020, and the interest had not been credited to them as at that date.

Note: The information given above is sufficient to answer part (a) (i) and (ii) of the question, and notes (h) and (i) below are pertinent to requirements (b) (i), (ii) and (iii) of the question.

(h) On 1 April 2020, Fowles Limited agreed to purchase the business on the following terms:
  (i) Amis to purchase one of the partnership's motor vehicles at an agreed value of £5,000, the remaining vehicles being taken over by the company at an agreed value of £30,000;
  (ii) the company agreed to purchase the plant and machinery at a value of £35,000 and the inventory at a value of £38,500;
  (iii) the partners to settle the trade accounts payable: the total amount agreed with the creditors being £16,000;
  (iv) the trade accounts receivable were not to be taken over by the company, the partners receiving cheques on 1 April 2020 amounting to £12,985 in total from the trade debtors in settlement of the outstanding debts;
  (v) the partners paid the outstanding office expense on 1 April 2020, and the landlord returned the rent paid in advance by cheque on the same day;
  (vi) as consideration for the sale of the partnership, the partners were to be paid £63,500 in cash by Fowles Limited, and to receive £75,000 in £1 ordinary shares in the company, the shares to be apportioned equally amongst the partners.

(i) Assume that all the matters relating to the dissolution of the partnership and its sales to the company took place on 1 April 2020.

Required:
(a) Prepare:
  (i) Amis, Lodge and Pym's income statement and profit and loss appropriation account for the year ending 31 March 2020;
  (ii) Amis, Lodge and Pym's current accounts (in columnar format) for the year to 31 March 2020 (the final balance on each account is to be then transferred to each partner's respective capital account);
  and
(b) Compile the following accounts:
  (i) the partnership realisation account for the period up to and including 1 April 2020;
  (ii) the partners' bank account for the period up to and including 1 April 2020; and
  (iii) the partners' capital accounts (in columnar format) for the period up to and including 1 April 2020.

Note: Detailed workings should be submitted with your answer.

(*Association of Accounting Technicians*)

35.6A Proudie, Slope and Thorne were in partnership sharing profits and losses in the ratio 3 : 1 : 1. The draft balance sheet of the partnership as at 31 May 2019 is shown below:

	£000 Cost	£000 Depreciation	£000 Net book value
Non-current assets			
Land and buildings	200	40	160
Furniture	30	18	12
Motor vehicles	60	40	20
	290	98	192
Current assets			
Inventory		23	
Trade accounts receivable	42		
Less Allowance for doubtful debts	(1)		
		41	
Prepayments		2	
Cash		10	
			76
Total assets			268
Current liabilities			
Trade accounts payable	15		
Accruals	3		
		18	
Non-current liabilities			
Loan – Proudie		8	
Total liabilities			(26)
Net assets			242
Capital accounts			
Proudie		100	
Slope		60	
Thorne		40	
			200
Current accounts			
Proudie		24	
Slope		10	
Thorne		8	
			42
Total capital			242

Additional information:

1 Proudie decided to retire on 31 May 2019. However, Slope and Thorne agreed to form a new partnership out of the old one, as from 1 June 2019. They agreed to share profits and losses in the same ratio as in the old partnership.

2 Upon the dissolution of the old partnership, it was agreed that the following adjustments were to be made to the partnership balance sheet as at 31 May 2019.

(a) Land and buildings were to be revalued at £200,000.

(b) Furniture was to be revalued at £5,000.

(c) Proudie agreed to take over one of the motor vehicles at a value of £4,000, the remaining motor vehicles being revalued at £10,000.

(d) Inventory was to be written down by £5,000.

(e) A bad debt of £2,000 was to be written off, and the allowance for doubtful debts was then to be adjusted so that it represented 5 per cent of the then outstanding trade accounts receivable as at 31 May 2019.

(f) A further accrual of £3,000 for office expenses was to be made.

(g) Professional charges relating to the dissolution were estimated to be £1,000.

3 It has not been the practice of the partners to carry goodwill in the books of the partnership, but on the retirement of a partner it had been agreed that goodwill should be taken into account. Goodwill was to be valued at an amount equal to the average annual profits of the three years expiring on the retirement. For the purpose of including goodwill in the dissolution arrangement when Proudie retired, the net profits for the last three years were as follows:

	£000
Year to 31 May 2017	130
Year to 31 May 2018	150
Year to 31 May 2019	181

The net profit for the year to 31 May 2019 had been calculated before any of the items listed in 2 above were taken into account. The net profit was only to be adjusted for items listed in 2(d), 2(e) and 2(f) above.

4 Goodwill is not to be carried in the books of the new partnership.

5 It was agreed that Proudie's old loan of £8,000 should be repaid to him on 31 May 2019, but any further amount owing to him as a result of the dissolution of the partnership should be left as a long-term loan in the books of the new partnership.

6 The partners' current accounts were to be closed and any balances on them as at 31 May 2019 were to be transferred to their respective capital accounts.

Required:

(a) Prepare the revaluation account as at 31 May 2019.

(b) Prepare the partners' capital accounts as at the date of dissolution of the partnership, and bring down any balances on them in the books of the new partnership.

(c) Prepare Slope and Thorne's balance sheet as at 1 June 2019.

(*Association of Accounting Technicians*)

35.7 Lock, Stock and Barrel have been in partnership as builders and contractors for many years. Owing to adverse trading conditions it has been decided to dissolve the partnership. Profits are shared Lock 40 per cent, Stock 30 per cent, Barrel 30 per cent. The partnership deed also provides that in the event of a partner being unable to pay off a debit balance the remaining partners will treat this as a trading loss.

The latest partnership balance sheet was as follows:

	Cost	Depreciation	
	£	£	£
Non-current tangible assets			
Freehold yard and buildings	20,000	3,000	17,000
Plant and equipment	150,000	82,000	68,000
Motor vehicles	36,000	23,000	13,000
	206,000	108,000	98,000
Current assets			
Land for building		75,000	
Houses in course of construction		115,000	
Inventory of materials		23,000	
Accounts receivable for completed houses		62,000	
			275,000
Total assets			373,000
Current liabilities			
Trade accounts payable		77,000	
Deposits and progress payments		82,000	
Bank overdraft		132,500	
Total liabilities			(291,500)
Net assets			81,500
Partners' capital accounts			
Lock		52,000	
Stock		26,000	
Barrel		3,500	
Total Capital			81,500

During the six months from the date of the latest balance sheet to the date of dissolution the following transactions have taken place:

	£
Purchase of materials	20,250
Materials used for houses in course of construction	35,750
Payments for wages and subcontractors on building sites	78,000
Payments to trade creditors for materials	45,000
Sales of completed houses	280,000
Cash received from customers for houses	225,000
Payments for various general expenses	12,500
Payments for administration salaries	17,250
Cash withdrawn by partners: Lock	6,000
Stock	5,000
Barrel	4,000

All deposits and progress payments have been used for completed transactions.

Depreciation is normally provided each year at £600 on the freehold yard and buildings, at 10 per cent on cost for plant and equipment and 25 per cent on cost for motor vehicles.

The partners decide to dissolve the partnership on 1 February 2020 and wish to take out the maximum cash possible, as items are sold. At this date there are no houses in course of construction and one-third of the land had been used for building.

It is agreed that Barrel is insolvent and cannot bring any money into the partnership. The partners take over the partnership cars at an agreed figure of £2,000 each. All other vehicles were sold on 28 February 2020 for £6,200. At the same date the inventory of materials was sold for £7,000, and the sale of the land realised £72,500. On 30 April 2020 the accounts receivable were paid in full and all the plant and equipment was sold for £50,000.

The freehold yard and buildings realised £100,000 on 1 June 2020, on which date all remaining cash was distributed.

There are no costs of realisation or distribution.

Required:

(a) Prepare a partnership income statement for the six months to 1 February 2020, partners' capital accounts for the same period and a balance sheet at 1 February 2020.

(b) Show calculations of the amounts distributable to the partners.

(c) Prepare a realisation account and the capital accounts of the partners to the final distribution.

(*Association of Chartered Certified Accountants*)

35.8A Grant and Herd are in partnership sharing profits and losses in the ratio 3 to 2. The following information relates to the year to 31 December 2018:

	Dr £000	Cr £000
Capital accounts (at 1 January 2018):		
Grant		300
Herd		100
Cash at bank	5	
Accounts payable and accruals		25
Accounts receivable and prepayments	18	
Drawings during the year: Grant (all at 30 June 2018)	40	
Herd (all at 31 March 2018)	40	
Non-current assets: at cost	300	
accumulated depreciation (at 31 December 2018)		100
Herd – salary	10	
Net profit (for the year to 31 December 2018)		60
Inventory at cost (at 31 December 2018)	90	
Trade accounts payable		141
Trade accounts receivable	223	
	726	726

→ *Additional information*:

1 The partnership agreement allows for Herd to be paid a salary of £20,000 per annum, and for interest of 5 per cent per annum to be paid on the partners' capital account balances as at 1 January in each year. Interest at a rate of 10 per cent per annum is charged on the partners' drawings.

2 The partners decide to dissolve the partnership as at 31 December 2018, and the business was then sold to Valley Limited. The purchase consideration was to be 400,000 £1 ordinary shares in Valley at a premium of 25p per share. The shares were to be issued to the partners on 31 December 2018, and they were to be shared between them in their profit-sharing ratio.

　　The sale agreement allowed Grant to take over one of the business cars at an agreed valuation of £10,000. Apart from the car and the cash and bank balances, the company took over all the other partnership assets and liabilities at their book values as at 31 December 2018.

3 Matters relating to the appropriation of profit for the year to 31 December 2018 are to be dealt with in the partners' capital accounts, including any arrears of salary owing to Herd.

Required:
(a) Write up the following accounts for the year to 31 December 2018:
　　(i) the profit and loss appropriation account;
　　(ii) Grant's and Herd's capital accounts; and
　　(iii) the realisation account.
(b) Prepare Valley's balance sheet as at 1 January 2019 immediately after the acquisition of the partnership and assuming that no further transactions have taken place in the meantime.

(Association of Accounting Technicians)

36

Company accounts

Learning objectives

After you have studied this chapter, you should be able to:

- explain how limited companies differ from sole traders and partnerships
- explain the differences between different classes of shares
- calculate how distributable profits available for dividends are divided between the different classes of shares
- explain the differences between shares and loan notes
- describe the purpose of a *Conceptual Framework* for financial reporting
- prepare the income statement for a company for internal purposes
- prepare the balance sheet for a company for both internal and external purposes
- explain what is shown in a statement of changes in equity
- explain what an audit report is
- explain how to present goodwill in company financial statements
- explain what fundamental ethical principles an accountant must follow

Introduction

In this chapter, you'll learn about the different types of companies that can exist and about the different types of long-term funds they can raise in order to finance their activities. You'll learn how to prepare the financial statements for companies and about the differences between the treatment of goodwill in company accounts and its treatment in the accounts of sole traders and partnerships.

36.1 Need for limited companies

Limited liability companies, more commonly referred to as **limited companies**, came into existence originally because of the growth in the size of businesses, and the need to have a lot of people investing in the business who would not be able to take part in its management.

Activity 36.1 Why do you think a partnership was not an appropriate form of business in this case?

The UK law governing companies, their formation and the duties relating to their members, directors, auditors and officials is largely contained in the Companies Act 2006. This Act consolidated the Companies Acts of 1985, 1989 and 2004. However much of the requirements concerning financial statements continue to be found in the 1985 Act.

36.2 Limited liability

The capital of a limited company is divided into **shares**. Shares can be of any nominal value – 10p, 25p, £1, £5, £10 or any other amount per share. To become a member of a limited company, or a **shareholder**, a person must buy one or more of the shares.

If shareholders have paid in full for their shares, their liability is limited to what they have already paid for those shares. If a company loses all its assets, all those shareholders can lose is their shares. They cannot be forced to pay anything more in respect of the company's losses.

Shareholders who have only partly paid for their shares can be forced to pay the balance owing on the shares, but nothing else.

Shareholders are therefore said to have 'limited liability' and this is why companies are known as 'limited liability' or, more usually, simply 'limited' companies. By addressing the need for investors to have limited risk of financial loss, the existence of limited liability encourages individuals to invest in these companies and makes it possible to have both a large number of owners and a large amount of capital invested in the company.

There are a few companies which have unlimited liability, but these are outside the scope of this book.

36.3 Public and private companies

In the UK, there are two main classes of company, the **public company** and the **private company**. Private companies far outnumber public companies. In the Companies Act, a public company is defined as one which fulfils the following conditions:

● Its memorandum (a document that describes the company) states that it is a public company, and that it has registered as such.
● It has an authorised share capital of at least £50,000.
● Minimum membership is one. There is no maximum.
● Its name must end with the words 'public limited company' or the abbreviation 'PLC'. It can have the Welsh equivalent ('CCC') if registered in Wales.

PLCs can, but don't have to, offer their shares for sale on the Stock Exchange. It is through the Stock Exchange that a large ownership base can be established.

A private company is usually, but not always, a smaller business, and may be formed by one or more persons. It is defined by the Act as a company which is not a public company. The main differences between a private company and a public company are that a private company

● can have an authorised capital of less than £50,000; and
● *cannot* offer its shares for subscription to the public at large, whereas public companies can.

This means that if you were to walk into a bank, or similar public place, and see a prospectus offering anyone the chance to take up shares in a company, then that company would be a public company, i.e. a PLC.

The shares that are dealt in on the Stock Exchange are all those of public limited companies. This does not mean that shares of all public companies are traded on the Stock Exchange. For various reasons, some public companies have either chosen not to, or have not been allowed to have their shares traded there. The ones whose shares are traded are known as 'quoted companies' meaning that their shares have prices quoted on the Stock Exchange. They have to comply with Stock Exchange requirements in addition to those laid down by the Companies Act and accounting standards.

Activity 36.2

Apart from not having to worry about complying with the Stock Exchange requirements, what other reasons can you think of that would explain why some PLCs do not wish to offer their shares on the Stock Market?

36.4 Directors of the company

The day-to-day business of a company is *not* carried out by the shareholders. The possession of a share normally confers voting rights on the holder, who is then able to attend general meetings of the company. At one of these general meetings, normally the **Annual General Meeting** or AGM, the shareholders vote for **directors**, these being the people who will be entrusted with the running of the business. At each AGM, the directors report on their stewardship, and this report is accompanied by a set of financial statements and other documents – the 'annual report'.

36.5 Legal status of a limited company

A limited company is said to possess a 'separate legal identity' from that of its shareholders. Put simply, this means that a company is not seen as being exactly the same as its shareholders. For instance, a company can sue one or more of its shareholders, and similarly, a shareholder can sue the company. This would not be the case if the company and its shareholders were exactly the same thing, as one cannot sue oneself. This concept is often referred to as the **veil of incorporation**.

Note: This is an extremely important concept. The most frequently cited example of the strength of the veil of incorporation is a case that went to the House of Lords in 1897. The case is known as *Saloman* v *Saloman & Co Ltd.* It involved a company formed by a Mr Saloman. The company was run by Mr Saloman in the same way as when he was operating as a sole trader. He received all the profits and made all the decisions. However, the *veil of incorporation* meant that the company was treated as completely separate from him. When the business failed owing a large amount of money, Mr Saloman did not have to pay for the business debts personally. The debts were the responsibility of the company, not of Mr Saloman. This was held to be the case even though Mr Saloman had lent some money to the company in the form of secured debentures (now called secured loan notes). This meant that any funds left in the company when it failed were first used to repay *those* loan notes (because they were 'secured' on the assets of the company) and the rest of the creditors (who were not 'secured') received nothing.

36.6 Share capital

Shareholders of a limited company obtain their reward in the form of a share of the profits, known as a **dividend**. The directors decide on the amount of profits which are placed in reserves (i.e. 'retained'). The directors then propose the payment of a certain amount of dividend from the remaining profits. It is important to note that the shareholders cannot propose a higher dividend for themselves than that already proposed by the directors. They can, however, propose that a lesser dividend should be paid, although this is very rare indeed. If the directors propose that no dividend be paid, then the shareholders are powerless to alter the decision.

The decision by the directors as to the amount proposed as dividends is a very complex one and cannot be fully discussed here. Such points as government directives to reduce dividends, the effect of taxation, the availability of bank balances to pay the dividends, the possibility of take-over bids and so on will all be taken into account.

The dividend is usually expressed as a percentage. A dividend of 10 per cent in Business A on 500,000 ordinary shares of £1 each will amount to £50,000. A dividend of 6 per cent in Business B on 200,000 ordinary shares of £2 each will amount to £24,000. A shareholder having 100 shares in each business would receive £10 from Business A and £12 from Business B.

There are two main types of shares:

1 **Preference shares.** Holders of these shares get an agreed percentage rate of dividend before the ordinary shareholders receive anything.

2 **Ordinary shares.** Holders of these shares receive the remainder of the total profits available for dividends. There is no upper limit to the amounts of dividends they can receive.

For example, if a company had 50,000 5 per cent preference shares of £1 each and 200,000 ordinary shares of £1 each, then the dividends could be payable as in Exhibit 36.1.

Exhibit 36.1

Year	1	2	3	4	5
	£	£	£	£	£
Profits appropriated for dividends	6,500	10,500	13,500	28,500	17,500
Preference dividends (5%)	2,500	2,500	2,500	2,500	2,500
Ordinary dividends	(2%)4,000	(4%)8,000	(5½%)11,000	(13%)26,000	(7½%)15,000
	6,500	10,500	13,500	28,500	17,500

The two main types of preference shares are non-cumulative preference shares and cumulative preference shares:

1 **Non-cumulative preference shares.** These can receive a dividend up to an agreed percentage each year. If the amount paid is less than the maximum agreed amount, the shortfall is lost by the shareholder. The shortfall cannot be carried forward and paid in a future year.

2 **Cumulative preference shares.** These also have an agreed maximum percentage dividend. However, any shortfall of dividend paid in a year can be carried forward. These arrears of preference dividends will have to be paid before the ordinary shareholders receive anything.

 Activity 36.3 Why do you think an investor might purchase preference shares rather than ordinary shares in a company?

Exhibit 36.2

A company has 500,000 £1 ordinary shares and 100,000 5 per cent non-cumulative preference shares of £1 each. The profits available for dividends are: year 1 £145,000, year 2 £2,000, year 3 £44,000, year 4 £118,000, year 5 £264,000. Assuming all profits are paid out in dividends, the amounts paid to each class of shareholder are:

Year	1	2	3	4	5
	£	£	£	£	£
Profits appropriated for dividends	145,000	2,000	44,000	118,000	264,000
Preference dividend (non-cumulative) (limited in Year 2)	5,000	2,000	5,000	5,000	5,000
Dividends on ordinary shares	140,000	–	39,000	113,000	259,000
	145,000	2,000	44,000	118,000	264,000

Exhibit 36.3

Assume that the preference shares in Exhibit 36.2 had been cumulative. The dividends would have been:

Year	1	2	3	4	5
	£	£	£	£	£
Profits appropriated for dividends	145,000	2,000	44,000	118,000	264,000
Preference dividend	5,000	2,000	8,000*	5,000	5,000
Dividends on ordinary shares	140,000	–	36,000	113,000	259,000
	145,000	2,000	44,000	118,000	264,000

*including arrears.

Note: This exhibit shows how much of the profit made in each year was paid out as dividend. The dividends are shown in the financial statements in the year they were paid, which may be a year later than the year in which the profit used to pay them was earned – see Section 36.12, especially Exhibit 36.5.

36.7 Share capital: different meanings

The term 'share capital' can have any of the following meanings:

1 **Authorised share capital.** Sometimes known as 'registered capital' or 'nominal capital'. This is the total of the share capital which the company is allowed to issue to shareholders.
2 **Issued share capital.** This is the total of the share capital actually issued to shareholders.

Note: Some students mix up these two terms and throw away marks in examinations as a result. In order to remember which is which, you only need to think about what the words 'authorised' and 'issued' mean.

If all of the authorised share capital has been issued, then 1 and 2 above would be the same amount.

3 **Called-up capital.** Where only part of the amount payable on each issued share has been asked for, the total amount asked for on all the issued shares is known as the called-up capital.
4 **Uncalled capital.** This is the total amount which is to be received in future relating to issued share capital, but which has not yet been asked for.
5 **Calls in arrears.** The total amount for which payment has been asked for (i.e. 'called for'), but has not yet been paid by shareholders.
6 **Paid-up capital.** This is the total of the amount of share capital which has been paid for by shareholders.

Exhibit 36.4 illustrates these different meanings.

Exhibit 36.4

1 Better Enterprises Ltd was formed with the legal right to issue 1 million shares of £1 each.
2 The company has actually issued 750,000 shares.
3 None of the shares has yet been fully paid up. So far, the company has made calls of 80p (£0.80) per share.
4 All the calls have been paid by shareholders except for £200 owing from one shareholder.

(a) Authorised or nominal share capital is:	1	£1 million.	
(b) Issued share capital is:	2	£750,000.	
(c) Called-up share capital is:	3	750,000 · £0.80 = £600,000.	
(d) Calls in arrears amounted to:	4	£200.	
(e) Paid-up share capital is:	(c)	£600,000 less (d) £200 = £599,800.	

36.8 Bonus shares

The issue of **bonus shares** appear to be outside the scope of syllabuses at this level. However, some examinations have included a minor part of a question concerned with bonus shares. All that is needed here is a very brief explanation only, leaving further explanations for a later stage in your studies.

Bonus shares are 'free' shares issued to shareholders without their having to pay anything for them. The reserves (e.g. retained profits shown in the balance sheet) are utilised for the purpose. Thus, if before the bonus issue there were £20,000 of issued share capital and £12,000 reserves, and a bonus issue of 1 for 4 was then made (i.e. 1 bonus share for every 4 shares already held) the bonus issue would amount to £5,000. The share capital then becomes £25,000 and the reserves become £7,000.

A fuller explanation appears in *Frank Wood's Business Accounting 2*. An issue of bonus shares is often referred to as a **scrip issue**.

36.9 Loan notes

You will recall the note about the veil of incorporation where loan notes had been issued to the owner of company. The term **loan note** is used when a limited company receives money on loan, and a document called a loan note certificate is issued to the lender. Interest will be paid to the holder, the rate of interest being shown on the certificate. (You will sometimes see them referred to as 'debentures', 'loan stock' or 'loan capital', but the correct term is 'loan note'.)

Interest on loan notes has to be paid whether profits are made or not. They are, therefore, different from shares, where dividends depend on profits being made. A loan note may be either:

● redeemable, i.e. repayable at or by a particular date; or
● irredeemable, normally repayable only when the company is officially terminated by going into liquidation. (Also sometimes referred to as 'perpetual' loan notes.)

If dates are shown on a loan note, e.g. 2016/2023, it means that the company can redeem it in any of the years covered by the date(s) showing, in this case 2016 to 2023 inclusive.

People lending money to companies in the form of loan notes will be interested in how safe their investment will be. Some loan notes are assigned the legal right that on certain happenings the holders of the loan notes will be able to take control of specific assets, or of the whole of the assets. They can then sell the assets and recoup the amount due under their loan notes, or deal with the assets in ways specified in the deed under which the loan notes were issued. Such loan notes are said to be 'secured' against the assets – this was the case in the veil of incorporation note in Section 36.5. (The term 'mortgage' loan note is sometimes used instead of 'secured'.) Other loan notes have no prior right to control the assets under any circumstances. These are known as 'simple' or 'naked' loan notes.

Activity 36.4 Why do you think a loan note might be 'secured' rather than being designated as a 'simple' loan note? (*Hint:* think about Mr Saloman.)

36.10 Goodwill

Companies can recognise goodwill arising on acquisitions as an intangible non-current asset. However, each year they must consider whether the value it is carried at has been impaired (i.e. has fallen), when this happens, the reduction must be shown in the profit and loss section of the income statement. The rules relating to this are to be found in IFRS 3 (*Business combinations*), IAS 36 (*Impairment of assets*) and IAS 38 (*Intangible assets*).

36.11 The conceptual framework

As you learned in Chapter 7, the *Conceptual Framework* indicates the concepts upon which financial statements are prepared and presented. In addition, it is used to guide the IASB when framing and developing new standards and when revising existing ones. However, it is an extremely difficult document to construct and its development is still on-going after decades of debate. The new exposure draft issued in early 2015 did not signal that it would soon be finalised. There is a great deal of debate between an exposure draft being issued and finalisation of any IASB pronouncement, never mind one this complex.

A sound *Conceptual Framework* ought to result in financial statements presenting a true and fair view of company performance and financial position. But the IASB faces great difficulty in finalising it because:

● Gaining consensus on an international scale is difficult – many countries that have adopted International standards have only done so after customising them to their own context and environment.
● The *Conceptual Framework* is being developed after standards in one form or another have been in use for decades. Many of those standards will need to be revised if there are significant changes in a new *Conceptual Framework*.
● Accountants are accustomed to the concepts they have been using throughout their careers and amending or removing any of them, or adding others, is unlikely to be met with universal acceptance.

Nevertheless, despite the flaws, having a conceptual framework sets a context within which all preparers of financial statements must operate. This leads to greater levels of understandability by users of those statements, and to greater consistency and comparability between periods and between entities, all of which are desirable for the primary stakeholders, the current and potential owners and creditors of the entities that produce them. At the time of writing, the revised conceptual framework is expected to be published around the end of 2017.

(You can read more about the IASB's *Conceptual Framework* at www.ifrs.org/projects/work-plan/conceptual-framework/)

36.12 Income statements of companies

The income statements of both private and public companies are drawn up in exactly the same way.

The trading account section of the income statement of a limited company is no different from that of a sole trader or a partnership. However, some differences may be found in the profit and loss account section. Two expenses that would be found only in company accounts are directors' remuneration and loan note interest.

Directors' remuneration

As directors exist only in companies, this type of expense is found only in company financial statements.

Directors are legally employees of the company, appointed by the shareholders. Their remuneration is charged to the profit and loss account.

Loan note interest

The interest payable for the use of the money borrowed is an expense of the company, and is payable whether profits are made or not. This means that interest on loan notes is charged as an expense in the profit and loss account. Contrast this with dividends which are dependent on profits having been made.

36.13 Statement of changes in equity

Unlike partnership income statements following the profit and loss account section of company income statements there is no section called the 'profit and loss appropriation account'. Instead, companies produce a **statement of changes in equity**. This shows separately:

(a) the retained profit for the period;
(b) distributions of equity (e.g. dividends) and contributions of equity (e.g. share issues);
(c) a reconciliation between the opening and closing carrying amount of each component of equity (i.e. share capital and **reserves**).

Taxation is shown as a deduction when arriving at retained profits on the face of the statement of profit or loss. This differs from its treatment in partnership and sole proprietor financial statements.

Exhibit 36.5 contains an example showing the changes in equity of a new business for its first three years of trading.

Exhibit 36.5

IDC Ltd has share capital of 400,000 ordinary shares of £1 each and 200,000 5 per cent preference shares of £1 each.

● The retained profits for the first three years of business ended 31 December are: 2018, £109,670; 2019, £148,640; and 2020, £158,220.
● Transfers to reserves are made as follows: 2018 nil; 2019, general reserve, £10,000; and 2020, non-current assets replacement reserve, £22,500.
● Dividends were paid for each year on the preference shares at 5 per cent and on the ordinary shares at: 2018, 10 per cent; 2019, 12.5 per cent; 2020, 15 per cent.

IDC Ltd
Statements of changes in equity (extracts)
(1) For the year ending 31 December 2018

	£
Retained profits	109,670
Less Dividends paid: Preference 5%	10,000
Ordinary 10%	40,000
	(50,000)
Retained profits carried forward	59,670

(2) For the year ended 31 December 2019

	£	£	£
Retained profits			148,640
Add Retained profits brought forward			59,670
			244,310
Less Transfer to general reserve		10,000	
Dividends paid:			
Preference dividend of 5%	10,000		
Ordinary dividend of 12.5%	50,000		
		60,000	
			(70,000)
Retained profits carried forward			174,310

(3) For the year ended 31 December 2020

	£	£	£
Retained profits			158,220
Add Retained profits brought forward			174,310
			332,530
Less Transfer to non-current assets replacement reserve		22,500	
Dividends paid:			
Preference dividend of 5%	10,000		
Ordinary dividend of 15%	60,000		
		70,000	
			(92,500)
Retained profits carried forward			240,030

36.14 The Balance Sheet

Prior to the UK Companies Act 1981, provided it disclosed the necessary information, a company could draw up its balance sheet and income statement for publication in any way that it wished. The 1981 Act, however, stopped this, and laid down the precise details to be shown. These are unchanged in the Companies Act 2006 and the current legal requirements are largely contained in the Companies Act 1985. International standards are not specific about the layout to adopt so UK companies tend to continue to use the Companies Act layouts. We will cover this topic in more detail in *Frank Wood's Business Accounting 2*.

Exhibits 36.6 and 36.7 present two versions of a balance sheet. They both comply with International GAAP. Exhibit 36.6 shows more detail. The detail that is omitted from Exhibit 36.7 would be shown separately as a note. Both these balance sheets would be prepared by companies for their own use rather than for their stakeholders, such as shareholders and creditors. **Balance sheets prepared for publication (i.e. for external users) contain much less detail and will be covered in detail in** *Frank Wood's Business Accounting 2*.

If you are asked in an examination to prepare a balance sheet for internal use and choose to present a balance sheet similar to Exhibit 36.7 you should include in a note the details from the layout as in Exhibit 36.6 that you have omitted from the balance sheet.

In *Frank Wood's Business Accounting 2* you will be told more about the differences between 'revenue reserves' and 'capital reserves'. The most important reason for the distinction has to do with deciding how much can be treated as being available for paying out to shareholders as dividends. 'Revenue reserves', which include the retained profits and the general reserve, can be treated as available for such dividends. 'Capital reserves', which will include revaluation reserves on property and land, and also some reserves (which you have not yet met) which have to be created to meet some legal statutory requirement, cannot be treated as available for payment of dividends.

A term which sometimes appears in examinations is that of 'fungible assets'. Fungible assets are assets which are substantially indistinguishable one from another.

Now, let's prepare two more balance sheets and an income statement for internal use.

Exhibit 36.6   Greater detail for internal use

Balance Sheet as at 31 December 2019

		Cost	Depreciation to date (b)	Net bookvalue
Non-current assets	(a)	£000	£000	£000
Goodwill		15,000	5,000	10,000
Buildings		15,000	6,000	9,000
Machinery		8,000	2,400	5,600
Motor vehicles		4,000	1,600	2,400
		42,000	15,000	27,000
Current assets				
Inventory			6,000	
Accounts receivable			3,000	
Bank			4,000	
				13,000
Total assets				40,000
Less Current liabilities				
Accounts payable		3,000		
Corporation tax owing		2,000		
			5,000	
Net current assets				
Non-current liabilities				
Six per cent loan notes: repayable 2018			8,000	
Total liabilities				(13,000)
Net assets				27,000
Equity				
Share capital				
Authorised 30,000 shares of £1 each	(c)			30,000
Issued 20,000 ordinary shares of £1 each, fully paid	(d)			20,000
Reserves	(e)			
Share premium	(f)		1,200	
General reserve			3,800	
Retained profits			2,000	
				7,000
Total equity	(g)			27,000

Notes:

(a) Non-current assets should normally be shown either at cost or alternatively at some other valuation. In either case, the method chosen should be clearly stated. As you will see in Exhibit 36.7, you could show the intangible non-current asset (goodwill) separately from the other non-current assets.

(b) The total depreciation from date of purchase to the date of the balance sheet should be shown.

(c) The authorised share capital, where it is different from the issued share capital, is shown as a note.

(d) Where shares are only partly called-up, it is the amount actually called up that appears in the balance sheet and not the full amount.

(e) Reserves consist either of those unused profits remaining in the retained profits, or those transferred to a reserve account appropriately titled, e.g. general reserve or non-current assets replacement reserve. These reserves are shown in the balance sheet after share capital under the heading of 'Reserves'.

(f) The share premium account is credited with the difference between the nominal value of shares issued and the issue price of those shares. For example, if a share has a nominal value of £1 and it is issued at a price of £3, £2 will be credited to the share premium account and £1 will be credited to the issued share capital account.

(g) The share capital and reserves should be totalled so as to show the book value of all the shares in the company. Either the term 'shareholders' funds' or 'members' equity' is often given to the total of share capital plus reserves.

Exhibit 36.7   Less detail for internal use

Letters in brackets (A) to (G) refer to notes following the balance sheet.

Balance Sheet as at 31 December 2019

		£000	£000	£000
Non-current assets				
Intangible assets	(A)			
Goodwill				10,000
Tangible assets	(B)			
Buildings			9,000	
Machinery			5,600	
Motor vehicles			2,400	
				17,000
				27,000
Current assets				
Inventory			6,000	
Accounts receivable			3,000	
Bank			4,000	
				13,000
Total assets				40,000
Current liabilities	(C)			
Accounts payable		3,000		
Corporation tax owing		2,000		
			5,000	
Total assets less current liabilities				
Non-current liabilities	(D)			
Loan notes			8,000	
Total liabilities				(13,000)
Net assets				27,000
Equity				
Called-up share capital	(E)			20,000
Share premium account	(F)			1,200
Other reserves				
General reserve				3,800
Retained profits				2,000
Total equity				27,000

Notes:

(A) Intangible assets are those not having a 'physical' existence; for instance, you can see and touch tangible assets under (B), i.e. buildings, machinery etc., but you cannot see and touch goodwill.

(B) Tangible non-current assets under a separate heading. Note that figures are shown net after depreciation. In a note accompanying the financial statements the cost and depreciation on these assets would be given.

(C) Only items payable within one year go under this heading.

(D) These loan notes are repayable in several years' time. If they had been payable within one year they would have been shown under current liabilities.

(E) An analysis of share capital will be given in supplementary notes to the balance sheet.

(F) One reserve that is not labelled with the word 'reserve' in its title is the share premium account. (Another is retained profits.) For various reasons (discussed fully in *Frank Wood's Business Accounting 2*) shares can be issued for more than their face (or 'nominal') value. The excess of the price at which they are issued over the nominal value of the shares is credited to a share premium account. This is then shown with the other reserves in the balance sheet.

A fully worked example

Exhibit 36.8

The following trial balance is extracted from the books of F. W. Ltd as on 31 December 2018:

Trial Balance as on 31 December 2018

	Dr £	Cr £
10% preference share capital		200,000
Ordinary share capital		700,000
10% loan notes (repayable 2022)		300,000
Goodwill at cost	255,000	
Buildings at cost	1,050,000	
Equipment at cost	120,000	
Motor vehicles at cost	172,000	
Provision for depreciation: buildings 1.1.2018		100,000
Provision for depreciation: equipment 1.1.2018		24,000
Provision for depreciation: motor vehicles 1.1.2018		51,600
Inventory 1.1.2018	84,912	
Sales		1,022,000
Purchases	439,100	
Carriage inwards	6,200	
Salaries and wages	192,400	
Directors' remuneration	123,000	
Motor expenses	3,120	
Business rates and insurances	8,690	
General expenses	5,600	
Loan note interest	15,000	
Accounts receivable	186,100	
Accounts payable		113,700
Bank	8,390	
General reserve		50,000
Share premium account		100,000
Interim ordinary dividend paid	35,000	
Retained profits 31.12.2017		43,212
	2,704,512	2,704,512

The following adjustments are needed:

(*i*)   Inventory at 31.12.2018 was £91,413.
(*ii*)   Depreciate buildings £10,000; motor vehicles £18,000; equipment £12,000.
(*iii*) Accrue loan note interest £15,000.
(*iv*)   Provide for preference dividend £20,000 and final ordinary dividend of 10 per cent.
(*v*)   Transfer £10,000 to general reserve.
(*vi*)   Write-off goodwill impairment of £30,000.
(*vii*) Authorised share capital is £200,000 in preference shares and £1 million in ordinary shares.
(*viii*) Provide for corporation tax £50,000.

The financial statements are shown below. First, there's an income statement for internal use. (The income statement for publication is greatly summarised and we will cover that topic in *Frank Wood's Business Accounting 2*.) This is followed by two versions of the internal balance sheet.

(a) Income Statement **for internal use only**, not for publication.

F. W. Ltd
Income Statement for the year ending 31 December 2018

		£	£
Revenue			1,022,000
Less Cost of goods sold:			
Opening inventory		84,912	
Add Purchases		439,100	
Add Carriage inwards		6,200	
		530,212	
Less Closing inventory		(91,413)	
			(438,799)
Gross profit			583,201
Less Expenses:			
Salaries and wages		192,400	
Motor expenses		3,120	
Business rates and insurances		8,690	
General expenses		5,600	
Directors' remuneration	(A)	123,000	
Loan note interest	(B)	30,000	
Goodwill impairment		30,000	
Depreciation: Buildings		10,000	
Equipment		12,000	
Motor vehicles		18,000	
			(432,810)
Profit for the year before taxation			150,391
Less Corporation tax			(50,000)
Retained profits			100,391
Note			
Ordinary share dividends paid	(C)	35,000	

Notes:

(A) Directors' remuneration is shown as an expense in the income statement.
(B) Loan note interest is an expense to be shown in the income statement.
(C) The final dividend of 10 per cent is based on the issued ordinary share capital and not on the authorised ordinary share capital. It is, therefore, £70,000. However, both it and the preference dividend of £20,000 should only be included as notes to the income statement. They should not be treated as current liabilities and should not appear in any financial statement. As only the interim ordinary dividend was paid during the year, this is the only one of these three dividend items that will appear in the statement of changes in equity.

(b) Balance sheet in greater detail for internal use.

Balance Sheet as at 31 December 2018

	Cost	Depreciation to date	Net book value
	£	£	£
Non-current assets			
Goodwill	255,000	30,000	225,000
Buildings	1,050,000	110,000	940,000
Equipment	120,000	36,000	84,000
Motor vehicles	172,000	69,600	102,400
	1,597,000	245,600	1,351,400
Current assets			
Inventory		91,413	
Accounts receivable		186,100	
Bank		8,390	
			285,903
Total assets			1,637,303
Current liabilities			
Accounts payable	113,700		
Loan note interest accrued	15,000		
Taxation	50,000		
		(178,700)	
Non-current liabilities			
10% loan notes		300,000	
Total liabilities			(478,700)
Net assets			1,158,603
Equity			
Share Capital		Authorised	Issued
		£	£
Preference shares		200,000	200,000
Ordinary shares		1,000,000	700,000
		1,200,000	900,000
Reserves			
Share premium		100,000	
General reserve		60,000	
Retained profits		98,603	
			258,603
Total equity			1,158,603

The proposed dividends should be shown in a note.

Note that the difference between the two balance sheets is solely that of detail. You should use whichever layout is more appropriate.

(c) Balance sheet in less detail for internal use.

F. W. Ltd
Balance Sheet as at 31 December 2018

Non-current assets		£	£	£
Intangible assets				
Goodwill				225,000
Tangible assets	(A)			
Buildings			940,000	
Equipment			84,000	
Motor vehicles			102,400	
				1,126,400
				1,351,400
Current assets				
Inventory			91,413	
Accounts receivable			186,100	
Bank			8,390	
				285,903
Total assets				1,637,303
Current liabilities				
Accounts payable		113,700		
Loan note interest accrued		15,000		
Taxation		50,000		
			178,700	
Non-current liabilities				
10% Loan notes			300,000	
				(478,700)
Total liabilities				1,158,603
Net assets				
Equity	(B)			
Called-up share capital	(C)			900,000
Share premium account				100,000
Other reserves				
General reserve				60,000
Retained profits				98,603
Total equity				1,158,603

The proposed dividends should be shown in a note.

(A) Notes to be given in an appendix as to cost, acquisitions and sales in the year and depreciation.

(B) Reserves consist either of those unused profits remaining in the appropriation account, or those transferred to a reserve account appropriately titled, e.g. general reserve, non-current assets replacement reserve, etc.
The closing balance of retained profits from the statement of changes in equity (not prepared for this example) is shown under reserves. These are profits not already appropriated, and therefore 'reserved' for future use.

(C) The authorised share capital, where it is different from the issued share capital, is shown as a note. Notice that the total figure of £1,200,000 for authorised capital is not included when adding up the balance sheet sides. Only the issued capital amounts are included in balance sheet totals.

36.15 True and fair view

When the financial statements of a company are published no one, neither the directors nor the auditors, ever states that 'the financial statements are correct'. This is because in preparing company financial statements many subjective estimates and judgements affect the figures. The valuation of inventory, or the estimates of depreciation, cannot be said to be 'correct', just as it is impossible to say that the allowance for doubtful debts is 'correct'. Only time will tell whether these estimates and judgements will turn out to have been 'correct'.

The expression that is used is that the financial statements give a **true and fair view** of the financial position and financial performance of the company.

36.16 IFRS 5: *Non-current assets held for sale and discontinued operations*

Accounting is not a static subject. Changes occur over the years as they are seen to be necessary, and also get general agreement as to their usefulness. Since the introduction of accounting standards over thirty years ago, the number of changes that practitioners and students have had to learn has increased at a very fast rate.

Suppose that you are considering the affairs of a business over the years. The business has not changed significantly, there have been no acquisitions, no discontinued operations, no fundamental reorganisation or restructuring of the business. In these circumstances, when comparing the financial statements over the years, you are comparing like with like, subject to the problem of the effects of inflation or deflation.

On the other hand, suppose that it has been decided to sell some non-current assets or to discontinue some of the operations of the business. When trying to see what the future might hold for the company, simply basing your opinions on what has happened in the past could be very misleading.

To help you to distinguish the past and the future, and to give you some idea as to what changes have occurred, IFRS 5 requires that:

● non-current assets held for sale are shown at the lower of carrying amount and fair value less selling costs;
● non-current assets held for sale are presented separately on the face of the balance sheet after current assets;
● non-current assets held for sale are not depreciated;
● gains or losses on the remeasurement of a non-current asset held for sale should be included in profit or loss from continuing operations;
● the results of discontinued operations are shown separately on the face of the income statement after the figure for profit for the period from continuing operations.

36.17 IAS 1 and financial statements

IAS 1 (*Presentation of financial statements*) was revised and reissued in 2007. In the revised standard, the balance sheet was renamed the 'statement of financial position'. However, 'balance sheet' is permitted also, and that is what we use in this book. It also changed the title of the 'cash flow statement' to 'statement of cash flows'. A new primary statement was also introduced: the statement of comprehensive income. It states that there are four primary statements:

● a statement of financial position (i.e. a balance sheet);
● a statement of comprehensive income;

● a statement of changes in equity;
● a statement of cash flows.

When a separate income statement is also presented, it is presented immediately before the statement of comprehensive income. In that case, the statement of comprehensive income starts with the profit or loss identified in the income statement. The difference in approach is cosmetic and the option to show a separate income statement simply enables continuation of use of the term 'income statement'.

As a minimum, **the statement of comprehensive income** must include line items presenting:

(*a*) revenue;
(*b*) finance costs;
(*c*) share of profits or losses of associates and joint ventures accounted for using the equity method;
(*d*) tax;
(*e*) the total of post-tax profit or loss on discontinued operations *plus* the post-tax gain or loss recognised on the measurement to fair value less costs to sell or on the disposal of the assets or disposal group(s) constituting the discontinued operations;
(*f*) profit or loss;
(*g*) each component of other comprehensive income classified by nature excluding amounts in (h);
(*h*) share of the other comprehensive income of associates and joint ventures accounted for using the entity method;
(*i*) total comprehensive income.

If a separate income statement is presented, it will contain items (a) to (f). Other comprehensive income comprises items that are not recognised in profit or loss, such as:

● changes in revaluation surplus;
● gains or losses arising from translating the financial statements of a foreign operation;
● gains and losses on remeasuring available-for-sale financial assets.

Total comprehensive income is the change in equity during a period other than those changes resulting from transactions with owners (i.e. holders of equity) in their capacity as owners (e.g. dividend payments).

The statement of changes in equity presents:

(*a*) total comprehensive income;
(*b*) the amounts of transactions with owners in their capacity as owners;
(*c*) for each component of equity, a reconciliation between the opening and closing carrying amount.

Either in the statement of changes in equity or in a note, the amount of dividend distributed to owners during the period must be shown, along with the related amount per share.

IAS 1 is covered in greater detail in *Frank Wood's Business Accounting 2*. In this book we are simply explaining some of its requirements. The overall effect is that financial statements prepared for publication (i.e. for external users) are very different from those produced for internal use. You will not be required to prepare a statement of comprehensive income in this book.

36.18 The Audit Report

The Companies Act requires that all companies other than dormant companies (i.e. companies that have not traded during the year) and small private companies be audited every year. ('Small' companies are exempt if they meet at least two of three conditions: annual turnover of no more than £10.2 million; assets worth no more than £5.1 million; no more than 50 employees.)

Auditors are appointed each year by the shareholders at the company annual general meeting (AGM). The auditors complete the report after examining the books and accounts and, in the report, they must say whether or not they agree that the accounts give a true and fair view. The report is presented to the shareholders at the same time as the financial statements are presented to them at the AGM. The content of the audit report is defined in sections 495 to 497 of the companies act 2006.

In preparing the audit report, the auditor must consider whether

● the accounts have been prepared in accordance with the Companies Act;
● the balance sheet shows a true and fair view of the state of the company's affairs at the end of the period and the income statement shows a true and fair view of the profit or loss for the period;
● proper accounting records have been kept and proper returns received from parts of the company not visited by the auditor;
● the accounts are in agreement with the accounting records;
● the directors' report is consistent with the accounts.

While smaller companies are exempt from the requirement to have their financial statements audited, they may still do so, if they wish.

Organisations that are not required to have their financial statements audited, such as sole traders, partnerships, clubs and societies, can still have their accounts audited. In this case, the audit is described as a *non-statutory audit*.

A qualified audit report indicates that the auditor is not satisfied that the financial statements present a true and fair view. When a company receives a qualified audit report, it acts as a signal to all stakeholders that something may be amiss. As such, it is a vitally important safeguard of the interests of the shareholders.

Contrary to what most of the public think, auditors do not guarantee to discover any fraud that may have occurred. That is not what the audit is for. Following such financial scandals as Tesco, Enron, the Maxwell affair, BCCI bank, Polly Peck and Barlow Clowes there has been pressure exerted upon the accounting profession to reconsider its position regarding the discovery of fraud when auditing the financial statements of a company.

36.19 Professional ethics

It is now recognised that accountants have a professional responsibility to be 'ethical'. This is a relatively new development. For many years, ethics were an informal element of the training of accountants. However, an apparently never ending stream of high-profile financial scandals since the 1960s has threatened the reputation of the accounting profession. As a result, the informal approach to ethics has been formalised in an attempt to stop such events occurring.

It is for this reason that some accountancy bodies now include a separate ethics course in their training. Others have embedded ethics into some of their courses and examinations. But, what does it mean to be 'ethical'?

Being ethical involves showing integrity, fairness, respect and openness in behaviour and attitude in all situations. Members of all professions have a responsibility to society because they have the specialist knowledge and expertise to deal with certain situations in a more informed way than those who are not so qualified. For accountants, their professional ethics are not just concerned with how an accountant should be in the workplace, they relate to how accountants should behave in all aspects of their public life.

Ethics apply not only to what an accountant does, and to his or her interaction with those who are not accountants. Ethics also apply to how accountants conduct themselves with each other and with those aspiring to be accountants. Managers and trainers of accountants have an ethical responsibility to present themselves as respectful, honest, and trustworthy; and to ensure that their accounting trainees embrace those same values.

The International Federation of Accountants is the world umbrella body for professional accountancy bodies. It has over 175 membership bodies and associate bodies in 130 countries representing more than 2.5 million accountants in public practice, education, government service, industry, and commerce. Its 2016 *Code of Ethics for Professional Accountants* forms the basis for many of the ethical codes applied by its member bodies. The IFAC Code is available at www. ethicsboard.org/iesba-code

In the IFAC Code, it is stated that a professional accountant must comply with the following fundamental principles:

(a) *Integrity* – to be straightforward and honest in all professional and business relationships.

(b) *Objectivity* – to not allow bias, conflict of interest or undue influence of others to override professional or business judgements.

(c) *Professional competence and due care* – to maintain professional knowledge and skill at the level required to ensure that a client or employer receives competent professional services based on current developments in practice, legislation and techniques and act diligently and in accordance with applicable technical and professional standards.

(d) *Confidentiality* – to respect the confidentiality of information acquired as a result of professional and business relationships and, therefore, not disclose any such information to third parties without proper and specific authority, unless there is a legal or professional right or duty to disclose, nor use the information for the personal advantage of the professional accountant or third parties.

(e) *Professional behaviour* – to comply with relevant laws and regulations and avoid any action that discredits the profession.

To supplement their ethical codes, accountancy bodies worldwide operate their own disciplinary code which establishes what steps may be taken should a member act unethically. These disciplinary codes are designed to protect non-accountants and to maintain the reputation of the profession and the demand for its services. Accountants found guilty of unethical behaviour risk the possibility of fines or even expulsion from their professional body.

 Activity 36.5   Do you think that such a system of self-regulation is appropriate?

Learning outcomes

You should now have learnt:

1 That limited companies exist because of the disadvantages and constraints arising from partnerships.

2 That a fully paid-up shareholder's liability is limited to the shares he or she holds in the company. Shareholders cannot then be asked to pay any other company debt from their private resources.

3 The difference between public and private companies.

4 That there are far more private companies than public companies.

5 The difference between a PLC and a company that is not a PLC.

6 That a limited company has a 'separate legal entity' from that of its members.

7 The difference between ordinary shares and preference shares.

8 How dividends are calculated.

9 The difference between shares and loan notes.

10 The contents of and purpose of a company's appropriation account.

11 That directors' remuneration is charged to the profit and loss account section of the income statement.

12 That loan note interest is charged to the profit and loss account section of the income statement.

13 That taxation is shown in the income statement.

14 That transfers to reserves and dividends are shown in the statement of changes in equity.

15 That the *Conceptual Framework* sets the context within which financial statements and accounting standards are prepared.

16 How to prepare company income statements for internal purposes.

17 How to prepare company balance sheets for both internal and external purposes.

18 How IAS 1 governs the preparation of financial statements prepared for publication.

19 That financial statements for publication differ greatly from those prepared for internal use.

20 The fundamental ethical principles that accountants must follow.

Answers to activities

36.1 Partnerships were not suitable for such businesses because:

● normally they cannot have more than 20 partners, not counting limited partners;
● if a partnership business fails, partners could lose part, or all, of their private assets to pay the debts of the business.

Limited companies do not have restrictions on the number of owners. Nor do the owners of limited companies generally run the risk of losing everything they own if the company fails.

36.2 There may be any number of explanations, including:

● they may not want a wide ownership base;
● they may feel that the costs of doing so are prohibitive;
● they may feel that there would not be sufficient demand for the shares to make it worthwhile;
● the directors may be concerned that it would make it easier for the company to be taken over;
● they may wish to wait until the Stock Market is at a higher level, i.e. they may wish to wait until they can maximise the amount they can sell the shares for when they first offer them for sale on the Stock Market;
● the Stock Market may be very volatile, making choosing a price at which to sell the shares very difficult – if the company gets it wrong, they may not sell all the shares they wanted to sell or they may not receive as much for each share as they could have done had they waited for the Stock Market to stabilise.

36.3 There is less risk for the investor. The annual preference dividend is known and it will be paid before any funds left over are used to pay a dividend on the ordinary shares. Even when an ordinary dividend is paid, it is not known in advance how much this will be, as it depends on how profitable the business has been over the financial period. It could be more than the preference dividend (which is normally the case) or it could be less. Although the preference dividend will often be at a lower rate than an ordinary dividend (i.e. a preference shareholder will receive less of a dividend for the same investment as an ordinary shareholder) the reduced risk results in some people preferring to purchase preference shares.

36.4 The lender may require it or the company may offer secured loan note status in order to attract funds at a more favourable rate of interest.

36.5 As with all professions, enforcement of a code of ethics in a manner which encourages outsiders to believe that accountancy bodies are serious on this issue is not simply a case of having a disciplinary code. Outsiders can be very sceptical about self-regulation, especially if accountants found guilty of unethical conduct are let off with a warning or a minor fine. This is a difficult situation to address: non-accountants lack the technical knowledge and expertise to interpret accounting practice and so are incapable of truly understanding many of the situations that may arise. Finding something more appropriate is difficult, if not impossible.

Review questions

36.1 The equity section of the balance sheet of Lyness Ltd as at 1 January 2020 was as follows:

	£000
Ordinary shares of 50p each	170
Share premium	110
General reserve	50
Retained profits	402
Total equity	732

During the year the following events occurred:

● In March 2020 the company paid the final dividend in respect of 2019 of 8 pence per share.
● In July 2020 it paid an interim dividend for 2020 of 2 pence per share.
● In November 2020 the company issued 100,000 new ordinary shares at a premium of 80 pence per share.

The company reported a profit after tax of £93,000 for 2020 and made a transfer of £20,000 to general reserve. The directors also proposed a final dividend of 13 pence per share in respect of 2020.

Required:
Prepare the Statement of Changes in Equity for Lyness Ltd for the year ended 31 December 2020.

36.2 Yakubo plc was incorporated in 2011. The company has an authorised share capital of 3 million ordinary shares of 1p each, and 1 million 3% preference shares of £1 each. One third of these ordinary shares and exactly one quarter of the preference shares are currently in issue.

The preference shares were issued at nominal value, but the ordinary shares were originally issued at a price of 49p per share. The company has traded successfully in its short life to date, and the market value of the ordinary shares currently fluctuates between £2.20 and £2.50.

The company's financial year end is 31 December. Ordinary dividends of 13p per share were paid in March 2019. This was the final dividend in respect of 2018. An interim ordinary dividend of 4p per share was paid in August 2019. A final dividend for 2019 of 16p per share has recently been proposed.

What were the total dividends paid during 2019 by Yakubo plc?

36.3 A balance sheet for Cuomo Ltd is to be drawn up from the following information as at 30 September 2020:

	£
Issued share capital: ordinary shares £1 each	85,000
Authorised share capital: ordinary shares of £1 each	1,000,000
3.75% loan notes (repayable 30 September 2025)	75,000
Buildings at cost	730,000
Motor vehicles at cost	148,000
Plant & equipment at cost	254,000

→

	£
Retained profits	487,400
Share premium account	115,000
Inventory	81,800
Accounts receivable	102,000
General reserve	90,000
Accounts payable	97,300
Accumulated depreciation: Buildings	127,000
Motor vehicles	87,000
Plant & equipment	117,000
Bank (balancing figure for you to ascertain)	?
Corporation tax payable	49,100

36.4 The following balances remained in the ledger of Lungox Ltd after preparation of the income statement for the year ended 31 December 2019:

	£000
Inventory	138
Accounts receivable	166
Issued ordinary shares of £1 each	80
4% preference shares of £1 each	50
Accounts payable	141
Balance at bank	18
General reserve	40
Retained profits at 1 January 2019	221
Profit for year to 31 December 2019	66
Non-current assets at cost less accumulated	547
depreciation	
5% loan notes, repayable 2029	150
Corporation tax payable	35
Share premium	96

During the year the preference dividend for 2018 was paid in full, along with ordinary dividends amounting to 10 pence per share. The directors also wish to transfer £15,000 to general reserve.

Required:
(a) An extract from the Statement of Changes in Equity for the year ended 31 December 2019, showing the movement in general reserve and retained profits.
(b) A balance sheet as at 31 December 2019.

36.5A Futurescope Ltd has an authorised capital of 200,000 3% preference shares of £1 each and 500,000 ordinary shares of 50p each. After preparation of the income statement for 2020, the following balances remained in the ledger:

	£000
Share capital: fully paid-up:	
Preference	20
Ordinary	130
Loan notes	116
Share premium account	78
General reserve	30
Retained profits at 1 January 2020	282
Net profit for 2020	43
Non-current assets	612
Current assets	191
Accounts payable	104

The directors recommend:
(*i*) that £12,000 be transferred to general reserve,
(*ii*) payment of the preference dividend,
(*iii*) an ordinary dividend of 10 pence per share.

Required:
Prepare a statement of changes in equity for 2020 and a balance sheet as at 31 December 2020.

36.6 The following details concern Terraxa Ltd in relation to its financial year ended 31 May 2020:

Trial balance as at 31 May 2020:

	Dr £	Cr £
Gas	27,435	
Dividends paid	4,280	
Sales		541,470
Carriage inwards	1,567	
Purchases	222,003	
Other operating expenses	81,221	
Accounts receivable	87,600	
Maintenance	18,289	
Accounts payable		56,769
Machinery: at cost	390,720	
Vans: at cost	314,460	
Machinery: accumulated depreciation at 1 June 2019		92,220
Vans: accumulated depreciation at 1 June 2019		72,000
Inventory as at 1 June 2019	18,424	
Cash at bank	374	
7% loan notes 2030–2032		173,000
Loan note interest paid	6,055	
Bad debt expense	15,598	
Allowance for doubtful debts at 1 June 2019		2,641
Ordinary shares of 10p each		55,000
Retained profits at 1 June 2019		194,926
	1,188,026	1,188,026

Additional information:
(*i*) The company's inventory was counted at 31 May 2020 and was valued at £19,404.
(*ii*) Depreciation is to be charged at the following rates per annum:
        Machinery: (reducing balance)   30%
        Vans: (straight-line)   20%
(*iii*) The amount shown for maintenance on the trial balance includes a payment of £8,580, which represents an annual maintenance contract to 31 March 2021.
(*iv*) Gas charges incurred for which no invoices have yet been received amount to a total of £5,335.
(*v*) The allowance for doubtful debts is to be set at 4% of accounts receivable.
(*vi*) The loan note interest is paid in two annual instalments and the second instalment needs to be provided for.
(*vii*) The corporation tax charge on the profit for the year is estimated to be £3,000.

Required:
Prepare, for internal use purposes, an income statement for the year ended 31 May 2020 and a balance sheet as at that date.

→ **36.7A**   On 1 June 2019 Latchford Construction plc had £3.6 million 4.5% loan notes in issue, interest being paid annually in two instalments on 31 August and 28 February.

On 1 October 2019 the company issued a further £1.1 million 3.0% loan notes, interest being paid annually in two instalments on 31 March and 30 September each year.

On 31 March 2020 Latchford Construction plc redeemed £1.5 million 4.5% loan notes, paying the interest due to that date.

On the basis of the above, what interest expense should appear in the company's Income Statement for its year ended 31 May 2020?

36.8   The following details concern Arkone plc regarding its financial year ended 31 March 2020:

Trial balance as at 31 March 2020:	Dr £	Cr £
Accounts receivable	96,000	
Business rates	26,340	
Accounts payable		68,339
Returns outwards		1,926
Dividends paid	30,630	
Inventory as at 1 April 2019	37,185	
Motor expenses	22,271	
General operating expenses	119,293	
Sales		795,286
Plant & equipment: at cost	445,500	
IT equipment: at cost	198,000	
Plant & equipment: accumulated depreciation at 1 April 2019		90,660
IT equipment: accumulated depreciation at 1 April 2019		62,400
Purchases	373,784	
Cash at bank	540	
5% loan notes 2030–2032		98,000
Loan note interest paid	2,450	
Bad debt expense	17,110	
Share premium		70,000
Allowance for doubtful debts at 1 April 2019		2,893
Issued ordinary share capital		75,000
Directors' remuneration	45,924	
Retained profits at 1 April 2019		150,523
	1,415,027	1,415,027

Additional information:
(i)   Inventory at the year end was valued at a cost of £38,913.
(ii) Depreciation is to be charged at the following annual rates:
   Plant & equipment: (reducing balance)   15%
   IT equipment: (straight-line)   25%
(iii) The amount shown for business rates on the trial balance includes a payment of £11,760, which represents twelve months' business rates to 30 November 2020.
(iv) Motor expenses incurred for which no invoices have yet been received amount to a total of £4,863.
(v)   The allowance for doubtful debts is to be revised to 4% of accounts receivable.
(vi) Interest on the loan notes is paid in two instalments each year, and the second instalment has not yet been paid.
(vii) The corporation tax charge on this year's profit is estimated to be £19,000.

Required:
Produce an income statement for the year ended 31 March 2020 and a balance sheet as at that date (both in an 'internal use' format, not for publication).

36.9A   The following is the trial balance of Tully Ltd as on 31 December 2020:

	Dr £	Cr £
Share capital issued: ordinary shares 20p		375,000
Accounts receivable and accounts payable	169,600	74,900
Inventory 31 December 2019	81,300	
Bank	17,900	
Premises at cost	265,000	
Machinery at cost	109,100	
Motor vehicles at cost	34,700	
Accumulated depreciation at 31.12.2019:		
Premises		60,000
Machinery		41,400
Motor vehicles		18,200
Sales		975,600
Purchases	623,800	
Motor expenses	4,300	
Repairs to machinery	3,600	
Sundry expenses	2,900	
Wages and salaries	241,500	
Directors' remuneration	82,600	
Retained profits as at 31.12.2019		31,200
General reserve		60,000
	1,636,300	1,636,300

Given the following information, you are to draw up an income statement for the year ending 31 December 2020, and a balance sheet as at that date:

(*i*)   Authorised share capital: £500,000 in ordinary shares of 20p.
(*ii*)   Inventory at 31 December 2020 £102,400.
(*iii*)   Motor expenses owing £280.
(*iv*)   Ordinary dividend proposed of 5 per cent.
(*v*)   Transfer £7,500 to general reserve.
(*vi*)   Provide for depreciation: motor vehicles and machinery 20% on cost; premises 5% on cost.

36.10   The following information regarding Bemaji Ltd relates to its year ended 28 February 2020:

Trial balance as at 28 February 2020:

	Dr £	Cr £
Dividends paid	61,810	
Purchases	433,903	
Sales		986,143
Returns outwards		2,951
Motor expenses	19,705	
Accounts receivable	102,000	
Rent	19,489	
Inventory as at 1 March 2019	43,104	
Accounts payable		85,747
Plant & equipment: at cost	579,660	
Motor vehicles: at cost	250,560	
Plant & equipment: accumulated depreciation at 1 March 2019		110,880
Motor vehicles: accumulated depreciation at 1 March 2019		61,440
Sundry operating expenses	108,476	
Cash at bank	1,092	
6% loan notes 2028–2030		150,000
Loan note interest paid	4,500	

Trial balance as at 28 February 2020 (continued):

	Dr £	Cr £
General reserve		22,600
Bad debt expense	24,310	
Share premium		46,000
Allowance for doubtful debts at 1 March 2019		4,093
Issued ordinary share capital		62,000
Rent received		7,070
Directors' remuneration	78,890	
Retained profits at 1 March 2019		188,575
	1,727,499	1,727,499

Additional information:
(i) The inventory was counted at 28 February 2020 and was valued at a cost of £44,201.
(ii) Depreciation is to be charged at the following annual rates:
   Plant & equipment: (reducing balance)   15%
   Motor vehicles: (straight-line)   20%
(iii) The amount shown for rent on the trial balance includes a payment of £6,120 which represents twelve months' rent to 31 October 2020.
(iv) Motor expenses incurred for which no invoices have yet been received amount to a total of £5,661.
(v) The allowance for doubtful debts is to be changed to 5% of accounts receivable.
(vi) The loan note interest is paid in two annual instalments and the second instalment needs to be provided for.
(vii) The corporation tax charge on the profit for the year is estimated to be £40,000.
(viii) The directors wish to transfer £7,000 to general reserve.

Required:
Prepare an income statement for the year ended 28 February 2020 as well as a balance sheet as at that date. Both statements should adopt an 'internal use' format.

36.11A   The following information concerns Hurmey plc in relation to its year ended 31 July 2020:

Trial balance as at 31 July 2020:

	Dr £	Cr £
Inventory as at 1 August 2019	53,010	
Wages & salaries	113,856	
Accounts payable		85,810
Returns outwards		2,928
Rent	19,757	
Utilities	20,479	
Purchases	523,735	
Accounts receivable	105,600	
Sales		1,138,555
Machinery: at cost	465,840	
Vans: at cost	278,580	
Machinery: accumulated depreciation at 1 August 2019		105,120
Vans: accumulated depreciation at 1 August 2019		63,900
Dividends paid	51,440	
Cash at bank	2,435	
7% loan notes 2025–2027		175,000
Loan note interest paid	6,125	
General reserve		34,100
Bad debt expense	25,174	
Share premium		77,000

Trial balance as at 31 July 2020 (continued):

	Dr £	Cr £
Allowance for doubtful debts at 1 August 2019		4,237
Premises: at cost	658,600	
Premises: accumulated depreciation at 1 August 2019		171,236
Ordinary shares of 50p each		67,000
4% preference shares of £1 each		54,000
Commissions received		7,958
Directors' remuneration	91,080	
Retained profits at 1 August 2019		428,867
	2,415,711	2,415,711

Additional information:
(*i*)   The inventory was counted at 31 July 2020 and was valued at a cost of £53,661.
(*ii*)   Depreciation needs to be charged at the following rates per year:

Premises:	(straight-line)	2%
Machinery:	(straight-line)	20%
Vans:	(reducing balance)	30%

(*iii*) The amount shown for rent on the trial balance includes a payment of £8,100 which represents twelve months' rent to 30 November 2020.
(*iv*)   Utilities charges incurred for which no invoices have yet been received amount to a total of £6,757.
(*v*)   The audit fee has been agreed at £18,000 and this needs to be provided for.
(*vi*)   The allowance for doubtful debts is to be set at 5% of accounts receivable.
(*vii*) The interest on the loan notes is paid in two instalments each year, and the second instalment needs to be accrued.
(*viii*) The corporation tax charge on this year's profit is estimated to be £33,000.
(*ix*)   The directors want to transfer £8,000 to general reserve.

Required:
An income statement for the year ended 31 July 2020 and a balance sheet as at that date, both in an internal use format (not for publication).

36.12   The trading section of the income statement for Brogia Ltd for the year ended 30 April 2019 has been completed. It showed a gross profit of £171,360.

The following balances remained in the books of account of Brogia Ltd at April 2019:

	£
Bank loan repayable 2028	60,000
Cash at bank	6,840
Inventory	98,240
Loan interest	1,800
Non-current assets	147,800
Operating expenses	84,090
Ordinary shares of 20p each	120,000
Provision for depreciation at 1 May 2018	48,800
Retained earnings	48,560
Share premium	20,000
Trade payables	89,309
Trade receivables	23,800

Additional information:

(i) It is the company policy to depreciate non-current assets using the reducing balance method at the rate of $33\frac{1}{3}\%$ per annum.

(ii) The bank loan was taken out in 2008 and interest is payable at the rate of 5% per annum.

(iii) The directors have been advised that there should be a provision for corporation tax for the year ended 30 April 2019. It is estimated that this should be 20% of the profit before tax.

(iv) On 25 April 2019 the directors paid a dividend of 4p per share. This has not been recorded in the books of account.

(v) On 29 April 2019 the directors issued 200,000 new ordinary shares at a price of 35p per share. The issue was fully subscribed, but has not been entered in the books of account.

Required:

(a) Complete the income statement for Brogia Ltd for the year ended 30 April 2019.

(b) Prepare the statement of changes in equity for the year ended 30 April 2019. A total column is not required.

(AQA AS Level)

36.13A The accountant of Fiddles PLC has begun preparing financial statements but the work is not yet complete. At this stage the items included in the trial balance are as follows:

	£000
Land	100
Buildings	120
Plant and machinery	170
Depreciation provision	120
Share capital	100
Retained profits brought forward	200
Accounts receivable	200
Accounts payable	110
Inventory	190
Operating profit	80
Loan notes (16%)	180
Allowance for doubtful debts	3
Bank balance (asset)	12
Suspense	1

Notes (i) to (vii) below are to be taken into account:

(i) The accounts receivable control account figure, which is used in the trial balance, does not agree with the total of the accounts receivable ledger. A contra of £5,000 has been entered correctly in the individual ledger accounts but has been entered on the wrong side of both control accounts.

A batch total of sales of £12,345 had been entered in the double entry system as £13,345, although individual ledger account entries for these sales were correct. The balance of £4,000 on sales returns account has inadvertently been omitted from the trial balance, though correctly entered in the ledger records.

(ii) A standing order received from a regular customer for £2,000, and bank charges of £1,000, have been completely omitted from the records.

(iii) A debtor for £1,000 is to be written off. The allowance for doubtful debts balance is to be adjusted to 1% of accounts receivable.

(iv) The opening inventory figure had been overstated by £1,000 and the closing inventory figure had been understated by £2,000.

(v) Any remaining balance on suspense account should be treated as purchases if a debit balance and as sales if a credit balance.

(vi) The loan notes were issued three months before the year end. No entries have been made as regards interest.

(vii) A dividend of 10% of share capital is to be proposed.

Required:

(a) Prepare journal entries to cover items in notes (i) to (v) above. You are NOT to open any new accounts and may use only those accounts included in the trial balance as given.

(b) Prepare financial statements for internal use in good order within the limits of the available information. For presentation purposes all the items arising from notes (i) to (vii) above should be regarded as material.

(Association of Chartered Certified Accountants)

36.14 On 1 February 2019 the equity section of the balance sheet of Zamilo plc was as follows:

	£
Issued share capital (ordinary shares of 10p each)	100,000
Share premium	190,000
General reserve	50,000
Retained profits	560,000
Total equity	900,000

During the year ended 31 January 2020 the company:

● made a 1 for 5 bonus issue of shares, making use of the share premium account
● reported a net profit after tax of £80,000
● paid dividends of £32,000
● made a transfer to general reserve of £10,000.

Required:
Prepare the Statement of Changes in Equity for Zamilo plc for the year ended 31 January 2020.

36.15 The chairman of a public limited company has written his annual report to the shareholders, extracts of which are quoted below.

Extract 1
'In May 2019, in order to provide a basis for more efficient operations, we acquired PAG Warehousing and Transport Ltd. The agreed valuation of the net tangible assets acquired was £1.4 million. The purchase consideration, £1.7 million, was satisfied by an issue of 6.4 million equity shares, of £0.25 per share, to PAG's shareholders. These shares do not rank for dividend until 2020.'

Extract 2
'As a measure of confidence in our ability to expand operations in 2020 and 2021, and to provide the necessary financial base, we issued £0.5 million 8% Redeemable Loan Stock, 2027/2030, 20 million 6% £1 Redeemable Preference Shares and 4 million £1 equity shares. The opportunity was also taken to redeem the whole of the 5 million 11% £1 Redeemable Preference Shares.'

Required:
Answer the following questions on the above extracts.

Extract 1
(a) What does the difference of £0.3 million between the purchase consideration (£1.7m) and the net tangible assets value (£1.4m) represent?
(b) What does the difference of £0.1 million between the purchase consideration (£1.7m) and the nominal value of the equity shares (£1.6m) represent?
(c) What is the meaning of the term 'equity shares'?
(d) What is the meaning of the phrase 'do not rank for dividend'?

→

Extract 2
(e)   In the description of the loan note issue, what is the significance of
    (*i*)   8%?
    (*ii*)   2027/2030?
(f)   In the description of the preference share issue, what is the significance of
    (*i*)   6%?
    (*ii*)   Redeemable?
(g)   What is the most likely explanation for the company to have redeemed existing preference
    shares but at the same time to have issued others?
(h)   What effect will these structural changes have had on the gearing of the company?[Author's Note]
(i)   Contrast the accounting treatment in the company's income statement of the interest due on
    the loan notes with dividends proposed on the equity shares.
(j)   Explain the reasons for the different treatments you have outlined in your answer to (*i*) above.

(*Association of Chartered Certified Accountants*)

Author's [Note]: Part (h) of the question is covered in the text in Section 41.4.

36.16   The directors of the company by which you are employed as an accountant have received
the forecast income statement for 2019 which disclosed a net profit for the year of £36,000.

This is considered to be an unacceptably low figure and a working party has been set up to
investigate ways and means of improving the forecast profit.

The following suggestions have been put forward by various members of the working party:
(a)   'Every six months we deduct income tax of £10,000 from the loan note interest and pay it over
    to the HM Revenue & Customs. If we withhold these payments, the company's profit will be
    increased considerably.'
(b)   'I see that in the three months August to October 2019 we have forecast a total amount of
    £40,000 for repainting the exterior of the company's premises. If, instead, we charge this amount
    as capital expenditure, the company's profit will be increased by £40,000.'
(c)   'In November 2019, the replacement of a machine is forecast. The proceeds from the sale of the
    old machinery should be credited to profit and loss account.'
(d)   'There is a credit balance of £86,000 on general reserve account. We can transfer some of this
    to the income statement to increase the 2019 profit.'
(e)   'The company's £1 ordinary shares, which were originally issued at £1 per share, currently have
    a market value of £1.60 per share and this price is likely to be maintained. We can credit the
    surplus £0.60 per share to the 2019 profit and loss account.'
(f)   'The company's premises were bought many years ago for £68,000, but following the rise in
    property values, they are now worth at least £300,000. This enhancement in value can be utilised
    to increase the 2019 profit.'
You are required, as the accounting member of the working party, to comment on the feasibility of
each of the above suggestions for increasing the 2019 forecast profit.

(*Association of Chartered Certified Accountants*)

36.17   Explain what you understand by the accounting term 'loan notes' and indicate the
circumstances under which a loan note issue would or would not be an appropriate form of financing.

(*Scottish Qualifications Authority*)

36.18A The trial balance exhibited below has been extracted from the nominal ledger of Unsworthy plc as at 31 December 2020:

	Dr £000	Cr £000
6% loan notes 2035		600
Staff wages & salaries	1,253	
Advertising	460	
Bad debt expense	159	
Bank		232
Freehold buildings at cost	1,640	
Freehold buildings: accumulated depreciation at 1/1/2020		760
Directors' remuneration	786	
Inventory at 1 January 2020	468	
Issued share capital: ordinary shares of 10p each		300
Freehold land at cost	692	
Royalties received		378
Loan note interest paid	28	
Overdraft interest paid	19	
Carriage inwards	74	
Dividends paid (paid in July 2020)	108	
Other operating expenses	665	
Machinery at cost	1,728	
Machinery: accumulated depreciation at 1/1/2020		948
Purchases	5,241	
Retained profits at 1 January 2020		924
Returns inwards	308	
Returns outwards		157
Sales		9,606
Share premium account		643
Trade payables		856
Trade receivables	922	
Rent and business rates	853	
	15,404	15,404

The following matters also need to be considered before preparing the financial statements of the company:

(1) Inventory at 31 December 2020 was counted and valued at a cost of £517,000.
(2) Depreciation is to be charged as follows:
   (a) Freehold buildings – 2.5% straight-line
   (b) Machinery – 15% reducing balance
(3) Rent and business rates include a payment of £195,000 in respect of rent for the quarter ending 31 January 2021.
(4) The audit fee for 2020 has recently been agreed at £95,000 and this needs to be provided for.
(5) During November 2020 the company made a 1-for-4 bonus issue of its 10p ordinary shares. The share premium account was intended to be used for the purposes of this. However, no entries whatsoever have been made in respect of the bonus issue.
(6) On 1 January 2020 Unsworthy plc had £500,000 8% loan notes in issue, interest being paid half-yearly on 30 June and 31 December. On 31 March 2020 the company redeemed all £500,000 of these loan notes at par, paying the interest due up to that date. On 1 April 2020 the company then issued £600,000 6% loan notes at par, interest being payable half-yearly on 30 September and 31 March.

(7) Two accounting errors have just been discovered that have not yet been corrected:
   (a) A purchase credit note for £16,000 from a supplier has been recorded twice by mistake during December 2020.
   (b) A contra entry (i.e. a 'set-off') of £7,000 needed between a receivable and a payable has not been recorded in the nominal ledger.
(8) The corporation tax due on the profit for the year is estimated to be £41,000 (this estimate is unaffected by the seven matters above).

Required:

Prepare the following financial statements, for internal use:
(i)   the Income Statement for the year ended 31 December 2020; and
(ii) the Balance Sheet as at 31 December 2020.

Purchase of existing partnership and sole proprietor businesses

Learning objectives

After you have studied this chapter, you should be able to:

- enter up the purchase of a business in the purchaser's books
- draw up the balance sheet of the purchaser after taking over the assets and liabilities of the vendor

Introduction

In this chapter, you'll learn how to record the entries in the accounting books when a sole proprietor or a partnership is taken over by individuals, sole proprietor businesses, partnerships and companies.

37.1 Types of purchase

You learnt in Chapter 33 that a sole trader's business may be sold as a going concern, rather than being broken up and its assets sold off one by one. The seller normally prefers to sell the business as a going concern, as more money is usually generated arising from the goodwill of the business. Buyers often prefer to purchase a going concern as it saves them all the problems of building markets and reputation.

In that chapter we also looked at the calculation of partnership goodwill when there was a change in the partners. We didn't consider what happens when a partnership is sold as a going concern. This happens relatively frequently. Now that you've learnt how to maintain partnership accounts, we're going to look further at the accounting treatment of sole proprietors being taken over as going concerns. While we will focus on sole proprietors, everything you will learn in this chapter applies also to partnerships when they are taken over as going concerns.

There are many ways in which a sole proprietor or a partnership may be taken over as a going concern. For example, an individual may purchase the business of a sole proprietor (this was the example used at the start of Chapter 33) or a sole proprietor may take over a partnership.

> **Activity 37.1**
>
> Think about this for a minute and then write down as many different entities (i.e. a person or persons, or a type of business) as you can think of that might purchase a sole proprietor business or a partnership as a going concern.

37.2 Value of assets bought in purchaser's books

It must not be thought that because the assets bought are shown in the selling firm's books at one value, that the purchaser must record the assets taken over in its own books at the same value – you learnt about recording changes in asset values in Chapter 43 when you looked at revaluation of partnership assets but, in that case, you were looking at what you do when you revalue the assets of a partnership that is continuing in business, not when it is sold.

When a business is sold, the seller has no need to revalue the assets and adjust the values shown in the balance sheet. However, the buyer really ought to show the assets (and liabilities) of the business it has taken over at their current values.

 Activity 37.2 Why does the seller not need to revalue the assets of the business and change the values shown in the balance sheet?

The values shown in the books of the purchaser are, therefore, those values at which it is buying the assets, such values being frequently quite different from those shown in the selling firm's books. As an instance of this, the selling firm may have bought premises many years ago for £10,000 which are now worth £50,000. The purchaser buying the premises will obviously have to pay £50,000 for them. It is, therefore, this value that is recorded in the books of the purchaser.

 Activity 37.3 Why would an accounting firm want to purchase another accounting firm?

37.3 Goodwill on purchase

As you might have guessed, when the total purchase price is *greater* than the new valuation made by the purchaser of the assets taken over, the difference is goodwill in the eyes of the purchaser. (The seller may have a very different view concerning the value of the assets.) This can be shown as:

	£
Total purchase consideration	90,000
Less New valuation of assets taken over (not usually the same values as per the old balance sheet)	(75,000)
Goodwill	15,000

The revised balance sheet of the purchaser will include goodwill as an intangible asset at the calculated figure. It will also include the assets bought at their new valuations.

37.4 Capital reserve on purchase

Where the total purchase price is *less* than the new valuations of the assets taken over, the difference can either be treated in the purchaser's sole proprietor or partnership books as **negative goodwill** or as a **capital reserve**. (Companies *must* reassess the values placed on the assets and liabilities and adjust them so as to eliminate the negative goodwill.) When treated as a capital reserve, it can be shown as:

	£
Total purchase consideration	55,000
Less New valuation of assets taken over (not usually the same values as per the old balance sheet)	(75,000)
Capital reserve	(20,000)

The new valuations of the assets will appear in the revised balance sheet of the purchaser. Any capital reserve arising will be shown in the capital section of the balance sheet.

37.5 Taking over a sole proprietor business

It is easier to start with the takeover of the simplest sort of business unit, that of a sole proprietor. Some of the balance sheet shown in this chapter will be deliberately simplified so that the principles involved are not hidden behind a mass of complicated calculations.

To illustrate the takeover of a business, given varying circumstances, the same business will be assumed to be taken over in different ways. The balance sheet of this business is that of A. Brown, as shown in Exhibit 37.1.

Exhibit 37.1

A. Brown
Balance Sheet as at 31 December 2019

	£	£
Non-current assets		
Fixtures		30,000
Current assets		
Inventory	8,000	
Accounts receivable	7,000	
Bank	1,000	
		16,000
Total assets		46,000
Current liabilities		
Accounts payable		(3,000)
Net assets		43,000
Capital		43,000

1 An individual purchases the business of a sole proprietor

(*a*) Assume that the assets and liabilities of A. Brown, with the exception of the bank balance, are taken over by D. Towers. He is to take over the assets and liabilities at the valuations as shown in Brown's balance sheet. The price to be paid is £52,000.

The opening balance sheet of Towers will be as shown in Exhibit 37.2.

Exhibit 37.2

D. Towers
Balance Sheet as at 1 January 2020

	£	£
Non-current assets		
Goodwill		10,000
Fixtures		30,000
		40,000
Current assets		
Inventory	8,000	
Accounts receivable	7,000	
		15,000
Total assets		55,000
Current liabilities		
Accounts payable		(3,000)
Net assets		52,000
Capital		52,000

As £52,000 has been paid for the net assets (assets less liabilities) valued at £30,000 + £8,000 + £7,000 − £3,000 = £42,000, the excess £10,000 represents the amount paid for goodwill.

(b) Suppose that, instead of the information just given, the same amount (£52,000) has been paid by Towers, but the assets were taken over at a value of Fixtures £37,000; Inventory £7,500; Accounts receivable £6,500.

The opening balance sheet of D. Towers would be as shown in Exhibit 37.3.

Exhibit 37.3

D. Towers
Balance Sheet as at 1 January 2020

	£	£
Non-current assets		
Goodwill		4,000
Fixtures		37,000
		41,000
Current assets		
Inventory	7,500	
Accounts receivable	6,500	
		14,000
Total assets		55,000
Current liabilities		
Accounts payable		(3,000)
Net assets		52,000
Capital		52,000

As £52,000 had been paid for net assets valued at £37,000 + £7,500 + £6,500 − £3,000 = £48,000 the excess £4,000 represents the amount paid for goodwill. The other assets are shown at their value to the purchaser, Towers.

2 A partnership acquires the business of a sole proprietor

Assume instead that the business of Brown had been taken over by M. Ukridge and D. Allen. The partners are to introduce £30,000 each as capital. The price to be paid for the net assets, other than the bank balance, is £52,000. The purchasers placed the following values on the assets taken over: Fixtures £40,000; Inventory £7,000; Accounts receivable £6,000.

The opening balance sheet of Ukridge and Allen will be as in Exhibit 37.4.

Exhibit 37.4

M. Ukridge and D. Allen
Balance Sheet as at 1 January 2020

Non-current assets	£	£
Goodwill		2,000
Fixtures		40,000
		42,000
Current assets		
Inventory	7,000	
Accounts receivable	6,000	
Bank*	8,000	
		21,000
Total assets		63,000
Current liabilities		
Accounts payable		(3,000)
Net assets		60,000
Capitals		
M. Ukridge		30,000
D. Allen		30,000
		60,000

*The bank balance is made up of £30,000 + £30,000 introduced by the partners, less £52,000 paid to Brown = £8,000.

The sum of £52,000 has been paid for net assets of £40,000 + £7,000 + £6,000 − £3,000 = £50,000. This makes goodwill to be the excess of £2,000.

3 Amalgamation of existing sole proprietor businesses

Now assume that Brown was to enter into partnership with T. Owens whose last balance sheet is shown in Exhibit 37.5.

Exhibit 37.5

T. Owens
Balance Sheet as at 31 December 2019

Non-current assets	£	£
Premises		20,000
Fixtures		5,000
		25,000
Current assets		
Inventory	6,000	
Accounts receivable	9,000	
Bank	2,000	
		17,000
Total assets		42,000
Current liabilities		
Accounts payable		(5,000)
Net assets		37,000
Capital		37,000

(a) If the two traders were to amalgamate all their business assets and liabilities, at the values as shown, the opening balance sheet of the partnership would be as in Exhibit 37.6 (remember that Brown's balance sheet is shown above in Exhibit 37.1).

Exhibit 37.6

A. Brown & T. Owens
Balance Sheet as at 1 January 2020

	£	£
Non-current assets		
Premises		20,000
Fixtures		35,000
		55,000
Current assets		
Inventory	14,000	
Accounts receivable	16,000	
Bank	3,000	
		33,000
Total assets		88,000
Current liabilities		
Accounts payable		(8,000)
Net assets		80,000
Capitals		
Brown		43,000
Owens		37,000
		80,000

(b) Suppose that instead of both parties agreeing to amalgamation at the asset values as shown, the following values had been agreed to:

Owens' premises to be valued at £25,000 and his inventory at £5,500; other items as per the balance sheet in Exhibit 37.6. Brown's fixtures to be valued at £33,000; his inventory at £7,200 and accounts receivable at £6,400. It is also to be taken that Brown has goodwill of £7,000 whereas Owens' goodwill was considered non-existent. Other items are as per the balance sheet in Exhibit 37.6.

The balance sheet will be at the revised figures, and is shown as Exhibit 37.7.

Exhibit 37.7

A. Brown & T. Owens
Balance Sheet as at 1 January 2020

	£	£
Non-current assets		
Goodwill		7,000
Premises		25,000
Fixtures		38,000
		70,000
Current assets		
Inventory	12,700	
Accounts receivable	15,400	
Bank	3,000	
		31,100
Total assets		101,000
Current liabilities		
Accounts payable		(8,000)
Net assets		93,100
Capitals		
Brown		51,600
Owen		41,500
		93,100

Brown's capital can be seen to be £43,000 + £3,000 (fixtures) − £800 (inventory) − £600 (accounts receivable) + £7,000 (goodwill) = £51,600.

Owens' capital is £37,000 + £5,000 (premises) − £500 (inventory) = £41,500.

4 A limited company acquires the business of a sole proprietor

In this book, only an elementary treatment of this topic will be considered. More complicated examples will be covered in *Frank Wood's Business Accounting 2*.

This time, D. Lucas Ltd is taking over Brown's business. For Brown, you need to use the balance sheet shown in Exhibit 37.1. Before the acquisition, the balance sheet of D. Lucas Ltd was as shown in Exhibit 37.8.

Exhibit 37.8

D. Lucas Ltd
Balance Sheet as at 1 January 2017

	£	£
Non-current assets		
Fixtures		36,000
Current assets		
Inventory	23,000	
Accounts receivable	14,000	
Bank	6,000	
		43,000
Total assets		79,000
Current liabilities		
Accounts payable		(11,000)
Net assets		68,000
Equity		
Preference shares		20,000
Ordinary shares		40,000
Retained profits		8,000
		68,000

(*a*) Assume that Brown's business had been acquired, except for the bank balance, goodwill being valued at £8,000 and the other assets and liabilities at balance sheet values. D. Lucas Ltd is to issue an extra 32,000 £1 ordinary shares at par and 18,000 £1 preference shares at par to Brown, in full settlement of the £50,000 net assets taken over.

Exhibit 37.9 presents the summarised balance sheet of the company before and after the acquisition. (Note that the increase in the accounts payable amount is shown as a negative adjustment as it increases the amount to be deducted from the assets.)

Exhibit 37.9

D. Lucas Ltd
Summarised Balance Sheet

	Before £	+ or − £	After £
Goodwill	–	+8,000	8,000
Fixtures	36,000	+30,000	66,000
Inventory	23,000	+8,000	31,000
Accounts receivable	14,000	+7,000	21,000
Bank	6,000		6,000
	79,000		132,000
Accounts payable	(11,000)	−3,000	(14,000)
	68,000		118,000

	Before £	+ or − £	After £
Capital and reserves			
Preference shares	20,000	+18,000	38,000
Ordinary shares	40,000	+32,000	72,000
Retained profits	8,000		8,000
	68,000		118,000

(*b*) If instead we assume that the business of Brown was acquired as follows:

The purchase price to be satisfied by Brown being given £5,000 cash and issue an extra 50,000 ordinary shares at par and £10,000 loan notes at par. The assets taken over to be valued at Fixtures £28,000; Inventory £7,500; Accounts receivable £6,500. The bank balance is not taken over.

Exhibit 37.10 shows the summarised balance sheet of the company after the acquisition. (Note that both the increase in the accounts payable amount and the loan notes are shown as negative adjustments as they increase the amount to be deducted from the assets.)

Exhibit 37.10

D. Lucas Ltd
Summarised Balance Sheet

	Before £	+ or − £	After £
Goodwill		+26,000	26,000
Fixtures	36,000	+28,000	64,000
Inventory	23,000	+7,500	30,500
Accounts receivable	14,000	+6,500	20,500
Bank	6,000	−5,000	1,000
	79,000		142,000
Accounts payable	(11,000)	−3,000	(14,000)
	68,000		128,000
Loan notes	–	−10,000	(10,000)
	68,000		118,000

	Before £	+ or − £	After £
Capital and reserves			
Preference shares	20,000		20,000
Ordinary shares	40,000	+50,000	90,000
Retained profits	8,000		8,000
	68,000		118,000

Goodwill is calculated: Purchase consideration is made up of ordinary shares £50,000 + loan notes £10,000 + bank £5,000 = £65,000.

Net assets bought are: Fixtures £28,000 + Inventory £7,500 + Accounts receivable £6,500 − Accounts payable £3,000 = £39,000.

Therefore, Goodwill is £65,000 − £39,000 = £26,000.

37.6 Business purchase account

In this chapter, to economise on space and descriptions, only the balance sheets have been shown. However, in the books of the purchaser the purchase of a business should pass through a Business Purchase Account.

This would be as follows:

Business Purchase Account

Debit		Credit	
Each liability taken over	(B)	Each asset taken over	(A)
Vendor: net amount of	(C)	at values placed on it,	
purchase price		including goodwill	

Vendor's Account (Name of seller/s)

Debit		Credit	
Bank (or share capital)	(D)	Amount to be paid	(C)
Amount paid		for business	

Various Asset Accounts

Debit			
Business purchase (value placed	(A)		
on asset taken over)			

Various Liability Accounts

		Credit	
		Amount of liability taken over	(B)

Bank (or Share Capital)

		Credit	
		Amount paid to vendor	(D)

Learning outcomes

You should now have learnt:

1 That assets purchased when a business is taken over are shown in the purchaser's balance sheet at their valuation, not at the value shown in the closing balance sheet of the seller.

2 That where a greater price is paid than the total valuation of identifiable net assets then the difference is shown as goodwill.

3 That where the purchase price is less than the total valuation of identifiable net assets then the difference is shown as a capital reserve or as negative goodwill (except for limited companies, which *must* remove it by amending the values of its assets and liabilities).

4 That a limited company may use shares or loan notes, as well as cash, to pay for the acquisition of another business.

5 How to enter up the purchase of a business in the purchaser's books.

6 How to draw up the balance sheet of the purchaser after taking over the assets and liabilities of the vendor.

Answers to activities

37.1 These include:

- an individual purchases the business of a sole proprietor;
- an existing sole proprietor buys the business of another sole proprietor;
- a partnership acquires the business of a sole proprietor;
- a partnership acquires the business of another partnership (this happens quite a lot in accounting partnerships);
- existing businesses of sole proprietors join together to form a partnership;
- a limited company takes over the business of a sole proprietor;
- a limited company takes over the business of a partnership.

37.2 Goodwill. The total amount received less the value of net assets shown in the balance sheet represents the goodwill paid by the purchaser. Adjusting the asset values first simply increases the accounting work to be done by the seller. (In a partnership, the change in value of the assets would need to be shared among the partners, and then followed by a similar series of entries to account for the goodwill.)

37.3 There could be many reasons, including:

- to gain the specialist expertise of the other firm – one may specialise in small business accounts and the other in tax. Combining them removes the need to pay a specialist when they need the expertise the other firm specialises in;
- to save money by relocating the staff of one firm into the offices of the other, enabling the existing offices of the other firm to be sold.

However, the most common reason is to achieve growth. The number of times over the last 20 or so years that the list by size of the largest accounting firms in the UK has changed is testimony to this drive for market dominance through growth.

Review questions

37.1

B Finlay
Balance Sheet as at 31 March 2019

	£	£
Non-current assets		
Premises		145,000
Current assets		
Inventory	47,000	
Accounts receivable	38,500	
Bank	900	
		86,400
Total assets		231,400
Current liabilities		
Accounts payable		(57,900)
Net assets		173,500
Capital		173,500

Required:

(a) The business of B. Finlay is taken over by J. Adams in its entirety. The assets are deemed to be worth the balance sheet values as shown. The price paid by Adams is £250,000. Show the opening balance sheet of Adams.

(b) Suppose instead that G. Hughes had taken over Finlay's business. He does not take over the bank balance, and values premises at £200,000 and inventory at £30,000. The price paid by him is also £250,000. Show the opening balance sheet of Hughes.

37.2A The balance sheets of two sole proprietors, Amy Adams and Brendan Ball, as at 31 March 2019 are presented below:

	Amy Adams		Brendan Ball	
	£	£	£	£
Non-current assets				
Buildings*		155,000		96,000
Machinery*		86,000		24,000
Motor vehicles*		37,000		17,000
Computer equipment*		12,000		–
		290,000		137,000
Current assets				
Inventory	20,600		14,000	
Trade receivables	30,100		27,000	
Prepayments	4,100		–	
Cash at bank	2,700		–	
Cash in hand	150	57,650	100	41,100
Total assets		347,650		178,100
Current liabilities				
Bank overdraft	-		3,240	
Trade payables	23,800		19,000	
Accruals	1,800		–	
Total liabilities		(25,600)		(22,240)
Net assets		322,050		155,860
Closing capital		322,050		155,860

*These amounts are all stated at cost less accumulated depreciation.

→

Brendan plans to emigrate to New Zealand and has therefore agreed to sell his business to Amy. Amy will take over Brendan's buildings, machinery, inventory, trade receivables and trade payables only.

Amy assesses the fair value of Brendan's buildings to be £125,000, his machinery £15,000 and his inventory at £10,000.

The agreed purchase price was £200,000. To finance the purchase Amy obtained a 10-year bank loan equal to 75% of the purchase price. One of the conditions of the loan was that Amy must contribute the other 25% from her own private funds.

The purchase price was paid in full on 1 April 2019.

On the same day Amy also:

- Disposed of one of her machines for £500. This machine had originally cost £13,000 and had accumulated depreciation of £11,000. Amy received the £500 in the form of a cheque which she banked straightaway.
- Purchased new computer equipment, paying £4,750 by means of a bank transfer.
- Wrote-off as irrecoverable a debt of £1,350 that was due from one of her credit customers.

Required:
(a) Draw up the Business Purchase Account in Amy's books.
(b) Prepare the Balance Sheet of Amy's business as at 1 April 2019 after all the transactions described above have been completed.

37.3 Spectrum Ltd is a private company with an authorised capital of £700,000 divided into shares of £1 each. 500,000 shares have been issued and are fully paid. The company has been formed to acquire small retail shops and establish a chain of outlets.

The company made offers to three sole traders and purchased the businesses run by Red, Yellow and Blue.

The assets acquired, liabilities taken over, and prices paid are listed below:

	Red £	Yellow £	Blue £
Premises	75,000	80,000	90,000
Delivery vans	7,000	–	10,000
Furniture and fittings	12,000	13,000	13,000
Inventory	8,000	7,000	12,000
Accounts payable	6,000	8,000	7,000
Purchase price	120,000	130,000	150,000

The company also purchased a warehouse to be used as a central distribution store for £60,000. This has been paid.

Preliminary expenses (formation expenses) of £15,000 have also been paid.

The company took over the three shops outlined above and started trading on 1 January 2018.

Approaches have also been made to Green for the purchase of his business for £100,000. Green has accepted the offer and the company will take over in the near future the following assets and liabilities:

	£
Premises	70,000
Inventory	18,000
Accounts payable	3,000

The transaction had not been completed on 1 January 2018 and Green was still running his own business.

Required:
(a) Prepare the opening balance sheet of Spectrum Ltd as at 1 January 2018.
(b) How would you advise Spectrum Ltd to finance the purchase of Green's business when the deal is completed?
(*Edexcel Foundation, London Examinations (University of London)*)

37.4 Dinho and Manueli are in partnership sharing profits and losses equally after interest of 10% on each partner's capital account in excess of £100,000. At 31 December 2018, the partnership trial balance was:

	Dr £	Cr £
Bank		56,700
Capital accounts: Dinho		194,000
Manueli		123,000
Accounts payable		85,800
Accounts receivable	121,000	
Equipment, at cost	85,000	
Long-term loan		160,000
Freehold property	290,000	
Accumulated depreciation on equipment		20,000
Inventory	143,500	
	639,500	639,500

On 31 December 2018, the partnership was converted to a limited company, Bin Ltd. All the partnership assets and liabilities were taken over by the company in exchange for shares in Bin Ltd valued at £304,000. The share capital was allocated so as to preserve the rights previously enjoyed by the partners under their partnership agreement.

The assets and liabilities and shares issued were all entered in the books of Bin Ltd at 31 December. In the company's books, the accounts receivable were recorded at £116,000 and the freehold property was valued at £260,000.

On 1 January 2019, Pa invested £120,000 in the company and was issued shares on the same basis as had been applied when deciding the share allocations to Dinho and Manueli – i.e. as if he had been an equal partner in the partnership.

Pa had previously been an employee of the partnership earning £40,000 per annum. The £120,000 he invested in the company had been earning interest of 6 per cent per annum from the bank. His salary will continue to be paid.

Assume that all profits will be paid as dividends. Ignore taxation.

Required:
(a) Prepare the partnership realisation account after the sale of the business to Bin Ltd had been completed and recorded in the partnership books.
(b) Prepare Bin Ltd's balance sheet as at 1 January 2019 after the purchase of shares by Pa.
(c) Calculate the minimum annual profit that Bin Ltd needs to make before it pays any dividends if Pa is to receive the same amount of income as he was receiving before buying shares in Bin Ltd.

part 9

AN INTRODUCTION TO FINANCIAL ANALYSIS

Introduction

This part deals with the identification of unknown figures needed in order to prepare financial statements, the maths all accountants need to know, and how to analyse and interpret financial statements.

Maths for accounting

After you have studied this chapter, you should be able to:

- explain why knowing how to do arithmetic and algebra is an essential skill in accounting
- describe a list of mathematical calculations that an accountant may make
- explain why it is important to always check the answer to any calculation
- explain the mathematics used for opening and closing adjustments to accounts
- explain the mathematics used for bad debts and allowances for doubtful debts
- explain the mathematics used for depreciation
- explain how to manipulate a formula to find a missing value for a variable in the formula
- explain why calculating a ratio is only the first step towards evaluating it
- explain how to calculate net revenue from a sales figure that includes VAT

Introduction

The ability to perform calculations is an essential skill of an accountant. The mathematics of accounting is mainly arithmetic and algebra. This chapter describes many of the common uses of this mathematics in financial accounting and shows how to do so efficiently and with success.

38.1 Why is it important that you know mathematics for accounting?

The answer to this question is very simple: mathematics is inseparable from accounting. Without mathematics, there would be no accounting as we know it. The need for accountants to know how to perform arithmetic is obvious. They need to know how to add, subtract, multiply, and divide. These are digital times, where computers are the accountant's principal tool and calculators are not far behind in second place. It is more the case now than ever before that accountants need to know when accounting information does not make sense, when a total is incorrect, when a calculation looks wrong. So, not only must accountants be very good at arithmetic, they also need to be good at mental arithmetic. They must be able to spot a possible error simply by looking at the numbers presented to them.

Is it assumed that simply by looking at the result of a calculation, an accountant can confirm that it is correct or that it is wrong? No, that would be impossible. Yet, we expect accountants to ensure the accuracy of the information they prepare for decision makers. A sole proprietor may ask his accountant what the depreciation on his non-current assets would be if he switched from straight line to reducing balance, and he expects a correct answer. The accountant opens her spreadsheet, enters the relevant data, selects the appropriate spreadsheet calculation functions, enters her own formulas, and out pops the answer. Simple, but is the answer correct? Maybe. . .

There are many ways in which it could be wrong. For example:

● the original data may have been entered into the spreadsheet incorrectly
● a wrong selection may have been made from the spreadsheet's list of available mathematical functions
● perhaps there is an error in one of the calculation formulas she wrote, a positive number may be being treated in calculations as though it is negative, a number may have been rounded to a whole number too early in the calculation process.

Errors may be caused by a human mistake. They may also occur because the software being used is not as reliable as it appears.

Spreadsheet software looks infallible but, sometimes, it uses algorithms (i.e. ways of performing calculations) that result in very small errors. For example, the correct answer may be 24,987 but the spreadsheet shows it to be 24,991. It is a small difference and probably not important. But, take the example of the mark on an exam. A correct answer of 49.501334 might be shown as 49.499976 by the spreadsheet and then rounded down to 49 by the spreadsheet instead of up to 50, resulting in an exam being failed when it should have been passed, and no one knows because everyone assumes that the spreadsheet performed the calculation correctly.

38.2 What mathematics do accountants need to know?

There is a long list of both general and specific mathematical calculations that accountants must be able to do. This requires that they are good at both arithmetic and algebra. Accountants need to be able to:

● add, subtract, multiply, and divide, ideally in their heads when the numbers are small
● calculate percentages, and know how to ensure that any rounding is done correctly
● calculate mark-ups and margins and not mix them up
● convert amounts from one currency to another
● discount amounts to provide an estimate of the current value of future cash flows
● perform calculations of depreciation, amortisation, impairment, revaluation, doubtful debts, accruals, prepayments, materiality, inventory valuation, discount, VAT, royalties, commissions, fair value, taxation, financial instruments, pensions, ratios, earnings per share, direct cost, indirect cost, allocation of cost, apportionment of cost, standard cost, variances from budgets, and many others.

And, for all the calculations they perform and for all the calculated numbers they look at, accountants must be able to interpret the answer, break it down into its constituent parts; know where all the numbers used to calculate it come from – what they represent.

For example, if an accountant looks at an income statement prepared for a partnership by her trainee accountant, she needs to be able to tell if all the calculations that were made to produce it are correct; and she needs to know if the numbers in the income statement make sense. Let's assume she knows that gross profit should be around 55 per cent of revenue, does a rough calculation in her head, and realises that it is over 60 per cent. It looks to her as if it is too high, so she investigates the elements within the cost of goods sold and discovers that the trainee has entered the opening inventory as £12,900 instead of £19,200. This leads her to look at the balance sheet.

Activity 38.1 Why would the accountant then look at the balance sheet?

If that reveals nothing, the accountant will look at the trial balance to see if the difference of £6,300 between what should have been entered (£19,200) and what was entered (£12,900) appears as one of the account balances. If it doesn't, the accountant may need to check all the account balances, one by one, until it is found.

Activity 38.2 What other obvious check could the accountant make?

These are some of the things an accountant must be able to do using mathematics. In some cases, they are beyond the scope of this book; for example, the last six items in the final bullet point above refer to things done in management accounting. However, all financial accountants at one time or another will be faced with having to deal with virtually all of the others.

Let's begin with the most basic mathematical skill needed by accountants: arithmetic.

38.3 Arithmetic

There is no possibility of anyone who cannot correctly perform basic arithmetic ever being a very successful accountant. Calculators, spreadsheets, and ERP systems like *SAP* will hide the weakness but, when mistakes are made and not identified, it will soon be revealed. The arithmetic needed is on two levels: performing the calculation, and checking the answer.

Doing the calculation

Firstly, you must be able to add, subtract, multiply, and divide. You must know how to do each of these quickly without any tools to help you: 5 times 8; 9 minus 13; 4 plus 7; 25 divided by 3. Most of us can do these pretty easily in our heads and know that the answer is correct. But accountants deal in much larger numbers:

(i)   2 million shares of 10p each – how much is that?
(ii) A dividend is declared of 7p on each of 675,000 shares – how much is that?
(iii) What proportion of a partnership do you own if you contributed £64,000 of the total capital of £185,000?
(iv) If you purchase inventory at different times for £3 per kilo, £3.20 per kilo, and £2.76 per kilo, what is the average cost of the inventory held at the end of the reporting period?

These four examples are of straightforward multiplication and division calculations that accountants are expected to do. The first three provide all the information needed. The fourth needs information about quantities before any calculations can be made. As well as doing the calculations and checking calculations, accountants need to be aware of the data required for every calculation they perform or check.

Addition and subtraction are much more straightforward, but everyone makes mistakes keying in long lists of numbers on a calculator or a keyboard.

Checking the answer

Here is a list of numbers you entered into your calculator and the total you can see on the screen:

2,473.90
1,526.81
3,488.20
7,823.18
Total: 15,315.09

It is not correct. You have keyed 2,476.90 into the calculator, hitting the '6' key instead of the '3'. It is a very easy mistake to make. Remember, you cannot see what you entered in the calculator any more. All you can see is the answer.

Activity 38.3 How do you avoid making mistakes of this type?

Let's assume the only tool available to you is your calculator. If it is a short list like the one above, first add up the final digits of the numbers to check that the final digit in the answer is correct. Do that in your head. Then, work from right to left across the columns, checking the arithmetic. Again, do it in your head. Alternatively, after checking mentally the columns you find easy to check, rekey the calculation into your calculator and see if the same answer is produced. If you have made a mistake, the chances of making the same mistake again are low, especially if you have a long list of numbers – more than maybe 10. When recounting or rekeying longer lists of numbers, switch the sequence when you repeat the calculation. Count bottom-up instead of top-down, or vice versa. Do this both when doing them in your head and when using a calculator. Always write down the answer. You are hoping to get the same answer as you had in one of your other attempts. You won't know you have done so if you do not have a note of the answers you get.

Many people have a habit of miskeying certain numbers, such as 6 instead of 3. Anyone who does so needs to recognise the problem and be careful to hit those problematic keys correctly. If you rekey everything a number of times and each time get a different answer, leave it and do something else for a while, or ask someone else to add up the list and then compare answers.

Activity 38.4 What is a far easier way to check your arithmetic with longer lists?

You can total short lists manually or in a calculator and check the answers mentally, or on paper, or by rekeying them. However, you will find it hard to do this with longer lists. So, in terms of addition and subtraction, if you have a short list of numbers, do it manually or use a calculator. If you have a longer list of numbers, use a spreadsheet. But, always, when you have an answer to any calculation **think for a moment and consider whether it looks sensible.**

If the total shown on your calculator for the small addition performed above was £25,312.09, your common sense should have told you that it was impossible for that number to be correct. Many accountants would notice such strangeness in the answer even if it were much closer to the correct answer. The scale of the answer needs to be correct and when you see a series of numbers that add to roughly £15,000 as these do, even an answer under £14,000 or just over £16,000 should start to ring alarm bells. The way to set yourself an estimate is to round each number to the nearest thousand. So, anything below 500 goes down and anything of 500 or more goes up. When this is done, the list of numbers goes mentally from:

$$2{,}473.90 + 1{,}526.81 + 3{,}488.20 + 7{,}823.18$$

to:

$$2 + 2 + 3 + 8 = 15$$

So, you would expect the answer to be around 15,000 and it is: 15,312.09

38.4 Mathematics for opening and closing expense adjustments

One of the most frequent calculations you will do in accounting is an adjusting entry for opening and closing accruals and prepayments, but there are many others. There are a few things that interfere with attempts to find the correct amount. The most common occurs when you get confused with the debits and the credits. Try to ignore them. Instead, consider what you are doing. Whatever you are doing, the adjustment will increase or decrease the balance on the account. **Think arithmetic, *not* debits and credits.**

If the adjustment is one that involves *increasing* the balance, calculate the adjustment and then enter it in the appropriate place in the account. **Now, you have done the calculation, you can think debits and credits.** If it is an account for an expense or an asset, the entry will be a debit. If it is anything else, the entry for the adjustment will be a credit.

If it is an adjustment that *decreases* a balance, the entries will be the opposite.

> **Activity 38.5** Would the entry for an increase in a liability account be a debit or a credit?

Imagine that you are given a list of adjustments to make to a trial balance. You may be given a variety of different adjustments to make. What you need to remember is that every adjustment is a simple arithmetical calculation. Try to focus on that. Logically, if you need to accrue an amount for an expense, the expense must be increased. If you need to make an adjustment for a prepayment, the expense must be decreased. Most adjustments are of one of these two types. Let's look at some examples.

Accrued expense adjustments

(*i*)   Rent unpaid at the period end is £400; you are told the amount. No calculation is needed.
(*ii*) Two months' rent is unpaid at the period end. The annual rent bill is £2,400. You need to calculate the amount of the accrual. If the rent for a year is £2,400 then the rent for one month is $1/12$ of the annual amount = £200. You must accrue 2 months' rent = 2 times £200 = £400.

You need to be careful when calculating the amount of the accrual. It is easy to press the wrong key on your calculator. Check the answer shown mentally. Does it look right?

Accrual adjustments are not difficult. They just take a bit of care. The balance on the above rent account will need to be increased by £400. It is an expense account, so the entry is a debit in the account and a credit to an account for accrued rent.

Prepaid expense adjustments

These can often be straightforward to do, but sometimes they are more complicated.

1 You are told the amount of the adjustment. For example, that business rates paid in advance at the period end are £300. No calculation is needed. (Business rates are a local tax set by the local government for a fixed amount each year. They are treated as a business expense.)

2 When it becomes more complicated, you need to know (i) what the financial period is for the business and, (ii) what period is covered by the amount paid. For example, if the year end for the business is 30 June and the period covered by the amount paid is for 3 months – June, July, and August – you know that the payment for 1 month should be included in your expense and that the payment for the 2 months after the period end should be treated as a prepayment.

For example, assume that the annual business rates bill is £900. The local government's year-end is 31 March. This means that the bill is for the 12 months ending on 31 March next year. You paid the whole amount due of £900 on 1 June. Your reporting period ends on 31 December. This means that you paid for 12 months but only nine of those months are included in your reporting period. So, you must treat $^9/_{12}$ of the payment as an expense and $^3/_{12}$ of the payment as a prepayment.

Looked at from another perspective, you should include $^9/_{12}$ of the payment as an expense in this year's income statement because 9 is the number of months that have passed of the 12-month period for which the payment was made. That means that you have prepaid the rest $= 1 - ^9/_{12} = ^3/_{12}$ of the amount you paid. That is, the prepayment is for $^3/_{12}$ of £900 = £225.

You should double check that you have identified the correct period to be used to calculate the prepayment. In this case, an easy check is to identify the months for which payment was made that occur after the end of the reporting period. In this case, they are January, February, and March = 3 months, which confirms you have used the correct number of months in your calculation of the prepayment.

> You should have noticed that these accrual and prepayment adjustments are not complicated. They only need you to think and then use very basic arithmetic to calculate the amounts involved. Once you have calculated the amount of an accrual, you debit the expense account (which increases the balance to the correct amount) and credit the account for that accrued expense, e.g. the accrued rent account. Accrual accounts go in the balance sheet under current liabilities. **The treatment of a prepayment is the opposite:** you credit the expense account (which reduces the balance to the correct amount) and you debit the prepaid expense account, e.g. the prepaid business rates account. Prepayment accounts go under the current assets in the balance sheet.

Opening accrual and prepayment account balances

This is where most students begin to find making adjustments for accruals and prepayments confusing. The trick is to treat this adjustment as a separate exercise from any period-end accrual or prepayment adjustment that you are making. Often, you can ignore these opening accruals and prepayments, apart from entering them into your T-account for the expense. In most of these examples, we'll use prepayments. **The approach for accruals is the opposite.**

a) The opening balance on a business rates account is a debit of £280. This is a prepayment from the previous reporting period. It belongs in the total of this year's expense. You do not need to do any calculations. Once the opening prepayment has been entered in the account, you will discover how much has been paid for business rates that may relate to this period. If there are no accruals or prepayments on the account at the end of the current period, the balance on the account is the amount that is included for business rates in the income statement.

Note: In examples like this, you need to discover whether the opening prepayment (or accrual) has been included in the account balance that you have been given. It will be obvious from the question.

b) The opening balance on a rent account is a credit for £150. This is an accrued amount from the previous reporting period. It means that of the payments made in this reporting period, £150 was paid to settle the amount due from the previous period. That £150 is not included in the total expense for this period. You do not need to do any calculation; however, you must enter the opening accrual as a credit in the account. If you then balance the account, you will discover how much has been paid for rent that may relate to this period. If there are no accrual or prepayments on the account at the end of the current period, the balance on the account is the amount that is included for rent in the income statement.

Most opening entries for accruals and prepayments are absorbed into the balance of the account at the end of the period. Once they have been entered into the T-account, you need only concern yourself with the resulting balance. For example:

c) Assume you have an opening prepayment of £600 on a rent account and that after you make the debit entry for the prepayment in the rent account the account has a balance of £1,500. Once you have made the entry for that opening prepayment, which is a debit in the expense account, you can then ignore it because it is included in the balance. If the rent for the year is £1,200 this is £300 less than your balance, so you have paid £300 in advance for next year. Your prepayment for this period is, therefore, £300.

d) Assume you have an opening prepayment of £300 on a rent account and the account has a balance of £1,700 after you make the debit entry in the T-account for the expense. This time, you are told that in the final month of the accounting period, rent totalling £1,200 was paid for 3 months. That is, it covered the rent due for the final month of this period and the first 2 months of the next period. To find the prepayment, you divide that payment (£1,200) by the number of months (3) and multiply the answer (£400) by the number of months in the next period for which you have already paid the rent (2). This gives you a closing prepayment of £800.

Note: In this example, you did not make any use of either the opening prepayment or the balance on the account when calculating the closing prepayment.

e) Assume that you have an opening prepayment of £450 on a rent account and the account has a balance before entering that prepayment of £1,650. Again, once you have made the entry for the opening prepayment, which is a debit in the expense account, you can ignore it. However, this time, you do not know what the annual rent should be. Instead, you are told that 2 months' rent has been paid in advance at the end of the reporting period. That is, the balance on the rent expense account is for 14 months, not 12. To discover the amount of the prepayment, you must first ensure that you have entered the opening prepayment into the T-account for the expense. Then, you divide the balance (£2,100) by the number of months it relates to (14). This gives a monthly rental expense of £150. You then multiply that by 2 to identify the amount of the prepayment, £300.

The important thing about involving opening accruals and prepayments in your calculations is to ensure that they have been entered in the appropriate expense account before the balance is calculated. If you do that, they should not affect your ability to perform calculations of closing accruals and prepayments.

Remember, an opening debit balance on an expense account is a prepayment – that is, an amount that was overpaid in the previous reporting period; and an opening credit entry on an expense account is an accrual – that is, an amount underpaid in the previous accounting period.

> Period end accrual and prepayment adjustments are not difficult to process. They just take a bit of care. If the adjustment is one that involves increasing the balance on the account, calculate the adjustment and then enter it in the appropriate place in the account. If it is an account for an expense or an asset, the entry will be a debit. If it is to any other type of account, the entry for the adjustment will be a credit. And, if the accrual or prepayment adjustment reduces the balance, you make a credit entry in expense accounts and asset accounts; and a credit entry if it is to any other type of account. The other side of each entry is to either an accrual account or a prepayment account, for example an accrued rent account or a prepaid rent account.

38.5 Mathematics for adjustments to accounts receivables

Another common adjusting entry performed by accountants is an adjustment to the amount shown in the balance sheet for accounts receivables, that is, debtors. There are two types: bad debt adjustments and allowance for doubtful debt adjustments.

● **Bad debt**: This is permanent; it reduces the balance on the debtor account, usually to zero.
● **Allowance for doubtful debts**: This is temporary; it adjusts the balance in a special purpose account called 'the allowance for doubtful debts account'. That adjustment made to that account may be an increase or a decrease. The resulting balance on the allowance account reduces the overall total of all accounts receivables in the balance sheet. No debtor account balance is changed.

Students often get these two types of adjustments mixed-up. Just as opening accrual and prepayment adjustments should be thought of separately from closing accrual and prepayment adjustments, so bad debts and changes in allowances for doubtful debts should be treated separately. **You always do the bad debt adjustment first.**

Bad debt adjustments

The calculations to be made for bad debts are usually very simple and easy to calculate. A bad debt means that the debt must be removed. This means that the debtor's account balance is reduced, usually to zero, by a credit entry for the bad debt. The total amount of all the accounts receivable obviously reduces by the same amount. The other side of the entry is a debit in an expense account, the 'bad debts account'. If only part of a debt is to be written-off as bad, you will be told the amount, e.g. £200. You simply reduce the balance on the account (and on the total accounts receivables) by that amount of £200 (by crediting the account of the debtor). And you debit the bad debt account with £200.

Doubtful debt adjustments

Doubtful debts are more complicated and often require that you calculate the amount to be used in the adjustment. However, there is very little variety in the range of calculations to be carried out. For example, assume that you are told that you must provide an allowance for 5% of outstanding accounts receivable at the period end.

Step 1: Write-off any bad debts.

Step 2: Calculate 5% of the remaining balance.

Let's say that is £500. This is the amount that should be the balance on the *Allowance for Doubtful Debts account*. You must then do another calculation.

Step 3: Discover what the balance on the allowance was at the end of the previous period. Let's assume it was £300.

Step 4: Calculate whether the new allowance of £500 is greater than or less than the previous allowance (£300).

Step 5: Make an adjusting entry to change the balance on the *Allowance for Doubtful Debts account* to the new balance (which you calculated in Step 2).

Step 6: Make a contra entry for that entry in an account called either the *Increase in Allowance for Doubtful Debts account* (an expense, therefore a debit entry) or in the *Decrease in Allowance for Doubtful Debts account* (a gain, therefore a credit entry)

In this case, the new allowance is greater by £200. It is an expense for the business, so you must make a debit entry for £200 in the *Increase in Allowance for Doubtful Debts account*. The other side of the entry is an adjusting entry to increase the balance on the *Allowance for Doubtful Debts account* by making a credit entry in that account for £200. **This account is a provision account – you are setting aside resources of the business in case some debtors fail to pay the amounts due.**

Sometimes you are not told the opening balance on the *Allowance for Doubtful Debts account*. Instead, you will be told the percentage allowance used previously (e.g. 3%) and the opening accounts receivable balance (e.g. £24,000). You will then need to calculate what the opening balance on the *Allowance for Doubtful Debts account* was. You do this by calculating 3% of £24,000 = £720.

This may be made more complex by telling you that the opening accounts receivable balance provided to you is *after* deducting the opening allowance for doubtful debts. In this case, you will need to do the following stepped calculation:

● Opening allowance divided by (1−% allowance) = opening accounts receivable before reducing it by the allowance.

  For example, if the opening accounts receivable balance after reduction for the allowance for doubtful debts was £190,000 and the allowance was 5%, you divide £190,000 by (1−0.05) = £190,00 ÷ 0.95 = £200,00.

● To calculate the figure for the opening allowance, you then either subtract the opening accounts receivable balance amount from the one you have just calculated, or multiply that answer by the percentage allowance (5%). To avoid mistakes, you should do both.

In the above example, £200,000 minus the original figure you received of £190,000 leaves £10,000. That is the opening allowance for doubtful debts. You can confirm it by calculating 5% of £200,000 = £10,000.

38.6 Mathematics for depreciation provisions

Every business is required to depreciate its non-current assets. There are two main methods: straight line and reducing balance.

● **Straight line:** annual depreciation = (cost − scrap value) ÷ years of useful economic life.
● **Reducing balance:** annual depreciation = cost × the percentage that reduces the net book value to the scrap value of the asset over its useful economic life.

Straight line

There are variants on the formula for the *straight line* method. For example, depreciation of a machine may be based on its estimated useful economic life; or it could be based on the estimated total number of units it will be able to produce before it has to be scrapped. Alternatively it may, for example, be based on the total time in actual use that it is estimated will be possible before it has to be scrapped. Irrespective of the basis used, the approach is a simple one to use and requires only that you are able to add, subtract, divide, and multiply; and that you remember to subtract the scrap value from the cost before doing the second stage of the calculation.

Sometimes you are told the depreciation percentage instead of the base for the measure – years, units, hours, and so on. When this happens, the annual depreciation = (cost − scrap value) × the percentage. So, a 20% depreciation rate on a machine that cost £3,000 and has a scrap value of £400 = (£3,000 − £400) × 20% = £2,600 × 20% = £2,600 × 0.20 = £520.

It is the same answer as the one you would get if you converted the percentage into the number of years of estimated useful economic life: 5. You can do this with any percentage if you find it easier to divide by the number of years than multiply by the percentage. All you need to do to convert the percentage to number of years is to calculate how many times the percentage divides into 100. For example, 25% is equivalent to (100 ÷ 25) years = 4 years.

Straight line involves very simple calculations. However, many students struggle when calculating percentage rates, and do so even more when calculating reducing balance depreciation.

Reducing balance

Reducing balance requires that you know how to calculate percentages. And that you know how to combine the percentage with the net book value. The problems faced can be separated into stages that may be encountered depending on the details of the calculation you are doing:

1 First, you need to know how to calculate a percentage.
2 You then need to know what to do with the answer.
3 You then need to know how to arrive at the total depreciation over a specific period.
4 And you need to know how to arrive at the net book value at the end of the same period.

Some find it difficult to use percentages and, instead of learning how to do it mentally, key the numbers into a calculator, press the % key when they think it is correct to do so, and blindly accept the result. When using a calculator, it is essential that you first estimate in your head what the answer should be and then consider whether the answer showing in the calculator could be correct. Many students put the decimal place in the wrong place, some make typos. **Failing to check a calculation you have done on a calculator is never a good idea.**

1 How to calculate a percentage

To calculate a percentage, you can adopt one of two approaches, as set out in Method A and B below. Let's illustrate them with an example. Imagine you had to calculate 36.5% of £5,700. **Note that in order to convert the 36.5% to a decimal, we move the decimal point two places to the left:**

(A) (36.5 × 5,700) ÷ 100

(B) 0.365 × 5,700

When students do this calculation on paper, many use Method A. Someone who has been taught to calculate percentages manually usually performs percentage calculations more accurately than someone who has not been taught to do so. Their most common error it to move the decimal place in the answer one step left instead of two, for example converting 208050 to 20805 instead of 2080.5.

When we do percentage calculations on a calculator, it is better to use Method B.

Unfortunately, many only learn to do the calculation on a calculator, which creates a false sense of confidence in the answer it produces, When Method A is used on a calculator, many students divide by 10 instead of 100, often because they miskey the number 100.

Another problem is that some students do not know that 36.5% is equivalent to 0.365 and enter 3.65 into the calculator. Finally, some do not know how to use the % button on the calculator and use it, blindly assuming what they are doing must be correct.

> The easiest way to calculate a percentage on a calculator is to first convert the percentage to a decimal. So, 36.5% is 0.365. Press the 'C' button to clear the memory of the calculator. Then enter 0.365, press the '×' key, and then enter 5700 followed by the '=' key. The correct answer of 2080.5 will be shown.

Whichever method you use, you must always stop to consider whether the answer it produces makes sense. That means you need an idea in your head of what the answer ought to be. A percentage of something cannot be greater than the number you start with; 50% is half the number you start with; and 10% is the same as the number you started with but with the decimal place moved one position to the left. These rules of thumb should help you to judge whether the answer of your calculation looks wrong.

2 What to do with the answer

On most occasions when you are asked to calculate reducing balance depreciation, it is not for the first year of ownership of the non-current asset. If you are asked to calculate the depreciation for a later year, the calculation involves reversing the percentage. Let's assume you are asked to calculate the depreciation for Year 3 on a machine that cost £4,000 and is being depreciated by 40% reducing balance. The steps to take are:

(a) Multiply £4,000 by $(1 - 0.4) = £4,000 \times 0.6 = £2,400 = $ Year 1 net book value
(b) Multiply £2,400 by $(1 - 0.4) = £2,400 \times 0.6 = £1,440 = $ Year 2 net book value

You now have the amount you need to depreciate by 40% in Year 3.

(c) Multiply £1,440 by $0.4 = £576 = $ Year 3 depreciation.

3 How to calculate the accumulated depreciation

You may have been asked to calculate the depreciation for Year 3 and also identity the total of the accumulated provision for depreciation account for the machine at the end of that year. To find that amount, you subtract the net book value at the end of the previous year (Year 2) from the cost of the machine. Then, add the Year 3 depreciation to that amount:

£4,000 − £1,440 = £2,560
£2,560 + £576 = £3,136 = the accumulated provision for depreciation on the machine at the end of Year 3.

4 How to calculate the net book value

You may have been asked to calculate the depreciation for Year 3 and also calculate the net book value at the end of that year. You can do this by subtracting the Year 3 depreciation from the net book value at the end of the previous year (Year 2):

£1,440 − £576 = £864 = the net book value at the end of Year 3.

5 How to check the answers to (3) and (4)

If you add the accumulated provision for depreciation to the net book value, you will find the original cost.

£3,136 + £864 = £4,000

38.7 Mathematics for analysis

The last line of the previous section is a formula. It shows the relationship between three things: accumulated provision for depreciation, net book value, and cost.

$$\text{Accumulated provision for depreciation} + \text{Net book value} = \text{Cost}$$

This formula can be rearranged, either as:

$$\text{Cost} - \text{Accumulated provision for depreciation} = \text{Net book value}$$

or as:

$$\text{Cost} - \text{Net book value} = \text{Accumulated provision for depreciation}$$

If you know two of these three values, you can identify the third. There are many examples of this type of relationship between accounting variables. You need to now how to manipulate formulas like this, so that you can find the numbers you do not have.

 Activity 38.6 Write down at least three formulas like these, each for a different group of accounting variables.

Did you notice the difference between the first four items in the solution to Activity 38.6 and the last two? The last two are ratios. You will learn about many different ratios in Chapters 39 and 41. Let's look at the two you have just seen:

$$\text{Current assets} \div \text{Current liabilities} = \text{Current ratio}$$

$$(\text{Current assets} - \text{Inventory}) \div \text{Current liabilities} = \text{Acid test ratio}$$

When accountants analyse accounting information, they usually begin with the balance sheet and the income statement. The accounting variables in these two ratios are all shown in the balance sheet. (You can also see the same figure for inventory in the trading account section of an income statement produced for internal use.) Calculating a ratio is not difficult, as long as you know what the ratio formula is, know where to obtain the appropriate data, and know how to add, subtract, divide and, less often, multiply. **What is difficult about calculating ratios is not the calculation, it is knowing what the answer from your calculation of a ratio is telling you.**

 Activity 38.7 Why is knowing how to interpret a ratio difficult?

This is where you begin to see how an accountant uses financial information. It involves a lot of factors that are not all numerical. Another word for 'numerical' is 'quantitative'. The other factors that an accountant considers may be 'qualitative'. Qualitative factors are descriptive; they can, for example, be good or neutral or bad or a mixture of these, and an accountant needs to now how to evaluate them in relation to the ratio results. They include things like how strong the competition is in the market, how price sensitive the market is, what competing goods/services you face in the market, and an assessment of what they imply for your ability to sell your goods and services. Combined, all the qualitative factors tell you whether the ratios you have calculated are good or bad.

Note: You cannot tell this immediately after you obtain the result of your ratio calculation. You must then consider any other relevant factors before drawing your conclusions about the goodness or badness of the result of your calculation.

In addition, you need to know how the value shown for each current asset and each liability was calculated – whether the value is itself a calculation; for example, accounts receivables will be shown in the balance sheet after deducting bad debts and then making an adjustment for any change in the allowance for doubtful debts. Inventory may be valued at cost, or at net realisable amount; it may be an estimate, it may be based on first-in-first-out (FIFO) or on average cost; it may include older items that may be close to becoming obsolete or deteriorating. Perhaps these adjustments were appropriate, perhaps they were not. Perhaps the method of calculation of the values was appropriate, perhaps it was not. Perhaps it is different from the method used by your competitors. If it is, it makes comparisons of the values and ratio results much more difficult.

In short, you need to consider a lot of things before drawing any conclusions about a ratio, including what is 'normal' in your industry and in your geographical location. It is, therefore, very important that you calculate each ratio correctly.

An accountant who can only calculate ratios but cannot interpret them is not a very good accountant. In fact, no-one can qualify as an accountant unless they can demonstrate this ability. It is one of the main things that makes an accountant worth employing. This is why you often find that accounting exams include essays and a request that you tell the examiner what a ratio is telling you. Ignoring those questions will not help you pass an exam.

Always attempt to answer these essay questions. In doing so, don't panic. Think about things that may be useful to consider in evaluating a ratio, list some, and then discuss how you would discover them and what you need to be careful about when you use them in any assessment you may make of a ratio. The answer to Activity 38.7 should give you sufficient things to think about in most cases.

When interpreting a ratio, think about the context of the business – products/services, industry, competition, markets, and so on – and about the characteristics of each of the variables in the ratio. If you do that, you should be able to score well in the essay you have been asked to write.

38.8 Mathematics for VAT

Another calculation that is often needed involves VAT. You will sometimes know only the gross amount of an item sold or purchased, but you need the net amount in order to arrive at the figure to include in the income statement. This figure is made up of the net amount plus VAT. To find the amount of VAT that has been added to the net amount, a formula capable of being used with any rate of VAT can be used.

$$\frac{\%\ \text{rate of VAT}}{100\ +\ \%\ \text{rate of VAT}} \times \text{Gross amount} = \text{VAT}$$

Suppose that the gross amount of sales was £3,300 and the rate of VAT was 20%. To find the amount of VAT and the net amount before VAT was added, you insert this information into the formula:

$$\frac{20}{100\ +\ 20} \times £3,300 = \text{VAT} = £550$$

What I've done here is show you the calculation for the VAT included in the sale price. How do you calculate the net amount, which is the amount you will include in the revenue line of your income statement?

Using what you see in the two boxes above, you can express the relationship between the gross amount of the sale, the VAT, and the net amount of the sale as a formula:

$$\text{Gross amount of a sale} - \text{VAT} = \text{Net amount of the sale}$$

or

$$£3,300 - £550 = £2,750$$

Therefore, the net amount was £2,750. To check your calculation is correct, add the VAT to the net amount of the sale. Your answer should be the gross amount of the sale.

38.9 In conclusion

Accounting depends on calculations: primarily arithmetic (add, subtract, divide, and multiply) and algebra (to help you manipulate a formula into a form that helps you discover what you are missing). But knowing how to do these calculations is only the beginning. You also need to ensure your data entry was correct, that the correct calculations were done, and that the answer makes sense. **Keeping a note of any working calculations you perform is essential.** Accountants will do that, and so should students. Accountants do it because they must ensure their answers are correct. So must you.

In addition, whenever you are asked to comment on something that has been calculated, you need to consider many other factors that may be relevant to your analysis. Only if you do that can you begin to draw sensible and relevant conclusions.

Learning outcomes

You should now have learnt:

1 Why knowing how to do arithmetic and algebra is an essential skill in accounting.

2 That there are many mathematical calculations that an accountant may make.

3 Why it is important to always check the answer to any calculation.

4 The mathematics used for opening and closing adjustments to accounts.

5 The mathematics used for bad debts and allowances for doubtful debts.

6 The mathematics used for depreciation.

7 How to manipulate a formula to find a missing value for a variable in the formula.

8 Why calculating a ratio is only the first step towards evaluating it.

9 How to calculate net revenue from a sales figure that includes VAT.

Answers to activities

38.1   The balance sheet cannot be in balance if an opening balance is incorrectly entered in this way. The only way the balance sheet could balance would be if a compensating error had occurred. That is, an error for the same amount but the opposite in kind, a debit as opposed to a credit. If that has not occurred, and the balance sheet is in balance, then the trainee must have done something else, such as using a suspense account to make it balance.

38.2   The accountant would also check to see if the amounts shown in the trial balance had been entered correctly in the financial statements. The trainee accountant may, for example, have realised that the balance sheet did not balance and simply changed one of the amounts in either the income statement or the balance sheet so that it did.

38.3   You could try being more careful and taking much longer, checking each number is correctly keyed before proceeding. However, that is not sensible use of your expensive time. It is much quicker to check the answers and then investigate any that are wrong.

38.4   If you need to check the arithmetic of a long list, rather than using a calculator, use a spreadsheet, where you can check each of the numbers you have entered. It is much easier to ensure you have the correct answer if you use a spreadsheet to sum lists of more than a few numbers.

38.5   It would be a credit.

38.6   There are many possibilities, including:

   (*i*)   Gross profit = Revenue − Cost of good sold
   (*ii*)   Net profit = Gross profit − Expenses
   (*iii*)   Owner's equity = Assets − Liabilities
   (*iv*)   Current assets − Current liabilities = Working capital
   (*v*)   Current assets ÷ Current liabilities = Current ratio
   (*vi*)   (Current assets − Inventory) ÷ Current liabilities = Acid test ratio

38.7   To interpret a ratio, you need to know what each variable or amount in the ratio represents. You also need to be able to set the ratio result in the context of the environment in which the entity operates. You need to know how the value shown for each current asset and each liability was calculated. In sum, you need to consider a lot of things before drawing any conclusions about a ratio, including what is 'normal' in your industry and in your geographical location.

Review questions

38.1   Why is being able to do arithmetic and algebra an essential skill for an accountant?

38.2A   Explain how to calculate a provision for depreciation using the reducing balance method.

38.3   Explain what information you would want in order to interpret some financial ratios you had calculated.

38.4A   Explain why it is important to keep notes of all the workings you use in a financial calculation.

38.5   Explain how to calculate the adjustments required to update an allowance for doubtful debts at the end of a reporting period.

38.6   Express the following relationships as formulas:
   (*a*)   Revenue, gross profit, and net profit.
   (*b*)   Opening inventory, closing inventory, purchases, and cost of sales.
   (*c*)   The balance brought forward on an expense account, the other transactions recorded in the expense account, the balance carried forward on the account, and the amount treated as an expense in the income statement.
   (*d*)   The opening balance on a sole proprietor's capital account, drawings, net profit, and the closing balance on the capital account.

Accounting ratios

Learning objectives

After you have studied this chapter, you should be able to:

- calculate some basic accounting ratios
- use accounting ratios to calculate missing figures in financial statements
- offer some explanations for changes in these ratios over time

Introduction

In this chapter, you'll learn about the relationship between mark-up and margin and how to use the relationship between them and sales revenue and gross profit to find figures that are missing in the trading account. You will also learn how to calculate the inventory turnover ratio and some explanations for why these ratios change over time.

39.1 The need for accounting ratios

We will see in Chapter 41 that accounting ratios are used to enable us to analyse and interpret accounting statements.

This chapter has been inserted at this point in the book so that you will be able to deal with the material in Chapter 40 which includes the drawing up of financial statements from incomplete records. The ratios described in this chapter will be sufficient for you to deduce the data needed to make the incomplete records into a complete set of records, so that you can then prepare the financial statements. Without the use of such accounting ratios, the construction of financial statements from incomplete records would often be impossible.

> **Activity 39.1** What do you think is meant by the term 'incomplete records'?

39.2 Mark-up and margin

The purchase cost, gross profit and selling price of goods or services may be shown as:

$$\boxed{\text{Cost Price } + \text{ Gross Profit } = \text{ Selling Price}}$$

When shown as a fraction or percentage of the *cost price*, the gross profit is known as the **mark-up**.

When shown as a fraction or percentage of the *selling price*, gross profit is known as the **margin**. We can calculate mark-up and margin using this example:

$$\text{Cost Price} + \text{Gross Profit} = \text{Selling Price}$$

$$£4 \quad + \quad £1 \quad = £5$$

$$\text{Mark-up} = \frac{\text{Gross Profit}}{\text{Cost Price}} \text{ as a fraction, or if required as a percentage, multiply by 100:}$$

$$\frac{£1}{£4} = \frac{1}{4}, \quad \text{or } \frac{1}{4} \times 100 = 25 \text{ per cent.}$$

$$\text{Margin} = \frac{\text{Gross Profit}}{\text{Selling Price}} \text{ as a fraction, or if required as a percentage, multiply by 100:}$$

$$\frac{£1}{£5} = \frac{1}{5}, \quad \text{or } \frac{1}{5} \times 100 = 20 \text{ per cent.}$$

Activity 39.2 Can you see a simple rule connecting mark-up to margin?

39.3 Calculating missing figures

Now we can use these ratios to complete trading accounts where some of the figures are missing. In all the examples in this chapter, we shall:

● assume that all the inventory in a business has the same rate of mark-up; and
● ignore wastages and theft of inventory.

Example 1

The following figures are for the year 2018:

	£
Inventory 1.1.2018	400
Inventory 31.12.2018	600
Purchases	5,200

A uniform rate of mark-up of 20 per cent is applied.

Required: find the gross profit and the sales figures.

Firstly, you prepare the trading account section of the income statement with the various missing figures shown as blank (or highlighted with a highlight pen, or with '?' inserted where the missing number should go):

Trading Account section of the Income Statement for the year ending 31 December 2018

	£	£
Sales		?
Less Cost of goods sold:		
Inventory 1.1.2018	400	
Add Purchases	5,200	
	5,600	
Less Inventory 31.12.2018	(600)	
		(5,000)
Gross profit		?

Answer:

It is known that:	Cost of goods sold + Gross profit	= Sales
and you know that you can use mark-up to find the profit, because:		
So:	Cost of goods sold + Percentage mark-up	= Sales
	£5,000 + 20%	= Sales
and Sales =	£5,000 + £1,000	= £6,000

The trading account section of the income statement can be completed by inserting the Gross Profit £1,000 and £6,000 for Sales.

Trading Account section of the Income Statement for the year ending 31 December 2018

	£	£
Sales		6,000
Less Cost of goods sold:		
Inventory 1.1.2018	400	
Add Purchases	5,200	
	5,600	
Less Inventory 31.12.2018	(600)	
		(5,000)
Gross profit		1,000

Example 2

Another business has the following figures for 2019:

	£
Inventory 1.1.2019	500
Inventory 31.12.2019	800
Sales	6,400

A uniform rate of margin of 25 per cent is in use.

Required: find the gross profit and the figure for purchases.

Trading Account section of the Income Statement for the year ending 31 December 2019

	£	£
Sales		6,400
Less Cost of goods sold:		
Inventory 1.1.2019	500	
Add Purchases	?	
	?	
Less Inventory 31.12.2019	800	?
Gross profit		?

Answer:

Moving items about:

Cost of goods sold + Gross Profit	= Sales	
Sales	− Gross Profit	= Cost of goods sold
Sales	− 25% margin	= Cost of goods sold
£6,400	− £1,600	= £4,800

Now the following figures are known:

		£	£
Sales			6,400
Less Cost of goods sold:			
Inventory 1.1.2019		500	
Add Purchases	(1)	?	
	(2)	?	
Less Inventory 31.12.2019		(800)	
			(4,800)
Gross profit			1,600

The two missing figures are found by normal arithmetical deduction:

$$\begin{array}{llr}
& \text{(2) less £800} & = £4,800 \\
& \text{Therefore (2)} & = £5,600 \\
\text{So that:} & \text{£500 opening inventory} + \text{(1)} & = £5,600 \\
& \text{Therefore (1)} & = £5,100
\end{array}$$

The completed trading account section of the income statement can now be shown:

Trading Account section of the Income Statement for the year ending 31 December 2019

	£	£
Sales		6,400
Less Cost of goods sold:		
Inventory 1.1.2019	500	
Add Purchases	5,100	
	5,600	
Less Inventory 31.12.2019	(800)	
		(4,800)
Gross profit		1,600

This technique is found very useful by retail stores when estimating the amount to be bought if a certain sales target is to be achieved. Alternatively, inventory levels or sales figures can be estimated given information as to purchases and opening inventory figures.

39.4 The relationship between mark-up and margin

As you learnt in Activity 39.2, both of these figures refer to the same gross profit, but express it as a fraction or a percentage of different figures. This connection through gross profit means that if you know one of the two (*mark-up* or *margin*) you will be able to determine the other.

You learnt a simple definition of this relationship in Activity 39.2. Now we'll take it further so that you can use the relationship in any situation.

If the mark-up is known, to find the margin take the same numerator to be numerator of the margin, then for the denominator of the margin take the total of the mark-up's denominator plus the numerator. For example:

Mark-up		*Margin*
$\dfrac{1}{4}$	$\dfrac{1}{4+1} =$	$\dfrac{1}{5}$
$\dfrac{2}{11}$	$\dfrac{2}{11+2} =$	$\dfrac{2}{13}$

If the margin is known, to find the mark-up take the same numerator to be the numerator of the mark-up, then for the denominator of the mark-up take the figure of the margin's denominator less the numerator:

Mark-up		*Margin*
$\dfrac{1}{6}$	$\dfrac{1}{6-1} =$	$\dfrac{1}{5}$
$\dfrac{3}{13}$	$\dfrac{3}{13-3} =$	$\dfrac{3}{10}$

Be sure that you learn this relationship. It is very often required in examinations.

39.5 Manager's commission

Managers of businesses are very often remunerated by a basic salary plus a percentage of profits. It is quite common to find the percentage expressed not as a percentage of profits before such commission has been deducted, but as a percentage of the amount remaining after deduction of the commission.

For example, assume that profits before the manager's commission was deducted amounted to £8,400 and that the manager was entitled to 5% of the profits remaining after the commission was deducted. If 5% of £8,400 was taken, this amounts to £420, and the profits remaining would amount to £7,980. However, 5% of £7,980 amounts to £399 so that the answer of £420 is wrong.

The formula to be used to arrive at the correct answer is:

$$\frac{\text{Percentage commission}}{100 + \text{Percentage commission}} \times \text{Profit before commission}$$

In the above problem this would be used as follows:

$$\frac{5}{100 + 5} \times £8,400 = £400 \text{ manager's commission.}$$

The profits remaining are £8,000 and as £400 represents 5% of it the answer is verified.

Activity 39.3 The same approach is taken when you want to know the VAT included in a bill you've paid. Assuming a VAT rate of 17.5%, what is the VAT when the total bill is £235?

39.6 Commonly used accounting ratios

There are some ratios that are in common use for the purpose of comparing one period's results with those of a previous period. Two of those most in use are the ratio of gross profit to sales, and the rate of **inventory turnover** (also known as 'stockturn').

Gross profit as percentage of sales

The basic formula is:

$$\frac{\text{Gross profit}}{\text{Sales}} \times \frac{100}{1} = \text{Gross profit as percentage of sales}$$

This represents the amount of gross profit for every £100 of sales revenue. If the answer turned out to be 15%, this would mean that for every £100 of sales revenue £15 gross profit was made before any expenses were paid.

This ratio is used as a test of the profitability of the sales. Just because sales revenue has increased does not, of itself, mean that gross profit will increase.

Activity 39.4 Spend a minute thinking about this and then write down why you think gross profit won't always increase if sales revenue increases.

Exhibit 39.1 illustrates this.

Exhibit 39.1

Trading Account sections of the Income Statements for the years ending 31 December 2016 and 2017

	2016		2017	
	£	£	£	£
Sales		7,000		8,000
Less Cost of goods sold:				
Opening inventory	500		900	
Add Purchases	6,000		7,200	
	6,500		8,100	
Less Closing inventory	(900)		(1,100)	
		(5,600)		(7,000)
Gross profit		1,400		1,000

In the year 2016 the gross profit as a percentage of sales was

$$\frac{1,400}{7,000} \times \frac{100}{1} = 20\%$$

In the year 2017 it became

$$\frac{1,000}{8,000} \times \frac{100}{1} = 12\frac{1}{2}\%$$

Sales had increased but, as the gross profit percentage had fallen by a relatively greater amount, the gross profit has fallen. There can be many reasons for such a fall in the gross profit percentage, including:

1 Perhaps the goods being sold have cost more, but the selling price of the goods has not risen to the same extent.
2 There may have been a greater wastage or theft of goods.
3 There could be a difference in how much has been sold of each sort of goods, called the sales mix, between the two years, with different kinds of goods carrying different rates of gross profit per £100 of sales.
4 Perhaps in order to increase sales, reductions have been made in the selling price of goods.

(The last reason was used in the answer to Activity 39.4, but any of these possible causes could have been used instead.) These are only some of the possible reasons for the decrease. The idea of calculating the ratio is to show that the profitability per £100 of sales has changed. The business would then try to find out why and how such a change has taken place.

As the figure of sales revenue less returns inwards is also known as 'turnover', the ratio is sometimes referred to as 'gross profit percentage on turnover'. However, the most frequently used names for it are 'gross profit on sales' and 'gross margin'.

Inventory turnover

If we always kept just £100 of inventory at cost which, when we sold it, would always sell for £125, and we sold this amount eight times in a year, we would make $8 \times £25 = £200$ gross profit. The quicker we sell our inventory (we could say the quicker we turn over our inventory) the more the profit we will make, if our gross profit percentage stays the same.

To check on how quickly we are turning over our inventory we can use the formula:

$$\frac{\text{Cost of goods sold}}{\text{Average inventory}} = \text{Number of times inventory is turned over within a period}$$

Activity 39.5 Spend a minute thinking about this and then write down why you think it might be useful to know how many times we turn over our inventory in a period.

It would be best if the average inventory held could be calculated by valuing the inventory quite a few times each year, then dividing the totals of the figures obtained by the number of valuations. For instance, monthly inventory figures could be added up and then divided by twelve. This would provide a far more meaningful figure for 'average' inventory. However, it is quite common, especially in examinations or in cases where no other information is available, to calculate the average inventory by using the figures for the opening inventory plus the closing inventory divided by two. Using the figures in Exhibit 39.1 we can calculate the inventory turnover for 2016 and 2017:

$$2016 \quad \frac{5{,}600}{(500 + 900) \div 2} = 8 \text{ times per year}$$

$$2017 \quad \frac{7{,}000}{(900 + 1{,}100) \div 2} = 7 \text{ times per year}$$

Instead of saying that the inventory turnover is so many times per year, we could say on average how long we keep inventory before we sell it. We do this by the formula:

To express it in months: $12 \div \text{Inventory turnover} = x \text{ months}$

To express it in days: $365 \div \text{Inventory turnover} = x \text{ days}$

From Exhibit 39.1:

	2016	2017

In months $\dfrac{12}{8} = 1.5$ months $\dfrac{12}{7} = 1.7$ months

In days $\dfrac{365}{8} = 45.6$ days $\dfrac{365}{7} = 52.1$ days

All the above figures are rounded to one decimal place.

When the rate of inventory turnover is falling it can be due to such causes as a slowing down of sales activity, or to keeping a higher amount of inventory than is really necessary. The ratio does not prove anything by itself, it merely prompts enquiries as to why it should be changing.

Current ratio

This ratio is current assets:current liabilities and indicates whether there are sufficient relatively liquid (i.e. convertible cash) assets to meet short-term debts when due. It is discussed in greater detail in Chapter 41.

This chapter has introduced ratios so as to help you understand the material in the next chapter.

In Chapter 41, we will return again to ratios, and cover the topic with a more advanced and detailed survey of what a range of ratios can be used for.

Learning outcomes

You should now have learnt:

1 That accounting ratios can be used to deduce missing figures, given certain assumptions.

2 That if the mark-up is known, the margin can easily be calculated.

3 That if the margin is known, the mark-up can easily be calculated.

4 How to calculate the gross profit on sales and inventory turnover ratios.

5 What may cause these ratios to change over time.

Answers to activities

39.1 Incomplete records exist where a business does not keep detailed accounting records. Perhaps it only operates a cash book, maybe not even that. In these circumstances, accountants have to construct the records that would have existed had a proper set of books been maintained, so that they can then prepare the financial statements. This involves working through invoices, receipts and bank records, plus any records the business has actually kept, and trying to identify and record what actually occurred during the period. Because of the logical relationships that exist between many of the items in financial statements, and because of the unambiguous rule of double entry, ratios defining the relationship between various items can be used to assist in this investigation. So, for example, if you know what inventory was held at the start, what was purchased and what inventory is left at the end, you can easily work out what was sold.

39.2 If you take mark-up and add one to the denominator (the bottom part of the fraction), you get the margin. This is *always* the case when the numerator (the top line) is 1.

39.3 You use the same formula but replace both the '5s' in the example with '17.5' and 'Profit before commission' with the total amount of the bill:

$$\frac{17.5}{100 + 17.5} \times £235 = £35$$

This is a *very* useful formula to know. You would be wise to remember it.

39.4 Gross profit may increase at the same rate as sales revenue because demand absorbed more units at the original price. This is normally the case if you make relatively small increases in the volume offered for sale when demand is currently exceeding supply. However, when sales volume increases, it is often partly because selling price has been reduced. Even though total sales volume has increased, sales revenue per unit is less than previously and so gross profit as a percentage of sales revenue will be lower than previously. Unless enough additional units are sold to recover the profit lost as a result of cutting the selling price, total gross profit will fall, not increase.

When a business is in trouble and cutting selling prices to try to make more profits by selling more units, it can often look as if it is doing much better if you only look at the sales revenue and gross profit figures. However, when you calculate the gross profit as a percentage of sales (i.e. the gross margin) and compare it with the previous gross margin, you can see that the business is possibly doing less well than before in terms of overall profitability.

39.5 It is useful to know as you can compare how quickly inventory is turning over now compared to the past. If it is turning over more slowly now (i.e. less times in a period than before), inventory levels may have grown higher, which may mean that the costs of holding inventory have risen. This rise in inventory levels may be due to our now buying more inventory every time we place an order – perhaps suppliers are offering discounts for larger orders. This may be good, or it may be bad. You need to investigate the situation and find out. Hence, checking the trend in inventory turnover alerts you to the possibility that costs may be rising and that they may exceed any savings being made. You can also check your rate of inventory turnover with those of your competitors, enabling you to detect whether your ordering and storing practices are significantly different from theirs. If they are, you would then investigate what is happening so as to ensure that you are not wasting resources unnecessarily.

Review questions

39.1 D. Staunton is a trader who sells all of her goods at 30% above cost. Her books give the following information at 31 December 2020:

	£
Inventory 1 January 2020	21,000
Inventory 31 December 2020	29,000
Sales for year	208,000

You are required to:
Prepare the trading account section of the Income Statement for D. Staunton for 2020.

39.2A Thomas Chan gives you the following information as at 31 March 2021:

	£
Inventory 1 April 2020	16,000
Purchases	90,000

His mark-up is 50% on 'cost of goods sold'. His average inventory during the year was £19,000. Draw up an income statement for the year ending 31 March 2021 assuming his net profit amounts to 12% of his sales.

39.3 J. Griffiths' business has a rate of inventory turnover of 7 times per year. Average inventory is £35,000. Mark-up is 40%. Expenses are 60% of gross profit.

You are to calculate:

(a) Cost of goods sold.
(b) Gross profit.
(c) Turnover.
(d) Total expenses.
(e) Net profit.

39.4A The following figures relate to the retail business of J. Daniels for the month of July. Goods sold fall into two categories, X and Y.

	Category X	Category Y
Sales	£15,000	£28,000
Gross profit margin	25%	30%
Total expenses as a percentage of sales	18%	18%
Annual rate of inventory turnover	9	14

You are to calculate for each category of goods:

(a) Cost of goods sold.
(b) Gross profit.
(c) Total expenses.
(d) Net profit.
(e) Average inventory at cost.

39.5   The following trading account is extracted from the income statement for the year ending 31 December 2018 and is given to you by the owner of the business, Mr. Malik:

	£	£
Sales		260,000
Less Cost of goods sold:		
Opening inventory	41,000	
Add Purchases	218,000	
	259,000	
Less Closing inventory	(49,000)	
		(210,000)
Gross profit		50,000

Mr. Malik says that he normally adds 30% to the cost of goods to fix the sales price. However, this year there were some arithmetical errors in these calculations.

(a)   Calculate what his sales would have been if he had not made any errors.
(b)   Given that his expenses remain constant at 9% of his sales, calculate his net profit for the year 2018.
(c)   Work out the rate of inventory turnover for 2018.
(d)   He thinks that next year he can increase his mark-up to 40%, selling goods which will cost him £240,000. If he does not make any more errors in calculating selling prices, you are to calculate the expected gross and net profits for 2019.

39.6A

Trading Account for the year ending 31 December 2019

	£		£
Inventory 1 January 2019	3,000	Sales	60,000
Purchases	47,000		
	50,000		
Inventory 31 December 2019	(4,500)		
Cost of sales	45,500		
Gross profit	14,500		
	60,000		60,000

R. Sheldon presents you with the trading account set out above.^{Author's note} He always calculates his selling price by adding 33$\frac{1}{3}$% of cost on to the cost price.

(a)   If he has adhered strictly to the statement above, what should be the percentage of gross profit to sales?
(b)   Calculate his actual percentage of gross profit to sales.
(c)   Give two reasons for the difference between the figures you have calculated above.
(d)   His suppliers are proposing to increase their prices by 5%, but R. Sheldon considers that he would be unwise to increase his selling price. To obtain some impression of the effect on gross profit if his costs should be increased by 5% he asks you to reconstruct his trading account to show the gross profit if the increase had applied from 1 January 2019.
(e)   Using the figures given in the trading account at the beginning of the question, calculate R. Sheldon's rate of inventory turnover.
(f)   R. Sheldon's expenses amount to 10% of his sales. Calculate his net profit for the year ending 31 December 2019.
(g)   If all expenses remained unchanged, but suppliers of inventory increased their prices by 5% as in (d) above, calculate the percentage reduction in the amount of net profit which R. Sheldon's accounts would have shown.

(*Edexcel, London Examinations: GCSE*)

Author's note: The trading account shown in the question has been prepared in an unconventional way. It is, in effect, a different form of presentation of the trading account section of the income statement. Do not, yourself, ever use this format when preparing an income statement.

39.7   L. Mann started business with £5,000 in the bank on 1 April. The business transactions during the month were as follows:

(*i*)   Took £300 out of the bank for petty cash
(*ii*)   Bought a second-hand van and paid by cheque £3,500
(*iii*) Bought goods on credit from A. Supplier for £2,500
(*iv*)   Sold goods for cash for £300
(*v*)   Sold goods on credit for £1,000 to B. Safe
(*vi*)   Returned faulty goods to A. Supplier £500
(*vii*) Paid sundry expenses of £50 in cash
(*viii*) Paid the rent of £500 by cheque
(*ix*)   Withdrew cash drawings of £500

Inventory at cost at 30 April was £1,250.

Required:
(*a*)   Prepare the ledger accounts recording the transactions.
(*b*)   Prepare the trial balance at 30 April.
(*c*)   Prepare an income statement for the month ending 30 April.
(*d*)   Prepare a balance sheet as at 30 April.
(*e*)   Calculate the percentages of:
    (*i*)   gross profit to sales
    (*ii*) net profit to opening capital.
(*f*)   Comment on:
    (*i*)   the relationship between drawings and net profit and why it is important that Mann keeps an eye on it
    (*ii*) working capital.

39.8A   Arthur deals in bicycles. His business position at 1 October was as follows:

Capital £3,369
Inventory £306 (3 × Model A bicycles @ £54 and 3 × Model B @ £48)
Balance at bank £3,063

Having established good relations with his supplier he is able to obtain bicycles on credit. He kept notes of all transactions during October which he then summarised as follows:

(*i*)   Purchased on credit from Mr Raleigh: 12 Model A at £54 and 10 Model B at £48. Total purchase £1,128.
(*ii*)   Sales for cash were: 11 Model A at £81 and 8 Model B at £72.
(*iii*) Paid rent by cheque £60, advertising £66 and miscellaneous expenses £12.
(*iv*)   Drawings were £150.

Arthur's valuation of the closing inventory was £456 as at 31 October.

Required:
(*a*)   Prepare a statement showing the bank transactions during October.
(*b*)   Check the closing inventory valuation.
(*c*)   Prepare a statement showing the gross profit and net profit for October and calculate the percentages of gross profit to sales and net profit to sales.
(*d*)   Prepare an income statement for the month of October together with a balance sheet as at 31 October.

39.9 The following information is available for the years 2017, 2018 and 2019:

	2017 £	2018 £	2019 £
Opening inventory	10,000	20,000	28,000
Purchases	70,000	86,000	77,000
	80,000	106,000	105,000
Less Closing inventory	(20,000)	(28,000)	(23,000)
Cost of sales	60,000	78,000	82,000
Sales	90,000	125,000	120,000
Gross profit	30,000	47,000	38,000

The inventory valuations used above at the end of 2017 and at the end of 2018 were inaccurate. The inventory at 31 December 2017 had been under-valued by £1,000, whilst that at 31 December 2018 had been over-valued by £3,000.

Required:
(a) Give the corrected figures of gross profit for each of the years affected by the errors in inventory valuation.
(b) Using the figures in the revised trading accounts, calculate for each year:
    (i) the percentage of gross profit to sales, and
    (ii) the rate of turnover of inventory.

Single entry and incomplete records

Learning objectives

After you have studied this chapter, you should be able to:

- deduce the figure of profits where only the increase in capital and details of drawings are known
- draw up an income statement and a balance sheet from records not kept on a double entry system
- deduce the figure for cash drawings when all other cash receipts and cash payments are known
- deduce the figures of sales and purchases from incomplete records

Introduction

In this chapter, you'll learn about single entry and incomplete records. You will learn how to use the accounting equation to identify the profit for a period when only the opening and closing capital figures and drawings are known. You will also learn how to find the figure for cash drawings or the figure for cash expenses when all other cash receipts and payments are known. And you will learn how to find the figures for purchases and sales from incomplete records.

40.1 Why double entry is not used

For every small shopkeeper, market stall, Internet café or other small business to keep its books using a full double entry system would be ridiculous. Apart from anything else, a large number of the owners of such businesses would not know how to write up double entry records, even if they wanted to.

It is more likely that they would enter details of a transaction once only, using a single entry system. Many of them would fail to record every transaction, resulting in incomplete records.

It is, perhaps, only fair to remember that accounting is supposed to be an aid to management – accounting *is not* something to be done as an end in itself. Therefore, many small firms, especially retail shops, can have all the information they want by merely keeping a cash book and having some form of record, not necessarily in double entry form, of their debtors and creditors.

However, despite many small businesses not having any need for accounting records, most do have to prepare financial statements or, at least, calculate their sales or profits once a year. How can these be calculated if the bookkeeping records are inadequate or incomplete?

Activity 40.1

What may cause these accounting statements and figures to need to be calculated?

(*i*) Profits
(*ii*) Sales
(*iii*) Financial statements

40.2 Profit as an increase in capital

From your knowledge of the accounting equation, you know that unless there has been an introduction of extra cash or resources into a business, the only way that capital can be increased is by making profits.

Identifying profits when opening and closing capital are known

If you know the capital at the start of a period and the capital at the end of the period, profit is the figure found by subtracting capital at the start of the period from that at the end of the period.

Let's look at a business where capital at the end of 2017 was £20,000. During 2018 there have been no drawings, and no extra capital has been brought in by the owner. At the end of 2018 the capital was £30,000.

$$\text{Net profit} = \begin{array}{c} \text{This year's} \\ \text{capital} \\ £30,000 \end{array} - \begin{array}{c} \text{Last year's} \\ \text{capital} \\ £20,000 \end{array} = £10,000$$

If drawings had been £7,000, the profits must have been £17,000:

$$\begin{array}{c} \text{Last year's Capital} + \text{Profits} - \text{Drawings} = \text{This year's Capital} \\ £20,000 \qquad + \quad ? \quad - \quad £7,000 \quad = \qquad £30,000 \end{array}$$

We can see that £17,000 profits is the figure needed to complete the formula:

$$£20,000 + £17,000 - £7,000 = £30,000$$

Identifying profits when you only have a list of the opening and closing assets and liabilities

In this case, you use the accounting equation.

Activity 40.2

What is the formula for the accounting equation? Write down both (*a*) the normal form and (*b*) the alternate form.

Exhibit 40.1 shows the calculation of profit where insufficient information is available to draft an income statement. The only information available is about the assets and liabilities.

Exhibit 40.1

H. Taylor has not kept proper bookkeeping records, but she has kept notes in diary form of the transactions of her business. She is able to give you details of her assets and liabilities as at 31 December 2018 and 31 December 2019:

At 31 December 2018
Assets: Van £6,000; Fixtures £1,800; Inventory £3,000; Accounts receivable £4,100; Bank £4,800; Cash £200.
Liabilities: Accounts payable £1,200; Loan from J. Ogden £3,500.

At 31 December 2019
Assets: Van (after depreciation) £5,000; Fixtures (after depreciation) £1,600; Inventory £3,800; Accounts receivable £6,200; Bank £7,500; Cash £300.
Liabilities: Accounts payable £1,800; Loan from J. Ogden £2,000.

Drawings during 2019 were £5,200.
You need to put all these figures into a format that will enable you to identify the profit. Firstly, you need to draw up a **statement of affairs** as at 31 December 2018. This is really just a balance sheet, but this is the name normally used when you are dealing with incomplete records.
From the accounting equation, you know that capital is the difference between the assets and liabilities.

H. Taylor
Statement of Affairs as at 31 December 2018

	£	£
Non-current assets		
Van		6,000
Fixtures		1,800
		7,800
Current assets		
Inventory	3,000	
Accounts receivable	4,100	
Bank	4,800	
Cash	200	
		12,100
Total assets		19,900
Current liabilities		
Accounts payable	1,200	
Non-current liability		
Loan from J. Ogden	3,500	
Total liabilities		(4,700)
Net assets		15,200
Capital[Note]		15,200

Note: The accounting equation tells you that this must be the figure to use.

You now draw up a second statement of affairs, this time as at the end of 2019. The formula of *Opening Capital + Profit − Drawings = Closing Capital* is then used to deduce the figure of profit.

H. Taylor
Statement of Affairs as at 31 December 2019

	£	£
Non-current assets		
Van		5,000
Fixtures		1,600
		6,600
Current assets		
Inventory	3,800	
Accounts receivable	6,200	
Bank	7,500	
Cash	300	
		17,800
Total assets		24,400
Current liabilities		
Accounts payable	1,800	
Non-current liability		
Loan from J. Ogden	2,000	
Total liabilities		(3,800)
Net assets		20,600
Capital		
Balance at 1.1.2019		15,200
Add Net profit	(C)	?
	(B)	?
Less Drawings		(5,200)
	(A)	

Deduction of net profit:
Opening Capital + Net Profit − Drawings = Closing Capital. Finding the missing figures (A), (B) and (C) by deduction:

(A) is the same as the total of the top half of the statement of affairs, i.e. £20,600;
(B) is therefore £20,600 + £5,200 = £25,800;
(C) is therefore £25,800 − £15,200 = £10,600.

To check:

Capital		
Balance at 1.1.2019		15,200
Add Net profit	(C)	10,600
	(B)	25,800
Less Drawings		(5,200)
	(A)	20,600

Obviously, this method of calculating profit is very unsatisfactory. It is much more informative when an income statement can be drawn up. Therefore, whenever possible, this 'comparisons of capital method' of ascertaining profit should be avoided and a full set of financial statements should be drawn up from the available records.

It is important to realise that businesses should have exactly the same income statements and balance sheets whether they keep their books by single entry or double entry. However, as you will see, whereas the double entry system uses the trial balance in preparing the financial statements, the single entry system has to arrive at the same answer by different means.

40.3 Drawing up the financial statements

The following example shows the various stages of drawing up financial statements from a single entry set of records.

The accountant has found the following details of transactions for J. Frank's shop for the year ended 31 December 2018.

(a) The sales are mostly on credit. No record of sales has been kept, but £61,500 has been received from persons to whom goods have been sold – £48,000 by cheque and £13,500 in cash.
(b) Amount paid by cheque to suppliers during the year = £31,600.
(c) Expenses paid during the year: by cheque: Rent £3,800; General Expenses £310; by cash: Rent £400.
(d) J. Frank took £250 cash per week (for 52 weeks) as drawings.
(e) Other information is available:

	At 31.12.2017	At 31.12.2018
	£	£
Accounts receivable	5,500	6,600
Accounts payable for goods	1,600	2,600
Rent owing	–	350
Bank balance	5,650	17,940
Cash balance	320	420
Inventory	6,360	6,800

(f) The only non-current asset consists of fixtures which were valued at 31 December 2017 at £3,300. These are to be depreciated at 10 per cent per annum.

We'll now prepare the financial statements in five stages.

Stage 1

Draw up a Statement of Affairs on the closing day of the earlier accounting period:

J. Frank
Statement of Affairs as at 31 December 2017

	£	£
Non-current assets		
Fixtures		3,300
Current assets		
Inventory	6,360	
Accounts receivable	5,500	
Bank	5,650	
Cash	320	
		17,830
Total assets		21,130
Current liabilities		
Accounts payable		(1,600)
Net assets		19,530
Financed by:		
Capital (difference)		19,530

All of these opening figures are then taken into account when drawing up the financial statements for 2018.

Stage 2

Prepare a cash and bank summary, showing the totals of each separate item, plus opening and closing balances.

	Cash	Bank		Cash	Bank
	£	£		£	£
Balances 31.12.2017	320	5,650	Suppliers		31,600
Receipts from debtors	13,500	48,000	Rent	400	3,800
			General expenses		310
			Drawings	13,000	
			Balances 31.12.2018	420	17,940
	13,820	53,650		13,820	53,650

Stage 3

Calculate the figures for purchases and sales to be shown in the trading account. Remember that the figures needed are the same as those which would have been found if double entry records had been kept.

Purchases: In double entry, 'purchases' are the goods that have been bought in the period irrespective of whether they have been paid for or not during the period. The figure of payments to suppliers must, therefore, be adjusted to find the figure for purchases.

	£
Paid during the year	31,600
Less Payments made, but which were for goods purchased in a previous year	
(accounts payable at 31.12.2017)	(1,600)
	30,000
Add Purchases made in the current year for which payment has not yet been made	
(accounts payable at 31.12.2018)	2,600
Goods bought in this year, i.e. purchases	32,600

The same answer could have been obtained if the information had been shown in the form of a total accounts payable account, the figure for purchases being the amount required to make the account totals agree.

Total Accounts Payable

	£		£
Cash paid to suppliers	31,600	Balances b/d	1,600
Balances c/d	2,600	Purchases (missing figure)	32,600
	34,200		34,200

Sales: The sales figure will only equal receipts where all the sales are for cash. Therefore, the receipts figures need adjusting to find sales. This can only be done by constructing a total accounts receivable account, the sales figure being the one needed to make the totals agree.

Total Accounts Receivable

	£		£
Balances b/d	5,500	Receipts: Cash	13,500
Sales (missing figure)	62,600	Cheque	48,000
		Balances c/d	6,600
	68,100		68,100

Stage 4

Expenses. Where there are no accruals or prepayments either at the beginning or end of the accounting period, then expenses paid will equal expenses used up during the period. These figures will be charged to the income statement.

On the other hand, where such prepayments or accruals exist, an expense account should be drawn up for that particular item. When all known items are entered, the missing figure will be the expenses to be charged for the accounting period. In this case, only the rent account needs to be drawn up.

Rent

	£		£
Bank	3,800	Profit and loss (missing figure)	4,550
Cash	400		
Accrued c/d	350		
	4,550		4,550

Stage 5

Now draw up the financial statements.

J. Frank
Income Statement for the year ending 31 December 2018

	£	£
Sales (stage 3)		62,600
Less Cost of goods sold:		
Inventory at 1.1.2018	6,360	
Add Purchases (stage 3)	32,600	
	38,960	
Less Inventory at 31.12.2018	(6,800)	
		(32,160)
Gross profit		30,440
Less Expenses:		
Rent (stage 4)	4,550	
General expenses	310	
Depreciation: Fixtures	330	
		(5,190)
Net profit		25,250

Balance Sheet as at 31 December 2018

	£	£
Non-current assets		
Fixtures at 1.1.2018		3,300
Less Depreciation		(330)
		2,970
Current assets		
Inventory	6,800	
Accounts receivable	6,600	
Bank	17,940	
Cash	420	
		31,760
Total assets		34,730
Current liabilities		
Accounts payable	2,600	
Rent owing	350	
Total liabilities		(2,950)
Net assets		31,780
Financed by:		
Capital		
Balance 1.1.2018 (per Opening Statement of Affairs)		19,530
Add Net profit		25,250
		44,780
Less Drawings		(13,000)
Total capital		31,780

40.4 Incomplete records and missing figures

In practice, part of the information relating to *cash* receipts or payments is often missing. If the missing information is in respect of one type of payment, then it is normal to assume that the missing figure is the amount required to make both totals agree in the *cash* column of the cash and bank summary. (This does not happen with bank items owing to the fact that another copy of the bank statement can always be obtained from the bank.)

Exhibit 40.2 shows an example where the figure for Drawings is unknown. The exhibit also shows the contra entry made in the cash book when cash receipts are banked.

Exhibit 40.2

The following information on cash and bank receipts and payments is available:

	Cash	Bank
	£	£
Cash paid into the bank during the year	35,500	
Receipts from debtors	47,250	46,800
Paid to suppliers	1,320	44,930
Drawings during the year	?	–
Expenses paid	150	3,900
Balances at 1.1.2017	235	11,200
Balances at 31.12.2017	250	44,670

Now, you need to enter this information in a cash book:

	Cash	Bank		Cash	Bank
	£	£		£	£
Balances 1.1.2017	235	11,200	Bank ¢	35,500	
Received from debtors	47,250	46,800	Suppliers	1,320	44,930
Cash ¢		35,500	Expenses	150	3,900
			Drawings	?	
			Balances 31.12.2017	250	44,670
	47,485	93,500		47,485	93,500

The amount needed to make the two sides of the cash columns agree is £10,265, i.e. £47,485 minus £(35,500 + 1,320 + 150 + 250). This is the figure for drawings.

Exhibit 40.3 shows an example where the amount of cash received from debtors is unknown.

Exhibit 40.3

Information on cash and bank transactions is available as follows:

	Cash	Bank
	£	£
Receipts from debtors	?	78,080
Cash withdrawn from the bank for business use (this is the amount which is used besides cash receipts from debtors to pay drawings and expenses)		10,920
Paid to suppliers	–	65,800
Expenses paid	640	2,230
Drawings	21,180	315
Balances at 1.1.2017	40	1,560
Balances at 31.12.2017	70	375

→

→

	Cash	Bank		Cash	Bank
	£	£		£	£
Balances 1.1.2017	40	1,560	Suppliers		65,800
Received from debtors	?	78,080	Expenses	640	2,230
Withdrawn from Bank ¢	10,920		Withdrawn from Bank ¢		10,920
			Drawings	21,180	315
			Balances 31.12.2017	70	375
	21,890	79,640		21,890	79,640

As it is the only missing item, receipts from debtors is, therefore, the amount needed to make each side of the cash column agree, £10,930, i.e. £21,890 minus £(10,920 + 40).

It must be emphasised that the use of balancing figures is acceptable *only* when all the other figures have been verified. Should, for instance, a cash expense be omitted when cash received from debtors is being calculated, this would result in an understatement not only of expenses but also, ultimately, of sales.

40.5 Where there are two missing pieces of information

Quite often, the only cash item for which there is some doubt is drawings. Receipts will normally have been retained for all the others.

If both cash drawings and cash receipts from debtors (or from cash sales) were not known, it would not be possible to deduce both of these figures separately. The only course available would be to estimate whichever figure was more capable of being accurately assessed, use this as if it were a 'known' figure, then deduce the other figure. However, this is a most unsatisfactory position as both of the figures are estimates, the accuracy of each one relying entirely upon the accuracy of the other.

Activity 40.3 Why is arriving at a figure for drawings that is as accurate as possible *very* important for the owner of a business?

40.6 Cash sales and purchases for cash

Where there are cash sales as well as sales on credit terms, then the cash sales must be added to sales on credit to give the total sales for the year. This total figure of sales will be the one shown in the trading account part of the income statement.

Similarly, purchases for cash will need to be added to credit purchases in order to produce the figure of total purchases for the trading account.

40.7 Inventory stolen, lost or destroyed

When inventory is stolen, lost or destroyed, its value will have to be calculated. This could be needed to justify an insurance claim or to settle problems concerning taxation, etc.

If the inventory had been valued immediately before the fire, burglary, etc., then the value of the inventory lost would obviously be known. Also, if a full and detailed system of inventory records were kept, then the value would also be known. However, as the occurrence of fires or burglaries cannot be foreseen, and many small businesses do not keep full and proper inventory records, the value of the inventory lost has to be calculated in some other way.

The methods described in this chapter and in Chapter 39 are used. Bear in mind that you are going to be calculating figures as at the time of the fire or theft, not at the end of the accounting period.

Let's now look at Exhibits 40.4 and 40.5. The first exhibit involves a very simple case, where figures of purchases and sales are known and all goods are sold at the same gross profit margin. The second exhibit is rather more complicated.

Exhibit 40.4

J. Collins lost the whole of his inventory in a fire on 17 March 2019. The last time that stocktaking had been done was on 31 December 2018, the last date of the balance sheet, when the inventory was valued at cost at £19,500. Purchases from then until 17 March 2019 amounted to £68,700 and sales in that period were £96,000. All sales were made at a uniform gross profit margin of 20 per cent.

First, the trading account section of the income statement can be drawn up with the known figures included. Then the missing figures can be deduced.

J. Collins
Trading Account section of the income statement for the period
1 January 2019 to 17 March 2019

		£		£
Sales				96,000
Less Cost of goods sold:				
Opening inventory		19,500		
Add Purchases		68,700		
		88,200		
Less Closing inventory	(C)	(?)		
			(B)	(?)
Gross profit			(A)	?

Now the missing figures can be deduced:

It is known that the gross profit margin is 20 per cent, therefore gross profit (A) is 20% of £96,000 = £19,200.

Now (B) + (A) £19,200 = £96,000, so that (B) is the difference, i.e. £76,800.

Now that (B) is known, (C) can be deduced: £88,200 − (C) = £76,800, so (C) is the difference, i.e. £11,400.

The figure for inventory destroyed by fire, at cost, is therefore £11,400.

Note: You should always do this calculation in the sequence shown (i.e. A then B then C).

Exhibit 40.5

T. Scott had all his inventory stolen from his warehouse on the night of 20 August 2020 along with many of his accounting records including his sales and purchases day books. The sales and purchases ledgers were found in the car park. The following facts are known:

(a) Inventory at the last balance sheet date, 31 March 2020, was £12,480 at cost.
(b) Receipts from debtors during the period 1 April to 20 August 2020 amounted to £31,745. Accounts receivable were: at 31 March 2020 £14,278, at 20 August 2020 £12,333.
(c) Payments to creditors during the period 1 April to 20 August 2020 amounted to £17,270. Accounts payable were: at 31 March 2020 £7,633, at 20 August 2020 £6,289.
(d) The gross profit margin on all sales has been constant at 25 per cent.

→

→

Before we can start to construct a trading account for the period, we need to identify the figures for sales and purchases. These can be found by drawing up total accounts receivable and total accounts payable accounts, sales and purchases figures being the difference on the accounts.

Total Accounts Receivable

	£		£
Balances b/d	14,278	Cash and bank	31,745
Sales (difference)	29,800	Balances c/d	12,333
	44,078		44,078

Total Accounts Payable

	£		£
Cash and bank	17,270	Balances b/d	7,633
Balances c/d	6,289	Purchases (difference)	15,926
	23,559		23,559

 Activity 40.4 You already did this for another example earlier in this chapter. Where?

The trading account section of the income statement can now show the figures so far known:

Trading Account section of the income statement for the period 1 April to 20 August 2020

		£	£
Sales			29,800
Less Cost of goods sold:			
Opening inventory		12,480	
Add Purchases		15,926	
		28,406	
Less Closing inventory	(C)	(?)	
	(B)		(?)
Gross profit	(A)		?

Gross profit can be found, as the margin on sales is known to be 25%, therefore (A) = 25% of £29,800 = £7,450.
Cost of goods sold (B) + Gross profit £7,450 = £29,800 therefore (B) is £22,350.
£28,406 − (C) = (B) £22,350 therefore (C) is £6,056.
The figure for cost of goods stolen is therefore £6,056.
The completed trading account is, therefore:

Trading Account section of the income statement for the period 1 April to 20 August 2020

		£	£
Sales			29,800
Less Cost of goods sold:			
Opening inventory		12,480	
Add Purchases		15,926	
		28,406	
Less Closing inventory	(C)	(6,056)	
	(B)		(22,350)
Gross profit	(A)		7,450

Learning outcomes

You should now have learnt:

1 The difference between a single entry system and a double entry system.

2 How to calculate net profit for a sole proprietor when you know the change in capital over a period and the amount of drawings during the period.

3 How to prepare an income statement and a balance sheet from records not kept on a double entry system.

4 How to deduce the figures for purchases and sales from a total accounts payable account and a total accounts receivable account.

Answers to activities

40.1 There is a range of possible reasons. Of the three examples shown here, the first must be done once a year, the second must be done from time to time, and the third is done on demand:

(*i*) Profits need to be calculated for the purpose of determining the income tax payable.

(*ii*) Turnover (i.e. sales) needs to be calculated in order to know whether or not the business needs to register for VAT.

(*iii*) Financial statements may be required by the bank.

40.2 (*a*) Capital = Assets − Liabilities
(*b*) Assets = Capital + Liabilities

40.3 Normal practice would be to try to get the owner to list all the cash withdrawn as accurately as possible and then use that figure for drawings. However, care needs to be taken to make this as accurate as possible because the Revenue and Customs (the UK tax authority) has very sophisticated data on the relationship between business income and expenditure and profitability, and also on level of income and standard of living enjoyed by a taxpayer. If the drawings are underestimated, this could have very serious repercussions for the owner.

40.4 This is exactly the same as what you did in Section 40.3 Stage 3.

Review questions

40.1 N. Alphonso started in business on 1 January 2018 with £10,000 in a bank account. Unfortunately, he did not keep proper books of account.

He must submit a calculation of profit for the year ending 31 December 2018 to the Inspector of Taxes. At 31 December 2018 he had inventory valued at cost £8,300; a van which had cost £9,000 during the year and which had depreciated during the year by 25%; accounts receivable of £11,620; expenses prepaid of £1,360; a bank balance of £4,110; a cash balance £50; trade accounts payable £9,470; and expenses owing £1,630.

His drawings were £600 cash each week.

Calculate his profit or loss for the year.

40.2 Stephanie Duke is a wholesaler whose accounting records are chaotic. You ascertain the following information:

(*i*) She draws £2,000 a month from the business for her living expenses.

(*ii*) In June 2020 her grandfather died and left her £5,500 in his will. Stephanie put the entire amount into her business.

(*iii*) The assets and liabilities of her business were as follows:

	31 December 2019	31 December 2020
	£	£
Non-current assets at valuation	140,000	154,000
Inventory at cost	53,200	59,100
Accounts receivable	68,500	70,400
Cash at bank	1,700	2,900
Accounts payable	72,300	80,600

Calculate the net profit for 2020 made by Stephanie.

40.3A B. Barnes is a dealer who has not kept proper books of account. At 31 October 2019 his state of affairs was as follows:

	£
Cash	210
Bank balance (not overdrawn)	4,700
Fixtures	2,800
Inventory	18,200
Accounts receivable	26,600
Accounts payable	12,700
Van (at valuation)	6,800

During the year to 31 October 2020 his drawings amounted to £32,200. Winnings from the Lottery of £7,600 were put into the business. Extra fixtures were bought for £900.

At 31 October 2020 his assets and liabilities were: Cash £190; Bank overdraft £1,810; Inventory £23,900; Accounts payable for goods £9,100; Accounts payable for expenses £320; Fixtures to be depreciated £370; Van to be valued at £5,440; Accounts receivable £29,400; Prepaid expenses £460.

Calculate the profit or loss made by Barnes for the year ending 31 October 2020.

40.4 The following is a summary of Ellie's bank account for the year ended 31 December 2019:

	£		£
Balance 1.1.2019	8,200	Payments to creditors for goods	136,200
Receipts from debtors	182,000	Rent	7,800
Balance 31.12.2019	12,800	Insurance	2,940
		Sundry expenses	1,260
		Drawings	54,800
	203,000		203,000

All of the business takings have been paid into the bank with the exception of £34,900. Out of this, Ellie has paid wages of £22,800, drawings of £2,800 and purchase of goods £9,300.

The following additional information is available:

	31.12.2018	31.12.2019
Inventory	20,600	23,000
Accounts payable for goods	23,400	26,200
Accounts receivable for goods	40,600	37,700
Insurance prepaid	910	1,020
Rent owing	570	–
Fixtures at valuation	3,700	3,400

You are to draw up a set of financial statements for the year ended 31 December 2019. Show all of your workings.

40.5A A. Bell has kept records of his business transactions in a single entry form, but he did not realise that he had to record cash drawings. His bank account for the year 2018 is as follows:

	£		£
Balance 1.1.2018	920	Cash withdrawn from bank	12,600
Receipts from debtors	94,200	Trade accounts payable	63,400
Loan from F. Tung	2,500	Rent	3,200
		Insurance	1,900
		Drawings	11,400
		Sundry expenses	820
		Balance 31.12.2018	4,300
	97,620		97,620

Records of cash paid were: Sundry expenses £180; Trade accounts payable £1,310. Cash sales amounted to £1,540.

The following information is also available:

	31.12.2017	31.12.2018
	£	£
Cash in hand	194	272
Trade accounts payable	7,300	8,100
Accounts receivable	9,200	11,400
Rent owing	–	360
Insurance paid in advance	340	400
Van (at valuation)	5,500	4,600
Inventory	24,200	27,100

You are to draw up an income statement for the year ending 31 December 2018, and a balance sheet as at that date. Show all of your workings.

40.6 On 1 May 2018 Jenny Barnes, who is a retailer, had the following balances in her books: Premises £70,000; Equipment £8,200; Vehicles £5,100; Inventory £9,500; Trade accounts receivable £150. Jenny does not keep proper books of account, but bank statements covering the 12 months from 1 May 2018 to 30 April 2019 were obtained from the bank and summarised as follows:

	£
Money paid into bank:	
Extra capital	8,000
Shop takings	96,500
Payments made by cheque:	
Paid for inventory purchased	70,500
Purchase of delivery van	6,200
Vehicle running expenses	1,020
Lighting and heating	940
Sales assistants' wages	5,260
Miscellaneous expenses	962

It has been discovered that, in the year ending 30 April 2019, the owner had paid into the bank all shop takings apart from cash used to pay (i) £408 miscellaneous expenses and (ii) £500 per month drawings.

At 30 April 2019:

£7,600 was owing to suppliers for inventory bought on credit.

The amount owed by trade accounts receivable is to be treated as a bad debt. Assume that there had been no sales on credit during the year.

Inventory was valued at £13,620.

Depreciation for the year was calculated at £720 (equipment) and £1,000 (vehicles).

You are asked to prepare an income statement for the year ending 30 April 2019. (Show all necessary workings separately.)

(*Edexcel Foundation, London Examinations: GCSE*)

40.7A   Bill Smithson runs a second-hand furniture business from a shop which he rents. He does not keep complete accounting records, but is able to provide you with the following information about his financial position at 1 April 2018: Inventory of furniture £3,210; Trade accounts receivable £2,643; Trade accounts payable £1,598; Motor vehicle £5,100; Shop fittings £4,200; Motor vehicle expenses owing £432.

He has also provided the following summary of his bank account for the year ended 31 March 2019:

	£		£
Balance at 1 April 2018	2,420	Payments of trade accounts payable	22,177
Cheques received from trade debtors	44,846	Electricity	1,090
Cash sales	3,921	Telephone	360
		Rent	2,000
		Advertising	1,430
		Shop fittings	2,550
		Insurance	946
		Motor vehicle expenses	2,116
		Drawings	16,743
		Balance at 31 March 2019	1,775
	£51,187		£51,187

All cash and cheques received were paid into the bank account immediately.
You find that the following must also be taken into account:

● Depreciation is to be written-off the motor vehicle at 20% and off the shop fittings at 10%, calculated on the book values at 1 April 2018 plus additions during the year.
● At 31 March 2019 motor vehicle expenses owing were £291 and insurance paid in advance was £177.
● Included in the amount paid for shop fittings were:
a table bought for £300, which Smithson resold during the year at cost, some wooden shelving (cost £250), which Smithson used in building an extension to his house.
Other balances at 31 March 2019 were:

	£
Trade accounts receivable	4,012
Trade accounts payable	2,445
Inventory of furniture	4,063

Required:
(a)   For the year ended 31 March 2019:
   (i)   calculate Smithson's sales and purchases,
   (ii) prepare his income statement.
(b)   Prepare Smithson's balance sheet as at 31 March 2019.

(Midland Examining Group: GCSE)

40.8   Although Janet Lambert has run a small business for many years, she has never kept adequate accounting records. However, a need to obtain a bank loan for the expansion of the business has necessitated the preparation of 'final' accounts for the year ended 31 August 2019. As a result, the following information has been obtained after much careful research:

1 Janet Lambert's business assets and liabilities are as follows:

As at	1 September 2018	31 August 2019
	£	£
Inventory	8,600	16,800
Accounts receivable for sales	3,900	4,300
Accounts payable for purchases	7,400	8,900
Rent prepaid	300	420
Electricity accrued due	210	160
Balance at bank	2,300	1,650
Cash in hand	360	330

2 All takings have been banked after deducting the following payments:

Cash drawings – Janet Lambert has not kept a record of cash drawings, but suggests these will be in the region of	£8,000
Casual labour	£1,200
Purchase of goods for resale	£1,800

Note: Takings have been the source of all amounts banked.

3 Bank payments during the year ended 31 August 2019 have been summarised as follows:

	£
Purchases	101,500
Rent	5,040
Electricity	1,390
Delivery costs (to customers)	3,000
Casual labour	6,620

4 It has been established that a gross profit of $33\frac{1}{3}\%$ on cost has been obtained on all goods sold.
5 Despite her apparent lack of precise accounting records, Janet Lambert is able to confirm that she has taken out of the business during the year under review goods for her own use costing £600.

Required:
(*a*) Prepare a computation of total purchases for the year ending 31 August 2019.
(*b*) Prepare an income statement for the year ending 31 August 2019 and a balance sheet as at that date, both in as much detail as possible.
(*c*) Explain why it is necessary to introduce accruals and prepayments into accounting.

(*Association of Accounting Technicians*)

40.9A Jean Smith, who retails wooden ornaments, has been so busy since she commenced business on 1 April 2018 that she has neglected to keep adequate accounting records. Jean's opening capital consisted of her life savings of £15,000 which she used to open a business bank account. The transactions in this bank account during the year ended 31 March 2019 have been summarised from the bank account as follows:

	£
Receipts:	
Loan from John Peacock, uncle	10,000
Takings	42,000
Payments:	
Purchases of goods for resale	26,400
Electricity for period to 31 December 2018	760
Rent of premises for 15 months to 30 June 2019	3,500
Rates of premises for the year ended 31 March 2019	1,200
Wages of assistants	14,700
Purchase of van, 1 October 2018	7,600
Purchase of holiday caravan for Jean Smith's private use	8,500
Van licence and insurance, payments covering a year	250

According to the bank account, the balance in hand on 31 March 2019 was £4,090 in Jean Smith's favour.

While the intention was to bank all takings intact, it now transpires that, in addition to cash drawings, the following payments were made out of takings before bankings:

	£
Van running expenses	890
Postages, stationery and other sundry expenses	355

On 31 March 2019, takings of £640 awaited banking; this was done on 1 April 2019. It has been discovered that amounts paid into the bank of £340 on 29 March 2019 were not credited to Jean's bank account until 2 April 2019 and a cheque of £120, drawn on 28 March 2019 for purchases, was not paid until 10 April 2019. The normal rate of gross profit on the goods sold by Jean Smith is 50% on sales. However, during the year a purchase of ornamental goldfish costing £600 proved to be unpopular with customers and therefore the entire inventory had to be sold at cost price.

Interest at the rate of 5% per annum is payable on each anniversary of the loan from John Peacock on 1 January 2019.

Depreciation is to be provided on the van on the straight line basis; it is estimated that the van will be disposed of after five years' use for £100.

The inventory of goods for resale at 31 March 2019 has been valued at cost at £1,900.

Accounts payable for purchases at 31 March 2019 amounted to £880 and electricity charges accrued due at that date were £180.

Trade accounts receivable at 31 March 2019 totalled £2,300.

Required:
Prepare an income statement for the year ending 31 March 2019 and a balance sheet as at that date.

(Association of Accounting Technicians)

40.10   David Denton set up in business as a plumber a year ago, and he has asked you to act as his accountant. His instructions to you are in the form of the following letter.

Dear Henry,

I was pleased when you agreed to act as my accountant and look forward to your first visit to check my records. The proposed fee of £250 p.a. is acceptable. I regret that the paperwork for the work done during the year is incomplete. I started my business on 1 January last, and put £6,500 into a business bank account on that date. I brought my van into the firm at that time, and reckon that it was worth £3,600 then. I think it will last another three years after the end of the first year of business use.

I have drawn £90 per week from the business bank account during the year. In my trade it is difficult to take a holiday, but my wife managed to get away for a while. The travel agent's bill for £280 was paid out of the business account. I bought the lease of the yard and office for £6,500. The lease has ten years to run, and the rent is only £300 a year payable in advance on the anniversary of the date of purchase, which was 1 April. I borrowed £4,000 on that day from Aunt Jane to help pay for the lease. I have agreed to pay her 10 per cent interest per annum, but have been too busy to do anything about this yet.

I was lucky enough to meet Miss Prism shortly before I set up on my own, and she has worked for me as an office organiser right from the start. She is paid a salary of £3,000 p.a. All the bills for the year have been carefully preserved in a tool box, and we analysed them last week. The materials I have bought cost me £9,600, but I reckon there was £580 worth left in the yard on 31 December. I have not yet paid for them all yet, I think we owed £714 to the suppliers on 31 December. I was surprised to see that I had spent £4,800 on plumbing equipment, but it should last me five years or so. Electricity bills received up to 30 September came to £1,122; but motor expenses were £912, and general expenses £1,349 for the year. The insurance premium for the year to 31 March next was £800. All these have been paid by cheque but Miss Prism has lost the rate demand. I expect the Local Authority will send a reminder soon since I have not yet paid. I seem to remember that rates came to £180 for the year to 31 March next.

Miss Prism sent out bills to my customers for work done, but some of them are very slow to pay. Altogether the charges made were £29,863, but only £25,613 had been received by 31 December. Miss Prism thinks that 10 per cent of the remaining bills are not likely to be paid. Other customers for jobs too small to bill have paid £3,418 in cash for work done, but I only managed to bank £2,600 of this money. I used £400 of the difference to pay the family's grocery bills, and Miss Prism used the rest for general expenses, except for £123 which was left over in a drawer in the office on 31 December.

Kind regards,
Yours sincerely,
David.

You are required to draw up an income statement for the year ending 31 December 2020, and a balance sheet as at that date.

(*Association of Chartered Certified Accountants*)

40.11 The following are summaries of the cash book and bank accounts of J. Duncan who does not keep his books using the double entry system.

Bank Summary	£	£
Balance on 1 January 2018		8,000
Receipts		
Accounts receivable	26,000	
Cash banked	4,100	30,100
		38,100
Payments		
Trade accounts payable	18,500	
Rent	1,400	
Machinery	7,500	
Wages	6,100	
Insurance	1,450	
Accounts receivable (dishonoured cheque)	250	
Loan interest	300	35,500
Balance on 31 December 2018		2,600

Cash Summary	£	£
Balance on 1 January 2018		300
Receipts		
Cash sales	14,000	
Accounts receivable	400	14,400
		14,700
Payments		
Drawings	9,500	
Repairs	300	
Electricity	750	
Cash banked	4,100	14,650
Balance on 31 December 2018		50

The following referred to 2018	£
Bad debts written-off	400
Discount received	350
Goods withdrawn by J. Duncan for own use	300
Credit note issued	1,200

The following additional information is available.

	1 January 2018 £	31 December 2018 £
Inventory	4,100	3,200
Machinery	12,600	15,900
Rent prepaid	200	
Rent owing		250
Accounts receivable	6,300	5,000
Accounts payable	2,400	2,500
Loan from bank at 8%	5,000	5,000
Loan interest owing		100

You are required to:
(*a*) Calculate the value of J. Duncan's capital on 1 January 2018.
(*b*) Prepare the Income Statement for the year ending 31 December 2018.

(*Scottish Qualifications Authority*)

→

40.12 Using the information in Review Question 40.11, prepare J. Duncan's balance sheet as at 31 December 2018.

40.13A The following are summaries of the cash book and bank accounts of P. Maclaran who does not keep her books using the double entry system.

Bank Summary	£	£
Balance on 1 January 2018		6,000
Receipts		
Accounts receivable	35,000	
Cash banked	2,200	37,200
		43,200
Payments		
Trade accounts payable	31,000	
Rent	1,100	
Machinery	3,400	
Wages	9,200	
Insurance	850	
Accounts receivable (dishonoured cheque)	80	
Loan interest	500	(46,130)
Balance on 31 December 2018		(2,930)

Cash Summary	£	£
Balance on 1 January 2018		60
Receipts		
Cash sales	9,700	
Accounts receivable	1,100	10,800
		10,860
Payments		
Drawings	6,600	
Repairs	1,400	
Electricity	570	
Cash banked	2,200	(10,770)
Balance on 31 December 2018		90

The following referred to 2018	£
Bad debts written-off	240
Discount received	600
Goods withdrawn by P. Maclaran for own use	1,200
Credit note issued	640

The following additional information is available.	1 January 2018	31 December 2018
	£	£
Inventory	2,300	5,400
Machinery	9,800	10,400
Rent prepaid		100
Rent owing	150	
Accounts receivable	8,100	9,200
Accounts payable	5,700	4,800
Loan from bank at 10%	7,000	7,000
Loan interest owing		200

You are required to:
(a) Calculate the value of P. Maclaran's capital on 1 January 2018.
(b) Prepare the Income Statement for the year ending 31 December 2018.

40.14A Using the information in Review Question 40.13, prepare P. Maclaran's balance sheet as at 31 December 2018.

40.15 A business prepares its financial statements annually to 30 April and stocktaking is carried out on the next following weekend. This year, 30 April was a Wednesday. Inventory was taken on 3 May and the inventory actually on the premises on that date had a value at cost of £124,620.

The following additional information is ascertained:

(i) The cash and credit sales totalled £2,300 during the period 1–3 May.
(ii) Purchases recorded during the period 1–3 May amounted to £1,510 but, of this amount, goods to the value of £530 were not received until after 3 May.
(iii) Sales returns during 1–3 May amounted to £220.
(iv) The average ratio of gross profit to sales is 20 per cent.
(v) Goods in the inventory at 30 April and included in stocktaking on 3 May at £300 were obsolete and valueless.

Required:
Ascertain the value of the inventory on 30 April for inclusion in the financial statements.

Analysis and interpretation of financial statements

Learning objectives

After you have studied this chapter, you should be able to:

- explain how the use of ratios can help in analysing the profitability, liquidity, efficiency and capital structure of businesses
- calculate the main accounting ratios
- interpret the results of calculating accounting ratios
- explain the advantages and disadvantages of the gearing of an organisation being high or low
- explain how the proportion of costs that are fixed and variable impacts profit at different levels of activity
- explain the relevance of IAS 1 and IAS 8, and accounting standards in general, to the preparation of financial statements

Introduction

In this chapter, you'll learn how to calculate and interpret the most commonly used accounting ratios. You'll learn how to assess an organisation's profitability, liquidity, efficiency, and capital structure using ratio analysis. In addition, you'll learn more about IAS 1 (*Presentation of financial statements*) and IAS 8 (*Accounting policies, changes in accounting estimates and errors*), of their importance, and of the importance of accounting standards in general to the preparation of financial statements.

41.1 The need for ratios

Without ratios, financial statements would be largely uninformative to all but the very skilled. With ratios, financial statements can be interpreted and usefully applied to satisfy the needs of the reader.

For example, let's take the performance of four companies, all dealing in the same type of goods:

	Gross profit	Sales
	£	£
Company A	200,000	848,000
Company B	300,000	1,252,000
Company C	500,000	1,927,500
Company D	350,000	1,468,400

Suppose you want to know which company gets the 'best' profit. Simply inspecting these figures and trying to decide which performance was the best, and which was the worst, is virtually impossible. To bring the same basis of comparison to each company we need some form of common measure. As you have already seen in Chapter 39, one measure commonly used is a ratio – the gross margin, i.e. the amount of gross profit on sales as a percentage. Applying this to these four companies, we find that their margins are:

	%
Company A	23.58
Company B	23.96
Company C	25.94
Company D	23.84

On this basis, Company C with a gross margin of 25.94% or, in other words, £25.94 gross profit per £100 sales, has performed better than the other companies.

41.2 How to use ratios

You can only sensibly compare like with like. There is not much point, for example, in comparing the gross profit percentage of a wholesale chemist with that of a restaurant.

Similarly, figures are only comparable if they have been built up on a similar basis. The sales figures of Company X, which treats items as sales *only when cash is received,* **cannot** be properly compared with those of Company Z, which treats items as sales *as soon as they are invoiced.*

Another instance of this could be that of inventory turnover, which you learnt about in Chapter 39. Let's compare two companies, Company K and Company L. They are both toy shops so would seem to be comparable. Both companies have annual sales revenue of £400,000. However, the average inventory of K is £50,000 whilst that of L is £20,000. Cost of sales for both companies is £200,000, so their inventory turnover ratios are:

$$\frac{\text{Cost of sales}}{\text{Average inventory}} \qquad \frac{K}{\dfrac{200,000}{50,000}} = 4 \qquad \frac{L}{\dfrac{200,000}{20,000}} = 10$$

It looks as though L has managed to turn its inventory over ten times during the year compared with K, four times. Is this true? Well, it depends. Let's imagine that K had a financial year end of 30 November, just before Christmas, so toy inventory would be extremely high; that L had a year end of 31 January when, following the Christmas sales, its inventory had dropped to the year's lowest level; and that at 30 November both this year and last year L also had inventory valued at £50,000. Can you see how the difference in the timing of the year end can affect this ratio significantly?

Ratios therefore need *very* careful handling. They are extremely useful if used and interpreted appropriately, and very misleading otherwise.

41.3 Users of ratios

As you know, there are a great many parties interested in analysing financial statements, including shareholders, lenders, customers, suppliers, employees, government agencies and competitors. Yet, in many respects, they will be interested in different things. There is not, therefore, any definitive, all-encompassing list of points for analysis that would be useful to all these stakeholder groups.

Nevertheless, it is possible to construct a series of ratios that together will provide all of them with something that they will find relevant and from which they can investigate further if necessary.

Ratio analysis is a first step in financially assessing an entity. It removes some of the mystique surrounding the financial statements and makes it easier to pinpoint items which it would be interesting to investigate further.

Exhibit 41.1 shows some categories of ratios and indicates some of the stakeholder groups that would be interested in them.

Exhibit 41.1

Ratio category	Examples of interested groups
Profitability	Shareholders, management, employees, creditors, competitors, potential investors
Liquidity	Shareholders, suppliers, creditors, competitors
Efficiency	Shareholders, potential purchasers, competitors
Shareholder	Shareholders, potential investors
Capital structure	Shareholders, lenders, creditors, potential investors

As you will see, some ratios belong in more than one of these categories.

41.4 Categories of ratio

Profitability ratios

1 Return on capital employed (ROCE)

This is one of the most important profitability ratios, as it encompasses all the other ratios, and because an adequate return on capital employed is why people invest their money in a business in the first place.

(a) Sole proprietors

In this chapter, we will use the average of the capital account as the figure for capital employed, i.e. (opening balance + closing balance) ÷ 2.

In Businesses C and D in Exhibit 41.2, both businesses have made the same amount of net profit, but the capitals employed are different.

Exhibit 41.2

Balance Sheets

	C	D
	£	£
Non-current assets + Current assets − Current liabilities	100,000	160,000
Capital accounts		
Opening balance	80,000	140,000
Add Net profit	36,000	36,000
	116,000	176,000
Less Drawings	(16,000)	(16,000)
	100,000	160,000

$$\boxed{\text{Return on capital employed (ROCE)} = \frac{\text{Net profit}}{\text{Capital employed}} \times 100}$$

therefore,

$$\overset{C}{\frac{36,000}{(80,000 + 100,000) \div 2}} \times \frac{100}{1} = 40\% \qquad \overset{D}{\frac{36,000}{(140,000 + 160,000) \div 2}} \times \frac{100}{1} = 24\%$$

The ratio illustrates that what is important is not simply how much profit has been made but how well the capital has been employed. Business C has made far better use of its capital, achieving a return of £40 net profit for every £100 invested, whereas D has received only a net profit of £24 per £100.

(b) Limited companies

There is no universally agreed definition of return on capital employed for companies. The main ones used are:

(i)   return on capital employed sourced from ordinary shareholders;
(ii) return on capital employed sourced from all long-term suppliers of capital.

Let's now look at each of these:

(i)   In a limited company this is known as **Return on Owners' Equity (ROOE)** or, more commonly, **Return on Shareholders' Funds (ROSF)**. From now on, we shall use the second of these terms, 'Return on Shareholders' Funds', but you will need to remember that when you see 'Return on Owners' Equity', it is the same as ROSF.
      The 'Return' is the net profit for the period. The term 'Shareholders' Funds' means the book value of all things in the balance sheet that describe the owners' capital and reserves. 'Owners' are the holders of the **ordinary** share capital. This is calculated: Ordinary Share Capital + all Reserves including Retained Profits.

(ii) This is often known simply as 'Return on Capital Employed' (ROCE). The word 'Return' in this case means net profit + any preference share dividends + loan notes and long-term loan interest. The word 'Capital' means Ordinary Share Capital + Reserves including Retained Profits + Preference Shares + Loan notes and Long-term Loans.

Given the following balance sheets and income statements of two companies, P Ltd and Q Ltd, the calculations of ROSF and ROCE can be attempted:

Balance Sheets as at 31 December

	P Ltd		Q Ltd	
	£	£	£	£
	2019	*2020*	*2019*	*2020*
Non-current assets	520,000	560,000	840,000	930,000
Net current assets	280,000	340,000	160,000	270,000
	800,000	900,000	1,000,000	1,200,000
10% loan notes	–	–	(120,000)	(120,000)
	800,000	900,000	880,000	1,080,000
Share capital (ordinary)	300,000	300,000	500,000	500,000
Reserves	500,000	600,000	380,000	580,000
	800,000	900,000	880,000	1,080,000

Income Statements for the year ending 31 December 2020 (extracts)

	P Ltd	Q Ltd
	£	£
Net profit	220,000	380,000
Dividends	(120,000)	(180,000)
	100,000	200,000

Return on Shareholders' Funds (ROSF)

P Ltd	Q Ltd

$$\frac{220,000}{(800,000 + 900,000) \div 2} \times \frac{100}{1} = 25.9\%$$

$$\frac{380,000}{(800,000 + 1,080,000) \div 2} \times \frac{100}{1} = 38.8\%$$

Return on Capital Employed (ROCE)

P Ltd	Q Ltd

Same as ROSF[Note 1] = 25.9%

$$\frac{380,000 + 12,000^{\text{Note 2}}}{(1,000,000 + 1,200,000) \div 2} \times \frac{100}{1} = 35.6\%$$

Note 1: The return on capital employed by all long-term sources of capital (in *Q Ltd's* case, the shareholders' funds and the debentures) is the same as the ROSF in the case of *P Ltd*, as it has no debentures.

Note 2: The loan note interest (i.e. 10% of £120,000 = £12,000) must be added back, as it was an expense in calculating the £380,000 net profit.

2 Gross profit as a percentage of sales

The formula is:

$$\frac{\text{Gross profit}}{\text{Sales}} \times 100$$

Go back to Chapter 39 to refresh your understanding of gross profit as a percentage of sales.

3 Net profit as a percentage of sales

The formula is:

$$\frac{\text{Net profit}}{\text{Sales}} \times 100$$

Liquidity ratios

You saw earlier in this section that the ratio called 'return on capital employed' is used to provide an overall picture of profitability. It cannot always be assumed, however, that profitability is everything that is desirable. It must be stressed that **accounting is used, not just to calculate profitability, but also to provide information that indicates whether or not the business will be able to pay its creditors, expenses, loans falling due, etc. at the correct times.** Failure to ensure that these payments are covered effectively could mean that the business would have to be closed down. Being able to pay one's debts as they fall due is known as being 'liquid'.

It is also essential that a business is aware if a customer or borrower is at risk of not repaying the amount due. New customers are usually vetted prior to being allowed to trade on credit rather than by cash. For private individuals, there are credit rating agencies with extensive records of the credit histories of many individuals. For a small fee, a company can receive a report indicating whether a new customer might be a credit risk. Similarly, information can be purchased concerning companies that indicates their solvency, i.e. whether they are liable to be bad credit risks.

The difference between these two sources of information is that, while the information on private individuals is based on their previous credit record, that of the companies is generally based on a ratio analysis of their financial statements.

When it comes to the liquidity of a business, both its own ability to pay its debts when due and the ability of its debtors to pay the amount they owe to the business are of great importance. Ratio analysis that focuses upon liquidity (or solvency) of the business generally starts with a look at two ratios (**liquidity ratios**) that are affected most by these two aspects of liquidity, the **current ratio** and the **acid test ratio**.

1 Current ratio

This compares assets which will become liquid within approximately 12 months (i.e. total current assets) with liabilities which will be due for payment in the same period (i.e. total current liabilities) and is intended to indicate whether there are sufficient short-term assets to meet the short-term liabilities.

$$\text{Current ratio} = \frac{\text{Current assets}}{\text{Current liabilities}}$$

When calculated, the ratio may be expressed as either a ratio to 1, with current liabilities being set to 1, or as a 'number of times', representing the relative size of the amount of total current assets compared with total current liabilities.

With *all* ratios, once you have performed the calculation, you need to decide what it tells you. To do so, there is no point in using a universal guide, such as '*the ratio should always lie between 1:1 and 2:1*'. Any such guidance is at best useless and at worst misleading. Instead, you need to consider the result in its context.

For example:

● What is the norm in this industrial sector? (For example, retailers are often below 1:1.)
● Is this company significantly above or below that norm?
● If so, can this be justified after an analysis of the nature of these assets and liabilities, and of the reasons for the amounts of each held?

You need to contextualise *every* ratio you calculate when you are trying to understand what the result means, not just this one.

2 Acid test ratio

This shows that, provided creditors and debtors are paid at approximately the same time, a view might be made as to whether the business has sufficient liquid resources to meet its current liabilities.

$$\text{Acid test ratio} = \frac{\text{Current assets} - \text{inventory}}{\text{Current liabilities}}$$

Activity 41.1   What is the difference between the formulae for the current ratio and the acid test ratio?

Exhibit 41.3 shows how two businesses may have similar profitability, yet their liquidity positions may be quite different.

Exhibit 41.3

		E			F
	£	£		£	£
Non-current assets		40,000			70,000
Current assets					
Inventory	30,000			50,000	
Accounts receivable	45,000			9,000	
Bank	15,000			1,000	
		90,000			60,000
Total assets		130,000			130,000
Current liabilities: accounts payable		(30,000)			(30,000)
Net assets		100,000			100,000
Capital					
Opening capital		80,000			80,000
Add Net profit		36,000			36,000
		116,000			116,000
Less Drawings		(16,000)			(16,000)
		100,000			100,000

Note: Sales for both *E* and *F* amounted to £144,000. Gross profits for *E* and *F* were identical at £48,000.

Profitability is the same for both businesses. However, there is a vast difference in the liquidity of the two businesses.

Current ratios

$$E = \frac{90{,}000}{30{,}000} = 3$$

$$F = \frac{60{,}000}{30{,}000} = 2$$

This looks adequate on the face of it, but let's look at the acid test ratio:

Acid test ratios

$$E = \frac{60{,}000}{30{,}000} = 2$$

$$F = \frac{10{,}000}{30{,}000} = 0.33$$

This reveals that *F* may be in trouble, as it will probably find it difficult to pay its current liabilities on time. **No matter how profitable a business is, unless it is adequately liquid it may fail.**

However, although a business should be adequately liquid, it is possible for it to have too high a current ratio or acid test ratio. If too many resources are being held as current assets, it would make these two ratios appear healthy, but those resources could have been used more profitably – you don't get any interest on inventory! Too high a balance in a current account at the bank also means that resources are being wasted.

Activity 41.2 Why is inventory omitted from the acid test ratio?

Efficiency ratios

1 Inventory turnover

Inventory turnover measures how efficient a business is at maintaining an appropriate level of inventory. When it is not being as efficient as it used to be, or is being less efficient than its competitors, this may indicate that control over inventory levels is being undermined.

A reduction in inventory turnover can mean that the business is slowing down. Inventory may be piling up and not being sold. This could lead to a liquidity crisis, as money may be being taken out of the bank simply to increase inventory which is not then sold quickly enough.

Note: In this chapter, we are classifying inventory turnover as an efficiency ratio. It is often also classified as a liquidity ratio.

For Exhibit 41.3 the cost of sales for each company was £144,000 − £48,000 = £96,000. If opening inventory had been E £34,000 and F £46,000 then, using the average of the opening and closing inventory, the inventory turnovers would have been:

$$\begin{array}{ccc} & E & F \\ \dfrac{\text{Cost of sales}}{\text{Average inventory}} & \dfrac{96,000}{(34,000 + 30,000) \div 2} & \dfrac{96,000}{(46,000 + 50,000) \div 2} \\[2ex] & = \dfrac{96,000}{32,000} = 3 \text{ times} & = \dfrac{96,000}{48,000} = 2 \text{ times} \end{array}$$

It appears that F's inventory may be too high, perhaps because it is having difficulty selling it compared with E. Or perhaps it is E that has a problem obtaining enough inventory. Either way, further investigation is needed.

2 Accounts receivable/sales ratio

The resources tied up in accounts receivable is an important ratio subject. Money tied up unnecessarily in accounts receivable is unproductive money. In the example in Exhibit 41.3 the **accounts receivable/sales ratio** can be calculated for the two companies as:

$$\begin{array}{ccc} & E & F \\ \text{Accounts receivable/sales} & 45,000/144,000 = 1:3.2 & 9,000/144,000 = 1:16 \end{array}$$

This relationship is often translated into the length of time a debtor takes to pay:

$$\begin{array}{cc} E & F \\ 365 \times \dfrac{1}{3.2} = 114 \text{ days} & 365 \times \dfrac{1}{16} = 22.8 \text{ days} \end{array}$$

Why Company E should have allowed so much time for its debtors to pay is a matter for investigation. Possibly the company was finding it harder to sell goods, and to sell at all was eventually forced to sell to customers on long credit terms. It could well be that E has no proper credit control system, whereas F has an extremely efficient one.

When the ratio is deteriorating (i.e. it is rising) this may signal liquidity problems.

Note: In this chapter, we are classifying accounts receivable/sales as an efficiency ratio. Like inventory turnover, it is often also classified as a 'liquidity ratio', as it can reveal both efficiency and liquidity issues. The next ratio, accounts payable/purchases, also provides this double aspect view.

3 Accounts payable/purchases ratio

Assuming that purchases for E amounted to £92,000 and for F £100,000 then the **accounts payable/purchases ratio** can be calculated for each as:

	E	F
Accounts payable/purchases	30,000/92,000 = 1:3.07	30,000/100,000 = 1:3.3

This also is often translated into the length of time we take to pay our creditors. This turns out to be:

$$E \qquad F$$

$$365 \times \frac{1}{3.07} = 119 \text{ days} \qquad 365 \times \frac{1}{3.3} = 110 \text{ days}$$

Shareholder ratios

These will include the following ratios. Note that 'price' means the price of the shares on the Stock Exchange.

1 Earnings per share (EPS)

The formula is:

$$\text{Earnings per share} = \frac{\text{Net profit after interest and tax and preference dividends}}{\text{Number of ordinary shares issued}}$$

This gives the shareholder (or prospective shareholder) a chance to compare one year's earnings with another in terms easily understood. Many people consider EPS to be *the* most important ratio that can be calculated from the financial statements.

2 Price/earnings ratio (P/E)

The formula is:

$$\text{Price/earnings ratio} = \frac{\text{Market price per share}}{\text{Earnings per share}}$$

This puts the price into context as a multiple of the earnings. The greater the P/E ratio, the greater the demand for the shares.

3 Dividend yield

This is found by the formula:

$$\text{Dividend yield} = \frac{\text{Gross dividend per share}}{\text{Market price per share}}$$

This measures the real rate of return by comparing the dividend paid to the market price of a share.

4 Dividend cover

This is found by the formula:

$$\text{Dividend cover} = \frac{\text{Net profit after tax and preference dividends}}{\text{Ordinary dividends paid and proposed}}$$

This gives the shareholder some idea as to the proportion that the ordinary dividends bear to the amount available for distribution to ordinary shareholders. Usually, the dividend is described as being so many times covered by profits made. If, therefore, the dividend is said to be *three times covered*, it means that one-third of the available profits is being distributed as dividends.

Capital structure ratios

Gearing

The relationship of equity shares (ordinary shares) to other forms of long-term financing (long-term loans plus preference shares) can be extremely important. Analysts are, therefore, keen to ascertain a ratio to express this relationship.

There is more than one way of calculating **gearing**. The most widely used method is as follows:

$$\frac{\text{Long-term loans} + \text{Preference shares}}{\text{Ordinary share capital} + \text{Reserves} + \text{Preference shares} + \text{Long-term liabilities}} \times 100$$

This formula is sometimes abbreviated to:

$$\frac{\text{Prior charge capital}}{\text{Total capital}} \times 100$$

which is exactly the same.

Long-term loans include loan notes. Total capital includes preference shares and ordinary shares, all the reserves and long-term loans.

Let's look at the calculations of the gearing of two small companies, *A Ltd* and *B Ltd* in Exhibit 41.4. Both have been trading for five years.

Exhibit 41.4

Year 5: items per balance sheet	A Ltd	B Ltd
	£	£
10% loan notes	20,000	200,000
10% preference shares	40,000	100,000
Ordinary shares	200,000	40,000
Reserves	140,000	60,000
	400,000	400,000

Gearing ratios:

$$A\ Ltd:\quad \frac{20{,}000 + 40{,}000}{20{,}000 + 40{,}000 + 200{,}000 + 140{,}000} \times \frac{100}{1} = 15\% \text{ (low gearing)}$$

$$B\ Ltd:\quad \frac{200{,}000 + 100{,}000}{200{,}000 + 100{,}000 + 40{,}000 + 60{,}000} \times \frac{100}{1} = 75\% \text{ (high gearing)}$$

Now let us look at how dividends are affected, given the same level of profits made before payment of loan note interest and preference dividends. All the profits made in these years are to be distributed.

→

→ *A Ltd: Low gearing*

		Year 6	Year 7	Year 8	Year 9
		£	£	£	£
Profits before deducting the following:		40,000	30,000	60,000	80,000
Loan note interest	2,000				
Preference dividend	4,000				
		(6,000)	(6,000)	(6,000)	(6,000)
Profits left for ordinary dividend		34,000	24,000	54,000	74,000
Rate of ordinary dividend		17%	12%	27%	37%

B Ltd: High gearing

		Year 6	Year 7	Year 8	Year 9
		£	£	£	£
Profits before deducting the following:		40,000	30,000	60,000	80,000
Loan note interest	20,000				
Preference dividend	10,000				
		(30,000)	(30,000)	(30,000)	(30,000)
Profits left for ordinary dividend		10,000	–	30,000	50,000
Rate of ordinary dividend		25%	–	75%	125%

A company with a high percentage gearing ratio is said to be *high geared*, whereas one with a low percentage gearing is said to be *low geared*. As you can see from the above example, the proportionate effect gearing has upon ordinary shareholders is far greater in a high geared company, ranging from 0 to 125 per cent dividend for B Ltd, whilst the range of ordinary dividends for A Ltd varied far less and lay between 17 and 37 per cent.

A high rate of debt (i.e. long-term loans and preference shares) means that in bad times very little might be left over for ordinary shareholders after payment of interest on the debt items and also preference dividends. In good times, however, the ordinary shareholders will enjoy a far higher return than in a low geared company.

This means that people investing in ordinary shares in a high geared company are taking a far greater risk with their money than if they had invested instead in a low geared company. It would have only required a drop of profits of £5,000 in Year 6 for B Ltd to find that there would be no ordinary dividends at all for Years 6 and 7. Such a drop in Year 6 for A Ltd would still have allowed a dividend of 12 per cent for both of Years 6 and 7. Investors therefore who are prepared to risk their money in the hope of large dividends would have chosen B Ltd, whilst those who wanted to cut down on their risk and be more certain about receiving dividends would choose A Ltd.

Changing the gearing of a company

The management might decide that for various reasons it would like to change the gearing of the company. It can do this as follows:

To reduce gearing

1 By issuing new ordinary shares
2 By redeeming loan notes
3 By retaining profits

To increase gearing

1 By issuing loan notes
2 By buying back ordinary shares in issue
3 By issuing new preference shares

Such changes will be influenced by what kinds of investors the company wishes to attract. A highly geared company will attract risk-taking buyers of ordinary shares, whilst a low geared company will be more attractive to potential ordinary shareholders who wish to minimise risk.

Other ratios

There are a large number of other ratios which could be used, far more than can be mentioned in a textbook such as this. It will depend on the type of company, exactly which ratios are the most important and it is difficult to generalise too much.

Different users of the financial statements will want to use the ratio analysis which is of vital concern to them. If we can take as an example a bank which lends money to a company, it will want to ensure two things:

(a) that the company will be able to pay interest on the loan as it falls due; *and*
(b) that it will be able to repay the loan on the agreed date.

The bank is therefore interested in:

(a) short-term liquidity, concerning payment of loan interest; and
(b) long-term solvency for eventual repayment of the loan.

Possible ratios for each of these could be:

(a) **Short-term liquidity ratios**, mainly the *acid test ratio* and the *current ratio,* already described.
(b) **Long-term solvency ratios**, which might include:

　(i) **Operating profit/loan interest.** This indicates how much of the profits are taken up by paying loan interest. Too great a proportion would mean that the company was borrowing more than was sensible, as a small fall in profits could mean the company operating at a loss with the consequent effect upon long-term solvency.
　(ii) **Total external liabilities/shareholders' funds.** This ratio measures how much financing is done via share capital and retained profits, and how much is from external sources. Too high a proportion of external liabilities could bring about long-term solvency problems if the company's profit-making capacity falls by a relatively small amount, as outside liabilities still have to be met.
　(iii) **Shareholders' funds/total assets (excluding intangibles).** This highlights the proportion of assets financed by the company's own funds. Large falls in this ratio will tend to show a difficulty with long-term solvency. Similarly, investors will want to see ratios suitable for their purposes, which are not the same as those for the bank. These will not only be used on a single company comparison, but probably with the average of the same type of ratios for other companies in the same industry.

41.5　The investor: choosing between shares and loan notes

The choice of an investor will always be related to the amount of acceptable risk. We can list the possible investments under the headings of risk.

Lowest risk

Loan note holders have their interest paid to them whether or not profits are made. This contrasts with shares, both preference and ordinary, where there have to be profits available for distribution as dividends.

In addition, should there be insufficient cash funds available to pay loan note interest, many loan notes give their holders the right to sell off some or all of the assets of the company, and to recoup the amount of their loan notes before anyone else has a claim. Such an investment does not have as much security as, say, government stocks, but it certainly ranks above the shares of that same company.

Medium risk

Preference shareholders have their dividends paid after the loan note interest has been paid, but before the ordinary shareholders. They still are dependent upon profits being available for distribution. If they are of the cumulative variety then any shortfall can be carried forward to future years and paid before any ordinary dividends are taken.

Highest risk

Ordinary shareholders have the highest risk. They must give way to both loan note holders and to preference shareholders for interest and dividends. However, should the remaining profits for distribution be very high then they may get a high return on their money.

41.6 Trend figures

In examinations, a student is often given just one year's accounting figures and asked to comment on them. Obviously, lack of space on an examination paper may preclude several years' figures being given; also, the student lacks the time to prepare a comprehensive survey of several years' financial statements.

In real life, however, it would be extremely stupid for anyone to base decisions on just one year's financial statements, if more information was available. What is important for a business is not just what, say, accounting ratios are for one year, but what the trend has been.

Given two similar types of businesses *G* and *H*, both having existed for five years, if both of them had exactly the same ratios in Year 5, are they both equally desirable as investments? Given one year's accounts it may appear so, but if one had all the five years' figures it may not give the same picture, as Exhibit 41.5 illustrates.

Exhibit 41.5

	Years	1	2	3	4	5 (current)
Gross profit as % of sales	G	40	38	36	35	34
	H	30	32	33	33	34
Net profit as % of sales	G	15	13	12	12	11
	H	10	10	10	11	11
Net profit as % of capital employed	G	13	12	11	11	10
	H	8	8	9	9	10
Current ratio	G	3	2.8	2.6	2.3	2.0
	H	1.5	1.7	1.9	1.0	2.0

From these figures *G* appears to be the worse investment for the future, as the trend appears to be downwards. If the trend for *G* is continued it could be in a very dangerous financial situation in a year or two. Business *H*, on the other hand, is strengthening its position all the time.

Of course, it would be ridiculous to assert that *H* will continue on an upward trend. One would have to know more about the business to be able to judge whether or not that could be true.

However, given all other desirable information, trend figures would be an extra important indicator.

41.7 Fixed and variable costs

Some costs will remain constant whether activity increases or falls, at least within a given range of change of activity. These costs are called **fixed costs**. An example of this would be the rent of a shop which would remain at the same figure whether sales increased 10 per cent or fell 10 per cent. The same would remain true of such things as rates, fire insurance and so on.

Wages of shop assistants could also remain constant in such a case. If, for instance, the shop employed two assistants, then it would probably keep the same two assistants, on the same wages, whether sales increased or fell by 10 per cent.

Of course, such fixed costs can only be viewed as fixed in the short term. If sales doubled, then the business might well need a larger shop or more assistants. A larger shop would also certainly mean higher rates, higher fire insurance and so on, and with more assistants the total wage bill would be larger.

Variable costs, on the other hand, will change with swings in activity. Suppose that wrapping materials are used in the shop, then an increase in sales of 10 per cent should see 10 per cent more wrapping materials used. Similarly an increase of 10 per cent of sales, if all sales are despatched by parcel post, should see delivery charges increase by 10 per cent.

Some costs could be part fixed and part variable. Suppose that because of an increase in sales of 10 per cent, telephone calls made increased by 10 per cent. With telephone bills the cost is often in two parts, one for the rent of the phone line and the second part corresponding to the actual number of calls made. The rental charge would not change in such a case, and therefore this part of telephone expense would be 'fixed' whereas the calls part of the cost could increase by 10 per cent.

This means that the effect of a percentage change in activity could result in a greater or lesser percentage change in net profit, because the fixed costs (within that range of activity) may not alter.

Exhibit 41.6 shows the change in net profit in Business A, which has a low proportion of its expenses as 'fixed' costs, and in Business B, in which the 'fixed' costs are a relatively high proportion of its expenses.

Exhibit 41.6

Business A

	£	£	(a) If sales fell 10% £	£	(b) If sales rose 10% £	£
Sales		500,000		450,000		550,000
Less Cost of goods sold		(300,000)		(270,000)		(330,000)
Gross profit		200,000		180,000		220,000
Less Expenses:						
Fixed	30,000		30,000		30,000	
Variable	130,000		117,000		143,000	
		(160,000)		(147,000)		(173,000)
Net profit		40,000		33,000		47,000

Business B

	£	£	(a) If sales fell 10% £	£	(b) If sales rose 10% £	£
Sales		500,000		450,000		550,000
Less Cost of goods sold		(300,000)		(270,000)		(330,000)
Gross profit		200,000		180,000		220,000
Less Expenses:						
Fixed	120,000		120,000		120,000	
Variable	40,000		36,000		44,000	
		(160,000)		(156,000)		(164,000)
Net profit		40,000		24,000		56,000

The comparison of percentage changes in net profit therefore works out as follows:

	Business A	Business B
Decrease of 10% sales:		

$$\frac{\text{Reduction in profit}}{\text{Original profit}} \times \frac{100}{1} \qquad \frac{7,000}{40,000} \times \frac{100}{1} = 17.5\% \qquad \frac{16,000}{40,000} \times \frac{100}{1} = 40\%$$

Increase of 10% sales:

$$\frac{\text{Increase in profit}}{\text{Original profit}} \times \frac{100}{1} \qquad \frac{7,000}{40,000} \times \frac{100}{1} = 17.5\% \qquad \frac{16,000}{40,000} \times \frac{100}{1} = 40\%$$

You can see that a change in activity in Business *B*, which has a higher fixed expense content, results in greater percentage changes in profit: 40% in *B* compared with 17.5% in *A*.

41.8 Limitations of accounting statements

Financial statements are only partial information. They show, in financial terms, what has happened *in the past*. **This is better than having no information at all, but much more information is needed to fully understand the present situation.**

First, **it is impossible to sensibly compare two businesses which are completely unlike one another solely by looking at their financial statements.** To compare a supermarket's figures with those of a chemical factory would be rather pointless. It would be like comparing a lion with a lizard.

Second, **there are a whole lot of factors that the past-focused financial statements do not disclose.** The desire to keep to the money measurement concept, and the desire to be objective, both dealt with in Chapter 7, exclude a great deal of desirable information.

> Go back to Chapter 7 to refresh your understanding of the money measurement concept and objectivity.

Some typical desirable information can be listed but, beware, the list is indicative rather than exhaustive.

(*a*) What are the future plans of the business? Without knowing this, making an investment in a business would be sheer guesswork.

(*b*) Has the firm got good quality staff?

(*c*) Is the business situated in a location desirable for such a business? A shipbuilding business situated a long way up a river which was becoming unnavigable, to use an extreme example, could soon be in trouble.

(*d*) What is its position as compared with its competitors? A business manufacturing a single product, which has a foreign competitor which has just invented a much improved product which will capture the whole market, is obviously in for a bad time.

(*e*) Will future government regulations affect it? Suppose that a business which is an importer of goods from Country *X*, which is outside the EU, finds that the EU is to ban all imports from Country *X*?

(*f*) Is its plant and machinery obsolete? If so, the business may not have sufficient funds to be able to replace it.

(*g*) Is the business of a high-risk type or in a relatively stable industry?

(*h*) Has the business got good customers? A business selling largely to Country *Y*, which is getting into trouble because of shortage of foreign exchange, could soon lose most of its trade. Also if one customer was responsible for, say, 60 per cent of sales, then the loss of that one customer would be calamitous.

(*i*) Has the business got good suppliers of its needs? A business in wholesaling could, for example, be forced to close down if manufacturers decided to sell direct to the general public.

(*j*) Problems concerned with the effects of distortion of accounting figures caused by inflation (or deflation).

You can see that the list would have to be an extremely long one if it was intended to cover all possibilities.

41.9 IAS 1: *Presentation of financial statements*

The way in which accounting information is presented in financial statement is governed by IAS 1. It lays down the statements that must be produced and what they contain. It will be covered in detail in *Frank Wood's Business Accounting 2*. Some aspects were covered briefly in Section 36.16.

41.10 IAS 8: *Accounting policies, changes in accounting estimates and errors*

Users of financial statements issued by organisations want to analyse and evaluate the figures contained within them. They cannot do this effectively unless they know which accounting policies have been used when preparing such statements.

Accounting policies

Accounting policies are defined in IAS 8 as:

> *the specific principles, bases, conventions, rules and practices applied by an entity in preparing and presenting financial statements.*

Accounting policies, therefore, define the processes whereby transactions and other events are reflected in the financial statements. The accounting policies selected should enable the financial statements to give a true and fair view and should be consistent with accounting standards and with relevant legislation.

When selecting an accounting policy, its appropriateness should be considered in the context of four characteristics that financial information must possess:

- **Relevance** – Does it produce information that is useful for assessing stewardship and for making economic decisions?
- **Reliability** – Does it reflect the substance of the transaction and other events that have occurred? Is it free of bias, i.e. neutral? Is it free of material error? If produced under uncertainty, has prudence been exercised?
- **Comparability** – Can it be compared with similar information about the entity for some other period or point in time?
- **Understandability** – Is it capable of being understood by users who have a reasonable knowledge of business and economic activities and accounting?

The financial information must also reflect economic reality and be neutral, prudent and complete. In addition, accounting policies must be applied consistently to 'similar transactions, events and conditions'.

Changes to accounting policies

Changes can only be made if required by a standard or if they result in reliable and more relevant information. Where the change is voluntary, it must be applied retrospectively and items restated.

Estimation techniques

Estimation techniques are the methods adopted in order to arrive at estimated monetary amounts for items that appear in the financial statements. Changes in accounting estimates relate to the carrying amount of an asset or liability or the amount of the periodic consumption of an asset. Where a change in an accounting estimate gives rise to changes in assets or liabilities, or relates to an item of equity, it is recognised by adjusting the carrying amount of the asset, liability or equity item in the period in which the change of estimate occurred.

Activity 41.3

From your knowledge of accounting, what do you think these methods may include? Think about this for a minute and then write down as many examples of estimation techniques as you can think of.

Examples of accounting policies

● The treatment of gains and losses on disposals of non-current assets – they could be applied to adjust the depreciation charge for the period, or they may appear as separate items in the financial statements.
● The classification of overheads in the financial statements – for example, some indirect costs may be included in the trading account section of the income statement, or they may be included in administration costs in the profit and loss account section of the income statement.
● The treatment of interest costs incurred in connection with the construction of non-current assets – these could be charged to profit and loss as a finance cost, or they could be capitalised and added to the other costs of creating the fixed assets (this is permitted by the relevant accounting standard).

Identifying whether an accounting policy has changed

This is done by considering whether any of three aspects have changed:

● **Recognition** – some items may be recognised in more than one way. For example, expenditure on developing new products may be recognised either as a profit and loss expense or as an asset in the balance sheet.
● **Presentation** – how something is presented in the financial statements. For example, where certain indirect costs appear in the income statement.
● **Measurement basis** – the monetary aspects of the items in the financial statements, such as the basis of valuation of inventory, say FIFO or LIFO.

If any of these three aspects have changed, this represents a change in accounting policy. If they haven't, something else has occurred, for example, the estimation technique in use. If depreciation was changed from straight line to reducing balance this would be **a change in estimation technique**, not a change in accounting policy. On the other hand, a decision to switch from valuing stock using FIFO to LIFO would constitute **a change in accounting policy** as the measurement basis would have changed.

41.11 Further thoughts on concepts and conventions

In Chapter 7, you were introduced to the concepts and conventions used in accounting. Since then, further chapters have consolidated your knowledge on specific points.

In recent years there has been a considerable change in the style of examinations in accounting at all levels. At one time nearly every examination question was purely computational, requiring you to prepare financial statements, draft journal entries, extract a trial balance and so on. Now, *in addition* to all that (which is still important) there are quite a lot of questions asking such things as:

● Why do we do it?
● What does it mean?
● How does it relate to the concepts and conventions of accounting?

Such questions depend very much on the interests and ingenuity of examiners. They like to set questions worded to find out those who can understand and interpret financial information, and eliminate those who cannot and simply try to repeat information learned by rote.

The examiners will often draw on knowledge from any part of the syllabus. It is therefore impossible for a student (or an author) to guess exactly how examiners will select questions and how they will word them.

An example of this is where the examiner could ask you to show how different concepts contradict one another. Someone who has just read about the concepts, and memorised them, could not answer this unless they had thought further about it. **Think about whether or not you could have answered that question before you read further.**

One instance is the use of the concept of consistency. Basically it says that one should keep to the same method of entering an item each year. Yet if the net realisable value of stock is less than cost, then the normal method of showing it at cost should be abandoned and the net realisable value used instead. Thus, at the end of one period, inventory may be shown at cost and at the end of the next period it will be shown at net realisable value. In this case the concept of prudence has overridden the concept of consistency.

Another instance of this is the practice of calculating profit based on sales whether they have been paid for or not. If the prudence concept were taken to extremes, then profit would only be calculated on a sale when the sale had been paid for. Instead, the realisation concept has overridden the prudence concept so you recognise a sale when it is reasonably certain that it will be paid for.

Review Questions 41.11 to 41.20 are typical examination questions which obviously relate to concepts and conventions, and to a general understanding of the subject.

41.12 Some other accounting standards

As well as the accounting standards that you have read about in this book, there are some other standards which may appear in your examinations. We will cover them briefly here.

IAS 38: *Intangible assets*

Money spent on research and development presents a problem for accountants. You could argue that:

● Such costs are incurred so that profits can be earned in the future, and should therefore be carried forward to those future periods.
● Just because you have incurred such costs, you cannot be certain about future profitability occurring. It should therefore be written off as an expense in the period when the costs are incurred.

The costs can be divided between:

● **Research.** This is carried out to advance knowledge or application of knowledge.

Examples include:

● searching for new knowledge;
● search for revaluation of and final selection of applications of research findings or other knowledge;
● search for alternative materials, devices, products, processes, systems or services;
● formulation, design, evaluation and final selection of possible alternatives for new and improved materials, devices, products, processes, systems or services.

● **Development.** Work undertaken to develop research that creates an asset that will generate probable future economic benefits.

IAS 38 requires that all research expenditure must be recognised as an expense when it is incurred. However, development costs, subject to satisfying technical and commercial feasibility being confirmed, may be capitalised as an intangible asset and carried forward to future periods.

IAS 10: *Events after the reporting period*

The balance sheet is supposed to reflect the financial position of an organisation at the balance sheet date. However, between the balance sheet date and the date when the financial statements are authorised for issue, events may occur which mean that the financial statements will need to be amended.

The events can be divided between:

● **Adjusting events.** When these exist, the financial statements must be amended. Examples would include settlement of a court case, information indicating that an asset was impaired at the date of the balance sheet, and the discovery of fraud or errors which show that the financial statements are incorrect.
● **Non-adjusting events.** These do not lead to amendments to the financial statements, but they may be shown as notes accompanying the financial statements. Examples would include changes in the market value of investments and dividends proposed.

IAS 37: *Provisions, contingent liabilities and contingent assets*

A provision may be defined as:

a liability of uncertain timing or amount.

A provision should only be recognised when an entity has a present obligation as a result of a past event *and* it is probable that an outflow of resources embodying economic benefits will have to occur *and* a reasonable estimate can be made of the amount involved.

A contingent liability may be defined as:

either a possible obligation arising from past events whose existence will be confirmed only by the occurrence of one or more uncertain future events not wholly within the entity's control; or a present obligation that arises from past events but is not recognised because it is not probable that an outflow of resources embodying economic benefits will be required to settle the obligation or the amount of the obligation cannot be measured with sufficient reliability.

An example of this could be where a legal action is being carried on, but the case has not yet been decided. For instance, a company may have been sued for £10 million damages, but the case is not yet over. The company may or may not have to pay the damages, but the case is so complex that it has no way of knowing.

A contingent asset may be defined as:

a possible asset arising from past events whose existence will be confirmed only by the occurrence or non-occurrence of one or more uncertain events not wholly within the entity's control.

Neither contingent liabilities nor contingent assets should be recognised. This is consistent with the prudence concept. A contingent liability should be disclosed.

Small and medium-sized entities and accounting standards

More than 95 per cent of all companies are small or medium sized. The UK has had an FRSSE (Financial Reporting Standard for Smaller Entities) for many years. It provided a simplified version of the body of UK accounting standards and is for use by 'smaller entities', i.e. small companies and other organisations that would be classified as 'small' if they were companies.

The FRSSE was replaced in 2015 by FRS 105 (*The financial reporting standard applicable to the micro-entities regime*). In 2009, the IASB issued an IFRS for small and medium-sized entities. It reduces disclosure requirements and simplifies recognition and measurement requirements and is only 15 per cent of the length of the extant body of international standards.

Learning outcomes

You should now have learnt:

1   That comparing the trends to see if the ratios are getting better or worse as each period passes is essential for proper control. Prompt action needs to be taken where the trend in a ratio is deteriorating.

2   The importance of interpreting ratios in their context: that is, against those of other similar businesses or against the same ratios calculated for the same organisation using data from other time periods.

3   That a business must be both profitable *and* sufficiently liquid to be successful. One factor without the other can lead to serious trouble.

4   That careful credit control to ensure that the accounts receivable/sales ratio is not too high is usually essential to the well-being of any business.

5   That gearing affects the risk factor for ordinary share investors. High gearing means greater risk whilst low gearing means lower risks.

6   How to calculate and interpret the most commonly used ratios.

7   The relevance of ratio analysis to an assessment of liquidity, efficiency, profitability and capital structure.

8   That the relative amounts of fixed and variable costs can affect profit significantly when there are swings in business activity.

9   The importance of IAS 1 and IAS 8, and accounting standards in general, to the preparation of financial statements.

Answers to activities

41.1   The only difference in the items involved between the two ratios is that the acid test (or 'quick') ratio does not include inventory. Otherwise, it is identical to the current ratio, comparing current assets *other than inventory* to current liabilities.

41.2   Inventory is omitted as it is considered to be relatively illiquid, because, depending on prevailing and future market forces, it may be impossible it to convert it to cash in a relatively short time.

41.3   All depreciation methods and methods used to estimate doubtful debts are the main ones we have encountered so far in this book. However, we've also looked at asset revaluation, another aspect of accounting for which the methods adopted in arriving at the valuation would be considered estimation techniques. Basically, any method used to arrive at an *estimated* figure shown in the financial statements is an estimation technique. So, to answer the question fully, you need to make a list of all those items that appear in financial statements that are estimates. The methods used to arrive at the value used for those figures are all estimation techniques. This would include, for example, the method used in order to arrive at the proportion of an electricity bill spanning the period end that belongs in the period for which the financial statements are being prepared. More obviously estimates may be required for bad debts, inventory obsolescence, and the useful lives or consumption pattern of non-current assets.

Review questions

41.1   Calculate the inventory turnover ratio if average inventory is £85,000 and cost of sales is £595,000.

41.2   Calculate return on capital employed for a sole proprietor whose net profit was £49,000 and whose capital employed was £245,000.

41.3   Calculate gross profit as a percentage of sales if gross profit was £159,800 and sales were £470,000.

41.4   Calculate net profit as a percentage of sales if net profit was £31,520 and sales were £394,000.

41.5   (a)   Calculate the current ratio if current assets are £78,000 and current liabilities are £62,000.
  (b)   If inventory is £29,000, what is the acid test ratio?

41.6   If accounts receivable are £78,000 and sales are £493,000, how many days does the average debtor take to pay?

41.7   If accounts payable are £49,000 and purchases are £396,000, how many days does the business take on average to pay its creditors?

41.8   From the following information, calculate:
  (a)   Earnings per share;
  (b)   Price/earnings ratio;
  (c)   Dividend yield; and
  (d)   Dividend cover.

  (i)   Net profit after interest and tax = £248,000.
  (ii)   Number of ordinary shares issued = 800,000.
  (iii)   Market price per share = £3.72.
  (iv)   Dividend per share = 16p.
  (v)   Ordinary dividends for the year = £128,000.

41.9   If prior charge capital = £95,000 and total capital = £233,000 what is the gearing?

41.10 You are to study the following financial statements for two businesses that operate in the same industry and then answer the questions which follow.

Financial Statements

	Business J		Business K	
	£	£	£	£
Income Statements				
Sales		472,000		695,000
Less Cost of goods sold				
Opening inventory	51,000		62,000	
Add Purchases	264,000		401,000	
Less Closing inventory	(64,000)	(251,000)	(50,000)	(413,000)
Gross profit		221,000		282,000
Less Depreciation	12,000		16,000	
Wages, salaries and commission	135,000		151,000	
Other expenses	36,000	(183,000)	47,000	(214,000)
Net profit		38,000		68,000
Balance Sheets				
Non-current assets				
Equipment at cost	120,000		160,000	
Less Depreciation to date	(50,000)	70,000	(30,000)	130,000
Current assets				
Inventory	64,000		50,000	
Accounts receivable	68,000		123,000	
Bank	15,000	147,000	5,000	178,000
Total assets		217,000		308,000
Current liabilities				
Accounts payable		(66,000)		(99,000)
Net assets		151,000		209,000
Financed by:				
Capitals				
Balance at start of year		148,000		221,000
Add Net profit		38,000		68,000
Less Drawings		(35,000)		(80,000)
Total capital		151,000		209,000

Required:

(a) Calculate the following ratios for each business:
   (i) gross profit as percentage of sales;
   (ii) net profit as percentage of sales;
   (iii) expenses as percentage of sales;
   (iv) inventory turnover;
   (v) rate of return of net profit on capital employed (use the average of the capital account for this purpose);
   (vi) current ratio;
   (vii) acid test ratio;
   (viii) accounts receivable days;
   (ix) accounts payable days.

(b) Comment on the ratios you have calculated in (a) and suggest some possible reasons for the differences and similarities between the businesses indicated by your figures.

→ **41.11A** Study the following financial statements of two companies and then answer the questions which follow. Both companies are wholesalers of household products. The values shown are in £000s.

	Abraxas Ltd		Buscema Ltd	
	£000	£000	£000	£000
Income Statements				
Sales		3,300		2,700
Less Cost of goods sold				
Opening inventory	410		216	
Add Purchases	2,340		1,697	
Less Closing inventory	(460)		(233)	
		(2,290)		(1,680)
Gross profit		1,010		1,020
Less Expenses				
Wages and salaries	712		569	
Directors' remuneration	85		175	
Other expenses	147		168	
		(944)		(912)
Net profit		66		108
Balance Sheets				
Non-current assets				
Equipment at cost	474		210	
Less Depreciation to date	(212)		(52)	
		262		158
Vans	213		117	
Less Depreciation to date	(85)		(55)	
		128		62
		390		220
Current assets				
Inventory	460		233	
Accounts receivable	524		106	
Bank	8		21	
		992		360
Total assets		1,382		580
Less Current liabilities				
Accounts payable		(744)		(179)
Net assets		638		401
Equity				
Issued share capital		260		80
Retained profits		378		321
Total equity		638		401

Required:

(a) Calculate the following ratios for both Abraxas Ltd and Buscema Ltd:
   (i)   gross profit as percentage of sales;
   (ii) net profit as percentage of sales;
   (iii) expenses as percentage of sales;
   (iv) inventory turnover;
   (v)   rate of return of net profit on capital employed (for the purpose of this question only, take capital as being total of share capitals + reserves at the date of the balance sheet);
   (vi) current ratio;
   (vii) acid test ratio;
   (viii) accounts receivable days;
   (ix) accounts payable days.

(b) Comment briefly on the performance of the two companies based on the ratios you have calculated, suggesting possible reasons for your observations.

41.12 Durham Limited had an authorised capital of £200,000 divided into 100,000 ordinary shares of £1 each and 200,000 8 per cent preference shares of 50p each. The following balances remained in the accounts of the company after the income statement had been prepared for the year ending 30 April 2019.

	Debit £	Credit £
Premises at cost	86,000	
General reserve		4,000
Ordinary shares: fully paid		100,000
8% Preference shares: fully paid		50,000
Electricity		100
Cash at bank	13,100	
Retained profits 1 May 2018		14,500
Accounts receivable and accounts payable	20,000	12,900
Net profit (year ending 30 April 2019)		16,500
Machinery and plant at cost	60,000	
Provision for depreciation on machinery and plant		40,000
Inventory	60,000	
Allowance for doubtful debts		4,000
Insurance	900	
Preference share dividend paid	2,000	
	242,000	242,000

The Directors have recommended:
  a transfer of £5,000 to general reserve;
  an ordinary dividend of £0.15p per share; and that the
  unpaid preference share dividend be paid.

(a) Prepare an appropriate extract from the statement of changes in equity for year ending 30 April 2019.
(b) Prepare the balance sheet as at 30 April 2019, in a form which shows clearly the **working capital** and the **shareholders' funds.**
(c) Identify and calculate:
   (i) one ratio indicating the firm's profitability;
   (ii) two ratios indicating the firm's liquidity position.
(d) Make use of your calculations in (c) above to comment on the firm's financial position.
(e) Name two points of comparison which are not available from the information above in this question but which could make your comments in (d) above more meaningful.

(*Edexcel Foundation, London Examinations: GCSE*)

41.13 The summarised accounts of Hope (Eternal Springs) Ltd for the years 2018 and 2019 are given below.

Income Statements for the years ending 31 December

	2018 £000	2018 £000	2019 £000	2019 £000
Sales		200		280
Less Cost of sales		(150)		(210)
Gross profit		50		70
Less				
Administration expenses	38		46	
Loan note interest	–		4	
		(38)		(50)
Net profit		12		20

Balance Sheets as at 31 December

	2018		2019	
	£000	£000	£000	£000
Non-current assets at cost *less* depreciation		110		140
Current assets				
Inventory	20		30	
Accounts receivable	25		28	
Bank	–		5	
		45		63
Total assets		155		203
Current liabilities				
Accounts payable	15		12	
Bank	10		–	
	25		12	
Non-current liabilities				
8% loan notes	–		50	
Total liabilities		(25)		(62)
Net assets		130		141
Equity				
Ordinary share capital		100		100
Retained profits		30		41
Total equity		130		141

Inventory at 1 January 2018 was £50,000.

Required:

(a) Calculate the following ratios for 2018 and 2019:
- (i) Gross profit: Sales
- (ii) Inventory turnover
- (iii) Net profit: Sales
- (iv) Quick ('acid test')
- (v) Working capital
- (vi) Net profit: Capital employed

(b) State the possible reasons for and significance of any changes in the ratios shown by your calculations.

(Midland Examining Group: GCSE)

41.14A Laura has recently inherited £50,000 and has been investigating the possibility of buying shares as an investment. She is, initially, looking to maximise her income.

She has researched two companies and has provided the following information based on the latest financial statements for the year ended 30 April 2019:

	Stabilo plc	Gogro plc
Current market price	£2.40	£1.40
Share price high-low last 52 weeks*	High – Low	High – Low
	£2.50 – £2.35	£1.45 – £0.60
Dividend per share	9.6p	10.5p
Dividend yield	4%	7.5%
Dividend cover	4 times	0.8 times
Earnings per share	25p	10p
Price earnings ratio	9.6	14
ROCE	6.8%	10.4%
Gearing	40%	125%

*this shows the highest and lowest price that the shares were bought and sold in the previous 52 weeks.

Balance sheet extracts for property, plant and equipment:

	Cost £m	Depreciation to date £m	NBV £m
Stabilo plc	250	50	200
Gogro plc	45	30	15

Required

Evaluate both businesses from an investor's point of view and advise Laura which company would be best for her to buy shares in.

(AQA A Level)

41.15A Alistair is concerned about the performance of his business. He has decided to assess the performance using ratio analysis.

He is able to provide the following information extracted from his income statement for the year ended 30 April 2018 in order to calculate ratios relating to profitability.

	£
Cash sales	10,000
Credit sales	185,000
Cash purchases	45,000
Credit purchases	80,000
Cost of sales	130,000
Gross profit	65,000
Operating expenses	55,250
Profit for the year	9,750

Required

(a) Calculate the gross profit mark-up.
(b) Calculate the gross profit margin.
(c) Calculate the profit in relation to revenue ratio.

Alistair is particularly concerned about the liquidity of his business. He allows his credit customers 30 days' credit. On average his suppliers also give him 30 days' credit. He has calculated the following ratios for the accounting years 2015–2018:

Ratio	2015	2016	2017	2018
Receivable days	60 days	50 days	45 days	40 days
Payable days	20 days	25 days	30 days	33 days
Inventory turnover	12 times	11 times	8 times	5 times

(d) Assess the performance of Alistair's business in relation to liquidity. Use the ratios provided by Alistair above.

(AQA AS Level)

→

→ **41.16**   The trading inventory of Joan Street, retailer, has been reduced during the year ending 31 March 2020 by £6,000 from its commencing figure of £21,000.

A number of financial ratios and related statistics have been compiled relating to the business of Joan Street for the year ending 31 March 2020. These are shown below alongside comparative figures for a number of retailers who are members of the trade association to which Joan Street belongs:

	Joan Street	Trade association
	%	%
Net profit as % net capital employed[Author's Note]	15	16
$\dfrac{\text{Net profit}}{\text{Sales}}$	9	8
$\dfrac{\text{Sales}}{\text{Net capital employed}}$	$166^2/_3$	200
$\dfrac{\text{Non-current assets}}{\text{Sales}}$	45	35
Working capital ratio:		
$\dfrac{\text{Current assets}}{\text{Current liabilities}}$	400	$287^1/_2$
Acid test ratio:		
$\dfrac{\text{Bank + Accounts receivable}}{\text{Current liabilities}}$	275	$187^1/_2$
$\dfrac{\text{Gross profit}}{\text{Sales}}$	25	26
Accounts receivable collection period:		
$\dfrac{\text{Accounts receivable} \times 365}{\text{Sales}}$	$36^1/_2$ days	$32^{17}/_{20}$ days
Inventory turnover (based on average inventory for the year)	10 times	8 times

Joan Street has supplied all the capital for her business and has had no drawings from the business during the year ending 31 March 2020.

Required:
(a) Prepare the income statement for the year ending 31 March 2020 and balance sheet as at that date of Joan Street in as much detail as possible.
(b) Identify two aspects of Joan Street's results for the year ending 31 March 2020 which compare favourably with the trade association's figures and identify two aspects which compare unfavourably.
(c) Outline two drawbacks of the type of comparison used in this question.

(*Association of Accounting Technicians*)

Author's Note: take the closing figure at 31 March 2020.

41.17A Harold Smart, who is a small manufacturer trading as Space Age Projects, is very pleased with his recently completed financial results which show that a planned 20 per cent increase in turn-over has been achieved in the last accounting year.

The summarised results relating to the last three financial years are as follows:

Year ended 30 September		2018	2019	2020
		£	£	£
Sales		90,000	100,000	120,000
Cost of sales		(74,000)	(75,000)	(92,000)
Gross profit		16,000	25,000	28,000
Administrative overheads		(3,000)	(5,000)	(6,000)
Net profit		13,000	20,000	22,000

As at 30 September	2017	2018	2019	2020
	£	£	£	£
Non-current assets:				
At cost	155,000	165,000	190,000	206,000
Provision for depreciation	(42,000)	(45,000)	(49,000)	(53,000)
	113,000	120,000	141,000	153,000
Current assets:				
Inventory	3,000	4,000	7,000	30,000
Accounts receivable	14,000	19,000	15,000	10,000
Balance at bank	2,000	1,000	3,000	–
	19,000	24,000	25,000	40,000
Current liabilities:				
Accounts payable	5,000	4,000	6,000	9,000
Bank overdraft	–	–	–	2,000
	5,000	4,000	6,000	11,000

Since 30 September 2017, Harold Smart has not taken any drawings from the business.

Harold Smart has been invited recently to invest £150,000 for a five-year fixed term in government loan stock earning interest at 12 $\frac{1}{2}$ per cent per annum.

Note: Taxation is to be ignored.

Notwithstanding his response to these financial results, Harold Smart is a very cautious person and therefore has asked a financial consultant for a report.

Required:
(a) A schedule of six accounting ratios or measures of resource utilisation covering each of the three years ended 30 September 2020 of Space Age Projects.
(b) As financial consultant prepare a report to Harold Smart on the financial results of Space Age Projects given above including comments on the alternative future actions that he might take.

Note: Reports should utilise the information given in answers to part (a) of this question.

(Association of Accounting Technicians)

→ **41.18** Business A and Business B are both engaged in retailing, but seem to take a different approach to this trade according to the information available. This information consists of a table of ratios, shown below:

Ratio	Business A	Business B
Current ratio	2 : 1	1.5 : 1
Quick assets (acid test) ratio	1.7 : 1	0.7 : 1
Return on capital employed (ROCE)	20%	17%
Return on shareholders' funds (ROSF)	30%	18%
Accounts receivable turnover	63 days	21 days
Accounts payable turnover	50 days	45 days
Gross profit percentage	40%	15%
Net profit percentage	10%	10%
Inventory turnover	52 days	25 days

Required:
(a) Explain briefly how each ratio is calculated.
(b) Describe what this information indicates about the differences in approach between the two businesses. If one of them prides itself on personal service and one of them on competitive prices, which do you think is which and why?

(*Association of Chartered Certified Accountants*)

41.19A You are given summarised information about two firms in the same line of business, A and B, as follows.

Balance Sheets at 30 June	A £000	A £000	B £000	B £000
Land		80		260
Buildings	120		200	
Less: Depreciation	(40)		–	
		80		200
Plant	90		150	
Less: Depreciation	(70)		(40)	
		20		110
		180		570
Inventory	80		100	
Accounts receivable	100		90	
Bank	–		10	
		180		200
		360		770
Accounts payable	110		120	
Bank	50		–	
	160		120	
Loan (10% p.a.)	100	(260)	130	(250)
		100		520
Capital at start of year		100		300
Add: Profit for year		30		100
		130		400
Less: Drawings		(30)		(40)
		100		360
Land revaluation		–		160
		100		520
Sales		1,000		3,000
Cost of sales		400		2,000

Required:

(a) Produce a table of eight ratios calculated for both businesses.

(b) Write a report briefly outlining the strengths and weaknesses of the two businesses. Include comment on any major areas where the simple use of the figures could be misleading.

(Association of Chartered Certified Accountants)

41.20 The following letter has been received from a client. 'I gave my bank manager those audited accounts you prepared for last year. But he says he needs more information before he will agree to increase my overdraft. What could he possibly want to know that he can't get from those accounts? If they are not good enough why bother to prepare them?'

Required:

Outline the major points which should be included in a reply to this letter.

(Association of Chartered Certified Accountants)

41.21 An acquaintance of yours, H. Gee, has recently set up in business for the first time as a general dealer.

The majority of his sales will be on credit to trade buyers but he will sell some goods to the public for cash.

He is not sure at which point of the business cycle he can regard his cash and credit sales to have taken place.

After seeking guidance on this matter from his friends, he is thoroughly confused by the conflicting advice he has received. Samples of the advice he has been given include:

The sale takes place when:

(i) 'you have bought goods which you know you should be able to sell easily';
(ii) 'the customer places the order';
(iii) 'you deliver the goods to the customer';
(iv) 'you invoice the goods to the customer';
(v) 'the customer pays for the goods';
(vi) 'the customer's cheque has been cleared by the bank'.

He now asks you to clarify the position for him.

Required:

(a) Write notes for Gee, setting out, in as easily understood a manner as possible, the accounting conventions and principles which should generally be followed when recognising sales revenue.

(b) Examine each of the statements (i) to (vi) above and advise Gee (stating your reasons) whether the method advocated is appropriate to the particular circumstances of his business.

(Association of Chartered Certified Accountants)

41.22 The annual final accounts of businesses are normally prepared on the assumption that the business is a going concern.

Required:

Explain and give a simple illustration of:

(a) the effect of this convention on the figures which appear in those final accounts.

(b) the implications for the final accounts figures if this convention were deemed to be inoperative.

(Association of Chartered Certified Accountants)

→

→ **41.23** One of the well known accounting concepts is that of materiality.

Required:
(a) Explain what is meant by this concept.
(b) State and explain three types of situation to which this concept might be applicable.
(c) State and explain two specific difficulties in applying this concept.

(*Association of Chartered Certified Accountants*)

41.24 State three classes of people, other than managers and owners, who are likely to need to use financial accounting information. Discuss whether you think their requirements are compatible.

(*Association of Chartered Certified Accountants*)

41.25 A business produces a standard manufactured product. The stages of the production and sale of the product may be summarised as follows:

Stage	A	B	C	D
Activity	Raw material	WIP-I	WIP-II	Finished product
	£	£	£	£
Costs to date	100	120	150	170
Net realisable value	80	130	190	300
Stage	E	F	G	H
Activity	For sale	Sale agreed	Delivered	Paid for
	£	£	£	£
Costs to date	170	170	180	180
Net realisable value	300	300	300	300

Required:
(a) What general rule do accountants apply when deciding when to recognise revenue on any particular transaction?
(b) Apply this rule to the above situation. State and explain the stage at which you think revenue will be recognised by accountants.
(c) How much would the gross profit on a unit of this product be? Why?
(d) Suggest arguments in favour of delaying the recognition of revenue until Stage H.
(e) Suggest arguments in favour of recognising revenue in appropriate successive amounts at Stages B, C and D.

(*Association of Chartered Certified Accountants*)

41.26
(a) In accounting practice a distinction is drawn between the terms 'reserves' and 'provisions' and between 'accrued expenses' and 'accounts payable'.

Required:

Briefly define each of the four terms quoted and explain the effect of each on the preparation of accounts.

(b) While preparing the final accounts for year ending 30 September 2019, the accountant of Lanep Lighting Ltd had to deal with the following matters:
   (i) the exterior of the company's premises was being repaired. The contractors had started work in August but were unlikely to finish before the end of November 2019. The total cost would not be known until after completion. Cost of work carried out to 30 September 2019 was estimated at £21,000;
   (ii) the company rented a sales showroom from Commercial Properties plc at a rental of £6,000 per annum payable half yearly in arrears on 1 August and 1 February;

(*iii*) on 3 October 2019 an invoice was received for £2,500 less a trade discount of 30 per cent, from Lucifer Ltd for goods for resale supplied during September 2019;

(*iv*) the directors of Lanep Lighting Ltd have decided that an annual amount of £5,000 should be set aside, starting with year ending 30 September 2019, for the purpose of plant replacement.

Required:
State the accounting treatment which should be accorded to each of the above matters in the Lanep Lighting Ltd income statement for year ending 30 September 2019 and balance sheet at that date.

(Association of Chartered Certified Accountants)

41.27 Bradwich plc is a medium-sized engineering company whose shares are listed on a major Stock Exchange.

It has recently applied to its bankers for a 7-year loan of £500,000 to finance a modernisation and expansion programme.

Mr Whitehall, a recently retired civil servant, is contemplating investing £10,000 of his lump sum pension in the company's ordinary shares in order to provide both an income during his retirement and a legacy to his grandchildren after his death.

The bank and Mr Whitehall have each acquired copies of the company's most recent annual report and accounts.

Required:
(*a*) State, separately for each of the two parties, those aspects of the company's performance and financial position which would be of particular interest and relevance to their respective interests.
(*b*) State, separately for each of the two parties, the formula of four ratios which would assist in measuring or assessing the matters raised in your answer to (*a*).

(Association of Chartered Certified Accountants)

41.28 Explain what you understand by the accounting term 'capital gearing', showing clearly the benefits of, and the potential problems associated with, high gearing.

(Scottish Qualifications Authority)

41.29A What benefits can result through the use of ratios and what limitations should be imposed on any conclusions drawn from their use?

part 10

AN INTRODUCTION TO MANAGEMENT ACCOUNTING

Introduction

This part introduces the management accounting side of accounting and looks at how costs can be gathered and utilised in decision-making within an organisation.

42

An introduction to management accounting

Learning objectives

After you have studied this chapter, you should be able to:

- explain why cost accounting is needed for there to be an effective management accounting system
- explain why the benefits of operating a costing system should always outweigh the costs of operating it
- explain what characteristic must exist before anything can be described as information
- explain why different costs are often needed when making decisions about the future compared to those that are used to calculate profit in the past
- explain which costing approach is the relevant one to use when considering a change in what and/or how much is produced
- explain what is meant by marginal cost and why selling prices should always exceed it
- explain why budgets are prepared
- describe the role of management accountants in the budgetary process
- describe the relationship between financial accounting data and management accounting data

Introduction

In this chapter, you'll learn about the importance of data being suitable for the purpose for which it is to be used and of the need for information to be useful. You'll learn how costs are recorded and of two of the most used approaches to costing. You'll also learn about systems of costing and of the importance of budgeting, not just to business but also to the role of the management accountant. Finally, you will learn about how management accounting data often forms the basis of data used in financial accounting.

42.1 Background

So far, you have learnt about bookkeeping and the preparation of financial statements. In accounting, these are the two components of what is known as **financial accounting**. The information that is produced by financial accounting is usually historical, backwards-looking and, mainly, for the use of decision-makers external to the organisation to which the data relates. You learnt about the sort of things that are done with this information in Chapter 41.

Activity 42.1 What sort of things are done with this information?

There is a second side to accounting. This one looks forwards and the output from it is used by decision-makers within the organisation. It also consists of two components: one where costs are recorded and one where the data is processed and converted into reports for managers and other decision-makers. The cost recording component is called **cost accounting** and the processing and reporting component is called **management accounting**, which is also the name used to refer to this side of accounting. It is also sometimes referred to as 'managerial accounting'.

42.2 Cost accounting

Cost accounting is needed so that there can be an effective management accounting system. Without a study of costs such a system could not exist. Before entering into any detailed description of costs it is better if we first ask what use we are going to make of information about costs in the business.

This can best be done by referring to something which is not accounting, and then relating it to accounting. Suppose that your employer asked you to 'measure the distance between Manchester and London without using the internet', but walked away from you without giving any further information. As you thought about the request the following thoughts might go through your head:

1 *How* is the distance to be measured? – e.g. by road, rail, plane or train.
2 The *costs* and *benefits* of obtaining the information – how much can you spend finding out the information without making it cost more to find out than will be saved by knowing the information we seek?
3 What is the *purpose* for which the measurement will be used? – e.g. to travel there by car, to walk there, to have goods shipped there by train or by road.

The lesson to be learnt from this is that measurement depends entirely on the use that is to be made of the data. Too often businesses make measurements of financial and other data without looking first at the use that is going to be made of it. In fact, it could be said that 'information' is useful data that is provided for someone.

Data given to someone that is not relevant to the purpose required is just not information. Data provided for a particular purpose that is completely wrong for the purpose, is worse than no data at all.

At least when there is no data, the manager knows that the best that can be done is to guess.

When useless data is collected it has cost money to collect, in itself a waste of money. Second, it is often assumed to be useful and so misleads a manager into taking decisions that are completely inappropriate. Third, it clogs up the communication system within a business, so that other data is not acted on properly because of the general confusion that has been caused.

When looking at costs, you need to consider the following:

1 What is the data on costs wanted for?
2 How are the costs to be measured? and
3 The cost of obtaining costing data should not exceed the benefits to be gained from having it.

When it is known what the costs are for, and how much is to be spent on studying them, the appropriate method for measuring them can be decided.

42.3 Costs

There are many classifications of cost. Let's briefly summarise those that you already know about.

Historical costs

These are the foundation of financial accounting. Exhibit 42.1 shows costs flowing through the financial accounting system.

Exhibit 42.1

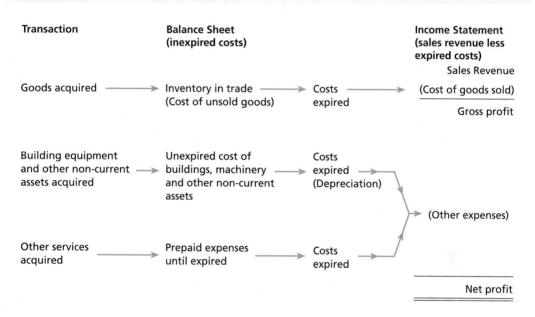

Transaction	Balance Sheet (inexpired costs)		Income Statement (sales revenue less expired costs)
			Sales Revenue
Goods acquired ⟶	Inventory in trade (Cost of unsold goods) ⟶	Costs expired ⟶	(Cost of goods sold)
			Gross profit
Building equipment and other non-current assets acquired ⟶	Unexpired cost of buildings, machinery and other non-current assets ⟶	Costs expired (Depreciation)	
			(Other expenses)
Other services acquired ⟶	Prepaid expenses until expired ⟶	Costs expired	
			Net profit

Product costs

These are the costs attributed to the units of goods manufactured. They are charged up to the cost of goods manufactured in the trading account, and would normally be part of the valuation of unsold goods if the goods to which they refer had not been sold by the end of the period. Product costs are therefore matched up against revenue as and when the goods are sold and not before.

Period costs

Period costs are those of a non-manufacturing nature and represent the selling and distribution, administration and financial expenses. They are treated as expenses of the period in which they were incurred irrespective of the volume of goods sold.

Combining all this, you arrive at the manufacturing accounts you covered in Chapter 29. Exhibit 42.2 shows the flow of costs through to finished products.

Exhibit 42.2

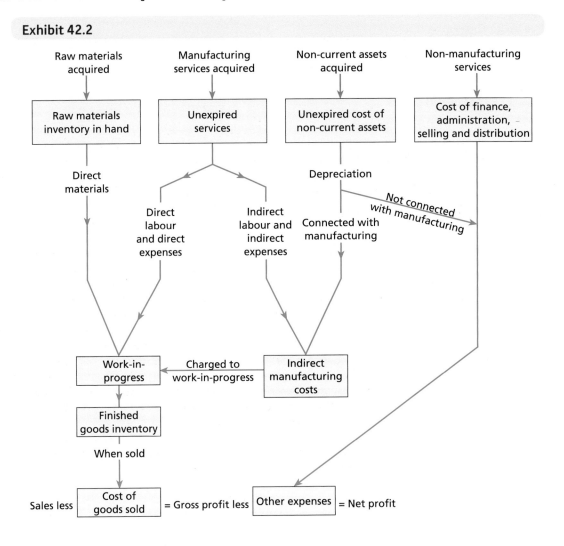

This, therefore, is what you use costs information for in financial accounting – to produce the information you need in order to prepare the financial statements. In management accounting, there is a different emphasis, some of which overlaps with the needs of financial accounting but some of which is for something quite different.

For example, most businesses want to know how much each item has cost to make. This means that the total costs for the whole business are not sufficient, and so these costs must be analysed further. They also want to know what costs are likely to be in the future. Again, more analysis is needed. Cost accounting is the process of measuring and recording all these costs.

Many advantages are gained by having a cost accounting system that provides this detail of cost information. When armed with the cost information that management accounting techniques can provide, managers and other internal decision-makers are far more able to make sensible decisions about what should be done to aid the progress of the business towards its objectives.

For example, imagine trying to decide which item to stop producing out of twelve items made by a business if you have little information as to the amount each item contributes towards the profitability of the business. Very often the solution will be that a new layout in the factory is needed; special training given to certain employees; changes made in the system of remunerating employees; and so on. The information provided by accounting is, therefore, only one part of the whole story for any problem requiring a decision to be made. Sometimes *it will be the least important information* available, as far as the decision-maker is concerned.

42.4 Cost control

One of the most important features of cost accounting is its use for control purposes, meaning, in this context, the control of expenditure. But control of expenditure is possible only if you can trace the costs down to employees who are responsible for such costs. A convenient and frequently adopted approach to collecting costs is through **cost centres** – production or service locations, functions, activities or items of equipment. Costs are collected from cost centres for individual **cost units** – units of product or service. For example, in a manufacturing business, all direct materials, direct labour and direct expenses are traced to cost centres. (In this case, they may be known as 'product centres'.)

A cost centre may be a single machine used for jobbing work, i.e. quite a lot of separate jobs performed specially to conform with the customer's specifications. It could, however, be a group of similar machines or a production department. Thus, if a business makes metal boxes on one machine, all the costs incurred directly relating to that machine (cost centre) would be gathered and then shared (allocated) among all the metal boxes (cost units) made by that machine.

By comparison, factory indirect expenses are 'indirect' and so cannot be traced (or it is not worthwhile tracing them) to product centres. Instead, these are traced to cost centres which give service rather than being concerned with work directly on the products. Such cost centres are, therefore, known as 'service centres'. Examples of service centres would be the factory canteen or the maintenance department. The costs from these service centres will then need allocating to the product centres in a logical fashion – for example, canteen costs may be allocated to product cost centres according to the number of employees working at each of them.

In practice, there are a number of possible ways of allocating costs to cost centres. What must not be lost sight of is the endeavour to trace costs to a person responsible for the expenditure so that the costs can be controlled.

42.5 Costing approaches

There are a number of ways costs can be gathered and collated. The two most commonly used are **absorption costing** and **marginal costing**.

Absorption costing

This involves allocating all direct costs and factory indirect expenses to products. The factory indirect expenses are seen as adding to the value of work-in-progress and, therefore, to finished goods. The production cost of any article is thus comprised of direct materials, direct labour, any direct expenses and a share of factory indirect expense.

After the financial year end, it is possible to look back and calculate exactly what the factory indirect expenses were. This means that this figure is used when calculating the valuation of the closing inventory. For a business which had produced 1,000 units, of which 200 units have not yet been sold, with a total production cost of £100,000, the closing inventory valuation becomes:

$$\frac{\text{Unsold units}}{\text{Total units produced}} \times \text{Production cost of goods completed} = \frac{200}{1,000} \times £100,000$$

$$= £20,000 \text{ closing inventory valuation}$$

Cost data is, however, used for purposes other than that of valuing inventory. The question is, therefore, often asked as to whether or not this method is suitable for all costing purposes. The short answer is that it is not.

Marginal costing

Where costing is used which takes account of only the variable cost of products rather than the full production cost, this is known as marginal costing. By ignoring the fixed costs, it is possible to see how much something contributes towards the profitability of a business. So, for example, if an order was received to buy 100 tables from a business for £65 each and the absorption cost of a table, £70, was considered, the order might be rejected, but if marginal costing was used and the marginal cost was £60, the order might be accepted as every table sold would contribute £5 towards the overall profitability of the business. Whether it is or not will depend upon whether there is any spare production capacity.

When using marginal costing for decisions like this, care needs to be taken that over all the decisions taken, sufficient additional income is generated to pay for all the fixed costs that are ignored by marginal costing.

42.6 Costing systems

Having decided which costing approach to adopt, you then need to decide which costing system to adopt. The one you choose will depend upon how your products or services are produced. There are two main types of costing system, **job costing** and **process costing**.

Job costing

This is used when production consists of separate jobs. For instance, where a Rolls-Royce is made to each customer's specifications, each car can be regarded as a separate job. When a job is long-term, the term 'project costing' is often used.

Job costing also applies where batches of items are made. For example, a jam bottling company may make jam in batches of 10,000 bottles and then switch over to making a different type of jam for the next batch. A printer may print a batch of 2,000 copies of a book. The 'job' can thus be one item or a batch of similar items. When a batch is involved, it is usually referred to as 'batch costing'.

Process costing

Process costing is used where production is regarded as a continuous flow. It is applicable to industries such as oil, paint manufacturing, steel, textiles, and food processing, where production is repetitive and continuous. For example, an oil refinery where crude oil is processed continually, emerging as different grades of petrol, paraffin, motor oil, etc., would use process costing, as would a salt works where sea water is pumped into the works and the resulting product is slabs or packets of salt. Another example would be a car manufacturer that produced one model of car for an extended period.

Overall

Job costing treats production as a number of separate jobs being performed, each of which needs to have costs allocated to it. Process costing, on the other hand, sees production as a continuous flow and no attempt is made to allocate costs to specific units being produced because the same thing is being produced continuously. As a result, costs per unit produced can always be calculated by dividing the costs for the period by the number of units produced.

Activity 42.2

For which of the following would you use job costing and for which would you use process costing? Split the job costing ones between job, batch and project costing.

Newspaper printing
School meals
A film in a cinema
Making a film
Manufacturing computer memory chips
A play in a theatre
Egg production
Building a space satellite

42.7 Budgeting and budgetary control

Management accounting is concerned with providing information for planning and control so that organisations can achieve their objectives. One of the central supporting devices of both of these aims is budgeting.

When a plan is expressed quantitatively it is known as a **budget** and the process of converting plans into budgets is known as **budgeting**.

The budgeting process may be quite formal in a large organisation with committees set up to perform the task. On the other hand, in a very small business the owner may jot down the budget on a piece of scrap paper or even on the back of a used envelope. Some even manage without writ-ing anything down at all – they have done the budgets in their heads and can easily remember them.

The methodology of budgetary control is probably accountancy's major contribution to management. Budgets are drawn up by management and recorded by management accountants. Actual results are compared against the budgets by the management accountants who pass reports to management concerning the extent to which budgets are being met. This enables managers to control activities and to step in and stop situations where the budget is being ignored or overlooked.

When budgets are being drawn up, two main objectives must be uppermost in the minds of management and management accountants – that budgets are for planning and for control. Management accountants must, therefore, operate a system of budgeting that enables these two aims to be achieved. They do so mainly through a system called variance analysis, which compares actual data to budgeted data and endeavours to identify what has given rise to any differences that are found. For example, if the gross profit on an item is lower than was budgeted, this could be because costs have risen or because the selling price has fallen. The management accountant uses special formulae to pinpoint the cause and passes the information to management so that they can exercise control if required.

42.8 Other aspects of management accounting

Management accounting is, therefore, all about gathering costs appropriately so that businesses can take appropriate decisions relating to manufacturing and selling their goods and services. Management accountants are primarily involved in establishing the costs incurred in producing the output of a business and in maintaining a budgeting system that provides managers with the capability to plan and control activity and so meet the objectives of the organisation.

Apart from the activities mentioned already in this chapter, management accountants are also involved in preparing any information of a financial nature that managers and other decision-makers require and which is not considered part of the role of the financial accountant. This can range from identifying the cost of a component part to the expected returns on a twenty-year project to build a chain of hotels. Their work can be much more varied than that of a financial accountant, and they are not tied by any rules and regulations concerning either how they perform calculations or how they present information.

However, as much of the cost information they produce is also used in the financial accounting system, they do need to ensure that their cost data are capable of being used in that medium. As it is easier to simply have one set of costs for an entire business, rather than one calculated for the management accountants and one calculated for the financial accountants, most management accountants follow the rules relating to cost determination that financial accountants are obliged to follow.

Learning outcomes

You should now have learnt that:

1 Cost accounting is needed for there to be an effective management accounting system.

2 The benefits of operating a costing system should always outweigh the costs of operating it.

3 Information is data prepared for a purpose. To qualify as 'information', the 'information' must be useful.

4 Different costs will often be needed when making decisions about the future than were used when calculating profit in the past.

5 Marginal cost, not absorption cost, is the relevant cost when considering a change in what and/or how much is produced.

6 Selling prices should exceed marginal costs. (Almost the only exception to this would be where a product was being promoted as a 'loss leader'.)

7 In the long term, the total of all the differences between revenue and marginal cost must exceed the fixed costs of the business.

8 Budgets are prepared in order to guide the business towards its objectives.

9 Budgets should be drawn up within the context of *planning* and *control*.

Answers to activities

42.1 It is used for ratio analysis, particularly for trend analysis and benchmarking against appropriate comparators such as the previous year's figures or the equivalent figures relating to competitors.

42.2 *Job costing*
Newspaper printing (batch)
School meals (batch)
A film in a cinema (job)
Making a film (project)
A play in a theatre (job)
Building a space satellite (project)

Process costing
Manufacturing computer memory chips
Egg production

Review questions

42.1 What makes information useful?

42.2 What is the difference between absorption costing and marginal costing?

42.3 What is the difference between job costing, batch costing, project costing, and process costing?

42.4 What are the two main objectives of budgeting?

42.5 What role do management accountants play in the budgetary process?

Multiple choice questions: Set 5

Now attempt Set 5 of multiple choice questions. (Answers to all the multiple choice questions are given in Appendix 2 at the end of this book.)

Each of these multiple choice questions has four suggested answers, (A), (B), (C) and (D). You should read each question and then decide which choice is best, either (A) or (B) or (C) or (D). *Write down your answers on a separate piece of paper.* You will then be able to redo the set of questions later without having to try to ignore your answers.

MC81 Given opening accounts receivable of £11,500, Sales £48,000 and receipts from debtors £45,000, the closing accounts receivable total should be

(A) £8,500
(B) £14,500
(C) £83,500
(D) £18,500

MC82 In a Sales Ledger Control Account the Bad Debts written off should be shown in the account

(A) As a debit
(B) As a credit
(C) Both as a debit and as a credit
(D) As a balance carried down

→

MC83 If cost price is £90 and selling price is £120, then

(*i*)   Mark-up is 25 per cent
(*ii*) Margin is 33 $\frac{1}{3}$ per cent
(*iii*) Margin is 25 per cent
(*iv*) Mark-up is 33 $\frac{1}{3}$ per cent

(A) (i) and (ii)
(B) (i) and (iii)
(C) (iii) and (iv)
(D) (ii) and (iv)

MC84 Given cost of goods sold £16,000 and margin of 20 per cent, then sales figure is

(A) £20,160
(B) £13,600
(C) £21,000
(D) £20,000

MC85 If opening inventory is £3,000, closing inventory £5,000, sales £40,000 and margin 20 per cent, then inventory turnover is

(A) 8 times
(B) 7 $\frac{1}{2}$ times
(C) 5 times
(D) 6 times

MC86 If accounts payable at 1 January 2019 were £2,500, accounts payable at 31 December 2019 £4,200 and payments to creditors £32,000, then purchases for 2016 are

(A) £30,300
(B) £33,700
(C) £31,600
(D) £38,700

MC87 Given opening capital of £16,500; closing capital as £11,350; and drawings of £3,300, then

(A) Loss for the year was £1,850
(B) Profit for the year was £1,850
(C) Loss for the year was £8,450
(D) Profit for the year was £8,450

MC88 A Receipts and Payments Account is one

(A) Which is accompanied by a balance sheet
(B) In which the profit is calculated
(C) In which the opening and closing cash balances are shown
(D) In which the surplus of income over expenditure is calculated

MC89 Prime cost includes

(*i*)   Direct labour
(*ii*) Factory overhead expenses
(*iii*) Raw materials consumed
(*iv*) Direct expenses

(A)   (i), (ii) and (iii)
(B)   (ii), (iii) and (iv)
(C)   (i), (iii) and (iv)
(D)   (i), (ii) and (iv)

MC90   Which of the following should be charged in the income statement?

(A)   Office rent
(B)   Work-in-progress
(C)   Direct materials
(D)   Carriage on raw materials

MC91   In the Manufacturing Account is calculated

(A)   The production costs paid in the year
(B)   The total cost of goods produced
(C)   The production cost of goods completed in the period
(D)   The gross profit on goods sold

MC92   The recommended method of departmental accounts is

(A)   To allocate expenses in proportion to sales
(B)   To charge against each department its controllable costs
(C)   To allocate expenses in proportion to purchases
(D)   To charge against each department its uncontrollable costs

MC93   Where there is no partnership agreement then profits and losses

(A)   Must be shared in the same proportion as capitals
(B)   Must be shared equally
(C)   Must be shared equally after adjusting for interest on capital
(D)   None of these

MC94   If it is required to maintain fixed capitals then the partners' shares of profits must be

(A)   Debited to capital accounts
(B)   Credited to capital accounts
(C)   Debited to partners' current accounts
(D)   Credited to partners' current accounts

MC95   You are to buy an existing business which has assets valued at Buildings £50,000, Motor vehicles £15,000, Fixtures £5,000 and Inventory £40,000. You are to pay £140,000 for the business. This means that

(A)   You are paying £40,000 for Goodwill
(B)   Buildings are costing you £30,000 more than their value
(C)   You are paying £30,000 for Goodwill
(D)   You have made an arithmetical mistake

MC96   Assets can be revalued in a partnership change because

(A)   The law insists upon it
(B)   It helps prevent injustice to some partners
(C)   Inflation affects all values
(D)   The depreciation charged on them needs to be reversed

→

→

MC97 Any loss on revaluation is

(A) Credited to old partners in old profit-sharing ratios
(B) Credited to new partners in new profit-sharing ratios
(C) Debited to old partners in old profit-sharing ratios
(D) Debited to new partners in new profit-sharing ratios

MC98 In a limited company which of the following is shown in the statement of changes in equity?

(*i*) Loan note interest
(*ii*) Dividends paid
(*iii*) Transfers to reserves
(*iv*) Directors' remuneration

(A) (i) and (ii)
(B) (ii) and (iii)
(C) (i) and (iv)
(D) (ii) and (iv)

MC99 The Issued Capital of a company is

(A) Always the same as the Authorised Capital
(B) The same as Preference Share Capital
(C) Equal to the reserves of the company
(D) None of the above

MC100 A company wishes to pay out all available profits as dividends. Net profit is £26,600. There are 20,000 8% Preference shares of £1 each, and 50,000 Ordinary shares of £1 each. £5,000 is to be transferred to General Reserve. What Ordinary dividends are to be paid, in percentage terms?

(A) 20 per cent
(B) 40 per cent
(C) 10 per cent
(D) 60 per cent

Answers to review questions

Note: All the answers are the work of the author. None has been supplied by an examining body. The examining bodies accept no responsibility whatsoever for the accuracy or method of working in the answers given.

Note: In order to save space, in most cases brackets have not been entered to indicate negative numbers. Also, £ signs have been omitted from columns of figures, except where the figures refer to £000, or where the denomination needs to be specified.

1.1
(a) 12,000   (b) 37,300   (c) 35,800   (d) 52,400
(e) 58,600   (f) 83,700

1.3
(a) Asset   (b) Asset   (c) Asset   (d) Liability
(e) Asset   (f) Liability

1.5
Wrong Assets: Loan from K. Jones; Bank overdraft;
Wrong Liabilities: Delivery van; Computer equipment; Machinery; Cash in hand.

1.7
Assets: Van 8,750; Market stall 2,400; Computer 490; Inventory 12,300;
Bank 1,440; Cash 200 = total 25,580
Liabilities: Loan 3,000; Account payable 8,200 = total 11,200
Capital: 25,580 − 11,200 = 14,380.

1.9

E. McNiven
Balance Sheet as at 31 December 2019

Non-current assets		
Equipment	17,890	
Motor vehicle	9,250	27,140
Current assets		
Inventory	15,260	
Accounts receivable	11,380	
Cash at bank	920	
		27,560
		54,700
Current liabilities		
Accounts payable		(14,700)
		40,000
Capital		40,000

1.11

	Assets	Liabilities	Capital
(a)	− Bank	− Accounts payable	
(b)	− Cash		
	+ Fixtures		
(c)	+ Inventory	+ Accounts payable	
(d)	+ Cash		
(e)	+ Cash	+ Loan from J. Walker	
(f)	+ Cash		
	− Accounts receivable		
(g)	− Inventory	− Accounts payable	
(h)	+ Computer equipment		
	− Bank		

1.13

T. Ross
Balance Sheet as at 7 May 2019

Non-current assets		
Fixtures	18,600	
Motor vehicle	8,200	
Computer	690	27,490
Current assets		
Inventory	4,750	
Accounts receivable	7,100	
Bank	1,360	
Cash	150	13,360
		40,850
Current liabilities		
Accounts payable		(11,050)
		29,800
Capital		29,800

2.1

		Debit		Credit	
1	Cash	Debit Cash account		Credit Capital account	400
2	Cash in US dollars	Debit Cash US$ account		Credit Capital account	280
3	Cash in the bank	Debit Bank account		Credit Capital account	900
4	Cash in the bank in euros	Debit Bank € account		Credit Capital account	350
5	Computer	Debit Computer account		Credit Capital account	710
6	Mobile phone	Debit Mobile phone account		Credit Capital account	590
7	Office furniture	Debit Office furniture account		Credit Capital account	840
8	Printer	Debit Printer account		Credit Capital account	160
9	Delivery van	Debit Delivery van account		Credit Capital account	2,950
10	Goods for sale	Debit Goods for sale account		Credit Capital account	12,300
11	Amount due from J. Gidman	Debit J. Gidman account		Credit Capital account	560
12	Amount due from K. Bailey	Debit K. Bailey account		Credit Capital account	230
13	Loan from bank	Debit Capital account		Credit Loan from bank account	

Capital account

	6,000

Loan from bank account

	6,000

2.2

Cash account

400	

Cash in US dollars account

	280

Cash in the bank account

900	

Cash in the bank in euros account

	350

Computer account

710	

Mobile phone account

	590

Office furniture account

840	

Printer account

	160

Delivery van account

2,950	

Goods for sale account

	12,300

Amount due from J. Gidman account

560	

Amount due from K. Bailey account

	230

2.3 The *Item exchanged* and the *Form of settlement*.

2.4 The debt owed to the business by the customer.

2.5 The debt you owe the supplier.

2.6 The loan from the bank [i.e. the debt you owe the bank].

2.7 Cash, cash, Cash in bank.

2.8
1 A Form of settlement given is a credit.
2 A Form of settlement recived is a debit.
3 The entry for the Item exchanged is the opposite to the entry for the Form of settlement.

2.9

Debit	Credit
Debit Cash account	Credit Customer receivable account
Debit Supplier payable account	Credit Cash account
Debit Bank account	Credit Loan from bank account

2.10

Debited	Credited	Debited	Credited
(a) Computers	Timeless	(b) B. Burt	Capital
(c) Bank	T. Robb	(d) Loan: I. Simms	Cash
(e) Timeless	Computers	(f) Bank	P. Bell
(g) Van	Tangle Motors		

2.12

Bank

Debit		Credit	
(1) Capital	15,000	(2) Office furn.	2,800
(23) Jevons	750	(5) Car	4,950
		(15) TVC	1,260
		(31) Machinery	710

Capital

Debit		Credit	
		(1) Bank	15,000

Office furniture

Debit		Credit	
(2) Bank	2,800	(8) Jevons	750

Machinery

Debit		Credit	
(31) Bank	710		

Motor vehicles

Debit		Credit	
(5) Bank	4,950		

TVC Ltd

Debit		Credit	
(15) Bank	1,260	(3) Computers	1,260

Jevons & Co

Debit		Credit	
(23) Bank	750	(8) Off. furn.	750

Computer equipment

Debit		Credit	
(3) TVC	1,260		

2.13

Cash

Debit		Credit	
(1) Capital	17,500	(2) Bank	9,400
(28) Bank	130	(25) Equipment	200

Capital

Debit		Credit	
		(1) Cash	17,500

Office furniture

Debit		Credit	
(5) Dream	2,100	(18) Dream	260

Van

Debit		Credit	
(8) Bank	5,250		

Equipment

Debit		Credit	
(25) Cash	200		
(12) Pearce & Sons	2,300		

Bank

Debit		Credit	
(2) Cash	9,400	(8) Van	5,250
(30) F. Brown	4,000	(26) Dream	1,840
		(28) Cash	130

Dream Ltd

Debit		Credit	
(18) Office furn.	260	(5) Office furn.	2,100
(26) Bank	1,840		

Pearce & Sons

Debit		Credit	
		(12) Equipment	2,300

F Brown (Loan)

Debit		Credit	
		(30) Bank	4,000

3.1

	Debited	Credited
(1)	Cash	Sales
(2)	Vehicles	F. Smith
(3)	Cash	Computer
(4)	J. Lilly	Sales
(5)	M. Peel	Returns outwards
(6)	Purchases	F. Day
(7)	Bank	Sales
(8)	W. Brown	Returns outwards
(9)	Returns inwards	I. Gray
(10)	Purchases	T. Gow

3.3

Cash

Debit		Credit	
(1) Capital	3,800	(3) Purchases	480
(10) Sales	172	(25) J. Gill	960
(31) A. Prince	292		

Purchases

Debit		Credit	
(3) Cash	480		
(7) J. Gill	1,200		
(18) F. Genesis	1,460		

Sales

Debit		Credit	
		(10) Cash	172
		(24) A. Prince	292

Returns outwards

Debit		Credit	
		(14) J. Gill	240
		(21) F. Genesis	104

A. Prince

Debit		Credit	
(31) Cash	292	(24) Sales	292

J. Gill

Debit		Credit	
(14) Returns	240	(7) Purchases	1,200
(25) Cash	960		

F. Genesis

Debit		Credit	
(21) Returns	104	(18) Purchases	1,460

Capital

Debit		Credit	
		(1) Cash	3,800

3.5

Bank

Debit		Credit	
(1) Capital	20,000	(25) B. Brown	1,924
(6) Cash	200	(29) Aberdeen Cars	9,100

Cash

Debit		Credit	
(2) D. Rupert (Loan)	5,000	(6) Bank	200
(4) Sales	1,910	(20) Purchases	770
(24) Sales	110	(31) Office furn.	365
(28) Capital	2,500		

Sales

Debit		Credit	
		(4) Cash	1,910
		(8) H. Rise	1,530
		(10) P. Taylor	341
		(14) G. Farm	535
		(14) R. Sim	262
		(24) Cash	110

Purchases

Debit		Credit	
(3) B. Brown	1,530		
(3) I. Jess	4,162		
(11) B. Brown	560		
(20) Cash	770		

Returns outwards

Debit		Credit	
		(15) B. Brown	94
		(19) I. Jess	130

Returns inwards

Debit		Credit	
(12) H. Rise	65		
(26) G. Farm	34		

Aberdeen Cars

Debit		Credit	
(17) Van	9,100	(29) Bank	9,100

Van

Debit		Credit	
(17) Aberdeen Cars	9,100		

Office furniture

Debit		Credit	
(18) J. Winter	1,800	(27) J. Winter	180
(31) Cash	365		

J. Winter Ltd

Debit		Credit	
(27) Office furn.	180	(18) Office furn.	1,800

Capital

Debit		Credit	
		(1) Bank	20,000
		(28) Cash	2,500

B. Brown

Debit		Credit	
(15) Returns	94	(3) Purchases	1,530
(25) Bank	1,924	(11) Purchases	560

I. Jess

Debit		Credit	
(19) Returns	130	(3) Purchases	4,162

D. Rupert (Loan)

Debit		Credit	
		(2) Cash	5,000

P. Taylor

Debit		Credit	
(10) Sales	341		

G. Farm

Debit		Credit	
(14) Sales	535	(26) Returns	34

H. Rise

Debit		Credit	
(8) Sales	1,530	(12) Returns	65

R. Sim

Debit		Credit	
(14) Sales	262		

4.5

(A) Bought motor vehicle £5,000, paying by cheque.
(B) Paid off £4,000 creditors in cash.
(C) Lee lent us £150,000, this being paid into the bank.
(D) Bought land and buildings £125,000, paying by cheque.
(E) Debtors paid cheques £80,000, being paid into bank.
(F) Land and buildings worth £300,000 were sold for £300,000, the proceeds being paid into the bank.
(G) Loan from Lee repaid out of the bank.
(H) Creditors £8,000 paid in cash.
(I) Inventory costing £17,000 sold for £12,000 on credit. Loss of £5,000 shown deducted from Capital.

4.1

Bank

(1) Capital	31,000	(3) Fixtures		480
(21) Rent received	480	(24) Van		16,400

Cash

(1) Capital	4,000		
(5) Sales	600	(10) Rent	800
		(12) Stationery	180
		(30) Wages	1,220
		(31) Drawings	1,020

Purchases

(2) A. Cliff	1,160
(6) S. Bell	1,300

Sales

		(5) Cash	600
		(23) R. Coat	3,200

Fixtures

(3) Bank	480

Rent

(10) Cash	800

Capital

		(1) Bank	31,000
		(1) Cash	4,000

A. Cliff

(18) Returns out	164	(2) Purchases	1,160

S. Bell

		(6) Purchases	1,300

R. Coat

(23) Sales	3,200

Rent received

		(21) Bank	480

Stationery

(12) Cash	180

Returns out

		(18) A. Cliff	164

Van

(24) Bank	16,400

Wages

(30) Cash	1,220

Drawings

(31) Cash	1,020

4.2

Capital

		(1) Cash	30,000

Cash

(1) Capital	30,000	(3) Rent	1,740
(11) Sales	940	(4) Bank	25,000
		(20) B repairs	156
		(28) Purchases	940
		(30) Motor exps	432

Bank

(4) Cash	25,000	(7) Stationery	170
		(27) T. Lamb	620
		(29) Van	7,000

Purchases

(2) T. Lamb	700
(28) Cash	940

Sales

		(5) R. Still	384
		(11) Cash	624
		(17) R. Davis	424

Stationery

(7) Bank	170

Returns outwards

		(14) T. Lamb	80

Computer

(31) S. Tims	1,460

Rent

(3) Cash	1,740

Building repairs

(20) Cash	156

Motor expenses

(30) Cash	432

Van

(29) Bank	7,000

T. Lamb

(14) Returns out	80	(2) Purchases	700
(27) Bank	620		

R. Still

(5) Sales	384	(22) Returns in	62

R. Davis

(17) Sales	424		

Returns inwards

(22) R. Still	62

S. Tims

		(31) Computer	1,460

5.1

B. Flyn

(1) Sales	810	(10) Returns	124
(4) Sales	134	(24) Cash	440
		(31) Balance c/d	380
	944		944
(1) Balance b/d	380		

F. Start

(4) Sales	480	(31) Balance c/d	720
(31) Sales	240		
	720		720
(1) Balance b/d	720		

F. Lane

(1) Sales	1,100	(18) Bank	1,100

T. Fey

(1) Sales	413	(10) Returns	62
		(20) Bank	351
	413		413

5.2

J. Wilson

(10) Returns	65	(1) Purchases	240
(28) Cash	300	(15) Purchases	210
(30) Balance c/d	85		
	450		450
		(1) Balance b/d	85

J. Fry

(10) Returns	140	(1) Purchases	1,620
(30) Balance c/d	1,480		
	1,620		1,620
		(1) Balance b/d	1,480

P. Todd

(30) Returns	39	(1) Purchases	390
(30) Balance c/d	821	(3) Purchases	470
	860		860
		(1) Balance b/d	821

P. Rake

(19) Cash	290	(3) Purchases	290

5.3

B. Flyn

Date	Details	Dr	Cr	Balance
May 1	Sales	810		810 Dr
May 4	Sales	134		944 Dr
May 10	Returns		124	820 Dr
May 24	Cash		440	380 Dr

F. Lane

Date	Details	Dr	Cr	Balance
May 1	Sales	1,100		1,100 Dr
May 18	Bank		1,100	0

T. Fey

Date	Details	Dr	Cr	Balance
May 1	Sales	413		413 Dr
May 10	Returns		62	351 Dr
May 20	Bank		351	0

F. Start

Date	Details	Dr	Cr	Balance
May 4	Sales	480		480 Dr
May 31	Sales	240		720 Dr

5.4

J. Wilson

Date	Details	Dr	Cr	Balance
Jun 1	Purchases		240	240 Cr
Jun 10	Returns	65		175 Cr
Jun 15	Purchases		210	385 Cr
Jun 28	Cash	300		85 Cr

P. Todd

Date	Details	Dr	Cr	Balance
Jun 1	Purchases		390	390 Cr
Jun 3	Purchases		470	860 Cr
Jun 30	Returns	39		821 Cr

J. Fry

Date	Details	Dr	Cr	Balance
Jun 1	Purchases		1,620	1,620 Cr
Jun 10	Returns	140		1,480 Cr

P. Rake

Date	Details	Dr	Cr	Balance
Jun 3	Purchases		290	290 Cr
Jun 19	Cash	290		0

5.5

J. Bee

(1) Sales	1,040	(24) Bank	900
		(28) Cash	80
		(30) Balance c/d	60
	1,040		1,040
(1) Balance b/d	60		

T. Day

(1) Sales	1,260	(12) Returns	190
(8) Sales	340	(30) Bal c/d	1,410
	1,600		1,600
(1) Bal b/d	1,410		

J. Soul

(1) Sales	480	(12) Returns	25
		(30) Balance c/d	455
	480		480
(1) Balance b/d	455		

L. Hope

(8) Sales	480	(30) Bank	480

D. Blue

(20) Bank	780	(2) Purchases	780

F. Rise

(17) Returns	12	(2) Purchases	1,020
(30) Balance c/d	1,100	(10) Purchases	92
	1,112		1,112
		(1) Balance b/d	1,100

P. Lee

(30) Balance c/d	560	(2) Purchases	560
	560		560
		(1) Balance b/d	560

R. James

(17) Returns	84	(10) Purchases	870
(26) Bank	766		
(30) Balance c/d	20		
	870		870
		(1) Balance b/d	20

J. Bee, T. Day and J. Soul are debtors.
F. Rise, P. Lee and R. James are creditors.

6.1

Capital

31.5 Bal c/d	800	1.5 Bank	800
	800		800
		1.6 Bal b/d	800

Loan – HBSC

31.5 Bal c/d	2,000	3.5 Bank	2,000
	2,000		2,000
		1.6 Bal b/d	2,000

Machinery

5.5 Bank	2,500	31.5 Bal c/d	2,500
	2,500		2,500
1.6 Bal b/d	2,500		

Purchases

9.5 Bank	200	31.5 Bal c/d	900
11.5 M. Ball	700		
	900		900
1.6 Bal b/d	900		

Sales

31.5 Bal c/d	1,400	13.5 Bank	380
		15.5 N. Chadwick	470
		17.5 J. Vaughan	550
	1,400		1,400
		1.6 Bal b/d	1,400

J. Vaughan

17.5 Sales	550	21.5 Returns in	60
		31.5 Bal c/d	490
	550		550
1.6 Bal b/d	490		

Returns inwards

21.5 J. Vaughan	60	31.5 Bal c/d	60
	60		60
1.6 Bal b/d	60		

6.1 (Cont'd)

Bank

1.5 Capital	800	5.5 Machinery	2,500
3.5 Loan – HBSC	2,000	7.5 Advertising	75
13.5 Sales	380	9.5 Purchases	200
25.5 N. Chadwick	170	19.5 Drawings	110
		23.5 M. Ball	300
		31.5 Electricity	145
		31.5 Bal c/d	20
	3,350		3,350
1.6 Bal b/d	20		

Advertising

7.5 Bank	75	31.5 Bal c/d	75
	75		75
1.6 Bal b/d	75		

M. Ball

23.5 Bank	300	11.5 Purchases	700
31.5 Bal c/d	400		
	700		700
		1.6 Bal b/d	400

N. Chadwick

15.5 Sales	470	25.5 Bank	170
		31.5 Bal c/d	300
	470		470
1.6 Bal b/d	300		

Drawings

19.5 Bank	110	31.5 Bal c/d	110
	110		110
1.6 Bal b/d	110		

Electricity

31.5 Bank	145	31.5 Bal c/d	145
	145		145
1.6 Bal b/d	145		

Trial balance as at 31 May

	Debit £	Credit £
Capital		800
Loan – HBSC		2,000
Bank	20	
Machinery	2,500	
Advertising	75	
Purchases	900	
M. Ball		400
Sales		1,400
N. Chadwick	300	
J. Vaughan	490	
Drawings	110	
Returns inwards	60	
Electricity	145	
	4,600	4,600

6.2

Cash

1.8 Capital	3,850	2.8 Bank	3,500
19.8 Sales	328	7.8 Purchases	323
		31.8 Bal c/d	355
	4,178		4,178
1.9 Bal b/d	355		

Bank

2.8 Cash	3,500	5.8 Machinery	2,500
24.8 G. Plover	2,000	29.8 D. Bellini	180
		30.8 Wages	530
		31.8 TVC	1,450
		31.8 Bal c/d	840
	5,500		5,500
1.9 Bal b/d	840		

Purchases

4.8 D. Bellini	414	11.8 Drawings	98
7.8 Cash	323	31.8 Bal c/d	639
	737		737
1.9 Bal b/d	639		

Sales

31.8 Bal c/d	923	10.8 J Adams	595
		19.8 Cash	328
	923		923
		1.9 Bal b/d	923

Computer equipment

22.8 TVC	1,450	31.8 Bal c/d	1,450
	1,450		1,450
1.9 Bal b/d	1,450		

TVC Ltd

31.8 Bank	1,450	22.8 Computers	1,450
	1,450		1,450

Drawings

11.8 Purchases	98	31.8 Bal c/d	98
	98		98
1.9 Bal b/d	98		

Capital

31.8 Bal c/d	3,850	1.8 Cash	3,850
	3,850		3,850
		1.9 Bal b/d	3,850

D. Bellini

12.8 Rets out	70	4.8 Purchases	414
29.8 Bank	180		
31.8 Bal c/d	164		
	414		414
		1.9 Bal b/d	164

Machinery

5.8 Bank	2,500	31.8 Bal c/d	2,500
	2,500		2,500
1.9 Bal b/d	2,500		

J. Adams

10.8 Sales	595	31.8 Bal c/d	595
	595		595
1.9 Bal b/d	595		

Loan: G. Plover

31.8 Bal c/d	2,000	24.8 Bank	2,000
	2,000		2,000
		1.9 Bal b/d	2,000

Returns outwards

31.8 Bal c/d	70	12.8 D. Bellini	70
	70		70
		1.9 Bal b/d	70

Wages

30.8 Bank	530	31.8 Bal c/d	530
	530		530
1.9 Bal b/d	530		

b) Trial balance as at 31 August

	Debit £	Credit £
Cash	355	
Capital		3,850
Bank	840	
D. Bellini		164
Purchases	639	
Machinery	2,500	
Sales		923
J. Adams	595	
Computer equipment	1,450	
Loan: G. Plover		2,000
Returns outwards		70
Drawings	98	
Wages	530	
	7,007	7,007

6.5

Capital

		£			£
30.4	Bal c/d	3,000	1.4	Bank	3,000
			1.4	Cash	500
		3,500			3,500
			1.5	Bal b/d	3,000

Cash

		£			£
1.4	Capital	500	30.4	Drawings	80
15.4	Sales	300	30.4	Bal c/d	720
		800			800
1.5	Bal b/d	720			

Purchases

		£			£
5.4	P. Thomas	475	30.4	Bal c/d	730
9.4	M. Wilkinson	255			
		730			730
1.5	Bal b/d	730			

Insurance

		£			£
7.4	Bank	120	30.4	Bal c/d	120
		120			120
1.5	Bal b/d	120			

E. Grant

		£			£
12.4	Sales	700	27.4	Ret inw'ds	80
			30.4	Bal c/d	620
		700			700
1.5	Bal b/d	620			

Returns outwards

		£			£
30.4	Bal c/d	50	22.4	M. Wilkinson	50
		50			50
			1.5	Bal b/d	50

Wages

		£			£
25.4	Bank	45	30.4	Bal c/d	45
		45			45
1.5	Bal b/d	45			

Drawings

		£			£
30.4	Cash	80	30.4	Bal c/d	80
		80			80
1.5	Bal b/d	80			

Bank

		£			£
1.4	Capital	3,000	6.4	Machinery	1,450
			7.4	Insurance	120
			20.4	P. Thomas	475
			25.4	Wages	45
			30.4	Bal c/d	910
		3,000			3,000
1.5	Bal b/d	910			

P. Thomas

		£			£
20.4	Bank	475	5.4	Purchases	475
		475			475

Machinery

		£			£
6.4	Bank	1,450	30.4	Bal c/d	1,450
		1,450			1,450
1.5	Bal b/d	1,450			

M. Wilkinson

		£			£
22.4	Ret outw'ds	50	9.4	Purchases	255
30.4	Bal c/d	205			
		255			255
			1.5	Bal b/d	205

Sales

		£			£
30.4	Bal c/d	1,325	12.4	E. Grant	700
			15.4	Cash	300
			24.4	E. Williams	325
		1,325			1,325
			1.5	Bal b/d	1,325

E. Williams

		£			£
24.4	Sales	325	30.4	Bal c/d	325
		325			325
1.5	Bal b/d	325			

Returns inwards

		£			£
27.4	E. Grant	80	30.4	Bal c/d	80
		80			80
1.5	Bal b/d	80			

M. Donnelly
Trial Balance as at 30 April

	Debit £	Credit £
Capital		3,500
Bank	910	
Cash	720	
Purchases	730	
Machinery	1,450	
Insurance	120	
M Wilkinson		205
E Grant	620	
Sales		1,325
Returns outwards		50
E Williams	325	
Wages	45	
Returns inwards	80	
Drawings	80	
	5,080	5,080

6.6

Bank

	£		£
Balance b/d	17,500	Central Council	2,500
Aardvarks	1,500	Klingon Corp	2,800
		Vehicle expenses	10,000
		Balance c/d	3,700
	19,000		19,000
Balance b/d	3,700		

Sales

	£		£
Balance c/d	6,500	Cash	5,000
		Aardvarks	1,500
	6,500		6,500
		Balance b/d	6,500

Cash

	£		£
Balance b/d	375.00	Spock	3,016.25
Sales	5,000.00	Balance c/d	2,358.75
	5,375.00		5,375.00
Balance b/d	2,358.75		

Spock

	£		£
Cash	3,016.25	Balance b/d	3,175
Discount	158.75		
	3,175.00		3,175.00

McCoy

	£		£
Balance c/d	500	Balance b/d	500
	500		500

Inventory

	£		£
Balance b/d	15,000	Cost of sales	500
Central Council	2,500	Cost of sales	250
		Balance c/d	16,750
	17,500		17,500
Balance b/d	16,750		

Aardvarks

	£		£
Sales	1,500	Bank	1,500
	1,500		1,500

Vehicle expenses

	£		£
Bank	10,000	Balance c/d	10,000
	10,000		10,000
Balance b/d	10,000		

6.6 (Cont'd)

Capital

Balance c/d	49,000	Balance b/d	49,000
	49,000		49,000
		Balance b/d	49,000

Fixtures

Balance b/d	20,000	Balance c/d	23,500
Klingon Corp	3,500		
	23,500		23,500
Balance b/d	23,500		

Cost of sales

Inventory	500	Balance c/d	750
Inventory	250		
	750		750
Balance b/d	750		

Discount received

Balance c/d	858.75	Spock	158.75
		Klingon Corp	700.00
	858.75		858.75
		Balance b/d	858.75

Scott

Balance c/d	200	Balance b/d	200
	200		200
		Balance b/d	200

Central Council

Bank	2,500	Inventory	2,500
	2,500		2,500

Klingon Corp

Bank	2,800	Fixtures	3,500
Discount	700		
	3,500		3,500

USS Enterprise
Trial Balance as at 31 October 2019

	Dr £	Cr £
Bank	3,700	
Capital		49,000
Cash	2,358.75	
Fixtures	23,500	
Inventory	16,750	
Cost of sales	750	
Sales		6,500
Discount received		858.75
Scott		200
McCoy		500
Vehicle expenses	10,000	
	57,058.75	57,058.75

7.1 See text.

7.2 See text.

7.3 See text.

7.4

(a) See text.

(b) The historical cost convention does not make the going concern convention unnecessary. Several instances illustrate this:

(i) Non-current assets are depreciated over the useful economic life of the assets. This presupposes that the business will continue to operate during the years of the assumed useful economic life of the assets.

(ii) Prepayments also assume that the benefits available in the future will be able to be claimed, because the business is expected to continue.

(iii) Inventory is also valued on the basis that it will be disposed of during the future ordinary running of the business.

(iv) The accruals concept itself assumes that the business is to continue.

All of this shows that the two complement each other. The examples indicate that financial statements prepared using the historical cost convention still require the going concern assumption too. There is no conflict between the two conventions.

(c) Shareholders want financial statements so that they can decide what to do with their shareholdings, whether they should sell their shares or hold on to them.

To enable them to decide upon their actions, they would really like to know what is going to happen in the future. To help them in this they would also like information which shows them what happened in the past. Ideally, therefore, they would like both types of report, those on the past and those on the future.

If they had a choice, the logical choice would be to receive a report on the future provided that it could be relied upon. The obvious problem with future estimates is that the future is unpredictable, so all forecasts will be inherently subjective and thus could not be relied upon.

9.1

Cash book

	Cash	Bank			Cash	Bank
(1) Capital	10,000			(2) Rent	1,000	
(3) G. Broad (Loan)		12,000		(4) J. Fine		1,800
(5) Sales	800			(9) A. Moore	300	
(7) F. Love		200		(16) Bank ¢	4,000	
(11) Sales		600		(19) R. Onions (Loan)		2,000
(15) P. Hood	700			(26) Motor expenses		460
(16) Cash ¢		4,000		(30) Cash ¢		320
(22) Sales		1,200		(31) Wages	1,200	
(30) Bank ¢	320			(31) Balances c/d	5,320	13,420
	11,820	18,000			11,820	18,000

690

9.3

Cash book

	Disct	Cash	Bank		Disct	Cash	Bank
(1) Balance b/d		620	7,142	(4) Rent			430
(2) G. Slick	13		247	(8) R. White	18		702
(2) P. Fish	16		304	(8) G. Green	24		936
(2) T. Old	21		399	(8) L. Flip	40		1,560
(6) F. Black: loan			5,000	(10) Motor expenses		81	
(12) J. Pie	2		88	(15) Wages		580	
(18) A. Pony	27		513	(21) Cash			400
(18) B. Line & Son	35		665	(24) Drawings		200	
(18) T. Owen	26		494	(25) W. Peat	5	155	
(21) Bank		400		(29) Fixtures			720
(31) Commission			120	(31) Balances c/d		4	10,224
(31) Total for month	140	1,020	14,972		87	1,020	14,972

Discounts allowed 140

Discounts received 87

9.5

Bank

	£		£
Balance b/d	40,000	Real Fine Ales	31,160
K. Hoskin	18,000	R. Goldthwaite	1,000
G. Carnegie	4,000	Balance c/d	29,840
	62,000		62,000
Balance b/d	29,840		

Discounts allowed

	£		£
K. Hoskin	2,000	Balance c/d	2,000

K. Hoskin

	£		£
Balance b/d	20,000	Bank	18,000
		Discount	2,000
	20,000		20,000

G. Carnegie

	£		£
Balance b/d	4,000	Bank	4,000

Discount received

	£		£
Balance c/d	1,640	Real Fine Ales	1,640

G. Vollmers

	£		£
Balance b/d	8,000	Bad debts expense	8,000

Real Fine Ales

	£		£
Bank	31,160	Balance b/d	32,800
Discount	1,640		
	32,800		32,800

Bad debts expense

	£		£
G. Volmers	8,000	Balance c/d	8,000

R. Goldthwaite

	£		£
Bank	1,000	Balance b/d	1,000

Petty Cash Book

Receipts		Total	Cleaning	Motor Expenses	Postage	Stationery	Travelling
300	(1) Cash						
	(2) Postage	18			18		
	(3) Travelling	12					12
	(4) Cleaning	15	15				
	(7) Petrol	22		22			
	(8) Travelling	25					25
	(9) Stationery	17				17	
	(11) Cleaning	18	18				
	(14) Postage	5			5		
	(15) Travelling	8					8
	(18) Stationery	9				9	
	(18) Cleaning	23	23				
	(20) Postage	13			13		
	(24) Motor service	43		43			
	(26) Petrol	18		18			
	(27) Cleaning	21	21				
	(29) Postage	5			5		
	(30) Petrol	14		14			
		286	77	97	41	26	45
286	(31) Cash						
	(31) Balance c/d	300					
586		586					

10.1

(a)–(c) See text.

(d) See text.

10.2
(a)

Petty Cash Book (June 2020)

Receipts		Total	Travel	Postage & stationery	Cleaning	Refreshments
32.17	(1) Balance b/d					
117.83	(2) Cash					
	(5) Postage stamps	17.57		17.57		
	(9) Coffee and biscuits	11.48				11.48
	(13) Taxi fares	18.00	18.00			
	(18) Stationery	22.16		22.16		
	(22) Cleaning	14.38			14.38	
	(23) Teabags	9.95				9.95
	(28) Train fares	38.75	38.75			
		132.29	56.75	39.73	14.38	21.43
132.29	(30) Cash	150.00				
282.29	(1) Balance c/d	282.29				

10.4 Fine Teas

Receipts	Date	Details	Total	Travel	Stationery	Postage	Miscellaneous	Repairs/Replacement
24.37	May 1	Balance b/d						
115.63	1	Cash						
	1	Bus fares	0.41	0.41				
	2	Stationery	2.35		2.35			
	4	Bus fares	0.30	0.30				
	7	Postage	6.50			6.50		
	7	Trade journal	0.95				0.95	
	8	Bus fares	0.64	0.64				
	11	Highlighter pens	1.29		1.29			
	12	Lightbulbs	5.42					5.42
	14	Parcel	3.45			3.45		
	15	Paper-clips	0.42		0.42			
	15	Newspaper	2.00				2.00	
	16	Photocopier repair	16.80					16.80
	19	Postage	1.50			1.50		
	20	Drawing pins	0.38		0.38			
	21	Train fare	5.40	5.40				
	22	Photo-paper	5.63		5.63			
	23	Display decorations	3.07				3.07	
	23	Pencil sharpener	1.14		1.14			
	25	Wrapping paper	0.78				0.78	
	27	String	0.61				0.61	
	27	Sellotape	0.75		0.75			
	27	Pens	0.46		0.46			
	28	Replacement part for printer	13.66					13.66
140.00	31	Bus fares	2.09	2.09				
64.00			76.00	8.84	12.42	11.45	7.41	35.88
76.00	31	Balance c/d	64.00					
140.00	June 1	Balance b/d	140.00					
	1	Cash						

(b) Briefly: to keep detail out of the cash book, to reduce the number of postings to expense accounts, and to enable the task of handling petty cash to be delegated to someone other than the main cashier. See text for more details.

(c) Notes and coins held on the premises will be extremely tempting to employees who may be inclined towards theft and fraud. If petty cash is not carefully monitored and controlled there will be a high risk of money being stolen; repeated thefts (even of small amounts) could amount to significant losses for the business.

(d) Advantages include:

(i) At any point in time, it is possible to check whether the amount of petty cash held plus the vouchers is equal to the imprest. If this is checked daily, for example, then if any cash is unaccounted for it will be detected immediately.

(ii) Total petty cash expenditure can be 'capped' because the petty cashier cannot disburse more than the float amount during any given period.

(iii) It helps ensure that the petty cash book will be kept up to date because the float amount should not be reimbursed until the vouchers for the period have been analysed and the petty cash book has been written-up.

(iv) The imprest system normally accommodates further controls such as specifying a maximum amount for any individual cash payment; ensuring that all vouchers are signed by a responsible person to authorise each payment; and (after the cash has been spent) attaching the receipt/bill for the payment to support each item of expenditure.

11.1

Sales Day Book

(1) P. Ryan	700
(3) T. Lee	320
(6) B. Cox	50
(10) P. Ryan	220
(17) J. Lock	960
(19) M. Gore	220
(27) C. Chen	95
(31) G. West	365
	2,930

Sales Ledger

P. Ryan			
(1) Sales	700		
(10) Sales	220		
T. Lee			
(3) Sales	320		
B. Cox			
(6) Sales	50		
J. Lock			
(17) Sales	960		
M. Gore			
(19) Sales	220		
C. Chen			
(27) Sales	95		
G. West			
(31) Sales	365		

General Ledger

Sales Account

(31) Total for month	2,930

11.3

Workings of invoices:

(1) F. Gray	3 rolls white tape × 10 =	30	
	5 sheets blue cotton × 6 =	30	
	1 dress length × 20 =	20	
		80	
	Less trade discount 25%	20	
			60
(4) A. Gray	6 rolls white tape × 10 =	60	
	30 metres green felt × 4 =	120	
		180	
	Less trade discount 33 1/3%	60	
			120
(8) E. Hines	1 dress length black silk × 20 =		20
(20) M. Allen	10 rolls white tape × 10 =	100	
	6 sheets blue cotton × 6 =	36	
	3 dress lengths black silk × 20 =	60	
	11 metres green felt × 4 =	44	
		240	
	Less trade discount 25%	60	
			180

(31) B. Cooper	12 rolls white tape × 10 =	120	
	14 sheets blue cotton × 6 =	84	
	9 metres green felt × 4 =	36	
		240	
	Less trade discount 33 1/3%	80	
			160

Sales Day Book

(1) F. Gray	60
(4) A. Gray	120
(8) E. Hines	20
(20) M. Allen	180
(31) B. Cooper	160
	540

Sales Ledger

F. Gray			
(1) Sales	60		
A. Gray			
(4) Sales	120		
E. Hines			
(8) Sales	20		
M. Allen			
(20) Sales	180		
B. Cooper			
(31) Sales	160		

General Ledger

Sales Account

(31) Total for month	540

11.5

Workings of purchases invoices

(1) A. Bell	4 DVD players × 30 =	120	
	3 mini hi-fi units × 180 =	540	
		660	
	Less trade discount 25%	165	
			495
(3) C. Gray	2 washing machines × 310 =	620	
	5 vacuum cleaners × 60 =	300	
	2 dishwashers × 190 =	380	
		1,300	
	Less trade discount 20%	260	
			1,040
(15) C. Donald	1 home ent. centre × 400 =	400	
	2 washing machines × 310 =	620	
		1,020	
	Less trade discount 25%	255	
			765
(20) F. Perry	6 external 1TB drives × 45	270	
	Less trade discount 33 1/3%	90	
			180
(30) S. Turner	4 dishwashers × 215	860	
	Less trade discount 20%	172	
			688

11.5 (*Cont'd*)

Purchases Day Book

(1) A. Bell		495
(3) C. Gray		1,040
(15) C. Donald		765
(20) F. Perry		180
(30) S. Turner		688
		3,168

(31) Total for month

General Ledger
Purchases Account

(31) 3,168

Purchases Ledger

A. Bell
(1) Purchases 495

C. Gray
(1) Purchases 1,040

C. Donald
(3) Purchases 765

F. Perry
(15) Purchases 180

S. Turner
(20) Purchases 688
(30) Purchases

11.7 **Purchases Day Book**

(1) Smith Stores		90
(23) C. Kelly		105
(31) J. Hamilton		180
		375

Purchases Ledger

Smith Stores
(1) Purchases 90

C. Kelly
(23) Purchases 105

J. Hamilton
(31) Purchases 180

General Ledger
Purchases Account
(31) Total for Month 375

Purchases Account

Sales Day Book

(8) A. Grantley		72
(15) A. Henry		240
(24) D. Sangster		81
		393

Sales Ledger

A. Grantley
(8) Sales 72

A. Henry
(15) Sales 240

D. Sangster
(24) Sales 81

General Ledger
Sales Account
(31) Total for month 393

11.9 (*a*) **Sales Day Book**

May 1	J. Swift		144
1	D. Brown		448
23	M. Peat		261
			853

(*b*)

Sales Ledger
J. Swift
May 1 Sales 144

D. Brown
May 1 Sales 448

M. Peat
May 23 Sales 261

Purchases Day Book

May 9	L. Syme		180
16	J. Wood		138
31	R. Gold		230
			548

Purchases Ledger
L. Syme
May 9 Purchases 180

J. Wood
May 16 Purchases 138

R. Gold
May 31 Purchases 230

(*c*)

Sales
May 31 Credit sales for the month 853

Purchases
May 31 Credit purchases for the month 548

(*d*) See text.

11.10 **Purchases Day Book**

(1) S. Dodd	216
(4) B. Line	324
(4) F. Town	322
(4) R. Pace	64
(4) T. Pang	130
(10) F. Town	90
(18) D. Ince	230
(18) P. Tago	310
(18) R. Scott	405
(18) N. Auld	220
(31) R. Pace	174
(31) J. Marsh	170
	2,655

Returns Outwards Day Book

(7) S. Dodd	58
(7) B. Line	63
(25) P. Tago	140
(25) F. Town	47
	308

Purchases Ledger

S. Dodd
(7) Returns 58 (1) Purchases 216

B. Line
(7) Returns 63 (4) Purchases 324

F. Town
(25) Returns 47 (4) Purchases 322
(10) Purchases 90

R. Pace
(4) Purchases 64
(31) Purchases 174

T. Pang
(4) Purchases 130

D. Ince
(18) Purchases 230

P. Tago
(25) Returns 140 (18) Purchases 310

R. Scott
(18) Purchases 405

N. Auld
(18) Purchases 220

J. Marsh
(31) Purchases 170

General Ledger

Purchases
2,655

Returns Outwards
(31) Total for month 308

(31) Total for month 2,655

11.12

Sales Day Book

(1)	T. Thompson	56
(1)	L. Rodriguez	148
(1)	K. Barton	145
(7)	K. Kelly	89
(7)	N. Mendes	78
(7)	N. Lee	257
(24)	K. Mohammed	57
(24)	K. Kelly	65
(24)	O. Green	112
(31)	N. Lee	55
		1,062

Purchases Day Book

(3)	P. Potter	144
(3)	H. Harris	25
(3)	B. Spencer	76
(9)	B. Perkins	24
(9)	H. Harris	58
(9)	H. Miles	123
(17)	H. Harris	54
(17)	B. Perkins	65
(17)	L. Nixon	75
		644

Returns Inwards Day Book

(14)	T. Thompson	5
(14)	K. Barton	11
(14)	K. Kelly	14
(28)	N. Mendes	24
		54

Returns Outwards Day Book

(11)	P. Potter	12
(11)	B. Spencer	22
(20)	B. Spencer	14
		48

Sales Ledger

T. Thompson
(1) Sales 56   (14) Returns 5

L. Rodriguez
(1) Sales 148

K. Barton
(1) Sales 145   (14) Returns 11

K. Kelly
(7) Sales 89   (14) Returns 14
(24) Sales 65

N. Mendes
(7) Sales 78   (28) Returns 24

N. Lee
(7) Sales 257
(31) Sales 55

K. Mohammed
(24) Sales 57

O. Green
(24) Sales 112

Purchases Ledger

P. Potter
(11) Returns 12   (3) Purchases 144

H. Harris
(3) Purchases 25
(9) Purchases 58
(17) Purchases 54

B. Spencer
(11) Returns 22   (3) Purchases 76
(20) Returns 14

B. Perkins
(9) Purchases 24
(17) Purchases 65

H. Miles
(9) Purchases 123

L. Nixon
(17) Purchases 75

General Ledger

Purchases
(31) Total for month 644

Returns Inwards
(31) Total for month 54

Sales
(31) Total for month 1,062

Returns Outwards
(31) Total for month 48

12.1

(a)	Motorbike	Dr	5,500	:	Lakeside Garage	Cr 5,500
(b)	Bad debts	Dr	347	:	T. Reason	Cr 347
(c)	UL Furniture Ltd	Dr	600	:	Office chairs	Cr 600
(d)	(i) Bank	Dr	190	:	J. Day	Cr 190
	(ii) Bad debts	Dr	110	:	J. Day	Cr 110
(e)	Drawings	Dr	60	:	Purchases	Cr 60
(f)	Drawings	Dr	40	:	Insurance	Cr 40
(g)	Trailer	Dr	1,700	:	C-Land Ltd	Cr 1,700

12.3

The Journal

(1)	Premises	34,000	
	Van	5,125	
	Fixtures	810	
	Inventory	6,390	
	Accounts receivable:		
	P. Mullen	140	
	F. Lane	310	
	Bank	6,240	
	Cash	560	
	Accounts payable:		
	S. Hood		215
	J. Brown		640
	Capital		52,720
		53,575	53,575
(14)	Van	4,850	
	Abel Motors		4,850

Purchases Day Book

(2)	S. Hood	145
(2)	D. Main	206
(2)	W. Tone	96
(2)	R. Foot	66
(22)	L. Mole	183
(22)	W. Wright	191
		887

Sales Day Book

(3)	J. Wilson	112
(3)	T. Cole	164
(3)	F. Syme	208
(3)	J. Allen	91
(3)	P. White	242
(3)	F. Lane	90
(9)	T. Cole	68
(9)	J. Fox	131
		1,106

Returns Outwards Day Book

(19)	R. Foot	6

Returns Inwards Day Book

(11)	J. Wilson	32
(11)	F. Syme	48
		80

12.3 (Cont'd)

Cash Book

	Disct	Cash	Bank		Disct	Cash	Bank
(1) Balances b/d		560	6,240	(1) Storage			40
(16) P. Mullen	7		133	(4) Motor expenses		60	
(16) F. Lane	20		380	(7) Drawings		150	
(16) J. Wilson	4		76	(24) S. Hood	18		342
(16) F. Syme	8		152	(24) J. Brown	32		608
				(24) R. Foot	3		57
				(27) Salaries			740
				(30) Business rates			140
				(31) Abel Motors			4,850
				(31) Balance c/d		350	204
	39	560	6,981		53	560	6,981

Trial Balance as at 31 May 2020

	Dr	Cr
D. Main		206
W. Tone		96
L. Mole		183
W. Wright		191
T. Cole	232	
J. Allen	91	
P. White	242	
J. Fox	131	
Capital		52,720
Storage	40	
Motor expenses	60	
Drawings	150	
Salaries	740	
Business rates	140	
Sales		1,106
Purchases	887	
Returns inwards	80	
Returns outwards		6
Premises	34,000	
Vans	9,975	
Fixtures	810	
Inventory	6,390	
Discounts allowed	39	
Discounts received		53
Bank	204	
Cash	350	
	54,561	54,561

Purchases Ledger

W. Wright

			(22) Purchases	191

L. Mole

			(22) Purchases	183

S. Hood

(24) Bank & disc	360	(1) Bal b/d	215
		(2) Purchases	145
	360		360

J. Brown

(24) Bank & disc	640	(1) Balance b/d	640

D. Main

			(2) Purchases	206

W. Tone

			(2) Purchases	96

R. Foot

(19) Returns	6	(2) Purchases	66
(24) Bank & disc	60		
	66		66

Sales Ledger

P. Mullen

(1) Bal b/d	140	(16) Bank & disct	140

F. Lane

(1) Bal b/d	310	(16) Bank & disct	400
(3) Sales	90		
	400		400

J. Wilson

(3) Sales	112	(11) Returns	32
		(16) Bank & disct	80
	112		112

T. Cole

(3) Sales	164		
(9) Sales	68		

F. Syme

(3) Sales	208	(11) Returns	48
		(16) Bank & disct	160
	208		208

J. Allen

(3) Sales	91		

P. White

(3) Sales	242		

J. Fox

(9) Sales	131		

General Ledger

Capital

			(1) Bal b/d	52,720

Storage

(1) Bank	40		

Motor Expenses

(4) Cash	60		

Drawings

(7) Cash	150		

Salaries

(27) Bank	740		

Business rates

(30) Bank	140		

Sales

			(31) Total for month	1,106

Purchases

(31) Total for month	887		

Return Inwards

(31) Total for month	80		

Return Outwards

			(31) Total for month	6

Premises

(1) Bal b/d	34,000		

Vans

(1) Bal b/d	5,125		
(14) Abel Motors	4,850		

Fixtures

(1) Bal b/d	810		

Inventory

(1) Bal b/d	6,390		

Discounts allowed

(31) Total for month	39		

Discounts Received

			(31) Total for month	53

Abel Motors

(31) Bank	4,850	(14) Van	4,850

13.1

(a) Style of invoice will vary.

Calculations:

	£
5 sets of golf clubs × £1,250	6,250
500 golf balls at £25 per 10 balls	1,250
5 golf bags at £370 per bag	1,850
	9,350
Less trade discount 30%	(2,805)
	6,545
Add VAT 20%	1,309
	7,854

(b)

Sales ledger of A. Cook

B. Pitt

	£
	7,854

Purchases ledger of B. Pitt

A. Cook

2020	£
March 1 Purchases	7,854

2020	
March 1 Sales	7,854

13.3

Sales Day Book

2019		Net	VAT
March 2	G. Bush	430	86
6	A. Gray	290	58
14	L. Rowe	560	112
31	S. Pegg	320	64
		1,600	320

Sales Ledger

G. Bush

(1) Sales 516

A. Gray

(8) Sales 348

L. Rowe

(19) Sales 672

S. Pegg

(31) Sales 384

General Ledger

Sales

(31) Credit sales for the month 1,600

Output VAT

(31) Sales Day Book: VAT content 320

13.4

Sales Day Book

	Net	VAT
(1) J. Royce	290	58
(4) D. Player and Co	440	88
(16) D. Player and Co	170	34
(31) N. Foster	110	22
	1,010	202

Purchases Day Book

	Net	VAT
(10) B. Hunter	360	72
(10) R. Dixon Ltd	230	46
(14) G. Melly	80	16
(23) G. Gooch	120	24
	790	158

Sales Ledger

J. Royce

(1) Sales 348

D. Player and Co

(4) Sales 528

(16) Sales 204

N. Foster

(31) Sales 132

Purchases Ledger

B. Hunter

(10) Purchases 432

R. Dixon Ltd

(10) Purchases 276

G. Melly

(14) Purchases 96

G. Gooch

(23) Purchases 144

General Ledger

Sales

(31) Credit sales for month 1,010

Purchases

(31) Credit purchases for month 790

Output VAT

(31) VAT in Sales Day Book 202

Input VAT

(31) VAT in Purchases Day Book 158

13.5

	£	£
Debit Bank		14,232
Credit Sales	11,860	
Credit Output VAT (20% of net sales value)	2,372	

13.6

		£
Output VAT payable to HMRC	£117,900 net × 20% VAT =	23,580
Input VAT reclaimable from HMRC	£88,140 including VAT × 1/6 =	(14,690)
Amount to be paid by the business to HMRC		8,890

13.8

£15 × 5/6 = £12.50 is net price excluding VAT at 20%.
Therefore £12.50 × 1.175 = £14.69 is the new price.

13.10

(a)

Sales Day Book

Date	Name and Details	List price less trade discount £		VAT £		Total £	
		£	p	£	p	£	p
2019 Mar	9 Neville's Electrical	576	–	57	60	633	60
	17 Maltby plc	3,000	–	300	–	3,300	–
	29 Neville's Electrical	368	–	36	80	404	80
		3,944	–	394	40	4,338	40

(b)

Neville's Electrical

2019		
Mar	9 Sales	633.60
	29 Sales	404.80

Maltby plc

2019		
Mar	17 Sales	3,300.00

Sales

2019		
Mar 31	Sales Day Book	3,944.00

Output VAT

2019		
Mar 31	Sales Day Book	394.40

(c)

Trial Balance as at 31 March 2019

	Dr	Cr
Neville's Electrical	1,038.40	
Maltby plc	3,300.00	
Sales		3,944.00
Output VAT		394.40
	4,338.40	4,338.40

14.1

I. Lamb

Income Statement for the year ended 31 October 2019

	£	£
Sales		100,250
Less Cost of goods sold:		
Purchases	60,400	
Less Closing inventory	15,600	44,800
Gross profit		55,450
Less Expenses:		
Salaries	29,300	
Motor expenses	1,200	
Rent	950	
Insurance	150	
General expenses	85	31,685
Net profit		23,765

14.2

G. Foot

Income Statement for the year ended 30 June 2019

	£	£
Sales		266,000
Less Cost of goods sold:		
Purchases	154,000	
Less Closing inventory	18,000	136,000
Gross profit		130,000
Less Expenses:		
Salaries and wages	52,000	
Rent	3,800	
Lighting and heating	700	
Insurance	3,000	
Motor expenses	4,600	
Sundry expenses	300	64,400
Net profit		65,600

14.5

(a)

Capital

30.9	Bal c/d	750		1.9	Capital...	Bank	750
		__750__					__750__
				1.10	Bal b/d		750

Loan – LloydWest

30.9	Bal c/d	3,000		3.9	Bank	3,000
		__3,000__				__3,000__
				1.10	Bal b/d	3,000

Van hire

5.9	Bank	320		30.9	Bal c/d	320
		__320__				__320__
1.10	Bal b/d	320				

Purchases

9.9	Bank	760				
11.9	J. Collins	570				
17.9	M. Pembridge	890		30.9	Bal c/d	2,220
		__2,220__				__2,220__
1.10	Bal b/d	2,220				

Sales

30.9	Bal c/d	2,700		13.9	Bank	930
				19.9	E. Barrett	1,770
		__2,700__				__2,700__
				1.10	Bal b/d	2,700

M. Pembridge

30.9	Bal c/d	890		17.9	Purchases	890
		__890__				__890__
				1.10	Bal b/d	890

Drawings

25.9	Bank	280		30.9	Bal c/d	280
		__280__				__280__
1.10	Bal b/d	280				

Bank

1.9	Capital	750		5.9	Van hire	320
3.9	Loan – LW	3,000		7.9	IT equip	2,200
13.9	Sales	930		9.9	Purchases	760
23.9	E. Barrett	590		21.9	J. Collins	450
				25.9	Drawings	280
				27.9	Wages	410
				30.9	Bal c/d	850
		__5,270__				__5,270__
1.10	Bal b/d	850				

IT Equipment

7.9	Bank	2,200		30.9	Bal c/d	2,200
		__2,200__				__2,200__
1.10	Bal b/d	2,200				

J. Collins

15.9	Returns out	120		11.9	Purchases	570
21.9	Bank	450				
		__570__				__570__

Returns outwards

30.9	Bal c/d	120		15.9	J. Collins	120
		__120__				__120__
				1.10	Bal b/d	120

E. Barrett

19.9	Sales	1,770		23.9	Bank	590
				30.9	Bal c/d	1,180
		__1,770__				__1,770__
1.10	Bal b/d	1,180				

Wages

27.9	Bank	410		30.9	Bal c/d	410
		__410__				__410__
1.10	Bal b/d	410				

(b)

Trial Balance at 30 September

	Debit £	Credit £
Capital		750
Bank	850	
Loan – LloydWest		3,000
Van hire	320	
IT equipment	2,200	
Purchases	2,220	
Sales		2,700
Returns outwards		120
M. Pembridge		890
E. Barrett	1,180	
Drawings	280	
Wages	410	
	__7,460__	__7,460__

(c)

Income Statement for the month ended 30 September

	£	£
Sales		2,700
Less Cost of goods sold		
Opening inventory	0	
Purchases	2,220	
Less Returns outwards	(120)	
Less Closing inventory	(570)	(1,530)
Gross profit		1,170
Less Expenses		
Van hire	320	
Wages	410	(730)
Net profit		440

15.1

I. Lamb
Balance Sheet as at 31 October 2019

Non-current assets		
Premises	47,800	
Motor vehicles	8,600	56,400
Current assets		
Inventory	15,600	
Accounts receivable	13,400	
Bank	8,200	
Cash	300	
	37,500	
		93,900
Current liabilities		
Accounts payable		8,800
		85,100
Capital		
Opening balance		65,535
Add Net profit		23,765
		89,300
Less Drawings		4,200
		85,100

15.2

G. Foot
Balance Sheet as at 30 June 2019

Non-current assets		
Buildings	84,800	
Fixtures	2,000	
Vans	16,000	102,800
Current assets		
Inventory	18,000	
Accounts receivable	31,200	
Bank	15,000	64,200
		167,000
Less Current liabilities		
Accounts payable		16,000
		151,000
Capital		
Opening balance		114,000
Add Net profit		65,600
		179,600
Less Drawings		28,600
		151,000

15.5

T. Smith
Balance Sheet as at 31 July 2020

Non-current assets		
Premises		160,000
Current assets		
Inventory	50,000	
Accounts receivable	4,000	
Cash and bank	8,300	62,300
		222,300
Current liabilities		
Accounts payable	14,000	
Non-current liability		
Mortgage loan	120,000	(134,000)
		88,300
Capital		
Opening balance		60,000
Capital introduced		8,000
Net profit		45,300
		113,300
Less Drawings		25,000
		88,300

15.7

Royston
Balance Sheet as at 30 September

	£	£
Non-current assets		
IT equipment		2,200
Current assets		
Inventory	570	
Accounts receivable	1,180	
Bank	850	2,600
		4,800
Current liabilities		
Accounts payable		(890)
Non-current liabilities		
Loan		(3,000)
Net assets		910
Opening capital		750
Add Profit for the month		440
Less Drawings for the month		(280)
Closing capital		910

16.1

B. Willis
Trading account part of the Income Statement for the year ending 31 January 2019

Sales		249,000
Less Returns in		7,470
		241,530
Less Cost of goods sold:		
Purchases	168,300	
Less Returns out	1,390	
	166,910	
Carriage inwards	3,470	
	170,380	
Less Closing inventory	25,630	144,750
Gross profit		96,780

16.3

G. Still
Income Statement for the year ending 30 September 2020

Sales		380,400
Less Returns in		1,540
		378,860
Less Cost of goods sold:		
Opening inventory		41,600
Add Purchases	188,430	
Less Returns out	3,410	
	185,020	
Carriage inwards	3,700	
		230,320
Less Closing inventory		44,780
		185,540
Gross profit		193,320
Less Expenses:		
Salaries and wages	61,400	
Warehouse rent	3,700	
Carriage out	2,100	
Insurance	1,356	
Motor expenses	1,910	
Office expenses	412	
Lighting and heating	894	
General expenses	245	72,017
Net profit		121,303

Balance Sheet as at 30 September 2020

Non-current assets		
Premises		92,000
Fixtures and fittings		1,900
Motor vehicles		13,400
		107,300
Current assets		
Inventory		44,780
Accounts receivable		42,560
Bank		5,106
		92,446
		199,746
Current liabilities		
Accounts payable		(31,600)
		168,146
Capital		
Opening balance		68,843
Add Net profit		121,303
		190,146
Less Drawings		22,000
		168,146

16.4

F. Sorley
Income Statement for the year ending 30 April 2020

Sales		210,420
Less Returns in		4,900
		205,520
Less Cost of goods sold:		
Opening inventory		9,410
Add Purchases	108,680	
Less Returns out	3,720	
	104,960	
Carriage inwards	840	
	115,210	
Less Closing inventory	11,290	103,920
Gross profit		101,600
Less Expenses:		
Salaries and wages	41,800	
Motor expenses	912	
Rent	6,800	
Carriage out	1,115	
Sundry expenses	318	50,945
Net profit		50,655

16.4 (Cont'd)

Balance Sheet as at 30 April 2020

Non-current assets		
Fixtures and fittings		912
Motor vehicles		14,400
		15,312
Current assets		
Inventory	11,290	
Accounts receivable	23,200	
Bank	4,100	
Cash	240	
	38,830	
	54,142	
Less Current liabilities		
Accounts payable		14,100
		40,042
Capital		
Opening balance		18,827
Add Net profit		50,655
		69,482
Less Drawings		29,440
		40,042

16.7 (a)

Cash

1.8	Capital	1,000	2.8	Bank	900
19.8	Sales	28	7.8	Purchs	55
			31.8	Bal c/d	73
		1,028			1,028
1.9	Bal b/d	73			

Bank

2.8	Cash	900	5.8	Vehicles	500
24.8	D. Watson	100	29.8	S. Holmes	24
			30.8	Wages	30
			31.8	Kingston	150
			31.8	Bal c/d	296
		1,000			1,000
1.9	Bal b/d	296			

Purchases

4.8	S. Holmes	78	11.8	Drawings	22
7.8	Cash	55	31.8	Bal c/d	111
		133			133
1.9	Bal b/d	111			

Sales

			10.8	D. Moore	98
31.8	Bal c/d	126	19.8	Cash	28
		126			126
			1.9	Bal b/d	126

Fixtures & fittings

22.8	Kingston	150	31.8	Bal c/d	150
1.9	Bal b/d	150			

Kingston Equipt Co

31.8	Bank	150	22.8	F&F	150
		150			150

Drawings

11.8	Purchases	22	31.8	Bal c/d	22
		22			22
1.9	Ba. b/d	22			

Capital

31.8	Bal c/d	1,000	1.8	Cash	1,000
		1,000			1,000
			1.9	Bal b/d	1,000

S. Holmes

12.8	Rets out	18	4.8	Purchases	78
29.8	Bank	24			
31.8	Bal c/d	36			
		78			78
			1.9	Bal b/d	36

Motor vehicles

5.8	Bank	500	31.8	Bal c/d	500
		500			500
1.9	Bal b/d	500			

D. Moore

10.8	Sales	98	31.8	Bal c/d	98
		98			98
1.9	Bal b/d	98			

Loan a/c: D. Watson

31.8	Bal c/d	100	24.8	Bank	100
		100			100
			1.9	Bal b/d	100

Returns outwards

31.8	Bal c/d	18	12.8	S. Holmes	18
		18			18
			1.9	Bal b/d	18

Wages

30.8	Bank	30	31.8	Bal c/d	30
		30			30
1.9	Bal b/d	30			

(b)

Trial balance as at 31 August:

	Debit	Credit
	£	£
Cash	73	
Capital		1,000
Bank	296	
S. Holmes		36
Purchases	111	
Motor vehicles	500	
Sales		126
D. Moore	98	
Fixtures & fittings	150	
Loan a/c: D. Watson		100
Returns outwards		18
Drawings	22	
Wages	30	
	1,280	1,280

16.7 (Cont'd)

(c) A. Joel

Income Statement for the month ended 31 August

	£	£
Sales		126
Less Cost of goods sold:		
Opening inventory	–	
Add Purchases	111	
less Returns outwards	(18)	
less Closing inventory	(28)	(65)
Gross profit		61
Less Expenses:		
Wages		(30)
Net profit		31

(d) A. Joel Balance Sheet as at 31 August

	£	£
Non-current assets		
Fixtures		150
Vehicles		500
		650
Current assets		
Inventory	28	
Receivables	98	
Bank	296	
Cash	73	
		495
Total assets		1,145
Current liabilities		
Payables		(36)
Non-current liabilities: Loan		(100)
Net assets		1,009
Opening capital		1,000
Add Net profit for the month		31
Less Drawings		(22)
Closing capital		1,009

16.9

Tangle

Income Statement for the year ending 30 April 2019

	£	£
Sales		71,600
Less Cost of sales		
Purchases	29,050	
Less Closing inventory	8,000	
		21,050
		50,550
Gross profit		
Less Expenses:		
Salaries	14,650	
Motor expenses	1,860	
Rent and business rates	2,500	
Insurance – Buildings	1,500	
– Vehicles	2,400	
		22,910
Net profit		27,640

Balance Sheet as at 30 April 2019

	£	£
Non-current assets		
Motor vehicles		20,000
Fixtures		35,000
		55,000
Current assets		
Inventory	8,000	
Accounts receivable	23,450	
Cash	1,000	
		32,450
		87,450
Less Current liabilities		
Accounts payable	19,500	
Bank	2,500	
	22,000	
Non-current liabilities:		
Loan	30,000	
		(52,000)
		35,450
Capital		
Opening balance	31,810	
Net profit	27,640	
	59,450	
Less Drawings	24,000	
		35,450

17.1
(a) Per text.
(b) Capital: (i), (ii), machine part of (v), (vi).
Revenue: (iii), (iv), drinks part of (v).

17.3
Capital: (a), (c), (e), (g); Revenue: (b), (d), (f).

17.5
Capital: (a), (b), (e).

17.7
Capital: (a), (c), (d), (f), (i), (l); Revenue: (b), (e), (g), (h), (i), (k).

17.9
£25,000 + 510 + 920 + 670 + 430 + 750 + 240 = £28,520

17.11

Wooden store shed

Balance b/d	850	Wooden store shed disposal	850

Office buildings

Balance b/d	179,500
Wages	109
Materials	109

Office buildings repairs

Wages	181
Materials	351

New brick-built store

Wooden store shed disposal	100
Materials	4,750
Wages	3,510
Direct expenses	85

Wooden store shed disposal

Wooden store shed	850	Bank	180
Bank	265	New store	100

17.13
Classifying something as a capital expense rather than a revenue expense increases non-current assets, reduces expenses and so increases net profit (and so also increases capital). This makes the business look more profitable than it would have been had the expenditure been classified instead as revenue expenditure. It also makes it look in a better financial state than it would have been (as non-current assets have increased). Misclassifying revenue expenditure as capital expenditure is misleading to users of the financial statements.

18.1
(i) FIFO Closing Inventory 280 × £32 = £8,960
(ii)

LIFO	Received	Issued	Inventory after each transaction	
Mar	400 × £30		400 × £30	12,000
Sept	300 × £32		400 × £30	12,000
			300 × £32	9,600
				21,600
Dec		420 × £40	280 × £30	8,400

(iii)

AVCO	Received	Issued	Average cost per unit inventory held	No. of units in inventory	Total value of inventory
Mar	400 × £30		£30	400	£12,000
Sept	300 × £32		£30.86	700	£21,600
Dec		420	£30.86	280	£8,641*

*rounded to nearest £

18.2

Trading Account for the year ending 31 December

	FIFO	LIFO	AVCO
Sales	16,800	16,800	16,800
Less Cost of sales			
Purchases	21,600	21,600	21,600
Less Closing inventory	8,960	8,400	8,641
	(12,640)	(13,200)	(12,959)
Gross profit	4,160	3,600	3,841

18.5
(a) (dates and calculations omitted)

Cash

Loan: School fund	200.00	Purchases	53.50
Sales	51.36		

Purchases

Cash	51.36

Sales

Cash	53.50

(b) Inventory valuation:

Break × 16p =	34	5.44
Brunch × 12p =	15	1.80
		7.24

Inventory

Trading account	7.24

18.5 (Cont'd)

(c)

Broadway School
Trading Account for the month ending 31 December 2019

Sales		53.50
Less Cost of sales		
Purchases	51.36	
Less Closing inventory	7.24	
		44.12
Gross profit		9.38

(d)

	Break	Brunch
Purchases (units)	240	108
Less Sold	200	90
Inventory should have been	40	18
Actual inventory	34	15
Missing items	6	3

If there have been no arithmetical errors, one can only assume that someone has stolen 6 Breaks and 3 Brunches.

18.6

(This is a brief answer showing the main points to be covered. In the examination the answer should be in report form and elaborated.)

1 For Charles Gray

(i) The concept of prudence says that inventory should be valued at lower of cost or net realisable value. As 50% of the retail price £375 is lower than cost £560, then £375 will be taken as net realisable value and used for inventory valuation.

(ii) The sale has not taken place by 30 April 2019. The prudence concept does not anticipate profits and therefore the sale will not be assumed. The gun should therefore be included in inventory, at cost price £560.

2 For Jean Kim

It appears that it is doubtful if the business can still be treated as a going concern.

If the final decision is that the business cannot continue, then the inventory valuation should be £510 each, as this is less than cost, with a further overall deduction of auction fees and expenses £300.

3 For Peter Fox

Inventory must be valued at the lower of cost or net realisable value in this case.

The cost to be used is the *cost* for Peter Fox. The historical cost concept requires that businesses use the actual original cost incurred by them in the past, not a cost that similar businesses might have paid for similar items. It is irrelevant what the cost may be for other distributors.

It would also be against the convention of consistency to adopt a different method. The consistency applies to Peter Fox, it is not a case of consistency with other businesses. Using selling prices as a basis is not acceptable to the vast majority of businesses.

18.8

(a) In one respect the consistency convention is not applied, as at one year end the inventory may be shown at cost whereas the next year end may see inventory valued at net realisable value.

On the other hand, as it is prudent to take the lower of cost or net realisable value, it can be said to be consistently prudent to consistently take the lower figure.

(b) Being prudent can be said to be an advantage. For instance, a shareholder can know that inventory is not overvalued: if it were, it would give him a false picture of his investment.

Someone to whom money is owed, such as a creditor, will know that the inventory in the balance sheet is realisable at least at that figure.

It is the knowledge that profits are not being overstated as a result of excessive values placed on inventory that gives outside parties confidence to rely on reported profits.

18.9

Cobden Ltd
Computation of inventory as at 31 May 2019

	Increase	Decrease
(a) No adjustment needed		
Cost lower than net realisable value	–	–
(b) Reduction to net realisable value		130
(c) Arithmetic corrected		126
(d) Omitted items	72	9
(e) Transposition error	2,010	
(f) Goods omitted	638	
(g) Hired item not to be included		347
(h) Samples to be excluded		63
(i) Sale or return items reduced to cost		184
(j) Goods held simply on sale or return		267
	2,720	1,126

Net increase		1,594
Inventory as originally computed		87,612
		89,206

20.1

Bad Debts

2020			2020		
May 31	T. Fox	840	Dec 31	Profit and loss	2,490
Sep 30	G. Pegg	930			
Nov 30	G. Swan	720			
		2,490			2,490

20.1 (*Cont'd*)

Allowance for doubtful debts

		2020	
		Dec 31 Profit and loss	947

Income Statement (extracts)

Bad debts	2,490
Increase in allowance for doubtful debts	947

Balance Sheet as at 31 December 2020 (extract)

Accounts receivable		47,350
Less: Allowance for doubtful debts		947
		46,403

20.2
(i)

Bad debts

2018		
Dec 31 Various	6,380	Dec 31 Profit and loss	6,380

Allowance for doubtful debts

Dec 31 Balance c/d	1,480	Jan 1 Balance b/d	1,300
		Dec 31 Profit and loss	180
	1,480		1,480

(*iii*)

Income Statement (extracts)

Bad debts	6,380
Allowance for doubtful debts	180

Balance Sheet (extract)

Accounts receivable	37,000	
Less allowance for doubtful debts	1,480	35,520

20.3
(i)

Bad Debts

2017			2017		
May 31 S. Gill	500		Dec 31 Profit and loss	900	
Oct 31 H. Black	400				900
	900				
2018			2018		
Jan 31 A. Tims	200		Dec 31 Profit and loss	1,200	
Jun 30 F. Dale	900				
Oct 31 J. Park	100				
	1,200				1,200

Allowance for Doubtful Debts

2017			2017		
Dec 31 Balance c/d	3,120		Dec 31 Profit and loss	3,120	
	3,120				3,120
2018			2018		
Dec 31 Balance c/d	3,480		Jan 1 Balance b/d	3,120	
			Dec 31 Profit and loss	360	
	3,480				3,480

(*ii*)

Balance Sheet (extracts)

		2017	
Accounts receivable		104,000	
Less Allowance for doubtful debts		3,120	100,880
		2018	
		116,000	
		3,480	112,520

20.5

Allowance for Doubtful Debts

2017			2017		
Dec 31 Balance c/d	770		Jan 1 Balance b/d	650	
			Dec 31 Profit and loss	120	
	770				770
2018			2018		
Dec 31 Balance c/d	980		Jan 1 Balance b/d	770	
			Dec 31 Profit and loss	210	
	980				980
2019			2019		
Dec 31 Profit and loss	330		Jan 1 Balance b/d	980	
Dec 31 Balance c/d	650				
	980				980

Income Statement Extracts for the year ending 31 December

2017

Gross profit	xxx
Less Expenses	
Increase in allowance for doubtful debts	120
Bad debts	3,320

2018

Gross profit	xxx
Less Expenses	
Increase in allowance for doubtful debts	210
Bad debts	2,150

2019

Gross profit	xxx
Add Reduction in allowance for doubtful debts	330
	xxx
Less Expenses	
Bad debts	3,490

20.7

(a)

Allowance for Doubtful Debts

2018			**2017**		
May 31 Profit and loss (W1)	2,600		Jun 1 Balance b/d	4,600	
31 Balance c/d	2,000				
	4,600			4,600	
			2018		
			Jun 1 Balance b/d	2,000	

(b)

Provision for Discounts Allowed

2018		
May 31 Profit and loss (W2)	1,194	

Workings

(W1) Allowance 1.6.2017 ... 4,600

Less Allowance 31.5.2018		
0.5% × 60,000		300
1% × 42,000		420
2% × 34,000		680
3% × 20,000		600
		2,000

Reduction in allowance ... 2,600

(W2) Accounts receivable liable for discounts	60,000
Less Allowance for doubtful debts	300
	59,700

Provision for discounts allowed 2% × 59,700 = 1,194

20.9

(days and months omitted)

(a)

Bad Debts

2016 Various	1,400	2016 Profit and loss	1,400
2017 Various	2,200	2017 Profit and loss	2,200
2018 Various	3,800	2018 Profit and loss	3,800

(b)

Bad Debts Recovered

2017 Profit and loss	210	2017 J. Sweeny	210
2018 Profit and loss	320	2018 Various accounts receivable	320

(c)

Allowance for Doubtful Debts

2016 Balance c/d	2,600	2016 Profit and loss	2,600
2017 Balance c/d	3,680	2017 Balance b/d	2,600
		Profit and loss	1,080
	3,680		3,680
2018 Profit and loss	80	2018 Balance b/d	3,680
Balance c/d	3,600		
	3,680		3,680

(d)

Income Statement (extracts)

(2016) Bad debts	1,400		
Allowance for doubtful debts	2,600		
(2017) Bad debts	2,200	(2017) Bad debt recovered	210
Allowance for doubtful debts	1,080		
(2018) Bad debts	3,800	(2018) Reduction in allowance for doubtful debts	80
		Bad debt recovered	320

20.10

(A) See text.
(B) See text.
(C) (1)

(i)

Allowance for Doubtful Debts

2017		**2017**	
Dec 31 Profit and loss	33	Jan 1 Balance b/d	750*
Balance c/d	717**		
	750		750

(ii)

Bad Debts

2017			2017		
	Accounts receivable – A. Stewart	900	Dec 31	Profit and loss	3,800
	Accounts receivable	2,300			
Dec 31	Accounts receivable – J. Smith	600			
		3,800			3,800

(c) (2) the net profit will increase by £33.
*3% 25,000 = 750; **3% 23,900

21.1

Straight Line

Cost	480
Yr 1 Depreciation*	140
	340
Yr 2 Depreciation	140
	200
Yr 3 Depreciation	140
	60

*480 − 60 = 420 ÷ 3 = 140

Reducing Balance

Cost	480
Y 1 Depn 50% of 480	240
	240
Yr 2 Depn 50% of 240	120
	120
Yr 3 Depn 50% of 120	60
	60

21.2

(a) Straight Line

Cost	26,660
Yr 1 Depreciation*	5,065
	21,595
Yr 2 Depreciation	5,065
	16,530
Yr 3 Depreciation	5,065
	11,465
Yr 4 Depreciation	5,065
	6,400

$$* \frac{26,660 - 6,400}{4} = 5,065$$

(b) Reducing Balance

Cost	26,660
Yr 1 Depn 30% of 26,660	7,998
	18,662
Yr 2 Depn 30% of 18,662	5,599
	13,063
Yr 3 Depn 30% of 13,063	3,919
	9,144
Yr 4 Depn 30% of 9,144	2,743
	6,401

21.3

(a) Reducing Balance

Cost	24,000
Yr 1 Depn 35% of 24,000	8,400
	15,600
Yr 2 Depn 35% of 15,600	5,460
	10,140
Yr 3 Depn 35% of 10,140	3,549
	6,591

(b) Straight Line

Cost	24,000
Yr 1 Depreciation*	6,000
	18,000
Yr 2 Depreciation	6,000
	12,000
Yr 3 Depreciation	6,000
	6,000

$$* \ 24,000 - 6,000 = 6,000$$

21.7

		Machines		
		A	B	C
2016	Bought 1.1.2016	4,000		
	Depreciation 12% for 12 months	480		
		3,520		
2017	Bought 1.9.2017		7,000	
	Depreciation 12% × 3,520	422		
	Depreciation 12% for 4 months		280	
		3,098	6,720	
2018	Bought 1.5.2018			2,000
	Depreciation 12% × 3,098	372		
	Depreciation 12% × 6,720		806	
	Depreciation 12% for 8 months			160
		2,726	5,914	1,840

2018 Total depreciation expense 372 + 806 + 160 = 1,338

21.8

Motor Vehicle

2016		
Jan 1	Trucks Ltd	12,000

Accumulated provision for depreciation on motor vehicles

2016			2016		
Dec 31	Balance c/d	3,000	Dec 31	Depreciation	3,000
2017			2017		
Dec 31	Balance c/d	5,250	Jan 1	Balance b/d	3,000
			Dec 31	Depreciation	2,250
		5,250			5,250

21.9

Ivor Innes
Balance Sheet as at 31 March 2018

Non-current assets		
Fixtures (7,600 − 600)		7,000
Current assets		
Inventory	19,000	
Accounts receivable (4,640 − 200)	4,440	
Bank	8,320	
Cash	700	
	32,460	
	39,460	
Current liabilities		
Accounts payable	(8,800)	
	30,660	
Capital		
Balance at start of year*	34,900	
Capital introduced	18,000	
	52,900	
Less: Net loss (balancing figure)	10,840	
Drawings	11,400	
	22,240	
	30,660	

* 840 + 7,600 + 5,500 + 17,800 + 8,360 − 5,200 = 34,900

21.12

(a) Reducing balance. Obsolescence probably very slow and not relevant.
(b) Straight line. Obsolescence very slow and probably not relevant.
(c) Straight line. Obsolescence depends on the market and growth at the business.
(d) Reducing balance (as it is likely to be more efficient in the early years of use and susceptible to obsolescence).
(e) Machine hours. Already obsolete.

21.14

Vans

2018			2018		
Jan 1 Bank	69,000		Dec 31 Balance c/d	213,000	
Aug 1 Bank	144,000				
	213,000			213,000	

Accumulated Depreciation: Vans

2018		2018	
Dec 31 Balance c/d	32,250	Dec 31 Profit and loss	32,250*

*69,000 × 25%	= £17,250	
144,000 × 25% × $^5/_{12}$	= 15,000	
	32,250	

21.15

(a)

Equipment

2017		2017	
Jan 1 Bank	800	Dec 31 Balance c/d	800
2018		2018	
Jan 1 Balance b/d	800	Dec 31 Balance c/d	3,800
Jul 1 Bank	2,400		
Oct 1 Bank	600		
	3,800		3,800
2019		2019	
Jan 1 Balance b/d	3,800	Dec 31 Balance c/d	3,800
2020		2020	
Jan 1 Balance b/d	3,800	Dec 31 Balance c/d	5,200
Apr 1 Bank	1,400		
	5,200		5,200

(b)

Accumulated Depreciation: Equipment

2017		2017	
Dec 31 Balance c/d	80	Dec 31 Profit and loss	80
2018		2018	
Dec 31 Balance c/d	295	Jan 1 Balance b/d	80
		Dec 31 Profit and loss	215*
	295		295
2019		2019	
Dec 31 Balance c/d	675	Jan 1 Balance b/d	295
		Dec 31 Profit and loss	380
	675		675
2020		2020	
Dec 31 Balance c/d	1,160	Jan 1 Balance b/d	675
		Dec 31 Profit and loss	485**
	1,160		1,160

* 800 × 10%	=	80
2,400 × 10% × $^1/_2$	=	120
600 × 10% × $^1/_4$	=	15
		215
** 3,800 × 10%	=	380
1,400 × 10% × $^3/_4$	=	105
		485

21.15 (Cont'd)

(c)

Balance Sheet Extracts

	31 December 2017			31 December 2019	
Equipment	800		Equipment	3,800	
Less Depreciation to date	80	720	Less Depreciation to date	675	3,125

	31 December 2018			31 December 2020	
Equipment	3,800		Equipment	5,200	
Less Depreciation to date	295	3,505	Less Depreciation to date	1,160	4,040

21.17

Plant

2017			
Jan 1 Bank	2,600	Dec 31 Balance c/d	4,700
Oct 1 Bank	2,100		
	4,700		4,700
2018			
Jan 1 Balance b/d	4,700	Dec 31 Balance c/d	4,700
2019			
Jan 1 Balance b/d	4,700	Dec 31 Balance c/d	7,500
Sep 1 Bank	2,800		
	7,500		7,500
2020			
Jan 1 Balance b/d	7,500	Aug 31 Disposals	2,600
		Dec 31 Balance c/d	4,900
	7,500		7,500

Accumulated Depreciation: Plant

2017			
Dec 31 Balance c/d	781	Dec 31 Profit and loss	781*

$2,600 \times 25\% = 650$
$2,100 \times 25\% \times {}^{3}/_{12} = 131.25$
781

2018			
Dec 31 Balance c/d	1,956	Jan 1 Balance b/d	781
		Dec 31 Profit and loss	1,175
	1,956		1,956
2019			
Dec 31 Balance c/d	3,364	Jan 1 Balance b/d	1,956
		Dec 31 Profit and loss	1,408*
	3,364		3,364

$*4,700 \times 25\% = 1,175$
$2,800 \times 25\% \times {}^{4}/_{12} = 233.33$
$1,408$

2020			
Aug 31 Plant disposals	2,383	Jan 1 Balance b/d	3,364
Dec 31 Balance c/d	2,639	Dec 31 Profit and loss	1,658*
	5,022		5,022

$* 2,600 \times 25\% \times {}^{8}/_{12} = 433.33$
$2,100 \times 25\% = 525$
$2,800 \times 25\% = 700$
$1,658$

Plant Disposals

2020			
Aug 31 Plant	2,600	Aug 31 Acc depn	2,383
Dec 31 Profit and loss	593	Aug 31 Bank	810
	3,193		3,193

Balance Sheet extracts

	2017	2018	2019	2020
Plant at cost	4,700	4,700	7,500	4,900
Less depn to date	781	1,956	3,364	2,639
	3,919	2,744	4,136	2,261

21.18

Machinery

2019			
Jan 1 Balance b/d	94,500	Dec 31 Machinery disposals	1,600
Dec 31 Bank	16,000	31 Balance c/d	108,900
	110,500		110,500

Office Furniture

2019			
Jan 1 Balance b/d	3,200	Dec 31 Balance c/d	3,660
Dec 31 Bank	460		
	3,660		3,660

Accumulated Depreciation: Machinery

2019			
Dec 31 Machinery disposals	1,280	Jan 1 Balance b/d	28,350
31 Balance c/d	48,850	Dec 31 Profit and loss	21,780
	50,130		50,130

Accumulated Depreciation: Office Furniture

2019			
Dec 31 Balance c/d	1,646	Jan 1 Balance b/d	1,280
		Dec 31 Profit and loss	366
	1,646		1,646

21.18 (Cont'd)

Machinery Disposals

2019		2019	
Dec 31 Machinery	1,600	Dec 31 Acc depn	40
31 Profit and loss: Gain on sale	40	31 Bank	1,280
			360
	1,640		1,640

Balance Sheet extract as at 31 December 2019

Machinery at cost		108,900
Less Depreciation to date		48,850
		60,050
Office furniture at cost		3,660
Less Depreciation to date		1,646
		2,014

21.20

(a) (i) Time factor (ii) Economic factors (iii) Deterioration physically (iv) Depletion.

(b) (i) Depletion (ii) Physical deterioration (iii) Time (iv) Not usually subject to depletion, but depends on circumstances (v) Economic factors, obsolescence for example (vi) Time factor.

(c)

Equipment

Balance b/d	135,620	Asset disposals	36,000
Bank	47,800	Balance c/d	147,420
	183,420		183,420
Balance b/d	147,420		

Accumulated Depreciation – Equipment

Asset disposals	28,224	Balance b/d	81,374
Balance c/d	90,858	Profit and loss	37,708
	119,082		119,082
		Balance b/d	90,858

Asset Disposals

Equipment	36,000	Accumulated depreciation	28,224
		Bank	5,700
		Profit and loss	2,076
	36,000		36,000

21.22

(a) (i) Straight line depreciation method

Non-current Asset

Year 1 Bank	10,000	Year 3 Asset disposals	10,000

Accumulated Provision for Depreciation

		Year 1 Profit and loss	2,000
Year 2 Balance c/d	4,000	Year 2 Profit and loss	2,000
	4,000		4,000
Year 3 Asset disposals	4,000	Year 3 Balance b/d	4,000

Asset Disposals

Year 3 Non-current asset	10,000	Year 3 Bank	5,000
		Year 3 Acc. provn for depn	4,000
		Year 3 Profit and loss	1,000
	10,000		10,000

(ii) Reducing balance method

Non-current Asset

Year 1 Bank	10,000	Year 3 Asset disposals	10,000

Accumulated Provision for Depreciation

		Year 1 Profit and loss	4,000
Year 2 Balance c/d	6,400	Year 2 Profit and loss	2,400
	6,400		6,400
Year 3 Asset disposals	6,400	Year 3 Balance b/d	6,400

Asset Disposals

Year 3 Non-current asset	10,000	Year 3 Bank	5,000
Year 3 Profit and loss	1,400	Year 3 Acc. provn for depn	6,400
	11,400		11,400

(b) (i) The purpose of depreciation is to apportion the cost of a non-current asset over the useful years of its life to the organisation.

The matching concept concerns the matching of costs against the revenues which those costs generate. If the benefit to be gained is equal in each year then the straight line method is to be preferred. If the benefits are greatest in Year 1 and then falling year by year, then the reducing balance method would be preferred. The impact of maintenance costs of the non-current asset, if heavier in later years, may also give credence to the reducing balance method.

(ii) The net figure at the end of Year 2 is the amount of original cost not yet expensed against revenue.

(c) The charge in Year 1 should be nil regardless of the depreciation method. The matching concept concerns matching costs against revenues. There have been no revenues in Year 1, therefore there should be no costs.

21.24 Your letter should include the following:

- Depreciation is an expense.
- It allows the expense of an asset to be spread over its useful economic life.
- It is only a book figure and therefore 'real' money is not set aside when you depreciate an asset.
- It is not a reserve, and never can be as there are no assets of the business underpinning it.

21.26

Machinery

Date	Detail	£	Date	Detail	£
2018			2018		
Jan 1	Bank	10,000	Dec 31	Balance c/d	16,000
July 1	Bank	6,000			
		16,000			16,000
2019			2019		
Jan 1	Balance b/d	16,000	Dec 31	Balance c/d	24,000
Mar 31	Bank	8,000			
		24,000			24,000
2020			2020		
Jan 1	Balance b/d	24,000	Oct 7	Machinery disposal	10,000
Nov 5	Bank	12,000	Dec 31	Balance c/d	26,000
		36,000			36,000
2021			2021		
Jan 1	Balance b/d	26,000	Feb 4	Machinery disposal	6,000
Feb 6	Bank	9,000	Oct 11	Machinery disposal	12,000
Oct 11	Machinery disposal	7,000	Dec 31	Balance c/d	24,000
		42,000			42,000

Accumulated provision for depreciation

Date	Detail	£	Date	Detail	£
2018			2018		
Dec 31	Balance c/d	3,200	Dec 31	Depreciation	3,200
2019			2019		
Dec 31	Balance c/d	8,000	Jan 1	Balance b/d	3,200
			Dec 31	Depreciation	4,800
		8,000			8,000
2020			2020		
Oct 7	Machinery disposal	4,000	Jan 1	Balance b/d	8,000
Dec 31	Balance c/d	9,200	Dec 31	Depreciation	5,200
		13,200			13,200

Accumulated provision for depreciation

Date	Detail	£	Date	Detail	£
2021			2021		
Feb 4	Machinery disposal	3,600	Jan 1	Balance b/d	9,200
Oct 11	Machinery disposal	2,400	Dec 31	Depreciation	4,800
Dec 31	Balance c/d	8,000			
		14,000			14,000

Machinery Disposal

Date	Detail	£	Date	Detail	£
2020			2020		
Oct 7	Machinery	10,000	Oct 7	Acc. provn for depn	4,000
			7	Bank	5,500
			Dec 31	Profit and loss (loss on sale)	500
		10,000			10,000
2021			2021		
Feb 4	Machinery	6,000	Feb 4	Acc. provn for depn	3,600
Oct 11	Machinery	12,000	4	Bank	3,000
			Oct 11	Acc. provn for depn	2,400
			11	Machinery	7,000
			Dec 31	Profit and loss (loss on disposal)	2,000
		18,000			18,000

X Y Ltd
Balance Sheet extracts as at 31 December

2020
	£	£
Machinery at cost		26,000
Less: Accumulated depreciation		9,200
		16,800

2021
	£	£
Machinery at cost		24,000
Less: Accumulated depreciation		8,000
		16,000

21.29

(a) (i) Straight line:
Cost £112,000 – trade-in £12,000 = £100,000
Per month £100,000 ÷ 48 = 2,083.33

2016	9 months	=		18,750
2017	12 months	=		25,000
2018	12 months	=		25,000
2019	12 months	=		25,000
2020	3 months	=		6,250
				100,000

21.29 (Cont'd)

(ii) Diminishing (reducing) balance:

	£
Cost	112,000
Depreciation 2016 (40%)	44,800
	67,200
Depreciation 2017	26,880
	40,320
Depreciation 2018	16,128
	24,192
Depreciation 2019	9,677
	14,515
Depreciation 2020	5,806
	8,709

(iii) Units of output (total £100,000):

			£
2016	4,000/20,000	=	20,000
2017	5,000/20,000	=	25,000
2018	5,000/20,000	=	25,000
2019	5,000/20,000	=	25,000
2020	1,000/20,000	=	5,000

(b) (i)

Machine

	£		£
2017		2017	
Jan 1 Balance b/d	112,000	Dec 31 Assets disposal	112,000
	112,000		112,000

(ii)

Accumulated Depreciation

	£		£
2017		2017	
Dec 31 Assets disposal	31,250	Jan 1 Balance b/d	18,750
		Dec 31 Profit and loss	12,500
	31,250		31,250

(iii)

Assets Disposals

	£		£
2017		2017	
Dec 31 Machine	112,000	Jun 30 Bank	80,000
		Dec 31 Depreciation	31,250
		31 Profit and loss	750
	112,000		112,000

22.1

(a)

Motor Expenses

	£		£
2016		2016	
Dec 31 Cash and bank	1,400	Dec 31 Profit and loss	1,600
31 Owing c/d	200		
	1,600		1,600

(b)

Insurance

	£		£
2016		2016	
Dec 31 Cash and bank	1,700	Dec 31 Prepaid c/d	130
		31 Profit and loss	1,570
	1,700		1,700

(c)

Computer Supplies

	£		£
2016		2016	
Dec 31 Cash and bank	900	Jan 1 Owing b/d	300
31 Owing c/d	400	Dec 31 Profit and loss	1,000
	1,300		1,300

(d)

Business Rates

	£		£
2016		2016	
Jan 1 Prepaid b/d	560	Dec 31 Prepaid c/d	560
Dec 31 Cash and bank	5,620	31 Profit and loss	5,620
	6,180		6,180

(e)

Rent Received

	£		£
2016		2016	
Jan 1 Owing b/d	380	Dec 31 Cash and bank	3,800
Dec 31 Profit and loss	3,840	31 Owing c/d	420
	4,220		4,220

22.3

Business Rates

	£		£
2018		2018	
Jan 1 Balance b/d	5,250	Dec 31 Profit and loss	6,200
Dec 31 Bank	1,550*	31 Prepaid c/d	600
	6,800		6,800

$*6,200 \times {}^{3}/_{12} = 1,550$

Packing Materials

	£		£
2018		2018	
Jan 1 Balance b/d	1,400	Dec 31 Profit and loss	3,600
Dec 31 Bank	4,000	31 Cash: Scrap	300
31 Owing c/d	900	31 Balance c/d	2,400
	6,300		6,300

22.8

(a)

D. Staunton

Income Statement for the year ended 30 September 2020

Sales		592,013
Less Cost of goods sold:		
Opening inventory	25,967	
Add Purchases	307,847	
Less Returns outwards	(2,064)	
Less Closing inventory	(26,424)	
		(305,326)
Gross profit		286,687
Less Expenses:		
Utilities	*(18,603 + 4,167)*	22,770
Business rates	*(19,978 − 3,920)*	16,058
Wages & salaries		136,163
Bad debt expense		13,192
Increase in allowance for doubtful debts		688
Depreciation expense:		
Equipment	*(188,760 − 74,100) × 0.3)*	34,398
Delivery vans	*(92,220 × 0.2)*	18,444
		(241,713)
Net profit		44,974

22.5

(a)

Insurance

2020			2020		
Jan 1 Prepaid b/d		1,236	Dec 31 Profit and loss		1,236
Dec 31 Bank		345	31 Prepaid c/d		345
		1,581			1,581
2021					
Jan 1 Prepaid b/d		345			

Wages

2020			2020		
Dec 31 Cash		15,000	Jan 1 Accrued b/d		306
31 Accrued c/d		419	Dec 31 Profit and loss		15,113
		15,419			15,419
			2021		
			Jan 1 Accrued b/d		419

Rent Receivable

2020			2020		
Dec 31 Profit and loss		2,741	Jan 1 In advance b/d		36
			Dec 31 Bank		2,600
			31 Arrears c/d		105
		2,741			2,741
2021					
Jan 1 Arrears b/d		105			

(b)

Income Statement (extract)

Insurance	1,236
Wages	15,113
Rent receivable	(2,741)

(c) (i) Expenses accrued increases the amount charged as expense for that period. It reduces the recorded net profit. It shows as a current liability in the balance sheet.

(ii) Income received in advance reduces the revenue to be recorded for that period. It reduces the recorded net profit. It shows as a current liability in the balance sheet.

(d) (i) To match-up expenses charged in the income statement with the expense cost used up in the period.

(ii) To match-up revenue credited to the income statement with revenue earned for the period.

22.8 (cont'd)

(b)

Balance Sheet as at 30 September 2020

	Cost	Acc Dep*	NBV
Assets			
Non-current assets:			
Equipment	188,760	108,498	80,262
(* Acc dep = 74,100 + 34,398)			
Delivery vans	92,220	79,164	13,056
(* Acc dep = 60,720 + 18,444)			
	280,980	187,662	93,318
Current assets:			
Inventory		26,424	
Accounts receivable	73,200		
less allowance for doubtful debts	(2,928)	70,272	
Prepayments (11,760 × 4/12)		3,920	
Bank		1,337	
Total assets		101,953	
		195,271	
Current liabilities:			
Accounts payable		62,165	
Accruals		4,167	
Total liabilities			(66,332)
Net assets			128,939
Opening capital			118,757
Add Net profit for the year			44,974
Less Drawings for the year			(34,792)
Closing capital			128,939

22.9

Rent

Aug 31 Balance b/d	4,400	Aug 31 Profit and Loss	4,800
31 Accrual c/d	400		
	4,800		4,800
		Sept 1 Accrual b/d	400

Rates

Aug 31 Balance b/d	1,600	Aug 31 Prepaid c/d	300
		31 Profit and loss	1,300
	1,600		1,600
Sept 1 Prepaid b/d	300		

Income Statement for the year ending 31 August 2018

Sales		40,900
Less Cost of goods sold		
Opening inventory	8,200	
Add Purchases	26,000	
	34,200	
Less Closing inventory	9,100	25,100
Gross profit		15,800
Less Expenses:		
Rent (4,400 + 400)	4,800	
Business rates (1,600 − 300)	1,300	
Sundry expenses	340	
Depreciation	1,800	
		8,240
Net profit		7,560

Balance Sheet as at 31 August 2018

Non-current assets		
Motor vehicles	9,000	
Less Accumulated depreciation (1,200 + 1,800)	3,000	6,000
Current assets		
Inventory	9,100	
Accounts receivable	1,160	
Prepayment	300	
Bank	1,500	12,060
		18,060
Current liabilities		
Accounts payable	2,100	
Accrual	400	(2,500)
		15,560
Capital		
Opening balance		19,700
Add Net profit		7,560
		27,260
Less Drawings		11,700
		15,560

22.11 *(a)*

Mr Khan

Income Statement for the year ended 30 September 2020

Sales			462,970
Less Cost of goods sold:			
Opening inventory		19,134	
Add Purchases		226,855	
Add Carriage inwards		2,229	
Less Closing inventory		(19,491)	
			(228,727)
Gross profit			234,243
Less Expenses:			
Gas	(20,005 + 4,786)	24,791	
Rent	(18,465 − 7,000)	11,465	
Wages & salaries		106,483	
Bad debt expense		13,408	
Increase in allowance for doubtful debts		700	
Depreciation expense:			
Machinery	(232,140 − 77,580) × 0.15	23,184	
Computers	(97,080 × 0.25)	24,270	
			(204,301)
Net profit			29,942

(b)

Balance Sheet as at 30 September 2020

Assets		Cost	Acc Dep*	NBV
Non-current assets				
Machinery	(* Acc dep = 77,580 + 23,184)	232,140	100,764	131,376
Computers	(* Acc dep = 54,600 + 24,270)	97,080	78,870	18,210
		329,220	179,634	149,586
Current assets				
Inventory			19,491	
Accounts receivable		74,400		
less allowance for doubtful debts		(2,976)	71,424	
Prepayments	(10,500 × 8/12 *months*)		7,000	
				97,915
Total assets				247,501
Current liabilities				
Bank overdraft		1,807		
Accounts payable		53,749		
Accruals		4,786		
Total liabilities				(60,342)
Net assets				187,159
Opening capital				191,319
Add Net profit for the year				29,942
Less Drawings for the year				(34,102)
Closing capital				187,159

23.1

Sales Ledger Control

Balances b/d	45,000	Returns inwards	1,900
Sales Day Book	32,000	Cheques and cash	29,800
		Discounts allowed	3,000
		Balances c/d	42,300
	77,000		77,000

23.3

Sales Ledger Control

2019		2019	
March 1 Balances b/d	18,000	March 31 Cash and bank	16,000
31 Sales	14,000	31 Discounts allowed	1,400
31 Balances c/d	60	31 Set-offs: Purchases ledger	120
		31 Balances c/d	14,540
	32,060		32,060

23.5

Purchases Ledger Control

Returns outwards	1,452	Balances b/d	19,420
Bank	205,419	Purchases Day Book	210,416
Petty cash	62		
Discounts received	1,721		
Set-offs against sales ledger	640		
Balances c/d	20,210		
	*229,504		*229,836
	332		

*Difference between two sides

Sales Ledger Control

Balances b/d	28,227	Returns inwards	3,618
Sales Day Book	305,824	Bank and cash	287,317
		Discounts allowed	4,102
		Set-offs against Purchase ledger	640
		Balances c/d	38,374
	334,051		334,051

23.6

Sales Ledger Control Account

Jan 1 Bal b/d	23,220	Cash from customers (excl £370)	146,610
Credit sales	162,540	Bad debt write-offs	4,770
		Discounts allowed	3,160
		Returns inwards	8,150
		Dec 31 Bal c/d	23,070
	185,760		185,760

Purchases Ledger Control Account

Discounts received	1,310	Jan 1 Bal b/d	16,400
Paid to credit suppliers	109,040	Credit purchases	114,800
Returns outwards	2,330		
Dec 31 Bal c/d	18,520		
	131,200		131,200

23.9

Total Accounts Receivable Account

Balance b/d	26,555	Cash (600,570 − 344,890)	255,680
Credit sales	268,187	Discounts allowed	5,520
		Set-offs against payables	70
		Bad debts	780
		Returns inwards	4,140
		Balances c/d	28,552
	294,742		294,742
Balances b/d	28,552		

Total Accounts Payable Account

Cash (503,970 − 14,440)	489,530	Balances b/d	43,450
Discounts received	3,510	Credit purchases	496,600
Set-offs against receivables	70		
Returns outwards	1,480		
Balances c/d	45,460		
	540,050		540,050
		Balances b/d	45,460

Note: The Allowance for doubtful debts does not affect the control accounts.

23.10

(a) To ensure an arithmetical check on the accounting records. The agreement of the total of individual accounts payable balances with that of the balance on the control account provides that check.

If the control account and the ledger are kept by separate personnel, then a check on their work and honesty is provided.

(b) (i) Increase £198 (ii) Decrease £100 (iii) No effect
(iv) Decrease £400 (v) Decrease £120.

(c) Accounting software will automatically enter two figures in different directions and will then confirm it in total fashion. As such there may seem at first sight to be no need for control accounts.

However, there is still the need to check on the accuracy of data input. It is important that both the skill and the honesty of the programmer are checked. Users will also still expect to see accounts for 'total receivables' and 'total payables' rather than having to add together the individual personal accounts on each ledger. Control accounts provide convenient 'at a glance' totals.

Accordingly there will still be a need for control accounts.

23.11

(a) See Section 23.1.
(b) See Section 23.5.

24.1

Bank Reconciliation as at 31 December 2019

Cash at bank as per cash book	5,300
Add: Credit transfers	245
	5,545
Cash at bank per balance sheet	5,545
Less: uncredited bank deposits	970
	4,575
Add: unpresented cheques	1,640
Cash at bank per bank statement	6,215

Note for students

Both in theory and in practice you can start with the cash book balance working to the bank statement balance, or you can reverse this method. Many teachers have their preferences, but this is a personal matter only. Examiners sometimes ask for them using one way, sometimes the other. Students should therefore be able to tackle them both ways.

24.3

(a)

Cash Book

2019			2019		
Dec 31 Balance b/d	1,535		Dec 31 Bank charges	49	
Dec 31 J. Watt	251		31 Balance c/d	1,737	
	1,786			1,786	

(b)

Bank Reconciliation Statement as on 31 December 2019

Balance per cash book	1,737
Add Unpresented cheque	125
Less Bankings not yet on bank statement (366 + 412)	(778)
Balance per bank statement	1,084

or

Bank Reconciliation Statement as at 31 December 2019

Balance per bank statement	1,084
Add Bankings not yet on bank statement (366 + 412)	778
Less Unpresented cheque	125
Balance per cash book	1,737

24.5

(a)

Cash Book (bank columns)

2018			2018		
Dec 31 Balance b/d	1,500		Dec 31 Bank charges	30	
31 Dividends	240		31 RAC	70	
31 HM Revenue & Customs	260		31 Loan repayment	200	
31 Deposit account	1,400		31 Balance c/d	3,100	
	3,400			3,400	

(b)

Bank Reconciliation Statement as on 31 December 2018

Balance per cash book	3,100
Add Unpresented cheques (250 + 290)	540
	3,640
Less Bankings not on statement	690
Balance per bank statement	2,950

24.7

Cash Book

2019			2019		
Mar 31 G. Frank	88		Mar 31 Balance b/d	4,195	
31 Balance c/d	4,158		31 TYF	32	
			31 Bank charges	19	
	4,246			4,246	

Bank Reconciliation Statement as at 31 March 2019

Overdraft per cash book	(4,158)
Less Bankings not yet in bank statement	(192)
Add Unpresented cheques	504
Overdraft per bank statement	(3,846)

24.9

(a)

Balance per Cash Book at 31 October		(554)
Less: Bank charges	136	
Sundries cheque	44	
Cheque returned – Jones	80	
Rates standing order	150	
Incorrect entry	6	(416)
		(970)
Add Dividends received not entered	62	
Error in calculation of opening balance	50	112
Corrected Cash Book balance		(858)

(b)

George Ltd

Bank Reconciliation Statement as at 31 October

Balance per bank statement*	(1,353)
Add Outstanding lodgements	762
	(591)
Less Unpresented cheques	(267)
Balance per cash book	(858)

* This is the balancing figure.

25.1

	£000
Net profit for the year	227
Depreciation	58
Increase in inventory	(29)
Decrease in accounts receivable	45
Decrease in accounts payable	(36)
Net cash flow from operating activities	265

25.3

	£000
Disposal working:	
Proceeds	59
Net book value disposed of (balancing figure)	(47)
Profit on disposal	12

Non-current assets at NBV T-account working

	£000		£000
Bal b/d	460	NBV disposed of (above)	47
Acquisitions (bal fig)	72	Dep'n expense for year	68
		Bal c/d	417
	532		532

25.6

(a)

Malcolm Phillips

Statement of Cash Flows for the year ending 30 April 2019

	£000
Operating activities	
Profit from operations	8,500
Adjustments for:	
Depreciation	200
Operating cash flows before movements in working capital	8,700
Increase in inventory	(2,800)
Decrease in accounts receivable	500
Increase in accounts payable	200
Cash generated by operations	6,600
Tax paid	–
Interest paid	–
Net cash from operating activities	6,600
Investing activities	
Payments to acquire tangible non-current assets	(3,000)
Net cash used in investing activities	(3,000)
Financing activities	
Capital introduced	2,000
Drawings	(8,000)
Net cash used in financing activities	(6,000)
Net decrease in cash and cash equivalents	(2,400)
Cash and cash equivalents at beginning of year	1,500
Cash and cash equivalents at end of year	(900)
Bank balances and cash	(900)

(b) (i) $\dfrac{7,500}{30,000} \times \dfrac{100}{1} = 25\%$ (ii) $\dfrac{22,500}{(3,100 + 5,900) \div 2\%} = \dfrac{22,500}{4,500} = 5$

25.7

D. Duncan
Statement of Cash Flows for the year ending 31 December 2020

Operating activities		
Profit from operations		23,240
Adjustments for		
Depreciation	1,800	
Profit on sale of tangible non-current asset	(620)	
Increase in allowance for doubtful debts	200	
		1,380
		24,620
Operating cash flows before movements in working capital		
Increase in inventory	(5,400)	
Decrease in accounts receivable (8,800 − 7,700)	1,100	
Increase in accounts payable	1,300	
		(3,000)
		21,620
Cash generated by operations		
Tax paid	–	
Interest paid	–	
Net cash from operating activities		21,620
Investing activities		
Receipts from sale of tangible non-current assets	3,820	
Net cash from investing activities		3,820
Financing activities		
Loan repaid to J. Fry	(2,500)	
Drawings	(22,630)	
Net cash used in financing activities		(25,130)
Net increase in cash and cash equivalents		310
Cash and cash equivalents at beginning of year		410
		720
Cash and cash equivalents at end of year		720
Bank balances and cash		720

26.1

(a) Error of omission – a credit purchase omitted from the books.
(b) Error of commission – a credit sale to J. Briggs entered in the account of H. Briggs.
(c) Error of principle – repairs debited to the asset account.
(d) Compensating errors – prepayments £15 too high and accruals £15 too high.
(e) Errors of original entry – a credit purchase for £100 recorded in the books as £10.
(f) Complete reversal of entries – payment of advertising debited to bank and credited to advertising.
(g) Transposition error – sales invoice for £263 entered as £236 in both ledger accounts.

26.2

To economise on space, all narratives for journal entries are omitted.

	Dr		Cr
(a) J. Trees	630	J. Trees	630
(b) Printer	846	D. Hogg	846
(c) Computers	389	Office expenses	389
(d) G. Lee	54	Sales	54
(e) Sales	340	Commissions rec'd	340
(f) Cash (needs double the amount)	260	A. Salmond	260
(g) Purchases	410	Drawings	410
(h) Discounts allowed	46	Discounts received	46

26.4

(a) 200 units × £2.62 = £524 *not* £5,240.
(b) (i) Inventory overstated by £4,716 (i.e. 5,240 − 524).
  (ii) Cost of goods sold understated by £4,716.
  (iii) Net profit overstated by £4,716.
  (iv) Current Assets overstated by £4,716.
  (v) Owner's Capital overstated by £4,716.

26.5

	Dr		Cr
(a) Sales	12,000	Capital	12,000
(b) Drawings	140	Sundry expenses	140
(c) Drawings	740	Rent	740
(d) Purchases	180	F. Smith	180
(e) Bank	1,240	Cash	1,240
(f) Bank	270	Cash	270
(g) G. Milne	205	N. Sturgeon	205
(h) Office expenses	70	Asset disposals	70

27.1

Suspense

	£		£
(i) Purchases	90	Balance b/d	71
(iii) Sales	54	(ii) Drawings	73
	144		144

27.2

(a)

The Journal (narratives omitted)

	Dr	Cr
(i) Suspense	1,205	
Sales		1,205
(ii) I. Blane	980	
I. Blank		980
Suspense	404	
(iii) Rent		404
Suspense	59	
(iv) Suspense		59
Discounts allowed	200	
(v) Sales		200
Computer disposals		

(b)

Suspense Account

Sales	1,205	Balance b/d	860
Discounts allowed	59	Rent	404
	1,264		1,264

(c) Net profit per financial statements | | 58,600 |

Add **(i)** Sales undercast | 1,205 |
  (iv) Discounts overcast | 59 | 1,264 |
| | 57,336 |
Less **(iii)** Rent undercast | | (404) |
Corrected net profit | | 59,460 |

Note: **(v)** has no effect on net profit. Sales are reduced by £125 but the loss on disposal of office equipment is reduced by £125 too.

27.4

Item	If no effect State 'No'	Debit side exceeds credit side by	Credit side exceeds debit side by
(i)	No		
(ii)	No		
(iii)	No		
(iv)		£520	
(v)			£212
(vi)			£380
(vii)	No		

27.5

Trial Balance as at 31 January 2019

	Dr	Cr
Drawings	19,500	
Inventory	8,410	
Accounts receivable	34,509	
(34,517 − 8)		
Furniture (2,400 + 407)	2,807	
Cash	836	
Returns inwards	2,438	
Business expenses	3,204	
Purchases (72,100 − 407)	71,693	
Discounts allowed	42	
Capital		7,845
Accounts payable		6,575
(6,890 − 315)		
Sales (127,510 + 90)		127,600
Discounts received		1,419
	143,439	143,439

27.6

(a) (i)

The Journal

	Dr	Cr
C. Thomas	450	
Thomasson Manufacturing Ltd		450
Suspense	100	
Telephone		100
Suspense	2,000	
Sales account		2,000
Machine repairs	390	
Machinery		390
Suspense	1,500	
Rent received*		1,500
Purchases account	765	
P Brooks		765

* Assumed not invoiced to Atlas Ltd

(ii) Computation of Corrected Profit for year ending 31 December 2018

Profit as originally reported		47,240
Add Telephone expense overstated	100	
Sales understated	2,000	
Rent received omitted	1,500	3,600
		50,840
Less Machinery repairs understated	390	
Purchases omitted	765	1,155
Corrected profit figure		49,685

(b) (i) Per text   **(ii)** Per text

27.8

(a)

Difference on Trial Balance Suspense

Per trial balance	2,513	J. Winters	
Discounts received	324	Wages	2,963
Discounts allowed	324		
	3,161		3,161

(b) Computation of Corrected Net Profit for year ending 30 April 2019

	−	+	
Net profit per draft accounts			24,760
(i) Discounts		648	
(ii) Wages	2,963		
(iv) Stationery prepaid		1,500	
(vi) Remittance	3,000		
	5,963	2,148	
			3,815
			20,945

Correct net profit
(iii) and (v) did not affect profit

(c) Per text

27.11

(a)

(i) Van	6,000	
Motor vehicle expenses		6,000
(ii) Fuel	250	
Drawings		250
(iii) B. Struton	300	
B. Burton Ltd		300
(iv) Drawings	750	
Business rates		750
(v) Drawings	720	
Wages		720
(vi) Purchases	500	
K. Jarman		500

(b)

Net profit per draft financial statements			23,120
Add (i)		6,000	
(iv)		750	
(v)		720	
		7,470	
		30,590	
Less (ii)		250	
(vi)		500	
		750	
		29,840	

27.12

(a)

(i) Suspense	10	
Sales		10
(ii) Discount allowed	2	
Suspense		2
(iii) Discount allowed	140	
Suspense		140
(iv) D. Bird	10	
Suspense		10
(v) Suspense	3	
J. Flyn		3

(b) The overall effect on the trial balance is that the following changes have been made:

	Dr	Cr
(i) Sales		10
(ii) and (iii) Discount allowed	142	
(iv) and (v) Accounts receivable	7	
(i) to (v) Suspense		139

27.14

Workings

(i) Purchases	10	
Suspense		10
(ii) A. Supplier	45	
Suspense		45
(iii) Plant and Machinery	70	
Repairs		70
(iv) Suspense	20	
S. Kane		20
(v) Sales	300	
Plant and Machinery disposals		300
(vi) Accounts receivable	60	
Suspense		60
(vii) Suspense	2	
B. Luckwood		2
(viii) Business rates	45	
Prepayments		45

(a)

Suspense

Balance	93	(i) Purchases	10
(iv) S. Kane	20	(ii) A. Supplier	45
(vii) B. Luckwood	2	(vi) Accounts receivable	60
	115		115

(b) (i) The suspense account is shown in the balance sheet, not the income statement. The following item increases net profit:

(iii)	70

The following items reduce net profit:

(i)	10
(viii)	45
	(55)
	15

Overall, net profit is increased by 15

Note: (v) has no effect on net profit. Sales are reduced by 300 and the loss on disposal of the plant and machinery is reduced by 300.

(ii) The following items are changed in the balance sheet:

	Dr	Cr
Suspense		93
(ii) Accounts payable	45	
(iii) Plant and Machinery	70	
(iv), (vi), (vii) Accounts receivable (60 − 20 − 2)	38	
(viii) Prepayments		45
		15
	153	153

Answers to Scenario Questions

SQ1 (a)

Picta Simpla

Income Statement for the year ending 30 June 2020

	£	£
Sales		258,100
Less Cost of goods sold		
Opening inventory	19,250	
Purchases	185,850	
	205,100	
Less: Closing inventory	50,150	
		154,950
Gross profit		103,150
Less Expenses		
Wages	14,500	
Advertising	15,500	
Postage and packing	7,250	
Rent	12,000	
Insurance	2,850	
Electricity	3,400	
Depreciation	800	
Stationery	1,350	
Telephone	3,450	
		61,100
Net profit		42,050

(b) Your note should explain that the business is a separate entity from him and so the cost of having a holiday has nothing to do with the business, but must be treated as drawings. It should also explain that drawings represent the amount of business assets taken out of the business by the owner for the owner's, not the business's, use. Drawings are *never* an expense of the business.

SQ2

(a)

Sleasy Cars

Balance Sheet as at 31 December 2019

	£	£	£	£
Non-current assets				
Land				5,000
Offices		500		
Less Depreciation		100		
			400	
Truck		5,000		
Less Depreciation		2,500		
			2,500	
				7,900
Current assets				
Inventory		21,000		
Accounts receivable and prepayments		1,900		
Cash		100		
				23,000
				30,900
Current liabilities				
Accounts payable and accruals	8,600			
Bank overdraft	6,400			
		15,000		
Non-curret liability		3,000		
				(18,000)
				12,900
Net assets				
Capital				
Opening balance*		15,500		
Add Net profit*		8,400		
		23,900		
Less Drawings		11,000		
				12,900

*5,000 + 10,000 + 500 = 15,500

*23,500 − 500 − 100 − 3,000 − 2,500 − 500 − 2,000 − 400 − 5,000 − 1,500 + 400 = 8,400

(b)

	Dr	Cr
Office overvalued: Net profit	500	
Office		500
Office depreciation: Net profit	100	
Depreciation – Office		100
Land overvalued: Net profit	5,000	
Land		5,000
Provision for long-term liability: Net profit	3,000	
Non-current liability		3,000
Depreciation on truck: Net profit	2,500	
Depreciation – Truck		2,500
Car overvalued: Net profit	500	
Inventory		500
Bad debt: Net profit	2,000	
Accounts receivable		2,000
Accruals: Net profit	400	
Accruals		400
Prepayment: Prepayment	400	
Net profit		400
Car overvalued: Net profit	1,500	
Inventory		1,500

SQ3

Mr Jones

Income Statement for the year ending XXX

	£	£
Sales		430,000
Less Cost of goods sold		
Opening inventory	6,520	
Purchases	305,500	
Carriage in	2,100	
	314,120	
Less Closing inventory	7,000	
		307,120
Gross profit		122,880
Less: Expenses		
Rent	5,350	
Business rates	2,800	
Insurance	400	
Postage	250	
Stationery	1,002	
Advertising	200	
Salaries and wages	10,500	
Bad debts	400	
Allowance for doubtful debts	112	
Depreciation	15,000	
		36,014
Net profit		86,866

Balance sheet as at XXX

	£	£	£
Non-current assets			
Equipment			150,000
Less: Depreciation			50,000
			100,000
Current assets			
Inventory	7,000		
Accounts receivable	4,608		
Prepayment	200		
Cash in hand	120		
		11,928	
			111,928
Current liabilities			
Accounts payable	9,600		
Bank overdraft	2,743		
Accrual	366		
			(12,709)
			99,219
Net assets			
Capital			
Balance			43,353
Net profit			86,866
			130,219
Less Drawings			31,000
			99,219

SQ4

(a)

Mr Try

Income Statement the year ending 30 June 2020

	£	£
Sales		17,644
Less Expenses		
Repairs	230	
Miscellaneous	110	
Insurance (350 – 50)	300	
Accounting fees (250 – 250 + 275)	275	
Postage and stationery	50	
Depreciation	375	
Allowance for doubtful debts	110	
Bank charges	45	
		1,495
Net profit		16,149

(b)

Balance Sheet as at 30 June 2020

	£	£	£
Non-current assets			
Ladders and equipment		750	
Less: Depreciation		375	
			375
Current assets			
Cleaning materials and cloths	3,400		
Accounts receivable	110		
Prepayments	50		
Bank	2,345		
Cash	35		
		5,940	
			6,315
Current liabilities			
Accounts payable	100		
Accruals	320		
		(420)	
			5,895
Capital			
Balance at 1 July 2019		346	
Net profit		16,149	
		16,495	
Less Drawings		10,600	
			5,895

(c) Your letter should explain that consumables are items purchased with the intention of using them in the short term, after which they will either have been used up (e.g. printer ink) or no longer usable (e.g. carbon paper). The ladders do not fall into the category of consumables. They were purchased for use in the long term, in this case, more than one accounting period. As such, they are non-current assets and must be depreciated.

SQ5 (a)

B's Casuals

Income Statement for the year ending 30 June 2020

Sales		260,040
Less: Cost of goods sold		
Opening inventory	21,500	
Purchases	68,500	
Carriage in	5,200	
	95,200	
Less: Closing inventory	22,500	
		72,700
Gross profit		187,340

	£
Less: Expenses	
Wages	24,500
Business rates	9,950
Bad debt	2,000
Advertising	1,040
Insurance	2,850
Electricity	3,400
Depreciation	15,800
Stationery	1,350
Telephone	3,450
	64,340
	123,000

(b) *Balance Sheet as at 30 June 2020*

Non-current assets		
Factory and Machinery	400,000	
Less Depreciation	115,000	
		285,000
Computer	4,000	
Less Depreciation	2,400	
		1,600
		286,600
Current assets		
Prepayments:		
Insurance	650	
Telephone	200	
Cash in hand	600	
		1,450
		288,050
Current liabilities		
Accounts payable	3,500	
Rates Accrual	2,450	
Electricity Accrual	500	
Loan from Mrs Baldwin	600	
		(7,050)
		281,000
Capital		
Balance at 1 July 2019		213,000*
Net profit		123,000
Less Drawings		(55,000)
		281,000

*balancing figure

(c) You need to explain how the accrual system operates and why it is used (see text Section 7.8). You also need to explain that drawings are assets withdrawn from the business for the owner's personal use, which is what his 'wages' and his home cinema system purchase are. Drawings are *never* expenses of a business.

28.1
Balgreen Bowling Club
Income and Expenditure Account for the year ending 31 December 2019

Income		
Collections at matches		17,200
Profit on refreshments		22,000
		39,200
Less Expenditure		
Rent for green (4,800 − 1,200)	3,600	
Printing and stationery (200 + 80)	280	
Secretary's expenses	320	
Repairs to equipment	280	
Groundsman's wages	16,000	
Miscellaneous expenses	240	
Depreciation of equipment (7,200 × 10%)	720	21,440
Surplus of income over expenditure		17,760

Balance Sheet as at 31 December 2019

Non-current assets		
Equipment (6000 + 1200)	7,200	
Less Depreciation	720	6,480
Current assets		
Prepayment	1,200	
Cash	21,760	22,960
		29,440
Current liabilities		
Expenses owing		(80)
Net assets		29,360
Financed by:		
Accumulated fund		
Opening balance (6,000 + 5,600)		11,600
Add Surplus of income over expenditure		17,760
		29,360

28.3
Happy Haddock Angling Club
(a)
Income and Expenditure Account for the year ending 31 December 2018

Income:		
Subscriptions		3,500
Visitors' fees		650
Competition fees		820
Snack bar profit (see workings)		1,750
		6,720
Less Expenditure:		
Rent and rates	1,500	
Secretarial expenses	240	
Loan interest	260	
Depreciation on games equipment	400	2,400
Surplus of income over expenditure		4,320

Workings: Snack bar profit: 6,000 − (800 + 3,750 − 900) − 600 = 1,750

(b)
Balance Sheet as at 31 December 2018

Non-current assets		
Clubhouse buildings (12,500 + 8,000)		20,500
Games equipment	2,000	
Less Depreciation	400	1,600
		22,100
Current assets		
Snack bar inventory	900	
Bank	700	1,600
		23,700
Current liabilities		
Subscriptions received in advance	380	
Loan from bank	5,500	(5,880)
		17,820
Financed by:		
Accumulated fund		
Opening balance (see workings)		13,500
Add surplus for year		4,320
		17,820

Workings: 200 + 800 + 12,500 = 13,500

28.5

(a)

Accumulated fund 1 August 2018

Equipment	975
Inventory of prizes	38
Arrears of subscriptions	65
Cash and bank	210
	1,288

Less Subscriptions in advance	10	
Prizes suppliers	58	68
		1,220

(b)

(i)

Subscriptions

In arrears b/d	65	In advance b/d		10
In advance c/d	37	Cash		1,987
Income and expenditure	1,980	In arrears c/d		85
	2,082			2,082

(ii)

Competition prizes

Inventory b/d	58	Accounts payable b/d	38
Cash	46	Inventory c/d	270
Accounts payable c/d	272	Cost of prizes given	68
	376		376

(c)

Miniville Rotary Club

Income and Expenditure Account for the year ending 31 July 2019

Income		
Subscriptions		1,980
Ticket sales	437	
Less Cost of prizes	272	165
Donations received		177
		2,322
Less Expenditure		
Rent (1,402 − 500)		902
Visiting speakers' expenses		1,275
Secretarial expenses		163
Stationery and printing		179
Donations to charities		35
Depreciation		195
		2,749
Excess of expenditure over income		427

Balance Sheet as at 31 July 2019

Non-current assets			
Equipment at cost		1,420	
Less Depreciation		640	780
Current assets			
Inventory of prizes		46	
Arrears of subscriptions		85	131
			911
Current liabilities			
Accounts payable for prizes	68		
Advance subscriptions	37		
Bank overdraft	13		(118)
			793
Accumulated fund			
Balance at start of year			1,220
Less Excess of expenditure over income			427
			793

28.6

(a)

Café operations:			
Takings			4,660
Less Cost of supplies:			
Opening inventory		800	
Add purchases (1,900 + 80)		1,980	
		2,780	
Less Closing inventory		850	1,930
			2,730
Wages			2,000
Profit			730
Sports equipment:			
Sales			900
Less Cost of goods sold:			
Opening inventory		1,000	
Add Purchases (1,000 × 50%)		500	
		1,500	
Less Closing inventory *(see note)*		900	600
Profit			300

Note: To find closing sports equipment inventory: 900 is sales at 50% mark-up on cost so cost of sales is 600. By arithmetical deduction closing inventory is found to be 900.

28.6 *(cont'd)*

(b)

Subscriptions

Owing b/d	60	In advance b/d Cash: 2017	120
		Cash: 2018	40
Income and expenditure	1,280	2018	1,100
		2019	80
In advance c/d	80	Owing c/d	80
	1,420		1,420

Life Subscriptions

	220	Balance b/d	1,400
Income and expenditure (11 × 20)		Cash	200
Balance c/d	1,380		
	1,600		1,600

(c)

Happy Tickers Sports & Social Club
Income and Expenditure Account for the year ending 31 December 2018

Income:

Subscriptions (1,280 + 220)		1,500
Profit on café operations		730
Profit on sports equipment		300
		2,530

Less Expenditure

Rent	1,200	
Insurance (900 × $^{12}/_{18}$)	600	
Repairs to roller ($^1/_2$ × 450)	225	
Sports equipment net cost (*see* note 1)	486	
Depreciation of roller ($^1/_2$ × 200)	100	2,611
Excess of expenditure over income		81

Balance Sheet as at 31 December 2018

Non-current assets

Share in motor roller at cost	1,000	
Less Depreciation to date	500	500
Used sports equipment at valuation		700
		1,200

Current assets

Inventory of new sports equipment (*see* note 2)	900
Inventory of café supplies	850
Subscriptions owing	80
Carefree Conveyancers: owing for expenses	225
Prepaid expenses (200 rent + 150 insurance)	350

Balance Sheet as at 31 December 2018 (continued)

Cash and bank (*see* note 3)		754	3,159
			4,359
Current liabilities			
Café suppliers		80	
Advance subscriptions		80	160
Non-current liabilities			
Life subscriptions		1,380	
			(1,540)
			2,819
Accumulated fund			
Opening balance		2,900	
Less Excess of expenditure		81	
			2,819

Notes:

Used Sports Equipment

1 Inventory b/d	700	Cash	14
Transferred from purchases	500	Income and expenditure a/c	486
		Inventory c/d	700
	1,200		1,200

2 b/d 1,000 + bought (1,000 × $^1/_2$)500 = 1,500 – sold 600 = 900

3 b/d 1,210 + receipts 6,994 – paid 7,450 = 754

(d) To most people probably the best description of the item would be 'deferred income', i.e. income paid in advance for future benefits.

It could, however, be described as a liability of the club. The club in future will have to provide and finance amenities for life members, but those members do not have to pay any more money for them. This is therefore the future liability to provide these services without further payment.

29.1

Loose Tools

2018		2018	
Jan 1 Balance b/d	6,000		
Various Bank	8,000	Dec 31 Manufacturing	4,200
Various Wages	1,300	31 Balance c/d	12,000
Various Materials	900		
	16,200		16,200
2019		**2019**	
Jan 1 Balance b/d	12,000		
Various Bank	4,000	Dec 31 Manufacturing	6,000
Various Wages	1,600	31 Balance c/d	12,800
Various Materials	1,200		

Loose Tools

2020			2020		
		18,800			18,800
Jan 1 Balance b/d	12,800		Various Bank: Refund	320	
Various Bank	7,200		Dec 31 Manufacturing	7,420	
Various Wages	1,000		31 Balance c/d	14,600	
Various Materials	1,340				
	22,340			22,340	

29.2 Manufacturing and Trading Account for 2020

Sales		406,120
Less: Cost of goods sold		
Opening inventory of raw materials	24,600	
Purchases of raw materials	165,400	
Carriage in of raw materials	9,100	
	199,100	
Closing inventory raw materials	31,300	
Cost of materials consumed	167,800	
Direct expenses		
Salaries and wages (151,400 − 44,500)	106,900	
Factory direct expenses	730	
Prime cost	275,430	
Indirect expenses		
Salaries and wages	44,500	
Rent and rates (3,000 × 3/4)	2,250	
Light and heat	4,900	
Repairs to machinery	3,400	
Depreciation – machinery	5,600	
Insurance – plant and machinery	860	
	336,940	
Add Opening work-in-progress	20,200	
	357,140	
Less Closing work-in-progress	23,400	
Production cost of goods produced	333,740	
Add Opening inventory of finished goods	18,600	
	352,340	
Less Closing inventory of finished goods	29,200	
	323,140	
Gross profit	82,980	

29.4

Z. Varga
Manufacturing Account and Income Statement for the year ending 31 December 2020

Opening inventory raw materials		50,800
Add Purchases		183,070
Add Carriage inwards		3,920
		237,790
Less Closing inventory raw materials		57,800
Cost of raw materials consumed		179,990
Direct labour		168,416
Prime cost		348,406
Factory overhead expenses		
Rent $^{3}/_{4}$	7,800	
Fuel and power	16,240	
Depreciation: Machinery	20,400	44,440
		392,846
Add Opening work-in-progress		62,200
		455,046
Less Closing work-in-progress		49,200
Production cost of goods completed		405,846
Sales		637,244
Less Cost of goods sold		
Opening inventory finished goods	46,520	
Add Production cost of goods completed	405,846	
	452,366	
Less Closing inventory finished goods	57,692	394,674
Gross profit		242,570
Less Expenses:		
Office salaries	66,838	
Rent $^{1}/_{4}$	2,600	
Lighting and heating	8,840	
Depreciation: Office equipment	4,600	82,878
Net profit		159,692

29.5

Manufacturing Account and Trading Account part of the Income Statement for the six months ending 30 September 2020

Raw materials		
Opening inventory		2,990
Purchases		15,630
Carriage in		126
		18,746
Less Closing inventory		4,200

Manufacturing Account and Trading Account part of the Income Statement for the six months ending 30 September 2020 (continued)

(a) Cost of *raw materials consumed*		14,546	
Direct wages		48,648	
(b) *Prime cost of production*		63,194	
Indirect expenses			
Factory general expenses	7,048		
Depreciation – Factory equipment	4,200		
Rent and business rates	2,100	13,348	
		76,542	
		3,900	
Add Opening work-in-progress		80,442	
		3,600	
Less Closing work-in-progress		76,842	
(c) *Production cost of finished goods*		112,410	
Sales			
Less Cost of goods sold			
Opening inventory of finished goods	15,300		
Add Production cost of finished goods	76,842		
	92,142		
Less Closing inventory of finished goods	17,700	74,442	
Gross profit		37,968	

29.7

E. Wilson
Manufacturing Account and Income Statement for the year ending 31 December 2020

Opening inventory of raw materials		13,260
Add Purchases		57,210
		70,470
Less Closing inventory of raw materials		14,510
Cost of raw materials consumed		55,960
Manufacturing wages (72,100 + 550)		72,650
Prime cost		128,610
Factory overhead expenses:		
Factory lighting and heating	7,220	
General expenses: factory	8,100	
Rent of factory	6,100	
Depreciation: Machinery	3,000	24,420
Production cost of goods completed		153,030
Sales		194,800
Less Cost of goods sold:		

Manufacturing Account and Income Statement for the year ending 31 December 2020 (continued)

Opening inventory of finished goods		41,300
Add Production cost of goods completed		153,030
		194,330
Less Closing inventory of finished goods		44,490
		149,840
Gross profit		44,960
Less Expenses:		
Office salaries	17,740	
General expenses: office	1,940	
Office rent (2,700 − 140)	2,560	
Office heating and lighting	1,490	
Sales reps' commission	11,688	
Delivery van expenses	1,760	
Depreciation: Office equipment	600	
Van	1,200	38,978
Net profit		5,982

Balance Sheet as at 31 December 2020

Non-current assets	Cost	Depreciation	Net
Machinery	40,000	14,400	25,600
Office equipment	9,000	1,400	7,600
Van	6,800	1,800	5,000
	55,800	17,600	38,200

Current assets			
Inventory: Finished goods	44,490		
Raw materials	14,510		
Accounts receivable	34,200		
Prepaid expenses	140		
Bank	16,142	109,482	
		147,682	
Current liabilities			
Accounts payable	9,400		
Expenses owing	550	(9,950)	
		137,732	
Capital			
Opening balance		155,950	
Add Net profit		5,982	
		161,932	
Less Drawings		24,200	
		137,732	

29.8

Mendip Ltd
Manufacturing Account and Income statement for
the year ending 30 June 2010

Raw materials		
Opening inventory		20,000
Purchases		130,100
		150,100
Less Closing inventory		22,000
Cost of raw materials consumed		128,100
Direct wages (63,000 − 15,700)		47,300
Direct factory expenses		9,100
Prime cost of production		184,500
Factory overheads		
Rates	3,000	
Heat and light	6,500	
Supervision	15,700	
Depreciation: Plant and machinery	10,500	35,700
Production cost of finished goods		220,200
Sales		317,500
Less: Cost of goods sold		
Opening inventory of finished goods	38,000	
Production cost of finished goods	220,200	
	258,200	
Less Closing inventory of finished goods	35,600	222,600
Gross profit		94,900
Less: Office salaries	36,300	
Directors fees	6,700	
Selling expenses	11,000	54,000
Net profit		40,900

Note: The dividends are not charged against revenue in the calculation of net profit. They are an appropriation of profit.

29.10

(a)

Jane Seymour
Manufacturing Account and Income Statement for
the year ending 31 July 2019

Direct materials purchased	43,000	
Less Closing inventory	7,000	36,000
Direct factory wages		39,000
Prime cost		75,000
Factory overhead expenses:		
Indirect factory wages	8,000	
Machinery repairs	1,600	
Rent and insurance (11,600 − 800) × $\frac{2}{3}$	7,200	
Light and power (5,000 + 1,000) × $\frac{2}{3}$	4,000	
Loose tools (9,000 − 5,000)	4,000	
Motor vehicle running expenses (12,000 × $\frac{1}{2}$)	6,000	
Depreciation: Plant and machinery	6,000	
Motor vehicles (7,500 × $\frac{1}{2}$)	3,750	40,550
		115,550
Less Closing work-in-progress		12,300
		103,250
Transfer of goods manufactured to trading account		95,000
Loss on manufacturing		8,250
Sales		170,000
Less Goods manufactured transferred	95,000	
Closing inventory	10,000	85,000
Gross profit		85,000
Less Administrative staff salaries	31,000	
Administrative expenses	9,000	
Sales and distribution staff salaries	13,000	
Rent and insurance (11,600 − 800) × $\frac{1}{3}$	3,600	
Motor vehicle running expenses (12,000 × $\frac{1}{2}$)	6,000	
Light and power (5,000 + 1,000) × $\frac{1}{3}$	2,000	
Depreciation: Motors (7,500 × $\frac{1}{2}$)	3,750	68,350
Net profit in trading		16,650
Loss on manufacturing		8,250
Overall net profit		8,400

(b) *Conservatism*. The valuation of inventory or work-in-progress does not include any element of expected future profit.

Matching. All of the prepayments and accruals adjusted for are examples of matching expenses against the time period(s) in which the revenue that they generate is recognised, as also are the depreciation charges.

Going Concern. When valuing inventory and work-in-progress, it has been assumed that the business is going to carry on indefinitely, and that they will be sold in the normal course of business rather than being sold because of cessation of activities.

30.1

SJD Sports Stores

Departmental Trading Account for the year ending 30 June 2019

	Footwear		Clothing		Equipment	
Sales		621,000		419,000		328,000
Less Cost of good sold:						
Opening inventory	69,000		56,000		47,000	
Add Purchases	404,000		287,000		185,000	
Less Closing inventory	77,000	396,000	48,000	295,000	53,000	179,000
Gross profit		225,000		124,000		149,000

30.2

J. Horner

Departmental Income Statement for the year ending 31 August 2020

	A		B	
Sales		75,000		50,000
Less Cost of goods sold:				
Opening inventory	1,250		1,000	
Add Purchases	51,000		38,020	
	52,250		39,020	
Less Closing inventory	1,410	50,840	912	38,108
Gross profits		24,160		11,892
Less Expenses:				
Wages	7,200		6,800	
Picture framing costs	300		–	
General office salaries	7,920		5,280	
Fire insurance	144		216	
Lighting and heating	248		372	
Repairs to premises	70		105	
Internal telephone	12		18	
Cleaning	72		108	
Accountancy charges	894		596	
General office expenses	306	17,166	204	13,699
Net profits/(losses)		6,994		(1,807)

31.1

Jack's Books (dates ignored)

Joint Venture with Wellie

TVs	3,000	Sales	8,300
Repairs	1,600		
Profit and loss	405		
Cash to Wellie	3,295		
	8,300		8,300

Wellie's Books

Joint Venture with Jack

Office rental	900	Cash: from Jack	3,295
Advertising	300		
Packaging materials	90		
TV	1,600		
Profit and loss	405		
	3,295		3,295

Memorandum Joint Venture Account

TVs	4,600	Sales	8,300
Repairs	1,600		
Office rental	900		
Advertising	300		
Packaging materials	90		
Profit on venture			
Jack $^{1}/_{2}$ 405	810		
Wellie $^{1}/_{2}$ 405			
	8,300		8,300

31.3

Bull's Books

Joint Venture with Craig and Finch

Rent	600	Balance c/d	1,503
Labour: Planting	260		
Labour: Fertilising	180		
Sundries	19		
Labour	210		
Fertiliser	74		
Profit and loss	160		
	1,503		1,503
Balance b/d	1,503	Cash: from Finch	1,503

Craig's Books

Joint Venture with Bull and Finch

Plants	510	Balance c/d	639
Motor expenses	49		
Profit and loss	80		
	639		639
Balance b/d	639	Cash: from Finch	639

Finch's Books

Joint Venture with Bull and Craig

Labour: Lifting	416	Sales	2,916
Sale expenses	318		
Profit and loss	40		
Balance c/d	2,142		
	2,916		2,916
Cash: to Bull	1,503	Balance b/d	2,142
Cash: to Craig	639		
	2,142		2,142

Memorandum Joint Venture Account

Rent	600	Sales	2,916
Labour: Planting	260		
Labour: Fertilising	180		
Labour: Sundry	210		
Labour: Lifting	416		
Fertiliser	74		
Motor expenses	49		
Plants	510		
Sale expenses	318		
Sundries	19		
Profit shared: Bull $^4/_7$	160		
Craig $^2/_7$	80		
Finch $^1/_7$	40	280	
	2,916		2,916

32.1

Gow, Short and Hill

Appropriation Account for the year ending 31 July 2019

Net profit b/d		230,000
Less Salaries: Short	70,000	
Hill	40,000	110,000
		120,000
Interest on capitals: Gow	4,800	
Short	3,200	
Hill	2,000	10,000
		110,000
Balance of profits		
Shared: Gow $^3/_{11}$	30,000	
Short $^4/_{11}$	40,000	
Hill $^4/_{11}$	40,000	110,000

32.3

Dunn and Outram

Profit and Loss Appropriation Account 2018

Net profit			90,000
Profit shared	Dunn	45,000	
	Outram	45,000	
			90,000
			90,000

Profit and Loss Appropriation Account 2019

Net profit			110,000
Salaries	Dunn	20,000	
	Outram	30,000	
Interest on capital	Dunn	8,000	
	Outram	3,500	
Profit shared	Dunn	24,250	
	Outram	24,250	
			110,000
			110,000

Profit and Loss Appropriation Account 2020

Net profit			50,000
Salaries	Dunn	20,000	
	Outram	30,000	
Interest on capital	Dunn	8,000	
	Outram	3,500	
Loss shared	Dunn	(5,750)	
	Outram	(5,750)	
			50,000
			50,000

Current Account – Dunn

2018			2018		
Drawings		26,000	Profit share		45,000
Bal c/d		19,000			
		45,000			45,000
2019			2019		
Drawings		24,000	Bal b/d		19,000
Bal c/d		47,250	Salary		24,000
			Interest on capital		8,000
			Profit share		24,250
		71,250			71,250
2020			2020		
Loss share		5,750	Bal b/d		47,250
Drawings		22,000	Salary		20,000
Bal c/d		47,500	Interest on capital		8,000
		75,250			75,250
			2021		
			Bal b/d		47,500

Current Account – Outram

2018			2018		
Drawings		32,000	Profit share		45,000
Bal c/d		13,000			
		45,000			45,000
2019			2019		
Drawings		28,000	Bal b/d		13,000
Bal c/d		42,750	Salary		30,000
			Interest on capital		3,500
			Profit share		24,250
		70,750			70,750
2020			2020		
Loss share		5,750	Bal b/d		42,750
Drawings		34,000	Salary		30,000
Bal c/d		36,500	Interest on capital		3,500
		76,250			76,250
			2021		
			Bal b/d		36,500

32.4

Blair, Short and Steel
Appropriation Account for the year ending 31 December 2020

Net profit b/d			111,100
Add Interest on drawings: Blair		400	
Short		300	
Steel		200	900
			112,000
Less Interest on capitals: Blair		3,000	
Short		2,000	
Steel		1,500	6,500
Salaries: Short		20,000	
Steel		25,000	45,000	51,500
			60,500
Balance of profits			60,500
Shared: Blair 70%		42,350	
Short 20%		12,100	
Steel 10%		6,050	60,500

Balance sheet as at 31 December 2020 (extracts)

Capital Accounts: Blair		100,000	
Short		50,000	
Steel		25,000	175,000

Current Accounts:	Blair	Short	Steel
Opening balances	18,600	9,460	8,200
Add Interest on capital	3,000	2,000	1,500
Salaries	20,000	25,000	
Share of profits	42,350	12,100	6,050
	63,950	43,560	40,750
Less Interest on drawings	400	300	200
Drawings	39,000	27,100	16,800
	24,550	16,160	23,750	64,460

32.8

Considerations

(a) *Legal position re Partnership Act 1890*: Partners can agree to anything. The main thing is that of mutual agreement. The agreement can either be very formal in a partnership deed drawn up by a lawyer or else it can be evidenced in other ways.

The Act lays down the provisions for profit sharing if agreement has not been reached, written or otherwise.

(b) As Bee is not taking an active part in the running of the business he could be registered as a limited partner under the 1907 Limited Partnership Act. This has the advantage that his liability is limited to the amount of capital invested by him; he can lose that but his personal possessions cannot be taken to pay any debts of the firm.

As Bee is a 'sleeping partner' you will have to decide whether his reward should be in the form of a fixed amount, or should vary according to the profits made. In this context you should also bear in mind whether or not he would suffer a share of losses if they occurred.

If he were to have a fixed amount, irrespective as to whether profits had been made or not, then the question arises as to the amount required. This is obviously a more risky investment than, say, government securities. He therefore would naturally expect to get a higher return.

Bee would probably feel aggrieved if the profits rose sharply, but he was still limited to the amounts already described. There could be an arrangement for extra payments if the profits exceeded a given figure.

Cee is the expert conducting the operations of the business. He will consequently expect a major share of the profits.

One possibility would be to give him a salary, similar to his current salary, before dividing whatever profits then remain.

(c) Dee is making himself available, as well as bringing in some capital. Because of this active involvement he will affect the profits made. It would seem appropriate to give him a salary commensurate with such work, plus a share of the profits.

(d) *Interest on capital*: Whatever is decided about profit sharing, it would seem appropriate for each of the partners to be given interest on their capitals before sharing the balance of the profits.

(e) Finally, it would be sensible to consider charging each partner interest on any drawings they take. This should deter partners from taking unnecessary drawings, and compensate the others if one partner takes out far more than the rest.

32.9

Frame and French
Income Statement and Profit and Loss Appropriation Account for the year ending 30 September 2019

Sales			363,111
Less Cost of goods sold:			
Opening inventory		62,740	
Add Purchases		210,000	
		272,740	
Less Closing inventory		74,210	198,530
Gross profit			164,581
Add Reduction in allowance for doubtful debts			150
			164,731
Less Salaries and wages (57,809 + 720)		58,529	
Office expenses (4,760 + 215)		4,975	
Carriage outwards		3,410	
Discounts allowed		620	
Bad debts		1,632	
Loan interest		3,900	
Depreciation: Fixtures	600		
Buildings	5,000	5,600	78,666
Net profit			86,065
Add Interest on drawings: Frame		900	
French		600	1,500
			87,565
Less Interest on capitals: Frame		5,000	
French		3,750	8,750
Salary: Frame			30,000	38,750
Balance of profits			48,815
Shared: Frame		29,289	
French		19,526	48,815

Balance Sheet as at 30 September 2019

	Cost	Depn	N.B.V.
Non-current assets			
Buildings	210,000	55,000	155,000
Fixtures	8,200	4,800	3,400
	218,200	59,800	158,400
Current assets			
Inventory		74,210	
Accounts receivable	61,400		
Less Allowance for doubtful debts	1,250	60,150	
Bank		6,130	
			140,490
			298,890
Current liabilities			
Accounts payable	26,590		
Expenses owing (215 + 720)	935	27,525	
Non-current liabilities			
Loan from P. Prince		65,000	(92,525)
			206,365

			N.B.V.
Financed by			
Capital Accounts: Frame		100,000	
French		75,000	175,000

	Frame	*French*
Current Accounts		
Opening balances	4,100	1,200
Add Interest on capital	5,000	3,750
Salary	30,000	–
Balance of profit	29,289	19,526
	68,389	24,476
Less Drawings	31,800	28,200
Interest on drawings	900	600
	35,689	(4,324)

	N.B.V.
	31,365
	206,365

32.11

Sage and Onion
Income Statement and Profit and Loss Appropriation Account for the year ending 31 December 2020

Sales (508,000 − 6,000)			502,000
Opening inventory		75,000	
Purchases (380,000 + 3,000)		383,000	
Carriage in		21,500	
		479,500	
Returns		12,000	
		467,500	
Closing inventory	68,000		
Drawings (500 + 630)	1,130	69,130	
Gross profit			398,370
			103,630
Discounts received			1,000
			104,630
Expenses			
Salaries (42,000 + 900)		42,900	
Office expenses		7,500	
Carriage out		3,000	
Adverts		5,000	
Discount allowed		1,200	
Rent and rates (2,800 − 200)		2,600	
Bad debt		1,400	
Depreciation − Fixtures and fittings		1,500	
Increase in allowance for doubtful debts		400	
			65,500
Net profit			39,130
Add Interest on drawings (360 + 280)		640	
Interest on current account		30	
			39,800
Less Interest on capital (5,000 + 2,500)		7,500	
Interest on current account		100	
Salaries (12,000 + 8,000)		20,000	
			27,600
Balance of profits			12,200
Shared: Sage		6,100	
Onion		6,100	
			12,200

Balance Sheet as at 31 December 2020

Non-current assets			
Freehold – Cost			50,000
Fixtures and fittings – Cost		15,000	
– Depreciation		4,500	10,500
			60,500
Current assets			
Inventory		68,000	
Accounts receivable (52,400 – 2,400)		50,000	
Prepayments		200	
Bank		31,600	149,800
			210,300
Current liabilities			
Accounts payable (33,300 + 3,000)		36,300	
Accruals		900	
VAT		8,700	(45,900)
			164,400
Financed by			
Capital Accounts			
Sage			100,000
Onion			50,000
			150,000

Current Accounts	Sage	Onion
Balance b/d	2,000	(600)
Interest on capital	5,000	2,500
Interest on current account	100	(30)
Salaries	12,000	8,000
Profit	6,100	6,100
Drawings/Int/Goods	(15,860)	(10,910)
	9,340	5,060

	14,400
	164,400

32.13

Reid and Benson
Income Statement for the year ending 31 December 2021

Sales	541,750	
Less Returns	800	540,950
Purchases	291,830	
Less Returns	330	
	291,500	
Carriage inwards	3,150	
	294,650	
Less Closing inventory	1,500	293,150
Gross profit		247,800
Less Expenses		
Staff salaries	141,150	
Rent	2,500	
Compensation payments	10,000	
General expenses	9,500	
Bad debts	1,150	
Increase in allowance for doubtful debts	1,500	
Depreciation	7,400	
Insurance (1,000 + 1,500 – 150)	2,350	175,550
Net profit transferred to Appropriation Account		72,250

Appropriation Account for the year ending 31 December 2021

Net profit		72,250
Less salary – Reid		18,000
		54,250
Add Interest on Drawings – Reid	1,050	
– Benson	550	1,600
		55,850
Less Interest on Capital – Reid	3,750	
– Benson	2,500	6,250
		49,600
Less Interest on Current a/c – Reid	250	
– Benson	200	450
		49,150
Balance of profits		
Shared – Reid		29,490
– Benson		19,660
		49,150

33.1

Balance Sheet as at 31 December 2021

Non-current assets

Fixtures and fittings	74,000	
Less Accumulated depreciation	19,400	54,600

Current assets

Inventory	1,500	
Accounts receivable (137,500 − 1,500)	136,000	
Prepayments	150	
Cash	400	
	138,050	
	192,650	

Current liabilities

Accounts payable	(23,400)
	169,250
	125,000

Financed by:

	Reid	Benson
Capital Accounts	75,000	50,000
Current Accounts		
Balance b/d	5,000	4,000
Salary	18,000	–
Interest on drawings	(1,050)	(550)
Interest on capital a/c	3,750	2,500
Interest on current a/c	250	200
Share of profit	29,490	19,660
Drawings	(17,000)	(20,000)
Balance c/d	38,440	5,810
		44,250
		169,250

33.1

(a)

Goodwill

Balance Sheet as at 31 March 2019

Goodwill	24,000
Other assets	100,000
	124,000
Capitals: Vantuira (30,000 + 7,200)	37,200
Aparecida (20,000 + 4,800)	24,800
Fraga (50,000 + 12,000)	62,000
	124,000

(b)

Goodwill Workings

	Before		After		Loss or Gain		Action needed	
Vantuira	3/10	7,200	1/2	12,000	Gain	4,800	Debit Vantuira	4,800
Aparecida	1/5	4,800	1/8	3,000	Loss	1,800	Credit Aparecida	1,800
Fraga	1/2	12,000	3/8	9,000	Loss	3,000	Credit Fraga	3,000
		24,000		24,000				

Balance Sheet as at 1 April 2019

Net assets		100,000
		100,000
Capitals Vantuira (30,000 − 4,800)		25,200
Aparecida (20,000 + 1,800)		21,800
Fraga (50,000 + 3,000)		53,000
		100,000

33.3

(a)

Goodwill		Dr	40,000
Capitals	Black	Cr	20,000
	Smart	Cr	20,000
Cash		Dr	70,000
Capital	King	Cr	70,000

(b)

Balance Sheet

Goodwill	40,000
Non-current and current assets (other than cash)	160,000
Cash	71,000
	271,000
Current liabilities	(41,000)
	230,000
Capitals Black	90,000
Smart	70,000
King	70,000
	230,000

(c)

Capitals	Black	Dr	20,000
	Smart	Dr	7,500
	King	Dr	12,500
Goodwill		Cr	40,000

33.5

(a)

Capital Accounts (£000)

	Wilson	Player	Sharp	Titmus			Wilson	Player	Sharp	Titmus
Bal c/d	73	108	62	30		Bal b/d	57	76	38	30
						Cash				
						Goodwill	16	32	24	–
	73	108	62	30			73	108	62	30

(b)

Goodwill 72,000; Other assets except cash 200,000; Cash 32,000; Capital as in (a); Accounts payable 31,000.

33.6

The senior partner's objection is a correct response. The money does not belong to the new partner once it has been paid.

This is because a new partner becomes an owner of part of the business, and this includes a part of the goodwill. This payment is specifically for that part of the goodwill. The goodwill was created by previous partners, and this is where the new partner buys his share from them. The £10,000 will be credited to the old partners in their old profit sharing ratio.

If C, the new partner, has paid £10,000 for one-fifth of the goodwill, then total goodwill is £50,000. Should the business be sold at a future date, and the goodwill realise £50,000, then C would receive one-fifth of the proceeds, i.e. £10,000, thus getting his money back. This illustrates the fairness of the accounting treatment of his original payment for goodwill. If anything had been credited to his account from this original payment for goodwill then he would have received that in addition. Obviously this would be unfair.

33.7

(a)

Stone, Pebble & Brick trading as Bigtime Building Supply Company
Profit and Loss Appropriation Account for the year ending 31 March 2019

	Apr–Dec	Jan–Mar
Net profit	27,225	9,075
Less Interest on Stone's loan	—	385
	27,225	8,690
Less Interest on capitals: Stone		250
Pebble		200
Brick		125
Less Salary: Brick		2,125
Balance of profits shared:		
Stone	1/3 9,075	1/2 2,995
Pebble	1/3 9,075	3/10 1,797
Brick	1/3 9,075	1/5 1,198
	27,225	5,990

(b)

Capitals

	Stone	Pebble	Brick		Stone	Pebble	Brick
Goodwill adjustment*		2,000	6,000	Balances b/d	26,000	18,000	16,000
Transfer to loan	14,000			Goodwill adjustment*	8,000		
Balances c/d	20,000	16,000	10,000				
	34,000	18,000	16,000		34,000	18,000	16,000

Current Accounts

	Stone	Pebble	Brick		Stone	Pebble	Brick
Drawings	8,200	9,600	7,200	Interest on capital	250	200	125
Balances c/d	4,120	1,472	5,323	Salary			2,125
				Share of profits:			
				Apr–Dec	9,075	9,075	9,075
				Jan–Mar	2,995	1,797	1,198
	12,320	11,072	12,523		12,320	11,072	12,523

*Note:

Goodwill:

	Value of goodwill taken over	Elimination of goodwill	Net effect
Stone	30,000	22,000	8,000 Cr
Pebble	20,000	22,000	2,000 Dr
Brick	16,000	22,000	6,000 Dr
	66,000	66,000	—

34.1

(a)

Buildings

Balance b/d	175,000	Balance c/d	250,000
Revaluation: Increase	75,000		
	250,000		250,000

Motor Vehicles

Balance b/d	43,000	Revaluation: Reduction	13,000
		Balance c/d	30,000
	43,000		43,000

Inventory

Balance b/d	15,900	Revaluation: Reduction	1,900
		Balance c/d	14,000
	15,900		15,900

Office Fittings

Balance b/d	4,700	Revaluation: Reduction	1,700
		Balance c/d	3,000
	4,700		4,700

Revaluation

Motor vehicles	13,000	Buildings		75,000
Inventory	1,900			
Office fittings	1,700			
Profit on revaluation				
Cox	29,200			
Fox	17,520			
Lock	11,680	58,400		
		75,000		75,000

Capitals

	Cox	Fox	Lock		Cox	Fox	Lock
Balances c/d	169,200	97,520	56,080	Balances b/d	140,000	80,000	44,400
				Profit on revaluation	29,200	17,520	11,680
	169,200	97,520	56,080		169,200	97,520	56,080

(b) Balance Sheet as at 1 January 2019

Non-current assets		
Buildings at valuation		250,000
Motor vehicles at valuation		30,000
Office fittings at valuation		3,000
		283,000
Current assets		
Inventory at valuation	14,000	
Accounts receivable	22,200	
Bank	3,600	
		39,800
		322,800
Capitals:		
Cox		169,200
Fox		97,520
Lock		56,080
		322,800

34.3

(a)

Revaluation*

Premises	90,000	Premises	120,000
Plant	37,000	Plant	35,000
Inventory	62,379	Inventory	54,179
Allowance for doubtful debts	3,000		
Profit on revaluation			
Alan $\frac{1}{2}$	8,400		
Bob $\frac{1}{3}$	5,600		
Charles $\frac{1}{6}$	2,800	16,800	
	209,179		209,179

*Just the net increases/decreases could have been recorded. Either method is acceptable.

Goodwill

			Goodwill cancelled		
Capitals: Alan $\frac{1}{2}$	21,000		Capitals: Alan $\frac{3}{7}$	18,000	
Bob $\frac{1}{3}$	14,000		Bob $\frac{2}{7}$	12,000	
Charles $\frac{1}{6}$	7,000		Don $\frac{2}{7}$	12,000	
	42,000			42,000	

Capitals

	Alan	Bob	Charles	Don		Alan	Bob	Charles	Don
Goodwill	18,000	12,000	–	12,000	Balances b/d	85,000	65,000	35,000	–
Retirement			42,000		Goodwill	21,000	14,000	7,000	–
Balances c/d	88,000	67,000		67,000	Cash				79,000
	106,000	79,000	42,000	79,000		106,000	79,000	42,000	79,000

Current Accounts

	Alan	Bob	Charles	Don		Alan	Bob	Charles	Don
Balance b/d		2,509			Balance b/d	3,714		4,678	
Retirement			7,478		Profit on Revaluation	8,400	5,600	2,800	
Cash	9,023				Cash				3,091
Balances c/d	3,091	3,091		3,091					
	12,114	5,600	7,478	3,091		12,114	5,600	7,478	3,091

Charles: Retirement

Car	3,900	Capital	42,000
Cash	53,578	Current	7,478
Balance c/d	20,000	Loan	28,000
	77,478		77,478

Bank

Don: Capital	79,000	Balance b/d	4,200
Don: Current	3,091	Retirement – Charles	53,578
Balance c/d	5,710	Repaid Alan – Capital	21,000
		Current	9,023
	87,801		87,801

(b) **Alan, Bob and Don**
Balance Sheet as at 30 June 2019

Non-current assets		
Premises		120,000
Plant		35,000
Vehicles (15,000 – 3,900)		11,100
Fixtures		2,000
		168,100
Current assets		
Inventory	54,179	
Accounts receivable (34,980 – 3,000)	31,980	
Cash	760	
	86,919	
		255,019
Current liabilities		
Accounts payable	19,036	
Bank overdraft	5,710	
	24,746	
Loan – Charles	20,000	
		44,746
		210,273
Capital		
Alan	67,000	
Bob	67,000	
Don	67,000	
		201,000
Current account		
Alan	3,091	
Bob	3,091	
Don	3,091	
		9,273
		210,273

34.5
(a)

Revaluation

Capital account:		Freehold premises	2,000
Gain on revaluation		Machinery and tools	900
A	4,000	Investments	1,100
B	4,000	Goodwill	8,000
C	4,000		
	12,000		12,000

Bank

Balance b/d	12,100	Capital account: A	18,900
Capital account:		Balance c/d	9,200
B	10,000		
C	6,000		
	28,100		28,100

Capital Accounts

	A	B	C
Balance b/d	20,000	17,000	25,000
Revaluation	4,000	4,000	4,000
New capital		10,000	6,000
Investment	(5,100)		
Bank	(18,900)		
	NIL	31,000	35,000

B and C
Balance Sheet as at 31 December 2020

Non-current assets		
Goodwill		8,000
Freehold premises		18,000
Machinery and tools		16,000
		42,000
Current assets		
Inventory	16,000	
Accounts receivable	12,800	
Bank	9,200	
	38,000	
		80,000
Current liabilities		
Accounts payable		(14,000)
		66,000
Financed by:		
Capital Accounts – B		31,000
– C		35,000
		66,000

35.1

Realisation

Buildings	150,000	Cash: Accounts receivable	20,900
Tools and fixtures	11,600	Buildings	139,000
Accounts receivable	22,300	Tools and fixtures	5,000
Cash: Expenses	1,950	Discounts	700
		Loss on realisation: Adrian	10,125
		Thomas	10,125
	185,850		185,850

Capital Accounts

	Adrian	Thomas		Adrian	Thomas
Loss on realisation	10,125	10,125	Balance b/d	108,000	59,300
Cash	97,875	49,175			
	108,000	59,300		108,000	59,300

Cash

Balance b/d	1,800	Realisation expenses	1,950
Accounts receivable	20,900	Accounts payable	17,700
Buildings	139,000	Capitals: Adrian	97,875
Tools	5,000	Thomas	49,175
	166,700		166,700

35.2

(a)

Realisation account

Non-current assets	185,000	Trade payables	8,900
Inventory	31,600	Pugh: vehicle taken over	22,000
Trade receivables	14,850	Bank (non-current assets)*	150,000
Bank (paid to payables)	8,624	Bank (inventory)	25,280
Bank (dissolution expenses)	1,951	Bank (receivables)	11,875
		Loss on realisation to capital a/cs:	
		Mears $^5/_{10}$	11,985
		Pugh $^3/_{10}$	7,191
		Stafford $^2/_{10}$	4,794
	242,025		242,025

*The 'fair value' of a non-current asset is essentially the price it could be sold for, which implies that £150,000 is the amount that would have been received. The 'value in use' is clearly not relevant here because the partnership is dissolving and the assets will definitely not be in use by the business!

(b)

Partners' capital accounts

	Mears	Pugh	Stafford		Mears	Pugh	Stafford
Current a/cs	19,500	-	-	Balances b/d	25,000	84,000	56,000
Pugh: vehicle	-	22,000	-	Current a/cs	-	31,704	36,136
Loss on realisation	11,985	7,191	4,794	M's deficiency	-	6,485	-
M's deficiency cleared**	-	3,891	2,594	to be cleared			
Bank: to close	-	82,622	84,748				
	31,485	115,704	92,136		31,485	115,704	92,136

**Pugh 6,485 x 84/140 = 3,891; Stafford 6,485 x 56/140 = 2,594 (proportions based on the ratio of Pugh & Stafford's capitals as on the most recent balance sheet, as in Garner v Murray).

(c)

Bank

Non-current assets sold	150,000	Balance b/d	9,210
Inventory sold	25,280	Paid to payables	8,624
Collected from receivables	11,875	Dissolution costs paid	1,951
		Capital a/cs, to close:	
		Pugh	82,622
		Stafford	84,748
	187,155		187,155

35.5

(a) (i)

Amis, Lodge and Pym

Income Statement and Profit and Loss Appropriation Account for the year ending 31 March 2020

Sales			404,500
Less Cost of goods sold:			
Opening inventory		30,000	
Add Purchases		225,000	
Add Carriage inwards		4,000	
		259,000	
Less Closing inventory		35,000	
			224,000
Gross profit			180,500
Add Bank interest		750	
Discounts received		4,530	5,280
			185,780
Less Office expenses (30,400 + 405)		30,805	
Rent, rates, light and heat (8,800 − 1,500)		7,300	
Carriage outwards		12,000	
Discounts allowed		10,000	
Increase in allowance for doubtful debts		295	
Depreciation: Motor		15,000	
Plant		20,000	95,400
Net profit			90,380
Add Interest on current accounts and drawings:			
Amis		1,000	
Lodge		900	
Pym		720	2,620
			93,000
Less Salary – Pym		13,000	
Interest on capitals: Amis	8,000		
Lodge	1,500		
Pym	500	10,000	23,000
			70,000
Balance of profit			
Shared:			
Amis 50%		35,000	
Lodge 30%		21,000	
Pym 20%		14,000	70,000

35.7

(a)

Lock, Stock and Barrel
Income Statement for the six months ending February 2020

	£	£
Sales of completed houses		280,000
Less Costs of completing houses		
Houses in course of construction at start	115,000	
Materials used	35,750	
Land used (75,000 × 1/3)	25,000	
Wages and subcontractors	78,000	253,750
Gross profit		26,250
Less Administration salaries	17,250	
General expenses	12,500	
Depreciation: Freehold yard and buildings	300	
Plant and equipment (6/12 × 10%)	7,500	
Vehicles (25% × 6/12)	4,500	42,050
Net loss		15,800
Shared: Lock 40%	6,320	
Stock 30%	4,740	
Barrel 30%	4,740	15,800

Capitals

	Lock	Stock	Barrel		Lock	Stock	Barrel
Drawings	6,000	5,000	4,000	Balances b/d	52,000	26,000	3,500
Loss shared	6,320	4,740	4,740	Balance c/d			5,240
Balances c/d	39,680	16,260	8,740				
	52,000	26,000	8,740		52,000	26,000	8,740

Lock, Stock and Barrel
Balance Sheet as at 1 February 2020

	Cost	Depreciation	
Non-current tangible assets			
Freehold land and buildings	20,000	3,300	16,700
Plant and equipment	150,000	89,500	60,500
Motor vehicles	36,000	27,500	8,500
	206,000	120,300	85,700
Current assets			
Inventory of land for building		50,000	
Inventory of materials		7,500	
Accounts receivable for completed houses		35,000	
Total assets		92,500	
			188,200
Less Current liabilities			
Trade accounts payable		52,250	
Bank overdraft		75,250	
Total liabilities			(127,500)
Net assets			50,700
Financed by:			
Capitals: Lock			39,680
Stock			16,260
Barrel			(5,240)
			50,700

(a) (ii)

Current Accounts

	Amis	Lodge	Pym		Amis	Lodge	Pym
Balances b/d				Balances b/d			13,000
Drawings	1,000	500	400	Salary			15,000
	25,000	22,000	15,000	Interest on capital	8,000	1,500	500
Interest on drawings	1,000	900	720	Balance of profits	35,000	21,000	14,000
Transfer to capital	16,000		11,380	Transfer to capital		900	
	43,000	23,400	27,500		43,000	23,400	27,500

(b) (i)

Realisation

	£		£
Motors (80,000 − 35,000)	45,000	Discount on accounts payable	500
Plant (100,000 − 56,600)	43,400	Amis: Motor	5,000
Accounts receivable (14,300 − 715)	13,585	Bank: Accounts receivable	12,985
Inventory	35,000	Fowles Ltd (75,000 + 63,500)	138,500
Profit on realisation			
Amis 50%	10,000		
Lodge 30%	6,000		
Pym 20%	4,000	20,000	
	156,985		156,985

(b) (ii)

Bank

	£		£
Balance b/d	4,900	Office expenses	405
Realisation: Accounts receivable	12,985	Accounts payable	16,000
Rent rebate	1,500	Capital: Amis	76,000
Fowles Ltd	63,500		
Capitals: Lodge	4,900		
Pym	4,620		
	92,405		92,405

(b) (iii)

Capital Accounts

	Amis	Lodge	Pym		Amis	Lodge	Pym
Current a/c			5,000	Balances b/d		900	
Fowles Ltd	16,000		11,380	Current a/c	80,000	15,000	
Shares	25,000	25,000	25,000	Realisation	10,000	6,000	4,000
Realisation: Motor	5,000			Bank		4,900	4,620
Bank	76,000						
	106,000	25,900	25,000		106,000	25,900	25,000

(b) Amounts distributable to partners:

On 28 February there was only (6,200 + 7,000 + 72,500 − 75,250)10,450, hence there was nowhere near enough to pay off the accounts payable, and so payment to partners could not be made.

On 30 April we treat it as though no more cash will be received.

(c) First distribution

	Lock	Stock	Barrel
Capital balances before dissolution	39,680	16,260	(5,240)
Loss if no further assets realised			
(85,700 + 92,500 − 6,000 − 6,200 −			
7,000 − 72,500 − 35,000 − 50,000) = 1,500			
Loss shared in profit/loss ratios	(600)	(450)	(450)
	(2,000)	(2,000)	(2,000)
	37,080	13,810	(7,690)
Barrel's deficiency shared profit/loss ratio	4,394	3,296	7,690
Paid to partners	32,686	10,514	–

Second and final distribution

	Lock	Stock	Barrel
Capital balances before dissolution	39,680	16,260	(5,240)
Profit finally ascertained			
100,000 − 1,500 = 98,500			
Shared	39,400	29,550	29,550
	79,080	45,810	24,310
Less Distribution and cars	34,686	12,514	2,000
Final distribution (100,000)	44,394	33,296	22,310

36.1

Lyness Ltd
Statement of Changes in Equity for the year ended 31 December 2020

	Ordinary shares £000	Share premium £000	General reserve £000	Retained profits £000	Total equity £000
Opening balance	170	110	50	402	732
Shares issued	50	80	–	–	130
Profit for year	–	–	–	93	93
Dividends paid	–	–	–	(34)	(34)
Transfer to general reserve	–	–	20	(20)	–
Closing balance	220	190	70	441	921

36.2

	£
1m ord shares in issue: 17p paid (13 + 4) in 2019 on each	170,000
250,000 prefs in issue: £1 par val × 3% = 3p divi per share	7,500
Total dividends paid during 2019	177,500

(The fact that ordinary dividends have been paid indicates that the preference shareholders have also been paid. Ordinary dividends cannot be paid without paying the preference dividend. The only reasonable assumption to make is that the equivalent of one year's preference dividend will have been paid during 2019.)

36.3

Cuomo Ltd
Balance Sheet as at 30 September 2020

	Cost	Acc dep	
Non-current assets			
Buildings	730,000	127,000	603,000
Plant & equipment	254,000	117,000	137,000
Motor vehicles	148,000	87,000	61,000
	1,132,000	331,000	801,000
Current assets			
Inventory		81,800	
Accounts receivable		102,000	
Cash at bank (difference)		14,000	197,800
			998,800
Current liabilities			
Accounts payable		97,300	
Corporation tax payable		49,100	
		146,400	
Non-current liabilities			
Loan notes		75,000	(221,400)
			777,400
Equity			
Called up share capital			85,000
Share premium			115,000
General reserve			90,000
Retained profits			487,400
Total equity			777,400

36.4

Lungox Ltd
Balance Sheet as at 31 December 2019

Non-current assets		547
Current assets		
Inventory	138	
Accounts receivable	166	
Bank	18	322
		869
Current liabilities		
Accounts payable	141	
Corporation tax payable	35	
	176	
Non-current liabilities		
5% loan notes	150	(326)
		543
Ordinary share capital		80
Preference share capital		50
Share premium		96
General reserve		55
Retained profits		262
		543

743

Lungox Ltd
Extract from Statement of Changes in Equity for the year ended 31 December 2019

	General reserve	Retained profits
Opening balance	40	221
Profit for the year	-	66
Transfer to general reserve	15	(15)
Preference dividends paid	-	(2)
Ordinary dividends paid	-	(8)
	55	262

36.6

Balance Sheet as at 31 May 2020

		Cost	Acc Dep*	NBV
Assets				
Non-current assets				
Machinery	(*Acc dep = 92,220 TB + 89,550 above)	390,720	181,770	208,950
Vans	(* Acc dep = 72,000 TB + 62,892 above)	314,460	134,892	179,568
		705,180	316,662	388,518
Current assets				
Inventory			19,404	
Accounts receivable		87,600		
less allowance for doubtful debts		(3,504)	84,096	
Prepayments	(**8,580 payment × 10/12 months paid in advance)		7,150	
Cash at bank			374	
				111,024
Total assets				499,542
Current liabilities				
Accounts payable		56,769		
Accruals	(6,055 unpaid interest + 5,335)	11,390		
Corporation tax payable		3,000		
			71,159	
Non-current liabilities				
Loan notes			173,000	
Total liabilities				(244,159)
Net assets				255,383
Equity				
Ordinary share capital				55,000
Retained profits	(194,926 + 9,737 − 4,280)			200,383
Total equity				255,383

Terraxa Ltd
Income Statement for the year ended 31 May 2020

Sales		541,470
Less Cost of goods sold:		
Opening inventory	18,424	
Add Purchases	222,003	
Add Carriage inwards	1,567	
Less Closing inventory	(19,404)	
		(222,590)
Gross profit		318,880
Less Expenses:		
Gas (27,435 per TB + 5,335 accrued)	32,770	
Maintenance (18,289 per TB − 7,150 prepaid **)	11,139	
Other operating expenses	81,221	
Bad debt expense	15,598	
Increase in allowance for doubtful debts	863	
Depreciation expense:		
Machinery ((390,720 − 92,220) × 0.3 reducing balance)	89,550	
Vans (Cost 314,460 × 0.2 straight-line)	62,892	
		(294,033)
Operating profit		24,847
Less Interest expense		(12,110)
Profit before tax		12,737
Less Corporation tax expense		(3,000)
Profit for the year		9,737

Arkone plc
Income Statement for the year ended 31 March 2020

Sales		795,286
Less Cost of goods sold:		
Opening inventory	37,185	
Add Purchases	373,784	
Less Returns outwards	(1,926)	
Less Closing inventory	(38,913)	
		(370,130)
Gross profit		425,156
Less Expenses		
Motor expenses (22,271 per TB + 4,863 accrued)	27,134	
Business rates (26,340 per TB − 7,840 prepaid**)	18,500	
General operating expenses	119,293	
Directors' remuneration	45,924	
Bad debt expense	17,110	
Increase in allowance for doubtful debts	947	
Depreciation expense:		
Plant & equipment ((445,500 − 90,660) × 0.15 reducing balance)	53,226	
IT equipment (Cost 198,000 × 0.25 straight-line)	49,500	
		(331,634)
Operating profit		93,522
Less Interest expense		(4,900)
Profit before tax		88,622
Less Corporation tax expense		(19,000)
Profit for the year		69,622

Balance Sheet as at 31 March 2020

	Cost	Acc Dep*	NBV
Assets			
Non-current assets			
Plant & equipment (*Acc dep = 90,660 TB + 53,226 above)	445,500	143,886	301,614
IT equipment (*Acc dep = 62,400 TB + 49,500 above)	198,000	111,900	86,100
	643,500	255,786	387,714
Current assets			
Inventory		38,913	
Accounts receivable	96,000		
less allowance for doubtful debts	(3,840)	92,160	
Prepayments (**11,760 payment × 8/12 months paid in advance)		7,840	
Cash at bank		540	
			139,453
Total assets			527,167
Current liabilities			
Accounts payable		68,339	
Accruals (2,450 unpaid interest + 4,863)		7,313	
Corporation tax payable		19,000	
		94,652	
Non-current liabilities			
Loan notes		98,000	
Total liabilities			(192,652)
Net assets			334,515
Equity			
Ordinary share capital			75,000
Share premium			70,000
Retained profits (150,523 + 69,622 − 30,630)			189,515
Total equity			334,515

36.10

Bemaji Ltd
Income Statement for the year ended 28 February 2020

Sales		986,143
Less Cost of goods sold:		
Opening inventory	43,104	
Add Purchases	433,903	
Less Returns outwards	(2,951)	
Less Closing inventory	(44,201)	
		(429,855)
Gross profit		556,288
Add Other income:		
Rent received		7,070
		563,358
Less Expenses		
Motor expenses (19,705 per TB + 5,661 accrued)	25,366	
Rent (19,489 per TB − 4,080 prepaid **)	15,409	
Sundry operating expenses	108,476	
Directors' remuneration	78,890	
Bad debt expense	24,310	
Increase in allowance for doubtful debts	1,007	
Depreciation expense:		
Plant & equipment (579,660 − 110,880) × 0.15	70,317	
Motor vehicles (Cost 250,560 × 0.2 straight line)	50,112	
		(373,887)
Operating profit		189,471
Less Interest expense		(9,000)
Profit before tax		180,471
Less Corporation tax expense		(40,000)
Profit for the year		140,471

Balance Sheet as at 28 February 2020

		Cost	Acc Dep*	NBV
Assets				
Non-current assets				
Plant & equipment (*Acc dep = 110,880 + 70,317)		579,660	181,197	398,463
Motor vehicles (*Acc dep = 61,440 + 50,112)		250,560	111,552	139,008
		830,220	292,749	537,471
Current assets				
Inventory			44,201	
Accounts receivable		102,000		
less Allowance for doubtful debts		(5,100)	96,900	
Prepayments (**6,120 payment × 8/12 months paid in advance)			4,080	
Cash at bank			1,092	
				146,273
Total assets				683,744
Current liabilities				
Accounts payable		85,747		
Accruals (4,500 unpaid interest + 5,661)		10,161		
Corporation tax payable		40,000	135,908	
Non-current liabilities				
Loan notes			150,000	
Total liabilities				(285,908)
Net assets				397,836
Equity				
Ordinary share capital				62,000
Share premium				46,000
General reserve (22,600 + 7,000)				29,600
Retained profits (188,575 + 140,471 − 61,810 − 7,000)				260,236
Total equity				397,836

36.12

Brogia Ltd
Income Statement for the year ended 30 April 2019

Gross profit	171,360
Operating expenses	(84,090)
Depreciation expense (147,800 − 48,800) × 1/3	(33,000)
Operating profit	54,270
Interest expense (60,000 × 5%)	(3,000)
Profit before tax	51,270
Corporation tax expense (51,270 × 20%)	(10,254)
Profit for the year	41,016

Brogia Ltd
Statement of Changes in Equity for the year ended 30 April 2019

	Share capital	Share premium	Retained profits	Total equity
Opening balance	120,000	20,000	48,560	188,560
Shares issued (working 1)	40,000	30,000	–	70,000
Profit for the year	–	–	41,016	41,016
Dividends paid (working 2)	–	–	(24,000)	(24,000)
Closing balance	160,000	50,000	65,576	275,576

Working 1: 200,000 new shares × 20p nominal value = £40,000; 200,000 new shares × 15p premium = £30,000

Working 2: 600,000 shares in issue as at 25 April × 4p = £24,000

36.14

Note: £100,000 in ordinary shares of 10p each = 1,000,000 ordinary shares of 10p each.

Bonus issue 1-for-5 new 10p shares issued 'for free' = 1,000,000 × 1/5 = 200,000 new shares of 10p = £20,000 of new share capital issued 'for free'

Zamilo plc
Statement of Changes in Equity for the year ended 31 January 2020

	Ordinary shares £	Share premium £	General reserve £	Retained profits £	Total equity £
Opening balance	100,000	190,000	50,000	560,000	900,000
Shares issued	20,000	(20,000)	–	–	–
Profit for year	–	–	–	80,000	80,000
Dividends paid	–	–	–	(32,000)	(32,000)
Transfer to general reserve	–	–	10,000	(10,000)	–
Closing balance	120,000	170,000	60,000	598,000	948,000

36.15

Extract 1

(a) The amount paid for goodwill.
(b) The excess represents share premium.
(c) Equity shares generally means ordinary shares. See text for a fuller description of ordinary shares
(d) That although issued in 2019 a dividend will not be paid on these shares in that year. The first year that dividends could be paid is 2020.

Extract 2

(e) (i) A rate of 8% per annum interest will be paid on them, irrespective of whether profits are made or not.
  (ii) These are the years within which the loan stock could be redeemed, if the company so wished.
(f) (i) This is the rate per annum at which preference dividends will be paid, subject to there being sufficient distributable profits.
  (ii) That the shares could be bought back by the company.
(g) Probably because there was currently a lower interest rate prevailing at the time of redemption and the company took advantage of it.
(h) Large amounts of both fixed interest and fixed dividend funds have resulted in a raising of the gearing.
(i) Loan note interest gets charged before arriving at net profit. Dividends are an appropriation of profits in the period in which they are actually paid. Dividends do not appear in the income statement at all.
(j) Shareholders are owners and help decide appropriations. Loan note holders are external lenders and interest expense has to be paid.

36.16

(a) This is incorrect. The tax portion has to be counted as part of the total cost, which is made up of loan note interest paid plus tax. Holding back payment will merely see legal action taken by the HM Revenue & Customs to collect the tax.

(b) This cannot be done. The repainting of the exterior does not improve or enhance the original value of the premises. It cannot therefore be treated as capital expenditure.

(c) This is not feasible. Only the profit on the sale of the old machinery, found by deducting net book value from sales proceeds, can be so credited to the profit and loss account. The remainder is a capital receipt and should be treated as such.

(d) This is an incorrect view. Although some of the general reserve could, if circumstances allowed it, be transferred back to the retained profits, it could not be shown as affecting the operating profit for 2019. This is because the general reserve was built up over the years before 2019.

(e) This is not feasible. Changes in the market value of shares in issue are not reflected in the company's books at all. The share capital has to be maintained at nominal value as per the Companies Act. A share premium cannot be credited in this fashion, and even if it could, it would still have to be credited to the *share premium account* and not the profit and loss account.

(f) Incorrect. Although the premises could be revalued the credit for the increase has to be to a capital reserve account (known as 'revaluation reserve.'). This cannot then be transferred to the credit of the profit and loss account.

36.17

See text. Points to be made include that there must be an expectation that sufficient profits will be made in future to make the loan note interest payments when due; also, there may be cheaper sources of finance available; also, if secured loan notes are to be issued, there must be sufficient assets available to act as security over the issue. Gearing is also an issue to be considered – see text.

37.1

Balance Sheet as at 31 March 2019

	(a) J. Adams	(b) G. Hughes
Goodwill	76,500	39,400
Premises	145,000	200,000
Inventory	47,000	30,000
Accounts receivable	38,500	38,500
Bank	900	–
	307,900	307,900
Accounts payable	(57,900)	(57,900)
	250,000	250,000
Capital	250,000	250,000

37.3 (a)

Spectrum Ltd
Balance Sheet as at 1 January 2018

Non-current assets		
Goodwill (note 1)		94,000
Premises (75,000 + 80,000 + 90,000 + 60,000)		305,000
Delivery vans (7,000 + 10,000)		17,000
Furniture and fittings (12,000 + 13,000 + 13,000)		38,000
		454,000
Current assets		
Inventory (8,000 + 7,000 + 12,000)	27,000	
Bank (note 2)	25,000	
		52,000
Current liabilities		
Accounts payable (6,000 + 8,000 + 7,000)		(21,000)
		485,000
Equity		
Issued 500,000 shares £1		500,000
Retained profits		(15,000)
		485,000

Notes:

1 Goodwill: Red – paid 120,000

Net assets taken over		
75,000 + 7,000 + 12,000 + 8,000 – 6,000 =	96,000	24,000
Yellow – paid	130,000	
Net assets taken over		
80,000 + 13,000 + 7,000 – 8,000 =	92,000	38,000
Blue – paid	150,000	
Net assets taken over		
90,000 + 10,000 + 13,000 + 12,000 – 7,000 =	118,000	32,000
		94,000

2 Bank: Shares issued 500,000

Less: Preliminary expenses	15,000	
Warehouse	60,000	
Red	120,000	
Yellow	130,000	
Blue	150,000	475,000
		25,000

(b) Spectrum Ltd can issue part or the remainder of the authorised capital, i.e. 700,000 – 500,000 = £200,000. Alternatively, given the company has no borrowings it could raise the £100,000 by issuing loan notes or obtaining a bank loan.

37.4 (a)

Dinho and Manueli
Realisation Account

Property	290,000	Accounts payable	85,800
Equipment	65,000	Bank	56,700
Inventory	143,500	Loan	160,000
Accounts receivable	121,000	Bin Ltd	304,000
		Loss: Dinho	6,500
		Manueli	6,500
	619,500		619,500

(b)

Bin Ltd

Goodwill [write-downs (30,000 + 5,000) − realisation loss (13,000)]   22,000

Property	260,000
Equipment	65,000
Inventory	143,500
Accounts receivable	116,000
Bank (120,000 − 56,700)	63,300
Accounts payable	(85,800)
	584,000
	(160,000)
	424,000
Loan	
Ordinary Share Capital	300,000
10% Preference shares (D = 87,500; M = 16,500; P = 20,000)	124,000
	424,000

(c) (salary as before, therefore not relevant; earnings on savings were 120,000 @ 6% = 7,200; preference dividend will be 20,000 @ 10% = 2,000, therefore, 5,200 needed from profit after preference dividend. Profit must be 3 × 5,200 = 15,600 + the total preference dividend of 12,400 = 28,000.

38.1 See Section 38.1.
38.3 See Section 38.7.
38.5 See Section 38.5.
38.6 See Section 38.7.

39.1

D. Staunton
Trading Account part of the Income Statement for the
year ending 31 December 2020

Sales			208,000
Less Cost of goods sold:			
Opening inventory		21,000	
Add Purchases		168,000	
		189,000	
Less Closing inventory	(D)	29,000	
	(C)		160,000
Gross profit	(B)		48,000
	(A)		

Missing figures found in the order (A) to (D).

(A) Mark-up is 30%. So sales represent 130% of cost.
208,000 × $^{30}/_{130}$ = 48,000 gross profit

(B) 208,000 − 48,000 = 160,000

(C) 160,000 + 29,000 = 189,000

(D) 189,000 − 21,000 = 168,000

39.3

(a) We know that

$$\frac{\text{Cost of goods sold}}{\text{Average inventory}} = \text{Rate of inventory turnover}$$

Substituting $\frac{x}{35,000} = 7$

x = Cost of goods sold = 245,000.

(b) If mark-up is 40%, gross profit is 40% of the cost of sales = 98,000.

(c) Turnover is (a) + (b) = 245,000 + 98,000 = 343,000.

(d) 60% × 98,000 = 58,800.

(e) Gross Profit − Expenses = Net Profit = 39,200.

39.5

(a) Sales = 210,000 + (30% × 210,000) = 273,000.

(b) 50,000 − (9% × 260,000) = 26,600.

(c) $\dfrac{210,000}{(41,000 + 49,000) \div 2} = 4.67.$

(d) Gross profit is 40% × 240,000 = 96,000.

Sales are 240,000 + 96,000 = 336,000.

Expenses are 9% of sales = 30,240.

Net profit = 96,000 − 30,240 = 65,760.

39.7

(a)

Capital

Balance c/d	5,000	Bank	5,000
	5,000		5,000
		Balance b/d	5,000

Bank

Capital	5,000	Cash	300
		Van	3,500
		Rent	500
		Balance c/d	700
	5,000		5,000
Balance b/d	700		

Cash

Bank	300	Sundry Expenses	50
Sales	300	Drawings	500
		Balance c/d	50
	600		600
Balance b/d	50		

Van

Bank	3,500	Balance c/d	3,500
	3,500		3,500
Balance b/d	3,500		

Purchases

A. Supplier	2,500	Balance c/d	2,500
	2,500		2,500
Balance b/d	2,500		

A. Supplier

Returns	500	Purchases	2,500
Balance c/d	2,000		
	2,500		2,500
		Balance b/d	2,000

Sales

Balance c/d	1,300	Cash	300
		B. Safe	1,000
	1,300		1,300
		Balance b/d	1,300

B. Safe

Sales	1,000	Balance c/d	1,000
	1,000		1,000
Balance b/d	1,000		

Returns out

Balance c/d	500	A. Supplier	500
	500		500
		Balance b/d	500

Sundry Expenses

Cash	50	Balance c/d	50
	50		50
Balance b/d	50		

Rent

Bank	500	Balance c/d	500
	500		500
Balance b/d	500		

Drawings

Cash	500	Balance c/d	500
	500		500
Balance b/d	500		

(b)

L. Mann
Trial Balance as at 30 April

Bank	700	
Cash	50	
Van	3,500	
Purchases	2,500	
Accounts receivable	1,000	
Sundry expenses	50	
Rent	500	
Drawings	500	
Capital		5,000
Accounts payable		2,000
Sales		1,300
Returns out		500
	8,800	8,800

(c)

Income Statement for the month ending 30 April

Sales		1,300
Purchases	2,500	
– Returns out	500	
	2,000	
– Closing inventory	750	
Cost of sales		1,250
Gross profit		550
Less Expenses		
Sundry expenses	50	
Rent	500	550
Net profit		0

(d)

Balance Sheet as at 30 April

Non-current assets		
Van		3,500
Current assets		
Inventory	1,250	
Accounts receivable	1,000	
Bank	700	
Cash	50	
	3,000	
		6,500
Current liabilities		
Accounts payable		(2,000)
		4,500
Capital		5,000
Less Drawings		500
		4,500

(e)(i) $\dfrac{550}{1,300} = 42.3\%$

(ii) $\dfrac{0}{5,000} = 0\%$

(f)(i) As there has been neither a profit nor a loss, the £500 drawings are eating into capital. This is not a good sign. Drawings must not exceed net profit in the long term, or the business will fail.

(ii) Working capital is £1,000. The current ratio is 1.5, which ought to be adequate, though this would need to be confirmed by comparison with other businesses operating in the same sector.

39.9 (a)

	2017	2018	2019
Opening inventory	10,000	21,000	25,000
Purchases	70,000	86,000	77,000
	80,000	107,000	102,000
Less Closing inventory	21,000	25,000	23,000
Cost of goods sold	(59,000)	(82,000)	(79,000)
Sales	90,000	125,000	120,000
Gross profit	31,000	43,000	41,000

(b) (i)

Gross profit/sales

2017
$$\frac{31,000}{90,000} = 34\%$$

2018
$$\frac{43,000}{125,000} = 34\%$$

2019
$$\frac{41,000}{120,000} = 34\%$$

(ii)

$$\text{Inventory turnover} = \frac{\text{Cost of goods sold}}{\text{Average inventory}}$$

2017
$$\frac{59,000}{(10,000 + 21,000) \div 2} = 3.8 \text{ times}$$

2018
$$\frac{82,000}{(21,000 + 25,000) \div 2} = 3.6 \text{ times}$$

2019
$$\frac{79,000}{(25,000 + 23,000) \div 2} = 3.3 \text{ times}$$

40.1

N. Alphonso
Balance Sheet as at 31 December 2018

Non-current assets		
Van at cost	9,000	
Less Depreciation	(2,250)	6,750
Current assets		
Inventory	8,300	
Accounts receivable	11,620	
Prepaid expenses	1,360	
Bank	4,110	
Cash	50	25,440
Less Current liabilities		
Trade accounts payable	9,470	
Expenses owing	1,630	(11,100)
		21,090
Capital		
Cash introduced	10,000	(C)
Add Net profit for the year		(B)
		(A)
Less Drawings (600 × 52)		(31,200)
		21,090

Missing figures (A), (B) and (C) deducted in that order. (A) to balance is 21,090, thus (B) has to be 52,290 and (C) becomes 42,290.

40.2

Opening capital = 140,000 + 53,200 + 68,500 + 1,700 − 72,300 = 191,100

Closing capital = 154,000 + 59,100 + 70,400 − 2,900 − 80,600 = 205,800

Therefore:

Opening capital	191,100
Add Capital introduced	5,500
Add Net profit for 2020 (balancing figure)	33,200
Less Drawings	(24,000)
Closing capital	205,800

40.4

Workings:

Purchases	Bank	136,200
	Cash	9,300
		145,500
− Opening creditors		23,400
		122,100
+ Closing creditors		26,200
Purchases for year		148,300

Sales	Banked	182,000
	Cash	34,900
		216,900
− Opening debtors		40,600
		176,300
+ Closing debtors		37,700
Sales for year		214,000

Opening Capital:

Bank	8,200	
Inventory	20,600	
Accounts receivable	40,600	
Insurance prepaid	910	
Fixtures	3,700	74,010
Less Accounts payable	23,400	
Rent owing	570	23,970
		50,040

Ellie
Income Statement for the year ending 31 December 2019

Sales			214,000
Less Cost of goods sold:			
Opening inventory		20,600	
Add Purchases		148,300	
		168,900	
Less Closing inventory		23,000	145,900
Gross profit			68,100
Less Expenses:			
Wages		22,800	
Rent (7,800 − 570)		7,230	
Insurance (2,940 + 910 − 1,020)		2,830	
Sundry expenses		1,260	
Depreciation: Fixtures		300	34,420
Net profit			33,680

Balance Sheet as at 31 December 2019

Non-current assets			
Fixtures at valuation		3,700	
Less Accumulated depreciation		300	3,400
Current assets			
Inventory		23,000	
Accounts receivable		37,700	
Prepayments		1,020	61,720
			65,120
Current liabilities			
Trade accounts payable	26,200		
Bank overdraft	12,800		(39,000)
			26,120
Capital			
Opening balance			50,040
Add Net profit			33,680
			83,720
Less Drawings (2,800 + 54,800)			57,600
			26,120

40.6

Jenny Barnes
Income Statement for the year ending 30 April 2019

Sales*			102,908
Less: Opening inventory		9,500	
Purchases (70,500 + 7,600)		78,100	
		87,600	
Less: Closing inventory		13,620	73,980
Gross profit			28,928
Less: Expenses:			
Sales assistants' wages		5,260	
Vehicle running expenses		1,020	
Bad debts		150	
Miscellaneous expenses**		1,370	
Light and heat		940	
Depreciation: Equipment		720	
Vehicles		1,000	10,460
Net profit			18,468

*Sales 96,500 + takings in cash later spent 6,408
(drawings 6,000 + expenses 408)
**Bank 962 + cash 408 = 1,370

40.8

(a)

Accounts Payable Control

Bank	101,500	Balances b/d	7,400
Cash	1,800		
Balances c/d	8,900	Purchases (difference)	104,800
	112,200		112,200

(b)

Janet Lambert

Income Statement for the year ending 31 August 2019

Sales (deduced – as margin is 25% = 4 × gross profit)		128,000
Opening inventory	8,600	
Add Purchases (104,800 – 600 drawings)	104,200	
	112,800	
Less Closing inventory	16,800	
Cost of goods sold		96,000
Gross profit (33 1/3% of Cost of goods sold)		32,000
Less: Casual labour (1,200 + 6,620)	7,820	
Rent (5,040 + 300 – 420)	4,920	
Delivery costs	3,000	
Electricity (1,390 + 160 – 210)	1,340	17,080
Net profit		14,920

Balance Sheet as at 31 August 2019

Current assets		
Inventory	16,800	
Accounts receivable	4,300	
Prepayments	420	
Bank	1,650	
Cash	330	23,500
Current liabilities		
Accounts payable	8,900	
Expenses owing	160	(9,060)
		14,440
Capital:		
Opening balance (Working 1)		7,850
Add Net profit		14,920
		22,770
Less Drawings (Working 2 + 600)		8,330
		14,440

Workings:

(1) Opening capital. Inventory 8,600 + Accounts receivable 3,900 + Prepaid 300 + Bank 2,300 + Cash 360 = 15,460 – Accounts payable 7,400 – Accruals 210 = 7,850.

(2) Cash drawings. Step (A) find cash received from sales. Accounts receivable b/d 3,900 + Sales 128,000 – Accounts receivable c/d 4,300 = 127,600 cash received.

Step (B) find cash banked. Balance b/d 2,300 + cash received? – payments 117,550 = balance c/d 1,650. Therefore, cash banked? = 116,900.

Step (C) draw up cash account:

Balance b/d	360	Labour	1,200
Sales receipts	127,600	Purchases	1,800
		Banked	116,900
		Drawings (difference)	7,730
		Balance c/d	330
	127,960		127,960

(c) Per text.

40.10

David Denton

Income Statement for the year ending 31 December 2020

Work done: Credit accounts	29,863	
For cash	3,418	33,281
Less Expenses:		
Materials (9,600 – 580)	9,020	
Secretarial salary	3,000	
Rent (300 – 75)	225	
Rates (180 – 45)	135	
Insurance (800 – 200)	600	
Electricity (1,122 + 374 estimated)	1,496	
Motor expenses	912	
General expenses (1,349 + 295)	1,644	
Loan interest (4,000 × 10% × 3/4)	300	
Increase in allowance for doubtful debts	425	
Accounting fee	250	
Depreciation of lease (650 × 3/4)	487	
Depreciation: Equipment	960	
Van (3,600/4)	900	1,860
		20,354
Net profit		12,927

Balance Sheet as at 31 December 2020

	Cost	Depreciation	
Non-current assets			
Lease	6,500	487	6,013
Equipment	4,800	960	3,840
Vehicle	3,600	900	2,700
	14,900	2,347	12,553
Current assets			
Inventory		580	

Balance Sheet as at 31 December 2020 (continued)

Accounts receivable (29,863 − 25,613)	4,250		
Less Allowance for doubtful debts	425	3,825	
Prepaid expenses (75 + 200)		275	
Bank (see workings)		6,084	
Cash		123	10,887
			23,440
Less Current liabilities			
Trade accounts payable	714		
Interest owing	300		
Accountancy fee owing	250		
Rates owing	135		
Electricity owing	374	1,773	
			(5,773)
Less Loan			4,000
			17,667
Financed by:			
Capital			
Introduced (6,500 + 3,600)		10,100	
Add Net profit		12,927	
		23,027	
Less Drawings (4,680 + 280 + 400)		5,360	
			17,667

Workings:
Bank (6,500 + 25,613 + 2,600 + 4,000) = 38,713 − 4,680 − 280 − 6,500
− 300 − 3,000 − 8,886 − 4,800 − 1,122 − 912 − 1,349 − 800 = 6,084

40.11

(a)

J. Duncan
Capital on 1 January 2018

Bank		8,000
Cash		300
Inventory		4,100
Machinery		12,600
Rent prepaid		200
Accounts receivable		6,300
		31,500
Accounts payable	2,400	
Loan	5,000	
		(7,400)
		24,100

(b)

J. Duncan
Income Statement for the year ending 31 December 2018

Sales			40,450
Less: Sales returns			1,200
			39,250
Less: Cost of Sales			
Opening inventory		4,100	
Add: Purchases		18,950	
		23,050	
Less: Withdrawn by the owner	300		
Less: Closing inventory	3,200	3,500	
			19,550
Gross profit			19,700
Add: Discount received			350
			20,050
Less: Expenses			
Rent (1,400 + 200 + 250)		1,850	
Bad debts written-off		400	
Wages		6,100	
Insurance		1,450	
Loan interest (300 + 100)		400	
Depreciation		4,200	
Repairs		300	
Electricity		750	
			15,450
Net profit			4,600

Workings:
Sales 26,000 − 250 + 14,000 + 400 − 6,300 + 5,000 + 1,200 + 400 = 40,450
Purchases 18,500 − 2,400 + 2,500 + 350 = 18,950
Depreciation = balancing figure.

40.12

J. Duncan
Balance Sheet as at 31 December 2018

Non-current assets		
Machinery at 1 January 2018		12,600
Add: Additions		7,500
Less: Depreciation (balancing figure)		4,200

J. Duncan
Balance Sheet as at 31 December 2018 (continued)

Current assets
Inventory		3,200	
Accounts receivable		5,000	
Bank		2,600	
Cash		50	15,900
			10,850
			26,750

Current liabilities
Accounts payable		2,500	
Accrued charges:			
Loan interest	100		
Rent	250	350	
		2,850	

Non-current liabilities
Bank loan 8%		5,000	
			(7,850)
			18,900

Capital account
Opening balance		24,100
Add: Net profit		4,600
Less: Drawings (9,500 + 300)		9,800
		18,900

40.15

Inventory value per stocktake on 3 May	124,620
Less Purchases (1,510 − 530)	980
	123,640
Less Sales returns (222 @ 80%)	176
	123,464
Less Obsolete inventory	300
	123,164
Add Inventory sold (2,300 @ 80%)	1,840
Value of inventory on 30 April	125,004

41.1 $\dfrac{595,000}{85,000} = 7$ times

41.2 $\dfrac{49,000}{245,000} \times 100 = 20\%$

41.3 $\dfrac{159,800}{470,000} \times 100 = 34\%$

41.4 $\dfrac{31,520}{394,000} \times 100 = 8\%$

41.5 (a) $\dfrac{78,000}{62,000} = 1.3{:}1$

(b) $\dfrac{(78,000 - 29,000)}{62,000} = 0.79{:}1$

41.6 $\dfrac{78,000}{493,000} \times 365 = 57.7$ days

41.7 $\dfrac{49,000}{396,000} \times 365 = 45.2$ days

41.8 (a) $\dfrac{\text{(i)}}{\text{(ii)}} = \dfrac{248,000}{800,000} = 31$ p

(b) $\dfrac{\text{(iii)}}{\text{(a)}} = \dfrac{3.72}{0.31} = 12$

(c) $\dfrac{\text{(iv)}}{\text{(iii)}} = \dfrac{0.16}{3.72} = 4.3\%$

(d) $\dfrac{\text{(i)}}{\text{(v)}} = \dfrac{248,000}{128,000} = 1.94$ times

41.9 $\dfrac{95,000}{233,000} = 40.8\%$

41.10

	Business J	Business K

(a) (i) Gross profit %

$\dfrac{221,000}{472,000} \times 100 = 46.8\%$ $\dfrac{282,000}{695,000} \times 100 = 40.6\%$

(ii) Net profit %

$\dfrac{38,000}{472,000} \times 100 = 8.1\%$ $\dfrac{68,000}{695,000} \times 100 = 9.8\%$

(iii) Expenses %

$\dfrac{183,000}{472,000} \times 100 = 38.8\%$ $\dfrac{214,000}{695,000} \times 100 = 30.8\%$

(iv) Inventory turnover

$\dfrac{251000}{(64000 + 51000) \div 2} = 4.4 \text{ times}$ $\dfrac{413000}{(62000 + 50000) \div 2} = 7.4 \text{ times}$

(v) Return on capital

$\dfrac{38,000}{(148,000 + 15,000) \div 2} = 25.4\%$ $\dfrac{68,000}{(221,000 + 209,000) \div 2} = 31.6\%$

(vi) Current ratio

$\dfrac{147,000}{66,000} = 2.23\text{:}1$ $\dfrac{178,000}{99,000} = 1.8\text{:}1$

(vii) Acid test ratio

$\dfrac{83,000}{66,000} = 1.26\text{:}1$ $\dfrac{128,000}{99,000} = 1.29\text{:}1$

(viii) Accounts receivable days

$\dfrac{68,000}{472,000} \times 365 = 52.6 \text{ days}$ $\dfrac{123,000}{695,000} \times 365 = 64.6 \text{ days}$

(ix) Accounts payable days

$\dfrac{66,000}{264,000} \times 365 = 91.3 \text{ days}$ $\dfrac{99,000}{401,000} \times 365 = 90.1 \text{ days}$

(b) J earns a higher gross margin. Perhaps it sells higher price, premium or branded products, while K's strategy may be higher volume, lower price goods.

But K converts a higher percentage of sales into net profit, indicating that it has much better control of its running costs. K appears to own higher value equipment, which might be helping it operate more efficiently.

K turns over its inventory much faster again indicating it may be selling popular, low margin products. J's inventory level is also increasing, which suggests it is possible that it has some rather slow-moving items in stock. The current and acid test ratios for both businesses are fairly high. The high current ratio of J in particular again suggests that its inventory level may be excessive. Perhaps K has offered more generous credit terms in order to attract customers and boost sales.

J is collecting money from customers in less than 2 months. Perhaps K has offered more generous credit terms in order to attract customers and boost sales.

But both companies appear to be taking 3 months to pay suppliers. If so, there is a danger that some suppliers might become disgruntled and refuse to sell to these businesses.

It would certainly help to know exactly what industry these two businesses operate in. Historic information concerning their performance over recent years would also be useful.

41.12

(a)

Durham Limited

Statement of Changes in Equity (extract) for the year ending 30.4.2019

	Retained Profits	General Reserve
Opening balance	14,500	4,000
Net profit for the year	16,500	–
Transferred to general reserve	(5,000)	5,000
Preference dividend paid	(2,000)	–
	24,000	9,000

(b)

Balance Sheet as at 30.4.2019

Non-current assets			
Premises at cost		86,000	
Machinery and plant at cost	60,000		
Less Accumulated depreciation	40,000	20,000	106,000
Current assets			
Inventory		60,000	
Accounts receivable	20,000		
Less Allowance for doubtful debts	4,000	16,000	
Prepayments		900	
Bank		13,100	90,000
			196,000
Current liabilities			
Accounts payable		12,900	
Expenses owing		100	(13,000)
			183,000
Equity			
Ordinary shares		100,000	
8% preference shares		50,000	150,000
General reserve			9,000
Retained profits			24,000
Shareholders' funds			183,000

(c) (i) *Return on Capital Employed (ROCE)*
This is the amount of profit earned compared with the amount of capital employed to earn it. Calculated:

$$\frac{\text{Net profit}}{\text{Average of shareholders' funds}} \times \frac{100}{1} = \frac{16,500}{(168,500 + 183,000) \div 2} \times \frac{100}{1}$$
$$= 9.39\%$$

(ii) *Current Ratio*
This calculates how well the current assets can finance current liabilities. Calculated:

$$\frac{\text{Current assets}}{\text{Current liabilities}} = \frac{90,000}{13,000} = 6.9{:}1$$

Acid Test Ratio
This calculates whether the business has sufficient liquid resources to meet its current liabilities. Calculated:

$$\frac{\text{Current assets} - \text{inventory}}{\text{Current liabilities}} = \frac{30,000}{13,000} = 2.3{:}1$$

(d) ROCE. The return of 9.39 per cent would appear to be adequate, but we cannot really comment further without more information.
Current Ratio. A figure of 2 : 1 is often reckoned as adequate. In this case a 6.9 : 1 figure is more than adequate.
Acid Test Ratio. All current liabilities can be met and the ratio is therefore adequate.

(e) 1 Previous years' figures.
2 We would need to know ratios for other similar businesses.

41.13

(a) (i) Gross profit: Sales

2018
$$\frac{50}{200} \times \frac{100}{1} = 25\%$$

2019
$$\frac{70}{280} \times \frac{100}{1} = 25\%$$

(ii) Inventory turnover

2018
$$\frac{150}{(50 + 20) \div 2} = 4.29$$

2019
$$\frac{210}{(20 + 30) \div 2} = 8.4$$

(iii) Net profit: Sales

2018
$$\frac{12}{200} \times \frac{100}{1} = 6\%$$

2019
$$\frac{20}{280} \times \frac{100}{1} = 7.14\%$$

(iv) Quick ratio

2018
$$\frac{25}{25} = 1$$

2019
$$\frac{33}{12} = 2.75$$

(v) Working capital (current ratio)

2018
$$\frac{45}{25} = 1.8$$

2019
$$\frac{63}{12} = 5.25$$

(vi) Net profit: Capital employed

2018
$$\frac{12}{130} \times \frac{100}{1} = 9.23\%$$

2019
$$\frac{20}{191} \times \frac{100}{1} = 10.47\%$$

(b) (Brief answer, but you should write more in an exam)
(i) No change.
(ii) Increase caused by lowering average inventory; also probably better sales management.
(iii) An increase in sales, without a larger increase in expenses, has led to a better return.
(iv) Issue of loan notes has improved the cash situation and therefore the quick ratio.
(v) Net current assets have increased largely due to issue of loan notes, although partly offset by non-current assets bought.
(vi) Increasing sales, good control of expenses, and better inventory turnover brought about better ROCE.

41.16

Joan Street
Income Statement for the year ending 31 March 2020

Sales		(W3)	240,000
Cost of sales			
Opening inventory			21,000
Add Purchases	(W6)	174,000	
	(W7)	195,000	

Joan Street

Income Statement for the year ending 31 March 2020 (continued)

			180,000
Less Closing inventory	15,000	(W1)	
Gross profit		(W2)	60,000
Sundry expenses		(W5)	38,400
Net profit		(W4)	21,600

Balance Sheet as at 31 March 2020

Non-current assets		(W9)	108,000
Current assets			
Inventory		15,000	
Accounts receivable	(W8)	24,000	
Bank	(W14)	9,000	
		(W13)	48,000
			156,000
Current liabilities		(W13)	12,000
Net assets		(W12)	144,000
Financed by:			
Capital:			
Opening balance		(W11)	122,400
Add Net profit			21,600
		(W10)	144,000

Worwkings (could possibly find alternatives)

(W1) As average inventory 21,000 + 15,000 ÷ 2 = 18,000 and inventory turnover is 10, this means that cost of sales = 18,000 × 10 = 180,000

(W2) As gross profit is 25% of sales, it must therefore be $33\frac{1}{3}$% of cost of sales

(W3) As (W1) is 180,000 and (W2) is 60,000 therefore sales = (W1) + (W2) = 240,000

(W4) Net profit = 9% of sales = 21,600

(W5) Missing figure, found by arithmetical deduction

(W6) and (W7) Missing figures – found by arithmetical deduction

(W8) $\dfrac{\text{Accounts receivable (?)} \times 365}{\text{Sales}} = 36\frac{1}{2}$, i.e.

$\dfrac{? \times 365}{240,000} = 36\frac{1}{2}$, by arithmetic

Accounts receivable = 24,000. Proof $\dfrac{24,000 \times 365}{240,000} = 36\frac{1}{2}$

(W9) 45% × 240,000 = 108,000

(W10) Knowing that net profit 21,600 is 15% of W10, so W10 = 21,600 × 100/15 = 144,000

(W11) Missing figure

(W12) Put in after (W11)

(W13) If Net current assets ratio is 4, it means a factor of current assets 4, current liabilities 1 = Net current assets 3 which is (W12 − W9) = 36,000, current assets therefore:

4/3 × 36,000 = 48,000

and current liabilities

1/3 × 36,000 = 12,000

(W14) Is new missing figure.

(b) Question asked for two favourable aspects and two unfavourable aspects but four of each are given here

Favourable: Inventory turnover, liquidity, net current assets, net profit on sales

Unfavourable: Gross profit to sales, accounts receivable collection, return on capital employed, turnover to net capital employed.

(c) Drawbacks include:

(i) No access to trends over recent years.

(ii) No future plans etc. given.

(iii) Each business is often somewhat different.

(iv) Size of businesses not known.

41.18

(a) (i) Current ratio: by dividing current assets by current liabilities.

(ii) Quick assets ratio: by dividing current assets less inventory by current liabilities.

(iii) Return on capital employed (ROCE): can have more than one meaning. One in common use is net profit divided by capital plus long-term liabilities (e.g. loans), and shown as a percentage.

(iv) Return on shareholders' funds (ROSF): net profit divided by capital, shown as a percentage.

(v) Accounts receivable turnover: Accounts receivable divided by sales multiplied by 365.

(vi) Accounts payable turnover: Accounts payable divided by purchases multiplied by 365.

(vii) Gross profit percentage: Gross profit divided by sales, expressed as a percentage.

(viii) Net profit percentage: Net profit divided by sales.

(ix) Inventory turnover: Cost of goods sold, divided by average inventory, expressed in days.

(b) (This part of the question tests your ability to be able to deduce some conclusions from the information given. You have to use your imagination.)

First, an assumption, we do not know relative sizes of these two businesses. We will assume that they are approximately of the same size.

A has a higher current ratio, 2 to 1.5, but the quick assets ratio shows a much greater disparity, 1.7 to 0.7. As inventory is not included in the quick assets ratio, it can be deduced that B has relatively greater inventory. Expected also from these ratios is that A has high amounts of accounts receivable, this being seen because accounts receivable turnover is three times as great for A as for B. We are told that both businesses are retailers so it is somewhat surprising that both appear to be selling significant amounts on credit.

The return on shareholders' funds (ROSF) is much greater for A than for B, 30 per cent to 18 per cent, but the ROCE is not that different, 20 per cent to 17 per cent. This shows that A has far more in long-term borrowings than B. The ROCE indicates that A is somewhat more efficient than B, but not by a considerable amount.

Gross profit percentage is far greater for A than B, but net profit percentage is the same. Obviously, A has extremely high operating expenses per £100 of sales.

The last ratio shows that inventory in A lies unsold for twice as long a period as for B.

A summary of the above shows that A has lower inventory, a higher figure for accounts receivable, sells at a slower rate, and has high operating expenses. B has more inventory, and sells its goods much quicker but at lower prices as shown by the gross profit percentage.

All the evidence points to A being a firm which gives emphasis to personal service to its customers. B on the other hand emphasises cheap prices and high turnover, with not as much concentration on personal service.

41.20

(There is no set answer. In addition, as a large number of points could be mentioned, the examiner cannot expect every aspect to be covered.)

The main points which could be covered are:

(i) The financial statements are for last year whereas, in fact, the bank is more interested in what might happen to the business in the future.

(ii) The financial statements are usually prepared on a historic cost basis. These therefore do not reflect current values.

(iii) The bank manager would want a cash budget to be drawn up for the ensuing periods. This would give the manager an indication as to whether or not the business will be able to meet its commitments as they fall due.

(iv) The bank manager wants to ensure that bank charges and interest can be paid promptly, also that a bank loan or overdraft will be able to be paid off. He will want to see that these commitments can still be met if the business has to cease operations. This means that the market value of assets on cessation, rather than the cost of them, is of much more interest to the bank manager.

To say that the financial statements are 'not good enough' is misleading. What the manager is saying is that the financial statements do not provide him with what he would really like to know. One could argue that there should be other types of financial statements drawn up in addition to those drawn up on a historic basis.

41.21

(a) The basis on which financial statements are prepared is that of 'accruals'. By this it is meant that the recognition of revenue and expenditure takes place not at the point when cash is received or paid out, but instead at the point when the revenue is earned or the expenditure is incurred.

To establish the point of recognition of a sale, several criteria are necessary:

(i) The product, or the service, must have been supplied to the customer.

(ii) The buyer must have indicated willingness to pay for the product or services and have accepted liability to do so.

(iii) A monetary value of the goods or services must have been agreed to by the buyer.

(iv) Ownership of the goods must have passed to the buyer.

(b) (i) This cannot be recognised as a sale. It does not comply with any of the four criteria above.

(ii) This also cannot be recognised as a sale. Neither criterion (i) nor (iv) has been covered.

(iii) If this was a cash sale, all of the above criteria would probably be achieved on delivery, and therefore it could be appropriate to recognise the sale.

If it was a credit sale, if the invoice was sent with the goods and a delivery note stating satisfaction by the customer is signed, then it would also probably be appropriate to recognise the sale.

(iv) Usually takes place after the four criteria have been satisfied. If so, the sale should be recognised.

(v) In the case of cash sales this would be the point of recognition.

In the case of credit sales it would depend on whether or not criteria (a) (i) and (iv) had also been satisfied.

(vi) This would only influence recognition of sales if there was serious doubt about the ability of the customer to pay his/her debts.

41.22

Obviously there is no set answer to this question. However, the following may well be typical:

(a) If the business is going to carry on operating, then the going concern concept comes into operation. Consequently, non-current assets are valued at cost, less depreciation to date. Inventory is valued at lower of cost or net realisable value. The 'net realisable value' will be that based on the business realising inventory through normal operations.

(b) Should the business be deemed as a case for cessation, then the going concern concept could not be used. The values on non-current assets and inventory will be their disposal values. This should be affected by whether or not the business could be sold as a whole or whether it would have to be broken up. Similarly, figures would be affected by whether or not assets had to be sold off very quickly at low prices, or sold only when reasonable prices could be achieved.

It is not only the balance sheet that would be affected, as the income statement would reflect the changes in values.

41.23

(a) See text, Chapter 7.

(b) Various illustrations are possible, but the following are examples:

(i) Apportionment of expenses between one period and another. For instance, very rarely would very small inventories of stationery be valued at the year end. This means that the stationery gets charged against one year's profits even though it may not all have been used up in that year.

(ii) Items expensed instead of being capitalised. Small items which are, in theory, capital expenditure will often be charged up to an expense account.

(iii) The value of assets approximated, instead of being measured with absolute precision.

(c) (i) An illustration could be made under (b) (iii). An inventory of oil could well be estimated; the true figure, if known, might be one or two litres out. The cost of precise measurement would probably not be worth the benefit of having such information.

(ii) What is material in one company may not be material in another.

41.24

No set answer. Question is of a general nature rather than being specific. A variety of answers are therefore acceptable.

The examiner might expect to see the following covered (this is not a model answer):

(a) Different reports needed by different outside parties, as they have to meet different requirements. Might find they therefore include:

(i) for bankers – accounts based on 'break-up' value of the assets if they have to be sold off to repay loans or overdrafts;

(ii) for investors – to include how business has fared against budgets set for that year to see how successful business is at meeting targets;

(iii) for employees – include details of number of employees, wages and salaries paid, effect on pension funds;

(iv) for local community – to include reports showing amounts spent on pollution control, etc.

And any similar instances.

(b) The characteristics of useful information have been stated in *The Framework for the Preparation and Presentation of Financial Statements* (see Section 7.9), and the accounting reports should be measured against this.

(c) Presentation (additional) in form of pie charts, bar charts, etc., as these are often more easily understood by readers.

41.25

(a) Accountants follow the realisation concept when deciding when to recognise revenue on any particular transaction. This states that profit is normally regarded as being earned at the time when the goods or services are passed to the customer and he/she incurs liability for them. For a service business it means when the services have been performed.

(b) The stage at which revenue is recognised could be either F or G. The normal rule is that the goods have been despatched, not delivered. For instance the goods may be shipped to Australia and take several weeks to get there.

Exactly where this fits in with F or G in the question cannot be stipulated without further information.

(c) If F is accepted as point of recognition, then £130 will be gross profit. If G is accepted as point of recognition the gross profit recognised will be £120.

(d) The argument that can be advanced is to take the prudence concept to its final conclusion, in that the debtor should pay for the goods before the profit can be recognised.

Until H is reached there is always the possibility that the goods will not be paid for, or might be returned because of faults in the goods.

(e) If the goods are almost certain to be sold, it could give a better picture of the progress of the firm up to a particular point in time if profit could be recognised in successive amounts at stages B, C and D. This would be more likely to be the approach if the company was in (say) the construction industry rather than manufacturing.

41.26

(a) A 'provision' is a liability that is uncertain in timing or amount. An example would be where a company offers a one-year warranty on the goods it sells. The company can only estimate how many customers will claim under this warranty, so would set up a 'provision' for the expected cost of meeting warranty claims. Being a one-year warranty, this provision would be shown under 'current liabilities'.

A 'reserve' is a component of equity other than share capital. A company will have a number of different reserves, such as 'share premium', 'general reserve' and 'retained profits'. The 'retained profits' reserve, for example, represents the accumulated net profits that the company has earned but not paid out as dividends.

Accrued expenses are those accruing from one day to another, but not paid at the year end. Such items as rates, electricity, telephone charges will come under this heading.

Accounts payable represent persons to whom money is owed for goods and services.

Provisions, accrued expenses and accounts payable would all be taken into account before calculating net profit. Reserves do not interfere with the calculation of net profit, as they are appropriations of profit or, as in the case of capital reserves, do not pass through the profit and loss account.

(b) (i) Provision made for £21,000. Charge to profit and loss and show in the balance sheet under current liabilities.

(ii) Accrued expenses, $^2/_{12}$ £6,000 = £1,000. Charge to profit and loss account and show as current liability in the balance sheet.

(iii) Account payable £1,750. Bring into purchases in trading account and show as current liability in the balance sheet.

(iv) Reserve £5,000. Transfer from retained profits to plant replacement reserve and show the transfer in the statement of changes in equity and in the balance sheet under *reserves*.

41.27

(a) *The bank*

The bank will be interested in two main aspects. The first is the ability to repay the loan as and when it falls due. The second is the ability to pay interest on the due dates.

41.28
See text.

42.1
See text.

42.2
See text.

42.3
See text.

42.4
See text.

42.5
See text.

Mr Whitehall
He will be interested in the expected return on his investment. This means that recent performance of the company and its plans will be important to him. In addition the possible capital growth of his investment would be desirable.
(b) *Note:* For your information; more than four ratios for bank are given below despite you having being asked for four.

Bank

Long-term ability to repay loan

(*i*) Shareholders' equity/Total assets
(*ii*) Loan capital/Shareholders' equity
(*iii*) Total liabilities/Shareholders' equity
(*iv*) Operating profit/Loan interest.

Short-term liquidity

(*i*) Liquid assets/Current liabilities.
(*ii*) Current assets/Current liabilities.

Mr Whitehall

Return on investment

(*i*) Price per share/Earnings per share
(*ii*) Dividend per share/Market price per share
(*iii*) Profit for the year/Dividends paid.
(*iv*) Profit for the year/Number of ordinary shares in issue.

Answers to multiple choice questions

Set 1 (pp. 81–4)

1	(C)	**2**	(D)	**3**	(B)	**4**	(C)	**5**	(A)
6	(C)	**7**	(C)	**8**	(A)	**9**	(C)	**10**	(A)
11	(B)	**12**	(D)	**13**	(B)	**14**	(D)	**15**	(B)
16	(C)	**17**	(C)	**18**	(A)	**19**	(D)	**20**	(C)

Set 2 (pp. 171–4)

21	(A)	**22**	(B)	**23**	(A)	**24**	(D)	**25**	(C)
26	(A)	**27**	(D)	**28**	(A)	**29**	(C)	**30**	(A)
31	(C)	**32**	(D)	**33**	(C)	**34**	(C)	**35**	(D)
36	(B)	**37**	(A)	**38**	(B)	**39**	(C)	**40**	(C)

Set 3 (pp. 341–3)

41	(A)	**42**	(C)	**43**	(A)	**44**	(D)	**45**	(A)
46	(A)	**47**	(B)	**48**	(C)	**49**	(D)	**50**	(C)
51	(A)	**52**	(D)	**53**	(C)	**54**	(C)	**55**	(D)
56	(C)	**57**	(A)	**58**	(A)	**59**	(B)	**60**	(C)

Set 4 (pp. 435–8)

61	(B)	**62**	(A)	**63**	(D)	**64**	(A)	**65**	(C)
66	(A)	**67**	(D)	**68**	(D)	**69**	(B)	**70**	(A)
71	(D)	**72**	(C)	**73**	(D)	**74**	(B)	**75**	(B)
76	(C)	**77**	(D)	**78**	(A)	**79**	(B)	**80**	(C)

Set 5 (pp. 636–8)

81	(B)	**82**	(B)	**83**	(C)	**84**	(D)	**85**	(A)
86	(B)	**87**	(A)	**88**	(C)	**89**	(C)	**90**	(A)
91	(C)	**92**	(B)	**93**	(B)	**94**	(D)	**95**	(C)
96	(B)	**97**	(C)	**98**	(B)	**99**	(D)	**100**	(B)

Glossary

Absorption costing (Chapter 42): The method of allocating all factory indirect expenses to products. (All fixed costs are allocated to cost units.)

Account (Chapter 2): Part of double entry records, containing details of transactions for a specific item.

Account payable (or Creditor) (Chapter 1): A person to whom money is owed for goods or services.

Account receivable (or Debtor) (Chapter 1): A person who owes money to a business for goods or services supplied.

Accounting (Chapter 22): The process of identifying, measuring and communicating economic information to permit informed judgements and decisions by users of the information.

Accounting cycle (Chapter 12): The sequence in which data is recorded and processed until it becomes part of the financial statements at the end of the period.

Accounting policies (Chapter 41): Those principles, bases, conventions, rules and practices applied by an entity that specify how the effects of transactions and other events are to be reflected in its financial statements.

Accounts (or **final accounts**) (Chapter 16): This is a term previously used to refer to statements produced at the end of accounting periods, such as the income statement and the balance sheet. Nowadays, the term 'financial statements' is more commonly used.

Accounts payable/purchases ratio (Chapter 41): A ratio assessing how long a business takes to pay creditors.

Accounts receivable/sales ratio (Chapter 41): A ratio assessing how long it takes debtors to pay their debts.

Accruals basis (or **Accruals concept**) (Chapter 7): The concept that profit is the difference between revenue and the expenses incurred in generating that revenue.

Accrued expense (Chapter 22): An expense for which the benefit has been received but which has not been paid for by the end of the period. It is included in the balance sheet under current liabilities as 'accruals'.

Accrued income (Chapter 22): Income (normally) from a source other than the main source of business income, such as rent receivable on an unused office in the company headquarters, that was due to be received by the end of the period but which has not been received by that date. It is added to accounts receivable in the balance sheet.

Accumulated depreciation account (Chapter 21): The account where depreciation is accumulated for balance sheet purposes. It is used in order to leave the cost (or valuation) figure as the balance in the non-current asset account. (It is sometimes confusingly referred to as the 'provision for depreciation account'.)

Accumulated fund (Chapter 28): A form of capital account for a non-profit-oriented organisation.

Acid test ratio (Chapter 41): A ratio comparing current assets less inventory with current liabilities.

Allowance for doubtful debts (Chapter 20): An account representing an estimate of the expected amount of debts at the date of the balance sheet which may not be paid.

Amortisation (Chapter 21): A term used instead of 'depreciation' when assets are used up simply because of the passing of time.

Assets (Chapter 1): Resources owned by a business.

AVCO (Chapter 18): A method by which goods used are priced out at average cost.

Bad debt (Chapter 20): A debt that a business will not be able to collect.

Balance brought down (Chapter 5): The difference between both sides of an account that is entered below the totals on the opposite side to the one on which the balance carried down was entered. (This is normally abbreviated to 'balance b/d'.)

Balance carried down (Chapter 5): The difference between both sides of an account that is entered above the totals and makes the total of both sides equal each other. (This is normally abbreviated to 'balance c/d'.)

Balance sheet (Chapter 1): A statement showing the assets, liabilities and capital of a business.

Balance-off the account (Chapter 5): Insert the difference (called a 'balance') between the two sides of an account and then total and rule off the account. This is normally done at the end of a period (usually a month, a quarter or a year).

Bank cash book (Chapter 9): A cash book that only contains entries relating to payments into and out of the bank.

Bank reconciliation statement (Chapter 24): A calculation comparing the cash book balance with the bank statement balance.

Bank statement (Chapter 9): A copy issued by a bank to a customer showing the customer's current account maintained at the bank.

Bookkeeping (Chapter 1): The process of recording data relating to accounting transactions in the accounting books.

Books of original entry (Chapter 8): Books where the first entry recording a transaction is made. (These are sometimes referred to as 'books of prime entry'.)

Budget (Chapters 1 and 42): A plan quantified in monetary terms in advance of a defined time period – usually showing planned income and expenditure and the capital employed to achieve a given objective.

Business entity concept (Chapter 7): Assumption that only transactions that affect the firm, and not the owner's private transactions, will be recorded.

Capital (Chapter 1): The total of resources invested and left in a business by its owner.

Capital expenditure (Chapter 17): When a business spends money to buy or add value to a non-current asset.

Capital reserve (Chapter 37): An account that can be used by sole traders and partnerships to place the amount by which the total purchase price paid for a business is less than the valuation of the net assets acquired. Limited companies cannot use a capital reserve for this purpose. Sole traders and partnerships can instead, if they wish, record the shortfall as negative goodwill.

Carriage inwards (Chapter 16): Cost of transport of goods into a business.

Carriage outwards (Chapter 16): Cost of transport of goods out to the customers of a business.

Cash (Chapter 25): Cash balances and bank balances, plus funds invested in 'cash equivalents'.

Cash book (Chapter 8): A book of original entry for cash and bank receipts and payments.

Cash equivalents (Chapter 25): Temporary investments of cash not required at present by the business, such as funds put on short-term deposit with a bank. Such investments must be readily convertible into cash, or available as cash within three months.

Casting (Chapter 26): Adding up figures.

Close off the account (Chapter 5): Totalling and ruling off an account on which there is no outstanding balance.

Compensating error (Chapter 26): Where two errors of equal amounts, but on opposite sides of the accounts, cancel each other out.

Consistency (Chapter 7): Keeping to the same method of recording and processing transactions.

Contra (Chapter 9): A contra, for cash book items, is where both the debit and the credit entries are shown in the cash book, such as when cash is paid into the bank.

Contribution (Chapter 30): The surplus of revenue over direct costs allocated to a section of a business.

Control account (Chapter 23): An account which checks the arithmetical accuracy of a ledger.

Cost centre (Chapter 42): A production or service location, function, activity or item of equipment whose costs may be attributed to cost units.

Cost unit (Chapter 42): A unit of product or service in relation to which costs are ascertained.

Credit (Chapter 2): The right-hand side of the accounts in double entry.

Credit note (Chapter 11): A document sent to a customer showing the allowance given by a supplier in respect of unsatisfactory goods.

Creditor (or **Accounts payable**) (Chapter 1): A person to whom money is owed for goods or services.

Current assets (Chapter 15): Assets consisting of cash, goods for resale or items having a short life.

Current liabilities (Chapter 15): Liabilities to be paid for within a year of the date of the statement of financial position.

Current ratio (Chapter 41): A ratio comparing current assets with current liabilities.

Day books (Chapter 8): Books in which credit sales, purchases, and returns inwards and outwards of goods are first recorded. The details are then posted from the day books to the ledger accounts.

Debit (Chapter 2): The left-hand side of the accounts in double entry.

Debit note (Chapter 11): A document sent to a supplier showing the allowance to be given for unsatisfactory goods.

Debtor (or **Accounts receivable**) (Chapter 1): A person who owes money to a business for goods or services supplied to him.

Depletion (Chapter 21): The wasting away of an asset as it is used up.

Depreciation (Chapter 21): The part of the cost of a non-current asset consumed during its period of use by the firm. It represents an estimate of how much of the overall economic usefulness of a non-current asset has been used up in each accounting period. It is charged as a debit to profit and loss and a credit against non-current asset accounts in the general ledger.

Direct costs (Chapter 29): Costs that can be traced to the item being manufactured.

Directors (Chapter 36): Officials appointed by shareholders to manage the company for them.

Discounts allowed (Chapter 9): A deduction from the amount due given to customers who pay their accounts within the time allowed.

Discounts received (Chapter 9): A deduction from the amount due given to a business by a supplier when their account is paid before the time allowed has elapsed. It appears as income in the profit and loss part of the trading and profit and loss account.

Dishonoured cheque (Chapter 24): A cheque which the writer's bank has refused to make payment upon.

Dissolution (Chapter 35): When a partnership firm ceases operations and its assets are disposed of.

Dividends (Chapter 36): The amount given to shareholders as their share of the profits of the company.

Double entry bookkeeping (or **Double entry**) (Chapter 2): A system where each transaction is entered twice, once on the debit side and once on the credit side.

Drawings (Chapter 4): Funds or goods taken out of a business by the owners for their private use.

Dual aspect concept (Chapter 7): The concept of dealing with both aspects of a transaction.

Equity (Chapter 1): Another name for the capital of the owner.

Error of commission (Chapter 26): Where a correct amount is entered, but in the wrong person's account.

Error of omission (Chapter 26): Where a transaction is completely omitted from the books.

Error of original entry (Chapter 26): Where an item is entered, but both the debit and credit entries are of the same incorrect amount.

Error of principle (Chapter 26): Where an item is entered in the wrong type of account, e.g. a fixed asset in an expense account.

Estimation techniques (Chapter 41): The methods adopted in order to arrive at estimated monetary amounts for items that appear in the financial statements.

Exempted businesses (Chapter 13): Businesses which do not have to add VAT to the price of goods and services supplied to them. They cannot obtain a refund of VAT paid on goods and services purchased by them.

Expenses (Chapter 4): The value of all the assets that have been used up to obtain revenues.

Factoring (Chapter 11): Selling the rights to the amounts owing by debtors to a finance company for an agreed amount (which is less than the figure at which they are recorded in the accounting books because the finance company needs to be paid for providing the service).

FIFO (Chapter 18): A method by which the first items to be received are said to be the first to be sold.

Final accounts (or **accounts**) (Chapter 16): This is a term previously used to refer to statements produced at the end of accounting periods, such as the income statement and the balance sheet. Nowadays, the term 'financial statements' is more commonly used.

Financial statements (Chapter 16): The more common term used to refer to statements produced at the end of accounting periods, such as the income statement and the balance sheet (sometimes referred to as 'final accounts' or simply 'the accounts').

Fixed capital accounts (Chapter 32): Capital accounts which consist only of the amounts of capital actually paid into the partnership.

Fixed costs (Chapter 41): Expenses which remain constant whether activity rises or falls, within a given range of activity.

Float (Chapter 10): The amount at which the petty cash starts each period.

Fluctuating capital accounts (Chapter 32): Capital accounts the balances of which change from one period to the next.

Folio columns (Chapter 9): Columns used for entering reference numbers.

***Garner* v *Murray* rule** (Chapter 35): If one partner is unable to make good a deficit on his/her capital account, the remaining partners will share the loss in proportion to their last agreed capitals, not in the profit/loss sharing ratio.

Gearing (Chapter 41): The ratio of long-term loans and preference shares shown as a percentage of total shareholders' funds, long-term loans, and preference shares.

General ledger (Chapter 8): A ledger for all accounts other than those for customers and suppliers.

Going concern concept (Chapter 7): The assumption that a business is to continue for the foreseeable future.

Goodwill (Chapter 33): An amount representing the added value to a business of such factors as customer loyalty, reputation, market penetration and expertise.

Gross loss (Chapter 14): Where the cost of goods sold exceeds the sales revenue.

Gross profit (Chapter 14): Where the sales revenue exceeds the cost of goods sold.

Historical cost concept (Chapter 7): Assets are normally shown at cost price.

Impersonal accounts (Chapter 8): All accounts other than debtors' and creditors' accounts.

Imprest system (Chapter 10): A system where a refund is made of the total paid out in a period in order to restore the float to its agreed level.

Income and expenditure account (Chapter 28): An account for a non-profit-oriented organisation to find the surplus or loss made during a period.

Income statement (Chapter 14): The financial statement in which the calculations of gross profit and then net profit are presented.

Indirect manufacturing costs (Chapter 29): Costs relating to manufacture that cannot be economically traced to the item being manufactured (also known as 'indirect costs' and, sometimes, as 'factory overhead expenses').

Input tax (Chapter 13): VAT added to the net price of inputs (i.e. purchases).

Inputs (Chapter 13): Purchases of goods and services.

Intangible asset (Chapter 33): An asset, such as goodwill, that has no physical existence.

Interest on capital (Chapter 32): An amount at an agreed rate of interest which is credited to a partner based on the amount of capital contributed by him/her.

Interest on drawings (Chapter 32): An amount at an agreed rate of interest, based on the drawings taken out, which is debited to the partners.

Inventory (Chapter 1): Goods in which the business normally deals that are held with the intention of resale. They may be finished goods, partly finished goods or raw materials awaiting conversion into finished goods which will then be sold.

Inventory turnover (Chapter 39): The number of times inventory is sold in an accounting period. (Also known as 'stockturn'.)

Job costing (Chapter 42): A costing system that is applied when goods or services are produced in discrete jobs, either one item at a time, or in batches.

Joint ventures (Chapter 31): Business agreements under which two businesses join together for a set of activities and agree to share the profits.

Journal (Chapter 8): A book of original entry for all items not contained in the other books of original entry.

Liabilities (Chapter 1): Total of funds owed for assets supplied to a business or expenses incurred not yet paid.

LIFO (Chapter 18): A method by which goods sold are said to have come from the last lot of goods received.

Limited company (Chapter 36): An organisation owned by its shareholders, whose liability is limited to their share capital.

Limited partner (Chapter 32): A partner whose liability is limited to the capital he or she has put into the firm.

Liquidity ratios (Chapter 41): Those ratios that relate to the cash position in an organisation and hence its ability to pay liabilities when due.

Loan note (Chapter 36): Loan made to a company for which a formal certificate has been issued to the lender by the company.

Loss (Chapter 3): The result of selling goods for less than they cost.

Manufacturing account (Chapter 29): An account in which production cost is calculated.

Margin (Chapter 39): Profit shown as a percentage or fraction of selling price.

Marginal costing (Chapter 42): An approach to costing that takes account of the variable cost of products rather than the full production cost. It is particularly useful when considering utilisation of spare capacity.

Mark-up (Chapter 39): Profit shown as a percentage or fraction of cost price.

Materiality (Chapter 7): That something should only be included in the financial statements if it would be of interest to the stakeholders, i.e. to those people who make use of financial accounting statements. It need not be material to every stakeholder, but it must be material to a stakeholder before it merits inclusion.

Measurement basis (Chapter 41): The monetary aspects of the items in the financial statements, such as the basis of the inventory valuation, say FIFO or LIFO.

Memorandum joint venture account (Chapter 31): A memorandum account outside the double entry system where the information contained in all the joint venture accounts held by the parties to the joint ventures are collated, the joint venture profit is calculated and the share of profit of each party is recorded in order to close off the account.

Money measurement concept (Chapter 7): The concept that accounting is concerned only with facts measurable in monetary terms, and for which purpose measurements can be used that obtain general agreement as to their suitability.

Narrative (Chapter 12): A description and explanation of the transaction recorded in the journal.

Negative contribution (Chapter 30): The excess of direct costs allocated to a section of a business over the revenue from that section.

Negative goodwill (Chapter 37): The name given to the amount by which the total purchase price for a business a limited company has taken over is less than the valuation of the assets at that time. The amount is entered at the top of the non-current assets in the balance sheet as a negative amount. (Sole traders and partnerships can use this approach instead of a capital reserve.)

Net current assets (Chapter 22): Current assets minus current liabilities. The figure represents the amount of resources the business has in a form that is readily convertible into cash. Same as working capital.

Net loss (Chapter 14): Where the cost of goods sold plus expenses is greater than the revenue.

Net profit (Chapter 14): Where sales revenue plus other income, such as rent received, exceeds the sum of cost of goods sold plus other expenses.

Net realisable value (Chapter 18): The value of goods calculated as their selling price less expenses before sale.

Nominal accounts (Chapter 8): Accounts in which expenses, revenue and capital are recorded.

Nominal ledger (Chapter 8): Another name for the general ledger.

Non-current assets (Chapter 15): Assets which have a long life bought with the intention to use them in the business and not with the intention to simply resell them.

Non-current liabilities (Chapter 15): Liabilities that do not have to be paid within 12 months of the date of the balance sheet.

Objectivity (Chapter 7): Using a method that everyone can agree to based on some clear and indisputable fact.

Obsolescence (Chapter 21): Becoming out-of-date.

Ordinary shares (Chapter 36): Shares entitled to dividends after the preference shareholders have been paid their dividends.

Output tax (Chapter 13): VAT added to the net price of outputs (i.e. sales).

Outputs (Chapter 13): Sales of goods and services.

Partnership (Chapter 32): A business in which two or more people are working together as owners with a view to making profits.

Partnership salaries (Chapter 32): Agreed amounts payable to partners in respect of duties undertaken by them.

Personal accounts (Chapter 8): Accounts for creditors and debtors.

Petty cash book (Chapter 10): A cash book for small payments.

Posting (Chapter 9): The act of transferring information into ledger accounts from books of original entry.

Preference shares (Chapter 36): Shares that are entitled to an agreed rate of dividend before the ordinary shareholders receive anything.

Preliminary expenses (Chapter 36): All the costs that are incurred when a company is formed.

Prepaid expense (Chapter 22): An expense which has been paid in advance, the benefits from which will be received in the next period. It is included in the balance sheet under current assets as 'prepayments'.

Prime cost (Chapter 29): Direct materials plus direct labour plus direct expenses.

Private company (Chapter 36): A limited company that must issue its shares privately.

Private ledger (Chapter 8): A ledger for capital and drawings accounts.

Process costing (Chapter 42): A costing system that is applied when goods or services are produced in a continuous flow.

Production cost (Chapter 29): Prime cost plus indirect manufacturing costs.

Profit (Chapter 3): The result of selling goods or services for more than they cost.

Profit and loss account (Chapter 14): An account in which net profit is calculated that is summarised and included in a separate edition of the income statement.

Prudence (Chapter 7): Ensuring that profit is not shown as being too high, that assets are not shown at too high a value and that the financial statements are neutral: that is, that neither gains nor losses are understated or overstated.

Public company (Chapter 36): A company that can issue its shares publicly, and for which there is no maximum number of shareholders.

Purchased goodwill (Chapter 33): The difference between the amount paid to acquire a part or the whole of a business as a going concern and the value of the net assets owned by the business.

Purchases (Chapter 3): Goods bought by the business for the prime purpose of selling them again.

Purchases day book (Chapter 8): Book of original entry for credit purchases. Also called the purchases journal.

Purchases invoice (Chapter 11): A document received by a purchaser showing details of goods bought and their prices.

Purchases ledger (Chapter 8): A ledger for suppliers' personal accounts.

Real accounts (Chapter 8): Accounts in which property of all kinds is recorded.

Realisation concept (Chapter 7): Only profits and gains realised at the date of the balance sheet should be included in the income statement. For a gain to be realised, it must be possible to be reasonably certain that it exists and that it can be measured with sufficient reliability.

Receipts and payments account (Chapter 28): A summary of the cash book of a non-profit-oriented organisation.

Reduced rate (of VAT) (Chapter 13): A lower VAT rate applicable to certain goods and services.

Reducing balance method (Chapter 21): A method of calculating depreciation based on the principle that you calculate annual depreciation as a percentage of the net-of-depreciation-to-date balance brought forward at the start of the period on a non-current asset.

Registered business (Chapter 13): A business that has registered for VAT. It must account for VAT and submit a VAT Return at the end of every VAT tax period.

Reserves (Chapter 36): Accounts to which profits are transferred for use in future years.

Residual value (Chapter 21): The net amount receivable when a non-current asset is put out of use by the business.

Return on capital employed (Chapter 41): Net profit as a percentage of capital employed, often abbreviated as ROCE.

Return on owners' equity (Chapter 41): Net profit as a percentage of ordinary share capital plus all reserves, often abbreviated as ROOE. The more common term in use for this is 'return on shareholders' funds'.

Return on shareholders' funds (Chapter 41): Net profit as a percentage of ordinary share capital plus all reserves, often abbreviated as ROSF and more commonly used than the alternative term, return on owners' equity.

Returns inwards (Chapter 16): Goods returned by customers. (Also known as 'sales returns'.)

Returns inwards day book (Chapter 8): Book of original entry for goods returned by customers. Also called the returns inwards journal or the sales returns book.

Returns outwards (Chapter 16): Goods returned to suppliers. (Also known as 'purchases returns'.)

Returns outwards day book (Chapter 8): Book of original entry for goods returned to suppliers. Also called the returns outwards journal or the purchases returns book.

Revaluation account (Chapter 34): An account used to record gains and losses when assets are revalued.

Revenue (Chapter 4): The financial value of goods and services sold to customers.

Revenue expenditure (Chapter 17): Expenses needed for the day-to-day running of the business.

Sale or return (Chapter 18): Goods passed to a customer on the understanding that a sale will not occur until they are paid for. As a result, these goods continue to belong to the seller.

Sales (Chapter 3): Goods sold by the business in which it normally deals that were bought with the prime intention of resale.

Sales day book (Chapter 8): Book of original entry for credit sales. Also called the sales journal.

Sales invoice (Chapter 11): A document showing details of goods sold and the prices of those goods.

Sales ledger (Chapter 8): A ledger for customers' personal accounts.

Separate determination concept (Chapter 7): The amount of each asset or liability should be determined separately.

Shareholders (Chapter 36): Individuals or entities holding one or more shares in a company.

Shares (Chapter 36): The division of the capital of a limited company into parts.

Stakeholders (Chapter 1): Those goups, entities and individuals who base decisions upon financial statements and other information relating to the entity of which they are stakeholders.

Standard cost (Chapter 18): What you would expect something to cost.

Standard rate (of VAT) (Chapter 13): The VAT rate usually used.

Standard-rated business (Chapter 13): A business that charges VAT at the standard rate on its sales.

Statement (Chapter 11): A copy of a customer's personal account taken from the supplier's books.

Statement of affairs (Chapter 40): A statement from which the capital of the owner can be found by estimating assets and liabilities. Then it is the equivalent of the balance sheet.

Statement of cash flows (Chapter 25): A statement showing how cash has been generated and disposed of by an organisation. The layout is regulated by IAS 7.

Statement of changes in equity (Chapter 36): A statement reconciling the opening and closing carrying amounts at each class and type of equity.

Stocktaking (Chapter 18): The process of physically identifying the inventory on hand at a given point in time.

Straight line method (Chapter 21): A method of calculating depreciation that involves deducting the same amount every accounting period from the original cost of a non-current asset.

Subjectivity (Chapter 7): Using a method that other people may not agree to, derived from one's own personal preferences.

Substance over form (Chapter 7): Where real substance takes precedence over legal form.

Super profits (Chapter 33): Net profit less the opportunity costs of alternative earnings and alternative returns on capital invested that have been foregone.

Suspense account (Chapter 27): An account in which you can enter the amount equal to the difference in the trial balance while you try to find the cause of the error(s) that resulted in the failure of the trial balance to balance.

T-account (Chapter 2): The layout of accounts in the accounting books.

Time interval concept (Chapter 7): Financial statements are prepared at regular intervals.

Total cost (Chapter 29): Production cost plus administration, selling and distribution expenses and finance expenses.

Trade discount (Chapter 11): A deduction in price given to a trade customer when calculating the price to be charged to that customer for some goods. It does not appear anywhere in the accounting books and so does not appear anywhere in the financial statements.

Trading account (Chapter 14): An account in which gross profit is calculated that is part of the income statement.

Transposition error (Chapter 26): Where the characters within a number are entered in the wrong sequence.

Trial balance (Chapter 6): A list of account titles and their balances in the ledgers, on a specific date, shown in debit and credit columns.

True and fair view (Chapter 36): The expression that is used by auditors to indicate whether, in their opinion, the financial statements fairly represent the state of affairs and financial performance of a company.

Unpresented cheque (Chapter 24): A cheque which has been given to a creditor but which has not yet been received and processed by the writer's bank.

Unregistered business (Chapter 13): A business that ignores VAT and treats it as part of the cost of purchases. It does not charge VAT on its outputs. It does not need to maintain any record of VAT paid.

Value added tax (VAT) (Chapter 13): A tax charged on the supply of most goods and services.

Variable costs (Chapter 41): Expenses which change in response to changes in the level of activity.

Working capital (Chapter 22): Current assets minus current liabilities. The figure represents the amount of resources the business has in a form that is readily convertible into cash. Same as net current assets.

Work-in-progress (Chapter 29): Items not completed at the end of a period.

Zero rate (of VAT) (Chapter 13): The VAT rate (of zero) that applies to supply of certain goods and services.

Zero-rated business (Chapter 13): A business that only supplies zero-rated goods and services. It does not charge VAT to its customers but it receives a refund of VAT on goods and services it purchases.

Index

Bold page numbers are definitions. They may be in the glossary, in the text, or both.

A glosssary of accounting terms is on page **764**